SPEAKING OF MONKS: *From* BENARES TO BEIJING

The volume contains essays by various authors from all over the world on different aspects of Indian and Chinese civilization. Also Buddhism both as a philosophy and religion. Topics covered include the role of women in Chinese religion, biographical writing in the tradition of Jainism in India and attitude towards language and translation in Indian Buddhism.

SPEAKING OF MONKS:
From
BENARES TO BEIJING

KOICHI SHINOHARA
&
PHYLLIS GRANOFF

New Age Books

ISBN: 81-7822-235-3

First Indian Edition: Delhi, 2006

First published in Canada by Mosaic Press Ltd.

Published by
NEW AGE BOOKS
A-44, Naraina Industrial Area, Phase-I
New Delhi 110 028 (INDIA)
Email: nab@vsnl.in
Website: www.newagebooksindia.com

Printed in India
at Nice Printing Press
3, Rashid Market Extension, New Delhi-110051

Contents

Introduction

The first, by Phyllis Granoff, Considers religious biographies of two Jain monks from Northwest India, who were important patriarchs of a medieval reform movement.

India and China both produced a rich biographical literature about which relatively little is known. We began our project with two basic objectives: to acquaint ourselves with at least some of this rich literature, and to see if there was something about the dynamics of biography writing in religious communities that common across divergent cultures.

As our investigation proceeded, we began to focus our attention on the local contexts in which biographies of monks were written and preserved. The two essays in this book deal with religious biographies, and tangentially autobiographies, and the shared context in broad general terms might be described as a religious environment in which distinctive groups were forming or consolidating their authority. In both cases biographies of the founders or a later charismatic leader were written as an important part of an effort to define and solidify distinctive religious communities. Each essay is a detailed study of specific biographies, and of the concrete circumstances that surrounded the composition of the biographies.

The medieval Jain community was divided into a number of competing and mutually exclusive monastic lineages that claimed the exclusive support of monks (Jinadatta) and of a later figure of the mature tradition (Jinaprabha) that one dominant concern of the biography lay in establishing the legitimacy of the authorities.

All of the biographies we studied made ample use of miracle stories. In a remarkably parallel fashion the discussion of Jain biographies shows how both Jinaprabha and Jinadatta became the subject of a number of miracle stories, stories that were extremely libile, andhad a life of their own outside the biographies. The miracle stories in the biographies of these two Indian monks gave life to what was the dominant biographical emphasis, the close support these monks had obtained from secular authorities.

Both studies also show that biographies in India could sometimes draw upon autobiographical writings, letters, memoirs, and personal religious poetry. The study of Jain biographies includes a traslation and discussion of a memoir and a translation of a parts of a very personal religious poem. The essay also deals with some of the conventions of autobiographical writing in medieval India. Both essays points out the complexity of the biographical and autobiographical process and treat the issue of the "image" of the monk that emerges through that process, an image that often reflects the practical political and sectarian needs of the community.

The study of Jain biographies in particular raised three issues that deserve detailed study. The first concerns the relationship between the normative picture of the monk that emerges in the Jain canon and the didactic story telling tradition that develops from the canon. The issue is discussed in brief in some of the notes to the essay that appear here, but it requires further work. A second major topic is autobiographical writing in medieval India. Realizing that Jinaprabha wrote a memoir and Jinadatta wrote very personal poetry, Phyllis Granoff searched for and found a significant body of religious autobiographical process. The essay in this volume indicates how common religious language can be adopted by an author with new emphases; Jinadatta uses images that are often found in Jain canonical writings and indeed in Buddhist biographies of the Buddha. But he uses them in new and different ways. We may learn a great deal about the differences and similarities between Jainism and Buddhism as religious systems from a comparison of Jain and Buddhist biographical sources.

In closing, then, we hope that these essays will interest readers for the questions that they raise, both those answered and those unanswered.

Jinaprabhasūri and Jinadattasūri: Two Studies from the Śvetāmbara Jain Tradition

Phyllis Granoff
McMaster University

Speaking of their fellow monks, in institutional histories in brisk and sometimes fulsome prose accounts of their deeds, or in carefully crafted idealized biographies in the baroque language of courtly poetry; in fast-paced recountings of miracle stories and wondrous acts in service of the faith, or in the gentle language of praise in hymns and songs, was something that medieval Śvetāmbara Jain monks did often. They wrote of their present and former teachers and the older leading philosophers, scholars and charismatic leaders of the faith in a number of different languages, literary forms and styles.

Many medieval biographies are often preserved as parts of larger compositions, *gurvāvalis* or *paṭṭāvalis* that are histories of a given lineage of monks. The *paṭṭāvalis* were products of the period when local groups of monks assumed prominence and the religious community was divided into exclusive lines of monks or *gacchas* to which lay followers in turn owed their allegiance. Written both in Sanskrit and Prakrit, *paṭṭāvalis* have been preserved as independent written texts and in inscriptions and colophons to manuscripts. The *paṭṭāvalis* all share a definite sectarian purpose in that they were all written to establish the legitimacy of a given line of monks. They do so by transmitting the history of the patriarchs of their group, recounting in each case the succession from teacher to student and thus the continuation of the monastic line.[1] They also glorify their own group, detailing the victories of the patriarchs over rivals and the many conversions they made to their group. Many of these deeds involve miracles, and the accounts of the monks in a *paṭṭāvali* range from sober diary-like descriptions of ceremonies performed and places visited to lively and colorful miracle stories. Within a *paṭṭāvali* the biographies of individual monks may also considerably in length and over time individual biographies will change and grow, with miracle stories proving certainly the most labile and creative components of these texts.[2]

In addition to these biographies which constitute institutional history there are many other biographies of monks and of lay followers, called *prabandhas,* that were brought together in diverse collections. Unlike the *paṭṭāvalis* the majority of the *prabandha* collections have no obvious specific sectarian bias, but gather together stories about important monks and kings who had various sectarian affiliations.[3] Indeed some of the biographies in these collections are of non-Jains whose stories were famous in medieval India. Whether written in Sanskrit or in Prakrit all of these *prabandhas* are usually colloquial in style. Miraculous and dramatic happenings tend to dominate these texts and give them their particular flavor, while relatively little attention is given to lists of places visited or images consecrated. In contrast to the *paṭṭāvalis* we read little of consecration of images and pilgrimages, of money lavished on a ceremony of tonsure or the installation of a patriarch. By and large the cast of characters in the *prabandhas* is also different from those who figure in the major *paṭṭāvalis,* although stories of a famous monk widely told in the *prabandhas* can occasionally appear attached to a different monk in a *paṭṭāvali.*[4]

A third type of medieval biographical writing is to be found in ornate poetry compositions that obey closely the norms set for the courtly Sanskrit poem. There were only some prominent monks, particularly in certain lineages, whose lives became the subject of these long elaborate courtly poems that were more often reserved for the lives of the original founders of Jainism, the *tīrthaṅkaras.*[5]

Finally, many monks were celebrated in vernacular hymns and poems that in their simplicity and brevity are the direct antithesis of the courtly poems. The hymns and songs celebrating medieval monks vary in tone; some are closest in content and tone to the soberer biographies of the official histories, while others are closer to the miracle stories that dominate the *prabandhas* and some of the insitutional biographies.[6]

Taken as a whole all of this literature about monks is as varied in content as it is in style. It is a literature that spans many centuries, beginning most likely in the eleventh century A.D. and extending into the present time.[7] It is written in a number of different languages and must have served many purposes, from public record to private devotions.[8] Nonetheless, when set against the other dominant types of literature that speak of monks and that existed until the medieval period and will continue throughout medieval times, it is clear that there is something distinctive in all of this new discourse about monks.

This paper is an effort to understand that discourse and to investigate what were the various modes in which medieval Śvetāmbara Jains spoke of monks when they wrote biographies.[9] It is a study of biographies that come from the sectarian biography tradition and thus it examines the various ways in which monks were spoken about in a sectarian context, a sub-set of the total and varied corpus of biography writing that exists for medieval Śvetāmbara Jainism. The paper considers multiple biographies of two Kharataragaccha monks, Jinaprabhasūri of a splinter group in the fourteenth century, and the eleventh-twelfth century monk Jinadattasūri, who is considered one of the most important early figures in the Kharatara lineage.[10]

The paper does at times also step beyond this more limited mandate of investigating the conventions of sectarian biography writing, for we are fortunate in having documents about both of these monks that are not sectarian biographies; indeed they are not biographies at all. Both monks in fact wrote about themselves and we may add to what others said about them their own accounts.[11]

Jinaprabhasūri wrote an account of his deeds in his *Vividhatīrthakalpa*, a text in which he assembled many stories about the holy places of Jainism.[12] His account is written in the third person and is more of a memoir than an autobiography, if one allows that autobiography must deal with inward reflection as well as external events.[13] By contrast Jinadatta wrote poignantly about the psychological isolation of the monk who would pit himself against the majority and seek the purity of the monastic life. While he does not use the first person and the language of his text is recognizable as closely adhering to certain well-established conventions, his writing nonetheless affords us powerful insight into how he viewed his mission.[14] Both monks were also eulogized by others during their life times in texts that have come down to us.[15] In addition, both must have been charismatic leaders, for around each of them there developed distinctive clusters of miracle stories and new stories about them continued to be written many centuries after their death.[16] Finally, there exists for Jinadatta a kind of "counter-biography" written by a polemicist from an opposing school. It is particularly interesting in that it illustrates the importance biography could have in sectarian disputes; to destroy the authority of a rival group it was necessary not only to refute their specific doctrines by logical argument. Sometimes it was even necessary to rewrite whole genealogies or to recast miracle stories that enhanced the prestige of a given monk so that he would appear ridiculous in the public eye.[17] For both Jinaprabha and Jinadatta we thus have a wide range of comparable material which should reveal at least the range of possible modes of speaking about two of the Kharataragaccha's best known monks.[18] A study of the various biographies written about these two sectarian leaders should give us invaluable insight into the dynamics of sectarian biography writing in medieval Jainism and its distinctive characteristics.

I. Jinaprabhasūri

A. Jinaprabhasūri, *Kanyānayanīyamahāvīrapratimākalpa*, from the *Vividhatīrthakalpa*, 22, pp. 45-47.

Having bowed down to Mahāvīra, who is steadfast and immovable as the mountain of the Gods, the abode of innumerable wonderful qualities, I shall say something of the events associated with the image of Māhavīra in the city Kaṇṇāṇaya.

The image of Mahāvīra in the city of Kaṇṇāṇaya which is in the realm of the Colas was commissioned by the lay devotee Māṇadeva, who was the younger nephew of Jinapatisūri and a resident of the city of Vikkamapura. It was consecrated on a Thursday, which coincided with the full moon and the tenth day of the month of Āsāḍha in the year 1233 Vikrama, by the Glorious Jinapatisūri, who in fact belongs to my own lineage. The image,. made of marble and moonstone, is twenty-three parvans in size and when struck gently against a persôn's finger nails it resounds like a fine bell. This image, it was revealed once in a dream, when brought into contact with a certain mineral compound of earth, is capable of effecting miracles. The community of the faithful worshipped the image for a long time, in fact until the year 1248. In that year after the light of the lineage of the Cāhuyāṇa, the Glorious King Pṛthivīraja, had been killed by Sulṭan Sāhavadīna, the pious Jain lay follower, the honored merchant Rāmadeva, sent a letter to the community of the faithful in which he said, "The Muslims have taken over the kingdom. You must keep the image of Mahāvīra in hiding." They concealed the image in a heap of sand in a village called Kayaṃvāsatthala, named after the local ruler, Kayaṃvāsa, who was the ornament of the Dāhima lineage. The image remained there until the year 1311 when a terrible famine took place.

The sculptor Jojao, unable to support himself, set out from Kaṇṇāṇaya with his family for a place that had not been hit by famine. Thinking that they ought not to attempt to travel too far on the first day, he stopped for the night in Kayaṃvāsatthala. In the middle of the night a god spoke to him in his dream, saying, "There is an image of the Lord Mahāvīra exactly so many furlongs from the place where you are sleeping. You must not go any further. You will find a means to support yourself and your family right here." As soon as he woke up, in a flurry of activity he had his children dig up that place. And then he beheld that image. Delighted, he went to the town to inform the Jain community. With great fanfare the community installed the image in a temple. They worshipped it morning, noon, and night. On many an occasion it was left unharmed, spared the depredations of the Muslims. And the Jain community supported that sculptor and his family. The faithful Jains looked everywhere for the halo that belonged to the image but could not find it. It was obviously lying buried somewhere underground. They assumed that it would have written on it an inscription and the date that the image had been made.

Once, when they were bathing the image, they noticed that sweat was dripping from it. No matter how many times they wiped it clean with care and devotion, the image would not stop sweating. They realized then that some calamity would soon befall them. On the very next morning the army of the Jaṭṭhua Rajputs attacked. The army surrounded the city on all sides. It was then that they realized the great power of the image, which remained in worship right up to the year 1385.

In that year the feudal lord of the city Āsī, belonging to the lineage of Allavia, wicked in intentions, took all the Jain monks and nuns and all the faithful lay Jains captive. The stone image of the Lord Pārśvanātha was smashed to bits. But the image of Mahāvīra, unharmed, was loaded onto a wagon and taken to Delhi where it was placed in the treasure house of the Sultan in Tugulakābād. It was kept captive by the Muslims, who wanted to wait and see what the Sultan would tell them to do with it when he returned. In time the Glorious Mahammad Sultan reached Joginīpura from the city of Devagiri.

In the meantime, in the course of his monastic wanderings, the Glorious Jinaprabhasūri, who had succeeded the Glorious Jinasiṃhasūri, the ornament of the Kharatara lineage, as head of the Kharatara community, chanced to come to the city of the Sultan, Delhi. Now one day, when the ruler had gathered an assembly of learned men in his court and asked of them who was most wise, the scholar of astrology, Dhārādhara, praised Jinaprabhasūri. The great king at once sent him to bring the monk to him with all due respect. This was the evening of the second day of the bright fortnight of the month Poṣa. The king met with the monk. He bade him take a seat near him and inquired respectfully of his welfare; he listened to the monk's words of blessing, words that showed his cleverness and originality as a poet. The two talked together alone there until late in the night. The monk slept there that night and as soon as the sun rose he was once again summoned into the presence of the king. The king was so pleased with the monk that he wanted to give him a thousand cows and much money, an excellent garden and hundreds of fine cloths, a hundred blankets and many fragrant substances like sandalwood and camphor. At this the monk said, "A monk may not accept such gifts." And enlightening the great king on this point, he refused all those gifts.

But then he reconsidered, for he feared that the great king might become angry with him, and he accepted after all some blankets and clothing when the king kept pressing him to take those gifts. The king then had him engage in debates with scholars who had come from many distant lands. When this was over the king had two great elephants brought. On one elephant the king seated the master Jinaprabha, and on the other sat the Glorious Jinadeva, the learned teacher. And as the eight kinds of drums that belonged to the Sultan were resounding, as conch shells were blown, as sounds of horns and trumpets filled the air, as bards recited their verses, the monk Jinaprabhasūri along with all the members of the Jain community and representatives of all the four castes, was given a formal send off so that he might return to his retreat.

The lay devotees celebrated his return with great pomp and splendour. They gave many great gifts in the service of the faith. Then the Great Muslim overlord presented the community with a decree that granted safety from harm to all of the Śvetāmbara Jain community. The master, Jinaprabhasūri, sent copies of it to the Jain community everywhere. In this way the Faith was made to prosper.

On another occasion the master, Jinaprabhasūri, asked the king for a decree that would guarantee the safety of the great Jain holy places like Śatruñjaya, Girinar and Phalavaddhi. And as ṣoon as it was asked for it was granted by the ruler of the whole world. He sent that decree to all of the holy places. And as soon as the master Jinaprabhasūri requested it of him, the king of kings released from bondage many prisoners.

Now on one Monday the master Jinaprabhasūri arrived at the palace just as it was beginning to rain. The Sultan came to greet him. The great king commanded his nobleman, Malikkakāfūr, to wipe the mud off the master's feet with a fine white cloth. And when the monk had given his blessings and praised the king with finely wrought verses that he then explicated for him, the great king marvelled at his cleverness and was delighted. He knew that this was the perfect moment, and so he asked the king for the image of Lord Mahāvīra, explaining to him everything about it. And the lord who ruled the entire world unchallenged gave him that image after chatting with him about many different things. He had it brought from the treasure house at Tugulakābād. In front of the entire assemblage of his courtiers he had the image brought before him, borne there quickly on the shoulders of his equestrian nobles, and after he had a good look at it he handed it over to the monk Jinaprabhasūri. With great rejoicing and much fanfare the image was welcomed into the community and all of the faithful then together placed the image in a temple known as the Malikatājdīn Sarai. The master Jinaprabhasūri performed the ritual of sprinkling powder over the image after reciting some sacred words to consecrate the powder. The image was worshipped with much ceremony.

After that, in accordance with a command from the great king, he left the Glorious Jinadevasūri there in Delhi with other monks and himself departed for the territory of Mahārāṣṭra. The great king sent with him such things as he might need,fine seats, bulls,camels,horses and carts. And all along his way the monk Jinaprabhasūri stopped at various cities and there strengthened the cause of the faith, and everywhere he was honored by the community and he himself did honor to the marvellous holy sites. And in time he reached the city Devagiri.

He was welcomed into the city by the community of the faithful and honored by them. And in the city Paiṭṭhāna there was an image of the Lord made in his life time and one of Suvrata. The leaders of the community Jagasīha, Sāhaṇa and Malladeva and other faithful lay devotees made a festival for those images.

After that, Jinadevasūri paid the great king a visit in his army encampment in Delhi. He was shown great respect by the king. The king gave him a separate section of the city. They called it the Sultan's Sarāi. And he instructed that four hundred families of pious Jains should live there. And there that ruler of this evil age even had made a hall for worship and a temple. And in that temple that very image of the Lord Mahāvīṛa from Kaṇṇyāṇa was installed. Even members of other religious communities worship that image morning, noon and night, and both Digambara and Śvetāmbara Jains do the same.

"Seeing the great deeds that Muhammad Shah did in the service of the Jain faith, people thought that perhaps this was not the evil age after all.

And that image of Mahāvīra which wards off all harm, Mahāvīra who had destroyed all the defilements, will be glorious for all time, as long as the sun and moon shall shine.

This account of the events surrounding the image of Mahāvīra from the city of Kaṇṇaṇāya has written down by the lord of ascetics, the disciple of the lord of ascetics Jinasiṃha."

This description of Jinaprabha's activities in the court of Delhi appears in the *Vividhatīrthakalpa*, a compendium of such short accounts about the many holy places of Jainism, that was in fact written by Jinaprabhasūri himself during the first decades of the fourteenth century. The *Vividhatīrthakalpa* contains sections in Sanskrit and Jaina Maharashtri, the language of our passage. It contains verse and prose accounts, and is highly varied in style. There are a few sections of the *Vividhatīrthakalpa* that are explicitly said to have been written by people other than Jinaprabhasūri, and in those cases the text clearly says who the author was. The next passage that we will consider here is one of the few sections with a different author and its introductory verse clearly identifies the author as Vidyātilaka, disciple of Saṃghatilaka. Scholars have assumed that with the exception of these few passages in which a different author is named, Jinaprabhasūri was responsible for the final redaction of the whole of the *Vividhatīrthakalpa*.[19] Given the fact that he identifies the author of the Kanyānayana section as the distinguished pupil of Jinasiṃhasūri and the leader of the monks, both of which designations fit himself, it seems to me without doubt that we should understand this passage as autobiographical, that is, as the author telling about things that happened to himself. It remains now to examine the manner in which the text invites us to draw this conclusion and the possible models that a medieval monk may have had when he came to speak of his own deeds.

The account of Mahāvīra at Kanyānayana may be divided into two parts. The first section deals with the history of the image of Mahāvīra, and the second deals with the deeds of the monk Jinaprabhasūri.[20] I shall focus my attention on this second section on Jinaprabhasūri. Perhaps the most striking feature about the account of Jinaprabhasūri in this passage is that there is nothing intrinsic to it that would indicate that the Jinaprabha named as the main actor in the text was actually also it author. The account is of an author telling of his own deeds and yet it is entirely written in the third-person.[21]

The only internal evidence that the Jinaprabha, whose deeds are celebrated here, is also the author of the passage comes from two verses that frame the entire vernacular prose account. The verse at the beginning explicitly states "I will tell ..." and the verse at the end then glosses the "I" by closing, "this account has been written by the king of monks, the disciple of Jinasiṃhasūri, himself a king of monks". The "I", we learn, is Jinasiṃhasūri's disciple, and that disciple of Jinasiṃhasūri was as distinguished as his teacher. Both are called "lord of monks". Jinaprabhasūri in the prose passage is explicitly said to be the monk who succeeded to the high office as head of the community that Jinasiṃhasūri held, and it is as Jinasiṃhasūri's disciple and successor that Jinaprabha is known in the tradition in all of the biographies that recount his deeds. It seems natural, therefore, to identify "the lord of monks, disciple of Jinasiṃhasūri", who is the author of the passage, with Jinaprabhasūri, the main actor in the text. The verses, then, establish that the third-person account is in fact at the same time a first-person account, and that the author of the text is in fact writing about himself.

This is not the only section in the *Vividhatīrthakalpa* in which Jinaprabhasūri begins with a statement, "I will relate the account of such and such a place", then gives the actual account and finally concludes with another verse in which he names himself and glosses the "I" of the opening verse, saying, "this section about such and such a place was written down by Jinaprabhasūri". The style of the section on Kanyānayana translated here is consistent with a more general practice that Jinaprabhasūri followed for many of the sections or individual *kalpā* in the work; the only difference is that instead of naming himself, the "I" of the first verse, directly as simply Jinaprabhasūri, he names himself as the disciple of Jinasiṃhasūri. In fact this deviation provides some clue for uncovering what might have served as the model for Jinaprabhasūri in his autobiographical account of his own recovery of the Mahāvīra image of Kanyānayanatirtha. For the first question that aries from our texts is what is the precedent for a monk speaking of his own deeds and what are the possible pre-existing literary models that Jinaprabha might have exploited in writing his memoir. What would have motivated him when he went to record his own deeds to record them entirely in the thrid-person, following the third-person format so closely that he even speaks of himself in honorifics?[22]

There does exist a well-established convention in medieval India writing in which an author of a text speaks of himself. This is in a *praśasti* or colophon that appears at the end of a text. In such a colophon an author may do a number of things. He usually begins by giving a detailed history of his lineage, either his family lineage if he is not a monk, or his monastic lineage if he is a monk.

The author speaks of himself in this lineage as primarily a student of a particular teacher, and it is as such that he most clearly identifies himself. He may then describe the circumstances of the composition of his work, and finally make a prayer that his work will bring peace and pleasure to its readers.[23] But even more telling for the present ivestigation is the observation that may *praśastis* combine both third-person accounts with a first-person statement that identifies the prime actor of the text with the author himself. We will return to this point below.

If we assume that Jinaprabhasūri in his account of his own activities is following the format known for the *praśasti*, we can understand many of the peculiarities of his writing. We can understand both why he prefers to designate himself as the disciple of his teacher, rather than with his own given monastic name, Jinaprabha, and why he utilizes the third-person for a description of his own deeds. The author of a text in talking about himself in a *praśasti* did both these things; spoke with emphasis on his lineage and his role as the disciple of his teacher, and used the third-person to describe his own deeds.[24]

We may also understand where Jinaprabhasūri might have found a precedent for capping his third-person verse, and calling our attention in this way to the fact that the person who is being talked about objectively by name and third-person pronouns, is actually the "I", the speaker of the text. There are many *praśastis* that similarly switch between third-person and first-person. Such passages may rely most heavily on the third-person, which they use for the description of the lineage and even for the description of the circumstances of the composition of the text, but they will add a statement in the first-person that makes clear that the third-person is also the "I", the speaker of the *praśasti.* The effect of this contiguous usage of third-person naming and first-person identifying verse is that we see the author of the *praśasti* in two distinct guises that are then harmonized. We see the author first not as subject or author at all, but as an objectively named person in the public domain, a member of a recognized group or lineage or family who acts in a totally public, shared context. We are then suddenly reminded that at the same time he is the speaker of the text, and that what he is relating may also be private facts. An example from an actual *praśasti* might help to make clear both the literary conventions of such colophons which I would see as the formal model for Jinaprabhasūri's own "memoir", and the blend of objectivity and interiority that they involve.

One of the most interesting examples of the harmonization of objective third-person reporting with first-person frame verse is in the colophon to the *Dharmābhayudaya Mahākāvya,* a poem that celebrates the deeds of the Jain minister Vastupāla, written by the monk Udayaprabha in the thirteenth century A.D. This colophon also comes from Jinaprabhasūri's own world, in that it is a Jain text that celebrates the deeds of famous Jains, much as his own *Vividhatīrthakalpa* does. In the colophone to the *Dharmābhyudaya Mahākāvya,* its author, Udayaprabha gives his monastic lineage up to his teacher, Vijayasena, whom he praises in verse 8. He then tells how the demi-god Kappardin and the goddess Aṃbā appeared to a pupil of Vijayasena in a dream and told the pupil to write the deeds of Vastupāla. The god and goddess address the pupil directly, and what they say is quoted by Udayaprabha. They call him by the second-person pronoun, "you" and they call him by name, Udayaprabha. This is the first indication we have that the pupil of Vijayasena named in the lineage sequence is Udayaprabha, whom we know to be the author of the *Dharmābhayudaya Mahākāvya.* We then learn that after this vision, early the next morning, this Udayaprabha goes to his teacher and gets his permission to do as the dream vision commanded him; we are told that Udayaprabha proceeds to write the account of the deeds of Vastupāla. Thus far the *praśasti* has been in the third-person, with the exception of the direct quote of the command of the demi-god and goddess. Udayaprabha by this point has referred to himself both as Udayaprabha and as the pupil of Vijayasena. Initially he spoke of himself only as Vijayasena's pupil, which is in keeping with the conventions of describing monastic lineage; his own name appeared first in the divine vision. When we come to verse 13, however, we suddenly encounter a first-person pronoun. "How shall I praise the greatness of Naracandrasūri," Udayaprabha now asks, and he explains his debt to this Naracandrasūri, "for although I have written this poem, by correcting its flaws Naracandrasūri has made it famous." The identification between the author of the passage and its chief actor is finally made explicit; although Udayaprabha had described his actions in the third-person, even his dream vision is conveyed to us in the third-person, these lines toward the end of the colophon make it clear that the author of the *praśati* text was also its prime actor. The vision appeared to Udayaprabha, Udayaprabha wrote the text in keeping with the instructions of the vision and after securing the permission of his teacher, and Udayaprabha is the "I", the one who is telling what happend to himself and how he came to write his book.[25]

Udayaprabha's colophon is not an isolated example of the use of third-person discourse with a final identification of the third-person named with an "I", the speaker of the colophon. It is normal in such cases for an "I" to appear after an account written totally in the third-person, concerning that "I", often detailing his history in the form of his lineage, and his deeds.[26] In addition it is worth noting that a combination of a third-person and first-person statement is not entirely confined to *praśastis* in medieval Indian writing. A hymn to Śāntinatha written by Munisundarasūri, for example, shows a first-person plea to the Jina, "May The Lord of the Jinas, Śānti, whose greatness is praised by Munisundarasūri, protect me" (verse 21). Cleverly embedded in the verse is the identificationof the formally named monk, Munisundarasūri, the author of the hymn, and the expressed "I". The poem then concludes with a verse that identifies the author in the specific language of his lineage and confirms the identification suggested in verse 21, "This was written by the disciple who had obtained perfection in the mantra of the Gaṇadhara through the graciousness of his teacher Somasundarasūri, who was the head of the community of monks and was like the moon to the sky of the Tapāgaccha" (verse 14).[27]

It is not difficult to see that Jinaprabhasūri's technique in his own account of his deeds, if not consciously modeled on the style of a *praśasti* like Udayaprabha's *praśasti*, is nonetheless remarkably similar to Udayaprabhasūri's text both in style and tone, and belongs to a recognizable style of writing about the self in medieval India. Jinaprabha has reversed the sequence of the third-person and the "I" normally observed in such *prasastis,* beginning with the "I" and closing with the third-person, but he has followed the practice of the colophon in several important ways. In keeping with the emphasis in a colophon on monastic lineage he has identified himself primarily as the student of his teacher, and more importantly in his account of his role in the rescue of the Mahāvīra from Kaṇṇaṇaya and his other activities he has kept strictly to the third-person, just as Udayaprabha did even when telling of his dream-vision. Jinaprabha's account of his deeds, told here in the third-person with a first-person verse added, is thus not an isolated example of a monk talking about himself as both himself and another, an belongs with other such texts like Udayaprabha's *praśasti*.[28]

In fact there is some indication that Jinaprabhasūri's extended use of the conventions of *praśasti* in writing a longer "memoir" was not an isolated act. Jinaprabhasūri was not the only medieval Jain monk who wrote about his own activities in a Muslim court outside the context of a *praśasti*, but keeping closely to its literary conventions. Several centuries after Jinaprabhasūri, the monk Siddhicandra wrote a biography of his teacher, Bhānucandra, who frequented the court of Akbar. Siddhicandra took his biography of his teacher as the occasion to write about his own activities at Akbar's court as well, and just as Jinaprabhasūri had done before him, he wrote of himself in the third-person and much in the manner of a *praśasti*. Siddhicandra was much less hesitant than Jinaprabhasūri was about using honorifics and epithets of praise to describe himself, and it is instructive to compare his account of himself in the *Bhānucandraganicarita* with his briefer self-characterizations in the various *praśastis* to his many works. The similarities in content and style are remarkable.[29]

Medieval India, thus, clearly had established specific conventions for talking about oneself, amongst which was the format of the *praśasti*. Both Jinaprabha and Siddhicandra followed that format carefully, with only subtle modifications.[30] How many other monks wrote about themselves in this literary style remains to be determined; nonetheless it is undeniable that at least some monks talked about themselves openly and unselfconsciously, with established literary conventions at their disposal to do so.

If we turn now from how Jinaprabhasūri talks about himself to the question of what he says about himself several aspects of his account seem significant, particularly in the light of what others will say of him. While Jinaprabha does not hesitate to relate the supernatural or miraculous events associated with the image of Mahāvīra, his own deeds are ordinary by comparison and told in a matter of fact way. Jinaprabha first attracts the attention of the Muslim ruler because of his reputation for intelligence. When they meet he pleases the Muslim ruler by his skill and cleverness in poetry. This fact is mentioned twice in the text. It is noted when Jinaprabha has his first meeting with the king and it is then repeated when Jinaprabha asks the king for the image of Mahāvīra. The text indeed indicates that it was because his clever panegyric and the skilful explanation that he gave of it so pleased the king that Jinaprabha thought the moment ripe for asking for the return of the image. This is a familiar *topos* in Jain biographies; Siddhasena wins over Vikramāditya with clever verses, for example.[31] The monk soliciting a Muslim ruler for the return of a magical image is also a familiar *topos* in medieval Indian hagiographies in general. Rāmānuja seeks the return of a famous Viṣṇu image from the Muslim ruler in Delhi.[32] There is no hint of anything out of the ordinary, which is remarkable given that other accounts of Jinaprabhasūri will attribute the king's initial interest in the monk to Jinaprabha's wondrous displays of magic, and they will also describe the return of the image as the result of Jinaprabha's supernatural powers.

Finally it is worth remarking that Jinaprabha explicitly states that the image of Mahāvīra was eventually moved by Jinadevasūri and that it was worshipped by the Śvetāmbaras and the Digambaras as well as by people of other faiths. He also says that he secured for the Śvetāmbara community in general a proclamation that allowed them freedom of worship. We shall see that in the late biographies of Jinaprabhasūri he is regarded as a particular friend to the Tapāgaccha, whom the Kharatara monks otherwise heartily opposed, and it is stressed that he was a friend to all Jains. At the same time his miracles take on an increasingly anti-Muslim cast in these later biographies.

Jinaprabhasūri's own account of his activities is definitely not anti-Muslim, although it tells in a straightforward way of the Muslim attacks on Jain villages and of Muslim destruction of other Jain images. It concludes with a verse in praise of the generous tolerance of the Muslim ruler and a positive assessment of his contributions to the Jain cause. For this reason I am inclined to regard the anti-Muslim tone of later biographies as alien to Jinaprabhasūri's own account.[33]

At the same time Jinaprabha's text is notably un-sectarian in the Jain context; there is no indication that Jinaprabha as a Kharatara monk was hostile to other Jain groups, and he speaks of his activities as benefitting all the Śvetāmbaras. Perhaps there was something in his own attitude and its catholicity that promoted at least the later retelling of his biography in which this Kharatara monk appears as a champion and friend to all of his fellow Jains. It is also worth noting that a similar inclusive attitude towards other Jains marks the later Kharataragaccha biographies in the standard Sanskrit biography collection, the *Kharataragacchabṛhadgurvāvali*. Part of this text was compiled by Jinapāla, who closely followed an earlier text, the commentary to the *Gaṇadharasārdhasātaka* of Saṅghatilaka that was composed in 1239 A.D. The sectarian bias of this part of the text is marked; Kharatara monks are depicted again and again as defeating rival Jains. The late Kharatara biographies, however, emphasize that all Jains participated in the pilgrimages that were organized and conducted by the Kharatara lay leaders, and that all Jains joined the ceremonies that the Kharatara monks performed.[34] They tend to focus on an external enemy, the Muslims, when they speak of conflict at all. Jinaprabha's own statement of his activities in this passage on the Kanyānayana Mahāvīra may be seen to share the tone of other contemporary biographical accounts of Kharatara monks in its desire to embrace the entire Jain community, while at the same time it lacks their notably anti-Muslim stance.

B. Jinaprabhasūri, the *Vividhatīrthakalpa*, no. 51, pp.95-97, *Kanyānayamahāvīrakalpapariśeṣaḥ, "An Addendum to the Account of the Mahāvīra from Kanyānayana"*, by Vidyātilaka, the disciple of Saṅghatilaka.

"And now the monk Vidyātilaka, following the instructions of Saṅghatilakasuri, has something to add to the 'Account of the Mahāvīra of Kaṇṇānaya."

The chief head of the monastic community, the Glorious Jinaprabhasūri, prevented the Muslims from destroying the temples made by the Jain lay devotees Pethaḍa, Sahajā, and Acala in the glorious city of Daulatāvād, by showing them an edict of the Muslim overlord that granted freedom of worship to the Jains. He performed many great deeds that redounded to the glory of the Jain faith. He preached the Jain doctrine to those desirous of receiving it, and instructed ascetics in the various penances that are taught in the holy scriptures, both canonical and extra-canonical. He taught a variety of disciplines, logic, grammar, poetry, drama and rhetoric, even to pupils who came from Jain sects other than his own. He robbed the famed debaters, all of them so many mighty warriors of debate, of their much vaunted pride, and thus passed a good three years.

Now it so happened once that in the glorious city Joginīpura the Glorious Ruler Mahammad Shah on some occasion or other had summoned many a wise man to his court and as they were discussing important matters of religion as was their wont, Mahammad Shah desired clarification on some point and he remembered the excellent qualities of the master, Jinaprabhasūri. And so he said, "If only Jinaprabhasūri, head of the monks, could now grace my court with his presence, then I know that he would be able to remove all the thorns of doubt from my mind with the greatest of ease. For I think that even the preceptor of the Gods, Bṛhaspati, has taken refuge in the heavens where there was none to contest him and fled this earth, defeated by the light of Jinaprabhasūri's intellect."

Now Tājalamalikka, a feudal officer who had come from Daulatāvād, heard the master's excellent qualities being praised like this by the king, and always one to seize the right moment, he prostrated himself before the king and proclaimed, "O Great King! That great man is there in Daulātāvad. But the water at that place does not agree with him very well and he has become extremely thin." These words only made the king remember even more intensely the greatness of the master and he instructed that nobleman," O Noble sir! Go quickly and have an edict written out at the secretariat. Send the edict at once, so that the leader of the monks may come here again right away, supplied with all that he needs for his journey."

And he did just that and sent the edict. In time the edict reached the Divan of Daulatāvād. And humbly the chief citizen of the city, the Glorious Kutulakhan, announced that an edict had come from the Great Lord for the leader of the monks and that the Great Lord desired that the monk should come to the city Delhi. Within ten days, when the moon was in the twelfth day of its bright fortnight, in the month of Jyeṣṭha, when all had been made ready, the master departed; he was given a great send-off, and he was accompanied by many faithful Jains, laymen and monks. And wherever he passed through along the way, there was much rejoicing, and as he went he broke the pride of the Age of Evil, by doing so much good, and he struck wonder in the hearts of the people and their leaders in every district that he crossed through. He brought back to the holy sites something of their former liveliness and was honored at every step by crowds of learned Jain monks of the rank of teacher, who rushed to see him, jostling each other in their eagerness. And so it was that in the course of his journey he arrived at the glorious fortified city of Allavapura in the territory of Rāyabhūmi.

Now the most excellent disciple of Jinaprabhasūri, the Glorious Jinadevasūri, adorned with many excellent qualities, was a valued presence in the court of the ruler there, and fearing that the infidels would become jealous of the way that Jinaprabhasūri was sure to spread the Jain faith and that they might then do him some harm, Jinadevasūri went directly to the ruler who issued an edict protecting Jinaprabhasūri, and he ushered Jinaprabhasuri into the royal presence. And Jinaprabhasūri, supplied with all he needed at the command of the king, greatly strengthened the cause of the Jain faith, and after a stay of a month and a half in Allāvapura, he finally left that city.

And in the glorious great city of Siroha the ruler there too provided Jinaprabhasūri with ten pieces of cloth, of the finest quality, soft and smooth to the touch. In time Jinaprabhasūri reached the outlying areas of the capital city of the heroic Hammīra.

And at last, on the second day of the bright half of the month of Bhādrapada, the ruler of the monks, the chief among the monks, surrounded by a host of ascetics, learned monks with the rank of teacher, and lay followers, who gathered around him in great devotion and at the very sight of him felt themselves to be the most blessed of men, indeed felt as if they had bathed in a veritable lake of the nectar of immortality, that Jinaprabhasūri came to adorn the royal court. At the very instant that he entered the king's court, the Glorious Mahammad, the Ruler of the World, seemed almost to step forward to greet him as he lifted his eyes that were brimming over with joy to gaze on Jinaprabhasūri. And in a soft and gentle voice he asked the monk how he had fared. And the Lord of the Earth affectionately kissed the hand of the monk and pressed it against his heart with great tenderness. In return, the master gladdened the mind of the king by offering him a blessing phrased in highly original language, words that had just come to him at that very moment. The monk was sent with great fanfare to a hall that the Jains used for worship and that had enormous rooms. And the Lord of the Earth instructed some of the Hindu rulers and his own feudal lords, the Glorious Dīnāra and others, to go with the monk. Hundreds and thousands of lay Jains, who had been yearning to see him for a long time, bowed down to him as he went. The townspeople, who had also been eager to see him all this time, thronged the streets. And all the other subjects of the Muslim Lord, peoples from the outlying districts as well, gathered. And as members of the caste of bards sang his praises; as the regions of the heavens were resounding with the loud sounds of every conceivable musical instrument, lutes, drums, cymbals, auspicious conch shells, much to the delight of the king; as Brahmins honored him in the words of the Vedas; as musicians and young happily married ladies chanted auspicious chants, he reached the assembly hall belonging to the Jains that was in the area of the city known as the Glorious Suratāṇa Sarāi.

And there the men amongst the lay devotees performed in his honor a ceremony of welcome. And on the third day of the bright half of the fortnight in the month of Bhādrapada, in a great and joyous ceremony organized by everyone in the lay community, he recited the Glorious Pajjosavaṇākappa. And letters arrived from everywhere inviting him to come. The Jain community for miles around rejoiced in his presence. And he had many Jains released from the king's prisons on payment of a fine; and others, to, in his compassion, he had freed from the prisons; and he gave succor and made others give succor to those who were in want. And in many different ways he furthered the cause of the Jain faith.

Thus was Jinaprabhasūri ever vigilant in strengthening the cause of the Jain faith as he defeated many an opponent in debate at the court of the king. And in time the four months of the rainy season came to an end and as they entered the month of Phālguna, the mother of the Sultan, whose name was Magadūmaī Jahāṃ, was due to arrive from Daulatāvād, and so the Sultan set off with a completely equipped army to meet her, and he fervently requested that Jinaprabhasūri accompany him, and so the Jain monk too set out. At a place called Vadathūṇa the Sultan met his mother. The Great King gave many gifts to all the people in a magnificent ceremony. Everyone was provided with exquisite clothes and excellent blankets. In time, with much fanfare, they reached the capital. The master, Jinaprabhasūri, was honored with gifts of clothes and fragrant unguents. And when the moon entered the twelfth day of its bright fortnight for the month of Caitra, in the shadow of a building donated by the Great Muslim Ruler, Jinaprabhasūri conducted a ceremony at which he ordained five new monks.[35] And he performed various rituals like the placing of the garland and granting of true faith. The costs of the ceremony were defrayed by the lay disciple, Madana, the son of Thiradeva. On the thirteenth day of the bright fortnight of the month of Āṣāḍha thirteen new images were installed with great ceremony. No expense was spared in those rituals by those who had commissioned the images, particularly by the lay disciple Ajayadeva, the son of Mahārāya.

And then one day the Lord of the Earth thought that it must be difficult for Jinaprabhasūri to come from so far when he desired his company; and so he gave to him a new building complex right next to his own palace, with so many splendid buildings. And he instructed the Jain community to take up residence there. The ruler himself named the section the "Bhaṭṭāraya Sarāi", the "Quarter belonging to the Lord of the Monks". There the Great Muslim Lord had a temple to Mahāvīra constructed, along with a great hall for worship and ceremonies for the faithful. And in the thirteenth year of the calendar as the Muslims reckon it, on an auspicious moment of the seventh day of the dark half of the month Āṣāḍha, as a great festival was celebrated at the command of the Ruler of the Earth, with songs and dance and music, with the King himself offering words of benediction, the Lord of Monks entered the ceremonial hall. And many wise men were honored with suitable gifts. The poor and wretched of the earth were rescued from their misery with lavish presents.

When the month of Mārgaśīrṣa arrived Jinaprabhasūri once more accompanied the Sultan, this time as he set off on a conquest of the Eastern regions. And at every stop Jinaprabhasūri furthered the cause of the Jain faith by such righteous acts as having prisoners set free. He restored the holy place of Mahurā. The foremost of the Brahmins were honored with gifts and presents. And then the Muslim Ruler began to think that the monk had indeed kept his promise to accompany him and by now must be suffering by having to stay in army encampments for so long. And so when they reached the city Āgarā he sent the monk back to the capital with the feudal ruler of Khoj, whose name was Lord Jahām. The lord of the monks took with him an edict that allowed him to make a pilgrimage to the Glorious Hastināpura and returned to his own quarters. He gathered around him the community of the faithful, monks, nuns, lay women and lay men, and he formally installed as leader of the pilgrimage the lay devotee Bohittha, the son of Cāhaḍa. And on an auspicious moment the master set out on his pilgrimage to Hastināpura, accompanied by a great retinue that included monks with the rank of teacher. And at every place the devotee Bohittha organized great festivities.

They reached the holy site and celebrated their auspicious arrival. There the master installed and consecrated new images of the Tīrthaṅkaras Śānti, Kunthu and Ara, and an image of Aṃbādevī, all in different temples. And a formal ritual of honoring the lay devotees with gifts was carried out by the leader of the pilgrimage Bohittha and other lay men. The indigent were honored with gifts of clothing, food, and betel leaves. And on the tenth day of the bright fortnight of the monthof Vaiśākha, as soon as he had returned from his pilgrimage, the master Jinaprabhasūri with great ceremony installed the famous image of Mahāvīra, which had the power to ward off all misfortunes, in a monastery that had been built at the orders of the Muslim King. And there it is still worshipped by the Jain community. And once the Muslim ruler had returned from his victorious conquest, festival after festival was celebrated in the many Jain temples. The Glorious Lord of the Whole World honored the master Jinaprabhasūri with gift after gift, each one greater than the next. And with every day banners of glory were raised aloft by the Glorious Lord of the Whole World of Monks as he strengthened the cause of the Jain faith. And the Śvetāmbaras and the Digambaras travelled in every corner of the realm without any danger or threat, holding in their hands edicts of safe passage from the Muslim Lord. And everywhere his army had conquered, the Muslim Lord, pleased with Jinaprabhasūri, the ornament of the Kharatara lineage of monks, by an edict ensured the safety of Jain holy sites, like the Glorious Śatruñjaya, Girinar and Phalavardhi. And with such great deeds Jinaprabhasūri emulated the accomplishments of those great monks who had preceded him, the Glorious Pādalipta, Mallavādī, Siddhasena Divākara, Haribhadrasūri and Hemacandrasūri. What more need I say, for everyone can see how the Lord of Men, the Muslim ruler, won over by the excellent qualities of the master Jinaprabhasūri, performs so many services for the Jain faith.

Every morning as the sun rises the auspicious sounds of conch shells reverberate from the many Jain temples; in the temple to Mahāvīra the faithful carry out rituals and worship ceremonies at which every conceivable musical instrument resounds. Everywhere around the glorious image of Mahāvīra the air is thick with the dust of fragrant powders, of camphor and sandalwood, scattered over the image in worship. And just as monks did when the Hindus ruled, and the times were not so evil, Jinaprabhasūri roams freely, spreading the Jain faith. And the leading philosohers of all the other religious schools with their disciples throw themselves at his feet like servants. They await his every word like supplicants. And followers of other religious wait patiently at his door to serve him, eager to be admitted into his presence, desirous of their own welfare in this world and in the next. And the master Jinaprabhasūri goes often to the court of the Muslim ruler, whenever he is summoned. He persuades the king to release his prisoners. He never ceases to amaze the king with his words that abound in logic and substantiate the teachings of the Jina. At every step this monk, whose behavior is exemplary and who performs great deeds, enhances the Jain cause. He brightens the world with the moon beams of his glorious deeds, and his mind is as pure as the water of the Ganges. He brings the world to life with the revivifying nectar of his words. Both those who agree with his philosophical position and those who hold to other views respectfully carry out his wishes, just as obedient servants of a king dutifully and humbly carry out the king's commands. And this leader of the monks, the supreme head of the community, discourses on the Jain system of thought and all the other system in a novel and unique manner.

Such is the greatness of the deeds that he does in service of the faith, and so little is my own intellect, and so only a sampling of those wonderful acts could be related by me, though they are still continuing as I write. May he live for ever so many years; may he continue to advance the cause of the Jain teachings, this most excellent of monks!

Thinking that to praise even a fraction of the great deeds of the Glorious Jinaprabhasūri would further the cause of the faith, I have told this addendum to the account of the Mahāvīra at Kaṇṇāṇaya."

Vidyātilaka, disciple of Saṃghatilaka, clearly describes his account of the deeds of Jinaprabhasūri as a continuation of or addendum to Jinaprabha's own description of some of his activities that formed the section of the *Vividhatīrthakalpa* on the Mahāvīra of Kaṇṇāṇaya. It is, however, much more than a simple continuation of Jinaprabha's text and differs significantly from it in style and in emphasis.

Vidyātilaka employs two distinct styles of writing which he keeps neatly apart. In fact his text can be divided into two sections simply on the basis of the way in which Vidyātilaka has described Jinaprabhasūri and his deeds. One mode of writing that Vidyātilaka exploits is already familiar to us from Jinaprabhasūri's own account; when he comes to detailing what Jinaprabhasūri actually did Vidyātilaka uses short, simple sentences and few compounds, and offers us a matter-of-fact direct statement of events. This is the language of the simple story, the *Hitopadeśa,* for example, and is a mode of writing that was often favoured by medieval authors either for didactic stories or in the writing of the accounts of famous monks. Many of the *prabandhas* in Rājaśekhara's *Prabandhakosá* are an excellent example of this kind of writing.

The second style that Vidyātilaka employs brings us nearer to the world of the formal encomium. With its honorifics, its majestic similes, its long sentences and more complicated compounds it is a language closer to that known from celebratory inscriptions and panegyrics, benedictory verses and the ornate poetic compositions, which in the Jain tradition were often written to praise the deeds of the Tīrthaṅkaras. Vidyātilaka begins in this more formal style, setting the tone for his later matter-of-fact recitation of Jinaprabhasūri's actual deeds. In this more ornate mode Vidyātilaka speaks in glowing honorifics of Jinaprabhasūri, and utilizes compound sentences to dazzle the reader with the sheer abundance of Jinaprabha's many wonderful deeds. Before turning to a consideration of the actual content of Vidyātilaka's account it is instructive to consider these points of style.

While reference has been made above to the fact that Jinaprabhasūri, speaking of himself in the third-person, occasionally referred to himself with an honorific epithet, by and large his prose was unembellished and even the honorific phrases he used were simple and modest. He called himself, for example, the lord of monks, *muninda,* which he also called his teacher. As much as an honorific, this term can also be understood as a simple statement of a title: both Jinaprabha and his teacher held the office of chief monk of their branch of the Kharatara group; both were in fact kings or rulers over the other monks. Jinaprabhasūri also prefaced his own name with the honorific *Siri*, but in a way that made his use of the term highly nuanced. For one, the prefix *siri* was so widely used in Jinaprabhasūri's time before proper nouns that it is possible that its honorific implications may have been quite blunted. *Siri* may have well served as a neutral marker placed by convention before a person's name, much like our "Mr", and much as it is used today in modern Indian languages. In any case the strength of the honorific as Jinaprabha has used it is greatly reduced by the fact that in the same sentence he has also referred to his teacher but in much more expansive terms. For his teacher he uses the words."*KharayaragacchālaṅkārasiriJinasiṃhasūri*", the Glorious Jinasimhasūri, the Ornament of the lineage of Kharatara monks." His own name, preceded by the bare *Siri,* seems considerably less distinguished.

Jinaprabhasūri's account also conveys the impression that he is humble and modest about his own deeds. To a great extent this impression is derived from the way in which he describes those deeds. In medieval India there was a clearly marked attitude towards discourse that associated the ornate and difficult, the complex and arcane with the learned culture of the court, and the simple and the readily understandable with the ignorant masses.[36] More specifically the classical Indian author also had available to him clear rules for what was the fitting subject for these different types of writing. The subject of the drama, for example, by definition was noble in character, compassionate, chaste, soft-spoken, and heroic.[37] The hero of the courtly poem or *mahākāvya* had to meet similar specifications, for the fit subject of a *mahākāvya* was a celebrated historical personage or a god.[38] There was no such restriction on the simple prose tale, and common experience in fact revealed that the subjects of stories told in simple language were far more varied and modest; animals, rogues, and fools could all be fitting subjects for the simple prose story, but never for the ornate poem.

A natural corollary to all of this discussion was that the type of language used in a description of someone's deeds was a strong indication of the way in which the author was conceptualizing his subject; if the deeds of a person were the subject of an ornate courtly poetic composition, this meant by definition that the person who was the hero of the poem exemplified all the traits required of such a hero in the texts on rhetoric. The very way in which language was used was already a judgement about the way in which a reader was to interpret the deeds described.[39]

While much of the speculation about the fitting subject for the courtly poem and the drama took place in non-Jain writings, there is no doubt that the Jains saw themselves as participating in the general high culture of the day.[40] Both Jains and non-Jains accepted the same standards for judging works of literature and sought to meet them. Perhaps nowhere is this more clear than when a Jain monk, Devavimalagaṇi, sets out to write a biography of another Jain monk, Hīravijaya, in the form of a courtly poem and consciously seeks to emulate that most celebrated of medieval Sanskrit compositions, Śrī Harṣa's *Naiṣadhacarita.* In his commentary Devavimalagaṇi takes great pains to point out the many resemblances his verses have to verses in the *Naiṣadha;* he often illustrates how his own use of rare words finds a precedent in Śrī Harṣa's poem, and by so doing indicates that his work is in no way inferior to Śrī Harṣa's acclaimed masterpiece.[41] Jinaprabhasūri's writing by contrast is untouched by any traces of the baroque language of the *mahākāvya,* and at least to me as a reader this fact contributes to the impression that he is modestly describing his own deeds.

Vidyātilaka, on the other hand, in addition to offering a matter-of-fact account of Jinaprabha's activities, brings into his text something of the atmosphere of the more learned courtly literary composition. For the start of the account he uses a much more studied and self-conscious prose which in its rhetorical devices, its parallelism and its preference for longer compounds, belongs less to the mode of casual story telling and more to the various types of formal compositions composed to honor great men. Vidyātilaka is also more generous with honorific terms.

In the very first sentence of his account Vidyātilaka calls Jinaprabhasūri "*bhaṭṭāraya*", an honorific title reserved for the chief pontiff of a monastic group, and a title that Jinaprabha never uses for himself. In addition, this long and complex sentence can be broken up into several shorter sentences.[42] All but one of the resulting five sentence fragments ends with a participle, implying that the actions in each fragment are to be understood as taking place at the same time. Each unit of this larger sentence relates one deed or type of deed that Jinaprabhasūri performed in service of the faith.

In the first small unit, the only unit to end in a continuative and not a participle, thus implying that the action of this fragment preceded the action described in the rest of the sentence, Jinaprabha is said to have secured an edict from the Muslim lord and prevented the destruction of certain Jain temples. By marking this activity as distinct from the other actions that the sentence will describe, Vidyātilaka from the start brackets for special consideration Jinaprabha's dealings with the Muslim overlord and his role in protecting the Jain community from the threat of Muslim attacks. In fact Vidyātilaka will focus on the close relationship between Jinaprabha and the Muslim ruler throughout this account.

The sentence then continues, stating first in general terms that Jinaprabha furthered the Jain cause in wonderful ways. It then proceeds to specify; he preached the doctrine to those eager to hear of it, taught penances to monks and nuns, instructed monks of various Jain lineages in the various disciplines, many of which are wholly secular in content, and finally, he was a great debater who defeated many a rival in debate.

The list encompasses most of the many roles for the Jain monk that are envisioned in the different texts that talk about monks. Preaching, teaching, debating are all roles well known from canonical stories and later didactic stories about monks. In addition in the canon and didactic stories monks, particularly the Tīrthaṅkaras, often give penances to other monks and nuns.[43] The role to which Vidyātilaka calls particular attention, securing the protection of the ruler, most notably a non-Jain ruler, assumes importance in these medieval biographies of monks, and is not as notable in other types of writing about monks. Some of the medieval biographies seek to justify the role of the monk at court by reference to an earlier tradition, and others as we shall see is the case with later accounts of Jinaprabhasūri, are at best ambivalent or judge negatively the very presence of the monk at court.[44]

The overall effect of the sentence, with its piling up of individual potentially independent units, and its careful naming of several major roles ascribed to monks in medieval texts, is to impress on the reader at the very start of the account both the great extent and the comprehensive nature of Jinaprabhasūri's activities. It also in its more formal tone conveys something of the seriousness of the subject, the great deeds of the monk; even recording and telling those deeds, Vidyātilaka himself tells us at the very end of the account, is itself a service to the faith.

Vidyātilaka continues to use the complex sentence as he introduces us to Jinaprabhasūri's deeds and this style of writing reaches its culmination in an expansive sentence in which we finally see Jinaprabhasūri reaching the court of the Muslim ruler and receiving the honors that are his due. This complex sentence is in marked contrast to the manner in which the actions of other characters have been portrayed up to this point in the text. Early in the account, for example, a feudal lord is sent to fetch Jinaprabhasūri, and what he does is described in the same choppy short sentences that Jinaprabhasūri had used to describe his own activities and that I believe is more associated with the commonplace events in a simple story. The last complex sentence of the text, the sentence which describes Jinaprabhasūri proceeding to the hall in the Sultan Sarāi, is nearly three lines long: we hear how the monk was praised by bards, serenaded by musical instruments, offered worship by Brahmins and sung to by lovely women and musicians. The piling up of sentence upon sentence without a break makes the importance of the occasion almost palpable. It is difficult not to come away with a sense of the splendour and the excitement of the event. From the opening sentence, with its running account of all of Jinaprabhasūri's roles, to this long sentence describing the honor accorded him, we thus gain a clear sense of the greatness of the monk and his reputation. The style of the text then changes, after we have been sufficiently alerted to the nature of the hero, a fit subject for such ornate language, and his deeds.

For the remainder of the text Vidyātilaka uses a different style of writing, the shorter sentences that we are familiar with from Jinaprabhasūri's own account. There is a definite sense that we are dealing with discrete events, facts substantiated by names of lay disciples who financed the ceremonies named, and dates of when the ceremonies were held. The remainder of the text reads much like a catalogue of travels and rites performed by Jinaprabhasūri; we encounter the monk as a participant on a pilgrimage, in his role as head of the religious community who can ordain other monks, and in his ritual role in which he installs images and performs ceremonies. The monks as pilgrim and the monk as ritual specialist are prominent in some medieval accounts of monks, and providing a detailed account of pilgrimages, ceremonies and expenses for the ceremonies is one mode of biography writing in medieval Jainism.[45]

The concluding paragraph of the text brings together the two styles that Vidyātilaka has thus far employed, the long sentences with their overtones of seriousness and their implied praise of their subject, and the short sentences in which the monk's specific deeds were depicted. Vidyātilaka in concluding his account of Jinaprabhasūri brings back the complex sentence, though on the whole he keeps to a sentence of modest length, longer than the sentences used to describe Jinaprabhasūri's deeds, but shorter by far than the complex sentences of the opening paragraph and the arrival of Jinaprabha in the Sultan Sarāi. At the same time he employs the self-conscious poetic images of the formal language of inscriptions and the great poems of praise to the Tīrthaṅkaras. Jinaprabhasūri's mind is pure like the water of the Ganges; his glory is white like moon beams and makes the world pure. Such language is a common feature of hymns and benedictory verses, and it is with such a benedictory verse that Vidyātilaka actually closes, a prayer for Jinaprabhasūri's long life.[46] With this prayer, Vidyātilaka also tells us that Jinaprabhasūri was still alive when he wrote this account of his deeds.

When we turn to a consideration of the content of Vidyātilaka's description of Jinaprabhasūri's deeds it is also clear that just as the two accounts differ in style they differ in emphasis. Jinaprabhasūri seemed almost hesitant about his relationship with the Muslim ruler; at least he indicated that he was aware of the possible objections to a monk receiving lavish gifts from a king. He explicitly appends to his statement that he received presents from the king a justification for his accepting the gift: he feared that the king would be angry at him if he refused his largesse. Vidyātilaka shows no such discomfort at the idea that Jinaprabha was richly rewarded by the king. He lists the lavish presents that Jinaprabha received and nowhere does he mention that Jinaprabha was reluctant to accept the gift. Jinaprabha's reaction to being a monk at court will be a crucial issue in the later biographies; some will have Jinaprabha repent of his close involvement in the life of the court, while others will continue to celebrate that fact and will, like Vidyātilaka, emphasize repeatedly just how much the king favoured the monk.

Jain-Muslim relations are a central theme in each of the accounts, but here too there are significant differences. Jinaprabhasūri was neither hostile to the Muslim ruler from whom he rescued the Mahāvīra image, nor was he overly partial to him. Indeed by introducing his account with a history of the Mahāvīra image which centers around the persecution of Jains and the destruction of Jain holy sites by the Muslims, Jinaprabhasūri at least asks his readers to remain aware of the potential threat that the Muslims were to Jain security.

By contrast Vidyātilaka has only praise for the Muslim Lord. There is no mention of persecutions, only of patronage to the Jain faith. In the conclusion of his account Vidyātilaka even remarks that the many great deeds that the Muslim Lord did for Jainism are known to all. There is a sense in which after the first section of the text in which Jinaprabhasūri is brought to court the account becomes as much a glorification of the religious donations of the Muslim king as it is a description of Jinaprabhasūri's accomplishments.

Later biographies will treat this topic very differently; increasingly they will depict the Muslim ruler in a negative light. Instead of keeping the Mahāvīra carefully in his treasury, the Muslim ruler will lay it on the floor of a mosque where Muslims desecrate it daily by stepping all over it. To the complex issue of whether a monk should be at court at all will be added whether a Muslim ruler can be a trustworthy patron. In all the biographies of monks in Muslim courts there is never any question of converting the Muslim ruler to Jainism as there is with Hindu kings, and the tendency over time with Jinaprabhasūri's biographies will be to paint a darker and darker picture of Muslim antagonism to Jainism.[47]

Finally, it is also significant for any discussion of the various ways of speaking about monks in medieval Jain texts to note that Vidyātilaka like Jinaprabhasūri does not attribute Jinaprabhasūri's success at court to his ability to perform miracles. It is his learning and his skill in composing poetry that impress the king. We will see that this was not the only interpretation of Jinaprabhasūri's securing royal favour. Another account written probably not long after Vidyātilaka's and by a student of Jinaprabhasūri indicates that it was as a magician and wonder worker that Jinaprabhasūri gained entree into Muslim court society.

C. Jinaprabhasūri, in the *Vṛddhācāryaprabandhāvali,* pp. 93-96.

Jinasiṃghasūriprabandha

Jinasimghasūri came to occupy the position held by Jinesvarasūri. He was always sunk in meditation, concentrating on the magic spell to the goddess Padmāvatī. Once, at the conclusion of his meditation, Padmāvatī spoke to him, "You have six months to live." The monk then said, "Appear to my students. Tell them who will occupy my position." Then Padmāvatī said, "Go to the city Mohilavāḍī. There is a wealthy and pious lay disciple named Mahādhara, who makes pure his lineage, which is known as Taṃvī. He has a son Rayaṇapāla. From the womb of his wife Khetalladevī has also come the child named Suhaḍapāla, endowed with every auspicious quality. He will occupy your position under the name Jinaprabhasūri; he will lead the monks and greatly enhance the cause of the Jain faith."

Hearing these words Jinasiṃghasūri went to that place. He was welcomed into the city by the lay disciples with much fanfare. Then the monk went to the home of the merchant Mahādhara. When he saw the teacher, Mahādhara took seven or eight steps towards him to greet him. He honored him and gave him a seat and said. "Blessed one! You have bestowed great favour on me by coming to my house. You must tell me why you have come." And then the master said, "O, noble man! I have come to your house in search of my disciple. Give me one of your sons." And the merchant agreed. He dressed all of his other sons up in their fine clothes and brought them before the monk. He said, "Choose the one who most pleases you." The master said, "These sons are all destined to have long lives. Let them stay in your home. Give me instead the little one, Suhaḍapāla." And this he did and when the time was most auspicious the child was ordained. The ordination took place in the year 1340; he taught the child and gave him the magic spell of Padmāvatī.

In time Jinaprabhasūri came to be the crest-jewel of learned men. In the year 1321, at an auspicious moment, Jinasimghasūri installed Jinaprabhasūri as his successor. Jinasimghasūri went to the world of the gods. Thus ends the account of Jinasimghasūri.

Jinaprabhasūriprabandha

Now the account of Jinaprabhasūri is told. Thus it was that Jinaprabhasūri came to occupy the position formerly held by Jinasiṃghasūri. And because of the merit that he had previously acquired the Goddess Padmāvatī appeared to him in person. One time the monk asked Padmāvatī, "Tell me, blessed lady! In what city will I become famous?" At that Padmāvatī said, "You should go to the seat of the Yoginīs in the city Delhi; there you will distinguish yourself. So go now!" And so the master began his journey.

In time he came to the city of the Yoginīs, and he stopped just outside the city in a place called Vāhāpura. Now one time the monk had gone to relieve himself when he was pursued by some ruffians, all of them believers in the false doctrine. They threw sticks and stones at him. And so the master said, "O Padmāvatī I have surely distinguished myself here!" At that Padmāvatī honored those assailants with their very own sticks and stones. Those ruffians took to their heels and went right to the ruler Mahammad Shah. They told him what had happend with the monk. The king was impressed and said, "Where is that fellow?" They told him, "We saw him just outside the city." He instructed his officers, "Go and bring him here so that I may see him." And so they went to the master and said, "Come, holy man, to see our king. Come with us!" And so it was that the teacher went as far as the palace gate, where he stopped.

The servants informed the king. And just at that very moment that they were talking to the ruler, the monk said to his pupils, "I am going to assume the Kuṃbhāsana yogic posture. When the Muslim king comes you must say, 'Here is our master'. He will say, 'Make him act normal.' At this you should grab a piece of wet cloth and put it on my shoulders." With these words the master sunk into meditation. He was fully immersed in his concentration and did not stir.

Mahammad Shah arrived on the scene and said to the disciples, "Where is your master?" They said, "You can see, he's right here." At this the Muslim Lord said, "Make him act normal." Then one of the students wet a piece of cloth and with it revived him. The monk returned to consciousness and blessed the Muslim Lord with the traditional words of blessing, that he came to know the Jain teachings. The two began to chat.

The Muslim Lord said, "Master! I have a queen, Bālāde, who is as dear to me as my own life. She has been possessed by some demi-god. She will not get dressed nor will she take care of herself. Please, come see her and cure her. I summoned all sorts of magicians and wizards and healers, but she threw sticks and stones at all of them." And so the monk went. When he saw the queen he shouted, "Hey! You scounderal! What do you want here? Go and leave her alone." The spirit said, "Where shall I go? This is a perfect house for me." The master said, "There's no other house anywhere?" It said, "Not one as nice as this!" At that the master summoned the protecting deity Meghanātha and said, "Get rid of him!" And so Meghanātha oppressed the possessing demi-god terribly. That demi-god announced, "I'm starved. Give me something to eat." "What shall I give you?" And so it said, "I like things like violence and murder." The master said, "Don't you dare utter such words in my presence! Now I will tie you up once and for all." And the master began to recite a spell. Then the demi-god said, "Master! You are supposed to have compassion for all living creatures. Why are you causing me so much pain?" The monk said, "Leave this place." The demi-god said, "Give me something." He said, "What shall I give you?" "Give me some wheat flour with ghee and molasses."

Then the Muslim ruler spoke up, "I'll give it to him." The master asked. "How will we know that you have truly gone?" That one said, "When I leave, a branch from that fig tree over there will fall. That is how you will know." And that is exactly what happened that night. In the morning the queen Bālāde was fine again. When he saw that the Muslim king was overjoyed. He said, "Beloved, what would have happended to you if that monk had not come?." When she heard these words she said, "My lord! He is like a father to me. Whenever he comes you must personally rise to greet him and give him half of your throne to sit upon!" The king agreed to do exactly as she said.

The king used to go to visit the monk. And he would bring the monk to his own place. He gave him half of his throne. And so the time passed, agreeable and pleasant. In the meantime the unrighteous and unbelieving Muslims spread their control over the whole world.

Now at this juncture there arrived on the scene one Rāghavaceyaṇa from Benaras. He was thoroughly learned in all the fourteen knowledges and he knew how to recite spells. He showed up one day to meet the king. The king honored him greatly. And from then on he was always hanging around the king. Once when he was there the full court was in session. The monk Jinaprabha, this Rāghavaceyaṇa and others were frittering away the time talking about all sorts of things. It suddenly occurred to Rāghavaceyaṇa, "Why don't I get rid of this awful Jinaprabha by blaming him for something." And with this in mind he used his magic powers to remove the ring from the finger of the Muslim Lord and stealthily stuck it in Jinaprabhasūri's dust broom without his realizing what was going on. But Padmāvatī told the monk what had happened, " Rāghavaceyaṇa wants to make you look guilty of stealing. He has taken the king's signet ring from him and hidden it in your dust broom. Be careful." And so Jinaprabhasūri took the ring and hid in the robe of Rāghavaceyaṇa's disciple without their noticing what he was doing. Mahammad Shah then noticed that his signet ring was gone. He looked high and low, but he couldn't find that signet ring. The Muslim king said, "My ring was right here. Who has taken it?"

At this Rāghavaceyaṇa said, " King! That monk has it!?" The Muslim king began to search the monk. The monk said, " King! He has it." Rāghavaceyaṇa turned his robe inside out. The monk said, " King! His disciple has it." And there they saw the ring. The king took it and said to Rāghavaceyaṇa, " You're a fine one for telling the truth! You took the ring yourself and blamed it on Jinaprabhasūri." Rāghavaceyaṇa was miserable. He went straight home.

On another occasion the sixty-four Yoginīs took on the form of Jain women lay disciples and appeared before the monk in order to trick him. They observed all the appropriate behaviour and sat down to hear the monk discourse on the sacred texts. Padmāvatī told the monk, " These women are really the sixty-four Yoginīs who have come to trick you." The monk took a good look at them. He saw that they were staring at him with unblinking eyes, totally absorbed in his discourse. At that the monk put a spell on them that paralysed them all. When the lecture was over all the lay disciples, men and women, set off for home. When those ladies went to get up their seats were stuck to them. The monk said, " It is time for the teacher to go about his business. Please, bid him your respectful farewells!" Then they said, "Master! We really came here to trick you. But instead you tricked us! Show us your kindness and release us." The monk said, "If and only if you will make me a promise will I release you."Tell us what you wish." "If you promise that you will never trouble any monk who is the chief monk of my lineage when he comes to your sacred territory, then I will release you." They all agreed. And so he released them and they went back to their own place. And so the masters can go anywhere and the Yoginīs do not bother them. They stand by the promise they once made.

One day the monk was in the king's court. A tribesman from Khorasan, skilled in magic, just showed up there. He walked right in and threw his own turban up into the air. He said to the Muslim king, "Lord! Is there anyone in your court who can get my turban down?" The king looked around at those in the court. At that point the monk said to Mahammad Shah, "See king, what I can do to him!?" And with that the monk threw his own dust broom up into the air. It knocked that turban right down. Then that tribesman made a water jug that a woman was carrying on her head stand still in mid-air. He told the Muslim king what he had done. Again the monk made the pot shatter and the water in it stayed in the very shape of the pot. The Muslim king said, " Make the water drip." And he did just that. The tribesman was humbled.

On another occasion when they were all assembled in the court the king asked. "Let those wise men here tell me how I will leave for Revādī tomorrow." All of them thought hard, then, and they wrote their answer on a piece of paper and gave the papers to the king. The king said, "Monk! You too must give me an answer." The monk then also gave his reply, using all his wits. The king took all those answers and hid them in his shirt. He thought, "What can I do to make liars out of them all!" And so he broke through the wall.[48] He went out and amused himself. He summoned the monk and all the others to gather at one particular place. The king said to them all, "Read me what each of you has written." And so each of them read what he had written. He said to the monk, "Read me what you wrote." And so the teacher read out, " He will break out through a wall, amuse himself for awhile and then take a rest under the fig tree." When he heard this the Muslim ruler was amazed. "Why, this teacher is like God Himself. Even the gods attend on him."

Again the ruler said, "This fig tree is so lovely and its shade is so cool. Make the tree follow me wherever I go." And he did just that. After they had gone about five miles the monk said, "King! Give the tree leave to go back to its own place." The king dismissed the tree.

On another occasion the Muslims had taken away the image of Mahāvīra from Kannāṇapura and it was lying face down at the gate to the king's palace. Everyone was walking all over it. Now Jinaprabhasūri came there. He saw the image lying like that. He went inside and announced to the Muslim king, " King! I have something to ask of you. Grant me this wish." The king said, " Ask and it shall be given." And so he asked for the image of Mahāvīra that was lying at the palace gate. And so the Muslim Lord had the image brought before him. He saw that it was exquisitely beautiful. And he said to the monk, " I will not give it to you." At this the monk said, " I have come here for nought." And the ruler said, " If you can make it speak then I will give it to you." The monk said, "If you will worship it and honor it properly then it speak." The Muslim king did just that. He gathered all the necessary things for worship and then he folded his hands together in reverence and he said, "Grant me your favour. Speak!" At that the Mahāvīra image extended its right hand and spoke,

"May the glorious teachings of the Jinas be victorious! May the beloved of the king prosper and be happy! May Shah Mahammad reign victorious on earth! May the monk Jinaprabhasūri be victorious!"

When the master explained to him what the verse meant, the Muslim Lord was delighted. He said, " Tell me, what can I give it?" The monk said, " This god likes fragrant substances," At this the Muslim lord said, " I give the two villages, Kharaha and Mātaṇḍa." The Jain lay disciples are always swooping down on those villages to get incense there. The Sultan had a temple built for the image.

The ascetic Rāghavaceyaṇa was defeated. The King's ring was hidden on the person of Rāghavaceyaṇa's disciple. He showed the power of investing a lifeless body with life. He took the Sultan to Śatruñjaya and made him the leader of the group of Jain pilgrims. A silk-cotton tree was made to rain down milk. The dark half of the fortnight was turned into the bright half of the fortnight.

A verse says: In the city Khaṇḍelapura in the year 1340 Jaṅgalaya, a devotee of Śiva, was converted to Jainism.

This is what happened. Once some people from Khaṇḍela, devotees of Viṣṅu, were earning their living by trading in things like molasses. They had been carrying our their business for some time. They had lots of raw molasses. Some servants were ordered to make wine from the molasses. And so they made wine and began to sell it. People bagan to call them wine makers. Now some of them, following the admonitions of the master, stopped making intoxicating drinks. Others were unwilling to stop making liquor and went right on with their business. That was when Jinaprabhasūri, following the instructions of Padmāvatī, brought Jaṅgalagūtta to see the truth.

Although this account and the one written by Vidyātilaka may very well have been written around the same time, we need not start with an analysis of style or subtle differences in attitude to establish the fact that they are clearly totally different modes of talking about the same monk. All three accounts we have been discussing were written in the vernacular. Two of them, that by Jinaprabhasūri himself and the one by Vidyātilaka, are largely matter of fact description of Jinaprabhasūri's deeds and do not relate any stories of miracles that the monk performed. In both of them Jinaprabhasūri appears at the court of the king as a learned and gifted scholar, capable of writing complex verse and familiar with all the traditional branches of courtly learning.

The monk as courtier is certainly a familiar figure in the medieval biography, but that is not the only guise in which a monk may appear at court. The monk as magician and tantric wizard, reviving the dead, curing possessed princes and queens, performing minor feats of magic, is also a familiar figure both in the medieval biography and in the medieval didactic story.

Some monks are always one or the other, courtier or magician; Bappabhaṭṭi, for example is always the courtier; Pādaliptasūri by contrast, is always the magician. And then there are monks like Jinaprabhasūri who are both to the tradition. Curiously, when Vidyātilaka compared Jinaprabhasūri to past Jain monks he included in his list Pādalipta, Hemacandra, Siddhasena and Haribhadra.

Hemacandra could also be both wizard and courtier, Siddhasena was capable of magic feats and pleasing the king with verses, and Haribhadra was known both as philosopher and as wizard, capable of making his defeated Buddhist opponents fly through the air and land in his cauldrons of oil. Vidyātilaka, then, in his choice of monks with whom he compared Jinaprabhasūri, would seem to have been aware that Jinaprabhaūri was not only the courtier he chose to write about, but also like the other monks in this list, a wizard.

It is not always possible to understand why one account will adhere to one model of the monk and another to a different model. Vidyātilaka's account is included in a text that is also largely a collection of miracle stories about holy places and images; clearly an account of a holy man's miracles would not have been at all out of place in such a context. The choice of which role the monk is to be depicted as playing is apparently not determined by any general contrast between vernacular/popular/magician and Sanskrit/learned/courtier. All of our texts are in the vernacular.

The determining factor is similarly not lay/monastic author or audience. All of our texts were written by monks, and although we do not know the intended audience in every case, a single text, for example the *Kharataragacchabṛahadgurvāvali,* written by a monk at the behest of a lay man, may vary in its use of miracle stories. The same may be said of the many *prabandhas,* written by monks for lay patrons. In these collections there may be the biography of a Bappabhaṭṭisūri, who is not particularly a miracle worker, and a Nāgārjuna, a tantric alchemist. This is true across sectarian lines and even over several centuries; the sixteenth century Tapāgaccha poem celebrating the deeds of the monk Lakṣmīsagarasūri, again written at the request of a lay Jain by a monk, has verses that celebrate the various heads of the monastic group, but by no means are miracle stories associated with every monk.[49] All of this suggests that the fact that a text was written at the express wishes of a lay patron does not account for the presence or absence of miracle stories. It indicates that there are other factors which governed the existence of cycles of miracle stories.[50]

It is also not prudent to consider the telling of miracle stories as a phenomenon that resulted as time distanced the biography writer from his subject. There are again too many biographies without miracles and too many contemporary accounts of kings, for example, who were regarded as divine incarnations within their life time. Telling stories of the supernatural powers a monk possessed could also be important in building his reputation while he was alive.[51]

My reading to date leads me to the conclusion that miracle stories tended to cluster around relatively few figures in the various monastic lineages. In the Kharataragaccha texts numerous miracle stories were told of Jinadatta and Jinaprabhasūri, for example, while in the Tapāgaccha Mānatuṅga and Dharmaghoṣa were the subject of many miracle tales. By contrast, despite the prominence of a monk like Hīravijaya in the Tapāgaccha, the main accounts of his life are relatively free of miracle stories.[52] This suggests that in fact some monks in the tradition were charismatic figures around whom miracle stories soon collected.[53]

When we turn to an actual analysis of these miracle stories, it is clear that Jinaprabha's miracles are often hostile in tone and involve some degree of aggression. This may be a reflection of an attitude that is evidenced very early in Indian religious traditions; Buddhist texts, for example, explicityly state that the performing of miracles is something that can be sanctioned in few cases, one of which is when a contest with heretics demands a display of supernatural power.[54] In Jain texts as well Mahāvīra contends with opponents by the use of often deadly supernatural power, and the *Āvaśyaka* tradition tells of a famous contest between Rohagutta, the sixth schismatic of the Jain community, and a monk/magician who challenges him.[55] There is thus a clear tradition of magic contests and miracles as aggressive acts.

From the very beginning the *Vṛddhācāryaprabandhāvali* biography sets the stage for the kind of miracles the Jinaprabhasūri will perform with their aggressive tone. Jinaprabhasūri is first assaulted by unbelievers, "ruffians", or as the text puts it "aṇāriyas", non-Aryans, which is a standard pejorative epithet applied to the Muslims. His miracle, performed by Padmāvatī on his behalf, involves assaulting the assaulters. The whole incident is described with a lightness and a touch of humor, both characteristic of miracle stories about monks. Jinaprabhasūri has been promised by the goddess that he will achieve greatness in Delhi and it is on the basis of her words that he has gone there. When he is attacked by some Muslims at a most inopportune moment he upbraids the goddess with sharp words, reminding her of her promise and chiding her at its sorry result. It is these moments in the miracle story biographies that give them so much warmth and make them so human, when the monk reacts to his situation as indeed we too might react. Despite the extraordinary nature of many of the feats he will perform, he is not as distanced from us as might be expected, brought close to our emotional world with descriptions like this one of the monk's own psychological reaction to the events around him.

The second miracle recalls the conversion miracles of Rajput princes related in many stories that tell of the origins of the Jain clans, and is also violent and aggressive.[56] The victim is a demi-god possessing a princess and while it may be true that he is not intended to attract much sympathy, nonetheless he is hard pressed by Jinaprabhasūri and must remind him in crisp words that it ill befits Jinaprabhasūri as a monk who has vowed to treat all creatures with compassion to mistreat even a wicked demi-god. Again their exchange is humorous; it also highlights the dramatic tension in a biography such as this one between the normative duties of a monk and the normative description of a monk on the one hand and the monk in his role as miracle-worker and wizard, on the other hand. Normative accounts of a monk and the behavior appropriate for a monk of course emphasize the monk's compassion to all living beings; there is something of the forbidden in Jinaprabhasūri's routing of the demi-god, as there is in many of his miracles and his reactions to aggressors. Some of this tension is no doubt dissipated by the humorous way in which it is here openly acknowledged, the mad and by nature immoral demi-god citing religious ideals to serve his own ends, a scenario that recalls the many funny stories in the Indian tradition of the hypocritical but clever aggressor teaching religion to his prey from texts like the *Hitopadeśa* and *Pañcatantra*.

The next sets of miracles are similarly conducted in an agonistic setting and are particularly important for any consideration of the development that the miracle story biography of Jinaprabhasūri will undergo. These miracles also alert us to another well-established story-type that may have contributed to the form Jinaprabhasūri's miracle story biography takes at this point. Jinaprabha was first introduced to us as a tantric adept; he engages in tantric meditation (Kuṃbhāsana) and recites *mantras* or spells to the Goddess Padmāvatī. It is as a tantric adept that he cures the queen of possession, reciting his spells once more. But in the next scene, when Rāghavaceyaṇa comes to the king's court and Jinaprabha vies with him, Jinaprabhasūri acts not so much as tantric adept, muttering spells or performing special rituals; he outdoes his rival with a simple trick of conjuring. Rāghavaceyaṇa, about whom we know only that he comes from Benaras, is skilled in magic and is a Hindu, comes as a magician to the king's court and Jinaprabhasūri defeats him as a more skilled magician. The tribesman from Khorasan who appears slightly later is also a conjurer and is defeated at his own game. The fact that he comes from afar, from beyond the pale of Indian civilization, may be another clue to the nature of the type-scene we have here: a magician comes to court, performs feats of conjuring and thereby makes the king realize the true nature of things and accept the true religion.

One of the best known stories of the magician in the king's court comes from the *Yogavāsiṣṭha.* This is the story of King Lavaṇa, who is sitting on his throne when a magician enters his court and waves his wand. The king then sees a man from Sindh appear, leading a horse. With this King Lavaṇa's adventures begin; he will experience life as an untouchable, see himself about to commit suicide and then wake up right back in his throne hall. He will have the unusual experience of seeking and finding external verification for his visions induced by the magician and ultimately he will make an important conclusion about the nature of reality; the magician and his conjuring trick will lead him to a realization about what is the true religious vision.[57] Sindh occupies the same place in medieval Indian mental geography that Khorasan does, and when I read the story of Jinaprabha and the unexpected guest from Khorasan I was immediately reminded of the magician who appeared to Lavaṇa and caused the man from Sindh to lead the king on his journey.

The Jain story tradition tells remarkably similar stories about magicians who suddenly appear out of nowhere in a king's court and perform feats of conjuring that then ultimately lead the king to an awareness of a religious truth. Hemacandra in his *Triṣaṣṭiśalakāpuruṣacarita,* volume 2, chapter 6, tells of a magician who appeared at the court of a king. He is rebuked by the king who disparages magic and returns in the guise of an astrologer, a Jain, who knows the future. He predicts the end of the world much to the hilarity of the king's courtiers, all of whom are Brahmins and thus Hindu. The Brahmins have the king seize the Jain astrologer when the prediction does not seem to be coming true, but much to their shock and dismay, they then hear the roar of the ocean as it comes to flood the world. The entire capital city is submerged, and like Lavaṇa in the *Yogavāsiṣṭha,* this king too is about to commit suicide, when he comes to his senses and the magic vision dissipates. The Jain astrologer explains that he was the magician whom the king had mocked and sent away. The king for his part takes away from the whole experience a decidedly serious religious lesson, that is very much like Lavaṇa's lesson in the *Yogavāsiṣṭha:* he realizes that the magic vision has taught him nothing less than the very nature of visible reality. Transmigratory existence has no more substantiality than a conjurer's trick. Hemacandra tells one more story of a magician at a king's court who again performs a feat of conjuring and thus enlightens a king.

I believe that Jinaprabha's encounters with the magician Rāghavaceyaṇa and the tribesman of Khorasan are variants on this obviously popular theme. Like the astrologer/magician who predicts and causes to appear a vision of the end of the world, Jinaprabhasūri must perform his magic in an agonistic setting. Rāghavaceyaṇa, the Brahmin, is trying to destroy him by making him out to be a thief; the tribesman offers a general challenge to all the courtiers. The ultimate result of all of Jinaprabha's magic is also to impress the king with the greatness of the Jain religion, although one obvious difference is that Muslims never convert in the many stories the Jains told of them; they only stop their persecutions and come to respect individual monks or a particular non-Muslim doctrine.[58]

Rāghavaceyaṇa's appearance at court thus may be seen to provide a clue as to how we are to interpret much of the rest of the text which is an account of various miracles that Jinaprabhasūri performs. Rāghavaceyaṇa comes as magician and Jinaprabhasūri defeats him as magician. It is finally in this role that he will bring the king to his ultimate realization that a Jain monk is powerful and Jainism is great. Over the course of time, as we shall see, this overall image of Jinaprabhasūri will not change although his encounters become more highly tinged with anti-Muslim sentiments. The tribesman is replaced by a Mulla, and the king's acts are described as more overtly antagonistic to the Jains. Nonetheless Jinaprabha remains both tantric adept and court magician throughout the various transformations that his miracle stories undergo.

These two roles are evident in the other miracle stories that the biography relates. Jinaprabhasūri bests the sixty-four Yoginīs, a feat attributed to other Jain monks as well, and similar to the heroic conquests of meat-eating goddesses that medieval Vaiṣṇava leaders as well as Jain leaders are said to perform.[59] He then rescuses the Kaṇṇāṇayana Mahāvīra, an accomplishment that does not have the prominence it did in Jinaprabhasūri's own account of his deeds or in Vidyātilaka's text.

Jinaprabhasūri here succeeds in getting the image back only after he complies with the request of the king to perform a miracle and make the image speak. In late medieval stories of conflict between Muslims and non-Muslims the Muslim ruler is often said to demand of an image a miracle or he will destroy the image, Rāmānuja, when he goes to Delhi to rescue a Viṣṇu image, must make the image move; Aurangzeb demands of Śrīnāthjī that it display a miracle or move out of his territory.[60] Another detail that does not appear in Jinaprabhasūri or Vidyātilaka is that the image has been ill-treated. It is lying on the ground at the gate of the king's palace where unbelievers trod on it in the ultimate sign of disrespect. It is not always Muslims in medieval Jain stories who so abuse the image of the Jina; in the traditional biographies of Haribhadra it is Buddhists who seek to force two Jains studying with them in disguise to step on an image of the Jina.[61] The story of the rescue of the Mahāvīra is also one of the miracle stories that will develop as it is retold, again in the direction of increasing anti-Muslim sentiment.

The text continues with other miracles. One of the miracles, the conversion of the merchant from Khaṇḍela, is introduced by a verse which is then glossed with a prose account of the event. This may provide some indication of how miracle story biographies like the present one were compiled; the compiler would seem to have had at his disposal a number of stories that circulated independently and that could be added to other miracle stories to make a longer text. The individual stories may have also circulated as short verses to which prose narratives were appended; such a process of transmitting stories is as old as story-telling itself in India. One result of compiling miracle story biographies from individually circulating stories in this way is that it could produce an account that lacked organic unity; it was up to the compiler to go beyond simply stringing together stories and make a unified text.[62]

Our text exemplifies well the difference between the two modes of composition. From the beginning to the end of the miracle of recovering the Mahāvīra of Kaṇṇāṇayana we have a skilfully organized text written in a uniform style. What follows gives the impression that in addition to his own text the author had before him another manuscript or manuscripts which related miracle stories about Jinaprabhasūri, and that he was in some haste to append them. He summarizes in one sentence those stories that he had already told; thus he says, "The ascetic Rāghavaceyaṇa was defeated. The king's ring was hidden on the person of Rāghavaceyaṇa's disciple." He briefly mentions other feats he had not described and then gives a longer description of the conversion at Khaṇḍelapura. The story of Khaṇḍelapura is concluded with a brief statement that this is how Jinaprabhasūri then converted Jaṅgalagutta, following the instructions of Padmāvatī, but the biography as a whole has no conclusion.

The lack of a proper end to our text is not in fact typical of biographies in general. *Prabandhas* are very careful about their endings; they often have a summary statement, "in this way the monk furthered the cause of the faith", and they very often mention his death. In the *paṭṭavalis* the biography normally concludes with the death of one leader and the succession of the next leader. Even in this *Vṛddhācāryaprabandhāvali,* a biography like that of Jinasimhasūri, who was Jinaprabhasūri's teacher, (which is the only important fact told about him), ends carefully with the statement that Jinasiṃha died. Vidyātilaka concluded his account with a benedictory verse; the biography was written while its subject was still alive, and so Vidyātilaka did not have at his disposal the normal conclusion to both the monk's life and the account of that life: the monk's death. Jinaprabhasūri's own account concluded with the rescue of the image and a statement that the image is now worshipped with devotion and care. This too was fitting given the fact that Jinaprabha recorded his own acts as part of an account of a particular image.

The *Vṛddhācāryaprabandhavāli* in other biographies that are miracle stories does conclude the biography with a statement of the monk's death. When we look at the biography of Jinadatta, for example, we read, "Jinadattasūri lived out his full life-span and then went to heaven." The fact that Jinaprabha is the last monk whose life is told in the text and that the biography has no concluding statement might suggest in fact that Jinaprabha was still alive when the account was written. In any case there is no doubt that the miracle stories told of him continued to live and grow, and we may turn next to later accounts of Jinaprabha and his miraculous deeds.

D. Jinaprabhasūri, from the *Purātanaprabandhasaṃgraha,* introduction pp. 30-32

Two factions sprung up in the Kharatara lineage from the time of Jinasiṃhasūri, each with its own following. Now the Glorious Jinasiṃhasūri practiced asceticism for six months in a certain cemetery in order to propitiate the goddess Padmāvatī. Padmāvatī then appeared to him and said, "Why have you worshipped me?" He said, "Give me the power to enlighten the king." The goddess said, "You have only six months to live. What would you do with the power to enlighten the king even if I gave it to you? Instead go to Vāgaḍa. There in a certain village are ten brothers. One of them has a youngest son who is only seven or eight years old. He doesn't have all his toes and so he walks a bit funny. Enlighten him and ordain him as a monk. I will appear to him in person even if he offers me just a bit of worship. And he will be the one to enlighten the king; he will greatly further the cause of the Jain faith." And with those words the goddess disappeared.

And that monk did exactly as she had instructed him. He ordained that boy as a monk. And when his life was about to end he installed him in his own position knowing him to be a worthy successor. After that the boy studied under the Glorious Mallisena, the author of the *Syādvādamañjarī.* He was known as Jinaprabhasūri. Whenever there was anything he did not quite understand in his studies he would kind of drift into sleep and ponder whatever it was that was causing him trouble. And he would know the answer right away. And so they called him the "Cozing Sarasvatī, Goddess of Wisdom." Now this Glorious Jinaprabhasūri was so naturally brilliant that after he studied the books, even just a little, all he needed to do was doze off and he could write down whatever he had learnt and he fully comprehended its meaning. When his teachers saw him do this they gave him the title, "The One to Whom Saraswatī Appears in Person". In time he became the one to enlighten the supreme lord of the Muslims, Piroz Shah, And with his assistance he put the finishing touches on his teachers work, the *Syādvādamañjarī,* and corrected it. That is why in the colophon to the *Syādvādamañjarī* the author wrote, "the full fragrance of this composition has been made manifest by the help of the Glorious Jinaprabhasūri." Thus concludes the account of Jinaprabhasūri's origins.

Once when the Sultan was in his court and having a discussion about matters of religion with Jinaprabhasūri some Mullah appeared. He made his own cap float in the air. All the courtiers were amused and amazed. At that the king looked over at Jinaprabhasūri. The monk raised aloft his dust broom and made the Mullah's cap fall down. The dust broom stayed suspended in the air. The master then said, "Let's see who can make it come down." And no one could make it fall down. At that the master himself grabbed it with his right hand. On the second day a pot full of water was made to hang in the air. At that the master, with the permission of the Sultan, struck the pot with his dust broom and caused it to shatter. But the water stayed suspended in the air, in the shape of a sweet-meat. By that miracle the cause of the Jain faith was greatly enhanced.

One day the Sultan said, "O, courtiers! If you put a lump of sugar in what do you get a sweet taste?" They all gave the best answer that they could think of, but the king was not pleased at all. He then asked Jinaprabhasūri. "In your mouth." And that answer pleased him.

On another day he put his own signet ring under his couch, right in one of its legs, and said to the monk, "Where has my ring gone?" The monk said, "It's in the city of the Yoginīs." "But where?" "In the palace." "But where?" "In the king's court." "But where?" "In your couch." "But where?" "In one of the four legs." And at that he pulled off one of the legs and presented the ring to the king. The king was delighted.

One day the king asked, "What's the best flower in the world?" Each of the courtiers gave the best answer he could, but none pleased the king. The monk said, "The Vuṇi is the best, for it covers the shame of Lady Earth." For saying this the king bestowed on the monk the title, "Coverer of the Earth".

One day the Sultan got up and was proceeding to his living quarters with the monk. They were climbing the steps, but some of the infidels had placed an image of Lord Vīra on one of the steps. The monk would not put his foot on it. The Sultan asked, "Why did you not put your foot on that stone?" He said, "He is called Mahāvīra." The Sultan said, "If he has such a fancy name why does he just sit there, saying nothing?" The monk said, "Because, as it is said, the demons are often more powerful than the gods. Everyone who comes on hard times would behave much the same." At that the Sultan summoned his men to move the image away, but even a thousand men could not budge it. When the Sultan asked the monk what to do, he said, "If you go yourself and lift it up it will move, but not otherwise." The Sultan did as he was told and moved it. He had a lofty temple to the Jina constructed right in front of his own palace. He asked, "O, monk! If you ask this Glorious Vīra something, will he answer or not?" The monk said, "He can say all kinds of things." After that the Sultan concealed himself behind a curtain and said, "How many Sultans have there been in my city?" And the Vīra answered, giving their number, names, and dates of rule. At that the king was overcome with pleasure. He asked again, "How many of you are there?" The Vira said, "We are twenty-four in number, beginning with Ṛṣabha." At that the king was so pleased that he gave the Vīra five hundred coins and flowers and food every day. All of this had been accomplished by the power of the monk's meditation and nothing else. The king had a temple of Vīra built in his palace precincts so that he could bow down to the image from his own room.

One day while they were talking the monk happened to mention the power of the "Magic Diagram of Victory." At that the king had one made at the cost of five hundred coins. The Sultan asked, "What does it do?" The monk told him, "Wherever this diagram is placed no enemy can tread." At that the Sultan took a mouse and placed it under his umbrella so that it could not run away. He let a cat go at it, but the cat did not even step within the shadow of the umbrella. Another magic power that the diagram had was that if it was tied onto someone's body that person could not be wounded with any weapon. When the Sultan heard this he had a goat brought and the Diagram of Victory affixed to its body. Many men with swords struck at the goat but not one blow hit its mark.

One day the Sultan was about to set off to conquer the land of Gujarat. He asked the monk, "By what gate will I depart?" The monk wrote down his answer on a slip of paper with all the details, put it in a container, sealed the container and gave it to the king. He told him, "King, when you get outside the city Yoginīpura, open this container and read what I have written." The Sultan did exactly as he was told. He read there on that note, "He will break down the thirty-one sheaves of the fortress known as Kākara as he departs."[63] He was delighted by the way the monk had foreseen his plans.

He assembled all his army under a spreading mango tree that was rich in fruits and tender leaves and gave much shade, and then he set off. He said to the monk, "See how pleasing to the eyes this mango tree is!" The monk said, "You are right." At that the monk caused the tree to spread a long shadow, two paces long, over the Sultan, and he made the tree move with him. The Sultan asked the monk, "Monk! Why is this tree coming along with me?" The monk said, "The tree will only go back to its own spot if you give it leave to go, and not otherwise." And so the Sultan formally bade the tree take its leave and the mango went back to its own place.

Now that monk in the course of a few expeditions made his way to Marusthāli by way of such cities as Nāgapura. At every village the local women came out to honor both the monk and the Sultan with gifts of sandalwood, flower garlands, coconuts, and rice. When he saw all the local women he asked someone who was standing near him, "Why do these women wear no ornaments, fine clothes or pearls? Are they being punished by someone or have some bandits raided the village that they should now seem so bereft of splendour?" That man replied, "O Lord! This place is just plain poor. That's all there is to it and nothing else." At that the Sultan, wanting to help others, gave to each woman gold coins, and bowing to each in turn sent them home. In this way the two travelled, granting the wishes of every poor man and woman on their route, and eventually they reached the city of Pattana.

The army camped outside the city Jandharāla. The Glorious Jinaprabhasūri, on his way into the city of Pattana, stopped at the monastery of the Tapāgaccha monk, the Glorious Somaprabhasūri. The Glorious Somaprabhasūri began to praise him, saying that it was because of his greatness that the Jain faith was prospering. He replied, "I have failed to observe the strict life of a monk, night and day traipsing after the Sultan! I have no independence any more. You follow the correct behavior of a monk. The true behavior appropriate to a monk is preserved in your monastery."

As they were talking in this way it so happened that the monks had taken out their purses for cleaning. One monk saw that mice had nibbled away at his purse. When Jinaprabhasūri saw this he waved his dust broom in the air. All of the mice came scurrying from outside the monastery to sit at the monk's feet. The monk said, "Say there, mice! Not even a worm would think of doing harm to monks like these. Why have you troubled them? I don't want to bother any creature, myself, Let's do this. Let the guilty party come forward and let everyone else go home." He banished the guilty party, forbidding him to come inside the room. The guilty mouse went out the door and took off.

Jinaprabhasūri stayed in Pattana for a few days and then joined some merchants who were on their way to Surāṣṭra. On another occasion, the monk was asked, "Monk! What is most holy to the Hindus?" He said, "The silk-cotton tree that rains down milk". At that the Muslim Ruler, acting as head of the Jain congregation, organized a pilgrimage, and performing the proper rites of worship, raising aloft the flags and honoring the Jinas with appropriate ceremony, with a group of one thousand Jains he set off, and with Jinaprabhasūri he circumambulated the silk-cotton tree three times and stood underneath it. At that moment, by the power of the monk's meditation, the tree began to rain down milk mixed with saffron and camphor over the Sultan and the pilgrims. The Sultan was delighted and they proceeded together to Girnar.

When they got near the holy mountain the Sultan asked the monk, "What is so special about this holy place?" The monk said, "It cannot be broken or destroyed. It is made of diamond." At this the Sultan began to strike the mountain with a hammer so that sparks flew out; but he could not chip it. Delighted with its power, he covered the spot with gold coins and worshipped the Jina Nemi.

During the night some Muslim gathered all the images in one place and proceeded to fall asleep. He told a group of merchants. "If these things give me some sign during the night I will let them be; if not I will grind them to bits." And with those words he fell asleep. But because the times were unpropitious no miracle occurred. In the morning the Jains told the Sultan what the Muslim had said and done with the images. The Sultan summoned him and said. "Did those things say anything to you or not?" He replied, "Nothing. Not a word." At this the Sultan said, "They all came to me and begged me, saying, 'That wicked one is oppressing us. You must punish him." And the Sultan had him held; it was with great difficulty that the Jain community secured his release. In this way, going here and there, fulfilling all the desires of all the people, the Sultan finally reached Yoginīpura with the monk, and entered the city to much rejoicing and celebration.

The account of Jinaprabhasūri that has been published in the *Purātanaprabandhasaṃgraha* belongs to a late manuscript and nothing can be said of its actual date. It is clearly in the same vein as the account from the *Vṛddhācāryaprabandhāvali,* though the changes in the stories are telling. From the very start Jinaprabhasūri is said to be destined to win over the Muslim ruler to the cause of Jainism, and the account will continue to focus on the close relationship between the king and the monk. The identity of the Muslim ruler has also changed; Jinaprabnhasūri now wins over Firoz Shah, the successor to Mahammad Shah who had figured in our other accounts.[64]

The importance of Jinaprabha's acts at the Muslim court is underscored in the text by a small alteration in the familiar scene in which the teacher Jinasimhasūri prays to the Jain goddess Padmāvatī. In the *Vṛddhācāryaprabandhavāli* Jinasimhasūri prays to Padmāvatī is search of a worthy disciple to take over his role as head of the Kharatara monks; here he prays to be granted the power to convert the king. That power is to be given to Jinaprabha instead. We are then told something of the young Jinaprabhasūri's miraculous ability to learn, after which we come to the miracles at the Sultan's court.

There is no indication of how Jinaprabhasūri first caught the attention of the king and we enter the story in mid-stream. The first miracles are variants of the contest between the tribesman and Jinaprabhasūri that we have already seen. In addition the Hindu Rāghavaceyaṇa had disappeared while the incident with the king's ring is retained. Here it is the king himself who hides his own ring. The miracles focus on the contest between a Muslim holy man and a Jain monk for the patronage of the king. The tribesman is now a Mullah and with the disappearance of the character Rāghavaceyaṇa there is no Hindu ascetic to complicate the picture.

As the story continues we see Jinaprabhasūri engage in clever repartee with the king, much as the skilled courtier does, and then we come to the Mahāvīra incident. The Mahāvīra had formed the focus of Jinaprabhasūri's own account of his activities, and its identity had been clearly given in the *Vṛddhācāryaprabandhavāli.* Here it is an unnamed Mahāvīra, and the focus of the story is on its clever bantering with the king, particularly its ability to name the king's predecessors with all their appropriate titles. The king's acceptance of Jainism is also emphasized in this account; he not only has a temple built but he worships the image himself.

The remaining stories concern the travels that the monk and the Sultan undertake together, again emphasizing their close connection. There is one particular new story that is of interest in that it shows just how flexible these biographies could be, particularly the miracle story biographies. This is the account of the meeting between Jinaprabhasūri and a Tapagaccha monk. Jinaprabhasūri expresses regrets about his close relationship with the king and praises the purity of conduct displayed by the Tapāgaccha monk. This is an ironic reversal; the Kharataragaccha began as a reform sect and they were vehemently opposed to the laxity of monks like the Tapāgaccha monks, who were often close to secular authority. Things have become a bit topsy-turvy as we now find the Kharatara monk embarrassed by his close connections at court and holding up the Tapāgaccha monk as the true monk.

In fact at some point in time the Tapāgaccha adopted Jinaprabhasūri and began to weave their own versions of his miracle stories.[65] This is clearly one of their rewrites, and it is instructive to pause briefly to examine the other major Tapāgaccha account of Jinaprabhasūri, the stories told by Śubhaṣīla in his *Pañcaṣaṣṭirabandhasaṃbandha* which bears the date of 1464 A.D.

Śubhaśīlagaṇi begins his text with an account of sixteen incidents in the life of Jinaprabhasūri. Many of them we have already seen and others are simple variants on the miracles we have encountered; like the stories in the *Purātanaprabandhasaṃgraha* they are Jinaprabhasūri at the court of Firoz Shah and not Muhammad Tuqlak. A typical example of these stories might be the following. One day the Sultan asks the monk, "What am I going to eat today? The monk writes down the answer and seals it and tells the Sultan,

"Open this after you have eaten". Naturally the Sultan finds the correct answer and is amazed. The only story that seems significantly transformed is that of the Kaṇṇāṇayana Mahāvīra. The image is now said to have come from Kanhaḍa and it lies prone in a mosque where Muslims tread on it. This places increased emphasis on Muslim/Jain conflict, a general trend observable in other late accounts of Jinaprabha.[66]

Not all of the vignettes Śubhasīla gives are miracle stories; a few are examples of cleverness and quick wit and belong to the type of stories we find in the medieval commentaries to sutras, like Malayagiri's commentaries on the *Nandisutta* with its stories of clever Rohaka. In some of the stories Jinaprabhasūri is associated with a lay disciple Jagahasimha from the Ukeśa clan, and it is possible that at least some of the additional vignettes in Śubhasīla's text may have circulated in this family much as the clan conversion stories did.[67]

Jinaprabhasūri seems to have been so popular in Śubhaśīlagaṇi's circle that stories of him are told throughout this collection. In story 309 we learn more of how Jinaprabhasūri came to figure so importantly in this Tapāgaccha collection of biographies and miracle tales. We learn here that Jinaprabhasūri was the disciple not of Jinasimhasūri, the Kharatara monk, at all, but actually of Vijayasenasūri, the Tapāgaccha monk. Padmāvatī appears to Vijayasena and tells him that he has only six months to live. She agrees to manifest herself to his student, and there the problem begins. They agree that there is no suitable student in Vijayasena's lineage of monks. For this reason Padmāvatī sends him to get the seventh son of a merchant Jinadatta. He does as he is told and this little boy becomes the monk Jinaprabhasūri.

The framework of the story remains the same, but a significant change has now been made. The story of the teacher searching for the worthy disciple is slightly altered. In the Jinasiṃha/Jinaprabha succession we have two monks in the same lineage. Here a Tapāgaccha monk must look outside his lineage and adopt Jinaprabhasūri, who now becomes not the head of the Kharatara monks but the head of the Tapāgaccha.

Jinaprabhasūri as a Kharatara monk so highly regarded by the Tapāgaccha that he is written into their lineage is an exception, but there is at least one other case I know of where a Tapāgaccha monk attracted sufficient attention from a Kharatara monk to have prompted the Kharatara monk to write his biography. The Kharatara monks were aware of the high regard in which Jinaprabhasūri was held by the Tapāgaccha. A late Kharatara *paṭṭavali* notes that Jinaprabhasūri taught many mantras to the Tapāgaccha monks.[69]

Returning to the *Purātanaprabandhasaṃgraha,* Jinaprabhasūri continues his travels with the Sultan, who by now is the head of a Jain pilgrimage, and eventually they return to Delhi. The text concludes neatly with a statement summing up the account, and saying that after all their travels the Sultan and the monk were welcome home with great fanfare.

The *Purātanaprabandhasaṃgraha* account is typical of the late expansion of Jinaprabha's biography. What is expanded is the miracle stories, and they are told in such a way as to focus the center of events on the Muslim/Jain conflict. The monk becomes even closer to the Sultan, and he also champions the cause of a new Jain group altogether, the Tapāgaccha.

There are other late medieval sources for the life of Jinaprabhasūri, hymns and songs, some of which have been published.[70] By and large those that I have been able to see do not emphasize miracle stories and continue the conservative tradition of Jinaprabhasūri's biography that began with his own account and continued with the account of his contemporary Vidyātilaka. It is clear that of the types of biography it was the miracle story biography that had the most potential for growth and change and the most flexibility. It is also clear that despite the fact that the biographies of Jinaprabhasūri appear in sectarian histories, their main focus is not intra-group rivalry at all. The biographies of Jinaprabhasūri when they are concerned with religious rivalry look beyond the divisions within Jainism and make statements about the strength of Jainism as opposed to other religions. On this point they are far closer to the biographies in the non-sectarian *prabandhas* than to other sectarian biographies.[71]

We shall in the investigation of some of the accounts of Jinadatta find the same range of texts as are exemplified here, but we shall see that these texts are more obviously sectarian in nature in that they are often preoccupied with the tensions that existed between the Kharatara Jains and other Jain groups. We have a deeply personal statement from the monk himself, a statement by a disciple that is eulogistic but not far in tone from the monk's self characterization, and a range of later biographies, many of which are collections of miracle stories. It remains to see what they can offer us in the way of other models that were available to medieval writers when they came to speak of monks.

2. Jinadattasūri

A. Jinadattasūri, the monk in his own words.

"He is properly called a good master, who speaks the truth.
Before him opponents retreat in fear.
He cares for all living beings as he cares for himself.
Asked the way to release he gives an answer."

Upadeśarasāyana, 4

"Now many are the words of the different teachers.
And popularly accepted practice is like a river that follows its own course unchecked.

He who has no boat in the form of a good master is swept away.
Cast into the swift current of popular practice, he suffers."

Upadeśarasāyana, 6

"That river of popular practice is deep and dank, and in its midst swim ignorant creatures. It is difficult to traverse.
How can People cross it if they have no boat?
Few indeed are those who have a good boat and make it across.
They find happiness after happiness."

Upadeśarasāyana, 7

"Those who are without merit do not find a good master as their boat.
The masses slip into the river of popular practice and are carried off.
That river empties into the ocean of endless rebirth
where there is no trace of happiness".

Upadeśarasāyana, 8

"There are some who, though they may live a hundred years, do only evil.
Even if they somehow become Jain monks,
still they do not abstain from committing sins."

Upadeśarasāyana, 16

"Such a one boasts to foolish people in a great booming voice; he spends his time making idle predictions and engaging in debates with hair-splitting arguments.
He brags, 'I shall expound all of the words of the Jinas,
and what is more I can discourse on any subject in the world.' "

Upadeśarasāyana, 17

"He keeps the fasts according to rule,
and his body is filthy, as if his inner impurities have come to the surface for all to see.
He wrongly interprets and expounds the holy texts,
particularly as they concern the rituals of confession and respectful salutation."

Upadeśarasāyana, 18

"He does not understand what the real meaning of the holy words is.
He too has fallen into the ways of common practice and is swept away on its current.
If someone learned tries to stop him
he jumps up and beats him with a stick."

Upadeśarasāyana, 19

"The righteous one seeks to resolve doubts by means of the scriptures. The false one resolves things by cutting the righteous to bits with a sword.
Surrounded by followers of his own ilk,
such a one is shunned by the learned."

Upadeśarasāyana, 20

"He who is learned harbours no jealousy.
And the others, well, as long as they live they know nothing else.
Those who adhere to the true path are few indeed.
And they are turned out by the community, who treat them as if they were outcastes."

Upadeśarasāyana, 21

"At every step those false monks search for weak spots in the good master;
and he being without anger, ever calm, does not suffer from their assault.
Their disciples, like wild beasts,
are eager to sniff out the good master's sore spots."

Upadeśarasāyana, 22

"Even if in these wicked times kings should show the wicked monks favour and give over to them the pure temples of the good masters,
still, the righteous monks do not respond except by discussion and debate, even if the wicked ones should come after them with clubs."

Upadeśarasāyana, 24

"The gods who protect the Jain faith always look with favour on the righteous monks who are devoted to the feet of their holy teachers and who praise the five worthies of the Jain tradition.
And those gods ensure that the good monks are able to complete what they set out to do in the service of the faith".

Upadeśarasāyana, 25

"Should the righteous monk, acting in service of the faith, be attacked and respond with violence,
still he remains righteous and his cause is not harmed.
He will abide forever in the highest place."

Upadeśarasāyana, 26

"They say that there is only one chief monk, leader of the community, whom the Jains praised in their preaching as the chief of the disciples.

He has many excellent qualities, and he achieves many great things in the service of the faith."

Upadeśarasāyana, 41

"Although not yet fully enlightened, that leader of monks knows everything, just as it is, through the power of the Jina, his own teachers and the teachings. And so what he sees is what there is; what he envisions will come to pass."

Upadeśarasāyana, 42

"He always keeps in mind the true teachings of his own great masters.
He is ever reflecting in his mind on what is true.
He cannot be bested in debate even by the most clever arguments;
he does not flee in fear from those who would dispute with him."

Upadeśarasāyana, 44

"By his pure conduct he delights those who are virtuous.
He keeps at a distance those who cannot bear his presence.
The gods care for his welfare.
And yet few indeed are those unbiased men who do him honor."

Upadeśarasāyana, 45

"Day and night he has only this thought in mind:
'Somewhere the true teaching of the Jinas is being lost.
There are so many monks who teach and follow a false way.'
But those who praise him are too few indeed."

Upadeśarasāyana, 46

"People are always looking for his weak spots.
Falsely they accuse him and make him suffer.
But through the greatness of his true religion he escapes their net, and everywhere engages in righteous acts."

Upadeśarasāyana, 47

"And yet he is never angry at those who would do him harm;
he never forgets his spirit of forgiveness, nor does he blame those who would hurt him.
If they approach him he converses with them.
And if what they say has merit then he is pleased."

Upadeśarasāyana, 48

"He is humble and never takes pride in himself.
He is quick to praise others wherever he sees the least little thing that is

praiseworthy.
He thinks, 'If people like them could cross the ocean of rebirth, I would be happy to follow them in all things.' "

Upadeśarasāyana, 49

"This is what the chief of the monks thinks.
And yet those wicked ones ever seek to cause him distress.
People, carried away by false popular practice,
neither desire to see him nor consider the consequences."

Upadeśarasāyana, 50

"This master is honored by so few people,
We do not respect him in our community.
Why should we follow him,
why should we leave our own masters as others have done?"

Upadeśarasāyana, 51

"This is what people say who do not know the true path as it has been expounded by Jinavallabha and his followers, the correct rules for behavior and the true way of serving the good master. They have fallen from the right path.
And so the masses pick fights with those who follow the correct path of Jinavallabha and his followers,
and they destroy themselves for this world and the next."

Upadeśarasāyana, 52

"You can find many people who have pulled out the hair on their heads and become monks.
But they still act under the power of passion and hatred.
They read, recite and explain the sacred texts,
but they have no idea of their true meaning."

Kālasvarūpakulaka, 7

"They practice religion insisting that what they are doing was proclaimed by the Jinas.
They stray far from the true path, devoid of a good master, wrongly reading the scriptures.
They revere as their master the one who denies the true course,
And they applaud his followers."

Kālasvarūpakulaka, 18

"They worship that what has been explicitly declared
by the Jinas to be unfit for worship.

Few indeed are those in the world who seek and find real jewels.
The fools in this world cannot tell the difference."

Kālasvarūpakulaka, 19.

Like Jinaprabhasūri, whose biographies we have examined thus far, Jinadattasūri also spoke of himself, but in a very different context and with a very different voice. I have translated above a number of verses from two Apabhraṃśa poems of Jinadatta, the *Upadeśarasāyana* and the *Kālasvarūpakulaka*.[72] Neither of these two poems is an autobiography, in the sense of being a complete account by an author of his life, nor is either poem a memoir, an objective description by an author of some of his activities. And yet both are extremely revealing of how Jinadatta viewed his mission: how he himself conceptualized the role of the monk in society, and how he saw his own situation.

We know nothing of the circumstances of the composition of the *Upadeśarasāyana,* though scholars consider that it was composed in the second half of the twelfth century, towards the end of Jinadatta's career.[73] The *Kālasvarūpakulaka* in verse 25 addresses several people who are unnamed, and adds that they have already been taught the true path by someone named Cāhila. The commentary explains that the people Jinadatta is addressing are the sons of this Cāhila. Cāhila was a pious devotee of Jinadatta who lived in the capital city of Gujarat, Pattan. He had four sons, who though by nature pious, fell under the influence of the corrupt times in which they lived, and begged to differ with their father on points of religion. They also wished to break away from his control and live apart from him. Cāhila wrote to Jinadatta and asked for his assistance. That assistance came in the form of a long letter, the text of which was constituted by this *Kālasvarūpakulaka*. We learn from the commentary that the letter had the desired effect; the sons converted to the true path taught by Jinadatta and espoused by their father.[74]

At least one of our poems, then, is explicitly said to have been written to exhort several young men to keep to the true path and abandon a false course. Since the two poems are so close to each other in thought and language, it seems to me reasonable to conclude that they were also similar in intent. We have, then, in the *Upadeśarasāyana*, "The Teachings as Elixir" and the *Kālasvarūpakulaka,* to repent, leave behind him his false way and follow the true course.

Both poems are infused with a sense of how difficult that admonition may be to carry out. Jinadatta speaks bluntly about the fact that most people simply do what they see others do; they follow the easy way out and fall in with the crowd. Jinadatta uses very conventional language to express this dominant theme: the ways of the world are like a river, and most people go with the current (*anusrotas);* only the rare and courageous individual dares to go against the current (*pratisrotas*). The language of following the current or going against the current is familiar in Jain didactic texts. Jinadatta had available to him a well-established mode of speaking; it only remained for him to make a slight and highly significant alteration in meaning to create the powerful sense of himself and his mission that comes through in both of these poems. In what follows I shall discuss what the tradition before Jinadatta meant by these two terms, and then return to Jinadatta's understanding of those who go with the stream and those who go against it.

A clear point of reference within the Jain tradition for Jinadatta's language is the *Daśavaikālikasūtra,* verses 543 and 544. These verses describe how the majority of people flow with the current while the man who desires release must pit himself against the current. Flowing with the current, the path of least resistance, leads only to further rebirth, while going against the current leads to release.[75]

Haribhadra, who like Jinadatta, was also regarded by the tradition as a great reformer, has commented on this passage in the *Daśavaikālikasūtra,* and the image reappears in many of his work.[76] When we examine Haribhadra's commentary to the *Daśavaikālika* and other of his texts like the *Upadeśapada* with the commentary of Municandrasūri, we find that Haribhadra has used these two key words, *anusrotas* and *pratisrotas* conservatively, keeping to the meaning that they have in the *Daśavaikālika* itself, and very differently from the way in which Jinadatta uses them. In what follows I have chosen to concentrate on Haribhadra's understanding of the terms *anusrotas* and *pratisrotas* in his *Upadeśapada,* since it offers such a detailed and unambiguous discussion of these concepts.

Municandrasūri on the *Upadeśapada* tells us that there are two main ways in which the river of life, the *jīvanadī,* flows. It flows towards further rebirth, *saṃsāra srotas,* and it flows toward ultimate release, *nirvṛti srotas.* The flow towards further rebirth is also called *anusrotas,* because in the words of the commentator, it flows along with, *anu,* the functioning of the sense organs. The flow that leads to release is also called the *pratisrotas,* for it goes against, *prati,* the functioning of the sense organs. The masses follow the *anusrotas* and remain in the sphere of worldly existence. Only a few seek the religious life and go against the normal functioning of desires.[77] The contrast in Haribhadra, as it was in the *Daśavaikālika* itself, is between those who follow a religious life at all (*pratisrotas),* and those who remain addicted to sense pleasures (*anusrotas).*

Haribhadra is not seeking to establish a difference between true seekers and false monks within the Jain fold, as we shall see Jinadatta does when he uses these terms. Haribhadra's text itself is perfectly clear on this point, for in the very next verse Haribhadra proceeds to say that it is not true that all the people who have turned their backs on worldly desire (and are following the *pratisrotas)* have the good fortune to hear and trust the Jain teaching. The commentary further explains that this is why we see religious seekers who are clearly devoted to the pursuit of the ultimate religious goal and indifferent to worldly life (*pratisrotas)* and yet follow teachings other than those of the Jain doctrine. *Pratisrotas* thus means anyone who has made a choice for the religious life and in so doing has renounced the life of enjoying the sense pleasures.[78]

Haribhadra also makes it clear in his *Upadeśapada* that those who both choose the religious life and adhere to the true teachings of the Jinas are few indeed. In fact the masses follow non-Jain teachings. Haribhadra warns us,[79] "The majority of mankind follows that which is against the teachings of the Jina. But why should a man care what others do? For indeed those who seek their spiritual good are not at all in the majority."

Again,

"Those who seek jewels are few indeed in this world, as are those who would give them. You must learn to recognize those who seek the jewel that is the true religious doctrine and those who can give that jewel to them."

In glossing these verses the commentary cites a number of Hindu practices that violate the laws of the Jinas and yet are extremely popular religious practices as an example of the beliefs of the majority, those who do not seek the jewel. The practices cited include various forms of religious suicide, self-immolation, jumping off cliffs, and the like, practices that would have been particularly abhorrent to the Jains with their strong prohibitions against taking life. It is clear that for Haribhadra in the *Upadeśapada* and his commentator to go against the stream means to go against the pull of the sense organs and opt for the religious life; at the same time to be in the minority who seeks the true jewel means to be a Jain as opposed to a Hindu. Haribhadra's text has both a strong consciousness of Jainism as the true faith and a minority belief and a consciousness that even to seek the religious life at all is a rare event. In Haribhadra's *Upadeśapada* Jainism is the valued truth, the jewel that few seek, and those who take the religious course as opposed to being content with worldy life are said to go against the stream.

This interpretation of the followers of Jainism as the few who follow the true course in contrast to the masses, who are not Jains, is also consistent with what is found in a variety of later Jain texts. The *Karuṇavajrāyudha,* a short play attributed to Balacandra, a disciple of Haribhadra, repeats the same notion. A king laments that most people follow only what others do; believing in Hindu doctrines, they commit terrible sins in the name of religion with their blood sacrifices and other false practices. Few have the courage to deviate from common custom and seek the truth, the Jain doctrine.[80]

A short didactic poem of the thirteenth century that stands very much in the direct tradition of Jinadatta's poems under consideration here seems also to have preferred a more traditional definition of "following in the ways of the world" as keeping to whatever pattern of behavior was expected of a person on the basis of his caste or family. The poem was written by a Kharatara lay follower who like Jinadatta abhors the corruption of the monks he sees around him; and yet there is no indication in his usage of the phrase, "following in the ways of the world" that he intends thereby to contrast bad Jains with good Jains.[81] In addition, the jewel that is difficult to obtain is as it was for Haribhadra— the Jain doctrine in general, although it is here opposed to worldly knowledge and not other non-Jain religious doctrines.[82] The persistence of this standard traditional interpretation in a text so close to Jinadatta's in other respects highlights Jinadatta's originality in adapting traditional concepts to make his very personal statement.[83]

Jains were not alone in characrizing the man who found the true religion as a member of a select minority; Buddhist and Hindu texts make the same point. Buddhist texts speak of the religious life as difficult, "*pratisrotas*", going against the current, while the masses go with the current and accept a life of the senses.[84] As a Hindu example, roughly contemporary with the writings of Jinadatta that are being discussed here, we might consider the hymn to Śiva that is carved on a wall of the Amareśvara temple at Mandhata. In this hymn the poet poignantly tells his beloved Śiva, "In this round of births, few people, having obtained birth as human beings, truly righteous, worship you, while others pray to other gods. O Destroyer of the God of Love! Many may climb the magic mountain of jewels, but only some will have the good fortune to find there a precious gem! The rest will gather worthless rock quartz."[85] The same image appears in verses glorifying a particular holy place; he who would leave that holy place for another would throw away a precious jewel in deluded desire for something worthless.[86]

That Jinadatta is using all of this familiar language with a different meaning is immediately clear when we look at the verses that I have translated here. Let us consider the *Kālasvarūpakulaka,* verse 19. We recognize without difficulty that Jinadatta, saying that those who seek for jewels are few, could be quoting Haribhadra's *Upadeśapada* directly, were it not for the fact that the several hundred years between them have brought changes to the vernacular language that each monk employs. But if Haribhadra was contrasting Jains with Hindus when he used this imagery, the context of Jinadatta's verse makes it clear that Jinadatta is contrasting one group of Jains with another. Those people who do not seek the jewels and do not even know the difference between the jewels and worthless objects still consider themselves to be Jains. This is made explicit in the first line of verse 18, "They practice religion, insisting that what they are doing was proclaimed by the Jinas." Verse 19 is talking about the same group of wrong-headed people. For Jinadatta the true jewel is not Jainism, in general as opposed to Hinduism, as it was for Haribhadra, but his own interpretation of Jainsm, the Jainism of the Kharatara monks, as opposed to the Jainism of the majority of monks around him.

A similar change is observable in Jinadatta's use of the contrast between *anusrotas* and *pratisrotas,* the two terms with which this discussion began. Haribhadra in his *Upadeśapada* and his commentaries to a number of texts understood those who go with the flow to mean those who go with the flow of the sense organs, that is those who do not desire the religious life, while *pratisrotas* meant those who battled against the pull of the senses. For Jinadatta the crowd that goes with the current, *anusrotas,* is comprised of all of the Jain monks who disagree with him and all their lay followers. The contrast is not between the religious seeker (*pratisrotas)* and ordinary individual living an ordinary life (*anusrotas),* as it was in Haribhadra and the *Daśavāikalika,* but between the Jain monk who has the courage to break with the majority of monks (*pratisrotas*) and the great bulk of Jains who do not adhere to Jinadatta's beliefs (*anusrotas*).

In the *Upadeśarasāyana*, in verse 19 translated above, Jinadatta explicitly states that to this group that goes along with the current, to this *anusrotas*, belongs also the Jain monk who does not correctly interpret the texts and does not practice the rituals correctly. The commentator here understands Jinadatta to be speaking of a particular monk as well as in general terms. In verse 18 Jinadatta remarks of this monk that his body is dirty and it is as if the impurities of his soul have become manifest on his body for all to see. The word *mala*, dirt, perhaps suggested to the commentator that Jinadatta was referring to a monk who bore the epithet Maladhārī, "The Dirty One", and his followers. I would identify this Maladhārī with Maladhārī Hemacandra.[87]

It is odd that almost nothing is said about this Maladhārī Hemacandra in any of the traditional Jain biographies. His name does not figure in the various biographies of Jinadatta either. He was a contemporary of Jinadatta and a prolific writer. He is said to have been close to the court circles and to have been a royal minister before becoming a monk. Perhaps it was due to his influence that Jinadatta noted in the *Upadeśarasāyana,* verse 24, that his opponents received considerable royal patronage, even at the expense of Jinadatta and his followers.[88] In any case, it is clear that those who follow the *anusrotas*, or go with the stream, are both in the majority and Jain. They are monks as well as lay devotees, and what distinguishes them is that they do not seek nor do they know the true Jainism of Jinadatta and his followers. Jindatta thus does not contrast the religious life with the ordinary life when he uses the language *pratisrotas/anusrotas* as did Haribhardra. He uses traditional languages to draw a different contrast, between those Jains who know and practice the true religion of the Kharatara monks and those who do not. This sense of his own small group as a minority and the true standard bearers of Jainism colors all of his Apabhraṃśa poems.

In his *Caccarī*, an Apabhraṃśa poems that eulogizes his master Jinavallabha, and that like the *Upadeśarasāyana* and the *Kālasvarūpakulaka* offer vivid insight into Jinadatta's view of his mission. Jinadatta states clearly that their doctrine, which he calls *vidhiviṣaya* has been proclaimed by Jinavallabha by striking out against the common course that people follow (*lokapravāha*), the stream that is commonly chosen. The commentary gives a careful gloss so that we understand that the stream that the masses enter into is the Jainism in which they revere monks who do not accept the *vidhi* path and worship in temples that do not strictly conform to the Kharatara rules. Again in the next verse Jinadatta praises Jinavallabha because he was able to reject what the majority of people had blindly been following. In verse 26 of the *Caccarī,* in describing what the true doctrine promulgated by Jinavallabha was, Jinadatta explicitly states that it is a doctrine in which what is right, even if it is stated by only one man, is done and not that which violates the Jain teachings but is done by many. The commentary adds that what Jinadatta intends by the last line, something that is done by many and is not acceptable, is certain rituals that have been accepted in the Jain temples but that the Kharatara monks reject. In any case, we are reminded here too of the language of Haribhadra's *Upadeśapada*, enjoining us not to bother with what is done by the majority, and of Nemicandra's didactic poem cited earlier which at one point equated "following common custom" with preserving traditional caste obligations, religious rituals, and professions. The change that Jinadatta is making in his use of the phrase "*lokapravāha*", "current of common custom" is unmistakable; the majority for Jinadatta is the dominant group of Jain monks, the non-Kharatara monks, while for Haribhadra and his commentator and many later Jains the majority are not Jains and common custom meant something more like caste duty and inherited religious practices.

Jinadatta, then, speaks an older language with a distinctly new meaning. His sense of being in the minority is more than just a statement of a Jain in a predominantly non-Jain milieu. In fact what makes his situation so acute is his painful awareness of being in the minority amongst those whom he should be able to call his own. His voice is that of the lone reformer; the reception he meets from the world around him is hostile. The image of the monk Jinadatta that emerges in these texts recalls the monk as martyr who is known from a text like the *Uttaradhyayana* chapter 4 with its mention of the *vadha parīsaha*, of how a monk may even have to endure martyrdom in the service of his faith, and of the famous *Uvahaṇasuya* of the *Āyaraṅga,* in which we hear of Mahāvīra's suffering verbal and physical abuse.[89] Jinadatta in his consciousness of his own mission as a lone seeker, sometimes subjected to physical abuse, often scorned and little honored, but always aware of the correctness of his path, is by no means without parallel in the Jain tradition.

In addition, his conviction that there were so many Jain monks who were false monks and his understanding that his own mission was to cleanse his own group from within both have parallels in other texts in medieval Jainism. Indeed, texts that describe the behavior of monks often spoke about Jain monks who were false. Amitagati, a Digambara who was about a hundred years earlier than Jinadatta, even spoke of such a monk as *lokapariktikṛtādāra*, one who cared too much about what the average person believed.[90] There were also other reform movements in Jainism; Haribhadra is associated with one of the earliest attempts to reform lax monks and Jinadatta even cites Haribhadra by name as the original source for some of the reforms promulgated by Jinavallabha (*Caccarī*, 14).[91] Haribhadra in his *Viṃśativiṃśikā* like Jinadatta warns against watering down the teachings for fear that there will be few followers and enjoins following a strict course.[92] Indeed Jinadatta as he described the lonely monk had a precedent in his own teacher, Jinavallabha's famous *Samghapaṭṭaka*, which was something of a call to arms to the Kharatara monks. For here too we read of monks who have fallen into lax ways; of people too stupid to know better being led around by the monks; of a topsy-turvy world where people honor the false monks and abuse the good monks. For Jinavallabha as for Jinadatta after him the Jain community, monks and lay followers, was hopelessly corrupt.[93]

Jinadatta's particular contribution to the literature of protest and reform is the way in which he has so skillfully altered traditional discourse to describe his plight and the plight of his times. Jinadatta speaks clearly and loudly with this old language given new meaning, and the image of Jinadatta, the leader of the monks, that emerges could not be more clear.[94]

Jinadatta, about mid-way through the *Upadeśarasāyana*, speaks directly about what it is like to be the leader of the monks, the *yugapradhāna*. I have translated some of these verses above, verses 41 ff. Reviewing them will provide a neat conclusion to the discussion thus far; it is also well for us to remember as we read these verses that when he wrote this text Jinadatta was near the end of his career as the leader of the Kharatara community, the *yugapradhāna*. He is clearly referring to himself in these verses by his formal title, a practice that we have seen was common in medieval India.

Jinadatta in these verses clearly sees himself as by definition alone; only one monk in a generation can occupy this high office. He is secure in his knowledge, and protected by the gods that protect the Jain faith, he is destined to do many important acts that will spread the true teachings. He does not flee from those who seek to engage him in debate. He is honored by few and reviled by many but unmoved by both honor and rejection. He is always conscious that the true Jainism is in trouble and that his task is to defend it against the many who would distort its fundamental teachings.

Jinadatta may not have used an autobiography in the form in which Western scholars define that genre, but it is hard to imagine how we could have learned more about his sense of what he was doing, his mission and his loneliness in pursuit of that mission, than what he tells us in these verses. That he uses a traditional often cliched idiom to create new meaning is an important indication not only of his own literary creativity but also of the vitality of his tradition. Jinadatta's texts also served as the model for other similar exhortatory texts, and the strength of his idiom is apparent in its ability to withstand a gap of several hundred years and still convey vividly a deep sense of personal conviction.[95]

Finally, Jinadatta's texts, exhortatory and didactic as they are, may also serve to remind us that there exist many other texts in the medieval period which speak in conventional language and at the same time are also highly personal in their tone. Hymns and exhortatory texts often used the first person and convey vividly religious yearnings and a deep sense of personal unworthiness; hymns are in fact particularly noteworthy as the genre par excellance in which an author could speak openly in the first person of religious desires and feelings of insufficiency. In medieval Jainism hymn writing was a major activity; all of the leading monks have left us hymns and there are a number of famous hymns written by lay devotees. Jinadatta's texts that have been studied here are often close in tone to the medieval hymns in which a monk describes his feelings and his commitment of his faith.[96] They may serve to remind us that there is a rich and varied discourse about the self in medieval India that extends from didactic texts to hymns and that has yet to be fully studied.

B. Jinadattasūri, from the *Kharataragacchabṛhadgurvāvali,* pp. 14-20.

Now some time ago some learned nuns, who were disciples of the teacher, the Glorious Dharmadeva, who was himself a disciple of the Glorious Jineśvarasūri, were spending the rainy season in Dhavalaka. The pious lay devotee, the wife of Vāchiga, came with her son Bāhaḍa to hear the nuns preach. The nuns outdid themselves that day in expounding the true religion. Now these nuns also knew how to recognize auspicious and inauspicious marks on children. They could see on this child all the marks that indicated that he was destined to be a great leader of monks. They begged the mother to give him to them. What more need I say? They so greatly endowed her with faith in the teachings that she agreed to give them her son as a novice disciple. At the end of the four months of the rainy season the nuns informed the teacher Dharmadeva what they had done, "We have obtained an extremely worthy disciple, who will make a great leader of monks. Please tell us what you wish us to do." At that the monk, waiting until the omens were all propitious, went to join them. And when he saw the boy he knew that it was exactly as they had said. And so on a propitious day in the year 1141 the boy was formally accepted as a novice and given the name Somacandra. And Dharmadeva instructed one of the other monks, "Sarvadevagaṇi! You must look after this boy carefully and take him with you wherever you go and whatever you do, even when you go to attend to a call of nature, so that he will learn how a monk is to behave." He had been born in the year 1132. He learned to read the alphabet without being taught. The teacher Aśokacandra performed for him the ceremoney of initiation know as *utthāpanā.*

On the very first day of his initiation Sarvadevagaṇi took him with him when he went to relieve himself. Being just a child and not knowing very much, he stepped all over a patch of ground on which young plants had sprouted. To teach him a lesson the older monk took away his dust broom and his face cloth, the outward signs of his new vocation as an ordained monk, and said to him, "Go back home. Once a person has taken the vows of a monk he can't go stepping all over fields." "My teacher is not without right, but when I came here I also had a head full of hair. Give me my hair back and then I can go home." Now when he heard the boy say these words the teacher was amazed and thought, "He has got me there. There is absolutely nothing that I can say to that." And Sarvadevagaṇṇi reported the incident to the teacher Dharmadeva. And Dharmadeva thought, "He will surely be a worthy leader of the community."

Somacandra began to go all over the city of Pattan to learn the sciences of prognostication and omens and the casting of horoscopes. Now one day some haughty fellow saw him as he was on his way to see the master named Bhāvaḍa in order to learn how to cast horoscopes. He called out to Somacandra, "Hey, white-robed fellow! What are you carrying around your school note books for?" "So I can be sure to write down every detail of how you made a fool of yourself and how I got everything just right." When he heard this, the boastful challenger took to his heels without another word. Somacandra arrived at his destination. There were a number of students there, sons of influential political officials, all reciting horoscopes. It was a full-fledged school, fully in session. At one point the master decided to test him, "Say, Somacandra! You Jains have a hymns of praise that you call the *navakāra.* Now what kind of name is that? Is the syllable 'na' a negative and do you then mean a hymn in which the letter "*va*" never appears? It does, of course!" Somacandra then said, "No, teacher. The word *navakara* isn't the Sanskrit word that means "where there is no letter "*va*"; "*navakāra*" is a Prakrit word that means "*navakaraṇa*", "an act of reverence." The teacher knew that this one was too smart for him to get the best of in an argument. He had given the perfect answer.

On another occasion, when it happened to be the special day set aside when the monks would fast, confess their sins and pull out their hair, Somacandra was unable to attend the lessons. The system worked in this way. If any of the students was unable to attend class, then the teacher would not give the class. Now his fellow-students, the sons of influential officials, were all puffed up with their own importance, and they said, "Teacher, put a stone in his place and go on with the lesson!" The teacher complied with their request and taught. On the next day Somacandra showed up and said to the teacher, "Clever of you to have put the stone in my place. Now ask me everything that you taught them about reckoning horoscopes, and more. Surely the one who can answer is hardly as dull as a stone; that's best said of the people who called me a stone." "Somacandra, I know that you are like the rare fragrant musk of the musk deer, spreading your good qualities everywhere. But these fools pressed me to teach and so I did. Please forgive me."

The teacher Haricandra taught the learned Somacandra all the Jain doctrines. And he gave him a book containing magic spells and the very notebook that he himself had used when he had learned the sacred doctrines, so pleased was he with Somacandra. And the teacher Devabhadra, likewise delighted with him, gave him the stylus which he himself had used to write on a wood block his four religious narratives, his account of the life of Mahāvīra and other works. The learned Somacandragaṇi then wandered as a monk from village to village, possessing great knowledge, practicing meditation, pleasing to all, bringing much delight to the lay community.

Now while the learned Somacandra was thus travelling from place to place, Glorious Devabhadrasūri learned that the Glorious Jinavallabhasūri had passed away. He was greatly saddened at the news and he thought, "Alas! The monastic community was well served by him as its leader, but now we are alone." But soon it occurred to the Glorious Devabhadrasūri, "If I do not find a worthy successor to the Glorious Jinavallabha and install him formally as head of our community of monks, then I will have shown Glorious Jinavallabha little respect indeed." And the teacher began to consider who in their lineage would make a worthy successor to Jinavallabha. And as he pondered this the name of Somacandra leapt to his mind and he thought to himself, "He is a worthy successor to Jinavallabha. He delights the community of lay followers with his learning, his practice of meditation and his strict observance of the proper rules for behavior and all of the rituals." And so with the approval of all the others, he wrote a letter to Somacandra, saying, "You must come to Citrakūṭa where we will all be gathered, so that we may formally install you as the successor to Glorious Jinavallabha." This is what the Glorious Jinavallabha himself had desired, but because it had not been done right away, there were now many who were eager to succeed to Jinavallabha's position as head of the monastic community. But let us proceed with our account. Since they had written to him to come, the learned Somacandra and the teacher Devabhadra, too, journeyed to Citrakūṭa, in addition to all of those others who were scrambling for power.

Everyone there knew only that someone would be formally installed as the successor to the Glorious Jinavallabha. On the day before the ceremony was to take place the Glorious Devabhadra told the learned Somacandra in private, "in the glorious city of Citrakūṭa, in the temple to Mahāvīra that was consecrated by the Glorious Jinavallabha, in a ceremony that honors the Jain community and that has been organized by the pious lay devotee Sādhāraṇa, I shall install you as the successor of the Glorious Jinavallabha. By our reckoning tomorrow will be the auspicious moment." "That is all very well, but if you install me as his successor on that day then I will not live long. But if I am installed six days later, on Saturday at an auspicious moment, then I shall live long, spreading the teachings everywhere as I wander, while the community of the faithful who adhere to the teachings of the Glorious Jinavallabha, monks, nuns and lay men and women, will prosper and be strong in number." The Glorious Devabhadrasūri replied, "That is not too long to wait. I will do as you say." And so on the very day that he had specified, in the year 1169 in the month of Vaiśākha, in the bright half of the lunar fortnight, at Citrakūṭa, in a magnificent ceremony, Somacandra was formally installed as the leader of the monastic community, the successor to the Glorious Jinavallabha; and he was given the name Glorious Jinadattasūri. As evening came and the auspicious moment arrived, he returned to his lodgings to the sounds of the many musical instruments that were being played. The Glorious Devabhadrasūri approached him with all due deference and the proper deportment, paid him honor and then said, "You must preach." And he did then preach, and his preaching was so filled with apt examples from the holy scriptures, like so many showers of the nectar of immortality, that those who heard it, monks, nuns and laity alike, were delighted and said, "Lucky indeed was the teacher Devabhadra, who installed as head of the monks this worthy man. He has made into reality the desire of the Glorious Jinavallabha, who had said, 'You must install Somacandragaṇi as my successor." And Devabhadra told him, "You must travel outside the city of Pattana for a short while." "I shall do as you say."

On another occasion Jinaśekhara had done something that was in violation of his monastic vows and so the teacher Devabhadra had expelled him. Jinaśekhara had then gone out to the area where the monks were accustomed to relieve themselves and waited there. When the Glorious Jinadattasūri came out to attend to a call of nature he fell at his feet and said, "You must forgive my offense this once. I promise that I will never do anything like that again." The Glorious Jinadattasūri was an ocean of compassion. He took him back into the community of monks. Afterwards the teacher Devabhadra said to him, "You will regret what you have done. No good will come of it." Jinadattasūri said, "He is devoted to the Glorious Jinavallabha, and he does his best to follow all the rules correctly. What more can we ask of him?" At that the teacher Devabhadra was silent and went back whence he had come.

Now comes the description of Jinadatta's travels. Where should he go? He fasted three times in order to summon his holy teachers. And so it was that the Glorious teacher Harisiṃha came down to him from heaven. "Why have you meditated upon me?" "Where shall I go in my wanderings?" And so he received this instruction: "Go to Marusthalī and other places." And while he was there some Jains, Mehara, Bhokhara, Vāsala, Bharata and others, came to the town on business. Seeing the master Jinadatta and hearing his words, they were extremely joyful. They accepted him as their teacher. And Bharata remained there to serve as reader of the scriptures. The others all returned home and praised the teacher to their families. Even in their home town he thus gained some following.

From there he went to Nāgapur. There the Jain lay follower Dhanadeva paid him respect. And he said to Jinadatta, "If only you would do as I say, then everyone would honor you." Jinadatta then said, "Dhanadeva! In our religion a lay follower is to listen to his preceptor. It is nowhere said that a monk should listen to a lay follower! And you should not say that I will not be honored because I lack a suitable following. For it is said,

'Do not think that just because he has many hangers-on a man is honored in this world.

For see how the sow, surrounded by all her many young, still eats shit' Dhanadeva was not impressed. But though he was not impressed, some wise and discriminating people thought that what the teacher had said was absolutely right.

From there he went on to Ajmera. The pious **Jains** Āsadhara and Rāsala, among others, lived there. Jinadatta went to the temple in Vahada to worship the Jina. On one occasion another monk of the rank of teacher was there. This monk was lower in status than Jinadatta, but he did not offer the appropriate respectful greetings to Jinadatta on his arrival. At that Āsadhara and some of the other lay devotees said to the rude monk."What use is it if you go to a temple if you do not behave properly there?" And so that monk offered the proper respect to Jinadatta.

The lay devotees then informed King Anorāja, "King! Our teacher, the Glorious Jinadattasūri, has come." The king replied, "So he has come! What do you seek from me?" "King! We are looking for some portion of the earth where we can build our temples and halls to hold our ceremonies, and where the pious lay families can make their homes." Afterwards the king told them, "You may have the land at the foot of the mountain just south of here, and you are free to do with it as you wish. And you must present your teacher to me." The lay devotees told their great master, Jinadatta, what had happend. At this the master said, "You should summon the king and have him come here. Since he himself wants to see me it is best that he come to me." The king was summoned on a propitious day. He came and respectfully greeted that excellent master. Jinadattasūri recited a verse of blessing to the king,

"May the Gods Brahmā, Viṣṅu and Śaṅkara grant you prosperity, O King! They bring joy to those who worship them, and are most righteous, or if you prefer to read the Sanskrit adjective a different way, they bring joy to all who worship them and Brahmā rides on a swan, Viṣṅu sits on a snake, and Siva on his bull."

When he heard this verse the king was delighted. He said, "You must stay here forever." "Well said, O King! But it is our custom that we always wander from place to place to help people everywhere. But I shall come back here again and again so that I may see you and you may take pleasure in being with me." The king was indeed pleased with Jinadatta and he got up to take his leave. Afterwards Jinadattasūri said to Āsadhara,

"This is the time when a man may do good, so long as fickle fortune smiles on him. Bad times must always come; and when they do, what man can help another?"

"And so you must have images of Neminātha, Ṛṣabhanātha and Pārsvanātha made, to rival those at Stambhanaka, Śatruñjaya and Ujjayanta. You should make a temple with a shrine to Ambikā on the top floor and a place for the images of the Gaṇadharas on the ground floor."

After that he began to tour Vāgaḍa. He set off when the omens were propitious. Previously the people in this area had possessed great faith in the glorious Jinavallabhasūri ; they had heard that he had passed on and now they learned that the one who had succeeded to his position as head of the monks, who was endowed with excellent qualities, knowledge, and the skill of practicing meditation; who knew both the letter and the spirit of the words that had come from the lotus-like lips of the glorious Mahāvīra; who was conversant with all the doctrines that had been set down by the Gaṇadhara sudharmasvāmin; who was vigilant in performing the proper rituals, the one named Glorious Jubadhattasūri, who was like a Tīrthaṅkara himself, had come to their town in the course of his monastic wanderings. And when they all saw him they were filled with joy and reverence. And so it happened that some of them achieved right faith; some of them took the minor vows, and some took the full vows of monks, and all were delighted in their hearts. Many were ordained as monks. And it is said that on that occasion fifty women were ordained as nuns.

On that same occasion he installed Jinaśekhara into the position of *upādhyāya,* and accompanied by a few monks he left for Rudrapallī in the course of his wanderings. He wanted to bring pleasure to those of his faction who lived there. The local teacher, Glorious Jayadeva, along with some of his disciples, learned of this fact, namely that the Glorious Jindạttasūri, who had succeeded to the position of the Glorious Jinavallabhasūri and was endowed with every virtuous quality, in the course of his wanderings was coming to their country. And they were pleased. Formerly they had heard how the Glorious

Jinavallabhasūri had learned from the Glorious Abhayadevasūri the doctrine that monks ought not to live in spearate buildings made for their use and how that Glorious Jinavallabhasūri had accepted this doctrine. And they too had been inclined to the same viewpoint. Now the most excellent master had personally come to see them and so with their families they went out to greet him. They bowed to the Glorious Jinadattasūri with great respect. And he addressed them with such good and sweet words from the scriptures that they all conceived this desire, "May he alone be our true teacher in every rebirth that we have." On a propitious day they took vows. They did not look back, as the world emperor Sanatkumāra did not look back when he abandoned the world to become a monk.

Now the Glorious Jinaprabhasūri was known amongst these people for his ability to predict the future and see the unseen. He had gone to the territory held by the Muslims. One of the Muslims, knowing his reputation, asked him, "What do I have in my hand?" He thought carefully and replied, "I shall tell you. You have a piece of chalk and a hair." Now the Muslim did not know about the hair. He held out his hand. He could see that there was a strand of hair stuck to the chalk. The Muslim was pleased and took the monk's hand and kissed it, and praised him loudly saying, "Bravo! Bravo!" Now the monk knew that these Muslims were not to be trusted and he feared that they might harm him and so at night he fled by stealth and returned to his own country. When he got back he heard that the Glorious Jayadeva under the guidance of the Glorious Jinadatta had accepted the doctrine that monks should not dwell in temples and he too became inclined to do the same. But he knew that their doctrine was deep and hard. And so he used his special knowledge to determine who was the true leader of the monks. It told him that the Glorious Jinadatta was the true head of all the monks. He tried again and he got the same answer. On the third try he saw a fiery mass fall from the sky. He heard a voice. "If you want the true religion then accept this excellent master, Jinadattasūri, and practice religion." He did as he was told and was pleased and filled with true faith.

And the monk Vimalacandragaṇi, who adhered to the doctrine that it was indeed proper for monks to live in temples, came to know that these two teachers had accepted the opposite doctrine forbidding monks to live in temples under the tutelage of the Glorious Jindattasūri, who had the most excellent knowledge, and who had stopped there in the course of his monastic tour. And when he heard that, he too accepted Jinadatta's doctrine. On that same occasion Jinarakṣita and Śīlabhadra were ordained monks along with their mother who became a nun. Similarly the two brothers, Thiracandra and Varadatta, were ordained.

Now there was an ascetic named Jayadatta, who specialized in reciting magic spells. All of his ancestors had possessed power over certain magic spells. They were all destroyed by an angry goddess. This Jayadatta too was imperilled and the took refuge with the Glorious Jindattasūri and became a monk. Then the honourable one protected him from the goddess. There was also the case of Gunacandragaṇi, who similarly was ordained by the Glorious Jindattasūri. Previously he had been a lay devotee of Jainism and had been captured by the Muslims. They knew from reading his palms that the would make an excellent Keeper of the Treasury. Fearing that he would try to escape, they kept him in chains. He recited the Jain hymn of praise to the five holy ones 100,000 times. Through the power of that recitation his chains fell off. And then he crept away in the last watch of the night and made his way to the home of some old lady. Taking pity on him, the old lady hid him in her granary, and when the Muslims came in search of him they could not find him. In the dark of night he made his way back to his own country. He was deeply impressed by the greatness of the Jain faith and became a monk. Rāmacandragaṇi, along with his son Jīvānanda, heard the great teachings from a monk of another lineage and came to accept the commands of the Glorious Jindattasūri. Similarly Brahmacandragaṇi became a monk. From their group Jinarakṣita, Śthiracandra and some other monks and Śrīmati, Jinamati, Pūrṇaśrī and other nuns were sent to Dhārā to study how to cast horoscopes and read omens. And with the support of the lay community they were able to complete their studies.

The Glorious Jinadattasūri went alone to Rudrapallī. As he was making his way there he encountered a certain lay disciple in some village, who was possessed by a terrible demi-god, every single day; it was only on account of the great merit that this lay disciple had accumulated that by chance the Glorious Jinadattasūri happened to come that way. He told Jinadattasūri about his condition. The monk knew at once that the demi-god that was causing this disciple so much pain could be defeated with the right spells and rituals. And so he wrote his poem celebrating the deeds of the Kharatara monks before him, the *Gaṇadharasārdhaśataka*. He wrote it down and placed it in the disciple's hand; he told the disciple that he must fix his eyes and his heart on it. And the disciples did exactly as he was told. And when that demi-god arrived on the seene in order to cause the disciple terrible pain, he got as far as the man's bed. He could not touch his body because of the powers of the *Gaṇadharasārdhaśataka*. The next day he made it as far as the door to the room; what more is there to say?

Jinadattasūri reached Rudrapallī. The teacher Jinaśekhara and all of the lay disciples came out to meet him and with much fanfare they ushered him into the city. He brought 120 families there to the Glorious Teachings of the Jinas. He consecrated a temple to Pārśvanātha and one to Ṛṣabhanātha. The lay devotees reconfirmed their faith and vowed to abstain from evil deeds within certain limits. Some excellent lay devotees like Depālagaṇi took the full vows of monks. Having brought all of them such joy, he promised to send the teacher Jayacandra to them and set off once more for the West.

Jinadatta travelled to the country Vāgaḍa, specifically to the city Vyāghrapura. There he gave instructions to the Glorious Master Jayadevācārya and sent him on to Rudrapallī. Jinadatta himself remained in Vyāghrapura where he composed the *Caccarī*, a poem about the proper rules governing a temple as they were set down by the Glorious Jinavallabha. He wrote his work down and he sent it along to the lay disciples, Vāsala and the others, so that they might learn the correct doctrine. Now in the city of Vikrampura there was a hall set aside for the performance of Jain rituals near the home of one Saṇhiyā, the father of Devadhara. It was there that the lay devotees all gathered and sat down and opened the *Caccarī*. Devadhara, who was maddened with pride, made fun of the book, which was written in Prakrit. Scoffing at its title, "*Caccarī, Kaccarī,* silly nonsense!", he grabbed the book out of the hand of the man who was holding it and tore it right in two. He was out of control. There wasn't a thing anyone could do to stop him. His father came to hear of what he had done. He said, "He's a stubborn one, that boy of mine. But somehow he must be stopped." He wrote a letter to the Honourable Jinadatta and told him exactly what had become of the copy of the *Caccarī* that he had sent them. The Honourable Jinadatta pondered the letter for a while and then sent off another copy of the *Caccarī* with a note. This is what the note said, "Do not be harsh to Devadhara. He shall, by the grace of God and a good teacher, become a worthy member of our religious community." The second copy of the book arrived and with great deference those lay disciples opened it and began to read it. It brought them all great satisfaction and pleasure.

Now Devadhara thought to himself, "Although I ripped that book in two someone seems to have sent another copy of it. There's more here than meets the eye. I wonder what's written in it anyway. I guess I'll just have to have a look at it in secret when there's no one else around." When the lay devotees set the book down on the sacred stand and shut the door behind them and there was no one else left in the hall, then Devadhara snuck out of his own house. He climbed the roof of his house and then jumped over to the roof of the hall and got in that way even though the door was shut tight from the outside. He grabbed the book and the more he read the greater was the delight that filled his heart. He thought to himself, "All of this is clear and absolutely correct. There are just two points that I wonder about, the business that an image can be unfit for worship and the remark about women not being able to worship. I must ask about these later. I shall accept whatever answer I am given."

Now the people that the Honourable One had sent to Dhārā while he was in the country of Vāgaḍa were all assembled there, and he preached to them all. And then the teacher Jayadeva, whom he had ordained as a monk himself, was installed in the rank of Lord of the Monks, Munīndra. Ten monks were made Vācanācāryas, teachers of the scriptures. These were the monks Jinacakritagaṇi, Śīlabhadragaṇi, Sthiracandragaṇi, Brahmacandragaṇi,

Vimalacandragaṇi, Varadattagaṇi, Bhuvanacandragaṇi, Varanagagaṇi, Rāmacandragaṇi, and Maṇibhadragaṇi. The five, Śrīmati, Jinamati, Pūraṇaśrī, Jinaśrī and Jinaśrī, were made leading nuns, Mahattarās. There was a student of the teacher Harisiṃha, whose name was Municandra. He requested the Glorious Jindattasūri, "If some worthy disciple of mine should come to you, please confer upon him the rank of teacher. Ācārya." Jinadattasūri agreed. He installed a disciple of his, named Jayasiṃha, in the rank of Munīndra in the city of Citrakūta. And his disciple, Jayacandra, as made Munīndra when the congregation gathered in Pattan. He told them both, "You must act as befits your rank." And Jīivānanda was installed as Upādhyāya. Were I to go into detail about the various ranks conferred on every monk, there would be no end. And so I have just told about a few. He instructed each person in his duties and told each where he should travel, and then himself set out for Ajmera. He was welcomed into that city with great fanfare.

Now the lay disciples had made three temples and a shrine to Ambikā on a mountain there. At a propitious moment the Glorious Jinadattasūri performed the ceremony of sprinking consecrated powder when the main dedication was held. After that the lay disciples conducted the ritual of fixing the finial on the temple. Next, in Vikramapura, the lay disciple Devadhara, son of Saṇhiyā, had gathered together five families related to him, in order to honor the memory of his father; he told Āsadeva and the others, "I shall summon the Glorious Jinadattasūri and see that he stops here in the course of his travels. And I do not want any one of you to say anything unpleasant to him." The lay disciples all set out together and reached Nāgapur.

Now at that time there was one Devācārya, who was particularly famous. He heared that Devadhara, who was himself quite well known, had arrived there from Vikramapur. Soon after that Devācārya was sitting in the temple, about to expound the sacred texts. Devadhara, too,having washed his feet and made sure that he was sufficiently clean, went to the temple. He saluted the teacher, who asked after his welfare. Then Devadhara spoke up, "Teacher, what kind of a temple is it where a woman can enter at night?" Devācārya thought to himself "Somehow or other someone has whispered the magic words of the Glorious Jinadattasūri into his ears. He seems to have been completely won over." And having concluded this, he spoke, " Lay disciple ! You are right. It is not correct to permit a woman to enter a temple at night." Devadhara said, " Then why do you not put a stop to the practice?" The teacher said, "Everyone does it. I wouldn't know where to begin." Devadhara said, "Blessed one! Should that temple in which the teachings of the Jina are not respected and people come and go at will, ignoring the commands of the Jina, still be called the Jina's temple? Why not just call it the people's temple?" The teacher said, "Why can't we call it the temple of the Jina, when everyone can see that the Jina sits right there inside it?" Devadhara said, "Teacher! I admit that I am not very bright, and yet even I know that we cannot call a house a certain man's house if no one respects his commands there. Even if there is a stone image of the Jina inside your temple, if no one who comes there respects the commands of the Jina but just does whatever he pleases, how can we call that temple the Jina's temple? And you know this as well as I do, but you refuse to go against the stream; to the contrary you just swim along with everyone, beckoning others to follow you. I have nothing further to say to you. Good day!" And with those words Devadhara got up to leave.

The relatives that he had brought with him were imbued with faith in the *vidhi mārga,* the way of Jinadatta and his group. Along with all his relatives Devadhara reached Ajmera. With his heart full of faith he bowed down to the Glorious Jinadattasūri, and when Jinadattasūri learned why he had come he preached to them all. Devadhara had no doubt that his mission would succeed. He asked the Honourable One to come to Vikrampura. After performing splendid ceremonies for the consecration of the images of Ambikā and the Gaṇadharas in the temples at Ajmer, the Glorious Jinadattasūri accompanied Devadhara to Vikramapura. He converted many people there. He installed an image of Mahāvīra.

On his way to Ucca he converted a number of goblins; by comparison the conversion of the poeople of Ucca was a simple matter! From there he went to Navahara. And from there to Tribhuvanagiri, where he converted a king named Kumārapāla. He had many monks go there. He consecrated an image of Śāntinātha. In the course of his tour in Ujjaiyin he converted the Yoginīs.

Now once when he was about to enter the city of Citrakūta, some evil minded fellows threw a cobra in front of him, all tied up, so that he would think it an evil omen and go elsewhere. The singing dropped to a whisper and the musical instruments were muted. The lay disciples, thinking, "Today is not a propitious day," became dejected. At that the Glorious Jinadattasūri, his knowledge illuminating all things as the sun illumines the world, spoke up. "Why are you worried? This is a good omen. It was sent to tell us that just as this cobra is tied up, so will a similar fate meet each and every person who attempts to do us harm." And the monk resumed his walking. Those evil-minded fellows this time sent a woman who had had her nose cut off to meet him, again as an bad omen. With his skill at clever repartee, Jinadatta was able to chase her off.[97]

Thus have I set down some of the wonderful deeds of the Glorious Jinadattasūri, who did many miraculous things; who was always worshipped by the gods; who was an ocean of compassion; who had consecrated images of the Tīrthaṅkaras Vīra, Pārśva, Śānti, Ajita, and others, and temples and finials to temples in cities such as Dhārā and Gaṇapadra; who through the power of his own knowledge was able to see that the son of Rāsala, the lay disciple, should succeed him; who as the sun awakens the day lotuses to bloom, had awakened many good souls to the truth.

After this he was welcomed into the glorious city Citrakūta with much pomp and splendour. He performed many ceremonies, both to consecrate images and at other functions. Then in the year 1203 in the bright half of the month of Phālgun at Ajmer Jinacandrasūri was ordained as a monk. And then in the year 1205 on the sixth day of the bright half of the fortnight of the month of Vaiśākha, the Glorious Jinadattasūri, who possessed tremendous powers through all the spells, magic diagrams and tantric rites that he had mastered by means of his terrific austerities and meditation, practices that it would be impossible for an ordinary person to perform; whose teachings were like wishing jewels that granted every desire; this Jinadattasūri installed in his own position the Glorious Jinacandrasūri, who had many excellent qualities to delight the minds of the wise, qualities like excellent health, handsome stature, and the like; who was only nine years old, and who was like a sun in the sky of the Rāsala lineage. In the year 1211 in the month Āṣāḍha, in the dark half of the lunar fortnight, Jinadattasūri went to heaven.

If Jinadattasūri in his own words was the lone crusader, abused and scorned by the masses, ever alert to the perils that beset the true faith, the Jinadattasūri of the *Kharataragacchabṛhadgurvāvali* is a much more complicated figure. There are really several Jinadattasūris in this biography, not all of whom are entirely compatible. There is the Jinadattasūri was recognize from his poetry; this is the Jinadattasūri who is not greeted by a monk of lower rank and who refuses to stop spreading his unpopular teachings in order to gain a following. The encounter with Dhanadeva in which Jinadatta compares the monk with many followers to the disgusting sow with her litter is one of the most colorful incidents in the biography, and it creates an impression that is difficult to dispel. It also has rich associations in medieval didactic literature, and may have gained in effect by the strength of those associations.

Haribhadra, in his *Upadeśapada,* a text that we have already consulted in connection with Jinadatta, tells a story of a Jain monk Vijayasena.[98] Vijayasena comes to the city Garjanaka. His followers dream that a pig, surrounded by heroic young elephants comes to their hermitage. In the morning Vijayasena explains their dream to them: a wicked monk with honest and decent disciples will visit them. At that very moment an ascetic Rudradeva appears on the scene. A test reveals that as wicked as Rudradeva is, his disciples are virtuous. The story goes on as the teacher is reborn as a camel and the disciples become princes, but we need not pursue its plot further. The pig is the wicked monk in this story, and wicked disciples would have been piglets, while the good disciples are elephants. The story-teller who has Jinadattasūri recite his graphic verse about the sow surely would have known this famous account of Vijayasena that Haribhadra related. It was standard fare in the medieval didactic collections. The *Bhavabhāvanā,* of Maladhārī Hemacandra, who may even have been the monk Jinadatta attacks in his *Upadeśarāsayana,* mentions as an example of a bad rebirth Vijayasena who was reborn as a camel.[99]

In addition, popular Hindu story literature of the period knows the pig with its large litter as the counterpart of the wicked man with his large brood; Kṣemendra in his *Bṛhatkathāmañjarī* has a Brahman lady console the childless Queen Vāsavadattā, who has just seen the five sons of a potter-woman, with these words,

"The wicked are like pigs that lie on the road with their many offspring; but it takes a rare act of fate for a fortunate, great and courageous child to be born, and that does not happen in just any family."[100]

The lonely reformer of these episodes of the *Kharataragacchabṛhadgurvāvali* biography and Jinadatta's own poetry appears as well in a hymn that was written during Jinadatta's lifetime by a poet named Palha. The poem was written down in the year 1113 A.D., some years before Jinadatta's death in 1154 A.D., by Jinarakṣita, who calls himself a pupil of Jinadattasūri. He wrote the poem down in Dhara.[101] Palha tells how Jinadatta, who occupied the position as head of the community that had been held by Jinavallabha, was treated by the lay disciples with scorn, and how in these bad times people took a false teacher for a good master and a good master for a fool.[102] It is clear that Jinadatta's poignant description of himself was also how others might see him, both in his life time and after he was gone.

Consistent with this Jinadatta, the crusader and reformer, is the Jinadatta who is willing to forgive a monk his offense against a monastic rule on the grounds that the monk is loyal to the Kharatara viewpoint and to the teachings of Jinavallabhasūri. The Jinadatta of the poems stresses loyalty to the teacher and raises to the status of essential teachings a number of issues about temples, images, and rituals that distinguished the Kharatara monks from their opponents; it is these issues that assume prominence over the more familiar rules and regulations for monks and begin to define the "good monk" from the earrant monk. Indeed, in the Apabhraṃśa poems as we have seen above, monks who excel in asceticism, the normative practice of Jain monks, may be the object of scorn because they do not obey these other rules about temples, images and rituals that Jinadatta and his group see as the predominant determinants of the true religious practice.

In this connection it is perhaps useful to consider an earlier and parallel episode in Jinadatta's biography, when another young monk commits an offense and is also ultimately not expelled from the community. This young monk is Jinadatta himself, and the brief episode in the biography that seems on the surface to provide both a warm human touch, with the image of the child monk so clearly drawn, and a moment of humor with the boy's clever retort, would in fact be seized upon by his opponents to show Jinadatta's profound unsuitability for the monastic life.[103] The incident occurs early in Jinadatta's career as a monk, when he has just been ordained. The child monk commits an infraction against his monastic vows when he carelessly tramples on young plants, much to his teacher's dismay. Instead of confessing his wrong-doing, he is prepared with a witty answer when his teacher would defrock him. The young Jinadatta allows that his teacher is perfectly justified in demanding that he return to him his external signs of monkhood; he adds, however, that the teacher must in turn give back to Jinadatta the mark of his status before he became a monk: the hair that he had on his head before he ritually plucked it out to become a monk! The teacher is suitably won over by Jinadatta's wit and the incident is closed.

Among many possible interpretations of the newly ordained Jinadatta's wrong-doing and his bold reply, the one that seems most relevant to me is that the biography here makes a clear break with normative conceptions of the Jain monk. The essence of being a monk in the canonical texts is, after all, the five major vows, the first of which is the vow of abstaining from harming living creatures. In a text like the *Daśavaikālikasūtra* and its commentaries it is also emphasized that preparation for the vows involves careful confession of past wrong-doing and promise to abstain from such wrong doing in the future; protection of the vows involves again repeated vigilance and confession of inadvertent failings.[104] In this incident, not only does Jinadatta fail in his vow through carelessness; instead of confessing his sin in the accepted formulaic pronouncement of wrong-doing, he makes light of the whole affair by a clever reply that in effect stresses that he is a monk and that there is no going back. The remainder of the biography will define what being a monk meant in jinadatta's case, and we shall see that it has little to do with the traditional vows and confession and vigilance. It has more to do with public ceremony, standards of temple worship, ability to work miracles and to out-maneouver opponents in the very sectarian world of medieval Śvetāmbara Jainism.

Less intimately related to Jinadatta the reformer, but nonetheless vital to the definition of Jinadatta as a monk, is the Jinadatta we meet as the magician and tantric wizard. This Jinadatta cures a lay disciple of possession by writing his *Gaṇadharasārdhaśataka* and bests the Yoginīs. Both of these are standard feats for the medieval Tantric monk; Jinaprabhasūri had cured the Muslim queen of possession and also conquered the yoginīs of Delhi. A consideration of these acts in fact brings us back to the sub-genre of the miracle-story biography that we encountered in our study of Jinaprabhasūri.

There is a miracle story biography of Jinadattasūri in the *Vṛddhācāryaprabandhāvali,* which I have not translated because in spirit it is so similar to that of Jinaprabhasūri. In addition, many of the stories told there of Jinadatta are told elsewhere of other monks. I give below a brief summary of some of these incidents.

The miracle story biography of Jinadatta opens in mid-stream with a statement that Jinadatta, the chief monk, was staying in the city of Anahilapattan. A certain lay disciple named Sirināgadeva is uncertain as to who indeed was fit to be considered the chief monk. As a matter of fact in every monastic lineage monks were bragging that one of their members was the leading monk and really no one could decide which group had the best case! At this point, the layman Nāgadeva betook himself to Mt. Girnar and began a fast to propitiate the Jain Goddess Ambā. Ambā appeared to him and told him how she knew that he was uncertain as to the true identity of the chief of the monks. She told him that she had written some letters on his hand. All he needed to do was to go to each and every monastery and ask the monks to read them. The monk who could do so would be none other than the chief monk. Nāgadeva dutifully did as he was told, but he met with little success. Finally he presented himself before Jinadatta, the leader of the Kharatara monks. At first Jinadatta was reluctant to read the verse written on Nāgadeva's hand, since it was a verse in his own praise and a monk does not engage in such boastful talk. Instead of reading the verse himself, he scattered over Nāgadeva's hand some specially consecrated powder. Then he had one of his students recite the verse. It was thus that Nāgadeva came to have no doubt that Jinadatta was the true leader of monks.[105]

This story closely resembles the way in which Jinesvara is revealed to the people as the leader of the monks.[106] A lay-man bears a secret divine message that only the true leader of the monks can read. The story is given an added sectarian tone in Jinadatta's biography in that it is said that other monks from other lineage were aggressively claiming this title, but this is the only distinctive change in an otherwise familiar motif.

In the next incident Jinadattasūri conquers the sixty-four Yoginīs, exactly as we have seen Jinaprabhasūri do in his biography from the same collection. In the third incident, the corpse of a dead Brahmin is put in a Jain temple by the local Brahmins who want to create trouble for the Jains. Jinadattasūri, having the magic ability to enter another person's body, revives the corpse and has it move to the Brahmin temple. The Brahmins are suitably impressed and seek Jinadatta's forgiveness. He then has the corpse move to the cemetery, at which the Brahmins all convert to Jainism. This story is also associated with another monk, Jīvadevasūri, where the dead Brahmin is a dead cow.[107]

It should be clear from this summary that the miracle stories associated with Jinadatta in the *Vṛddhācāryaprabandhāvali* are extremely varied and probably derived from a variety of sources. They are not unique to Jinadatta, nor are they unique to the more general class of literature that I have been calling "sectarian biography". These stories are told of other monks in both sectarian and non-sectarian collections, and within the sectarian biographies they are told in Sanskrit and Prakrit, in biographies that are replete with miracles and in biographies that include miracle stories less frequently. The text is primarily of interest in warning us against making any hasty generalizations about religious biography in medieval Jainism beyond recognizing its richness and its flexibility.

In addition to the miracle stories that are preserved in the *Vṛddhācāryaprabandhāvali,* the poems sung of Jinadattasūri and collected in the *Aitihāsika Kavya Saṃgraha* tend to focus on miralce stories, which are also the core stories of the clan conversion accounts centering around Jinadatta.[108] It is clear even in his biography from the *Kharataragacchabrahadgurvāvali* that no account of the monk was conceivable without some mention of his miracles. The incident with the *Caccarī* also highlights a belief that was common in medieval Jain biographies, that hymns have great power. The *Caccarī* that acts as a talisman is a hymn to Jinavallabha.[109]

While Jinadatta certainly did not describe himself as a miracle worker, the existence of so many miracle stories about Jinadatta indicates that these texts saw nothing fundamentally incompatible between the monk as reformer and the monk as miracle worker. The greatest gap between the biographer's portrait of Jinadatta and his own self-portrayal is probably to be found not in Jinadatta the miracle-worker, but in a third role in which Jinadatta appears in the *Kharataragacchabṛhadgurvāvali* biography, Jinadattasūri as public figure, leader of the monastic community. In his official capacity Jinadatta travels, installs images, consecrates temples and spreads his teachings. Other official duties include insuring the continuity of the monastic community in its formal structure, and so we learn that Jinadatta installed monks and nuns in various positions in the monastic hierarchy. For the Kharatara biographers in general these are the noraml official duties of the head monk; he is a ritual specialist, he is responsible for maintaining the formal order of the community, which includes finding his own successor, and he is a teacher. The monk may also best challengers in debate, but this is not a role that is particularly ascribed to Jinadatta. In his official and public capacity Jinadattasūri is not the lone and abused reformer; his march resembles the triumphal procession; as he travels from city to city he is greeted and welcomed by exuberant crowds of the faithful. He is enormously successful in making conversions and we learn of vast numbers of families that the converted. We even hear that he converted a king, something that many celebrated monks indeed are said to have done.

As the text relates these official duties, its language becomes more formal and ornate. Sentence structure becomes more complex and compounds become longer and more studied. There is the same divergence in style, from simple story to ornate honorific prose that we observed in Vidyātilaka's account of Jinaprabhasūri. It is worth emphasizing that the formal language corresponds with the description of official ceremonies. Jinadattasūri's last official duty, his installation of Jinacandrasūri, is described in the most ornate language of all.

In summary, then, we have moved from Jinadatta's self portrait of the monk as lone reformer to a Sanskrit biography in which we may still catch a glimpse of the lone and outcaste monk, but in which we see more of the established and successful leader of a flourishing group of monks. We have also seen Jinadatta the miracle worker, one of a community of monks who perform miracles. These miracles play no role in the sectarian struggle within Jainism, but are directed towards members of other hostile faiths.

3. Conclusions

This paper was intended to show that there exist a variety of modes for speaking of monks in medieval India. Monks may speak of themselves, and the two examples discussed here have illustrated that when they do so they speak both in modes they inherit and in a language that has been used before them, but they can do so with a radically new voice. Their followers also speak of them, and have at their disposal many options indeed. Miracle stories, accounts of official acts, both exist and may intertwine. Biographies may also refer obliquely to didactic stories, but they have their own distinctive way of speaking, and only further studies of individual biographies can help us to understand all of the subtleties of their discourse.

This paper in its examination of the biographies of two sectarian leaders, I hope has shown that there are no easy generalizations about the discourse of medieval biography writing or even sectarian biography writing in Jainism. To consider the biographies of Jinadatta first, the Sanskrit biography of Jinadattasūri in the *Kharataragacchabṛhadgurvāvali* might seem at a hasty glance typical of a sectarian biography with its emphasis on the formal ceremonies Jinadatta performed and its attention to his official acts in his role as head of that community. It also might appear to be typically sectarian in that the contests Jinadatta holds are by and large with other Jain monks. At the same time, however, we have the many miracle stories associated with Jinadatta, which pay little heed to his official ceremonial roles, and have a far more universal flavor. These stories were also collected in a text that purports to be a sectarian history exactly as the Sanskrit history does; there is no indication that the group that preserved its history in this way regarded the Sanskrit text with its to us obviously "sectarian" concerns as a more definitive account of the lineage. Sectarian history or sectarian biography could emphasize intragroup conflict and public ceremonial roles within the Jain community or it might not; defining the sectarian biography is perhaps more easily done by reference to the non-sectarian biography or *prabandhas*. A medieval *prabandha* collection like the *Prabandhakośa* of Rājaśekhara will rarely tell of images installed and students promoted to certain positions, but the presence of these details was never a sine-qua-non of the sectarian biography writer.

Finally we must turn to Jinaprabhasūri, both to his memoir and to the biographies of him, again preserved in sectarian collections. Different in literary style from the biographies of Jinadatta, they also differ in content in many cases. They have little or no trace of intra-group politics but look towards a larger political arena. Only the miracle stories seem to converge.

In conclusion, it seems prudent to note the richness of possibility that exists in medieval sectarian biography writing; at this still preliminary stage of my research an exact characterization of medieval religious biography in Jainism still eludes easy reach. It is clear that if we were to isolate characteristics of the sectarian biography from the biography of Jinadatta in the *Kharataragacchabṛhadgurvāvali,* for example, we would ignore much of the rich discourse of monk in all of these other texts with their differing perspectives. The same could be said of any single text that this paper has explored.

The sectarian biography, like biography writing in general in medieval Jainism, is extremely flexible and always responsive to the exigencies of local circumstances and needs. It is this flexibility that is perhaps its defining characteristic and that is likely to have made it such an effective tool in medieval Jain religious teaching. In both form and content it had no restrictions; it could be courtly poem or racy tale; it could be bombastic eulogy or simple didactic hymn. And behind this diversity of literary form is a wide diversity of contents. There is no one sectarian leader, no one image of the chief monk. Courtier, miracle worker, scholar, ritual specialist, author, preacher, his deeds were celebrated in many forms and with many voices.

Notes

1. Indeed the seemingly simple act of including a particular monk in a given lineage may in and of itself prove to be an aggressive assertion of the authority of the lineage and a point of contention between rival groups. Such was the case with the inclusion of Abhayadeva in the Kharatara lineage. All the Kharatara *paṭṭāvalis* that I have read include Abhayadeva as a key figure in the lineage; Abhayadeva was the pupil of Jineśvara and the Kharatara *paṭṭāvalis* trace the origin of their group back beyond Jineśvara, but assert that their name "kharatara" was given to Jineśvara by the Gujarati king Durlabha, when Jineśvara defeated a rival at the king's court. The Tapāgaccha monks vigorously contest the inclusion of Abhayadeva in the Kharatara lineage. The Tapagāccha Dharmasāgara in his vigorous polemics against the Kharataras asserts categorically that one should never read the texts written by monks of other lineages which proclaim false teachings, and yet the Tapāgaccha monks read and studied the commentaries of Abhayadevasūri to the canonical texts. Dharmasāgara in a small polemical treatise entitled "*Mūlapuruṣavāda*", "The Debate Over the Founder", insists that the Kharataragaccha did not even appear until after Abhayadeva and that Abhayadeva therefore cannot be said to have been one of their group. The Kharataragaccha *paṭṭāvalis* become the focus of his attacks in very much the same way as did the doctrinal texts that these

monks have written. Dharmasāgara's text is published in the Āgamodaya Samiti Series, vol. 49, 1927.

2 There is little scholarship on the *paṭṭāvalis.* I have written about some of the biographies in the Kharatara texts in an article on the traditional biographies of Siddhasena published in the *Journal of Indian Philosophy,* part I in volume 17, 1989, pp.329-384 and Part II in vol.18, 1990, pp.261-304, and in an article on Jain biographies and clan histories, "Religious Biographies and Clan Histories Among the Svetāmbara Jains of North India" in *East and West,* vol.39, December, 1989, pp.195-217. I have also referred to some of the Kharatara biographies in my essay. "Going By the Book : The Role of Written Texts in Medieval Indian Sectarian Conflicts", in a festschrift for Professor J. Deleu that is being edited by Professor K. Watanabe. The article contains a partial translation of the biography of Jinadatta from the longer Kharatara collection that I translate in this paper. References to extant scholarship on the Kharatara biographies and to work that has been done on the general phenomenon of the rise of the different *gacchas* in Śvetāmbara Jainism may also be found in those articles. I have translated the biographies of Jineśvara from the *Kharataragacchabṛahadgurvāvali* and the *Vṛddhācāryaprabandhavāli* in a volume of Jain stories that I have edited under the title *The Clever Adulteress and the Hungry Monk,* Oakville, Ontario: Mosaic Press, 1990.

The collections of *paṭṭāvalis* that I have had access to are the following. *Khartaragacchabṛhadgurvāvali* edited with the *Vṛddhācāryaprabandhāvali* by Jina Vijaya Muni, Singhi Jain Series, vol.42, Bombay: Bharatiya Vidya Pitha, 1956 A.D. *Kharataragacchapaṭṭāvalisaṃgraha,* edited by Jinavijaya, Calcutta: Puran Chand Nahar, 1932. *Paṭṭāvalisamuccaya*, edited Muni Darśanavijaya, Viragam : Sri Caritra Smaraka Granthamala, 2 vols, 1933. The *Gurvāvali* of Munisundarasūri is a history of the deeds of the leading monks of the Tapāgaccha. It has been published on the Jaina Yashovijaya Granthamala, no. 4, Kashi: Candraprabha Press, 1905. The *Kharataragacchabṛhadgurvāvali* has been translated into Hindi by Mahāmahopādhyāy Vinayasāgara with an introduction by Agarchand Nahta as the first volume in the *Kharataragacha Kā Itihāsa*, Ajmer: Dada Jinadattasūri Astamahasatabdi Mahotsava Svagatakarini Samiti 1959. Some other paṭṭāvalis have been published in the *Jaina Aittihasika Kāvya Saṃgraha* by Agarchand Nahta and Bhanwarlal Nahta , Sri Abhaya Jaina Granthamala, Vol 8, Calcutta : Sankaradana Subhairaj Nahta 1938. The earliest Kharataragaccha Paṭṭāvali, the commentary of Sumatigaṇi to the *Gaṇadharasārdhaśataka*, dated 1239 AD. has only been published in part, in the introduction to the colume *Three Apabhraṃśā* Works of Jinadattasūri, edited by Lalchandra Bhagavandas Gandhi. Gaekwad's Oriental Seriers, vol. 37, Baroda, reprinted 1967.

3. They could nonetheless be used for sectarian purposes. Dharmasāgara in the treatise cited in note 1 turns to the *Prabhāvakacarita* for support of his

contention that Jineśvarasūri did not debate in the court of Durlabha and was not granted the epithet "Kharatara" by the king. See p.44. The *Prabhāvakacarita* is published in the Singhi Jain Series, vol.13, edited Jina Vijaya Muni, 1940. Jineśvarasūri appears in section 19, in the biography of Abhayadevasūri.

4. Thus we see Jinadatta in late Kharataragaccha *paṭṭāvalis* discovering magic books in a temple in Citrakūta, a feat associated in the *prabandhas* with Siddhasena. For details see my article on Siddhasena's biographies cited in note 2. I have written about some of the biographies in the *prabandhas* in the articles cited in note 2 and in the following articles, "Jain Biographies of Nāgārjuna: Notes on the Composing of a Biography in Medieval India", pp. 45-67 and "The Biographies of Āryakhapaṭacārya: A Preliminary Investigation into the Transmission and Adaptation of Biographical Legends", pp. 67-99 in the volume *Monks and Magicians: Religious Biographies in Asia* that I edited with Dr. Koichi Shinohara, Oakville, Ontario: Mosaic Press, 1988. I have also written on the biographies of Haribhadra in an article, "Jain Lives of Haribhadra: An Inquiry into the Sources and Logic of the Legends", *Journal of Indian Philosophy,* vol.16, 1988, pp.109-125. The major *prabandha* collections that I have used for this study are the following. *Prabandhacintamani* of Merutuṅga, edited Jinavijaya Muni, Singhi Jain Series, vol.1, Santiniketan, 1933. This has been translated into English by Tawney, *The Prabandhacintāmaṇi or Wishing-Stone of Narratives,* Calcutta: Asiatic Society, 1901. *Prabandhakośa* of Rājaśekhara, edited Jinavijaya Muni, Singhi Jain Series, vol.6, Santiniketan, 1935. I have translated some of the biographies from this text into English in *The Clever Adulteress* and there exists a complete Gujarati translation of the text by Hiralal Rasiklal Kapadia, Sri Forbes Gujarati Series, no. 18, 1934. *Prabhāvakacarita* of Prābhacandrasūri, edited Jinavijaya Muni, Singhi Jain Series, vol.13, Ahmedabad, 1940. *Purātanaprabandhasaṃgraha,* edited Jinavijaya Muni, Singhi Jain Series, vol.2, Santiniketan, 1936. *Shri Shubhasīla Gani's Panchashati Prabandha Saṃbandha,* edited Muni Shri Mṛgendra Muniji, with an introduction by Dr. Shri Harivallabh C. Bhayani, Surat: Suvasita Sahitya Prakasan, 1968.

5. The most famous of these compositions is the *Hīrasaubhāgya* of Devavimalagaṇi, published with an auto-commentary by the Nirnaya Sagara Press, Bombay, 1900, edited by Kashinatha Pandurang Parab. Other famous examples that I have used for this study are the following. *Digvijayamahākāvya* of Meghavijayagaṇi, edited by Pandit Ambarlal Premcandra Shah, Bombay: Bharatiya Vidya Pitha, Singhi Jain Series, vol.14, 1949; *Guruguṇaratnākara* of Somacaritragaṇi, edited in the Yashovijayagranthamala by Muni Indravijaya, Benaras: Dharmabhyudaya Press, Vira Samvat 2437; *Vijayadevasūrimāhātmya,* written by Śrī Vallabha Upādhyāy, edited by Jinavijaya, Jaina Sahitya Samshodak Granthamala, 1928. While all of these are independent poetic

compositions they differ considerabily from each other in style. The *Hīrasaubhāgya* conforms most closely to the standards of the Sanskrit *mahākāvya.* This type of biography seems to have been particularly favoured by the Tapāgaccha, a group that maintained close links with circles of political power and the culture of the court. I would note here that while the division I have made between *paṭṭāvali, prabandha,* and these *mahākāvyas* is no doubt useful it is by no means a rigid division. There exist histories of lineages that call themselves *prabandhas* (the *Vṛddhācāryaprabandhāvali* of a splinter group of the Kharataragaccha cited in note 2 is an example), and *paṭṭāvalis* written after the *Hīrasaubhāgya* cite that poem as their source (see the Tapāgaccha *paṭṭāvali* in the *Paṭṭāvalisamuccaya* of Muni Darśana Vijaya cited in note 2, pp. 71-77).

6. For this study I have relied primarily on the poems collected in the *Jaina Aitihāsika Kāvya Saṃgraha* cited in note 2. That some of these poems were used by monks for their own readings is clear from a colophon to a poem about Jinalabdhisūri which states that the manuscript was for the private devotions of the monk Jinabhadra. See the article by Agarchand and Bhanwarlal Nahta, "Kharataragaccha ke Ācāryoṃ Sambandhi Katipaya Ajñāta Aitihāsika Rācañaeṃ", in the *Śrī Mahāviravidyālaya Suvarṇamahotsava Grantha,* Bombay: Sri Mahavira Vidyalaya, 1968, pp. 24-36. There are also poems written by monks about their former teachers that are deeply emotional and fervent prayers, couched in the very language that these authors use to address their petitions to the *tīrthaṅkaras.* These poems usually do not deal with the specifics of the teacher's life, but with his power to destroy the petitioner's bad *karma* and lead him into the city of Release. Typical of such poems are those by the 16th century monk Samayasundarasūri on Śrī Jinakuśalasūri and some of the other late Kharatara leaders. See the *Samayasundarakṛtikusumañjali* edited by Agarchand and Bhanwarlal Nahta, Abhaya Jaina Granthamala no.15, Calcutta, 1956, pp. 349-417. Like the various Tīrthaṅkaras, these teachers also have sacred sites or *pīṭhas* where they are particularly powerful and to which pilgrimages are made. Samayasundara's poems are often addressed to the teacher at a specific site, and some enjoin worship of the teacher's footprints at specific times of the calendar year.

7. The origins of medieval biography writing are obscure. Scholars normally assume the first collections to have been either that of Bhadresvara in his *Kahavali,* still unpublished, or Hemacandra in his *Parisistaparvan.* For references see my paper on Haribhadra cited in note 4.

8. A Colophon to poems written about Jinalabdhisuri gives the information that the poems were part of a diverse collection of writing that the monk-Jinabhadrasūri kept together for his own private study. See the article by Agarchand and Bhanwarlal Nehta cited in note 6.

9. In my choice of the term "discourse" I have in mind the type of study that Philippe Lejeune has undertaken for autobiography. See *On autobiography*, Minneapolis : University of Minnesota Press, 1989, Particularly pp. 162-184. I should like to do a similar study of ways of conceptualizing monks' lives medieval Jainism and I envision this paper as a preliminary stage of a much fuller study.

10. The Kharatara monks regard their lineage as older than Jinadatta, while certain of their rivals consider that the Kharataragaccha was in fact founded by Jinadatta. See the remarks of Dharmasāgara a sixteenth century opponent of the Kharataragaccha in his *Śrīmahāvīravijñaptidvātrimśikā*, page 15 in the edition published under the title *dharmasāgaragranthasaṃgraha* in the Agamoddharaka Granthamala, volume 18, Calcutta 1961, edited by Munilābhasāgara. Dharmasāgara is adamant that Jinadatta founded the Kharatara sect. See also note 1, above.

11. Neither monk is unique in doing so. The subject of autobiographical writing in medieval India deserves far more attention than it has received to date. Mukund Lath, who translated the most extensive autobiography that is known from medieval India, the *Ardhakathānaka* of the lay Jain Banarsīdās, discusses the general subject of autobiography in India in his introduction to the translation, *Half a Tale : A Study in the Interrelationship between Autobiography and History,* Jaipur: Rajasthan Prakrit Bharati Sansthan, 1981. The text has also been edited by R.S. Sharma in *Indica,* Vol.vii, 1970, with a translation and some remarks. Mukund Lath concluded that autobiography was more an unfulfilled promise than a reality in medieval India; he singled out for particular notice Bāṇa and Daṇḍin as authors who wrote of themselves, albeit briefly. It is Lath's opinion that after Dandin there is no significant autobiographical expression in India (see p.xx). My own investigations have led me to the opposite conclusion, that in fact there is considerable interesting autobiographical writing in medieval India and that scholars need to look afresh at this writing.

For example, the *Bhānucandragaṇicarita* of Siddhicandra, which I will discuss again below, in fact contains a detailed autobiography of Siddhicandra. The text has been edited by Mohanlal Dalicandra Desai with a lengthy introduction on the Jains at the Moghul courts in the Singhi Jain Series, vol 15, Calcutta and Ahmedabad: Singhi Jain Granthamala, 1941. In his brief introduction to the work Vijaya Muni commented on the fact that the *Bhānucandragaṇicarita* is both biography of Bhānucandra and autobiography of Siddhicandra (p.vi). Desai also cites Samayasundara's own words that describe his encounter with the Emperor Akbar (p.13, note 14). There are in addition numerous confessional and devotional poems in medieval Jainism which are extremely personal and revealing of their author's state of mind. I hope in the future to study both the ritual of confession in medieval Jainism and the autobiographical confessional poems that I believe are related to it. I delivered a paper on the general subject of autobiographical writing in medieval Jainism at the 33rd ICANAS held in Toronto in August, 1990 that touches upon some of this material. The paper will be published in the conference proceedings and includes some of the translations of Jinadatta's *Upadeśarasāyana* that also appear here. I am also presently preparing a study of autobiographical narratives in didactic stories that includes an analysis of the autobiography the Śvetāmbara monk Siddharṣi wrote in the tenth century, the *Upamitibhavaprapañcakathā*.

Medieval Hinduism also provides many examples of autobiographical writings that deserve to be better known; in the Rādhāvallabha tradition, for example there is the *Svapnaprasaṅga* of Ananya Ali Jī, an autobiographical account in which dreams play a major role. Excerpts from the text are given in Vijayendra Snātak, *Rādhāvallabha Saṃpradāya: Siddhānta aur Sāhitya,* Delhi: National Publishing House, 1968, pp.482-483 and in Dr. Virendranāth Miśra's *Vrajbhāṣa Gadyasāhitya kā Vikās,* Delhi: Pandulipi Prakasan, 1982, p.165. Ananya Ali Jī and his work are discussed in Prabhudayāl Mitāl, *Vraj ke Dharma-saṃpradāyon kā Ithihāsa,* Delhi: National Book Publishing, 1968, p. 414. The text has been edited from Vrndavan, v.s.2009. I thank Dr. Alan Entwistle of University of Washington, Seattle, for sending me a copy.

The Śaṅkaradeva Vaiṣṇava tradition of Assam made extensive use of biographical writings and descriptions of the literature in secondary sources give ample indication that autobiographical writing also exists in medieval Assam. So for example we read of Cakrapāṇi, who told his own life in the last section of his biography of Śaṅkaradeva, much as Siddhicandra did in his account of Bhānucandra. See Dr. Kesavananda Dev Goswami, *Post-Śaṅkaradeva Vaiṣṇava Faith and Culture of Assam,* Sri Garib Dass Oriental Series, no. 79, Delhi: Sri Satguru Publications, 1988, p.208. Another example, Vidyānanda Ojhā gives an account of incidents in his own life in his biography of Purusottama and Caturbhuja Ṭhākur, and like Jinaprabhasūri uses the third-person in his autobiographical sections (Goswami, p.4).

In medieval Bengali writing Kṛttivāsa, the author of the *Rāmāyana* in Bengali, has left us with a detailed autobiography. He begins with a history of his ancestors and then speaks of himself in the same mixture of first and third-person discourse that characterize the account of Jinaprabhasuri that is studied in this paper: "Kṛttivāsa was born on a Sunday, the fifth day in the month of Māgh. At an auspicious moment I fell from my mother's womb to this earth. My father wrapped me in a clean cloth and took me onto his lap." The account continues with a description by Kṛttivāsa of his studies and accomplishments, culminating in his reception by the king of Gauda who was pleased with Kṛttivāsa's poetic talents. Kṛttivāsa is perhaps the least modest of medieval India autobiographers; he does not hesitate to tell us how Sarasvatī, the Goddess of Learning, possessed him and how through Her power he learned many languages without the slightest trouble. The autobiography is printed in the edition of Kṛttivāsa's *Rāmāyaṇa* edited by Upendranath Mukhopadhyaya, Calcutta: Vasumati Sahitya Mandir, n.d.

It is clear that a review of autobiographical literature in medieval India is a desideratum; standard sources on Europe maintain vigorously that "individualism", biography, autobiography and portraiture are uniquely Western conceptions (Colin Morris, *The Discovery of the Individual,* 1050-1200, London, SPCK, 1972, chapter 1), while no study exists of the Indian material that would easily contradict such unsubstantiated assertions. See also John Paul Eakin, *Fictions in Autobiography: Studies in the Art of Self-Invention,* Princeton: Princeton University Press, 1985 and Karl Weintraub, "Autobiography and Historical Consciousness", in *Critical Inquiry,* vol.1, 1975, pp.821-845.

12. Edited Jinavijaya Muni, Singhi Jain Series, vol.10, Santiniketan, 1934, no.22, pp.45-47. Jinaprabha describes his own deeds here in a section about the holy place called Kanyānayanatīrtha, which I translate in this paper.

13. See Karl Weintraub's distinction in his article cited above, "Autobiography and Historical Conciusness", in *Critical Inquiry,* vol.1, 1975, pp.821-845.

14. See the works of Jinadatta published in *Three Apabhraṃśa Works of Jinadattasūri,* cited note 2.

15. Vidyātilaka, the student of Saṃghatilaka, wrote an addendum to the section on Kanyānayanatīrtha. This appears as section 51, pp. 95-97. I have translated it in this paper. Jinaprabha was still alive when Vidyātilaka wrote this, for Vidyātilaka here offers a prayer for Jinaprabha's long life. Vidyātilaka is known as the author of a commentary to Haribhadra's *Ṣaddarśanasamuccaya* that he wrote in 1335 A.D. A manuscript of this commentary exists in Jaisalmer and the colophon describes Vidyātilaka as the student of Saṃghatilaka, exactly as he describes himself in the Kanyānayanatīrtha addendum. There is no question that the author of this addendum is the author of the commentary to the *Ṣaddarśanasamuccaya* and a contemporary of Jinaprabhasūri. See Muni Shri Puṇyavijayaji, *Catalogue of Sanskrit and Prakrit Manuscripts, Jesalmer Collection,* Ahmedabad: L.D. Institute of Indology, L.D. Series, 36, 1972, p. 325 for the colophon. Jinadatta was eulogized during his life time by a poet Palha. The text is published as appendix 4 in the volume *Three Apabhraṃśa Works of Jinadattasūri,* cited in note 2.

16. For Jinaprabhasūri the main sources have been extensively reviewed by Lalcandra Bhagavandas Gandhi in his book in Gujarati, *Śrījinaprabhasūri āne Sultān Mahammad,* Srisukhasagara Jnanabindu series volume 35, Lohavat (Marwar): Śrīnaharisagarsūri Jnanabhandar, 1939. I was able to get this book only after I finished writing the bulk of the paper; nonetheless I have benefitted from reading it. I was also only able to find the essay on Jinaprabhasūri by

Agarchand and Bhanwarlal Nahta after completing this paper. Their essay is included in the edition of Jinaprabhasūri's *Vidhimārgaprapā* that was published in the Sri Jinadattasūri-pracinapustakoddhara Fund, volume 44, edited by Jina Vijaya, and published from Surat in 1941. While the Nahtas have relied heavily on Gandhi's book they also have some new information about the biographies of Jinaprabhasūri, particularly about the location of places like Kanyānayanatīrtha that figure so prominently in the accounts of Jinaprabhasūri. Both Gandhi and the Nahtas accept that Jinaprabhasūri wrote a memoir in the form of the *Kanyānayanatīrthakalpa* that I have translated here. See pp. 24-25. On p. 38 Gandhi remarks on the fact that Jinaprabhasūri identifies himself only indirectly in the concluding verse of the memoir, something that I have interpreted as revealing the formal reliance of the memoir on the conventions of the *praśasti.* Gandhi prefers to understand Jinaprabha's hesitation to use his own name as evidence of his humility. The Nahtas on page 12 of their article on Jinaprabhasūri in the edition of the *Vidhimārgaprapā* accept the account of the *Kanyānayanatīrthakalpa* as an autobiographical account.

In addition to the accounts of him in the *Vividhatīrthakalpa,* my own study in the present paper is based on the biography of Jinaprabhasūri published in the introduction of the *Purātanaprabandhasaṃgraha,* pp. 30-32 which I have translated. This is from a late manuscript that can only be dated as before the 18th century. In addition I have read the poems in the *Jaina Aitihāsika Kāvya Saṃgraha,* cited in note 2, and the many short miracle tales in the *prabandha* collection of Śubhaśīlagaṇi cited in note 2. I have also used and translated the section in the *Vṛddhācāryaprabandhāvali.* This text, written most likely by a student of Jinaprabhasūri, may be the earliest of these miracle collections. See note 2 for publication details.

For Jinadatta the sources are extensive. The earliest major biography is that by Sumatigaṇi done in 1239 A.D., eighty-four years after Jinadatta's death. The biography in the standard Sanskrit history of the Kharatara school written by Jinapāla follows Sumatigaṇi's text almost word for word and was probably written not long after Sumatigaṇi's wrote his work. All of the late Kharataragaccha *paṭṭāvalis* include biographies of Jinadatta as does the *Vṛddhācāryaprabandhāvali* and there are numerous poems that celebrate his deeds as well. Miracle stories about Jinadatta appear in all of these texts and in another source: the vernacular stories that describe the origins of the various Jain clans. For details of the publication of the texts see note 2 of this paper and for information on the clan histories see my paper on clan histories and religious biographies cited in note 2. The book, *Yugapradhāna Śrī Jinadattasūri,* by Agarchand and Bhanwarlal Nahta provides an extremely useful overview of the stories told of Jinadatta. It has been published in the Sri Abhaya Jina Granthamala, vol.12, Calcutta: Sankardana Subhairaj Nahta, 1947.

17. The Tapāgaccha monk Dharmasāgarasūri does both of these things. He rejects the claim of the Kharataragaccha monks that their lineage includes Abhayadevasūri and he rewrites the biography of Jinadatta so that Jinadatta is made to appear ludicrous. In the autocommentary to the *Iiriyāpathikāṣattriṃśikā,* edited in the Agamodaya Samiti Granthamala, 49,1927, p.27 ff, on verse 25, Dharmasāgara relates how Jinadatta worshipped Cāmuṇḍā in order to increase his popularity. Jinadatta's biographies, on the other hand, extol the monk for his conquest and conversion of Cāmuṇḍā. Dharmasāgara also tells how Jinadatta was chastised by Śrī Hemācārya and fled on a camel. He lies to his followers when they ask him how he has travelled so quickly : he claims that he has used his magic power to make a camel carry him speedily. For this he is given the name "camel driver", a name that is clearly pejorative and makes him angry. In what follows on Jinadatta I shall attempt to identify his speicific opponent as Hemacandra Maladhārī : Dharmasāgara's Hemacandra is the Hemacandra assoicated with Kumārapāla. It is conceivable that he has confused the two monks. It is worth noting that Dharmasāgara's attempt to revile the Kharatara monks by rewriting their biographies is not without parallel in medieval sectarian conflicts in India. The followers of Madhva rewrite the biography of Śaṅkara in the Maṇimañjarī. See my article, "Holy Warriors: A preliminary study of some Biographies of Saints and Kings in the Classical Indian Tradition", *Journal of Indian Philosophy,* vol. 12, 1984, P.296. Dharmasāgara rewrites the histories of other groups and other monks; he also explicitly rejects their claims that their teachings were validated by visions of the Goddess of the Faith by calling such claims outright lies. See the *Īriyāpathikādṣatriṃśikā* p.27 on the same verse where Dharmasāgara calls Candraprabha's claim that Presiding Goddess of the Faith visited him in a dream a lie. Paul Dundas has written more extensively about Dharmasāgara attacks on the Kharatara accounts of their lineage. For futher information on the subject the reader is referred to his paper, "The Marginal Monk and the True Tīrtha", to be published in the Festschrift for Jozef Deleu cited in note 2.

18. Throughout its long history Jain literature had always spoken of monks, in the stories in the canonical texts, in texts devoted entirely to prescribing the proper behavior of a monk, and in the many didactic stories that monks wrote and told each other and their lay audiences, to give a few examples. This study begins with the working hypothesis that canonical stories and the didactic stories which are closely related to the canonical texts offer a mode of discourse about monks that is different from that exploited by the medieval biography writer. Actually to prove this hypothesis would require an in-depth study of the language used to describe monks in the canonical texts and didactic stories, particularly the stories that were contemporary to the medieval biographies. I have not yet made such a study and I have based my hypothesis on a random reading of stories in these sources.

My conclusions to date are that while some of the medieval accounts of monks may be found in didactic story collections and so might be considered to have grown from the important didactic story tradition of Śvetāmbara Jainism, even those accounts portrary monks in a light that is different from the image of the average monk that emerges from the didactic story with its strong links back to canonical stories. The description of monks in didactic stories, good monks, bad monks, struggling monks or monks who have fulfilled their purposes, share an emphasis on the religious vows that a monk takes and the ascetic practices that define him as a monk. For example, there are clear patterns for the behaviour of monks in a canonical text like the *Antagadadasāo*, where lay men hear the preaching, become monks, ask the permission of the teacher to do penance, perform a penance that is described with some specificity, and then reach their goal, being reborn in heaven with an assurance of release in the future. The pattern obtains for women as well as men. The language used to describe Indrabhūti in the *Uvāsagadasāo*, chapter 1 is also indicative of the emphasis on the asceticism of the monk; Indrabūti's physical appearance is described in terms that make clear his ability to perform asceticism and then there follows a number of adjectives describing his penances. The *Jñātādharmakathā*, 1, offers in its description of Meghakumāra the classical description of the monk that is closely followed in the didactic story tradition, where the monk's deportment is carefully described as he exercises strict control over the way he walks and speaks.

When we turn to the didactic stories, for example the many stories in the *Triṣaṣṭiśalākāpuruṣacarita* of Hemacandra, we see a similar emphasis on the monk's conquering desire and anger, practicing penance, exercising patience and forbearance (edited by Puṇyavijayaji in the Sri Jaina Atmananda Satabdi Series, no. 8, Bhavanagar: Sri Jaina Atmananda Sabha, 1950, book 2, sarga 1, vs.78-81) Later in the same chapter the monk is described as preserving the *samitis* in exactly the same terms used to describe Meghakumāra in the *Jñātādharmakathā*. There is a long passage from vs.265 that describes in detail the careful behavior of the monk in his eating and excreting, his attitudes towards heat and cold, thirst and hunger; we learn that he does not bathe nor fan himself; he does not respond when bitten by mosquitoes and does not grow angry when abused. Finally in the culmination of his career we read of his penance and his death by fasting.

If this description represents the normative account of a monk in a medieval didactic collection it is clear that the medieval biographies use a very different form of discourse. The medieval biographies have little to say of the proper deportment of monks, of how they eat and where they excrete; the medieval biography may describe an entire career without a mention of penance or the observation of a monastic vow. We do not read of monks enduring hardship from heat and cold but of monks engaged in triumphal marches, in grand ceremonies of pilgrimage and heated public debates in the courts of kings.

The death of the monk is often only perfunctorily mentioned in medieval biographies and few monks whose stories are told are explicityly said to achieve release; most, we learn simply go to heaven. Since descriptions of monks like those offered by Hemacandra in his *Triṣaṣṭiśālākapuruṣacarita* and in other later didactic texts are in fact contemporary with many of the medieval biographies it is not sufficient to view this change in language as primarily an historical change that is connected with changes in the role of monks in society. This is the view of S. Settar in his recent book, *Inviting Death: Indian Attitudes Towards the Ritual Death,* Leiden: E.J. Brill, 1989, Monographs and Theoretical Studies in Sociology and Anthropology in Honour of Nels Anderson, publication 38. Settar noted a change in the language of inscriptions in South Indian Jainism, the same kind of change in perspective that I would like to see in the alternatives of didactic story/canonical story as opposed to medieval biography. Settar noted that the early names of monks all emphasize their asceticism while a new language appears in the medieval period which emphasizes the close connection of the monk with political power and the public display of aggressive brilliance in debate. There is a close connection between the language of some of these inscriptions and the language of the medieval biography; for South Indian monks some of the most famous biographical stories in fact appear in a well-known inscription as well as in story collections. (For details of this inscription see my papers on Haribhadra and Siddhasena cited in notes 2 and 4).

I would prefer at this point in my understanding to regard the change as one of emphasis; the model of the monk as ascetic that pervades the canon and the didactic story continues throughout the medieval period but a different model (or different models) is preferred by biography writers. To the extent that medieval biographies have a distinctive mode of discourse they may be understood as loosely constituting a genre and we must look to other genres for the kind of information that we might have expected from a biography but did not find: information about the austerities and religious practices of the monks. The didactic story is not the only source of such information. There was in the medieval Jain community another specific mode of writing in which monks described their austerities and the religious practices of the lay community they directed. This is the *sāṃvatsarika patra,* a letter, which monks exchanged and which described in summary from but with meticulous detail the various austerities that everyone observed. There has been very little scholarship to date done on these marvellous documents; I would refer interested readers to the remarks by Agarchand and Bhanwarlal Nahta in their introduction to the volume, *Bikaner Jaina Lekha Saṃgraha,* in the Sri Abhaya Jain Granthamala, number 15, Calcutta: Nahta Brothers, Vira samvat, 2472, pp. 87 ff. The Nahtas also reproduce some letters of kings to monks, which also deserve to be better known. I hope in the future to study some of this documentation, but in the present paper I shall confine my efforts to studying the complexities of the discourse about monks which biography writers employed.

There is no question that this discourse exists in contrast to the widely-known mode of discourse in the didactic story; indeed specific biographies may even play upon the contrast. I think for example of the biography of the monk Vīrasūri in the *Prabhāvakacarita,* no.15, pp.127-132. Vīrasūri stops the night in the temple of a demi-god, Vallabhīnātha. Vallabhīnātha kills anyone who sleeps in his temple at night, and he makes every effort to put an end to Vīrasūri too. The terrible attacks he conjures up for the monk are immediately familiar: these are the vision the meditating devotees see in the *Uvāsagadasāo.* But instead of the expected denouement, the devotee enduring the visions or succumbing and then eventually prevailing and reaching his religious goal, we have a different conclusion. The monk conquers the non-Jain deity and gains him as a servant. Together they fly off to visit the magical realms and magical Jain images, and the monk even brings back some divine rice grains that the king of the Gods had offered to one of the Jains and in so doing amazes a king, furthers the cause of the faith and himself becomes greatly celebrated. The asceticism of the devotee who could endure terrible visions in his meditation becomes here a magical act of power through which the charismatic monk subdues a deity, gains his friendship, is able to perform further magical feats and convert kings.

This story of Vīrasūri also clearly points to a third large group of biographical writing that must be considered if we are to understand the special status of medieval biographies of monks. This is the biographies of the *tīrthaṅkaras,* the earliest of which are to be found in the *Āvaśyaka* commentaries. Like Vīrasūri, for example, Mahāvīra sojourns in temples of non-Jain deities and eventually receives their homage. While many of the story motifs that can be found in medieval biographies of monks also appear in the biographies of the *tīrthañkaras* my reading to date leads me to conclude that the *tīrthaṅkara* biographies are indeed a different group of writings with different emphases. While I must reserve any definitive comments for future research, I would say at this point that *tīrthaṅkara* biographies privilege stages in the lives of their subject that are absent from the biographies of most if not all medieval monks. The Jains stress that the *tīrthaṅkaras* in a past life acquired the special kind of karma that determined that they would become *tīrthaṅkara.* Biographies of *tīrthaṅkaras* relate in great detail these past lives and point out the particular life in which a *tīrthaṅkara* acquired his special *karma.* Biographies of medieval monks do not include accounts of past lives. The birth of the *tīrthaṅkara* is a special *topos* that is also absent from most biographies of medieval monks; another missing *topos* is the acquisition of the supernatural knowledges of Jainism: *avadhi, manaḥparyāya,* and *kevalajñāna.* Monks do not achieve *kevala jñāna* in the biographies written about them, while this is a central episode in the biography of a *tīrthaṅkara.* Biographies of the *tīrthaṅkaras* also stress their austerities; medieval monks are not primarily ascetics and there is much pageantry in their careers. In short, while biographies of *tīrthaṅkaras* and medieval monks may converge in their accounts of conversions and debates with heretics, at almost all the other points they are strikingly different. For a synoptic discussion of the biographies of the *tīrthaṅkaras* in the *Āvaśyaka* tradition see Nalini Balbir's recent thesis done at the Sorbonne. The thesis has a long section on the biographies of Mahāvīra and Ṛṣabha.

19. This is the underlying assumption of the discussion by Jina Vijaya Muni in his Hindi introduction to the text. John Cort has also discussed the text and translated many of the sections in the volume of Jain literature that I have edited, *The Clever Adulteress and the Hungry Monk,* cited in note 2.

20. The first section deserves careful study in its own right and I hope to return to it at a later date in a more general discussion of stories about miraculous images in medieval India. The passage is invaluable for what it tells us about how the medieval Jain tradition conceptualized the perfect, most efficacious image. In addition it shows close parallels to medieval Hindu accounts of images; for example, this image rings like a bell when struck. In the *Padmasaṃhitā,* a late Pāncarātra text, we learn that an image to be efficacious must be made from a masculine stone, which is there defined as a stone that resounds like fine bell metal when struck. See the *Padmasaṃhitā Kriyāpada,* 11.25 ff. The text has been edited by Smt. Seetha Padmanabhan and Prof. R.N. Sampath in the Pancaratra Parisodhana Parisad Series, no.3, Madras, 1974.

21. By contrast in the brief introductory paragraph about the Mahāvīra image the author does use a first-person pronoun once. This is in the very beginning in the description of the Mahāvīra image. It is stated simply that the image was consecrated by Jinapatisūri, whom he calls, "my former teacher". This statement is in fact corroborated by the *Kharataragacchabṛhadgurvāvali,* p.24, line 6 from the bottom. Jinapatisūri was not the direct teacher of Jinaprabhasūri, but the teacher of Jineśvara, who in turn was the teacher of Jinasimhasūri, Jinaprabhasūri's own teacher. Jinaprabhasūri here uses the term. "my former teacher" to mean an earlier teacher in my lineage. Given the very general nature of this reference, we still must wait until the end of the entire prose section before we learn that the author of the passage was in fact the leading disciple of Jinasiṃhasūri, namely Jinaprabhasūri, the main protagonist of the text as well. As I discuss in detail I would like to see in this delayed confirmation of the identity of author and actor and the use of third-person throughout the actual narrative dealing with his own acts a reliance on the medieval *praśasti* as a formal model.

In a recent work on Chinese autobiographical writing Pei-Yi Wu noted that Chinese autobiographical writing relied heavily on biography and also utilized the third-person. He sought to connect this with the well-known Chinese penchant for history writing; biography as history recorded external facts and autobiography, dependant on biography, also kept to a strict factual account in the third-person. See *The Confucian's Progress: Autobiographical Writings in Traditional China,* Princeton: Princeton Universtiy Press, 1990, particularly the first chapter. In the case of Jinaprabhasūri's account of his own deeds I would prefer to understand his use of the third-person in terms of a more specific reliance on the literary model of the *praśasti.* It is interesting to note that this type of writing also existed in traditional China. Pei-Yi Wu called it "authorial self-account" (p.42)

22. The use of honorifics in an autobiography would seem not to be confined to this short passage by Jinaprabha. Michael Aris in his study of the substantial autobiography of the Tibetan monk Pemalingpa, *Hidden Treasures and Secret Lives: A Study of Pemalingpa (1450-1521) and the Sixth Dalai Lama (1683-1706),* Indian Institute of Advanced Study, Shimla, Delhi: Motilal Banarsidass, 1988, p.20 noted that "Pemalingpa quite often commits the solecism of using honorific expressions towards himself, though this is probably as much a fault of expression as a reflection of the certainty of his divine role." In the present case of Jinaprabha I would prefer to regard the use of honorifics not as a solecism, but as perfectly consistent with the fact that what we have here is an author speaking of himself in the third-person and following strictly all the usual norms of third-person accounts. The question then turns to the origins of or at least the models for speaking about one's own deeds in the third person.

In addition there are numerous cases in which medieval Indian authors speak unhesitatingly of their own religious and intellectual accomplishments. For example, Jayaratha, the commentator to Abhinavagupta's *Tantrāloka,* follows Abhinavagupta's autobiography with one of his own in the concluding chapter of the text. In his concluding verses he praises himself unstintingly, saying that he has reached the ultimate state of merging into pure non-dual consciousness, and that there is no one on earth more learned than himself in the doctrines of the *Tantrāloka. See Tantrāloka,* vol.VIII, pp.3724-3725, in the new edition by R.C. Dwivedi and Navjivan Rastogi, Delhi: Motilal Banarsidass, 1987.

Even a brief acquaintance with the related literature warns us against judging Jayaratha's self-praise harshly and considering it a product of his arrogance. The existence of closely related examples where an author speaks unhesitatingly of his spiritual and intellectual gifts indicates that Jayaratha was following a recognized convention in so speaking of himself. A short text eulogizing Abhinavagupta, the *Gurunāthaparāmarśa* includes verses that describe the author's own spiritual accomplishments as well as praising Abhinavagupta, his *guru,* who helped him achieve his religious goals. See V. Raghavan, "The *Gurunāthaparāmarśa*" in *Abhinavagupta and His Works,* Varanasi:

Chaukhambha Oriental Research Series, vol.20, 1980, pp.1017. In the same volume Raghavan also mentions a text still in manuscript, the *Svātmapraśaṃsā,* in which an author describes his own spiritual achievements. See p.28. Abhinavagupta himself often described his own spiritual accomplishments. In the *Bhairava Stava,* or "Hymn to Bhairava", printed by K.C. Pandey on p.951-952 of his *Abhinavagupta: An Historical and Philosophical Study,* Varanasi: Chowkhamba Sanskrit Series Vol.1, 1963, Abhinavagupta describes how he has achieved realization of the truth that everything is non-different from God. In the short *Anubhavanivedanam,* also published by Pandey, p.953, Abhinavagupta describes his actual experience of the ultimate reality. It is clear that there exists a tradition in which religious aspirants speak openly of their experiences and of their achievements, often in verse. The subject deserves a detailed study.

23. The possible permutations and combinations of these basic elements deserve study. It would be extremely useful for any consideration of medieval Indian "autobiographical" writing to review in detail a number of *praśastis* and examine how authors describe themselves and the conditions under which they wrote. Also relevant are the types of Tantric texts discussed in the preceding note. Another related genre of "autobiographical" writing is the songs of vernacular saints and tantric poets, a genre that was beginning to achieve prominence when Jinaprabhasūri was writing. The Buddhist *caryāgītis,* for example, often combine an "I" statement with an identifying concluding line that names the poet by name. In contrast to Jinaprabha's text and the *praśasti* the balance in these poems is more heavily on the "I"; the verse is often a first-person statement with a third-person concluding line. In this they are closer to medieval hymns and exhortatory texts written in the first-person that will be discussed later in the treatment of Jinadatta's Apabhraṃśa poems. While it is unlikely that Jinaprabha read the *caryāgītis* themselves, it is possible that this general type of writing was known to him. This would have given him several models at least for the combination of third-person and first-person in speaking about himself, including *praśastis* and mystical songs. I hope in the future to return to the question of medieval Indian conventions for autobiographical writing and make a more detailed study of the literary models and their implications than I can do at present.

24. This use of the third-person to speak about oneself is not confined to *praśastis* as they appear in books; inscriptions in temples may do the same. Hans Bakker recently analyzed a number of interesting inscriptions from Ramtek in Maharashtra. He considered two of them to have been written on the same occasion of a pilgrimage to the holy site. The first inscription tells of Sarṅgadeva, whose praises are sung by a poet Trivikrama. The second inscription tells how the poet Trivikrama, son of Śrīdhara, son of Camuṇḍa, with his brother offered homage to Rāma. Bakker identified the poet Trivikrama

in the second inscription as the author as well as the actor in the inscription. Nonetheless, he speaks of himself only in the third-person. See Hans Bakker, " The Ramtek Inscriptions", *Bulletin of the School of Oriental and African Studies,* vol. LII, part 3, 1989, pp.470-473.

25. The *Dharmābhyudayamahākāvya* is edited by Muni Caturavijayaji in the Singhi Jain Series, vol. 4, Bombay: Bharatiya Vidya Pitha, 1949. The colophon appears on p.188-190.

26. Another problem that deserves study is the extent to which authors in fact introduced the first-person in their *praśastis;* it is clear that some *praśastis* do use the combination of first-person and third-person, but it would be interesting to know how prevalent the pattern actually was. For example, one text contemporary to jinaprabha's *Vividhatīrthakalpa,* the *Prabandhacintāmaṇi* of Merutuṅga exemplifies the pattern; it states in the third-person that someone, unnamed, made this text as a service to the wise and pious. There then intervenes a verse praisng the text and finally there follows a verse in which the author speaks with the first-person pronoun. The *praśasti* to the Apabhraṃśa *Kahākosa* of Muni Śrīcandra written in the 11th century combines the third-person description of the author, including honorific epithets, with a first-person verse in which the author begs the reader's indulgence for any errors he may have made. See the *Kahākosa,* edited H.L. Jain, Prakrit Text Society Series, no.13, Ahmedabad: Prakrit Text Society, 1969, pp.538-539. The *praśasti* to the *Navasāhasāṅkacarita* written by Padmagupta in the first decade of the eleventh century begins with a verse in the third-person in which the poet says that Padmagupta wrote this poem, having been granted special poetic wisdom through his faith in Rāma. The second verse then switches to the first-person. The poet turns to the king, whose deeds the poem celebrates, and asks, "Sindhurāja! Let this poem that I have written, of resplendent beauty, grace your ears like jewelled earrings." See page 288 of the text edited by Shastri Jitendrachandra Bharatiya, Varanasi: Vidyabhavan Sanskrit Granthamala, 66, 1963. By contrast the *Prabandhakośa* of Rājaśekharasūri, roughly contemporary to Jinaprabhasūri, uses only the third-person pronoun. Abhinavagupta's extended *praśasti,* which constitutes virtually the entire 37th chapter of the *Tantrāloka,* is written in the third-person, while his commentator, Jayaratha uses both third-person and first-erson for the account of his own family and his own deeds. A general study of a variety of these and other medieval *praśastis* would be a necessary first step in understanding the conventions and the patterns of discourse of speaking about oneself in medieval India.

27. The hymn is edited in the *pariśiṣta* to the *Mantrarāja Rahasya,* by Jinavijaya Muni, Singhi Jain Series, 73, Bombay: Bharatiya Vidya Pitha, 1980, p.117. We shall return to a consideration of hymns as a model in general for autobiographical writing in medieval India in the discussion of Jinadattasūri.

28. It is worth noting that the tradition of speaking of oneself in the third person is far more widespread than the formal writing of the *praśasti* and was common in ordinary everyday usage. A modern commentator to the Tantric text, the *Cidgaganacandrikā,* in discussing how all three persons refer in fact to the subject, the "I", cites the familiar example of a person, whose name might be Caitra, saying, "Caitra greets you", *Caitraḥ praṇamati,* in the third person, an elocution that is immediately recognized to mean, "I, Caitra, greet you." It may well be that this type of well-sanctioned practice underlies the *praśasti,* with its implicit "I" in the third person which may in addition be made explicit as in Udayaprabha's *praśasti.* See Pandit Raghunatha Miśra's *Kramaprakāśikā* to the *Cidgaganacandrikā,* Sarasvati Bhavana Granthamala, vol.115, Varanasi: Sampurnanad Sanskrit Vishvavidyalaya, 1980, p.123. While Tantric philosophy was dominant at the time in which Jinaprabhasūri wrote, I am reluctant to see in his choice of the third-person pronoun anyting more than a reliance on cmmon usage and the literary model of the *praśasti.* In addition, the early Buddhist tradition offers much material to the scholar who seeks to understand conventions employed in talking about yourself in early India. The *Apadāna,* for example, is written as a first-person account, and many of the *Thera and Therīgāthās* are also in the first-person. In the commentary to the verse of the Thera Dabba, the commentator has no hesitaton in stating that the author of the verse is speaking about himself, although he does so as if he were speaking about a third party; in glossing two pronouns he states, *"ubhayenapi annaṃ viya katvā attanameva vadati",* with both these words he refers to himself, speaking as if he were speaking of another person." See page 63 of the *Theragātha Atthakathā,* edited Dr. Angaraj Chaudhary, Nalanda: Nava Nalanda Mahavihara, 1976.

29. See the *praśastis* collected as an appendix to the *Bhānucandragaṇicarita* in the edition cited in note 11.

30. We shall see when we come to a consideration of Jinadatta's poems that this was by no means the only format in which medieval Indians could speak of themselves. Exhortatory didactic texts and hymns were two other types of writing in which an author spoke of himself, in these cases in the first-person and with greater attenton to his inner states than to any external events.

31. See my paper on Siddhasena, cited in note 2.

32. *Prapannāmrta* of Anantācārya, edited Svami Ramanarayanacarya, Varanasi: Somani Trust, Sam.2023, chapters 47 and 48. Like the later Jinaprabhasūri, Rāmānuja is mocked by the sultan when he asks for the return of the image and he must make the image act as if it were alive before he can secure its return. Rāmānuja makes the image come when he calls it, while Jinaprabhasūri, we shall see, makes the image speak. Both stories imply that the Muslim considers the image useless, dead, while to the faithful Hindu and Jain devotee it is not a mere lifeless stone.

33. The traditional sources are not always agreed on who the Muslim ruler was who honored Jinaprabhasūri. As Pandit Lalcand Bhagavan Gandhi notes in his book *Śrī Jinaprabhasūri āne Sultān Mahammad,* cited in note 16, a colophon to Jinaprabhasūri's *Tīrthakalpa* identifies the ruler clearly as Muhammad Tuglak (pp.22-23). Later texts associate Jinaprabhasūri with Firoz Shah, the successor to Muhammad Tuglak. According to Gandhi, p.59, the first author to place Jinaprabhasūri in the court of Firoz Shah was the Tapāgaccha monk Somadharmasūri who in 1446, some seventy-five years after Jinaprabhasūri, wrote his *Upadeśasaptati* in which he included an account of the miracles Jinaprabhasūri performed at the court of Firoz Shah. This account corresponds closely with that in the *Purātanaprabandhasamgraha.* Śubhasīlagaṇi in his collection of *prabandhas* also associates Jinaprabhasūri with Firoz Shah and not Muhammad Tuglak. This apparently later tradition of the miracles at Firoz Shah's court seems to be connected with the Tapāgaccha, as opposed to the earlier miracle story tradition recorded in the Prakrit *Vṛddhācāryaprabandhāvali,* by a student of Jinaprahasūri's and thus by the Kharataragaccha. The two traditions, however, are not separate independent lines of transmission of miracle stories; they show many similarities in their accounts.

It is interesting to note that the Jain respect for the tolerance of both these rulers is not borne out by other accounts of their religious policies. In particular Jain appreciation of the generosity of Firoz Shah is in direct contrast to Hindu accounts of this ruler, who was regarded as a staunch iconoclast and markedly intolerant man. See the remarks in Prabhudayāl Mītal, *Vraj ke Dharma-Sampradāyoṃ kā Itihāsa,* Delhi: National Publishing House, 1968, p.245-246. See also Firoz Shah's own self-glorification, which has been translated by N.B. Roy in *Islamic Culture,* XV, 1941, pp.449-469. The image that emerges from this small text is of a highly intolerant sovereign, who found his glorification in the destruction of all those whose religious beliefs differed from what he regarded as orthodox Islam. It is curious to note that Firoz Shah never mentions his relationship with the Jain monk Jinaprabhasūri. This silence raises definite questions as to the political motivation behind the many accounts of Jinaprabha at the court of Firoz Shah that I cannot answer at this stage of my knowledge. Pandit Lalcandra Bhagavan Gandhi discusses other contemporary Jain teachers who were said to have been honored by the Muslim rulers. See pp.109-116 of his owrk cited in note 16.

34. See pages 60,61,64 etc.

35. The phrase that appears in the text "*pātasāhidattasaibāṇachāyāe*" is obscure. Gandhi in his Gujarati translation of the text fond in *Śrī Jinaprabhasūri āne Sultāṇ Mahammad,* p.50, does not translate the word.

36. This clash in attitudes towards language and culture is part of the subject of Siddhasena's traditional biographies. See my paper in the *Journal of Indian*

Philosophy, cited in note 2. This attitude is clear in many of the biographies of other monks as well. For example, in Jinaprabha's own account of his deeds that we have been discussing it is not only Jinaprabha's skill in composing his verse to the king that attracts the ruler's attention; it is also the commentary he gives on the verse, a fact which implies that the verse was not fully comprehensible without this skilled explanation. The verse that makes the king wish to invite the monk to his court and makes the monk a fit member of courtly society is a verse that is neither simple, nor readily understandable. Similarly in the *Prabandhakośa* biography of Śrī Harṣa we learn that Śrī Harṣa praises the king and then explains his verse of praise in great detail. At this the courtiers and the king were delighted. *See Prabandhakośa,* p.55. I have translated this biography in *The Clever Adulteress,* cited in note 2.

37. See the *Daśarūpa* of Dhanañjaya 2.1. My edition lacks the title page. There is a discussion of the hero of the drama in Sylvain Lévi, *Le Theatre Indien,* Paris: College de France, second edition, 1963, pp.62ff.

38. See the discussion by S.D. Gyani, *Agni-purāṇa: A Study,* Varanasi: Chowkhambha Sanskrit Series, vol.XLII, p.46-47. Daṇḍin in his *Kāvyādarśa* 1.15-17 set the rules for the subject matter of the *Mahākāvya* and described the court poem in lofty terms: the court poem is not an idle amusement, but a serious literary work that can even lead a man to the accomplishment of the ultimate religious goal. See Daniel Ingalls, *An anthology of Sanskrit Court Poetry,* Cambridge: Harvard University Press, 1965, p.33.

39. For some of the discussion on the nature of the *nayāka* in Sanskrit poetry see the references in the two previous notes.

40. There is an interesting story in the biography of Hemacandra where a Brahmin, clearly jealous of Hemacandra's success with King Siddharāja, accuses him of being of little wit and stealing all his ideas from the Brahmins. In response to this Hemacandra composes his famous grammar, to prove that he could indeed be as original as any Brahmin scholar. See the *Prabandhacintāmaṇi,* p.59.

41. In the first sarga alone some of these references include 1.64;1.83; 1.99; 1.102; 1.106; 1.112.

42. Regrettably I have often translated these complex sentences by breaking them into their component parts. While the reader misses the fact that Vidyātilaka is writing in a certain style and must be told that, the sentence is at least still readable. I feared that to render many of these long sentences with connectives and not breaking them into full stops would have made the translation unwieldy.

43. See for example Hemacandra's *Trīṣaṣṭiśalākapuruṣacarita,* cited in note 18, 1.88; 1.92; 2.811; 2.873; 2.935-6; *Antagadadasāo,* where the Tīrthaṅkaras preach and instruct the new monks on penance. The *Bhāgavatīsūtra* recounts a number of debates that Mahāvīra has with leaders of other religious groups,

although the formal debate at the court of the king is clearly a medieval phenomenon and is not a part of the canonical texts.

44. The *Hīrasaubhāgyakāvya,* for example, takes great pains to establish a precedent for Hīravijaya as the teacher of the Emperor Akbar. The poem cites several times the precedent of the monk Bappabhaṭṭisūri, who was at the court of King Āma (17.84;17,198). Bappabhaṭṭisūri's biography appears in the various *Prabandha* collections and the *Śatruñjayamahākalpa,* a collection of stories about the pilgrimage site Śatruñjaya, to which Śubhaśilagani appended a long commentary in the mid-fifteenth century. It is the commentary that contains most of the stories. The text has been edited by Lābhasāgaragaṇi in the Agamoddhara Granthamala, 41, Ahmedabad, V.S.2026. The *Hīrasaubhāgya* also cites the example of Hemacandra, who frequented the court of Kumārapāla (11.1), and even finds a canonical parallel in the monk who taught the King Pradeśi in the *Rāyapaseniyasutta* (11.61). Attitudes towards the monk at court vary in the medieval biography texts and the subject deserves a full study. I hope in the future to focus my attention on the problem. I have written a short paper on the subject, "Authority and Innovation: A study of the Use of Similes in the Biography of Hīravijaya to Provide Sanction for the Monk at Court", published in *Jinamañjari,* vol.1, october 1990, pp. 48-61, unfortunately with many misprints.

45. For example some of the Sanskrit *Kharataragacchabṛhadgurvāvali* cited in note 2. See also the various Tapāgaccha biographies cited there. In particular the *Vijayapraśasti* emphasizes the rituals the monk performed and the contributions the lay community made to the ceremonies. The importance of pilgrimage in medieval Jainism is also vividly manifest in these biographies which spend so much time on describing the pilgrimages in which the monks took part. Didactic stories and canonical stories describe the monk as wandering from place to place, but not specifically as visiting sites sacred to the Jain tradition. The institution of pilgrimage and the monk as leading participant in a pilgrimage are more the concern of the medieval biography texts than the didactic stories of the same period in time. The *Vijayapraśati* is edited by Pandit Hargovinddas and Pandit Bechardas, Benaras: Yashovijaya Granthamala, no. 23, V.S. 2437.

46. Similes and their appropriateness in hymns of praise are a topic of serious discussion. Haribhadra in his *Lalitavistara* spends considerable time explaining the use of specific similes when applied to the Tīrthaṅkaras and defends them against objections. *Lalitavistara* edited in the Devacandra Lalbhai Jainapustakoddhara Series, no. 29, 1915, pp. 24 ff.

47. In the traditional accounts Siddhasena converts Vikramāditya and Hemacandra converts Kumārapāla, for example. The last biography of Jinaprabha that I translated here might possibly be regarded as an exception to this general rule.

48. The word in the text is not clear. I am supplying this translation from the other versions of the story that will be discussed below.
49. See the *Prabandhakośa* of Rājaśekhara and the *guruguṇaratnākara* of Somacaritra Gaṇi, edited by Muni Indravijaya, Benares: Dharmabhyudaya Press, vira samvat, 2437.
50. In support of the hypothesis that miracle stories were told about certain monks by both monks and lay people I would mention that there is no discussion that I know of from the scholastic tradition that disputes that monks or images work miracles and thus would lead to a conclusion that miracles were disparaged by monks. Monks often wrote hymns praising miraculous images and Jinaprabhasūri throughout his *Vividhatīrthakalpa* nowhere evidences any disbelief in the miracles he describes. In fact images that work miracles and monks that work miracles are analogous; a god is present to the image or monk and the god actually does the miraculous deeds. A denial of miracle-working powers on the part of a monk should involve a denial of miracle working powers for images, any yet there is no evidence that this was the case. Monks made pilgrimages to all the famous miracle working images in medieval times. There is thus no evidence that would allow us to assert that our biography of Jinaprabhasūri from the *Vṛddhācāryaprabandhāvali* with all of its miracles was a product of a different religious community and reflects a different religious background from the other accounts we have reviewed. At most we can say that it represents another mode of depicting a monk that was often used by those who wrote the accounts of monks. It depicts the monk as tantric adept, wizard, and miracle worker, and it was a way of speaking about monks that did not suit every monk in the tradition but that when employed produced rich, warm and often humorous accounts.
51. See may article, "Holy Warriors: A Preliminary Study of Some Biographies of Saints and Kings in the Classical Indian Tradition", *Journal of Indian Philosophy,* 12, 1984, pp. 291-303. On the question of the role of stories in building a monk's reputation see Michael Carrithers, *The Forest Monks of Śrī Laṅkā: An anthropological and Historical Study,* Delhi: Oxford University Press, 1983, p. 84.
52. The *Hīrasaubhāgya* does conclude with a catalogue of miracles that were observed at the monk's *stūpa.* This is important, I think; it indicates that it was not the genre of text, a *mahākāvya,* that inhibited the poet from describing miracles, but some other factor.
53. There is a medieval biography of the monk Vijayadeva, cited in note 5, in which the author states explicitly that he collected the miracle stories he has appended to the end of his poem from lay followers, but such an explicit association of miracles with lay worship seems to be an exception. This biography of the Tapagaccha monk Vijayadeva is also unusual in that it separates out the miracle stories, the examples of *devasāṃnidhya,* of how the

gods assisted the monk or acted on his behalf, from the rest of the biography. The poem is for the most part a straightforward account of Vijayadeva, the rituals he performs, the places he goes, until the last chapter, 19, verses 164 ff., in which the miracle stories are told together almost as an afterthought. By contrast most medieval biographies do not distinguish a supernatural event from what we might consider an ordinary event, either by the language or style in which the event is told or by positioning the miracle stories in a separate section. On miracle stories as equally the concern of monks I would cite the fact that the modern monk Śrī Rāmalāljigaṇi collected his miracle stories about the Kharatara leaders who converted the Rajput kings from monks. See his *Mahajanavaṃśavali,* Bombay: Nirnaya Sagara Press, 1900.

54. See the *Prātihāryasūtra in the Divyāvadāna*, number 12, pp. 88ff. of the edition by P.L. Vaidya from the Buddhist Sanskrit Text Series, Darbhanga: Mithila Institute, 1959.

55. See the contest between Gosala and Mahāvīra in the *Bhagavatī Sūtra,* 15, that eventually results in Gosala's death. For references see JozefDeleu, *Viyāhapannatti (Bhagavaī): The Fifth Aṅga of the Jaina Canon, Introduction, Critical Analysis, Commentary and Indexes.* Brugge: De Tempel, 1970. On Rohagutta see Ernst Leumann, "Die Alten Berichte von den Schismen der Jaina", *Indische Studien,* XVII, 1885, pp. 116-123.

56. I have discussed some of these stories in a paper "Religious Biographies and the Clan Histories of the Śvetāmbara Jains" published in *East and West,* vol. 39, 1989, pp. 195-217.

57. The story is retold in Wendy O'Flaherty, *Dreams, Illusion and other Realities,* Delhi: Motilal Banarsidass, 1987, chapter 4, pp. 132-134. I have discussed it and the related story of Gadhi in my paper, "The Yogavāsiṣṭha, the Continuing Search for a Context", in *New Horizons of Research in Indology,* Poona University Silver Jubilee Volume edited by Dr. V.N. Jha, Poona University, 1989, pp. 181-206.

58. This makes an interesting contrast with some late medieval Hindu accounts of Hindu/Muslim conflict, in which Muslim rulers are defeated and made to worship the Hindu deities. See for example Vipradāsa's *Manasā Maṅgal,* edited Sukumar Sen, Calcutta: Bibliotheca Indica, no.277, 1953, *pāla 5.*

59. In the same text Jinadattasūri defeats the sixty-four yoginīs who are regarded as extremely potent deities in the Delhi area. Ārya Khapaṭācārya in the story about him that is attached to the commentary to the *Bhaktāmarastotra* converts Cāmuṇḍā (see my paper in *Monks and Magicians* cited in note 4). Many Jain monks in didactic stories convert Cāmuṇḍā or related Hindu goddesses and force them to stop accepting blood-sacrifice. A famous example is the conversion of the royal clan goddess in the *Yaśodharacarita.* The version from the *Bṛhatkathākósa* of Harisena has recently been translated by Friedhelm Hardy in *The Clever Adulteress and the Hungry Monk,* mentioned in note 2.

For the Vaiṣṇava conversions of Hindu goddesses that likewise involve forcing the goddesses to renounce blood-offerings see the references in Prabhudayal Mītal, *Vraj Ke Dharma-sampradāyoṃ kā Ithihāsa,* Delhi:National Publishing House, 1968, p. 347.

60. For Rāmānuja see the *Prapannāmṛta* cited in note 32; on Śrīnāthjī see the *Śrīnāthjī Kī Prākathya Vārtā,* Nathdwara: Vidyavibhag Mandir Mandal, v.s. 2037, p. 36.

61. See my article on Haribhadra cited in note 4.

62. In an interesting study of the *Golden Legend* of Jacques de Voragine, Alain Boureau proposed to borrow the term "agglutinative" from linguistics to refer to a composition in which anecdotes are added to each other without any concern for their organic relationship. See alain Boureau, *La Legende Doree, Le Systeme narratif de Jacques de Voragine,* Paris: Les Editions du Cerf, 1984, p. 212. At the same time in his analysis of the collection as a whole, Boureau argues for a reading of the text as an organic unity, in which repetitions of episodes over a number of individual biographies gain in significance by the comparisons and contrasts implied (see pp. 239 ff.) In my own analysis of medieval Jain religious biographies, most notably in my paper on Siddhasena cited in note 2, I have tried to discover the organic unity of a single biography. In the present case of the miracle stories of Jinaprabhasūri I would prefer to regard the biography in the *Vṛddhācāryaprabandhāvali* as an exception to a more general hypothesis that single biographies will indeed integrate diverse episodes into a purposeful whole; perhaps this text with its abrupt ending was unfinished. I believe that it is possible to argue that the miracles up to the recovery of the Kannyānayanatīrtha image can be seen to show a certain logic; the series of miracles is framed by encounters with the Muslims, the main focus of the biography, while the intermediate miracles establish without doubt the credibility of Jinaprabhasūri as a magician and charmer of the king. The agglutinative anecdotes that follow, to borrow Boureau's terminology, reveal by contrast that the compiler's work was yet to be done.

63. This phrase was not entirely clear to me.

64. See note 33 for further comments on this change.

65. It is difficult to know exactly when the process of adopting Jinaprabhasūri into the Tapāgaccha actually began. In his study of Jinaprabhasūri entitled *Śrī Jinaprabhasūri āne Sultān mahammad,* p. 10, Lalcandra Bhagavandas Gandhi noted a reference to Jinaprabhasūri's involvement with the Tapagaccha in a commentary to Jinaprabha's *Siddhāntastava.* He surmised that the commentator was a member of the Tapāgaccha. The commentator states that Jinaprabhasūri was impressed with the growing fortunes of the Tapāgaccha, which was blessed by a boon from the Goddess Padmāvatī. For this reason he personally bestowed upon the Tapāgaccha monk Somatilakasūri copies of the many *stotras* that he

had written. About seventy-five years after the death of Jinaprabhasūri, the Tapāgaccha monk Somadharmagaṇi wrote the *Upadeśasaptati* in which he related many of the miracle stories associated the Jinaprabhasūri known from other sources. He also relates an encounter between Jinaprabhasūri and a Tapāgaccha monk Somaprabhasūri, very much like the one in the *Purātanaprabandhasaṃgraha.* Gandhi has translated the relevant section of the *Upadeśasaptati* into Gujarati. In a note he examines the evidence and concludes that there is little to support the historicity of their meeting. See pp.64-66.

66. This change is particularly interesting in light of the existence of several related stories which describe how Aurangzeb had the temple of Keśava in Mathura destroyed and the images brought to Agra where they were buried under the stairs of the mosque of Jahanara. See the reference in A.W. Entwistle, *Braj: Centre of Krishna Pilgrimage,* Groningen: Egbert Forsten, 1987, p.181. It is tempting to interpret the change in Jinaprabha's biography as a response to a similar environment and to want to date the text to the seventeenth century when Muslim policies reflected increased hostility towards non-Muslim religions. Such an hypothesis, however, requires further corroborating evidence. I am reluctant at the present state of my knowledge to speculate on the exact conditions that led to either of the basic changes in the miracle story biographies of Jinaprabhasūri: the increased hostility to the Muslims and the growing raprochement with the Tapāgaccha. It is clear that a variety of responses were possible to similar conditions. The biography of Bhānucandra, for example, describes an environment in which the Muslim overlord was generous in his patronage of the Tapāgaccha monks; in this it is reminiscent of Jinaprabhasūri's own positive assessment of the kindnesses Jains received from the Muslim rulers. At the same time the *Bhānucandragaṇicarita* is filled with incidents that clearly indicate that the level of hostility between the Kharatara and Tapāgaccha monks was high indeed. On many occasions the Tapāgaccha monks sought the intervention of the Muslim ruler to prevent their rivals in the Kharataragaccha from building temples or controlling major sites of pilgrimage. See the *Bhānucandragaṇicarita* cited in note 11, particularly chapter 4. Thus it would be hasty to conclude from Jinaprabhasūri's biographies that patronage from a Muslim ruler was associated with a reprieve from sectarian hostility and an effort to secure benefits for the Jain community at large, while hostility from the Muslims resulted in a feeling of sectarian rivalry.

67. See my paper on the clan conversion stories cited in note 2.

68. This is the *Vijayadevamāhātmya,* cited in note 5.

69. See the *paṭṭāvali* number 3 in the collection compiled by Jinavijaya and published by Puran Chand Nahar, Calcutta, 1932, p. 32. I would like to pursue the question of Jinaprabhasūri's relationship to the Tapāgaccha, but thus far have not succeeded in finding sufficient information.

70. See the *Aitihāsika Jaina Kāvya Saṃgraha,* cited in note 2, pp. 11, 13.

71. In an article on the biographies of Haribhadra I have noted as characteristic of the *prabandhas* an anachronistic hostility to Buddhism and suggested that this might have been a reaction to certain contemporary political factors, the Jains trying to maintain their prestige with Hindu rulers at a time when the Hindu community was becoming particularly xenophobic. I would also like to suggest that they were attempting to reduce the emphasis on intra-sectarian conflicts by focusing on general Jain triumphs over non-Jains. I have in my study of Siddhasena's biographies raised this last point in some detail. See "Jain Biographies of Haribhadra: An Inquiry into the Logic of the Legends", *Journal of Indian Philosophy,* vol.16, 1988, pp. 329-384, part I. Part II of the article appeared in vol.18, 1990, pp. 261-304.

72. There is much in these poems that deals with the specific points of disagreement between Jinadatta and the monks he criticizes. I have not translated those verses since I am more interested in what Jinadatta says about himself, about the monk who does follow the true path. It is nonetheless necessary to keep in mind that Jinadatta is very specific in these poems about what he does not like. The verses that I have translated, with their general exhortations, are balanced in both poems by verses that either give detailed instructions on proper behavior or attack specific practices.

73. See the Sanskrit introduction to the text, p.115.

74. There does exist a tradition of using letters as didactic texts in medieval India, although the genre has received inadequate scholarly attention to date. The only comprehensive study is of Buddhist letters preserved in Tibetan. See Siglinde Dietz, *Die Buddhistische Briefliterature Indiens,* Asiatische Forschungen, Band 84, Wiesbaden: Otto Harrassowitz, 1984.

75. *Dasaveāliyasutta* with Bhadrabahu's *Niryukti* and Agastyasiṃha's *Cūrṇi,* edited Muni Shri Punyavijayaji, Prakrit Text Society Series, no.17, Varanasi: Prakrit Text Society, 1973, pp.261-262.

76. Haribhadra's commentary is quoted in the edition of the *Pañcasūtrakam* of Cirantanācārya that has been edited by Muni Sri Jambuvijayaji, Delhi: Bhogilal Leherchand Institute of Indology, 1986, p.61. The same image appears in this *Pāncasūtraka,* and in his commentary to that passage Haribhadra cites the *Daśavaikālika sūtra* as scriptural authority.

77. *Śrī Upadesapadamahāgrantha,* edited Sri Pratapavijaya Gani in the Srimanmuktikamalajainamohanamala, no.19, Bombay: Nirnaya Sagara Press, 1923, p. 177.

78. The same usage of this image is to be found in the *Pravrajyāvidhanakulaka,* verse 22. The text is edited in the Agamodayasamiti Series as volume 49, 1927. Compare also the phrase, "*lokadiṭṭhi visayānukūlavāinī*", "ordinary people direct their gaze to make it flow comfortably along with the objects of the senses," in the *Vasudevahiṇḍi,* page 15, edited by Caturvijaya Muni and

Punyavijayamuni, first reprint, 1989, Ahmedabad: Gujarat Sahitya Akademi.

79. See page 38, verses 910-913.

80. *Karuṇāvajrāyudha,* edited by Muni Caturavijaya, Sri Jaina Atmananda Series, vol.56, Bhavnagar, 1916, p. 12.

81. See the *Ṣaṣtiśatakaprakaraṇa* of Nemicandra Bhaṇḍārī, verse 6, edited by Bhogilal J. Sandesara in the Pracina Gurjara Granthamala series, vol.1, from Maharaja Sayajirav Visvavidyalaya, Baroda, 1953, verse 6, p.9.

82. *Sastiśatakaprakaraṇa,* verse 16, p. 21.

83. In verse 32, however, Nemicandra uses the closely related phrase, *micchāpavāha,* "the flow of false doctrine" in a way that the context suggests directly parallels Jinadatta's use of *anusrotas* and *lokapravāha.* Verse 33 makes clear that the people swept away by the current of false belief nonetheless think themselves to be Jains. Similarly his verses 66, 68 and 91 leave no doubt that he is using the term *lokapravāha* exactly as Jinadatta used it before him to indicate the majority of Jains who follow a false path and false teachers. Nemicandra's text is an interesting point of comparison for Jinadatta's writing that are the focus of the present study. Nemicandra preserves all of the fire and commitment we feel in Jinadatta's writings and the poignant sense of the lone true believer. His biography is told by one of the commentators on the *Saṣṭiśatakaprakaraṇa,* Merusundara Upadhyaya, who belongs to the fifteenth century. Merusundara relates how Nemicandra sought diligently for a true teacher until he came to Pattan where he met Jinapatisūri and accepted the Kharatara teachings. We sense something of the fervor of the seeker in Nemicandra's text as we sense the devoted reformer in Jinadatta's text. What is perhaps most remarkable is the vitality and effectiveness of the language even after a lapse of several hundred years.

84. Two themes, the rarity of seeking the religious life and the difficulty of encountering the true faith, are in fact very common in exhortatory and didactic texts in all of Indian religions. For Buddhist parallels see the *Mūlasarvāstivādavinayavastu, Saṃghabhedavastu,* which in relating the biography of the Buddha, uses the term *pratisrotas* to explain why the Buddha is at first reluctant to teach. The Buddha says, *"pratisrotonugāmināṃ mārgaṃ gaṃbhīram atidurdṛśam",* "The path that goes against the current is deep and difficult to see." See the edition by R. Gnoli, *The Gilgit Manuscript of the Sanghabhedavastu,* part I, Rome: Instituto Italiano per il Medio ed Estremo Oriente, 1977, p. 129. Compare also the Pali *Mahāvagga,* p8 in the Nalanda Pali series. In a later text, the *Rāṣṭrapālaparipṛccha,* a prince describes himself as *"pratisrota"* while the whole world is *"anusrota".* See p. 149 of the edition in the *Mahāyānasūtrasaṃgraha* edited by P.L. Vaidya, Buddhist Sanskrit Texts, no. 17, Darbhanga: Mithila Institute of Post-graduate Studies and Research in Sanskrit Learning, 1961.

In Hinduism, the *Vivekacūḍāmaṇi* opens with verses that proclaim how difficult it is even to obtain human birth and how much more so it is to be born a man. Once born a man it is not easy to understand the true scriptures; the person who has achieved all this and yet does not exert himself for the religious life is a fool indeed. See *Śrī Śaṅkarācāryaviracitaprakaraṇagrantha,* Poona: Oriental Book Agency, 1952, p. 219. The second verse of Jinadatta's *Upadeśarasāyana* expresses exactly the same thought, "Do not waste this human birth that you have obtained with such difficulty. See to it that you cross over the ocean of rebirth. Do not give yourself over to passion and anger. Do not sully yourself with every possible flaw." Compare also Amitagati's *Subhāṣitasandoha, Dvādaśavidhatapaścaraṇaṣattrimśat,* verse 19, edited Pandit Balachandra Sidhant Shastri, Jivaraja Jaina Granthamala, 31, Sholapur. Jain Samskrti Samrakshaka Sangha, 1977, p. 232, and his *Śrāvakācāra,* 4.99, in the same series, vol.1 of *Śrāvakācāra Saṃgraha,* edited Pandit Hiralal, 1976. Outside Jainism, in fact medieval religious leaders repeatedly exhorted believers not to follow the ways of the world; see for example the *padas* of Dadu Dayal, in Monika TheilHorstmann, *Crossing the Ocean of Existence: Braj Bhasa religious poetry from Rajasthan, A Reader,* Wiesbaden: Otto Harrassowitz, 1983, p. 80.

85. The inscription is given in *Epigraphia Indica,* vol.XXV, no. 17, "Halāyudhastotra from the Amareśvara Temple", P.P. Subrahmanya Sastri, pp. 173-182, verse 10, p. 176. The inscription is dated 1063 A.D. The use of the image in this inscription might also be understood as in fact very close to what we find in Jinadatta. It is possible to see in this image a desire to promote sectarian religious interests over the interests of the larger religious group.

86. See for example a poem by the Hindi bhakta poet Dhruvadās in his *Vṛndāvan Līlā.* The poem is cited by Vijayendra Snatak, *Radhavallabha Sāṃpradāya: Siddhānta aur Sāhitya,* Delhi: National Publishing House, 1968, p. 223.

87. Perhaps some corroboration for this is to be found in the remarks of Dharmasāgara in his auto-commentary to his *Īriyāpathikāṣaṭtriṃśikā,* verse 25, where he tells the story of how Jinadatta was rebuked by Hemācārya and frightened fled for his life. Dharmasāgara identifies this Hemācārya with the preceptor of King Kumārapāla; I have suggested in note 17 that he may in fact be confusing two different monks who had the same name.

88. My information on Maladhārī Hemacandra comes from Sādhvī Samghamitra's *Jainadharma ke Prabhāvaka Ācārya,* Ladnun: Jaina Visva Bharati, 1986, pp. 626-633. I have not had much success in trying to find his texts.

89. For some comments on the *Uvahanasuya* and an English translation see Nathmal Tatia and Muni Mahendra Kumar, *Aspects of Jaina Monasticism,* Ladnun, Rajasthan: Jain Visva Bharati, 1981, pp. 97-107.

90. See *Yogasāraprābhṛta,* edited Sri Jugalkishor Mukhtar, Bombay: Bharatiya Jnanapitha, 1968, Jnanapitha Murtideva Jaina Granthamala, Sanskrit Grantha no.33, verse 18, section 8.

91. There is an excellent discussion on reform movements among Jain monks in the article by Nathuram Premi, "Vanavāsi aur Caityavāsi Saṃpradāya", published in *Jaina Sāhitya aur Itihāsa,* Bombay: New Bharata Printing Press, 1942, pp. 437-370.

92. Edited by K.V. Abhyankar, Pune: Aryabhusana Press, 1932, chapter 17, verse 16.

93. The *Saṃghapaṭṭaka* is published as an appendix in the edition of Jinadatta's Apabhraṃśa poems in the Gaekwad's Oriental Series. See in particular verses 16,24,29,32,33,35. Jinadatta in his poems and the authors of these related texts all share an extremely aggressive attitude towards other Jain monks and a readiness to condemn laxity in others while at the same time promoting their own cause. Their polemical stance raises an issue that many of the biographical and autobiographical writings of medieval Jain monks raise, namely the question of just what is the relationship between the image or self-image of the medieval monk and normative descriptions of monks on the canonical texts and the didactic stories. Jinadatta and his fellow reformist monks would seem to be ignoring the prohibition in the *Daśavaikālikasūtra,* 519, that warns a monk against saying of another that he is of bad conduct; the same verse also prohibits a monk from thinking that he is better than his peers. See also Devendra's *Dharmaratnaprakaraṇa,* verse 121, edited as Jaina Granthamala no. 3., Palitana 1906, pp. 167-168.

It may be relevant that Jinavallabha in the *Saṃghapaṭṭaka* often phrases his condemnation of the Jain religious community so as to place it in a traditionally acceptable discourse about the decline of the faith : the language of the decline of the world ages and the age of wickedness, the *duḥsamākāra.* See verses 28, 29, 30 in particular. Jinadatta also makes reference to commonly accepted beliefs in the declining world age in his *Upadeśarasāyana* verses 54-55. In my own subjective impression of these two texts, however, the discourse of the *duḥsamākāla* is far more obvious in Jinavallabha, while Jinadatta's text instead privileges images like thoses discussed in this paper which had traditionally been employed in a very different sense.

To return to the questin of the propriety of Jinadatta's open criticism of his fellow monks, it was, of course, commonly accepted that behavior condemned by a given text could be permitted in extreme circumstances to futher the cause of the faith (see the entry on *sāvajjācariya* in the *Abhidhānarājendrakośa);* nonetheless, it is evident that medieval biographical literature and autobiographical writing often speaks with a voice that is at variance with the extensive corpus of literature that sets down rules for the behavior of monks. That there were limits even to their exceptions to normative rules of behavior is perhaps implied by the case of Dharmasāgara, the Tapāgaccha polemicist who challenged the Kharatara account of its own history and in particular rewrote the biography of Jinadatta in a most unflattering manner (see notes 1 and 17 for details). Dharmasāgara's books seem to have been banned by the leaders of his own group, perhaps because they exceeded the acceptable limits of criticizing others, limits that must have been quite broad in the aggressively sectarian world of medieval Jainism. On the proscription of Dharmasāgara's writing see the comments of Desai in his introduction to the *Bhānucandragaṇicarita,* cited in note 11, p.63.

94. The existence of this literature of protest which I regard here as the broader context of Jinadatta's poems raises a number of interesting issues and deserves a full study. Colin Morris in his book *The Discovery of the Individual and Society* cited in note 11 regarded the popularity of satire and protest writing in middle ages as evidence of a growing sense of individuality and self-awareness, traits that he felt were largely confined to "Western" civilization. Jinadatta's writings offer a medieval Indian example of this genre, and I suspect that a fuller consideration of this type of writing in medieval India could lead to a compelling challenge to a facile contrasts berween "Western" and "Non-Western" notions of the self that still dominate scholarly writing today.

In addition it is necessary to note that Jinadatta's in not the only language of protest that existed in medieval India. The short Gujarati text, the *Ānandavimalasūrirāsa,* published in the *Aitihāsika Rāsa Saṃgraha,* vol. 3, edited by Sri Vijayadharmasūri, Bhavnagar, 1921, pp. 116-129, has a much gentler language. The monk, moved to action by the many abuses of manastic life that he witnesses, leaves his group to practice the true religion and be an example to others. Rather than dwelling on the loneliness of the reformer, this text celebrates Ānandavimalasūri's success in converting people to his reformed religion, and the *rāsa* is upbeat and cheerful in tone. Even the monk's accusations are gentle by comparison to those Jinadatta heaps on his fellow monks.

The 16th century monk Samayasundara in his *Guruduhkhitavacana* speaks with yet a different voice of protest. In these poems the elderly monk poignantly laments the fact that his students have all deserted him. He blames his neglect of the Jain Faith in a previous lifetime for their failure to serve him. See the *Samayasundarakṛtikusumāñjali* edited by Agarchand and Bhanwarlal Nahta, Abhaya Jaina Granthamala no.15, Calcutta, 1956, pp. 419-420 and the comments on the life of Samayasundara written for the volume by Mahāmahopādhyāya Vinayasāgara, p.28-32.

95. See my comments on Nemicandra's *Ṣaṣṭīṣatakaprakaraṇa* in note 83.

96. Pei-Yi Wu in his book on Chinese autobiographical writings cited in note 23 noted that writing in the first-person was confined to lyrical poetry in China, with biography and autobiography using the third-person (page 6). If

one were to attempt a similar categorization for medieval India surely the confessional hymn would occupy the niche that lyrical poetry has in classical china. I should like to return to this question in the future and study in greater detail the first-person hymn and its conventions of speaking about the self. The exhortatory text in which an author addresses his soul directly also provided another format in which a poet could speak about himself; an example of such a text in Digambara Jainism is the famous *Jīvasaṃbodhanapañcaviṃśati*, section 16 in the *Subhāṣitaratnasaṃdoha* of Amitagati, published most recently from Sholapur, Jivaraja Jaina Granthamala, 1977, or Guṇabhadra's *Ātmānuśāsana*, published in the Sanatana Jaina Granthamala, Bombay, 1905. These didactic texts also deserve to be studied as a group in order better to understand the various conventions that were utilized by medieval Indians to speak about themselves. Outside Jainism, there exist a number of hymns which convey vividly their author's sense of unworthiness in the manner of these Jain confessional hymns. Perhaps the most famous is the "Devyaparādhastotra" that has been attributed to Śaṅkara. There are also many deeply moving hymns in Sanskrit which express fervent religious emotion, for example hymns of yearning or longing, though most of these tend to be of a later date.

Finally, the realtionship between poems like Jinadatta's and the vernacular literature of medieval Indian is worthy of study. There is a sense in which Jinadatta's poetry stands at the beginning of a very long history of the vernacular exhortatory and confessional poem in North India. For example, a verse of Kabir's like the following verse, recalls closely Jinadatta's laments over the folly of the masses:

"Look, wise people, at the world's folly. If a man speaks the truth he is pursued and beaten; the world believes in phonies."

The verse is cited by Atul Chandra Mukhopadhyay, *Madhyayuger Santkabi*, Calcutta: Jijnasa, 1978, p. 23.

In a different vein, the Bengali verses of Balāram Dās, with their poignant lament of the author's foolish neglect of the true religion, are also heir to Jinadatta's verses and the type of Sanskrit hymn cited in this note in conveying a deep sense of the author's own personal experience of religion. For Balarām Dās see *Vaiṣṇava Padāvali,* edited Sri Harekrṣna Mukhopadhyay, Calcutta: Sahitya Samsad, revised edition 1980. Such late medieval poetry has usually been interpreted as a product of the social and political conditions of its time; it is clear that it has literary antecedents that go back much further.

97. The text is unclear to me at this point. The woman is speaking in a local dialect. The Hindi translation of the text cited above in note 2 does not translate their exchange.

98. *Upadesapāda,* p.159.

99. *Bhavabhāvana* of Maladhārī Śrīhemacandrasūri in the *Śrutaratnākara* edited by Muni Pradyumna Vijaya, Vol.1, Bombay: Syadvadamrta Prakasana

Mandir Trust, 1976, vs.201.
100. *Bṛhatkathāmañjari,* 4.1.39, reprint of the Kavyamala edition from New Delhi: Panini, 1982, p.106.
101. The poem is printed on pp.110-112 of the edition of Jinadatta's Apabhramṣá poems in the Gaekwad's Oriental Series.
102. Verses 4,8.
103. See Dharmasāgara's *Mūlapuruṣavāda,* p.44 cited in ntoe 1. Dharmasāgara here maintains that the fact that Jinadatta stepped on the young plants should be interpreted as a sign that in the future he would do harm to the Jain monastic community; that he acknowledged that his teacher was correct to demand the return of his monastic goods showed that his ordination would lead only to harm for the Jain teachings and for himself; and finally, that he demanded his hair back indicates that he recognized that the correct station in life for himself was that of a householder.
104. An excellent discussion of this with excerpts from the relevant commentaries is to be found in the Hindi notes in the edition by Muni Nathmal, Ladnun: Jain Visva Bharati, 1974, p.147. The note here stresses that the phrase used in the *Daśavaikālika* at this point to describe the monk, "*samyata-virata-pratihata-pratyākhyātapāpakarma*" is standard in the Jain *āgama;* it encapsulates the Jain doctrine that the essence of taking the five vows and thus of being a monk lies in three acts of repudiating wrong deeds: in confessing past wrong deeds *(pratikramaṇa)*; in promising not to do wrong in the future *(pratyākhyāna)* and in behaving in such a way that no wrong-doing is done in the present *(saṃvara).*
105. *Vṛddhācāryaprabhandhāvali,* p.91.
106. The story is told of Jineśvara in the *Kharataragacchabṛhadgurvāvali* and I have translated it in *The Clever Adulteress,* pp. 172-180. The fact that it appears in the Sanskrit history in one case and in a Prakrit collection in another should serve as a clear indication that we must not be at all rigid in defining the boundaries of vernacular/Sanskrit biographies. It also makes clear that we must excercise extreme caution in naming a collection like the *Vṛddhācāryaprabandhāvali* a "miracle collection" and defining it as different from a text like the *Kharataragacchabṛhadgurvāvali;* here the opening story in the so-called "miracle collection" is also prominently displayed in the Sanskrit biography of another monk.
107. I have translated the biography of Jivadevasūri from the *Prabandhakośa* of Rājaśekharasūri in *The Clever Adulteress,* pp.149-153.
108. See my paper on the clan conversion stories cited in note.
109. For references see my paper on Siddhasena cited in note 2.

Buddhaghosa's Penance and Siddhasena's Crime: Remarks on Some Buddhist and Jain Attitudes Towards the Language of Religious Texts

Phyllis Granoff
McMaster University

I. Introduction: The Philosophical Context of Buddhist and Jain Attitudes Toward Language

Early in its history Indian philosophy developed a concept of a "sacred language", a language appropriate to matters of ritual. Eventually the concept would be extended to require that the ritually correct language should also be the only language in which serious philosophical discussion should be held. To use that language incorrectly moreover involved sin, as did any other infraction of the strict rules governing ritual. The language was Sanskrit and its correct usage was determined by the instructions on grammar given by the grammarians. The most vociferous proponents of the viewpoint that there exists only one language, the Sanskrit language, which was to be used for ritual were naturally the grammarians and after them the Mīmāṃsakas.[1]

The exact parameters of the discussion often vary; the grammarians tended to prefer the more radical view that Sanskrit must be used at all times, even outside of a ritual context, while the Mīmāṃsakas were content to restrict the necessary use of Sanskrit to the sphere of ritual. In any case, both groups were agreed in arguing that Sanskrit was the only language that was capable of making its meaning known directly; it was therefore the only "true" language capable of directly fulfilling the function that we expect of a language, to communicate meaning. In the viewpoint of the grammarians and the Mīmāṃsakas Sanskrit was the *mūlabhāṣya*, the "root language" or "primary language". Its forms, as fixed by grammar, were invariant and so could be learned by children through observation. A child hearing a Sanskrit word on a number of occasions and watching the behaviour of the speaker and listener could infer the meaning of a Sanskrit word and then understand it correctly the next time it appeared in conversation. Other languages were regarded as misusages of Sanskrit, *apabhraṃśa*, deviations from the correct form, and in fact were seen to be variable. Learning these languages was made problematic in the theory of the grammarians precisely because the individual words exhibited infinite variety; hearing a word even a few times could not insure that a child would understand it in a new context; indeed, the chances were great that the word the child heard in the learning situation would not be used in precisely that form again. The only way these other languages could make known their meaning, under this theory, was through the intermediary of a fixed and invariable Sanskrit word which a listener would call to mind on hearing the aberrant non-Sanskrit term.

While it is possible to maintain that the notion of Sanskrit as the exclusive ritual language was developed independently of the lively debates between the Mīmāṃsakas and grammarians on the one hand, and other religious groups in India on the other hand, it is not difficult to see that their insistence on the use of Sanskrit as a sacred language would affect very greatly at least two other groups who did not use Sanskrit for their religious writings, the Buddhists and the Jains.[2] Even in their canonical texts, and more elaborately in the commentaries to the various *suttas* and other post-canonical writings, the Jains emphatically assert that local languages are as valid and as direct indicators of meaning as is Sanskrit. Indeed a late text states that only a person who is conversant in many local languages should be appointed to a leading position amongst the monks.[3] The sin that accrues to a person for the misuse of language has nothing to do with the language that is being spoken, but concerns the speaker's intention and the effects his words have on another. Thus cruel speech and lies bring sin, and not the fact that the language spoken is a language other than Sanskrit.[4] The Jains also directly counter the Mīmāṃsakas and grammarians in philosophical debates, where they argue cogently that the position of the grammarians and ritualists that only Sanskrit makes known its meaning directly is not logically demonstrable. They also mockingly offer that to insist that failure to use Sanskrit entails sin and correct use of Sanskrit implies merit could have unexpected results; a Sanskrit statement to kill a Brahmin would lead to merit while a Prakrit statement to give gifts to a Brahmin would be sinful! In addition medieval Jain philosophers counter that if there is a root language that is a primary denotator of meaning, that language is not Sanskrit at all, but Prakrit.[5] The Jains would also seem to have practiced what they preached, for throughout their history they used both vernacular languages and Sanskrit for religious purposes.

The Buddhists, like the Jains, also allowed the use of languages other than Sanskrit for religious texts and rituals.[6] And like the Jains their philosophers argued against the Mīmāṃsakas and the grammarians who spoke of one single ritual language and insisted that it be Sanskrit. Dharmakīrti, in his *Vādanyāya*, argues that all languages, Sanskrit, Prakrit, Apabhraṃśa, Dravidian, Andhran, function in exactly the same way to make known their meaning. All require that there exist a common understanding that a given word has a specific meaning and that a listener be familiar with the linguistic conventions of a particular language in order to derive meaning from it. Dharmakīrti also rejects the notion that speaking any particular language is meritorious while the use of some other language is inherently sinful.[7]

Both the Jains and Buddhists, then, give evidence for their rejection of the notion of a single sacred language, of the concept that Sanskrit is especially privileged because it alone of all languages functions directly to make known its meaning, and of the theory that some language is by nature meritorious while others are by nature wicked. These assertions amount to a thorough attack on the Mīmāṃsakas and grammarians, with their emphasis on the necessary use of Sanskrit in ritual, and other orthodox schools like the Naiyāyikas who followed them on this point.

The sources for the study of Buddhist and Jain attitudes towards language are many. To date scholars on the Buddhist side seem to have concentrated on passages in the canon and its commentaries, while Jain scholarship, particularly in the editing of the relevant texts, has also examined the philosophical context for Jain attitudes towards vernaculars. There is one other source of information about Buddhist and Jain attitudes towards language that has not yet been explored in any depth in this connection. This is religious biography, particularly the biographies of Siddhasena on the Jain side and of Buddhaghoṣa on the Buddhist side. Examining these biographies in fact suggests that while a reading of the Buddhist philosopher Dharmakīrti and the Jain philosopher Prabhācandra would lead to the conclusion that the Jains and Buddhists thought very much alike on the question of language, in fact at least some members of each community would not have agreed with each other. For in the stories told of him, Siddhasena is said to have sinned for wishing to translate the Jain sacred writings into Sanskrit, the language that the dominant group in India regarded as the sacred language par excellence, and he must undergo a penance for this outrage against the Jain faith. By contrast, one of Buddhaghoṣa's most celebrated deeds is that he rendered the commentaries that existed in Śrī Laṅkā in the local vernacular into Māgadhī, which we shall see some Buddhists regarded as the root language, and above all the sacred language of Buddhism. In some versions of the biography Buddhaghoṣa even goes so far as to burn the Sinhalese books. If Dharmakīrti could argue that all languages were equal and no one language had any special status, it is nonetheless evident that the biography of Buddhaghoṣa reveals a very different attitude towards language. One language is privileged: it is no longer Sanskrit, but the attitude towards language in general revealed by Buddhaghoṣa's biography is far closer to the attitude of the orthodox Mīmāṃsaka than to anything in the Buddhist or Jain tradition. This paper will look at the biographies of Buddhaghoṣa and Siddhasena and then conclude with some remarks about Buddhist and Jain views of language and the appropriateness of the stories the two traditions told of two of their most distinguished scholars.

II. The Biographies of Siddhasena and Buddhaghosa

Accounts of Siddhasena may be found in a number of Śvetāmbara sources. His biography figures in all of the major *prabandhas* and in some didactic story collections. To my knowledge the earliest written source is either the didactic story collection, the commentary of Āmradevasūri to the *Ākhyānakamaṇikośa*, which was written in 1134 A.D., or Bhadreśvara's *Kahāvali*, which may be as early as the twelfth century and which is somewhere in between a biography collection and a didactic story collection. Both of these texts are in Prakrit, while the later *prabandha* collections are in Sanskrit. My comments here shall be based on the text of Rājaśekharasūri in his Sanskrit *Prabandhakośa*, which is dated 1349 A.D. The incident of Siddhasena wishing to put the Jain sacred writings into Sanskrit is a central incident in all of the extant versions of his biography and is told in much the same manner in all of these accounts.[8]

Siddhasena is introduced to the reader as an arrogant Brahmin, extremely proud of his learning, and particularly adept in speaking Sanskrit. From the beginning the biography makes the question of language its central preoccupation. Siddhasena has made the rash pronouncement that he will become the disciple of anyone who defeats him in debate. He has heard of the great prowess of the Jain monk Vṛddhavādin and he rushes to confront him. Siddhasena meets Vṛddhavādin on the road and immediately challenges him to debate. Not averse to such a contest, Vṛddhavādin nonetheless hesitates, for a debate needs learned witnesses and indeed learned judges. Siddhasena, for his part, is unperturbed. He suggests that they take the village cowherds as their audience and that they allow them to settle the question of which of them will triumph. Vṛddhavādin agrees and Siddhasena, right there in the midst of a cow-pasture, begins to discourse elegantly in Sanskrit. He goes on and on, but at last when he finally falls silent, the cowherds have a chance to vent their disapproval. "The cowherds all said, 'He doesn't know anything. All he's done is to grunt and groan and shout and scream and give us a good earache. Who needs him?'" They turn to Vṛddhavādin, who always knew what any occasion demanded. He girded-up his loins, we are told, and began to sing in a wonderfully melodious voice, with a tune that was particularly popular amongst cowherds, and of course, not in Sanskrit but in their local dialect. That Vṛddhavādin had hit the right note in more than one sense is amply clear from the text, as it says,

"The cowherds were enraptured. They said, 'Vṛddhavādin truly knows everything. Why, just see how fine he sings!' And they made fun of Siddhasena, saying, 'Siddhasena talks rubbish.'"

And so it came to be that Siddhasena converted to Jainism. In keeping with his initial vow to become the disciple of the person who could best him in debate, he becomes the disciple of Vṛddhavādin and becomes a Jain monk.

The contest between Vṛddhavādin and Siddhasena has nothing to do with the content of their statements; it is decided on the basis of how they present their remarks. Siddhasena fails because he inappropriately speaks Sanskrit to the cowherds, and Vṛddhavādin triumphs because he correctly addresses the villagers in their own idiom, in their own vernacular dialect and in a style of oral performance that is accompanied by music and dance.[9] But Siddhasena will have much to endure before he is finally completely weaned from his yearning for Sanskrit and the Sanskrit intellectual tradition. This only comes through a series of incidents.

In the service of a king, Siddhasena falls victim to the seductive charms of the courtly culture. People begin to speak ill of the monk who is so fond of secular comforts, and his old teacher Vṛddhavādin comes to know of Siddhasena's close association with the royal court and his laxity as a monk. Vṛddhavādin goes in disguise to enlighten Siddhasena and the way in which he chooses to bring his erring disciple back to his senses is again critical. He uses in effect the same tool he had first used against the arrogant Brahmin Siddhasena. He recites before him an elementary Prakrit verse. Siddhasena fails to understand the verse, which in itself is surprising, and that leads him to infer that all is not as it seems. The man he has before him is no ordinary man; it is none other than his teacher Vṛddhavādin.

The odd fact that someone who is so learned would fail to understand such a simple verse also leads the reader to infer that what is happening here is not all that it seems, either. Defeat or victory have nothing to do with the content of statements made or with intelligence; the speaker of Sanskrit simply loses out to the speaker of Prakrit as we saw was exactly the case in the initial encounter between Siddhasena and Vṛddhavādin that had led to Siddhasena's conversion to Jainism.

Once more Siddhasena is abruptly shaken from his complacency and once more he follows Vṛddhavādin, the Jain monk and Prakrit speaker, from the court of the king, who was always regarded in classical India as the champion of the elite, Sanskritic culture.

Siddhasena's conversion from Sanskrit to Prakrit, however, is far from complete. The clash between Siddhasena, the representative of Sanskrit culture, and the Jain community, the champions of vernacular learning, must openly take place one more time before the two groups can find some common ground for compromise. This will take place in an incident that is usually placed near the end of Siddhasena's biography. The incident makes explicit what the biography had implied this far, namely that Siddhasena champions Sanskrit over Prakrit and that this is his flaw.

One day Siddhasena summons the members of the Jain community and offers to put all of the Jain sacred writings into Sanskrit. His fellow monks are furious at the suggestion. The text tells us, "They said, 'Do you think that the Great and Glorious Founders of the Faith, the Tīrthaṃkaras, and the monks who led the community after them only wrote their works in Ardha Māgadhī because they were incapable of writing them in Sanskrit? In speaking like this you have committed a grave offense that demands a grave penance.'" Siddhasena then agrees to accept a severe penance; he will wander incognito, not bearing the external marks of a Jain monk, the gauze over his mouth or the broom, and disguised as a Śaiva ascetic. The completion of his penance occurs when he performs a miracle in the presence of King Vikramāditya of Ujjain. Siddhasena causes the *liṅga* of Mahākāla to split open and an image of the Jain Tīrthaṃkara Pārśvanātha to appear. The instrument of his magic is his skill in language; Siddhasena recites some verses and the *liṅga* splits. It was commonly believed that certain words, particularly the words of hymns, carry magical powers.[10] But the text that Siddhasena recites was not in fact primarily a hymn. It is indeed in Sanskrit, but the *Dvātriṃśikā* is on the whole an extremely abstruse and difficult text of philosophy. I understand that this incident in a crucial way resolves the tension that the biography has been building up between Prakrit/ Jainism on the one hand and Sanskrit/ royal court/ Brahmins on the other. Siddhasena has done his penance for wanting to put the Jain sacred writings into Sanskrit. He performs a miracle at the end of that penance, reciting a text that is in Sanskrit, but which derives its power not from its erudition and its philosophical content, which may be considered a part of the learned Sanskrit culture, but from the magical force of all sacred words. Siddhasena may use Sanskrit now that he understands it has no privileged status.[11]

The incident concludes when King Vikramāditya is converted to Jainism and Siddhasena is welcomed back by the Jain community. But lest we think that Siddhasena is once more seduced into remaining with a king and enjoying the culture of the court, the text adds an incident in which Siddhasena cleverly manipulates the king to gain a favour for the Jain community and then states that Siddhasena voluntarily welcomed death, ending his career as a pious Jain monk.

This biography of Siddhasena, then, is centered around a conflict between language that is made clear at the very outset. Siddhasena the Brahmin, the elegant speaker of Sanskrit, must humble himself before the Jain monk, Vṛddhavādin, the singer of simple rustic Prakrit verses. In this initial incident, Sanskrit as the language of debate takes second place to Prakrit as the best means of communication. This victory for Prakrit that begins the biography is then extended; a Prakrit verse again triumphs when Siddhasena is at the court of a king and has become too involved in courtly culture for a Jain monk. Vṛddhavādin awakens Siddhasena to his duties with a simple Prakrit stanza. Here Prakrit is victorious over secular Sanskrit learning. Finally, in the episode where Siddhasena desires to put the Jain canon into Sanskrit there is no contest; it is stated at once outright that this is an offense against the Jain religion. Prakrit is also the language suited for religious texts. A compromise is reached, perhaps, when after his penance Siddhasena recites his Sanskrit verses and calls forth the image of a Jain Tīrthaṃkara. Sanskrit, with the right understanding of the place of language in religion, can have a powerful effect.

When we turn to the biographies of Buddhaghoṣa, we see at once that the preoccupation with language that marked the biography of Siddhasena is also a fundamental concern of the Buddhist biographer. Sources for the life of Buddhaghoṣa are as varied as those that exist for Siddhasena; I base my comments here on the *Buddhaghosuppatti* of Mahāmaṅgala, which may have been written in the fourteenth century in Burma.[12] Buddhaghoṣa's successful translation into Māgadhī of the Sinhalese commentaries to the Buddhist canonical works may be seen in many ways as the mirror-image of Siddhasena's misguided desire to translate the Jain canonical texts into Sanskrit.

There is ample evidence that long before the extant biographies of Buddhaghoṣa were written, at least amongst some Buddhists Māgadhī had achieved something of the status of a sacred language. Some Buddhists held Māgadhī to be privileged in exactly the same terms that the grammarians and Mīmāṃsakas had argued that Sanskrit was privileged, terms which Dharmakīrti had taken such pains to refute.[13] Most telling in this connection are the statements that Buddhaghoṣa himself makes. Buddhaghoṣa has comments on the nature of language in general and on the special status of Māgadhī in a number of places in his works, including the *Sammohavinodinī* on the *Vibhaṅga*, the *Samantapāsādikā* on the *Vinaya* and the *Visuddhimagga*. I consider here the passage from the *Visuddhimagga*, which has suffered considerably at the hands of translators.[14]

Buddhaghoṣa describes the *niruttipatisaṃbhidā*, "True knowledge of the nature of language", in a paragraph that I would translate roughly as follows:[15]

> "The term '*niruttipatisaṃbhidā*', 'true knowledge of the nature of language', means knowledge in full detail of the language of Māgadhī, which is the root language of all creatures, the natural language, and is considered to be the sacred language. And such a knowledge of what is the natural language takes the following form. As soon as a person hears something being said he knows at once that what has been said is either in the natural language or is not. When we gloss the technical term 'knowledge that arises when something is spoken in the natural language of our religious texts', we gloss the word 'spoken' by the synonyms 'uttered' or 'said'. We also gloss the term 'natural language' with the words 'usage that never changes'. And when such a natural language is spoken, uttered, that is, said, with respect to the special topics covered in the scriptures, a person skilled with 'true knowledge of the nature of language' knows at once whether what has been uttered is in fact the natural language or not. For a person who has perfected his true knowledge of the nature of language, as soon as he hears words like '*phasso*' and '*vedanā*', knows that these are utterances of the 'natural language', while as soon as he hears such words as '*phassā*' and '*vedano*', on the other hand, he knows that these are not utterances of the natural language."

If we return for a moment to the Mīmāṃsakas and the grammarians, Buddhaghoṣa's statements begin to assume a recognizable contour. The Mīmāṃsakas and the grammarians had argued that Sanskrit was the natural language, the root language, and that its usage was fixed once and for all by grammar. It was unvarying, which made it possible for children to learn Sanskrit, while vernaculars were varying and thus could not possibly express their meaning directly. Buddhaghoṣa has turned the argument around. He agrees, the natural language is grammatically fixed and unvarying. But then the examples he gives of the same words, once in their correct gender for examples of natural language, and once in incorrect forms as examples of something other than natural language, indicate that what he means by this root language is Māgadhī, correctly used. He also indicates that it is this language that is to be used with respect to topics covered in scriptures, much as the orthodox Hindus had argued for the exclusive use of Sanskrit in a ritual context.

In another context, in his comments in the *Sammohavinodinī* about the monk Tissadattathera, who could preach in many languages, Buddhaghoṣa makes clear that Māgadhī is always to be preferred for religious instruction because it is the easiest of all languages to grasp and offers instantaneous understanding. He also asserts that it was the language of the Buddha, a belief that no doubt led him to promote its usage as a sacred language and elevate it to the status that Sanskrit held for the orthodox Hindu community.[16] Buddhaghoṣa also asserts in his commentary to the *Vinaya*, the *Samantapāsādikā*, that Māgadhī was the language of the Buddha and that Buddhist texts should be in Māgadhī.[17] It is necessary to keep all of this in mind as we turn to the biography of Buddhaghoṣa and see how very differently the question of translating sacred texts is handled.

Like Siddhasena, Buddhaghoṣa begins life as a Brahmin. He is learned and proud of his learning. Like Siddhasena, he converts when an heretical monk, this time a Buddhist monk, bests him in an intellectual contest. But if Siddhasena's flaw is his addiction to Sanskrit learning, Buddhaghoṣa's is a more general arrogance. One day we learn that Buddhaghoṣa was puzzling over the question of who was the more learned, himself or his teacher. Furious at this lack of respect, the teacher calls him to task. To expiate this sin Buddhaghoṣa must journey to Śrī Laṅkā and translate the sacred texts into Māgadhī. He accepts this as his penance with the added proviso that he wishes first to convert his father to Buddhism before he departs.

Buddhaghoṣa journeys to Śrī Laṅkā; by prodigious acts of memory and through his deep learning he passes tests both human and divine and is permitted to carry out the task of translating the Sinhalese commentaries into Māgadhī. The Sinhalese commentaries are then burned, and as if to prove to the world that Māgadhī indeed was the correct choice for the translation and not Sanskrit, and that he has not eschewed Sanskrit because he is not capable of writing in Sanskrit, Buddhaghoṣa publicly demonstrates his proficiency in Sanskrit by reciting some Sanskrit verses. This ends his stay in Śrī Laṅkā, and our brief look into his biography.

It is clear that there is no conflict in the text over what is the correct language for the sacred texts; whereas Siddhasena vacillated between Sanskrit and Prakrit, and the biography set up and resolved a tension between the Sanskritic culture and the vernacular culture, Buddhaghoṣa's biography knows no such conflict. It is firmly on the side of a canonical language, Māgadhī. The vernacular works are burned. It substitutes Māgadhī for Sanskrit and allows that there is indeed a hierarchy of languages, with Māgadhī at the top and the other vernaculars beneath it. In so doing it comes to the opposite conclusion of Siddhasena's biography, in which the notion of a single canonical language is denied.

III. Conclusions: The Logic of the Legends

There is about these two biographies a certain remarkable fidelity to fact. It is not the type of fact that one expects from a biography; few would wish to defend the position that Siddhasena actually proposed to put the Jain sacred writings into Sanskrit and was required therefore to undertake a penance that ended with his miraculous manifestation of the image of Pārśvanātha at Ujjain. Equally few would wish to defend the position that Buddhaghoṣa was required by his teacher to journey to Śrī Laṅkā and put the commentaries into Māgadhī because he thought he knew more than his teacher. Nonetheless the fact is that Siddhasena seems indeed to have been committed to Sanskrit and Sanskrit learning: his texts display a remarkable mastery over Brahmanical learning and over the Sanskrit language. At the same time, however, as the biography indicates, Siddhasena also knew that Prakrit was a suitable vehicle for religious instruction. After all, his major philosophical work, the *Sanmatitarka* was written in Prakrit.

As for Buddhaghoṣa, there is no question that he espoused the view that Māgadhī was the language of the Buddha, the root language that lay behind all languages, and the language best suited for teaching the Buddhist doctrine. It seems fit indeed that it is to him that the tradition ascribed the accomplishment of rendering vernacular commentaries into Māgadhī. While an assessment of the influence that Buddhaghoṣa's theories of language might have had on others is clearly beyond the scope of this paper, it is clear from the references made earlier to Dharmakīrti in the *Vādanyāya* that not all Buddhists would have shared his views. Others hotly debated the very notion of a canonical or ritual language and that any one language was privileged over others. Indeed Buddhists were engaged in translation projects and encouraged translation of texts, although the fact that some authors felt compelled to defend the practice of translation seems to indicate a resistance to changing a text from one language into another.[18]

The Jains do not seem to have developed a theory of Māgadhī as the one sacred language as Buddhaghoṣa did, although it is certainly true that they occasionally speak of Māgadhī as the base language from which other languages evolved.[19] Indeed they always wrote in a variety of languages and encouraged their monks to learn local languages. It would seem that amongst the Buddhists and Jains, who shared so much in common in their reaction to the grammarians and Mīmāṃsakas in the debate over a scriptural language, Buddhaghoṣa's was a minority opinion, though one elegantly expressed both in his own works and in the stories that grew up around him.

Notes

1. E. Frauwallner has pointed out that the Mīmāṃsakas owe much to the grammarians for their understanding of the nature of sound. In an article, "Mīmāṃsāsūtra I,1,6.23" in *Wiener Zeitschrift für die Kunde Süd und Ost-Asiens, 5, 1961, pp. 113-124*, Frauwallner proposed that the Mīmāṃsakas did not originally hold to the doctrine that sound was eternal, but that they eventually adopted this doctrine from the grammarians. I would suggest that the same is true with regard to the debate over the use of Sanskrit as the single ritual language. Patañjali in the *Mahābhāṣya* vigorously argues for the use of precisely correct Sanskrit in a ritual context, with the concomitant assertion that misuse of Sanskrit involves sin. The argument seems very much intended to establish for the grammarian a foothold amongst the orthodox scholars by asserting that their skill in analyzing language was necessary for the ritualists in order correctly to perform rituals. There is no direct evidence that the argument is directed against any particular school, Buddhist, Jain or otherwise, although Madhav Deshpande in his interesting study of Indian attitudes towards language, *Sociolinguistic Attitudes in India : An Historical Reconstruction*, Ann Arbor: Karoma Publishers, 1979, p.18 and note 50, has identified an indirect reference to a Buddhist verse in the discussion about the function of grammar and the necessity of using correct Sanskrit. The topic deserves further study. In any case, in later times as we shall see below, the necessity of using Sanskrit as a sacred language would be used as one more argument against the Buddhists and Jains. See the *Vyākaraṇamahābhāṣya*, edited with Kaiyyaṭa's *Pradīpa* and Nāgojibhaṭṭa's *Bhāṣyapradīpoddyota*, by Vedavrata Vyākaraṇācārya, Gurukul Jhajjar, Harayana Sahitya Samsthan, 1962, pp.8-23 for a sense of the grammarian's arguments.

Bhartṛhari in the *Vākyapadīya* I.139-142 argues that only Sanskrit makes its meaning known directly, while the Sanskrit-based vernaculars, which he calls Apabhraṃśas, require the intermediary of a Sanskrit word. The *Vṛtti* of Vṛṣabhadeva on verse 139 cites the maxim, *śabdaprakṛtir apabhraṃśaḥ* "The Apabhraṃśas have as their base another language", and attributes it to the *Saṃgrahakāra*, or Vyādi, who precedes Patañjali. (*Vākyapadīya of Bhartṛhari with the Commentaries Vṛtti and Paddhati of Vṛṣabhadeva*, Kāṇḍa I, edited by K. A. Subramania Iyer, Poona: Deccan College Monograph Series, 1966, p.229). This would be the earliest reference that I know to the notion that Sanskrit is the root language. While Bhartṛhari can be read as advocating the view that any failure to use precisely correct Sanskrit leads to sin, even in a context outside of ritual, (see verses I.131 and I.132), it was clear that even amongst the grammarians themselves there was no agreement as to whether the notion of a "sacred language", the use of which led to merit and the misuse of which led to sin, implied that this was the case only during ritual or always. The *Padamañjarī* commentary to the *Kāśikā* on Pāṇini notes both views but advocates the more restricted understanding of Sanskrit as a sacred language, the use of which was required only in ritual. See the *Padamañjarī*, volume 1, page 13 of the edition *Kāśikāvṛtti*, edited by Dvārikādās Śāstrī and Śrīkālikāprasādaśukla, Varanasi: Prācyabhāratīprakāśa, 1965.

The Mīmāṃsakas, who were ultimately concerned mostly with matters of ritual, advocated the view that correct Sanskrit was required only in the context of ritual. See the *Bhaṭṭadīpikā*, cited by the *Mīmāṃsākośa* of Kevālananda Sarasvatī, Satara: Prajñā Pāṭhaśālā Maṇḍala, 1952, volume 6, page 3786 and the *Tantravārttika* on I.3.18, in the edition of Pandit Gaṅgādhara Śāstrī, Benaras Sanskrit Series, 1903, numbers 5, 7, 16, 23, 27, 29, 32, 34, 36, 39, 60, 62, and 72, pages 230, 239.

On the Mīmāṃsaka side, the necessity of conducting ritual in precisely correct Sanskrit was discussed at length in every major work, most notably of course Kumārila's *Ślokavārttika* and *Tantravārttika*. The discussion in the *Tantravārttika* is particularly interesting in that it raises a question that is less often debated by the grammarians, namely what languages are to be considered as Apabhraṃśas that require the intermediary of Sanskrit in order to make known their meaning, and what languages are actually prohibited during ritual. An opponent is allowed to argue that the prohibition against using *mleccha* speech in the ritual does not in fact refer to the Sanskrit-based Apabhraṃśas, but only to the non-Sanskritic languages, explicitly the Dravidian languages. The Siddhāntin replies this is an untenable viewpoint; all but precise grammatically correct Sanskrit is prohibited during ritual. The debate in the *Tantravārttika* also makes clear that the *pūrvapakṣa* is at least at times another Mīmāṃsaka, who resists the influence of the grammarians, and not necessarily a Buddhist or Jain. Kumārila often allows the *pūrvapakṣa* to take as his main opponent the grammarians and attack the notion that one can define a proper word as opposed to one that is improper. He returns then with the orthodox Mīmāṃsaka position, which insists that the science of grammar is necessary to the ritualist. See *Tantravārttika* under I.3.18. The discussion begins in the edition cited above on page 190 and the discussion on defining the *mleccha* language is on page 198.

Any further study of the complex issues involved in the discussion about language must offer a detailed analysis of these and other passages in the *Tantravārttika*. Deshpande's book cited earlier in this note is a beginning; he has at least sketched some of the Brahmanical, Buddhist and Jain attitudes towards language. Nonetheless I would take exception with his conclusions at a number of points. Deshpande regarded the main difference between Buddhist and Jain attitudes towards language as a question of which group was most committed to the use of Sanskrit. In fact I shall develop the theory in this paper that their difference, where it occurred, concerned the more fundamental issue of whether there is any one language that has the privileged status of being the sole language suitable for use in religious ritual and writing. I shall contend that the Jains answered on the whole in the negative while a minority of Buddhists answered in the affirmative. But at least in one important case the language that they chose to privilege was not in fact Sanskrit but Māgadhī. Deshpande argues that the Buddhists, particularly the Mahāyāna community, were far more committed to Sanskrit than the Jains because they drew their teachers from the

Brahmin community while the Jains did not (p. 56). He does not substantiate this claim and in fact the stories of Jain monks told in the various Jain *prabandhas* indicate that the Jains also drew their converts largely from the most educated class of society, the Brahmins, exactly as similar Buddhist stories say the Buddhists did. Deshpande does mention in passing the tension between Prakrit and Sanskrit in the biography of the Jain monk Siddhasena, something that this paper will discuss in detail. He is silent about Buddhaghoṣa, whose attitudes towards language will be a second focus of this paper.

2. By the time of Kumārila it is undeniable that the Mīmāṃsaka argues vehemently against the Buddhists and to some extent the Jains as well in practically every context. Thus in the *Tantravārttika* Kumārila heaps scorn on the Prakrit language of the Buddhist texts and uses the fact that they are written in this poor language to argue that they therefore cannot be true. In support of my contention that the doctrine of a sacred language might well have been developed by orthodox circles independently of any debate against the Buddhists and Jains, it is worth noting that Kumārila's attacks against specifically the Jain and Buddhist texts as written in Prakrit do not occur in the section devoted to demonstrating that Sanskrit as defined by the grammarians is the sacred language, but in a section on the authority of the *kalpasūtras*. The section is part of a general discussion of the nature of valid scripture. Kumārila remarks that since it has already been proved that Buddhist and Jain scriptures cannot be valid in the same way the orthodox *smṛti* literature is valid, the next supposition might be that they have the same kind of validity as the *kalpasūtras*. He first discusses how the *kalpasūtras* are necessary aids to the Vedic ritual and then proceeds to deny that kind of validity to the Buddhist and Jain scriptures. See the *Tantravārttika*, pages 162, 168-175. The Naiyāyikas also eventually use the argument for a sacred language against the Buddhists. Jayanta Bhaṭṭa in the *Nyāyamañjarī* would seem to be presenting a Buddhist as the *pūrvapakṣa* in his discussion of Sanskrit as a ritual language. I infer this from the fact that very early in the debate he has the *pūrvapakṣa* cite verses from Dharmakīrti's *Pramāṇavārttika*, 3.318;3.319b-3.320a. The *Pramāṇavārttika*, however, does not go into a debate against the grammarians. The *Nyāyamañjarī* edition that I am using is the Vizianagaram edition. Mine lacks the title page. The relevant section is pp.372-392. The edition of the *Pramāṇavārttika* I have used is the one edited by Svami Dvārikādās Śāstrī in the Bauddha Bharati Series, volume 3, Varanasi: Bauddha Bharati, 1968 and the relevant verses are pp. 356-357.

In addition the *Tattvopaplavasiṃha*, which attacks every doctrine of orthodox philosophy, not unexpectedly also attacks the concept of a sacred language and the notion that correct usage can be ordained by rules of grammar. The text has been edited in the Gaekwad's Oriental Series, volume LXXXVII, by Pandit Sukhalalji and the passage in question is from pp. 115-125. My edition lacks the title page.

Later as Hindu religious groups also began to use vernacular languages the debate against the necessity of using Sanskrit for religious texts would expand from a Buddhist-Jain vs. Mīmāṃsaka-grammarian debate to include such groups as the Śaivas like Abhinavagupta and the Southern Tamil authors. On the use of Prakrits in the *tantras* see Navjivan Rastogi, *The Krama Tantricism of Kashmir: Historical and General Sources*, vol.1, Delhi: Motilal Banarsidass, 1979, p. 8, which cites the *Mahārthamañjarīparimala* saying that Prakrit is the language best suited to teaching its doctrines. Rastogi notes that the Tripurā *tantras* also advocate the use of Prakrit instead of Sanskrit. The extent to which these later texts are indebted to Buddhist and Jain refutations of the notion of Sanskrit as a ritual language remains to be studied.

3. See the *Kharataragacchabṛhadgurvāvali* edited by Jina Vijaya Muni, Singhi Jain Series, number 42, Bombay: Bharatiya Vidya Bhavan, 1956, page 36.

4. The Jain emphasis on the validity of local languages is clear from their concept of *bhāsāsatta*, particularly the category of "true" speech that goes under the term *janapadasatya*, "the validity of local languages", and maintains that all languages are equally capable of making known their meanings and must be seen to be equally valid in their own local contexts. The term *janavayasatta* appears in the *Ṭhānaṅga Sutta*, 10.89. The text is edited by Muni Nathmal from Ladnun, Rajasthan: Jain Vishva Bharati, 1976 and the section is on p. 922. See also the numerous references given in the *Abhidhānarājendrakośa* of Vijayarājendra Suri, Delhi: B.R. Publishing Corporation, reprinted 1985, volume IV, p.1388 and volume V, pp. 1522-1556, and those in the *Jainalakṣaṇāvali: Jaina Pāribhāṣika Śabdakośa*, of Bālcandra Siddhānta Śāstrī, Delhi: Vira Seva Mandir Prakasan, 1973, vol.2, p.455. It is clear from the many citations in these works that the Jains are arguing not only for the validity of the Sanskrit based languages, but also for the Dravidian languages as well. The concept of improper speech, either false or ill-intentioned and speech that leads to the harm of other living beings is developed in the *Ṭhānaṅga Sutta*, 10.90, the *Dasaveālia Sutta*, chapter 7 and in the *Āyāraṅga Sutta*, 2.4.1. The *Dasaveālia* is edited by Muni Shri Punyavijayaji with the *Niryukti* and *Cūrṇi* in the Prakrit Text Series, vol.XVII, Ahmedabad, 1973. The *Āyāraṅga* is edited by Muni Jambuvijayaji with the *Niryukti* and the commentary of Śīlāṅkācārya in the Lala Sundarlal Jain Āgamagranthamālā, vol.1, Delhi: Motilal Banarsidass, 1978.

There are few exceptions to the Jain respect for the use of vernacular languages in all manner of religious undertaking, ritual, transmission of sacred texts, and even the philosophical debate, and for their insistence on the fact that correct grammar has nothing to do with merit. Nonetheless they did not mean to disregard the rules of grammar, as we see in Vādi Devasūri's *Pramāṇanayatattvālokālaṇkāra*, VIII.22, where the philosopher argues that in a debate speakers must use grammatically correct expressions. The text is published with an English translation by Harisatya Bhattacharya, Bombay: Jain Sahitya Vikas Mandal, 1967, and the passage is on page 643.

5. The Jain and indeed the Buddhist refutations often occur not in the wider context of a discussion of scripture or of the nature of language, but almost as an aside in the refutation of the Nyāya flaws of debate or *nigrahasthāna*, specifically the fault known as *aprāptakāla*, where the parts of an inference are

named out of sequence. (*Nyāyasūtra* 5.11). The Naiyāyika had traditionally argued that the parts of an inference require correct sequence; when a person hears them out of sequence he must first infer the correct order and then he understands the inference. The Naiyāyika used the case of understanding Prakrit words here as a supporting example of how a listener infers an underlying correct phenomenon first and from that gains meaning. It was this statement that gave the Jain the opportunity to challenge the whole notion of the orthodox Hindu philosopher that only Sanskrit had primary denotative capacity. The peripheral position of the debate in Jain and Buddhist sources reinforces my supposition that its original context was not as an attack against the Buddhists and Jains for using Prakrit as a scriptural language. The Buddhists and Jains directly refute the Mīmāṃsaka doctrine of *apauruṣeyatva*, that valid scripture is unauthored, a doctrine which directly attacked the validity of their scriptures. In comparison to their discussion of Sanskrit as a ritual language, they devote considerable attention to the refutation of the notion that scripture is unauthored. For a cursory Jain discussion of Sanskrit as the sacred language in the context of the refutation of the Nyāya *nigrahasthānas* see Prabhācandra's *Prameyakamalamārtaṇḍa*, edited by Mahendrakumar Sastri, Bombay: Nirnayasagara Press, 1941,p. 668. See also Vidyānandin's *Tattvārthaślokavārtika*, edited by Pandit Manoharlal, Bombay: Nirnaya Sagara Press,1918, p.290. By contrast Prabhācandra's *Nyāyakumudacandra* stands out for the fact that it deals in detail with the issue of a sacred language in a section of the text that is devoted to a consideration of the nature of language and the nature of scripture. The text is edited by Pandit Mahendra Kumar Nyayacarya in the Manik Chandra Digambara Jaina Granthamālā, number 39, Bombay: Manik Chandra Digambara Series, 1941, and the section is in volume 2, pp.757-767. The editor has provided extensive references to relevant Jain, Buddhist and Hindu texts on the subject of a sacred language from which I have benefitted greatly in this study.

6. The attitude of the early Buddhist community towards vernacular languages and the question of the use of Sanskrit versus vernacular languages has been the subject of much writing by modern scholars. It is not my intention here to do any more than give a few of the more prominent titles in which the issue of language has been discussed. It seems clear to me, despite the muddle of much that has been written on the subject, that like the Jains, the Buddhists used many languages and allowed for the use of vernaculars in a religious context. Works that deal with this subject include the following. Étienne Lamotte, *Histoire du Bouddhisme Indien*, Louvain: Institut Orientaliste, reprinted 1967, pp. 607 ff. Heinz Bechert, *Die Sprache der ältesten buddhistischen Überlieferung: The Language of the Earliest Buddhist Tradition, Symposien zur Buddhismusforschung, II*, Göttingen: Vandenhoeck and Ruprecht, 1980, particularly the articles "Sakāya Niruttiyā: Cauld kale het", by John Brough, pp. 35-43; "The Dialects in which the Buddha Preached", by K.R. Norman, pp. 61-78 and "Bu-ston on the Languages Used by Indian Buddhists at the Schismatic Period", by Akira Yuyama, pp. 175-182. Oskar von Hinüber, "Zur Geschichte des Sprachnamens Pāli", in *Beiträge zur Indien Forschung, Ernst Waldschmidt zum 80*

Geburtstag gewidmet, Berlin: Museum für Indische Kunst, 1977, pp. 237-247. Sylvain Lévi, "Sur la Recitation primitive des textes bouddhiques", *Journal Asiatique*, 1915, II, pp. 401-447. K.R. Norman, "The Role of Pāli in Early Sinhalese Buddhism", in Heinz Bechert, *Buddhism in Ceylon and Studies on Religious Syncretism*, Akademie der Wissenschaften in Göttingen, 1978, pp.31 ff. Lin Li-Kouang, *L'aide memoire de la vraie loi*, Paris, 1949, pp. 216 ff.

7. The text is edited in the Bauddha Bharati Series by Svami Dvārikādās Śāstrī as volume 4 from Varanasi in 1972. The relevant section is pp. 98-104. Like most of the Jain philosophy texts, this text also engages the Mīmāṃsaka and grammarian in the course of refuting the Nyāya definition of the flaw in debate known as *aprāptakāla*. The Jain and Buddhist arguments are substantially the same.

8. I have written a lengthy essay on the various biographies of Siddhasena which includes translations of the accounts in the *Ākhyānakamaṇikośa* and the *Prabandhakośa* and is entitled, "The Biographies of Siddhasena : A Study in the Texture of Allusion and the Weaving of a Group Image". Part I has been published in the *Journal of Indian Philosophy*, vol.17, 1989, pp. 329-384 and part II will appear in the same journal shortly. The *Prabandhakośa* is edited by Jina Vijayamuni in the Singhi Jain Series, volume 6, Santiniketan: Singhi Jaina Pitha, 1935 and Siddhasena's biography is pages 15-23.

9. That Vṛddhavādin sings and dances while Siddhasena discourses in Sanskrit introduces another element into their opposition. While we are not told in the *Prabandhakośa* what exactly Siddhasena says and we learn only that he rambled on and on, in the *Ākhyānakamaṇikośavṛtti* Siddhasena is directly quoted. He offers formal philosophical argument, a formal inference, in support of his contention that there is no Omniscient Being. See the *Ākhyānakamaṇikośa*, edited by Muni Śrī Puṇyavijayajī, Prakrit Text Society Series, no.5, Varanasi: Prakrit Text Society,1962, pp.171-172. It seems to me that when we consider the contrast in their presentation as well as the difference in the languages that Vṛddhavadin and Siddhasena employ, we may understand Vṛddhavādin as representing not only the vernacular culture as opposed to Sanskrit culture, but also the entire realm of orality over literacy, where orality teaches through verse and performance and literacy involves the more abstract thinking of the philosophical debate. For a discussion of oral culture as oriented around verse and performance as didactic devices and a discussion of the relationship between literacy and philosophy see the works of Eric A. Havelock. A useful introduction is his recent work *The Muse Learns to Write: Reflections on Orality and Literacy from Antiquity to the Present*, New Haven: Yale University Press, 1986, particularly chapter 8, "The General Theory of Primary Orality", pp. 62-78.

Jain biographies have much to say about the relative importance of oral transmission of teachings and book learning. I have some remarks on the primacy given to the written word among the Kharataragaccha in my paper on Siddhasena and in a paper that is soon to be published in the Festschrift for J. Deleu that is being edited by K. Watanabe.

10. See my references in the paper on Siddhasena cited above, notes 46 and 47. The belief is as ancient as speculation in religious texts in India. It was particularly prominent in medieval Jainism, where hymn-makers and hymns were given great honour. The *Bhaktāmarastotra* of Mānatuṅga, for example, gathered around itself numerous miracle tales which then were given the form of a commentary to the hymn. The text is edited by Hiralal Rasikdas Kapadia, in the Sheth Devachand Lalbhai Pustakoddhara Series, no. 79, Bombay, 1932.

11. It is also important to note that he uses Sanskrit not in the context of a philosophical debate, as he had at the outset of his career when he first encountered Vṛddhavādin, but in a type of oral performance. It is to be recalled that it was Vṛddhavādin the singer and dancer who first converted Siddhasena to Jainism, and it was suggested above in note 8 that Vṛddhavādin not only represents the Prakrit language but also the oral mode of teaching in this biography. Such an interpretation is supported by this incident in which we finally see Siddhasena emerge as the hero. For if he uses that tool of Brahmanical culture par excellence, the Sanskrit language, he does so here in a mode that is more compatible with the Jain/ vernacular culture as this biography so defines that culture than he did in his ramblings in the conversion debate. The abstract philosophical content of the *Dvātriṃśikā* is not at issue here nor is it relevant to Siddhasena's miracle; what is significant for the miracle is the mere oral recitation of his verses. Indeed all Siddhasena needs to do is utter one verse for smoke to come pouring out of the *liṅga*.

12. The text has been edited and translated by James Gray, London: Luzac and Company,1892. For information about the text see Gray's introduction and the brief comments by K.R. Norman in *Pāli Literature*, Wiesbaden: Otto Harrassowitz, in the series *History of Indian Literature*, vol. VII, page 145. On Buddhaghoṣa and other accounts of his life see Bimala Churn Law, *Buddhaghoṣa*, Bombay: Royal Asiatic Society, Monograph number 1, 1946, and Reverend Thomas Foulkes, "Buddhaghoṣa", *Indian Antiquary*, vol.19, April 1890, pp. 103-122. All of the Pāli accounts of Buddhaghoṣa, whether composed in Śrī Laṅkā or in Burma, are later than the Jain biographies of Siddhasena, which raises the question of direct influence. In addition the *Buddhaghosuppatti* weaves into the biography of Buddhaghoṣa an incident that had been associated with Śrī Harṣa in the *Prabandhakośa*. Both these remarkable men can reproduce verbatim an argument made in a langauge they cannot understand! (See chapter 5 in the *Buddhaghosuppatti* and *Prabandhakośa*, page 56; the story of Śrī Harṣa is translated in P. Granoff, ed. *The Clever Adulteress and Other Stories* (Oakville: 1990) 156-62). At this point in my research I am reluctant to argue for direct influence between the Jain *prabandhas* and the biography of Buddhaghoṣa. I prefer to see in the case of the Śrī Harṣa/Buddhaghoṣa parallel an example of a well-known and popular story that was told of many different people independently. Conceivably this story told of wise men who were gifted with language was told of many others as well; thus it is not necessary to look for direct borrowing. In the case of the rewriting of the canon into a canonical language I would also prefer to see between the Buddhists and the Jains a

similar preoccupation with the larger debate about sacred language in India rather than a direct reworking by the Buddhists of Jain material. In part I am doubtful that texts like the Jain *prabandhas* circulated much outside the Jain community, although I have no evidence to support this hypothesis.

13. K.R. Norman, "The Dialects in Which the Buddha Preached", cited above, has a number of citations from Buddhaghoṣa in which Māgadhī is said to be the root language. See pages 66ff. Oskar von Hinüber, *op.cit.*, p. 239, suggested that the earliest discussion of Māgadhī as the immutable natural language is to be found in the *Sammohavinodinī*, Buddhaghoṣa's commentary to the *Vibhaṅga*. The text is to be found in the Nalanda Pali Series, edited U.Dhammaratana, Patna: Nava Nalanda Mahavihara, 1961, pages 390-391.

14. Neither the translation of Pe Maung Tin, *The Path of Purity*, Pali Text Society 1975, reprint, page 511, nor that of Bhikku Nyayamoli, Colombo: A. Semage, 1964, p.485 correctly conveys the meaning of the passage. These are the only two translations I have had available to me. The edition of the *Visuddhimagga* that I am using is the one published in the Pali Granthamala series as volume 3, edited by Dr. Rewatadhamma, Varanasi, 1969. The passage is in volume 2, page 959.

15. I have altered slightly the order of sentences in order to unpack the tight construction and hopefully to highlight the sense of the passage. Instead of offering the technical definitions of terms such as *attha* and *dhamma*, which Buddhaghoṣa has just defined in the previous pages, I have used the loose phrase, "the special topics covered in the scriptures." I hoped thereby not to make the translation so technical or complicated that the main point would be lost.

16. *Sammohavinodinī*, pp. 390-391. The story itself is curious and seems hardly to fit Buddhaghoṣa's purpose of insisting that the object of the *nirutti-paṭisaṃbhidā* is the correct grammatical usage of Māgadhī. Nonetheless, if I understand the text correctly, the story does give Buddhaghoṣa the occasion to discuss his theory of Māgadhī as the root of all languages and as the natural language, the language that a feral child would naturally speak without being taught. Buddhaghoṣa turns the story of Tissadatta from one meant to illustrate that a monk could preach in any language to an illustration of the fact that all other languages are learnt by hard effort whereas knowledge of Māgadhī is inborn.

17. *Samantapāsādikā*, edited by Birbal Sharma, Patna: Nava Nalanda Mahavihara, 1967, volume 3, page 1297.

18. See *The Book of Zambasta*, R. Emmerick, London:Oxford University Press, London Oriental Series, volume 21, 1968, chapter 23, page 343. I am indebted to the article by Oskar von Hinüber cited earlier for this interesting reference.

19. See the *Nyāyakumudacandra*, page 764. See also the *Aupapatikasūtra* cited by K.R. Norman, "The Dialects in Which the Buddha Preached", page 66.

Taoist Thought in the *Kuan-tzu*

Kanaya Osamu
Tohoku University

The *Kuan-tzu*, which mainly deals with politics and economy, contains thoughts on a variety of topics. It is commonly known that this work exhibits a strong Taoist influence. In the present paper I will study the Taoist thought of the *Kuan-tzu* and show that it appears as a realistic and practical philosophy that has much in common with the so-called *tao-fa* thought found elsewhere. I shall also argue that this Taoist thought pervades the whole of the *Kuan tzu*.

The chapter in the *Kuan-tzu* in which the Taoist concept of *tao* appears most frequently is the "Nei-yeh p'ien". In that chapter *tao* is explained as a principle that "determines man's life and death as well as the success or failure of things"; it is also said that "though the world is replete with it, it cannot be discerned by people in general." This *tao* closely resembles the *tao* of Lao-tzu and Chuang-tzu. However, one distinctive characteristic of *tao* in the "Nei-yeh p'ien" is that it is conceived as something fluid which enters and dwells in man's mind. There is an influence of the concept of *ch'i* (ether) here. In other words, the concept of *tao* is used in the "Nei-yeh p'ien" in the same sense as are the ethereal concepts related to *ch'i*, namely, *ching*, *shên*, and *ling-ch'i*.

Tao, an objective entity existing in a fluid state on a cosmic scale, enters and abides in man's mind under certain conditions, such as when "the mind is at peace and the feelings are calm." Needless to say, this entering of the *tao* into the mind of man, as it is the indwelling of the fundamental principle, gives birth to a sage who is endowed with special abilities surpassing those of the man of ordinary mind.

Now such *tao* as described in the "Nei-yeh p'ien" is similar in nature to *shên* or *shên-ming* appearing in the "Hsin-shu shang-p'ien" in the same *Kuan-tzu*. "Hsin-shu shang-p'ien" stresses the predominance of the mind (*hsin*) over the sensory organs and teaches that *shên* or *shên-ming* comes and abides in the mind when the latter is in the state of inaction (*wu-wei*) and vacuous calmness (*hsü-*

ching); it puts the mind in an ideal state in which it can exhibit special power. This tallies with the line in the "Nei-yeh p'ien" stating that "*tao* will enter and abide in the mind when the mind is at peace and feelings are calm." Although it possible to say that *tao* and *shên* are two different concepts insofar as the terms used are different, it cannot be denied that they are at least linked through a common idea.

If we pay attention to the conceptual similarities it is clear that such statements as "if the form (*hsing*) is not right, virtue (*tê*) will never come", in the "Hsin-shu hsia-p'ien", and "Tao, when in heaven, is the sun, and when in man, it is the mind" in the "Shu-yen p'ien" are related to each other.

As it has already been pointed out, the concept of *tao* as a *ch'i*-like entity which circulates in a fluid state in the universe and enters and abides in man's mind also appears in certain parts of the "Jên-chien-shih" and "Chih-pei-yu" chapters of the *Chuang-tzu*. Those passages, however, are exceptional. *Tao* in the *Chuang-tzu* is in general conceived as ubiquitous and "to acquire *tao*" there means an "unconscious unity with *tao* in the state of self-oblivion." Aside from the above-mentioned exceptional passages, the *Chuang-tzu* does not teach that *tao* enters and abides in man's mind. The ethereal state of *tao*, therefore, may be said to be one of the distinctive aspects of the Taoist thought in the *Kuan-tzu*, as was noted by Fêng Yu-lan in his work, *Hsien-Ch'in Tao-chia san-pai ti tzu-jan-kuan ti i-t'ung* (A comparative study of the outlook of nature of the three schools of Taoism in the Pre-Ch'in period).

The linkage of *tao* and *ch'i* seen in the "Nei-yeh p'ien" and "Hsin-shu shang-p'ien" may be said to be a result of a more rationalistic way of understanding the Taoist concept of *tao*. *Ch'i* was originally thought to be an entity filling the universe in the state of a fluid and imparting life to all beings. Later, however, it came to be thought that there were two kinds of *ch'i*, good and evil, and further that there were *ching* or *ling-ch'i*, the very essence of *ch'i*. It was these concepts that were employed in the "Nei-yeh" and "Hsin-shu" chapters to give a rationalist interpretation to such conventional concepts as *shên* and *shên-ming*. It may be said that it was through such a process that the indwelling of *tao* in man's mind as the very essence of the universe or as the fundamental principle of the world came to be explained rationally.

In these sections of the *Kuan-tzu*, *tao* has hardly any religious character; nor is it based on any metaphysical system that stresses its nature as the fundamental cause of beings. It is rather conceived as a governing principle of the order penetrating the concrete movements and working of the universe and nature. This is the idea that is implied in such expressions as "*t'ien chih tao*" or "*t'ien-ti chih tao*" in other chapters of the *Kuan-tzu*. The respect for *tao* was at once respect for *t'ien* (heaven = nature). A notion of the interaction between heaven and man underlies the whole of the *Kuan-tzu*.

Now, changing the subject, let us next see the Taoist rules of life and way of government as given in the *Kuan-tzu*. Unlike the case of *tao*, descriptions regarding such topics, if we include brief fragmentary comments, are found scattered throughout the whole work. The problem here is to clarify their characteristics and how they are related to the work as a whole.

First, when we take up the "Nei-yeh p'ien" in which *tao* is discussed frequently, we find that the discussion on the rules of practical life centers on the rules for preserving health. It is quite natural, therefore, that a similar discussion is found also in the "Hsin-shu hsia-p'ien" whose descriptions overlap in many points with those in the "Nei-yeh p'ien". It is noteworthy, however, that this discussion is given far less weight in the "Hsin-shu hsia-p'ien" than in the "Nei-yeh" chapter.

The discussion about maintaining health appears also at the end of the "Pai-hsin p'ien", but its purport is avoidance of the evil effects of immoderate behaviour rather than preservation of health itself. This is all that will be said here about the positive discussion of the preservation of health in the "Nei-yeh p'ien", since it is, as shown above, quite exceptional in the whole of the *Kuan-tzu*.

What deserves more attention is the *tao-fa* thought seen in the "Hsin-shu shang-p'ien." The first half, the "Ching" section, of that chapter presents a kind of psychological view of the devices for receiving *shên* into one's mind, but the second half, the "Chieh" section, more or less features political thought. There we can find discussions on propriety (*li*) reminiscent of Hsün-tzu of the Confucian school, but there are also words giving weight to law (*fa*) and discussions of *fa* that are based on the Taoist view of *tao*. Moreover, the pursuit of the agreement between name and reality (the *ming-shih* theory) is discussed. From these facts it is surmised that the "Chieh" section of the "Hsin-shu shang-p'ien" is related also to Legalist (Fa-chia) thought. The difference, however, between the concept of *fa* in the "Hsin-shu shang-p'ien" and that of the Legalists is that the former is based on the Taoist concept of *tao*. "*Fa* based upon *tao*" here refers not to such a positive law as that propounded by Han Fei, but to a law close to the natural law which could blend with the Confucian view of morality.

The eclectic *tao-fa* thought came to draw attention for the first time when four chapters of old manuscripts including *Ching-fa* were unearthed at Ma-wang-tui. It was noted that the *tao-fa* thought in those old manuscripts was identical to the political thought that occupies an important place in the "Hsin-shu shang-p'ien": the words "*tao* gives birth to *fa*" in the *Ching-fa* tally with "*fa* derives from *ch'uan* (Perfect balance), and *ch'uan* derives from *tao*" in the "Hsin-shu shang-p'ien."

Furthermore, it gradually became clear that it is not only in the "Hsin-shu shang-p'ien" that this characteristic thought is discerned. There are words clearly expressing the *tao-fa* thought in such chapters in the *Kuan-tzu* dealing with *fa* as "Fa-fa p'ien", "Chün-ch'ên shang-hsia-p'ien", and "Pan-fa chieh p'ien". Lines expressing a similar thought, though not using the word *tao-fa*, are found in abundance in the whole work of *Kuan-tzu*.

As in the case of the Ma-wang-tui manuscripts, *tao* in the *Kuan-tzu* is conceived as a governing principle of the order of the universe and nature; the *tao-fa* thought in these works stresses the interrelations between heaven (nature) and man, regarding the former as the exemplar of the latter. In fact a stress upon the interrelations between heaven and man based upon the *tao-fa* thought is a theme that runs through all of the *Kuan-tzu*. The "Shih" and "Chiu-shou" chapters, which are closely related to the Ma-wang-tui manuscripts and to the "Hsin-shu shang-p'ien", basically conform with the *tao-fa* thought in that they teach as the way of government that one should follow the decree of heaven, earth, and nature. Words exhorting a man to follow nature are found all over the *Kuan-tzu*. Notable examples include the passage promoting agricultural production in the "Mu-min p'ien, ti-i" chapter at the outset of the *Kuan-tzu*, and the thought of "following heaven" in the "Hsing-shih p'ien, ti-êrh."

To sum up, the Taoist thought in the *Kuan-tzu* is realistic and practical, in keeping with the basic tenor of the entire *Kuan-tzu* which mainly deals with political and economic affairs. Even the concepts of "*tao*" and "*shên*" in the "Nei-yeh" and "Hsin-shu" chapters have a practical tone: *tao* and *shen* are thought to flow in the universe and, by entering and dwelling in his mind, to impart to man special powers for preserving health, conducting himself, and dealing with politics. Those chapters are not intended to give any metaphysical interpretation of *tao*.

What is most noteworthy in this context is the political thought that is based upon the eclectic *tao-fa* thought. This, together with the emphasis on the interrelation of heaven and man that underlies the *tao-fa* thought, is the distinguishing feature of the *Kuan-tzu*. The Taoist thought in the *Kuan-tzu* shows its strongest influence here. Another distinctive Taoist idea that needs to be mentioned is the concept of *tao* enveloping the universe. This idea is central to the discussion in the "Chou-hê p'ien", but a detailed discussion of this topic must be postponed to another occasion. In short, the *Kuan-tzu* mainly deals with practical matters concerning politics and economy, but underlying it is a kind of Taoist thought which provides the whole work with a philosophical background.

Reference: KANAYA Osamu, *Kanshi no kenkyū* (A study of the *Kuan-tzu*), Tokyo, Iwanami Shoten, 1987.

List of Characters

Chieh 解

Chih-pei-yo 知北遊

Ching 經

Ching-fa 經法

Chiu-shou 九守

Chou-hê p'ien 宙合篇

Chuang-tzu 莊子

Chün-chên shang-hsia-p'ien 君臣上下篇

ch'i 氣

ch'ing 精

ch'uan 權

Fêng Yu-lan 馮友蘭

fa 法

Fa-chia 法家

Fa-fa p'ien 法法篇

Han Fei 韓非

Hsien-Ch'in Tao-chia san-pai ti tzu-jan-kuan ti i-t'ung 先秦道家三派的自然觀的異同

Hsin-shu hsia-p'ien 心術下篇

Hsin-shu shang-p'ien 心術上篇

hsing 形

Hsing-shih p'ien ti-êrh 形勢篇第二

hsü-ching 虛靜

Hsün-tzu 荀子

Iwanami Shoten 岩波書店

Jên-chien-shih 人間世

Kanaya Osamu 金谷 治

Kanshi no kenkyu 管子的研究

Kuan-tzu 管子

Lao-tzu 老子

li 禮

ling-ch'i 靈氣

Ma-wang-tui 馬王堆

ming-shih 名實

Mu-min p'ien ti-i 牧民篇第一

Nei-yeh p'ien 內業篇

Pai-hsin p'ien 白心篇

Pan-fa chieh p'ien 版法解篇

Shên 神

shên-ming 神明

Shih 勢

Shu-yen p'ien 樞言篇

t'ien chih tao 天之道

t'ien-ti chih tao 天地之道

tê 德

tao-fa 道法

wu-wei 無為

Nirvikalpa-jñāna
Awareness Freed From Discrimination

Leslie S. Kawamura
The University of Calgary

This paper comprises a translation of Chapter VIII (*Adhi-prajñā*) of Asaṅga's *Mahāyāna-saṃgraha* together with Professor Gadjin M. Nagao's commentary on it.[1]

*VIII.1 [*Mahāyāna-saṃgraha-śāstra, *Asaṅga's text:]*

The superiority of [the learning of] the excellent training of mind (*adhicitta*) has been explained in the above manner. How is the superiority of [the learning of] the excellent training of wisdom (*adhiprajñā*) to be understood? That the superior quality of the excellent training of wisdom is non-discriminatory knowledge (*nirvikalpa-jñāna*) can be known through [the discussions on] its

1) essential nature (*svabhāva*),
2) basis (*āśraya*),
3) cause (*nidāna*),
4) objective-reference (*ālambana*),
5) form (*ākāra*),
6) response to criticisms (*codya-parihāra*),
7) foundation (*ādhāra, dhṛti*),
8) companion (*sahāya*),
9) maturation (*vipāka*),
10) flowing out (*niṣyanda*),
11) release (*niḥsaraṇa*),
12) reaching ultimacy (*niṣṭhā-gamana*),
13) praiseworthy qualities (*anuśaṃsa*) of [the knowledge that results from] preparatory practice (*prāyogika*), of [the knowledge] freed from discrimination (*nirvikalpa*), and of [the knowledge] obtained subsequently [after that] ([*tat-*]*pṛṣṭha-labdha*),

14) differentiation/distinctions (*prabheda*) [into three knowledges].

15) examples (*dṛṣṭānta*) [of the two knowledges—i.e. non-discriminatory knowledge and knowledge obtained subsequently,

16) effortlessly (*anābhoga* spontaneously) enacting (*kṛtya-anuṣṭhāna*), and

17) profundity/depth (*gāmbhīrya*).

From reflecting on the topics above, the superiority of *nirvikalpa-jñāna* should be known.

VIII.1 [NAGAO COMMENTARY:]

Among the three learnings of morality (*śīla*), meditation (*dhyāna*), and wisdom (*prajñā*), the third one, "the excellent [training of] wisdom" (*adhiprajñā*) is explicated in this text by the term *nirvikalpa-jñāna* (non-discriminatory knowledge). In this section, Asaṅga introduces 17 topics by which the nature, basis, etc. of that wisdom freed from discrimination is discussed. The 17 topics are explained in the following 25 verses that comprise the sections i.e., sections VIII.2 through VIII.18.

In topic 13 (VIII.14), *nirvikalpa-jñāna* is discussed fully in view of the three kinds of knowledges, but Vasubandhu's *Bhāṣya*[2] on this section [VIII.1] summarizes the three kinds of knowledges as follows.

The first one is called *nirvikalpa-jñāna* derived on the stage of preparatory practice (*prāyogika*); it is knowledge resulting from the investigation of non-discursiveness by means of reason. The second one is knowledge freed from discrimination; it is more commonly known as "basic non-discriminatory knowledge." The third one is knowledge that comes out of that basic knowledge; it is discriminatory and is called "knowledge acquired subsequently" (*pṛṣṭha-labdha-jñāna*). Two knowledges, the first one (which is the cause for the second one) and the third one (which is the effect of the second one), are discriminatory and function in the mundane world. Only the second one is truly non-discriminative and supra-mundane. What is ultimately aimed at is none other than the second one, "basic non-discriminatory knowledge," but insofar as the first one and the third one relate to it as its previous cause and its later effect, they are included in the knowledge freed from discrimination. In this manner, *nirvikalpa-jñāna* is discussed in view of three kinds.

The establishing of *nirvikalpa-jñāna* and, in particular, the establishing of the third knowledge acquired subsequently (although its seminal idea can be found in *Bodhisattva-bhūmi*[3]) are salient features of this text.

What is meant by the term *nirvikalpa-jñāna* is to be known through the discussions comprising this chapter. It is not an easy task to define the term, because, in spite of the fact that it refers, without doubt, to knowledge that lacks discrimination, the term "discrimination" (*vikalpa*: to construct or to divide) is understood in various ways. If one should say something about *nirvikalpa-jñāna*, it may be said that it is characterized as knowledge lacking the subject/object dichotomy; as lacking mistaken judgment: as not setting up something as a particular object; as the unity—i.e., the non-distinction between reality and wisdom; as equality and non-distinctiveness of all entities, etc.

Nirvikalpa-jñāna is explained at length in *Mahāyānasūtrālaṃkāra*. In the *Dharmadharmatāvibhāga*, it is discussed in conjunction with the "Ingress into the turn-about of the basis" (*āśraya-parāvṛtti*). It is perturbing that the idea does not appear in *Madhyāntavibhāga*. Aside from the present text, there is no other text that devotes a whole chapter to its discussion.

VIII.2 [Text: svabhāva*]*

Among those [topics], it is said that the essential nature (*svabhāva*) of *nirvikalpa-jñāna* is rid of the five aspects [of wrong views] (*pañcākāra-vivarjita*):

1) fully rid (*parivarjana*) of [the view that *nirvikalpa-jñāna* is] a lack of attention (*amanasikāra*),

2) fully rid of transgressing (*atikrama*) the stages accompanied by reflection and investigation (*savitarka-savicāra-bhūmi*),

3) fully rid of the tranquility (*upaśānti*) gained in [the meditation on] the cessation of consciousness and sensations (*saṃjñā-vedita-nirodha*),

4) fully rid of the belief in its nature as materiality (*rūpa-svabhāva*), and

5) fully rid of delineation in mind wherein reality is taken as an object (*tattvārtha-citrikāra*).

It should be known thus that *nirvikalpa-jñāna* is fully rid of these five aspects [of wrong views].

The way in which *nirvikalpa-jñāna* is established (*vyavasthāpita*) is as explained above, and in regard to this, [there are many] verses:

For the bodhisattvas, the essential nature of non-discriminative knowledge is rid of the five
aspects [of wrong views] and is rid of the delineation of taking hold of reality variously.[4]

VIII.2 [NAGAO COMMENTARY]

Here the first topic, the "essential nature" of *nirvikalpa-jñāna* is explained. The intrinsic nature of *nirvikalpa-jñāna* cannot be explained positively; it can be explained only negatively as "not that, not that." Therefore, here five expressions that can mislead one into thinking about or that are prone to make one misunderstand *nirvikalpa-jñāna* are given and each is then negated. By means of negation, there is an attempt to captivate *nirvikalpa-jñāna*.[5]

Of the five, no. (1) the view that *nirvikalpa-jñāna* is a lack of attention (*amanasikāra*), that is a thought-less and conception-less state, is negated (*parivarjana*). If it were the case that *nirvikalpa-jñāna* meant a termination of the thinking process, then to sleep soundly or to faint would also be a case of *nirvikalpa-jñāna* and people would gain this state without effort. No (2), "transgressing (*atikrama*) the stages accompanied by reflection and investigation (*savitarka-savicāra-bhūmi*)" can be accomplished by those who have entered the second *dhyāna* or higher *dhyāna* stages. It is a possibility for even worldly and non-Buddhist people and it can be accomplished by the sages of the small-vehicle, i.e., the śrāvakas. This cannot be *nirvikalpa-jñāna*. In the same manner, no. (3) "cessation of consciousness and sensation" (*saṃjñā-vedita-nirodha*), i.e., the meditation of cessation (*nirodha-samāpatti*), is a kind of no-mind meditation in which there is neither mind nor mental activities (cf. I.52). There is no meaning of wisdom either. As for no. (4), "its nature is materiality" (*rūpa-svabhāva*), this would be no-mind in a different sense; inanimate things (*jaḍa*) like trees and boulders are motionless and senseless, but it is not possible that they be *nirvikalpa-jñāna*. Finally, no. (5) "delineation wherein reality is taken as a particular object (*tattvārtha-citrīkāra*)," one gives free reign to erroneous investigation by repeatedly questioning whether reality is like this or whether reality is like that. Delineation is truly a process of discrimination. To be freed from a process of discrimination of this kind is *nirvikalpa-jñāna*.

The above comprises an explanation of the five aspects of wrong views and the freedom from them. Vasubandhu's *Bhāṣya*[6] adds that *nirvikalpa-jñāna* is similar to visual cognition in that visual consciousness is a direct perception and accordingly the eyes perceives its object, color/form, without discriminating (*avikalpa*) or variously delineating anything concerning its object.

These five aspects indicate what *nirvikalpa-jñāna* is not because No. 1) is not knowledge just as the ignorance of stupid people is not knowledge; No. 2) has not transcended the worldly concerns; No. 3) is no-mind and thus lacks any judgment; No. 4) is without life and is emotionless; and No. 5) is the reverse of non-discrimination. In comparison to these five, *nirvikalpa-jñāna* can be said 1) to be knowledge, 2) to transcend the world, 3) to be conscious and with sensations, 4) to be alive and have emotions, and 5) to be non-discriminating.

Many verses that summarize *nirvikalpa-jñāna* follow, but it should be pointed out that the verse in this section summarizes the five aspects discussed above. The last foot is an explanation of the fifth aspect and it also defines *nirvikalpa-jñāna*, because it is rid of the delineation of reality.

VIII.3 [Text: āśraya*]*

For the bodhisattvas, the basis for *nirvikalpa-jñāna* is not mind, yet it is mind,
because [*nirvikalpa-jñāna*] does not reflect on an object and yet is produced [from the mind].

VIII. 3 [NAGAO COMMENTARY]

The second of the 17 topics concerns the "basis" (*āśraya*) of *nirvikalpa-jñāna*. Through its discussion on whether the foundation or basis of *nirvikalpa-jñāna* is the mind (*cittam eva*) or not (*na tu cittaṃ*), this section reveals the self-contradictory position that the term *nirvikalpa-jñāna* implies. If *nirvikalpa-jñāna* is founded on the mind, since the mind is what reflects (i.e., discriminates), it would be a contradiction to claim it to be "non-discriminatory." On the other hand, if it be based upon that which is not the mind, for example some material thing, then it would be a contradiction to claim it to be knowledge. E. Lammotte read this passage, "le support (*āśraya*) du savior intuitif n'est ni pensée (*citta*) ni non-pensée (*acitta*)..."[7]

In response to this difficult problem, Asaṅga says, "is not mind, yet it is mind." Because *nirvikalpa-jñāna* "does not reflect upon an object" in the manner that the ordinary mind perceives things objectively, it does not have the mind as its basis; "and yet," because *nirvikalpa-jñāna*, gained from the long discipline of learning and practice, "is produced" from the mind, it has the mind as its basis.

VIII.4 [Text: **nidāna***]*

For the bodhisattvas, the cause of *nirvikalpa-jñāna* is the impressions gained through hearing
and [through] fundamental intense attention accompanied by [mind-]talk.

VIII.4 [NAGAO COMMENTARY]

The third of the 17 topics concerns the cause (*nidāna*). The "impressions gained by listening" (*śruta-vāsanā*) and also "fundamental intense attention" (*yoniśo-manasikāra*) accompanied by mind-talk (*sa-jalpa*) are the causes by which *nirvikalpa-jñāna* is produced. *Śruta-vāsanā* has been explained in I.45 *ff* as impressions of listening that flow out from the pure dharma-realm. Also, we have seen in III.1 *ff*, especially in III.7A, that the ingress into vijñapti-mātra is made possible when mind-talk, that is regarded as fundamental intense attention, arises with the impressions gained through listening functioning as its cause. Here we have the movement from "listening" to "fundamental intense attention" that is no other than the movement from "listening" to "reflecting" within the system of the three learnings of listening, reflecting, and practicing. This course of movement,

impressions gained by listening → mind-talk → fundamental intense attention

as the cause for ingress into *vijñapti-mātra*, has been explained in this section as the cause from which *nirvikalpa-jñāna* arises.

VIII.5 [Text: **ālambana***]*

For the Bodhisattvas, the objective-reference of *nirvikalpa-jñāna* is the inexpressibility
of the entities of reality; moreover, it is non-substantive and reality just-as-it-is.

VIII.5 [NAGAO COMMENTARY]

The fourth of the 17 topics concerns the objective-reference (*ālambana*) of *nirvikalpa-jñāna*. Because *nirvikalpa-jñāna* is a form of awareness, it must have some kind of objective-reference. Its objective-reference is summed up first as "the inexpressibility (*nirabhilāpyatā*) of the entities of reality (*dharma*)." This means that the objective-reference is of an inexpressible nature or the way of existence that is beyond expressions. Further, the meaning is augmented by the terms "non-substantive" (*nairātmya*) and "reality just-as-it-is" (*tathatā*). The first one, by referring to the non-substantiveness, the non-realness, of both the person and entities of reality, manifests the negative aspect expressed by *śūnyatā*. The latter one manifests the affirmative aspect, i.e., "reality as-it-is," revealed by the very existence of that negation. By these two aspects of negation and affirmation, the *Upanibandha* clarifies that what *nirvikalpa-jñāna* takes as its objective-reference is free of two misconceptions of (1) misconceiving what is non-existent as existent (*samāropa*) and (2) misconceiving what is really existent as non-existent (*apavāda*).

VIII.6 [Text: ākāra*]*

For the Bodhisattvas, the modus operandi of *nirvikalpa-jñāna* is one in which there is
no acquisition of a defining-characteristic with regard to an objective-reference to be known.

VIII.6 [NAGAO COMMENTARY]

The fifth of the 17 topics concerns the modus-operandi (*ākāra*) of *nirvikalpa-jñāna*. Here the term "modus-operandi" refers to the manner in which *nirvikalpa-jñāna* perceives its object. That object is "the objective-reference (*ālambana*) which is to be known (*jñeya*)," that is, reality as-it-is as explained in VIII.5 above. However, because *nirvikalpa-jñāna* does not discern the distinction between the subject as seer and the object as the seen, the two are equal and indistinct. That is to say, the subject becomes one with the object and reality as-it-is and awareness are in total union. In other words, the manner in which reality as-it-is presents itself and the modus-operandi of *nirvikalpa-jñāna* are in harmony and there is no characteristic difference between the two. The non-characterization of the objective-reference is expressed in the verse by the words, "there is no acquisition of a defining-characteristic" (*animitta*). The non-acquisition of a defining characteristic means that there is no perception of a subject and no perception of an object. Both are in harmony and without distinction; consequently, the awareness called, "*nirvikalpa-jñāna*" is a knowing in which there is no perception of a defining-characteristics of any kind. Therefore, to see without perceiving a defining-characteristic—i.e., the non-acquisition of a defining-characteristic—is the modus-operandi of *nirvikalpa-jñāna*.

VIII.7 [Text: codya-parihāra*]*

That which has the nature of origination from being a composite is discriminated; there is no other [object].

When letters are mutually combined together, they constitute a [meaningful] object. This refers to origination from being a composite. [1]

When expressions [of conceptual knowledge] do not exist, there is no knowledge regarding what is expressed.

Because [expression and the expressed] are contrary, there is no [knowledge of the expressed] in the expression; therefore, all things are beyond words. [2]

VIII.7 [NAGAO COMMENTARY]

The sixth of the 17 topics concerns response to criticisms (*codya-parihāra*). In this section, it is assumed that criticisms regarding the topics above are stated by the outsiders i.e., non-Buddhists, and it sets out to respond to them. The verses contain only the responses and not the criticisms. According to *Bhāṣya*[8], the criticisms concern the ideas expressed in VIII.5 above—i.e., if it is the case (as explained in VIII.5 above) that entities of reality are beyond expressions and cannot be perceived, then what is the objective-reference of discrimination, judgement, or perception? In what manner is the object of perception beyond expression? Verse [1] is a response to the first question and verse [2] is a response to the second.

Verse [1]: When words come together, concepts are established and our discriminative perception takes those concepts as its object of perception. The opening statement, "from being a composite (*sāṃyogika*)"—i.e., what is aggregated—refers to the statement, "letters are mutually combined together" of the third line, and when letters (*vyañjana*) mutually come together (*anyonya-saṃyoga*), the concepts of nouns and verbs are established as verbal expressions. A thing the nature (*svabhāva*) of which is an aggregation becomes the "meaningful object" (*sārthakatva*) of perception; therefore, to the question, "What is the objective-reference of our discrimination, judgement, and perception?" the response is "a composite is discriminated" and "there is no other (*anyathā*) [object]." In other words, it is not the case that some substantive existence is the object of perception.

And how is it that "all things are beyond words (*anabhilāpya, avācya*)?" Verse [2] responds to this question by using the two technical terms "expressions" (*abhidhāna*) and "what is expressed" (*abhidheya*). "Abhidhāna" refers to language and concepts, that is, name. "Abhidheya" refers to sense, that is, the meaningful object of perception. Our daily perceptions are based upon concepts, that is, upon expressions. Consequently, "when expressions [of conceptual knowledge] (*abhidhāna*) do not exist, there is no knowledge (*jñāna*) regarding what is expressed (*abhidheya*)." What does this mean? If the object of our perception was something that had substantive existence, then we should be able to comprehend an object without "expressions." However, if we lack the knowledge of expression by concepts, even if an object should exist substantively, knowledge with respect to that object would not arise. It follows that an object of perception is not something that exists substantively, but it is what is expressed through words (Verse [2]).

Now, if it should be asked whether the knowledge of an object is already included in the "expressions [of conceptual knowledge]" the response is that it is not the case. "Expression and the expressed are contrary (*viruddhatva*)," because they have different defining-characteristics (*lakṣaṇa*). They are contrary because the processes of expressing by means of concepts and of perceiving what is expressed by concepts as its objective-reference are operationally different from each other, one being "active" and the other "passive." The active "expression" cannot be the same as the passive "what is expressed." This is totally different from the fact that *nirvikalpa-jñāna* and *tathatā* are of one substance, because there is no discrimination between the "active" and the "passive." Consequently, "there is no knowledge regarding what is expressed."

The expression and the expressed constitute what we understand as our everyday, conventional perceptions and discriminations; however, no knowledge is found in them and therefore, viewed from the standpoint of ultimate reality, it is said that "all things are beyond words."

VIII.8 [Text: **ādhāra/dhṛti***]*

Nirvikalpa-jñāna is a foundation of the bodhisattva's practice
that is obtained after that, because it strengthen [the practice].

VIII.8 [NAGAO COMMENTARY]

The seventh topic refers to the foundation (*ādhāra/dhṛti*). The so-called "knowledge obtained subsequently" arises on the foundation (*ādhāra, dhṛti*) of *nirvikalpa-jñāna*. According to the commentary, the statement, "the bodhisattva's practice that is obtained after that (*tat-pṛṣṭha-labdha*)" in the verse, means that a bodhisattva's practice is a practice guided by the knowledge that follows after *nirvikalpa-jñāna*. Because *nirvikalpa-jñāna* "strengthens" that practice, it is "a foundation of the bodhisattva's practice." The word *ch'ih* affixed to all four Chinese translations—Buddha śānta, Paramārtha, Dharmagupta, and Hsüan-tsang, has the meanings "to support," "to uphold," "to sustain" and so on.

VIII.9 [Text: **sahāya***]*

For the bodhisattva, the companion of *nirvikalpa-jñāna* is expressed
in terms of the two paths comprised of the five perfections.

VIII.9 [NAGAO COMMENTARY]

The eighth of the 17 topics concerns the companion (*sahāya*). Here the relationship between the six perfections (*pāramitā*) and *nirvikalpa-jñāna* is explained. The word *sahāya* is used in the sense of a friend when in need, an attendant, a companion. *Nirvikalpa-jñāna* is treated as the sixth perfection (*prajñā*) and the other "five perfections" (*pañca-pāramitā-maya*) beginning with the perfection of giving (*dāna-pāramitā*) are considered to be its companion. This companion is said to be comprised (*maya*) of "two paths" (*mārga-dvaya*) to which the *Bhāṣya* (Vasubandhu's commentary) refers as the path of preparatory equipment (*saṃbhāra-mārga*) and the path of resource (*niśraya-mārga*). The first one is called "path of preparatory equipment," because one accumulates "roots of merits" by practicing the four perfections from the perfection of giving to the perfection of energy (*vīrya*). The second one is called "path of resource," because on the basis of the four former perfections, the perfection of wisdom (*prajñā-pāramitā*)—i.e., *nirvikalpa-jñāna* is attained with the perfection of meditative absorption (*dhyāna*) as its resource.[9]

VIII.10 [Text: **vipāka***]*

For the bodhisattvas, the ripening of the fruit of *nirvikalpa-jñāna* takes
place in
the two assemblies of the Buddha through practice and attainment.

VIII.10 [NAGAO COMMENTARY]

The ninth of 17 topics concerns the ripening of the fruit (*vipāka*). The next four verses (VIII.10-VIII.13) explain how *nirvikalpa-jñāna* functions in the steps from saṃsāra to liberation. That this and the following verse belong to the stage of saṃsāra is clearly indicated at the beginning of *Bhāṣya* when it states, "when the fruition of Buddhahood has not yet been attained"[10] (*Paramārtha-Bhāṣya* does not make this clear). This is also evidenced by the fact that the function, or cause and effect of *nirvikalpa-jñāna* is explained by using conventional worldly terms regarding cause and effect, such as, the "ripening of the fruit" (*vipāka*) used here and the "issuance of the fruit" (*niṣyanda*) discussed in the next verse.

Now, the term "ripening" refers to no other than the saṃsāric world—that is, emotions (*kleśa*) and actions (*karman*) of one's present moment of existence ripen into their respective fruits in the next moment of existence. However, insofar as the discussion is on the fruition of the function of *nirvikalpa-jñāna*, the term "ripening" cannot refer to saṃsāric existence; consequently, "the ripening of the fruit ... takes place in the two assemblies of the Buddha (*buddha-maṇḍala*)." The "two assemblies" refer to Buddha assembly of the transformation-body (*nairmāṇika-kāya*) and the Buddha assembly of the enjoyment-body (*sāṃbhogika-kāya*). When in one's effort to attain *nirvikalpa-jñāna* (that is, the first of the three non-discriminative knowledges discussed in VIII.19 below) "through practice" (*prayoga*), one gains the fruit of birth into the Buddha assembly of the transformation-body wherein one listens to the teachings of the Enlightened One. Or if one has already realized the "attainment" (*adhigama*) of *nirvikalpa-jñāna* (the second, basic knowledge discussed in VIII.19 below), then one is born into the Buddha assembly of the enjoyment-body. It should be noted that "attainment" has its various depth; thus, this indicates one form of Enlightenment, because as stated previously, this attainment takes place while one has not yet attained the full fruit of Buddhahood. In this manner, one can meet the Buddha in the next moment of existence by means of *nirvikalpa-jñāna* and one can join the two Buddha assemblies. This is the meaning of the passage, "the ripening of the fruit."

VIII.11 [Text: **niṣyanda***]*

For the bodhisattvas, the issuance [as the fruit] of *nirvikalpa-jñāna*
is thought to become more excellent (superior) as life goes on from
moment to moment.

VIII.11 [NAGAO COMMENTARY]

The tenth of the 17 topics concerns "issuance" (*niṣyanda*). The term "issuance" refers to the cause/effect relationship that obtains when the wholesome, unwholesome, or indifferent qualities flow out naturally and effect a similar wholesome, unwholesome, or indifferent quality. This form of causal relationship is different from that of the "cause/effect relation-ship of ripening." With regard to *nirvikalpa-jñāna* also, there is the idea of "issuance;" consequently, through one's birth in the Buddha assembly "as life goes on from moment to moment (*uttarottara-janman*)" or as one flows through from the first bodhisattva stage to the second, or from the tenth bodhisattva stage to Buddhahood, that *nirvikalpa-jñāna* "becomes more excellent (superior) (*viśeṣa-gamana*)." This is what is meant by the statement, "the issuance [as the fruit] of *nirvikalpa-jñāna*."

VIII.12 [Text: **niḥsaraṇa / niryāna***]*

For the bodhisattvas, release [from saṃsāra] by means of *nirvikalpa-jñāna* is [actualized] on the ten stages because of achievement and consummation.

VIII.12 [NAGAO COMMENTARY]

The eleventh of the 17 topics concerns release (*niḥsaraṇa / niryāna*). "Release" means that one is liberated from worldly concerns and attains final nirvāṇa and this "is actualized on the ten stages" (*daśa-bhūmi*) of the bodhisattva's practice. After eons of practice, there is the highest "achievement" (*prāpti*) of *nirvikalpa-jñāna* on the first stage of insight, but during the course of practice from the second through the tenth stages, that *nirvikalpa-jñāna* which had been attained is gradually brought to "consummation" (*niṣpatti*).

VIII.13 [Text: **niṣṭhā-gamana***]*

For the bodhisattva, *nirvikalpa-jñāna* reaches ultimacy
because the three pure bodies are attained and because unbounded power is attained.

VIII.13 [NAGAO COMMENTARY]

The twelfth of the 17 topics concerns "reaching ultimacy" (*niṣṭhāna*). That "*nirvikalpa-jñāna* reaches ultimacy," is explained by the two reasons of "because the three pure bodies (*śuddha-tri-kāya*) are attained (*lambhana*)" and "because unbounded power (*vaśitā-uttama*) is attained." Although the three bodies of the Buddha—*svabhāvika-kāya*, *sāṃbhogika-kāya*, and *nairmaṇika-kāya*—are attained on the first stage of the path, there still remains something impure there. Because the impurities are gradually removed as one progresses through the stages and *nirvikalpa-jñāna* becomes completely purified on the tenth stage, the verse states, "the three pure bodies are attained." Furthermore, even though the three bodies are there on the first stage, when the three bodies reach the tenth stage, "unbounded power is attained." The three bodies are explained in detail in Chapter X of this text. In that discussion, ten kinds of "unbounded powers" are explicated in view of explaining the highest, unbounded power.[11]

VIII.14 [Text: **anuśaṃsa***]*

Just like open-space [is not defiled by clouds etc.,] that *nirvikalpa-jñāna* is undefiled
by the various powerful evils owing to devotion and conviction. [1]
The undefiled state of that *nirvikalpa-jñāna*, like open-space, is freed from all obstructions
insofar as it is endowed with Achievement and consummation. [2]

The undefiled state of that *nirvikalpa-jñāna* like open-space, is free of all afflictions.

Even though it functions within the ordinary world, it is never defiled by worldly things. [3]

VIII.14 [NAGAO COMMENTARY]

The thirteenth of the 17 topic concerns the blessings (*anuśaṃsa*) of the three knowledges. The term "blessings" refers to blessings as derived from virtuous actions. From this section on, *nirvikalpa-jñāna* is divided into three kinds (the one resulting from practice, the one freed from discrimination, and the one obtained after the one freed from discrimination) and its virtues are explained from various aspects by means of examples. This division of *nirvikalpa-jñāna* into the three kinds of knowledges is introduced for the first time here in this section, but the text does not clearly indicate their respective names. The text simply uses the term *nirvikalpa-jñāna* in most instances, the three knowledges being grouped into one with the basic *nirvikalpa-jñāna* at their center. Only the *Bhāṣya* (see note 2) gives the division of the three knowledges and summarizes them in VIII.1. Here, in this section, a similar statement is repeated again.

The "blessings," that is, the virtues of *nirvikalpa-jñāna*, are that "it is like open-space" (*ākāśa*) and "it is undefiled" (*nirlipta*). Space has many qualities; its infinite expanse is used to exemplify the infinite expanse of *śūnyatā* and *dharma-dhātu*, and its fundamental purity is often used as a comparison for the purity of mind. Here, purity is used as an example for *nirvikalpa-jñāna*.

Verse one explains the undefiled state of the knowledge derived on the path of preparatory practice. It is said that *nirvikalpa-jñāna* "is undefiled by the various powerful evils" (*tīrva-pāpa*). Furthermore, it is stated that this is "owing to devotion and conviction." Although this first knowledge is knowledge gained through the religious practices of ordinary beings that take place before the "path of insight," insofar as it is knowledge that seeks after *nirvikalpa-jñāna*, it is not defiled by the evils of the past. The use of the words "devotion only (*śraddha-mātra*) and conviction (*adhimukti*)" in this context is worthy of notice. The fact that these two words are used probably indicates that this knowledge belongs to the level of the ordinary people; however, to link this knowledge directly with the practice of religion based on faith of the ordinary people is problematic, because it refers to *nirvikalpa-jñāna* and confidence-trust is spoken about in regard to that knowledge.

Verse two refers to the undefiled state of the fundamental *nirvikalpa-jñāna* which is "free of (*mukta*) all obstructions (*āvaraṇa*)." In regard to the statement, "endowed with (*upeta*) achievement (*prāpti*) and consummation (*niṣpatti*)," *nirvikalpa-jñāna* is achieved on the first bodhisattva stage and consummated on the tenth, as explained in section VIII.11 (release) previously.

Verse three explains the knowledge obtained after that *nirvikalpa-jñāna*. The knowledge obtained subsequently is knowledge that, departing from enlightenment, re-enters into the ordinary world after enlightenment is attained. Owing to great compassion, a bodhisattva takes on a new birth and always "functions (*vicaran*) in the ordinary world (*loka*)" and yet, like the lotus flower that blooms and is untouched by the murky water, the bodhisattva "is never defiled by worldly things (*loka-dharma*)" such as praise and blame, etc.

VIII.15 [Text: prabheda*]*

Just as a deaf-mute wishes to experience a thing; [just as] a deaf-mute has already experienced a
thing; [just as] a non-deaf-mute experiences a thing, just so are the three kinds of knowledges explained. [1]
Just as the dull-witted wishes to experience a thing; [just as] the dull-witted has experienced a thing;
[just as] the dull-witted experiences a thing, just so are the three kinds of knowledges explained. [2]
Just as the five [sensory organs] wish to experience a thing; [just as] the five have experienced a thing;
[just as] the mind experiences a thing, just so are the three kinds of knowledges explained. [3]
Just as one who is in the dark regarding treatises but wishes [to know] them and one who has experienced the
contents and meaning [of the treatises], just so are the three kinds of knowledges beginning with the one resulting from practice to be known in order. [4]

VIII.15 [NAGAO COMMENTARY]

The fourteenth of the 17 topics concerns the differentiation/distinction (*prabheda*) into three knowledges (*jñāna-traya*). In VIII.1, we encountered only the name, "*prabheda*" (differentiation according to distinction), but here the distinction of *nirvikalpa-jñāna* is clarified through the use of four examples. The words, "to experience a thing" means to take hold of some external thing; it simply means to perceive and refers to our world of ordinary perceptions and experiences. Perceptions and experiences are followed by the verbal expressions of the contents of those experiences. Thus the examples illustrated in verses one and two are stated in a manner of incorporating the two elements of the experience of a thing and the expression of the experience in words.

The "deaf-mute (*mūka*)" in verse one cannot speak, but "wishes (*iccha*) to experience a thing (*arthānubhāva*)." This illustrates the knowledge to be acquired on the stage of preparatory practice and is to be called the first *nirvikalpa-jñāna*. Another deaf-mute, though unable to speak, "has already experienced (*anubhūta*) a thing;" this illustrates the second *nirvikalpa-jñāna* as the basic non-discriminatory knowledge. The "non-deaf-mute," that is, one who is not a deaf-mute (*a-mūka*), can express in words what has been experienced fully; this illustrates the third *nirvikalpa-jñāna*, the one attained subsequently. In short, in knowledge derived on the stage of preparatory practice, one has not experienced anything and cannot express anything in words; in basic non-discriminating knowledge, one experiences all things but does not express them in words; in the knowledge that follows, one has already experienced things fully and expresses them in words.

The dull-witted (*mūḍha*), mentioned in verse two, is not versed in words and cannot create concepts; consequently, the dull-witted is unable to express anything in words. The rest is to be understood in the same manner as verse one above.

The "five [sensory organs] (*pañca-indriya*)," mentioned in verse three, refer to the five sensory organs of seeing (eyes), of hearing (ears), of smelling (nose), of tasting (tongue), and of touching (skin covering of the body) together with "the first five cognitions." In contrast to this, the "mind" (*manas*) mentioned in the verse refers to the sixth cognition (mental cognition, *mano-vijñāna*) or the organ (*manas*) for this cognition. Instead of the words, "to express" what has been experienced, here we find the words "to discriminate" things experienced. As the first five cognitions are direct perceptions, they are non-discriminative; that is, they are without intervention of thinking that is discriminative. In contrast, the "mind" (*manas*) or mental cognition (the sixth cognition) is no other than that which thinks and discriminates. Consequently, the five cognitions are contrasted with the mind respectively in view of the non-existence and existence of discrimination. Thus, the three knowledges are illustrated as follows. The first is the five cognitions that neither experience nor discriminate an external world; the second is the five cognitions that experience an external world but dare not (or cannot) discriminate it; the third is the mind that both experiences and discriminates an external world. Verse four contrasts the dull-witted one "who is in the dark (*avidita*) regarding treatises (*śāstra*)" and the learned one "who has experienced the contents and meaning (*dharmārtha-anubhūta/vid*)." According to the *Bhāṣya*, the word "contents" (*dharma*) means "only the words."[12] In contrast, "meaning" (*artha*) refers to the function of words. In this manner, *nirvikalpa-jñāna* of the stage of preparatory practice (*prāyogika*) is illustrated by the dull-witted who is in the dark regarding treatises but who seeks after them; the basic *nirvikalpa-jñāna* is illustrated by the learned one who has a thorough knowledge of words that comprise the contents of the treatises; knowledge obtained after that is illustrated by the learned one who not only is thoroughly versed in the contents of the treatises, but also is able to explain their meanings in all ways.

VIII.16 [Text: **dṛṣṭanta***]*

Nirvikalpa-jñāna is just like when one closes one's eyes;
knowledge obtained subsequently is just like when one opens one's eyes. [1]
Nirvikalpa-jñāna is to be known to be like open-space.
Just as the appearance of color/form [is infinite], therein, knowledge obtained subsequently is the same. [2]

VIII.16 [NAGAO COMMENTARY]

The fifteenth of the 17 topics concerns examples (*dṛṣṭānta*) of the two kinds of knowledges—*nirvikalpa-jñ āna* and [*tat-]pṛṣṭha-labdha*. Unlike the previous sections that aligned and compared the three knowledges, here only the "basic non-discriminatory knowledge" and "the knowledge obtained subsequently" are considered.

Verse one explains their distinctions and in verse [2] examples are explained. In other words, verse [1] distinguishes the two knowledges by comparing them to "when one closes ones eyes (*nimiñjita*)" and "when one opens ones eyes (*unmiñjita*);" verse two illustrates basic non-discriminatory knowledge "to be like open-space" and the knowledge obtained subsequently as "just like [the appearance of color/form (*rūpa-pratibhāsa*) [is infinite] therein."

In VIII.14, "open-space" was used in the sense of purity, but the *Bhāṣya* here gives four meanings for the term regarding which *Hsüan tsang* and Tibetan translations are closely aligned. The four meanings given for "open-space" are: 1) expansive (*sphuraṇa*), 2) stainless (*nirlepa*), 3) not self-contriving (*avikalpana*), and 4) not to be discerned by others (*avikalpya*).[13] *Gupta's* translation corresponds closely to these, but *Paramārtha's* translation is quite different.

"Knowledge obtained subsequently" refers to the situation in which all entities manifest their form in open-space (that is compared to basic *nirvikalpa-jñāna*). In other words, being developed from *śūnyatā*, their form exist *śūnyatā*. This knowledge obtained subsequently differs from basic non-discriminatory knowledge in that it discerns (discriminates) and is discerned (discriminated) by others. Basic non-discriminating knowledge is negative and transcendental. Knowledge obtained subsequently is affirmative and re-appears in the world of existence.

VIII.17 [Text: **kṛtyānuṣṭhāna**]

Just as the maṇi-jewel and the [heavenly] drums perform their own
respective acts [spontaneously] without discriminating,
So too Buddha activities occur always [spontaneously] in various ways
without distinguishing.

VIII.17 [NAGAO COMMENTARY]

The sixteenth of the 17 topics refer to 'effortlessly (*anābhogena*) enacting various acts (*kṛtyānuṣṭhāna*).' If *nirvikalpa-jñāna* that has been explained in the sections above is the fundamental essence of a Buddha, then it would be without discrimination (*vinā kalpam*) and therefore would not distinguish sentient beings. That being so, how could it benefit sentient beings? Such a question is assumed here, and this section is a response to it. If this question is to be related to the idea expressed in the statement, "Just like the appearance of color/form [is infinite] therein" of the previous section, it would take the following form. From a negative non-discriminatory knowledge (*nirvikalpa-jñāna*), how does the affirmative discrimination of existence called "color/form" arise in the knowledge obtained subsequently? The response to that is: 'naturally,' 'spontaneously,' or 'on its own accord.' Here the examples of the maṇi-jewel (*maṇi*) and heavenly drums or cymbals (*tūrya*) are given. The word "maṇi" refers to a wish-fulfilling gem (*cintā-maṇi*) that fulfills a person's wish spontaneously without distinguishing. The word "tūrya" refers to heavenly musical instruments of the (various) gods. Even when there is no one to strike the drums or cymbals, the sounds of music flow out of them spontaneously. The analogy of the maṇi-jewel and the heavenly instruments in regard to fact that the Buddhas and Bodhisattvas have no self-interest in their act of salvation is used to show that the activity of the Buddha (*buddha-kriyā*) and Bodhisattvas arises spontaneously on its own accord. Knowledge obtained after that *nirvikalpa-jñāna* is understood as an act of compassion towards sentient beings that arises spontaneously from *śūnyatā* (emptiness) and the negation of *nirvikalpa-jñāna*. In short, "knowledge obtained after *nirvikalpa-jñāna*" is śūnyatā enacting spontaneously.

VIII.18 [Text: **gāmbhirya***]*

[*Nirvikalpa-jñāna*] exists neither wherein [there is discrimination] nor in some other; it is neither
knowledge nor not knowledge. A knowing which is not distinct from what is known is non-discriminating. [1]
Because there is no entity [whatsoever] that is discriminated, it is taught [by the Buddha] that all Entities are by nature free of discrimination.
Therefore, knowing in such a manner is non-discriminative [knowledge]. [2]

VIII.18 [NAGAO COMMENTARY]

The seventeenth, i.e., the last of the 17 topics concerns profundity (*gāmbhīrya*). Being named "profundity," this section is naturally full of paradoxical expressions, and there are many points that are difficult to explain.

The *Bhāṣya*[14] gives two interpretations of the first verse:

(1) The perceptual-object of unreal imagination (*abhūta-parikalpa*) or of cognition (*vijñāna*) in general is of the other-dependent (*paratantra*) nature. This is testified, for instance, by the statement (II.16) that other dependent nature is taken as what is discerned (*parikalpya*), that is, as the object of discerning (*parikalpa*). Does *nirvikalpa-jñāna* also occur with such an existence as its object of perception or does it have something other? In response, the verse says that such an existence that is discriminated (*vikalpya*) is not the object of its perception, but there is no other object apart from it. The statement, "[*Nirvikalpa-jñāna*] exists neither wherein [there is discrimination] (*nāsti tasmin*)" means that because *nirvikalpa-jñāna* is non-discursive (*nirvikalpa*), it does not occur wherein there is discursive thought. However, *nirvikalpa-jñāna* is a knowledge that perceives the reality or suchness (*tathatā*) of all beings, that is, dharmatā (reality per-se) of all entities (*dharma*). Since *dharmatā* is not perceived separately from *dharma* and relates to it as 'neither one nor different,' when *nirvikalpa-jñāna* realizes reality per-se (*dharmatā*), its object is nothing

but *dharma*. This is the meaning of the statement, "nor in some other (*na cānyasmin*)."

Now another question is raised concerning the relationship between *nirvikalpa-jñāna* and knowledge (*jñāna*). If *nirvikalpa-jñāna* is knowledge, then how can it be said to be non-discriminatory (*nirvikalpa*)? If it is not knowledge, then *nirvikalpa* should not form a compound with *jñāna* as its last member. The response in the verse is the paradoxical statement, "it is neither knowledge (*na jñānaṃ*) nor not knowledge (*na cājñānaṃ*)." This means that since the basic *nirvikalpa-jñāna* is different from the other two knowledges, the knowledge on the stage of preparatory practice and the knowledge obtained subsequently, it is said to be "neither knowledge," but since it is an effect of the knowledge on the stage of preparatory practice and the cause for the knowledge obtained subsequently, is said to be "nor not knowledge."

(2) The second interpretation combines the two items above into one. It is expressed in the verse by the statement, "[*Nirvikalpa-jñāna*] exists neither wherein [there is discrimination], nor in some other." Because *nirvikalpa-jñāna* does not exist wherein there is discrimination, the verse states "It is neither knowledge" and because suchness (*tathatā*) or reality per-se (*dharmatā*) is not found "in some other" apart from wherein there is discrimination, the verse states "nor not knowledge."

Thus, *nirvikalpa-jñāna* is an 'equality-knowledge' in which there is no distinction between the seeing-subject and the object-seen. The verse concludes: "a knowing which is not distinct (*na viśiṣṭa*) from what is known (*jñeya*)," that is, knowledge which is of one substance with the object, "is non-discriminating (*nirvikalpaka*)." Asvabhāva's *Upanibandhana* adds: "A knowing that is not distinct from what is to be known" is compared to the relationship that obtains between open-space and color/form that appears therein[15] (cf. VIII.16, Verse 2).

Now, with regard to the second verse, there is a problem in interpreting the fourth line, but the first three lines give no problem. A certain sūtra quoted here in the verse explains that the Buddha "taught that all entities (*sarva-dharma*) are by nature (*prakṛtyā*) free of discrimination (*avikalpatva*)." And why is it that all entities are free of discrimination? The response is given in the first line thus, "Because there is no entity that can be discriminated (*vikalpya*)." The words "that can be discriminated" is contextually the same as the words 'an existence that is discriminated' (*vikalpya*) explained in the discussion on interpretation (1) above. Because what is discerned and conceptualized in the cognitive process is nothing other than what has been created through discrimination, it does not exist in reality. Whatever is established through discrimination or through the thought process cannot be said to have real or actual existence. In contrast, the entities truly existent are found only in knowledge (*jñāna*) that is non-discriminating (*nirvikalpa*). This is what the Buddha meant in the statement, "all entities are by nature free of discrimination."

However, if all entities are by nature free of discrimination, then people should not need to put forth the effort of going through religious practices in order to attain *nirvikalpa-jñāna*; they should be liberated just as they are. The response to this criticism is given in the fourth line, but it is interpreted differently by the different translators. According to the three translations by Paramārtha, Gupta, and Hsüan-tsang, the reason that people are not liberated just as they are is that they lack *nirvikalpa-jñāna* or that their knowledge is not *nirvikalpa* (both with the double negation, 'no nirvikalpa' and 'not nirvikalpa'). In contrast to this, the Tibetan translation, that has only one negative particle, states "therefore, knowing in such a manner is non-discriminative [knowledge]." Buddhaśānta's translation is very close to this in that it has only one negative particle. Thus the translations differ from each other.

The statement "knowing in such a manner" in the Tibetan translation means to know all entities in the manner that the Buddha explicated them and that is said to be *nirvikalpa-jñāna*. If we interpret this Tibetan translation to imply that people lack *nirvikalpa-jñāna* and thus cannot be liberated just-as-they-are, then it has the same intention as the other three Chinese translations. Consequently, after explicating that meaning, the *Bhāṣya* explains that only when one is awakened (enlightened) to *nirvikalpa-jñāna* there is liberation, but so long as it is not realized, there is no liberation.[16] The present translation has followed tentatively the Tibetan text, because it seems to be most conducive to keeping the verse form.

VIII.19 [Text: Three kinds of **Prāyogika-jñāna, Mūla-jñāna** *and Five kinds of* **tat-pṛṣṭha-labdha-jñāna***]*

Here, *nirvikalpa-jñāna* that results from practice (*prayogika-nirvikalpa-jñāna*) [on the stage of preparatory practice] is three-fold, on account of its divisions according to whether it arises (1) from a cause (*hetu*), (2) from being drawn out (*ākṣepa*), or (3) from repeated praxis (*abhyāsa*).

[The basic] *nirvikalpa-jñāna* is also three-fold, because it is *nirvikalpa-jñāna* by virtue of being (1) satisfaction (*saṃtuṣṭi*), (2) unperverted (*aviparyāsa*), and (3) without conceptual fabrication (*niṣprapañca*).

[The knowledge] obtained subsequently (*tat-pṛṣṭha-labdha*) to *nirvikalpa-jñāna*] is five-fold, because of its distinctions of careful observation (*vicāra*), (1) thorough penetration (*prativedha*), (2) repeated recollection (*anusmaraṇa*), (3) establishing [what is recalled as a teaching] (*vyavasthāna*), (4) integrating [all teachings] (*sambhinna[-ālambana]*), and 5) perfecting as one wishes (*samṛddhi*).

VIII.19 [NAGAO COMMENTARY]

The three knowledges—*nirvikalpa-jñāna* that results from practice on the stage of preparatory practice, basic *nirvikalpa-jñāna*, and knowledge acquired subsequently to the basic *nirvikalpa-jñāna*—are divided further into three or five kinds. The basis for these divisions differs in each case.

Nirvikalpa-jñāna that results from practice is distinguished according to the cause from which it arises (Parmārtha's *Bhāṣya* says 'with regard to cause'[17]).

(1) The first, "cause" (*hetu*), means the family line or lineage (*gotra*) into which one is born. Family lineage means, with respect to the mundane world, that one is endowed with a particular physical body and belongs to a special genealogy, and that this has been going on since time immemorial. In the same way, one who belongs to the bodhisattva family is one who has the qualification of being a receptacle to receive Buddhahood and this is understood to be the "cause." According to the *Upanibandha*,[18] *nirvikalpa-jñāna* that results on the stage of preparatory practice will arise in one who possesses this cause by virtue of meeting 'powerful condition.' (Here 'condition' is contrasted with 'cause;' by virtue of realizing that it is a powerful condition, it is ascertained that one has been in the Buddha-family.) (2) The second, "being drawn out" (*ākṣepa*), means that, in some case, knowledge resulting from practice is "drawn out" in the present life owing to the repeated praxis of the former life functioning as its cause. (3) The third, "repeated praxis" (*abhyāsa*), means that, in some case, knowledge resulting from praxis arises owing to the repeated praxis in the prsent life by each individual.

Basic *nirvikalpa-jñāna* is distinguished into three according to the kind of person who possesses it (Paramārtha's *Bhāṣya:* 'with regard to person'[19]). The first one is *nirvikalpa-jñāna* of the worldly or ordinary person. The second one is of the śrāvakas and others. The third one is of the bodhisattvas, and it is needless to say that only this one is the true *nirvikalpa-jñāna*.

(1) The first one is "non-discriminatory" in that an ordinary person gains "satisfaction" with a low level enlightenment and does not try to attain a higher state. Or the ordinary person, by means of the ordinary wisdom of hearing, thinking, and practice, attains the highest worldly state (*bhavāgra*), mistakes it for nirvāṇa, and, being satisfied, does not try to attain anything higher. (2) The second one is "non-discriminatory" in that the śrāvaka and other sages, who have already awakened to the "unperverted" suchness by realizing the impermanence, suffering, and so on of the world, do not fall again into erroneous discrimination of permanence, and so on. (3) The third one is "non-discriminatory" in that the bodhisattvas envisage all entities "without conceptual fabrication," fabrication being nothing more than an activity belonging to the world of conventional language.

Knowledge obtained subsequently is a discriminatory knowledge that is attained after the negation implicit in "basic *nirvikalpa-jñāna*" is realized. Its discriminatory process of careful observation (*vicāra*) is distinguished into five kinds according to its content (Paramārtha's *Bhāṣya*: 'with regard to events'[20]).

(1) As for the first, "careful observation of thorough penetration," thorough penetration (*prativedha*) refers to intuitive realization of truth (*abhisamaya*). Having arisen from the samādhi of *nirvikalpa-jñāna*, an awareness that 'I thoroughly penetrated such and such' occurs to the bodhisattva and he carefully

observes it. (2) The second, "its recollection (*anusmaraṇa*)" means not to forget what has been penetrated by recollecting it later. (3) The third, "establishing (*vyavasthāna*) [what is recalled as a teaching]" means to establish what was penetrated as a teaching and explain it to others. (4) The fourth, "the intergrating [all teachings]" (*sambhinna[-ālambana]*) means to comprehend the teachings by (synthesizing and) integrating all of them into one. This enables one to attain the turn-about of the basis (see III.12). (5) The fifth, "perfecting as one wishes" (*samṛddhi*) is so translated because Buddhaśānta translates the text here by the term *ch'êng-chiu* (perfection) and all the other three Chinese translations by the term *ju-i* (fulfilling as one wishes) and thus, it includes the meaning "mastery" (*vibhutva*). Mastery, in this context means, for example, if one so wishes one can change a piece of dirt into gold (refer to verse [4] in the following section) and this is the working of supernatural power (*ṛddhi*) that operates in the knowledge obtained subsequently after *nirvikalpa-jñāna*. The words "carefully observing" qualifies all of five topics, but in regard to the fifth, the *Bhāṣya* gives two possible interpretations: (1) carefully observing the fulfilling according to one's wishes and (2) carefully observing in order to fulfill according to one's wishes.[21]

VIII.20 [Text: Demonstration/proof of nirvikalpa-jñāna*]*

There are separate verses to demonstrate (prove *sādhaka*) *nirvikalpa-jñāna*:[22]

(1) Hellish beings, animals, man, heavenly beings—each according to one's ability thinks differently
about a single same thing; therefore, it is claimed that an object is not something effected.
preta-tiryaṅ-manuṣyāṇāṃ devānāṃ ca yathā-arhataḥ /
tulyavastu-manobhedād artha-aniṣpattir iṣyate / 1 /

(2) In regard to the past etc., also in a dream or two images, because objects of perception do not exist and because
[in such a case,] that [cognition itself] is taken as the objective referent [a world external does not exist].
atīta-ādau tathā svapne pratibimba-dvaye 'pi ca /
asann-ālambanatvāc ca tad-ālambana-yogataḥ / 2 /

(3) If an object of perception were effected as an object, then non-discriminating knowledge could not exist.
And on account of the non-existence of that, the attainment of Buddhahood also could not occur.
arthasya arthatva-niṣpattau jñānaṃ na syād akalpakam /
tad-abhāvāc ca buddhatva-prāptir naiva-upapadyate / 3 /

(4a) Because when a bodhisattva attains [mental] mastery, earth and so on are perceived as existing [just as
one wishes] owing to the strength of zealous application, and [so also] for a meditation practitioner,
bodhisattve vaśi-prāpte 'dhimukti-vaśād yataḥ /

tathā-bhāvaḥ pṛthivy-ādau dhyāyinām ca-upalabhyate / 4a /

(4b) and here because to a knowledgeable one who has attained calm and who has fulfilled his investigation

all dharmas become manifest just-as-they-are [as objects] when he is intensely attentive to them,

niṣpanna-vicayasya-iha dhīmataḥ śama-lābhinaḥ /

sarva-dharma-manaskāre tathā-artha-khyānato 'pi ca / 4b /

(4c) and again because, when the activity of knowing is non-discriminating, all objects do not become manifest;

therefore, you should know things [as such] do not exist! when it does not exist, its representation [also does not exist].

jñāna-cāre 'vikalpe hi sarvārtha-akhyānato 'pi ca /

artha-abhāva-upagantavyo vijñaptes tad-abhāvataḥ / 4c /

VIII.20 [NAGAO COMMENTARY]

The text opens with the statement, "to demonstrate (prove *sādhaka*) *nirvikalpa-jñāna*." The *Bhāṣya* also states that the explanation regarding *nirvikalpa-jñāna* ended with the last section; thus, from this section onward the text attempts to demonstrate *nirvikalpa-jñāna*. The sanskrit version of these verses can be found in *Abhidharmasamuccayabhāṣya* (see note 22); however, from where these verses originate cannot be established accurately.[23] As pointed out in II.14B, in the Tibetan translation these six verses appear both there in II.14B as well as here in this section; however, as attested to by the Chinese translations, these verses were found in the original text, in all probabilities, in this section only.

The ideas explained in these six verses have been discussed already in prose in II.14A (the section preceding II.14B). In that section, the knowledge by which the non-existent quality of the external world is known was divided into four. In order to parallel the discussion of the four in section II.14A, here, they have been indicated by the numbers in parentheses (1)-(4), the fourth one (4) being divided further into three, indicated by (a)-(c). It should be noticed, however, that whereas sections II.14A and 14B were devoted to the explication of *vijñapti-mātra* (hence, the non-substantial quality of the external world), here the six verses are used to demonstrate *nirvikalpa-jñāna*. Therefore, although an outline of the four knowledges has been presented in the previous sections from the viewpoint of *vijñapti-mātra*, here the four will be investigated especially in regard to how they demonstrate *nirvikalpa-jñāna*.

(1) The statement, "an object is not something effected" (verse 1, line 4), suggests the conclusion that what is perceived as the external world is non-substantive. Hellish beings see water as a plateau; animals see as pure water what man sees as filth; what man sees as pure water is seen by heavenly beings as impure. In this manner, the fact that "each according to one's ability thinks differently about a single same thing" demonstrates (proves) that what is perceived as the external world lacks determinate substantive qualities.

(2) Even though "the past" and "the future" do not exist substantively just as the Sautrāntikas claim, they are still cognized as real. Even though we are sleeping in a small room, we enjoy the wide expanse of the mountains and rivers "in a dream." We have "two images," the image we see in a mirror or the image we see in meditation. In such cases, "those objects of perception do not exist" substantively. Instead, cognition "itself," that is, what has been constructed as an object (of cognition) within the cognitive process becomes the "objective referent." In other words, "the past" and so on "possess that [cognition itself] as the objective referent." This means that the mind sees mind itself. In other words, the mind perceives the image that it has itself constructed. It is in this sense that cognition-only is established and what is perceived substantively as an external object does not exist.

(3) *Nirvikalpa-jñāna* is knowledge that arises in the negation of the substantive quality of an object. "If an object of perception were effected as an object," then the knowledge that discerns the reality of that object could not be a "non-discriminating knowledge." If non-discriminating knowledge did not exist and there was only discriminating knowledge, then "the attainment of Buddhahood" would become meaningless, because the claim for discriminating knowledge simply rejects the fundamental meaning underlying "wisdom" and "enlightenment" of Buddhahood.

(4) Here in (4a) to (4c) also, the manner in which the external world or the object appears is discussed. Division (4a) clarifies that "when a bodhisattva attains masteries, earth and so on are perceived as existing [as one wishes]," for example, as gold "owing to the strength of zealous application." When the knowledge obtained subsequently was discussed in the previous section (VIII.19), the fifth point, "perfecting," was interpreted to include the meaning of supernatural power of 'mastery' in terms of '*ju-i*' (fulfilling one's wishes). Here, in this context, the same super-natural power is at work.

The term "meditation practitioners" refers to the śrāvaka and others who have attained meditative practices fully; by virtue of this, the same supernatural power is obtained by them and the manner in which the external object appears is the same for them.

Division (4b) explains that when a bodhisattva "is intensively attentive to [the dharmas taught in the sūtras]," the meaning of the sūtras and the images of the buddhas "become manifest just-as-they-are."

In contrast to divisions (4a) and (4b) above that explain that objects become manifested, division (4c) explains that *nirvikalpa-jñāna* means that an object is not manifested. In all these cases, "the non-existent quality of the world" is exemplified and the statement found in the fourth foot of the first verse is simply highlighted.

The discussion up to this point can be considered to be a re-statement of a sūtra (on this point see II.14A). Finally, in (4c), pāda c and d, a conclusion is given. Although the statement, 'cognition-only exists, objects do not exist,' a statement fundamental to the Yogācāra Vijñānavāda school, can be established through the realization of "the non-existence of thing [as such]," it is further concluded that when a thing [as such] does not exist, "representation" of cognition also is non-existent. When the world that is to be represented by cognition (as its object) does not exist, "representation" itself loses its meaning and cannot be an object of cognition. This means that when an outer object does not exist, cognition-only also cannot be established (in *nirvikalpa-jñāna*).

VIII.21 [Text: nirvikalpa-jñāna/prajñā*]*

The perfection of wisdom (*prajñā-pāramitā*) and *nirvikalpa-jñāna* are not different (*nirviśiṣṭa*). It is, for example, as stated [in a sūtra]: "A bodhisattva dwells (*tiṣṭhati*) in the perfection of wisdom according to non-dwelling (*asthāna-yogena*) and then he fulfills (*paripūri*) the other [five] perfections (*pāramitā*) by means of intense practice (*bhāvanā*)."

How does the bodhisattva fulfill (*paripūri*) according to non-dwelling? By rejection (*parityāga*) of the five kinds of dwelling (*pañca-vidha-sthāna*). (1) Rejection of dwelling in the conceit of "I" (*ahaṃkāra-sthāna*) as held by the non-Buddhists (*tīrthika*). (2) Rejection of dwelling in the discriminating thought (*vikalpa-sthāna*) held by a bodhisattva who has not yet seen truth (*adṛṣṭa-tattva-bodhisattva*). (3) Rejection of dwelling in either of the two extreme views (*anta-dvaya-sthāna*) of saṃsāra and nirvāṇa. (4) Rejection of dwelling in the contentment (*saṃtuṣṭi-sthāna*) that the mere removal of the obstruction of afflictions (*kleśa-āvaraṇa-prahāṇa-mātra*) is sufficient. (5) Rejection of dwelling in a world of nirvāṇa without [afflictional] remainder (*nirupadhiśeṣa-nirvāṇa-dhātu-sthāna*) where the benefitting of sentient beings is disregarded (*sattva-artha-nirapekṣa*).

VIII.21 [Nagao Commentary]

Here it is made clear that *nirvikalpa-jñāna* is not different from the perfection of wisdom (*prajñā-pāramitā*) expounded in the Prajñāpāramitā Sūtras. It is also evident that the Yogācāra school considered the Prajñāpāramitā Sūtras as the most superior texts on which to base one's tenets. The statement, "dwells according to non-dwelling," in the passage quoted above reflects a convention found in the Prajñāpāramitā Sūtras—that is, the statement is paradoxical and contradictory. The term *nirvikalpa-jñāna* does not appear there, but the paradoxical statement, "dwelling according to non-dwelling," demonstrates what *nirvikalpa-jñāna* means. Accordingly, it reminds one of the modus operandi of *nirvikalpa-jñāna* which is to discriminate without discriminating.

Here, however, in order to dissolve the contradiction of dwelling without dwelling, the author explains in what a bodhisattva should not dwell, so that he can dwell properly—that is, the author explains what kind of dwelling is to be rejected. Dwelling in this context can mean 'dwelling happily in trust,' hence it can refer to one's own conviction or standpoint. There are five kinds of dwellings that belong to five kinds of persons and that are to be rejected. (1) The non-Buddhists dwell happily in the attachment to a belief in ātman. (2) A bodhisattva who has not understood reality as-it-is dwells in the thought in which he discriminates wisdom to be such and such. (3) Worldly people dwell happily in saṃsāra while the śrāvakas dwell happily in the thought of escaping from it and of aiming for nothing but nirvāṇa. (4) The śrāvakas dwell in the thought of removing the obstacles of afflictions without showing any interest in the removing of the obstacle of the knowlables. (5) Again, the śrāvakas, without placing importance on the practice of benefitting other fellow beings, dwell in the ultimate nirvāṇa, the nirvāṇa without remainder, in which afflictions are totally removed. Because these five dwellings are to be rejected, it is said that the bodhisattva dwells according to not dwelling.

VIII.22 [Text: śrāvaka's and bodhisattva's wisdom: distinctions]

What distinctions (*viśeṣa*) are there between the wisdom (*jñāna*) of a śrāvaka and that of a bodhisattva? It should be known that there are distinctions in view of five aspects (*ākāra*). (1) Distinction in view of non-discrimination (*nirvikalpa*): [unlike the śrāvaka,] the doctrines of psycho-physical constituents and others (*skandha-ādi-dharma*) are viewed without discrimination [by a bodhisattva]. (2) Distinction in view of not being restricted to small portions (*a-prādeśika*): [a bodhisattva, unlike the śrāvaka,] not being limited to small portions, pursues completely [the three matters of] penetrating into truth (*tattva-prativedha*), entering all modes of the knowables (*sarvākāra-jñeya-praveśa*), and performing for the sake of (*adhikṛtya*) [benefitting] all sentient beings. (3) Distinction in view of not residing (*anavasthita*): [a śrāvaka resides in nirvāṇa, but for a bodhisattva] nirvāṇa is not dwelt in (*apratiṣṭhita-nirvāṇa*). (4) Distinction in view of the infinite (*ātyantika*): [the virtues of a bodhisattva, unlike those of the śrāvaka are] inexhaustive (*a-kṣaya*) [and are working infinitely] even when a bodhisattva enters the nirvāṇa-domain (*nirvāṇa-dhātu*). (5) Distinction in view of having nothing higher (*niruttara*): there is not separately another particularly superior (*viśiṣṭa-tara*) vehicle (*yāna*) beyond that [bodhisattva-yāna, that is, the mahāyāna]. Here there is a verse:

> Those [bodhisattvas] who have acquired wisdom (*jñāna*), the nature of which is compassion and is sublime owing to the five kinds of distinctions,
> are said to acquire (*saṃpad*) quickly (*adūra*) [fortunes] worldly (*laukika*) and transworldly (*lokottara*).

VIII.22 [Nagao Commentary]

The distinction of the śrāvaka's and the bodhisattva's intuitive realization (*abhisamaya*) has been discussed already in III.15. The distinction of wisdom discussed in this section is closely aligned with those distinctions and the meanings overlap. Moreover, the five distinct aspects of wisdom has many points in common with the five rejections of dwelling discussed in the previous section.

(1) Unlike the śrāvakas who doctrinally systematize the teachings of the five psycho-physical constituents and others through intellectual analysis, the bodhisattvas observe the same teachings through the wisdom of *nirvikalpa-jñāna* that surpasses the common intellect. This characterizes the distinctive quality of

this wisdom. (2) In contrast to the śrāvaka whose understanding is fractional, that of the bodhisattvas is "not limited to a small portion." The reason for this is that a śrāvaka's "penetration into truth" consists of an understanding of the non-substantiality of the personality (*pudgala-nairātmya*) only while that of the bodhisattvas consists of the non-substantiality of both the personality and the entities (*pudgala-dharma-nairātmya*; cf. VII.8 §7). Among the "three matters" discussed above, the latter two are understood to be varieties of the first one, "penetration into truth." (3) As for nirvāṇa, the śrāvakas dwell in and cling to nirvāṇa, but the bodhisattvas do not. Therefore, the nirvāṇa of the bodhisattvas is called "nirvāṇa not dwelt in" (*apratiṣṭhita-nirvāna*) which is discussed in the next chapter (chapter IX) of this text. (4) The nirvāna of the śrāvakas is none other than an ultimate cessation, wherein wisdom comes to an end; but in the nirvāṇa of the bodhisattvas, the activity of dharmakāya is endless (according to *Upanibandha*[24]), and this means that on the basis of dharmakāya, enjoyment body (sambhoga-kāya) and transformed body (nirmaṇa-kāya) are active constantly and without limit. (5) The spiritual path of the śrāvakas has something higher above it insofar as the pratyekabuddha and bodhisattva vehicles are beyond it, but the bodhisattva vehicle, that is, the Mahāyāna, is without superior and there is nothing higher than that. Here the word "vehicle" is used in the meaning of "wisdom." The wisdom of the bodhisattva is distinguished from that of the śrāvaka owing to these five reasons and it is admirably superior.

In the verse, a bodhisattva's wisdom is said to be established on the basis of compassion and is superior by virtue of five aspects. Accordingly, a bodhisattva is able to completely accomplish the mundane and supermundane bliss.

VIII.23 [Text: The outcome/result]

When the bodhisattvas , having acquired the virtues (*guṇa-saṃpad*) of the excellent training of discipline (*adhiśīla*), the excellent training of mind (*adhicitta*), and the excellent training of wisdom (*adhiprajñā*), have attained masteries (*vibhutva*) over all fortunes (*dhana*) and others, why is it that [when, without doubt, the bodhisattvas generously share these fortunes and so on] sentient beings who suffer the pains of poverty (*upakaraṇa-vyasana[?]*) appear? The reason for this are:

(1) Sentient beings are seen to possess karma that hinder (*vibamdha-karma*) [the bodhisattva's act to bestow fortune, status, and so on upon them by means of his supernatural powers].

(2) If enjoyment is brought forth (*bhoga-upasaṃbhāra*) upon them, it is thought that this proves to be something that hinders (*antarāya*) the occurrence of the wholesome (*kuśala-dharma-utpāda*).

(3) If [on the other hand, enjoyment is not brought upon them and they suffer from poverty,] it is thought that they experience face to face (*abhimukha*) disgust (*saṃvega*) of this world.

(4) If enjoyment is brought upon them, this is thought to prove to be the cause (*hetutva*) for increasing the unwholesome (*akuśala-dharma-upacaya*).

(5) It is also thought that enjoyment brought upon them becomes the cause for harming (*ghātana*) other sentient beings much more than themselves (*bahutara-sattva*).

Here, there is a verse:

Acts (*karman*), hindrances (*pratibandha*) [to the wholesome], face to face experience (*abhimukhatva*) [of disgust], accumulation (*caya*) [of the unwholesome], and injury (*pīḍana*) [to others] are seen;
therefore, people are unable to acknowledge enjoyment [of fortunes and so on that are brought forth] by a bodhisattva.

VIII.23 [Nagao Commentary]

This section comprises the conclusion for chapters VI through VIII in which excellent training in the three learnings were discussed. As a result of the excellent training in the three learnings, a bodhisattva becomes a liberated person who "has mastery over all fortunes and so on." However, in spite of that, this section points out several cases in which sentient beings are not able to enjoy the benefits bestowed upon them by the bodhisattvas (cf. X.19A verse). If the bodhisattvas bestow all of the fortunes amassed by them upon sentient beings, then "why is it that the sentient beings suffer the pains of poverty?" The fact that sentient beings cannot enjoy the fortunes bestowed upon them is not the fault of the bodhisattva but is the fault of the sentient beings (cf. X.28A [7]) who are like a cracked dish that cannot be filled with water and house the reflection of the moon. When there is a flaw like a crack inherent in the sentient beings, the bodhisattva is unable to do anything. The fault of the sentient beings are explained as fivefold. Sentient beings possess "karma that hinder" the bestowing of fortune (reason no. 1 discussed in text above). So long as sentient beings possess these acts, even though a bodhisattva may have the supernatural power of bestowing fortunes, he cannot exercise that power positively. The *Upanibandha* quotes a verse which describes a mother who attempts to breast feed her child, but even though milk is plentiful and the mother wishes to feed her child, if the child's throat is clogged, there is nothing that the mother can do.[25] The *Bhāṣya* exemplifies this by the example of a man's ability to drink water from a river, but the hungry ghost's (preta's) inability to drink the water owing to its own karma.[26] Moreover, among the reasons why the Bodhisattva is unable to bestow fortunes is the fact that the bestowing of fortune becomes "hinderance to the wholesome" (reason no. 2) for the sentient beings, because it functions as "a cause for increasing the unwholesome" (reason no.4), and because it function as "a cause to harm others" (reason no. 5). These are all faults possessed by the sentient beings. If, on the other hand, fortune is not bestowed upon them, then they will "experience face to face the disgust of the world" (reason no. 3), and this leads people towards the wholesome. These four exemplify that "not to bestow" represents the bodhisattva's great compassion and the act of benefitting others. For these five reasons, it is said that there are "sentient beings who suffer the pains of poverty." Finally, the meanings are summarized in a single verse.

I would like to acknowledge the Sabbatical Leave Research Grant from the University of Calgary that made it possible to work personally with Professor Nagao in preparing this paper. I also wish to express my gratitude to Professor Nagao without whose guidance this English translation would not have been accomplished.

Notes

1. Professor Nagao's research into all aspects of Buddhism in India, China, and Tibet has been, in a sense, for the sake of accomplishing a definitive Japanese translation of Asaṅga's work. Consequently, it seems most appropriate that a small segment of his work appear as a contribution to Professor Yün-hua Jan's retirement volume as these two scholars have been life long colleagues. The translation of Asaṅga's text is marked by the roman numeral VIII to indicate the chapter; the arabic numbers that follow indicate the sub-divisions as devised by Professor Étienne Lamotte in his monumental work, *La Somme du Grand Véhicle d'Asaṅga (Mahāyāna-saṃgraha), Tome I and II* (Louvain: Bureaux du Muséon, 1938). Professor Nagao's study is indicated by the words "Nagao Commentary." It should be mentioned that the end notes appearing here have been added for the sake of this paper by me and that they are totally different from the extensive footnotes appearing in Professor Nagao's Japanese translation for which see note 11 below.

2. See, *Theg pa chen po bsdus pa'i 'grel pa* in *Sde Dge Tibetan Tripiṭaka*, hereafter *SDTT*, Tokyo: Sekai Seiten Kankō Kyōkai, 1980. Sems tsam 12. p 88, 175a.

3. See Unrai Wogihara ed. *Bonbun Bosatsuji-kyō (Bodhisattvabhūmi)*. Tokyo: Sankibo Buddhist Book Store, 1971. p. 38.

4. svabhāvo bodhisattvānāṃ pañcākāravivarjitaḥ /
jñānasya nirvikalpasya na bhūta-artha-vicitrakaḥ /
(The reconstucted sanskrit verse is by G.M. Nagao)

5. *SDTT*, Sems tsam 12. p 133, 266a-b.

6. *SDTT*, Sems Tsam 12, p. 88, 175b.

7. Ét. Lamotte, ibid. Tome II. p. 234.

8. *SDTT*, Sems tsam 12, p.88, 176a.

9. For a complete discussion, see *SDTT*, Sems Tsam 12, p. 88, 176b: lam gnyis ni tshogs lam dang / rten gyi lam mo // de la tshogs kyi lam ni sbyin pa dang / tshul khrims dang / bzod pa dang / brtson 'grus kyi pha rol tu phyin pa'o // rten gyi lam ni bsam gtan kyi pha rol tu phyin pa ste / gang gi phyir sngar bstan pa'i pha rol tu phyin pa las yang dag par byung ba'i dge ba'i rtsa ba dang / bsam gtan la brten nas rnam par mi rtog pa'i ye shes shes rab kyi pha rol tu phyin pa zhes bya ba de 'byung bar 'gyur bas so //

10. ibid. p. 88, 176b: sangs rgyas nyid ma thob kyi bar du .../

11. G.M. Nagao, *Shodaijōron—Wayaku to Chūkai*. Tokyo: Kōdansha Inc. 1982 (vol 1), 1987 (vol. 2). See vol. 2, Chapter X, section 3B, p. 322-325.

12. *SDTT*, Sems tsam 12, p. 89, 178a: 'dir chos ni ye ge tsam du bzhed do //

13. ibid., p. 89, 178b: nam mkha' bzhin du zhes bya ba ni / ji ltar nam mkha' khyab pa dang / ma gos pa dang / mi rtog pa dang / brtag par bya ba ma yin pa de bzhin du rnam par mi rtog pa'i ye shes kyang chos thams cad la ro gcig pa stong pa nyid kyis khyab pas na khyab pa'o // chos thams cad kyis ma gos pas na gos pa med pa'o // rang nyid kyis rnam par mi rtog pas na rnam par med pa'o // gzhan gyis brtags par bya ba ma yin pa nyid kyis rnam par brtag par

bya ba ma yin pa ste / rnam par mi rtog pa'i ye shes ni de ltar blta bar bya'o //

14. ibid., p. 89-90; 178b-179b.

15. *SDTT*, Sems tsam 12, p. 135, 269b-270a: shes bya dang ni khyad med pa'i // shes gang de nyid mi rtog nyid / ces bya ba ni gzung ba dang 'dzin par rnam par dbye bar yongs su chad pa med pa'i phyir 'di ni shes pa'o // 'di ni shes bya'o zhes khyad par med pa gang yin pa de ye shes de'i rnam par mi rtog pa nyid de / gang shes bya dang tha dad pa [270a] ma yin pa de ni nam mkha' dang snang ba bzhin no //

16. See *SDTT*, Sems tsam 12, p. 90, 179b.

17. *Taishō* (hereafter *T.*), vol. XXXI, p. 243c.

18. *SDTT*, Sems tsams 12, p. 135, 270a.

19. *T.* vol. XXXI. p. 243c.

20. *T.* vol. XXXI, p. 244a.

21. *SDTT*, Sems tsam 12, p. 90, 180b.

22. The following six sanskrit verses can be found in the *Abhidharma-samuccaya-bhāṣya*, N. Tatia, ed. Patna: Kashi Prasad Jayaswal Research Institute, 1976. p. 42, Section 41C(2)iii.

23. Refer to G.M. Nagao, op.cit., vol 1, II.14B note 1.

24. *SDTT*, Sems tsam 12, p. 136, 272b.

25. *SDTT*, Sems tsam 12, p. 137, 273a: / ma ni byis pa'i bu rnams la // nu zho blug par nus mod kyi // kha yi bu ga thums pa yi // bu la mas ni ji ltar bya /

26. This example of the hungry ghost is found in the Chinese version of the *Bhāṣya*. The Tibetan text has interpolated comments on three kinds of *rten-gnas* (= āśraya?) and on ten definitions with respect to whether a buddha comes or does not come into the world—ideas not related to topics in this chapter. The interpolation is from line 7, fol. 181b to line 3, fol. 182b in *SDTT*, Sems tsam 12, p. 91 and is from line 5, fol. 221a to line 5, fol. 222a in the Peking edition, vol.112, p. 304-305. Following this interpolation, the commentary resumes with comments on ideas found in chapter X section 28A[2]; consequently, this example cannot be found, at least in this section of the Tibetan text.

ART CRITICISM AND SOCIAL STATUS IN NORTHERN SONG CHINA: LIU DAOCHUN'S "GENRE THEORY" OF ART[1]

Charles H. Lachman
Dartmouth College

> ...nothing can be a reason why a painting is good or bad unless it is concerned with what can be looked at in the painting, unless it is concerned with what can, in some sense, be seen.[2]

(i) Introduction

The *Songchao minghua ping* ("Evaluations of Song Dynasty Painters of Renown"; hereafter SCMHP),[3] compiled before 1059 by Liu Daochun, has been rightly described as one of the "most important histories of tenth and early eleventh-century [Chinese] painting".[4] The work comprises a collection of biographies and critical comments for some ninety-one painters active between roughly 950 and 1050 C.E., although there are actually one hundred and ten entries in all, as some artists appear more than once.[5] These notices are divided into six categories as follows:

1. Figure painting (40 entries)
2. Landscape (18 entries)
3. Domestic and Wild Animals (19 entries)
4. Birds and Flowers (22 entries)
5. Demons and Spirits (4 entries)
6. Architecture (7 entries)

Each of these six subject categories is further divided into three "classes" (*pin*): the Inspired (*shen*), the Subtle (*miao*), and the Talented (*neng*); and in the case of Figure painters, each of these classes is then subdivided into "upper" (*shang*), "middle" (*zhong*), and "lower" (*xia*) grades. For painters of the Inspired classes, each entry is followed by an individual Evaluation (*ping*), while those who are ranked Subtle or Talented are evaluated in groups.

In terms of its basic structure, the SCMHP interweaves several strands from earlier critical systems. For instance, the practice of "grading" painters goes back at least as far as Xie He's (fl. 500-535) *Gu huapin lu* ("Old Record of Gradings of Painters"), one of China's earliest extant art-critical texts, while the tripartite Inspired-Subtle-Talented scheme can be traced back to the eight-century critic Zhang Huaiguan.[6] There are no known antecedents, however, for the subject-matter categories which Liu employs to organize his text, and one of the main points to be considered here is that an appreciation of the implications of this unique arrangement is crucial to an understanding of Liu's evaluative system and its place in the development of Chinese art theory. That is, whereas Western art criticism since the time of Alberti has usually concentrated on the formal properties of the art object itself, a review of early textual sources shows that Chinese criticism generally tends to view the work as an extension of its maker; accordingly, to evaluate the artifact is to evaluate the artist, and *vice versa*. A close analysis of the SCMHP, however, reveals that Liu Daochun's "genre theory" approach to evaluation implicitly challenged traditional assumptions about the relationship between social status and artistic quality, and suggests that some long-held opinions about the status of painters during the Five Dynasties (906-960)/ Northern Song (960-1127) period should perhaps be reconsidered.

(ii) The Position of the Artist in pre-Song Texts

Attaching names to specific works of art is far from a universal practice; indeed, the great bulk of the world's art production has been anonymous, and often remains so even within those "rare art traditions" where the assignation of authorship has evolved.[7] In China, for instance, the voluminous extant historical records yield fewer than one thousand names—and many of those are only names—of artists active during the entire Song period (960-1279),[8] while the SCMHP reports that over three thousand painters responded to the Emperor's summons when it came time to decorate the Taoist Palace of the Pristine Realm of Jade Clarity (*yuqing zhaoying gong*) in 1008.[9]

According to Kris and Kurz, the custom of linking the creator's name to his creation depends "not upon the greatness and perfection of his artistic achievement—even if this were objectively ascertainable—but upon the significance attached to the work of art".[10] In turn, once the work of art has been accorded such significance, a natural consequence is that a greater interest in the artist is thus generated, and it is precisely this interest in art and its makers that allows that artist's biography, as a literary category, to come into being.[11]

In comparison with the West, such interest was relatively slow to develop in China. In the fifth century C.E., for instance, the painter Wang Wei (415-443) lamented the fact that there was "no general appreciation of fine painting"—and by extension, no general appreciation for fine painters, either—among his contemporaries, whereas calligraphy was universally admired.[12] In part, this situation would soon change, however, inasmuch as "fine painting" did in fact come to be more generally appreciated; and although this heightened awareness was accompanied by a grater interest in (if not appreciation of) painters, as well, it is instructive to note the specific shape that this interest assumed for pre-Song writers, particularly with regard to their concern for the social status of the artist.

One of the first texts to speak to this point is not an art-historical or art-critical work, but belongs to the category of "family instructions" (*jiaxun*).[13] Among the earliest surviving examples of this genre, Yan Zhitui's (ca. 531-595) *Yanshi jiaxun*, or "Family Instructions of the Yan Clan", describes the position of the artists of the day in no uncertain terms:

> To find amusement in looking at the art objects of all times is particularly valuable and enjoyable. But, if your official position is not high enough, you are frequently ordered to paint for the government or for private friends, and this is a disgusting kind of service.[14]

Yan goes on to discuss the cases of three contemporary officials, and cites examples of the "shameful" treatment they received because of their artistic inclinations and talents. He asks, "If these three scholars had been ignorant of painting, simply engaging themselves in their original professions, would they have met such humiliation"?[15]

Moreover, such disdain was apparently not limited to painters, but extended to calligraphers (see above, Note 12) and to musicians, as well. Apropos playing the *pipa* (lute"), Yan cautions that:

> you should not allow yourself to have a reputation in this art, for then you will have to entertain nobles, sitting in a humble place and taking the insult of drinking the dregs and eating the cold remains.[16]

Zhang Yanyuan's *Lidai minghuaji* ("A Record of Famous Painters of all Ages"; hereafter LDMHJ),[17] China's earliest (847) full-fledged history of art (and a work that, as one scholar claims, "easily surpasses Vasari's *Lives*, written seven centuries later, in scope and sophistication")[18] also addresses itself to the issue of the artist's status. Zhang's earliest notices go back to Shi Huang (ca. 2400 B.C.E.), who is himself said to have served as a Minister at the Court of the Yellow Emperor (*Huangdi*);[19] and while such figures must be consigned to the realm of legend, beginning with the accounts for the Later Han period (25-220 C.E.) we are on somewhat firmer ground. Of the six painters listed for this period in the LDMHJ, Zhang mentions that one was Director of the Board of Sacrificial Worship,[20] one was a Prefect,[21] one became the Vice-president of a Board,[22] one rose to the rank of Minister,[23] and two served as Painters-in-Attendance (*daizhao*) at the Imperial Workshops.[24]

This emphasis on non-artistic achievement is not limited to Zhang's entries for the earlier periods, but persists up to, and through, his notices of "the present day", and virtually without exception. Nor among ninth-century writers is this emphasis unique to Zhang Yanyuan: Zhu Jingxuan's *Tanghchao minghua lu* ("A Record of Tang Dynasty Painters of Renown"), for example, written shortly before the LDMHJ, reflects a similar concern, as Zhu writes of Presidents and Vice-presidents of Boards, members of State Councils, and even a provincial Governor.[25] Concealed by all of this interest in prestigious ranks and titles, however, is the desire to make a sharp distinction between "artists"—that is, great men who happen also to paint—and mere "artisans", and also to illustrate what may result when the dividing line is blurred.

The classic illustration of this point is made in the following well-known story about Yan Liben (610-670):

> [Once] when Taizong was paying a visit to the Xuanwu Lake and saw some mandarin ducks at play, he summoned Liben to depict them. The attendants were so tactless as to shout, "Summon the master painter!" Liben was so deeply chagrined by this that he finally gave up painting, and warned the junior members of his family against making any study of the art.[26]

Referring to the vice-president of the Board of Justice as a "master painter" (*huashi*) was clearly construed as a slur of the highest order, which underscores the importance that was attached to distinguishing sharply between artist and artisan. Still, if Yan Liben had been summoned politely, he would have been summoned none the less. Thus, as texts such as the TCMHL and the LDMHJ make clear, artists in the Tang (even those with resounding titles) were still essentially at someone's beck and call; even the "incomparable" Wu Daozi (active ca, 710-760) was not permitted to execute a painting "unless there was an edict".[27] Though socially superior to artisans, even the greatest artists seem not to have enjoyed a significantly greater degree of artistic autonomy than their fifth-, sixth-, and seventh-century forerunners.

Several early anecdotes detail another aspect of the artist's circumscribed freedom; namely, the desire to please the public. Zhang Yanyuan, for instance, records the following about Dai Kuei (d. 396 C.E.):

> Since Kuei was inventive in the mechanical arts, he was also good at the casting of Buddha images, and also at the carving of them. Once he was working on a wooden image of Wuliangshou (Amitayus) which was sixteen feet tall, and the accompanying Bodhisattvas. Kuei considered that the ancient rules for making Buddhist images were primitive and clumsy, and that when this work was opened for public worship it would not move men's hearts. So, he would sit hidden behind a curtain and secretly listen to the discussions of the crowds who came to see it. Whatever praise or blame he heard he would immediately subject to detailed analysis, and after three years of intensive thought he finally completed the carving of the image.[28]

In a similar vein, Zhu Jingxuan relates that Zhou Fang (d. ca. 800) was once commissioned by the Emperor Dezong (r. 780-805) to execute a work at a monastery in Chang'an:

> When he brought down his brush, the populace of the capital came jostling each other to see, pushing their way to the garden of the temple. Among them were both wise men and simpletons; some talked of the excellence of the work, while others pointed out its flaws. The artist made revisions to suit their ideas, and in little more than a month, all criticism ceased.[29]

Such concern for the opinions of the public at large—and the corollary notion that the artist should conform to it—would have been unthinkable to the later artists who painted, so they claimed, to please themselves alone.

There are, to be sure, a few exceptions to the generalized portrait of the pre-Song artist that emerges from the foregoing, but they do indeed stand out as exceptions: Han Gan (d. after 781), for example, is recorded as having been ordered by the Tang emperor Xuanzong (r. 712-756) to use Chen Hong (active ca. 735-760) as his model for painting horses. When the Emperor found out that he had not done as told, and inquired why, Han Gan replied: "His Majesty's servant has taken his own models; namely all the horses in the Imperial stables."[30] Han's fortunate blend of flattery and artistic skill may have spared him the Emperor's wrath, but that this story is preserved at all testifies to the fact that while being commanded to paint a specific subject in a specific way was a common occurrence, asserting one's individuality and doing otherwise was certainly not.

There are other instances in the LDMHJ, mostly involving pre-Tang painters, where the artist appears at first glance to be more "assertive" and less concerned with status than most of the men discussed thus far. Dai Kuei, for example, "was summoned to take official positions at intervals throughout his life, but he never accepted any of them:,[31] nor did his son or grandson consent to serve in an official capacity.[32] Zong Ping (375-443), too, was offered several positions, but chose instead to spend his time among the mountains.[33] As a last example, there is Tao Hongjing (ca. 452-536), who resigned from office and took to the hills, calling himself the Hermit of Huayang. As Zhang reports:

> The Emperor Wu Di (r. 502-550) once wished to summon him for employment in the government, but the Hermit made a painting of two oxen, one being pulled along by a golden halter, and the other meandering off in search of water and grass. Wu Di understood his meaning, and did not pester him further with office or rank ... and gave him the unofficial title of Prime Minister in the Mountains.[34]

The first thing to note about the artists in the above examples is that they all come from "noble families", and that—for each of them—painting is but one among several accomplishments. A further common feature is that the "assertiveness" of the artist does not arise directly in conjunction with his art, as it did in the case of Han Gan, but arises, rather, in connection with his reluctance to take on an official governmental position. In these respects, all of these cases fit very neatly into the pattern that has been described as the "one socially acceptable form of escape" for the man who "found it impossible to meet the demands of Confucian conformity";[35] namely, withdrawing from society to live as a recluse.

But as the literary historian Li Chi has pointed out:

> ...as early as the time of Confucius the concept of the recluse had begun to change from a man who had renounced the world and had hidden himself in the wilderness to one who kept himself apart from the world of affairs and yet was anxious to make himself heard.[36]

Moreover, a great deal of prestige was accorded these high-minded souls who lived in "retirement", to the point that a ruler would often be "inclined to pay more heed to a recluse whom he had summoned to court than to ordinary officials".[37] Thus, the "refusal to serve" witnessed in the above examples was part and parcel of the behaviour expected of the recluse;[38] it cannot be taken as necessarily signifying lack of interest in status, nor should it be viewed as attesting to the artist's independence or individualism: as will be suggested below, it was not until the Song that these features would be indelibly added to the artist's portrait.

In short, Tang and pre-Tang textual sources indicate a growing public interest in both painting and painters, and manifest a particular concern for the question of the social status of the artist, as this alone, it would seem, could redeem the fact that a Gentleman was a painter at all. In general, even artists of rank were liable to be treated as artisans, and they themselves were much concerned with keeping a sharp line of demarcation between the two. Though there are instances that suggest that some artists displayed no lack of confidence in their social position, this was clearly not a common attitude among painters, and seems not be have been shared by the public at large.

Finally, it is interesting to note the parallels that can be discerned in Hans Frankel's analysis of the way in which writers of poetry and prose were viewed in the Tang. In his study of the biographical sections of the *Jiutangshu* ("Old History of the Tang Dynasty"), Frankel points out that one hundred and one writers are given biographies in a special "Garden of Letters" (*wenyuan*) section—a category that is ranked fairly low—and that the basis for inclusion in this group was not governed by literary criteria, as one might expect that it would have been.[39] He writes,

> To be sure, some of the best known poets and prose writers are included—men like Chen Zi'ang, Li Hua, Wang Wei, [and] Li Bo … but one misses others of equal stature, such as Zhang Yueh, Bo Juyi, and Li Deyu. The explanation … [is that] the latter were prominent statesmen, whereas the "Garden of Letters" is reserved for those who were famous only as literati, and this, in the view of the Confucian historiographer, is a shortcoming.[40]

Though brilliant and successful as writers, those who did not couple this with a high-ranking government position were thus consigned to a special category "reserved for those who fall short of the Confucian ideal of the well-rounded gentleman".[41] Being "only" a brilliant poet was certainly more acceptable than being "only" a brilliant painter, reflecting the relative worth accorded these two talents in the Tang, but neither accomplishment was highly enough regarded that it could stand completely on its own.

[iii] The Rise of the "Independent Artist"

Liu Daochun's entry for the Inspired landscapist Li Cheng (919-967) contains the following anecdote:

> During the Kaibao reign era (968-976),[42] a certain Sun Sihao extended invitations to masters from the four corners of the land. Although he was aware of the fact that a skilled artist like Li Cheng would not be easily persuaded, he still sent him a letter of invitation. Cheng replied: "I am a scholar by birth and have always known whom to avoid. By nature, I love mountains and rivers, but I wield a brush only for my own satisfaction. How could I go galloping off to the home a rich and powerful family to mingle with mere artisans?"[43]

This was not to be the end of the matter, however, as the tenacious Mr. Sun contrived to bribe an official in Li's hometown and thereby managed to procure several of his paintings. Sometime later, Li was in the capital and acceded to Sun's request that he at least pay a visit; upon his arrival, though, when he saw his paintings on display, he was "taken aback and thus departed in anger".[44]

Looking back on this account from a modern vantage point, there is a tendency, perhaps, to see it simply as providing more examples of the "persistent collector" and the "temperamental artist"—frequently encountered *topoi* for which countless citations, from both East and West, could be adduced.[45] And while these associations can never be completely left behind, it may be fruitful, nonetheless, to attempt to approach the text from the other side; that is to say, to come upon it from the point of view of the works that preceded it, such as those touched on above.

When looked at from this angle, a rather different picture emerges, though many of its components are familiar. (For instance, echoes of Yan Liben's umbrage at having been called a "master painter" may be heard clearly in Li's reply to Mr. Sun, confirming that the artist's sensitivity to being treated as an artisan had not been dulled.) But while a demonstration of the artist's self-confidence may not be totally without precedent, that this confidence is ultimately rooted in his view of himself as an artist, independent of any accomplishments outside of the realm of painting, is indeed a new note. Moreover, that other artists in the texts are frequently presented as sharing a similar attitude, and the Liu Daochun endorses their stance—Li Cheng, after all, is ranked as the "most Inspired" landscape painter in the SCMHP—seem particularly novel features when compared with the views that prevailed in the Tang period and earlier.

Also, and again in marked contrast to the situation presented in pre-Song texts, it is clear from the Li Cheng anecdote, and from many others, as well, that the nature of the artist/patron relationship has changed. Painters are now persistently courted by ardent admirers:

> —as soon as they heard that Sun Mengqing (act. mid 10th c.) desired to undertake a commission, the wealthy "would flock to his door and compete to be the first to secure a purchase";[46]
>
> —"people of wealth and rank would come to [Wu Zongyuan's] door daily";[47]
>
> —"Yuan Ai (act. late 10th c.) "earned a resounding reputation, and ministers and nobles competed for his brushwork";[48]

—"it reached the point where there was vying in the nobles' residences for portraits" by Yin Shi (act. ca. 1025-1050);[49]

—A wealthy southern merchant offered one hundred thousand cash to Gao Keming (act. 1st half 11th c.) to "commission a picture of 'A Spring Dragon Emerging from Hibernation'".[50]

Among other things, examples such as these indicate something of the degree to which both artists and artworks had generally increased in public esteem, a contention supported by much other evidence from the SCMHP. Not only are collectors shown going to great lengths in their attempts to secure certain paintings, but one also receives the impression that collecting is itself a more common activity than it had been in the past. In part, this last may be due to the fact that the gradual eclipse of figure painting by the landscape and bird-and-flower genres resulted in the greater availability of works that were more "portable" than those executed on large screens, or on monastery and temple walls. At the same time, burgeoning interest in painting no doubt stimulated the production of these more collectable formats (though which is cause and which effect is a moot point).

Other evidence from the SCMHP suggests that, to some extent, the motivation behind the urge to collect is connected to the issue of status—a phenomenon not infrequently associated with acquiring and commissioning works of art—and in several instances here, the "status" accrues not so much from the painting itself as from the fact that it was painted by the "right" artist. For example, Liu reports that the works of Wang You (act. late 10th c.) were so similar to those of the better known Zhao Chang (ca. 960-ca 1016) that they could hardly be distinguished one from the other; yet, whenever a family got hold of a work by Wang, "they would often regard it as if it were by Zhao",[51] with the implication being that some may not have been above conscious deception. And might this not account for the fact that the *Xuanhe huapu* catalogue lists one hundred and fifty-four pictures by Zhao Chang as belonging to the Emperor Huizong's (r. 1101-1126) Imperial collection—even though concurring with Liu's report that Zhao's works were very difficult to obtain, as the artist himself had tried to buy them back—while not a single Wang You is mentioned?[52]

In some respects, then, as the foregoing suggests, artist (and their works) were treated differently in the early years of the Song than they had been previously.[53] At the same time, of course, artists also *acted* differently, and themselves took new views of their creations. Corroboration for both of these points is amply provided in the SCMHP.

This new behaviour, as it were, manifests itself most clearly as a marked independence, already hinted at in the Li Cheng-Mr. Sun story. And if the pre-Song artist was necessarily compliant, his successor was increasingly willful: thus, although Wu Zongyuan was besieged with commissions, he was "rarely willing to accede" to these requests;[54] and even though Gao Keming was offered a large sum of money for a work, "he was not a common practitioner and resolutely would not yield" to such entreaties.[55]

Private collectors and patrons were not the only ones, however, to be confronted by such recalcitrance on the part of the artist, as there are instances in the SCMHP when even Imperial commands are greeted with defiance. Zhao Guangfu (act. late 10th c.), for instance, was appointed to the Imperial Academy but secretly fled;[56] as did Chen Yongzhi (act. early-mid 11th c.) when he became dissatisfied with the assignments he was given.[57] Likewise, Li Xiong (cat. ca 975-1000) refused to paint a silk fan on order from the Emperor, claiming that he could only paint on a large-scale.[58]

In terms of the artist's attitude toward his own paintings, there are indications in the SCMHP of a growing personal "attachment" for which there is little precedent in earlier sources. Something of this has already been seen in those cases above where a painter is reluctant to part with one of his works, and in the somewhat extreme example of Zhao Chang, who did not part lightly with his works to begin with, and then in his later years went so far as to try to buy back as many of them as he could.[59] This same sort of protective attitude can be seen in the entry for Yin Zhi: although he began a commissioned portrait, he never returned to finish it, much to the agitation of the family by whom he had been hired. When he learned that someone else had finally been asked to complete his rough sketch, he responded by saying, "To copy my sketches is alright, but having the colours applied [by someone else] is not something that I am willing to permit!"[60] Now, while a detailed investigation of the psychological roots of this phenomenon of the artist's attachment to his work would go far beyond the bounds of the present inquiry, it seems reasonable to surmise that it is the artist's new pride, spurred by public recognition of his accomplishments, that occasions this proprietary attitude toward his creations.

In all, if Tang and pre-Tang texts stress that the artist worked "on command", the SCMHP allows that the early Song painter worked "at will"; and if the former was "ordered" to execute commissions, the latter was frequently "begged": an oversimplification, to be sure, yet there can be little doubt that the "independent" artist of the SCMHP was both a social reality and a post-Tang creation. As will be seen below, however, this new artist existed side by side with more traditional practitioners, Liu Daochun's attitude towards whom will now be considered.

[iv] The Academy

> "Academy, Academic, Academism (Or Academicism)—the words mean 'bad' in the conversations of the art community, much worse than 'pretty' or 'decorative' or even 'sentimental'—they are about as dirty as polysyllables can get".[61]

Although the author of these words is referring to modern western attitudes towards the European tradition of Academies of art, they aptly characterise the stance that the Chinese literati would come to adopt toward their own tradition of the *tuhuayuan*. "By the end of the Ming dynasty", as Joseph Levenson writes, "...[p]ainters by *profession* [i.e. "academics"] were disparaged".[62]

Ironically, and in contrast to later developments, when the first European academies of art were founded in Renaissance Italy they were set up in opposition to the medieval Guild workshops and viewed as the vanguard of a new humanist sensibility. Though the contrast in China was certainly less marked, the earliest academies there, too, were viewed in a comparatively better light than were their later counterparts, even if they may never have been accused of standing at the forefront of new directions in art. Still, that so many of the various sovereigns during the Five Dynasties/Northern Song period took such an active interest in painting—manifest in their creation of these court-linked academies—was no doubt a contributing factor in the general rise in esteem that painting enjoyed in this period.

Some scholars have claimed that the Academy may have been an important historical factor in another sense, as well. As Wai-kam Ho writes:

> One cannot but be convinced that the rise of scholar-official painting was directly caused, stimulated, and conditioned by the conspicuous presence of the Academy. It was an inevitable antithesis in such a dialectical historical development.[63]

While the "inevitability" to which he refers may be questioned, his conclusion that scholar-official painting [*shidafu hua*] would have followed a different course of development had the Academy not existed is well warranted. For our purposes here, however, the central question that needs to be considered is that of the value which Liu Daochun attributed to Academic success; or to rephrase it, what is the correlation between Liu's evaluations and a painter's "official" rank?[64]

In the SCMHP, certainly, the presence of the Academy is pervasive. Of the ninety-one biographical entrants, more than a third (31)—including five who served the Southern Tang (937-974), Later Liang (907-923), and Shu (929-966) kingdoms—are mentioned as having received appointments. Of these, four later left the organization, and two declined to serve from the start. Moreover, of the thirty-six painters known to have entered the Academy during the reigns of Taizu (r. 960-976), Taizong, Zhenzong (r. 998-1023), and Renzong (r. 1023-1064), Liu devotes entries to twenty-six of them.[65]

Not surprisingly, far and away the greatest number of painters whom Liu connects with the Academy were known primarily as figure painters, while the rest are spread fairly evenly over the other five genres. This distribution may be tabulated as follows:

From a simple numerical point of view, then, Liu does not (on the surface at least) exhibit any traces of the anti-academic sentiments that later were common. But if he recognized that many painters connected with the Academies were well-deserving of notice, a closer look at the text reveals that they are nonetheless consistently denied his highest accolades. For example, two of the six Inspired academy members who appear in Table I are among the painters, mentioned above, who left the Academy, and if they are removed from the chart, four of the six subject-matter categories are left without a single Inspired painter to represent them. Moreover, of the four who remain (two painters of

	Inspired	Subtle	Talented	Totals
Figures	2	7	5	14
Landscapes	-	1	2	3
Animals	1	1	3	5
Birds/Flowers	2	1	1	4
Demons	1	-	-	1
Architecture	-	2	2	4
Totals	6	12	13	31

Table I

figures, and two of birds and flowers), not one is at the top of his class. Conversely, of the thirteen painters associated with the Academy who fall into Liu's lowest ranking, at least six were Painters-In-Attendance (*daizhao*)—the *highest* office a painter could hold.

This statistical reading of the place of the Academy in the SCMHP is bolstered by a number of factors. For one, and as will be discussed in more detail below, those artists who are presented as at odds with the strictures of Academic life are portrayed in a generally sympathetic manner and are certainly not criticized by Liu—if anything, their behavior is lauded. Also, Liu is not above the occasional veiled barb: for example, he reports that the Emperor Taizong was so taken with Xu Xi's (act. 3rd. quarter 10th c.) bird-and-flower paintings that all the official painters had to take them as a standard, though Xu himself, of course, is not reported to have had anything to do with the *tuhuayuan*.[66]

Liu's attitude toward the Academy, then, seems ambivalent at best. While he obviously does not ignore its members, nor fail to heap much praise on many of them, there is certainly no indication that the status of membership was in a painter's favor *vis-à-vis* Liu's evaluations. In fact, at the highest levels of evaluation at any rate, a happy association with the Academy may have affected one's ranking adversely.

[v] Status and Evaluation

While the foregoing indicates a certain antipathy toward Academic painters on the part of Liu Daochun, this does not, in and of itself, indicate his alignment with the traditional opposition: namely, the proponents of *shidafu hua*, or "scholar-official art". In the first place, the lines of combat had probably not yet been drawn in quite such terms at the time when Liu was writing. Moreover, an examination of his characterizations of the highest-ranked painters in each subject-matter divisions reveals that they do not appear to constitute any easily identifiable group:

FIGURES: Wang Guan (act. ca. 963-975) was from a poor family that could not afford to finance his studies; no mention is made of his ever having held an official position, or of any other scholarly accomplishments;[67]

LANDSCAPE: Li Cheng was descended from a long line of scholar-officials, and though he is reported to have taken the *jinshi* ("Doctor of letters") examination, he is not reported to have passed it, nor is it mentioned that he ever held an official post;[68]

ANIMALS: Very little is reported concerning the background of Zhao Guangfu, except that he was appointed to the painting Academy as an Apprentice (*xueshi*); but "he had no desire to accept this post and thus fled in secret";[69]

BIRDS AND FLOWERS: Xu Xi came from an honorable family of Jiangnan, but there is no mention of office or other such achievement;[70]

DEMONS AND SPIRITS: Li Xiong was "barely literate and disliked following conventions"; though he was appointed to the Academy, he disobeyed an imperial command and had to flee in secrecy to his native village;[71]

ARCHITECTURE: Guo Zhongshu (ca 930-977) was a Scholar of Broad Learning (*boshi*), and held a fairly high rank in the government of the Later Zhou (951-960) state; however, after Taizong came to power, he, too, disobeyed an Imperial command and was consequently banished to a remote outpost.[72]

In reading through these six accounts in the SCMHP, one of the most striking features is precisely the fact that the social standing of the artist enters the discussion obliquely, if at all; further, the same feature is discernible throughout the text. By contrast, comparable entries in earlier texts such as the TCMHL and the LDMHJ are much concerned with offices and titles; indeed, many entries in both of these texts consist of little more than the artist's name and rank. It is this, in fact, that defines the "artist" (a man of rank who also paints), as opposed to the "artisan" (one who only paints). As Zhang Yanyuan writes:

> From ancient times, those who have excelled at painting have all been men robed and capped and of noble descent, rare scholars and lofty-minded men who awakened the wonder of their own time and left behind them a fragrance that shall last a thousand years. This is not a thing that humble rustics from village lanes could ever do.[73]

In this context, it is interesting to note one modern art historian's claim that there was never any "sudden amelioration in the social status" of Chinese artists, since "[c]alligraphers and painters always enjoyed the highest possible social distinction, by virtue of the major accomplishment of literacy. It was inside the scholar caste, in the ranks of the civil administration, that the twin arts developed and reached maturity".[74] But if the artist is defined in terms of his social standing and official position to begin with, then the conclusion that artists always "enjoyed the highest possible social distinction" is obviously tautological. Moreover, as late as the Tang period, as has been seen in the case of Yan Liben, even artists of rank were not necessarily held in high esteem—as artists.

In addition, it has been seen above that there was a striking volte-face in the artist/patron relationship from the Tang to the Song, and that this can be taken as confirmation of the fact that public esteem for artists was on the rise. Thus, while the change was not, perhaps, so "sudden"—nor the cause so immediately apparent—as in the West, when the breakdown of the Guild system in the fifteenth century turned "artisans" into "artists", there was nonetheless a general amelioration in the social status of Chinese artists over the course of the tenth and eleventh centuries.[75]

In a certain sense, the culmination of this trend was sparked by Su Shi (1037-1101) and his circle who, in part through the equation of painting with poetry, took the last step in securing for painting a legitimate place among the pursuits of the scholar-official.[76] Such artists (i.e., scholar-officials), certainly, were in little danger of being subjected to the "humiliating" treatment that caused such grief for their Tang counterparts. Still, "social standing" remained a fundamental aspect of the definition of the artist for these theorists, and those who practiced the art under other circumstances (that is, other than as officials "lodging their interest" [*yuxing*] in painting in their leisure time) continued to be viewed with scorn.

This continued concern with the status of the artist can be detected in Guo Ruoxu's remarks that,

> the rare works of the past were mainly those by talented worthies of high position or by superior gentlemen in retirement...and their lofty and refined emotions were all lodged in painting. If a man's condition is high, his spirit-consonance [*qiyun*] cannot be but lofty.[77]

A similar sentiment is echoed by Deng Chun (act. mid 12th c.). In the Preface to his *Huaji* ("Painting Continued") he writes that, following Guo Ruoxu, he has "in a similar fashion specifically established the two categories of High Officials and Retired Scholars".[78] As he explains elsewhere in the same work,

> When Guo Ruoxu deeply despised common artisans, saying (of their work) 'although called "painting" it will not be painting', it was because they were only able to transmit the form and could not transmit the spirit. Therefore, 'animation through spirit consonance' is the first of the laws of painting, and Ruoxu was right when he only attributed it to those in high position or in retirement.[79]

While numerous other examples could be presented here, they would merely serve to underscore this same basic point; namely, that the late Northern Song spokesmen for scholar-officials' art were, *mutatis mutandis*, fundamentally in agreement with the earlier view that *only* men of a certain social standing could truly be artists, and with the corollary notion that being *only* an artist—or better, "painter"—excluded one from the start from membership in this élite group. Indeed, anyone who was only a painter was thus an "artisan" by definition.

It is against this background that the unorthodoxy of the stance adopted in the SCMHP can be viewed most clearly, inasmuch as Liu Daochun takes strong exception to both of these cardinal points of scholar-official art theory. To be sure, a number of "High Officials and Retired Scholars" do appear in the SCMHP, some of whom are graded very high in Liu's system, but throughout the text—and at the highest levels—are entries for painters whose only accomplishments are connected to their painting. Thus, while "rank" need not work against someone, neither is it alone sufficient to warrant high praise for him—as an artist.

Ultimately, for Liu Daochun, social standing alone, whether high or low, neither defines the "artist", nor determines his worth as an artist. (This latter, rather, is primarily based on the quality of the work itself.) In sum, espousing a view that departed radically from those of earlier theorists, and that would be rejected wholesale by those who were to follow him, Liu Daochun turned tradition on its head by boldly asserting that being a great artist made one, in some fundamental sense, a "great man".

[vi] Liu Daochun's "Genre Theory" of Art

To summarize briefly: From a broad historical point of view, evaluation in Chinese art criticism, like evaluation in Chinese literary criticism, was to a significant degree based on social factors. In early art-critical writings, this is manifested by a great concern for the official position and rank of the artist (who is opposed to the mere artisan); in later writings, the terms would change—to "amateur" and "professional"—but the concern for status would remain. Indeed, even the formal qualities of the work of art were seen through a social filter by literati theorists such as Guo Ruoxu: in their view, what matters in a painting is that it expresses *qiyun*; but *qiyun* is an innate characteristic of High Officials, Nobles, and recluses, and only their works, therefore, can be imbued with this quality.

In the SCMHP, however, evaluation is approached from an altogether different direction. In the first place, Liu Daochun shows himself to be essentially indifferent to the social background of the artist. While his biographical entries usually mention if someone held a particular office or title, and so on, there is no obvious correlation between these and the grade that a painter is assigned in the SCMHP, and it could be argued, in fact, that Liu includes such information merely to conform to the expected requirements of the "artist's biography" as a literary form. In any case, such data are confined to the biographical portions of the text, and do not appear in the discrete Evaluations, nor is such information ever called upon to account for artistic greatness.

Coupled with this indifference to the personal attributes of the artist is a correspondingly greater interest in, and emphasis upon, the formal qualities of the work of art. Thus, for Liu Daochun, the criteria appropriate to the valuation are those that are ultimately based in art. Lacking a large corpus of indubitably authentic works, it is impossible, of course, to be very precise about these standards of quality, but a constant factor in Liu's discussions is that no one feature of the work of art is treated as necessarily "decisive"; rather, his final arbitrations are based on the consideration of a complex web of factors. This general principle is further complicated by the fact that Liu establishes different criteria for different genres of painting; that is, since the various types of painting (based on subject matter) are postulated as having dissimilar ends, it follows that these cannot be achieved by identical means. Accordingly, neither can they be judged by constant standards.

The underlying premise of this approach to evaluation is that art is a fully legitimate and worthwhile pursuit, and that it is perfectly acceptable to be "only" a great artist. This theme is illustrated not only by the content of the SCMHP, but is revealed through and reinforced by the form of the text, as well. This contention is perhaps best illustrated by contrast: In the THJWZ, for instance, Guo Ruoxu adopts subject-matter divisions for his biographical entries for painters from the Five Dynasties on; however, within these groupings he also employs certain special categories for "princes, nobles, and scholar-officials", and for several "lofty-minded recluses". (Buddhist monks and Taoist masters also have a special place: the very end of each section.) In other words, despite the use of these divisions, the artist and his social status remain a central feature of Guo's accounts.

But for Liu Daochun, this division of material into subject-matter groups serves a very different function: by disregarding all social categories and by including separate Evaluations, the genre arrangement thus implicitly helps to assert the primacy of the work of art. This is further underscored by the fact that painters can appear in more than one grouping and with different rankings in each. Thus, the very structure of the SCMHP is itself a carrier of meaning, and the form and content of the text complement each other at every turn.

In conclusion, though the specific stylistic features upon which Liu bases his standards of quality must of necessity remain somewhat vague, it is nonetheless very clear that his general approach to the evaluation of painting was a dramatic departure from tradition; indeed, it is not too much to say that Liu's new "genre theory" of art, as embodied in the SCMHP, represents a radical moment in the history of Chinese art theory and art criticism. In light of this, it can be seen that the late Northern Song formulation of the relationship between social status and evaluation (which might be summed up by the phrase, "Only a great man can become a great artist") was not simply a benign refinement of Tang and pre-Tang views, but seems rather to have been a conscious rejection of the theories put forward by earlier Northern Song critics such as Liu Daochun.

Notes

1. For the sake of consistency, pinyin romanization is used throughout this essay, even within citations from works which originally used another system; all bibliographic references, however, retain their original orthography.
2. Paul Ziff, "Reasons in Art Criticism", in Joseph Margolis (ed.), *Philosophy Looks at the Arts* (New York: Scribner's, 1962), p. 162.
3. All references are to the translation in C. Lachman, *Evaluations of Sung Dynasty Painters of Renown: Liu Tao-ch'un's "Sung-ch'ao ming-hua p'ing"* (Leiden: E.J. Brill, 1989 [T'oung Pao monograph 16]).
4. Richard Barnhart, *The Marriage of the Lord of the River: A Lost Landscape by Tung Yüan* (Ascona: Artibus Asiae, 1970), p. 22 (note 38).
5. Hin Cheung Lovell erroneously writes that there are entries in the SCMHP for 110 painters, but this count overlooks the fact that 10 painters are given multiple entries; see her *An Annotated Bibliography of Chinese Painting Catalogues and Related Texts* (Ann Arbor: Center for Chinese Studies, 1973), p. 3. The recently published *Early Chinese Texts on Painting*, edited by Susan Bush and Hsio-yen Shih (Cambridge MA: Harvard-Yenching Institute, 1985), p. 367, states that there are 120 entries in the SCMHP, but there is no explanation for how this figure was derived.
6. Bush and Shih, *Early Chinese Texts*, p. 47. See W.R.B. Acker, *Some T'ang and pre-T'ang Texts on Chinese Painting*, vol. I (Leiden: E.J. Brill, 1954) for a translation and discussion of the *Gu huapin lu*.
7. See Joseph Alsop, *The Rare Art Traditions* (London: Thames and Hudson, 1982), pp. 181-183.
8. Yu Jianhua, *Zhongguo huihua shi* ["A History of Chinese Painting"], 2 vols., (Shanghai: Shang-wu, 1937), vol I, p. 168.
9. SCMHP, p. 26. A description of the construction of this shrine is provided by Suzanne Cahill, "Taoism at the Sung Court: The Heavenly Text Affair of 1008", *Bulletin of Sung and Yüan Studies* 16 (1980), p. 32.
10. Ernst Kris and Otto Kurz, *Legend, Myth, and Magic in the Image of the Artist: A Historical Experiment* [based on *Die Legend vom Künstler*, 1934] (New Haven: Yale University Press, 1979), p. 3. According to their analysis, this "urge to name the creator" generally indicates that "the work of art no longer serves exclusively a religious, ritual, or, in a wide sense, magic function", and that "its valuation has at least to some extent become independent of such connections" (p.4).
11. See Ernst Kris, *Psychoanalytic Explorations in Art* (New York: Schocken Books, 1964), p. 66.
12. Quoted in Max Loehr, "The Question of Individualism in Chinese Art", *Journal of the History of Ideas* 22.2 (April-June 1961), p. 147. That admiration for calligraphers was still perhaps less than universal, even a century or more later, is suggested in a passage from the late sixth-century *Yanshi Jiaxun* ["Family Instructions for the Yan Clan"] (discussed below):

Wang Bao was a man of eminent family background, brilliant talent and excellent knowledge...Because he was a master of calligraphy, he had a rough road among stone tablets and pillars, and toiled at service with brush and ink. Frequently he regretted this, saying, "If I were not a master of calligraphy, I should not be so harassed as I am today". (Quoted from Ssu-yü Teng, *Family Instructions for the Yen Clan* [Leiden: E.J. Brill, 1968], p. 99 [slightly revised]).

13. For a historical summary of this genre see Teng, *Family Instructions*, pp. ix-xiv.
14. Translation from *ibid*., p. 201 (slightly revised).
15. *Ibid*., p. 202.
16. *Ibid*., pp. 205-206.
17. Translated in W.R.B. Acker, *Some T'ang and pre-T'ang Texts on Chinese Painting*, 2 vols. (Leiden: E.J. Brill, 1954 and 1974); hereafter cited as *Tang Texts* I and II.
18. James F. Cahill, *Parting At the Shore* (Berkeley: University of California Press, 1982), p. 6.
19. *Tang Texts* II, p. 1.
20. *Tang Texts* II, p. 7.
21. *Tang Texts* II, p. 10.
22. *Tang Texts* II, p. 11.
23. *Tang Texts* II, p. 13.
24. *Tang Texts* II, p. 14.
25. See A.C. Soper (trans.), "T'ang Ch'ao Ming Hua Lu: Celebrated Painters of the T'ang Dynasty by Chu Ching-hsüan of T'ang", *Artibus Asiae* 21.3/4 (1958): 204-230; hereafter cited as TCMHL.
26. Translation from *ibid*., p. 213 (slightly revised).
27. *Tang Texts* II, p. 232.
28. *Tang Texts* II, p. 95. For an earlier version of this story, see A.C. Soper, *Literary Evidence for Early Buddhist Art in China* (Ascona: Artibus Asiae, 1959), pp. 19-21.
29. Translation from TCMHL, p. 211.
30. *Ibid*., p. 215.
31. *Tang Texts* II, p. 95.
32. *Tang Texts* II, p. 100.
33. *Tang Texts* II, p. 115.
34. *Tang Texts* II, p. 173.
35. James R. Hightower, "The Question of Individualism in Chinese Literature", *Journal of the History of Ideas* 22.2 (April-June 1961), p. 159.
36. Li Chi, "The Changing Concept of the Recluse in Chinese Literature", *Harvard Journal of Asiatic Studies* 24 (1963), p. 237.
37. *Ibid*., p. 240.
38. As Frederick Mote writes in "Confucian Eremitism in the Yüan Period", in A. Wright (ed.), *The Confucian Persuasion* (Stanford: Stanford University Press,

1960), the renunciation of public life was "the keystone of Chinese eremitism" (p. 204).

39. Hans Frankel, "T'ang Literati: A Composite Biography", in A. Wright and D. Twitchett (eds.), *Confucian Personalities* (Stanford: Stanford University Press, 1962), p. 67.

40. *Ibid.*

41. *Ibid.*

42. In his *Tuhua jianwen zhi* ("Experiences in Painting"; hereafter THJWZ), completed ca. 1080, Guo Ruoxu records the year of Li's death as 967—a date that is generally accepted as accurate—which would indicate that the text here is in error. Oddly enough, Guo himself repeats the mistaken reign era elsewhere in the same passage noted here. See A.C. Soper (trans.), *Kuo Jo-hsü's "Experiences in Painting" (T'u-hua chien-wen chih)*, (Washington, D.C.: American Council of Learned Societies, 1951), p. 46.

43. SCMHP, p. 56.

44. SCMHP, *ibid.*

45. See Kris and Kurz, *Legend, Myth, and Magic*, for numerous examples.

46. SCMHP, p. 21.

47. SCMHP, p. 27.

48. SCMHP, p. 47.

49. SCMHP, p. 49.

50. SCMHP, p. 60.

51. SCMHP, p. 87.

52. *Xuanhe huapu* ("Painting Catalogue of the Xuanhe Era"; hereafter (XHHP), preface dated to 1120, (Taibei: Shijie, 1974), p. 502.

53. This is not to suggest that this "different" treatment is manifested in every entry in the SCMHP, as there are many instances where painters are "commanded" to execute certain works; what I mean to call attention to, rather, is a general trend.

54. SCMHP, p. 27

55. SCMHP, p. 60.

56. SCMHP, p. 22.

57. SCMHP, p. 39.

58. SCMHP, p. 90.

59. SCMHP, p. 83.

60. SCMHP, p. 49.

61. Thomas Hess, "Some Academic Questions", in Thomas Hess and John Ashberry (eds.), *The Academy: Five Centuries of Grandeur and Misery, from the Caracci to Mao Tse-tung* (New York: Macmillan, 1967 [Artnews Annual 33]), p. 8.

62. Joseph R. Levenson, "The Amateur Ideal in Early Ch'ing Society: Evidence from Painting", in John Fairbank (ed.), *Chinese Thought and Institutions* (Chicago: University of Chicago Press, 1957), p. 323. Levenson's overall discussion of the "amateur ideal" should be read in light of James Cahill, "Style as Idea in Ming-Ch'ing Painting", in Maurice Meisner and Rhoads

Murphy (eds.), *The Mozartian Historian* (Berkeley: University of California Press, 1976), where exception is taken to many of its arguments.

63. Wai-kam Ho, "Aspects of Chinese Painting from 1100 to 1350", in *Eight Dynasties of Chinese Painting* (Cleveland: Cleveland Museum of Art, 1980 [exh. cat.], p. xxv.

64. Prior to the reign of Huizong, the "offices" held by Academy members were outside of the regular governmental ranks; see *ibid.*

65. These figures are based on information contained in the SCMHP, and on statistical tables compiled by Yu Jianhua; see his *Zhongguo huihua shi*, vol. 1, pp. 168-170.

66. SCMHP, pp. 78-79.

67. SCMHP, pp. 16-18.,

68. SCMHP, pp. 56-58.

69. SCMHP, p. 22.

70. SCMHP, pp. 78-79.

71. SCMHP, p. 90.

72. SCMHP, p. 93.

73. *Tang Texts* I, p. 153.

74. William Willetts, *Chinese Arts*, 2 vols. (Harmondsworth: Penguin Books, 1958), vol. 2, p. 514.

75. For a discussion of the artist/patron relationship in the West, and of how it was affected by the breakdown of the Guild system, see Rudolf and Margot Wittkower, *Born Under Saturn: The Character and Conduct of Artists* (London: Weidenfield and Nicholson, 1963), Chapter 2. In *The Rise of the Artist in the Middle Ages and the Early Renaissance* (London: Thames and Hudson, 1972), especially pp. 97-106, Andrew Martindale argues that too much has been made of the differences between Medieval and Renaissance artists, and claims that it is a lack of sources concerning Medieval painters that makes the contrast appear so sharp; however, what he seems to overlook is that it is precisely this lack of sources which demonstrates the low esteem in which artists were held in this period.

76. See Susan Bush, *The Chinese Literati on Painting: Su Shih (1037-1101) to Tung Ch'i-ch'ang (1555-1636)*, rev. ed., (Cambridge MA: Harvard University Press, 1978 [Harvard-Yenching Institute Studies 27]), pp. 22-28, for a succinct and trenchant analysis of this equation as it came to be made in the Northern Song period.

77. Quoted in Bush and Shih, *Early Chinese Texts*, pp. 95-96.

78. *Ibid.*, p. 131.

79. *Ibid.*, p. 132.

List of Characters

boshi 博士

Chen Hong 陳宏

Chen Yongzhi 陳用之

Dai Kuei 戴逵

daizhao 待詔

Deng Chun 鄧椿

Dezong 德宗

Gao Keming 高克明

Gu huapin lu 古畫品錄

Guo Ruoxu 郭若虛

Guo Zhongshu 郭忠恕

Han Gan 韓幹

Huangdi 黃帝

huashi 畫師

Huaji 畫繼

Huizong 徽宗

jiaxun 家訓

jinshi 進士

Jiutangshu 舊唐書

Kaibao 開寶

Li Cheng 李成

Li Xiong 李雄

Lidai mingghuaji 歷代名畫記

Liang 梁

Liu Daochun 劉道醇

miao 妙

neng 能

pin 品

ping 評

pipa 琵琶

qiyun 氣韻

Renzong 仁宗

shang 上

shen 神

Shi Huang 史皇

shidafu hua 士大夫畫

Shu 蜀

Siku quanshu zhenben 四庫全書珍本

Su Shi 蘇軾

Sun Mengqing 孫夢卿

Sun Sihao 孫四浩

Songchao minghua ping 宋朝名畫評

Taizong 太宗

Taizu 太祖

Tangchao minghua lu 唐朝名畫錄

Tao Hongjing 陶弘景

Tuhua jianwen zhi 圖畫見聞志

tuhuayuan 圖畫院

Wang Guan 王瓘

Wang Wei 王微

Wang You 王友

wenyuan 文苑

Wu Daozi 吳道子

Wu Di 武帝

Wu Zongyuan 武宗元

xia 下

Xie He 謝赫

Xu Xi 徐熙

Xuanhe huapu 宣和畫譜

Xuanzong 玄宗

xueshi 學士

Yan Liben 閻立本

Yan Zhitui 顏之推

Yanshi jiaxun 顏氏家訓

Yin Zhi 尹質

Yu Jianhua 俞劍華

Yuqing zhaoying gong 玉清昭應宮

yuxing 寓興

Yuan Ai 袁靄

Zhang Huaiguan 張懷瓘

Zhang Yanyuan 張彥遠

Zhao Chang 趙昌

Zhao Guangfu 趙光輔

Zhenzong 真宗

zhong 中

Zhongguo huihua shi 中國繪畫史

Zhou 周

Zhou Fang 周方

Zhu Jingxuan 朱景玄

Zong Ping 宗炳

Women in Chinese Religions: Submission, Struggle, Transcendence

Daniel L. Overmyer
University of British Columbia

"We women (*wo nü tzu*) are despised for troubling our mothers' bodies. Our parents must bring us up, but when a girl grows up she abandons her parents and is married to another."

"When a woman is married to a husband for her whole life she is controlled by him. All her joys and sorrows derive from him. After they are married she necessarily suffers the pains of childbirth, and cannot avoid the sin of offending the sun, moon, and starts with a flow of blood. Now I will speak to you in more detail about the sufferings women endure in childbirth."

Old nun's sermon, *Liu Hsiang pao chüan* (18th century),
(*chüan* 1, pp. 4b-5a, 6b-7a)

"What's the use of reading books [for the civil service examinations]? It is better to study the Way; profit lies therein... To be an official for one life is to gain enemies for 10,000 lifetimes. Every wrong [you do] will be avenged without ceasing. I am pointing out to you the path to the Western Land. I urge you, husband, to take the earliest opportunity to practice spiritual discipline."

Liu Hsiang to her husband, *Liu Hsiang pao-chüan*,
(*chüan* 1, pp. 41b-42a)

Introduction

The history of women in Chinese religions is long and complex, but a few facts are clear. As has been true in every traditional civilization, women in China were kept in an inferior social position. They were controlled by their fathers and husbands, denied status until they had male children, expected to do menial work, forced to welcome concubines, and in desperate situations sold for cash. In the process, however, many women became social entrepreneurs who established a degree of status and power for themselves, both within the family and in the marketplace. Chinese religions in general supported the established social hierarchy, with women near the bottom. Nonetheless, religious activities offered alterative consolation and status to women, outside the home, so that to this day many religious participants are women. Through ritual, scripture study, and moral acts women had access to a world of meaning partly their own, a world that provided support for most, and social transcendence for a few.

This paper is intended as an introduction to some of the roles women played in Chinese religions, as household ritualists, lay devotees of a deity, shamans, nuns, and sectarian teachers. In all of this the quantitative social and economic background should be kept in mind. In traditional China the overwhelming majority of women were poor, illiterate, and had to work hard every day to survive. This was true for men too, but women had the additional burdens of inferior status and the dangers of childbirth. The religious activities of most women were confined to worshipping their husband's ancestors and occasionally visiting a local temple to pray for healing or sons. For them such rituals were at best a temporary consolation with no social implications other than making it easier to stay where they were. Even if a woman were a pious lay Buddhist the values in sermons she might hear would emphasize frugality, obedience, chastity, acceptance of her lot, hope for paradise after death. For all but a few religion was socially conservative. The more active religious roles for women discussed in this paper should be understood against this background. They represented theoretical possibilities that were realizable only by a few, and even most of those had to define themselves over against men. If this ground theme is understood it will not need to be repeated in what follows.

The focus of this paper is on the participation of living women in Chinese religious activities. It is not directly concerned with related issues such as theories of a "feminine" principle in Taoist philosophy or the development of female deities. There is no doubt that women have been actively involved in a variety of cults and rituals throughout Chinese history, but records concerning them are few and scattered. It is important to distinguish what women actually did from theories composed by men that indicate a sexually balanced view of cosmic forces, such as *ch'ien* and *k'un* in the *I-ching* and *yang* and *yin* in Han thought. The *Tao-te ching* contains many statements praising non-interference, yielding, lowliness, and the virtues of water, all of them conventionally regarded as showing appreciation for the "feminine" side of existence, but of course all these virtues are simply expressions of what men would like women to be. Praising the Tao as mother of the world does not mean that one thinks highly of women, and indeed there is no hint of such appreciation in the *Tao-te ching*. The same is true of other philosophical Taoist books such as the *Chuang-tzu* or the *Huai-nan tzu*; they contain no consideration or appreciation of the role of living women. Other early philosophical texts are the same; it is assumed that women are necessary as wives, concubines, and mothers, but otherwise they are ignored. Their ritual roles are limited to assisting at sacrifices to their husband's ancestors. When Mencius states that all men have the potential for goodness, that's what he means: all men. The potential of women for moral self-cultivation is not denied, it is just not considered. The goal of such self-cultivation is better management of family and state, a role not open to women. Though there are some positive statements about mothers and wives, Chinese philosophy is almost entirely a discussion by and for men in their controlling intellectual, moral, and social roles. If women are mentioned at all it is to note the obedience they owe to parents, husband, and adult sons as part of the hierarchical order of society. Beyond that the spirit of philosophical discussion was set by a famous passage in *Analects 17:25:*

> The Master said, "In one's household, it is the women and the small men that are most difficult to deal with. If you let them get too close, they become insolent. If you keep them at a distance, they complain.[1]

One must maintain a critical perspective as well on the relationship of female deities to women participants in their cults. There have been three great national goddesses in the history of Chinese religions, the Queen Mother of the West (Hsi Wang-mu), Kuan-yin, and Ma-tsu (T'ien Hou). In addition, there have been a large number of lesser deities with more specific functions, such as healing and the bringing of (male) children. Women have been active worshippers of these deities, but their role as formulators and organizers is not clear. I know of no evidence that women wrote texts about these deities or established temples for them; indeed the role assigned to women in society at large would have prevented such activities. There is some evidence that princesses, courtesans, and prostitutes worshipped the Queen Mother of the West during the T'ang dynasty, but for the most part the Taoist tradition of this goddess was maintained by men. This is largely the case with other Taoist female deities and immortals as well; their beauty and power were praised by men; they are what men wanted to believe in and worship, but there is no necessary connection between their cults and attitudes toward living women. In China as elsewhere, that goddesses are worshipped does not mean that women are honored. On the contrary, goddesses can be projections of male desires and needs to a cosmic level, by-passing women on the way. Hence, this paper will concentrate on evidence for what women actually did in Chinese religions, both in general descriptions and in texts in which women are given active roles. This paper attempts a preliminary survey of its whole topic, to bring together what I know so far, and to clarify where further reading and research are needed. It will proceed by first discussing the evidence for women's religious activities in rough historical order, culminating in the most independent role women had, as teachers and leaders in early modern religious sects. Once the evidence is before us we can analyze, compare, suggest areas for further research, and attempt to draw lessons for today. This is a large task that I approach with diffidence but also with a conviction that it needs to be done.

The Shang and Mid-Chou Periods (c 1500-600 B.C.E.)

The first archaeologically verified kingdom in Chinese history was the Shang (c 1500-1050 B.C.E.), which arose due to technological innovation such as bronze casting, and the development of new forms of social and administrative control. The great majority of the population continued to live in semi-subterranean houses in small villages, employing stone tools in subsistence agriculture, as had been the case in the prehistoric period. The emergence of a hereditary royal clan made possible a new concentration of the surplus resources of this neolithic agricultural base. The specialized rulers, administrators, priests, and technicians who relied on these resources developed bronze metallurgy, writing, new techniques of divination, military weaponry and organization, and more elaborate architecture. Social stratification became much more pronounced, with political and economic power concentrated in the hands of a small hereditary elite.

Most of our records of Shang religion describe the activities of men, but in some cases aristocratic women are referred to as well. The wives or consorts of kings occasionally participated in rituals intended to exorcise harmful spirits. They also made formal announcements to ancestors of such events as a successful harvest or a plague of locusts. A third kind of ritual carried out by women was that of invocation to ancestral spirits to aid in childbirth, and to petition for male children, a theme oft repeated in later centuries. There are many references to palace ladies in oracle bone (divination) texts. Prayers are offered for their health and safe childbirth, and after death some were worshipped as ancestors themselves. The wives of subject rulers sometimes came to offer tribute to the Shang court. Fu Hao, a consort of King Wu Ting in the 13th century B.C.E., is described as a military leader who led attacks on neighboring tribes. Thus there is evidence that at least a few Shang women had active religious and social roles, perhaps more so than in later periods.

There is also a bit of evidence for female deities in the Shang, particularly an Eastern Mother (Tung-mu) and a Western Mother (Hsi-mu) who seem to have been deities in charge of directions. Oxen were sacrificed to them as they were to ancestors.[2]

The Chou succeeded the Shang in the eleventh century B.C.E. Early Chou society was dominated by hereditary aristocratic lineages who controlled land, taxation, military force, literacy, and ritual access to their own ancestors and deities. The agricultural population worked the land as serfs, bound to their lords by obligations to provide food, other material needs, and labor service.

The religious activities of the early Chou aristocracy were focussed on their ancestors, who were believed to reside in a celestial court presided over by T'ien, "heaven," the Chou high god. These ancestors had power to influence the prosperity of their descendants, their fertility, health, and longevity. Through ritual equation with deities of natural forces the ancestors could also influence the productivity of clan lands. In addition, royal ancestors served as intermediaries between their descendants and T'ien.

There are very few references to women as active participants in Chou religion; to get any sense at all of what they might have done I have turned to late Chou or Han (202 B.C.E.-220 C.E.) sources such as the *Li-chi* (Record of Rites), which was edited in the Han but includes earlier material. From such material it appears that Chou women could have three religious roles, as assistants in ancestor worship, as ritualists for a silk-worm cult, and as shamans or spirit-mediums.

There are several passages in the *Li-chi* that mention the role of the ruler's wife in assisting at ancestral sacrifices. Wives are described as bringing in the stands for sacrificial dishes, serving as representatives of their husbands' female ancestors, and supervising the raising of silkworms and the making of silk robes worn at sacrifices. Before ancestral rituals both the ruler and his wife were expected to purify themselves in a ten-day period of abstinence and mental concentration, to facilitate communion with the spirits. The cooperation expected of the wife in these rituals is well summed up in such passages as the following:

> In sacrificing, husband and wife had their several duties which they personally attended to... When the victim was introduced the ruler held it by the rope... the wives of the ruler's surname followed the wife with basins; she presented the purified liquid; the ruler held in his hand the knife with the bells; he prepared the lungs (to be offered to the personator [ritual representatives of the ancestor]), and his wife put them on the dishes and presented them. All this shows what is meant in saying that husband and wife had their parts which they personally performed.[3]

Shamanism in China most commonly took the form of deities and spirits possessing receptive human beings. Spirit mediums both female and male are mentioned in discussions of early Chou religion as participants in court rituals, responsible for invoking the descent of the gods, praying and dancing for rain, and for ceremonial sweeping to exorcise harmful forces. They were a subordinate level of officially accepted ritual performers, mostly women, who spoke on behalf of the gods to arrange for sacrifices. In conditions of extreme drought they could be exposed to the sun as an inducement to rain. Female mediums were called *wu*; a word etymologically related to that for dancing; male mediums were called *hsi*. In the state of Ch'u south of the center of Chou culture there were shamans believed able to practice "magic flight," that is, to send their souls on journeys to distant realms of deities and immortals.

Han historical sources indicate that by the third century B.C.E. there were shamans all over China, many of whom were invited by emperors to set up shrines in the capital. This was done in part to consolidate imperial control, but also to make available fresh sources of sacred power to support the state and heal illness. So, for example, in 201 B.C.E. Kao-tsu (r. 202-195 B.C.E.), the founding emperor of the Han, invited female spirit mediums from four important regions of the realm to sacrifice regularly in the palace; Emperor Wu (r. 141-87 B.C.E.) summoned shamans when he was ill, while one of his sons invoked such aid to determine his succession to the throne.

One of the most detailed discussions of early Chinese shamanism is by J.J.M. de Groot, who provides a variety of Chinese primary texts in his citations. One, from the *Kuo Yü* (Conversations of the States), compiled in the third century B.C.E., notes that some particularly upright and intelligent persons could be possessed by spirits (*shen*), and continues:

> When an intelligent spirit descends into them, in the case of men they are called *hsi*, while women are called *wu*. As functionaries they regulated the places for the position of the gods [at sacrifices], the order of their tablets, the [proper] sacrificial victims and implements [to be used], and the ceremonial dress to be worn in accord with the seasons.[4]

De Groot notes that, "As the Wu-ist priesthood consisted largely, probably, even principally, of women, we cannot wonder that its influence was prevalent to a great extent among the female sex." He goes on to cite a statement by the late Han scholar Wang Fu,

> The *Book of Poetry* criticizes a woman who did not twist her hemp, but sauntered in the marketplace, yet even now there are many who do not occupy themselves with providing food at home, or raising silkworms or weaving, but give priority to studying the occupations of shaman and invocator. Dancing to the sound of drums, they serve the spirits and thereby cheat the people and mislead women of the common folk.[5]

De Groot's subsequent discussion cites several other passages referring to female shamans, and includes a chapter on their activities in the Fujian province of his day, emphasizing their particular role of summoning deceased ancestors to ask about their well-being, and to petition their aid for descendants. This role is emphasized by Jack Potter as well in his article on Cantonese shamanism in the twentieth century, where he describes the mediums as "old ladies who speak to spirits." He summarizes their activities by saying that they,

> ...act as intermediaries between the villagers and the supernatural worlds of heaven and hell. Assisted by their familiar spirits, the [mediums] send their souls to the supernatural world, where they communicate with deceased members of village families. They also know how to recapture the souls of sick village children, and they can predict the future. They take care of the souls of girls who die before marriage, and protect the life and health of village children by serving as... fictive mothers [to take advantage of the shaman's authority over spirits].

Potter notes that several of the women he interviewed became shamans after some of their children had died. The spirits of these children were among their helpers.[6]

Though women continue to have a role in Chinese shamanism, it is clear that over the centuries this role has been reduced to the more limited and specialized function of intermediary for family spirits. It is male shamans who are possessed by the more important gods, and who carry out dramatic public exorcism rituals.[7]

Women in Taoism

Taoism is China's own "indigenous higher religion," characterized by the fifth century C.E. by a literate and self-perpetuating priesthood, a pantheon of celestial deities, complex rituals, and revealed scriptures in classical Chinese.

Most branches of Taoism eventually traced their origin to a new revelation from the Most High Lord Lao to Chang Tao-ling in 142 C.E., establishing him as "Celestial Master." He was empowered to perform rituals and write talismans that distributed this new manifestation of the Tao for the salvation of humankind. Salvation was available to those who repented of their sins, believed in the Tao, and pledged allegiance to their Taoist master. The master in turn established an alliance between the gods and the devotee, who then wore at the waist a list (register) of the names of the gods to be called on for protection. The register also served as a passport to heaven at death. Taoist ritual consists essentially of the periodic renewal of these alliances by confession, visualization, petition, and the offering of incense and sacred documents. Taoists texts are concerned throughout for moral discipline and orderly ritual and organization.

Though men still dominated the tradition, women had a more important role in the first centuries of Taoism than in any previous form of Chinese religion. Early Taoist texts are addressed to households, not just to men, unlike the male orientation of classical philosophy. To be sure, Taoist householders are assumed to be men, but women are included and sometimes specifically mentioned as participants. One fifth century text praises both the Celestial Masters and their wives as founders of the tradition. Another devotes several pages to instructing women in various stage of life. Writing of the Celestial Master tradition, Henri Maspero comments:

> Beginners were called the Sons and Daughters of the Tao: *tao-nan*, *tao-nü*. The higher rank was that of Man or Woman Wearing the Cap, *nan-kuan* or *nü-kuan*, and this was sometimes written with a character of the same pronunciation which signified Mandarin. Further progress gave the right to the title of Father or Mother of the Tao, *tao-fu* or *tao-mu*. As we see, all these ranks were accessible to women as well as to men; there seems to have been no difference between them, and religious life was open equally to the two sexes. However, for the title which seems to have been the highest, that of Divine Lord, *shen-chün*, no feminine equivalent has been found.[8]

There was also a Taoist tradition of sexual rituals that it was believed could bring immortality to women as well as men. There is evidence that during the T'ang dynasty (618-907 C.E.) some aristocratic women became Taoist nuns renowned for their piety. From this period as well there are also a number of biographies of women who became immortals.

However, the later Taoist texts I have read seem to be addressed more particularly to men. There are occasional references to Taoist families, but if women are mentioned at all it is to urge that they be avoided if they have recently given birth, or that they not be allowed to observe a male practitioner mixing alchemical potions. The chief exception to this that I know of is in the early Ch'üan-chen tradition in which several women attained positions of leadership.

Some of the more important references to women in early Taoist texts I have read are as follows:

1. *Cheng-i fa-wen T'ien-shih chiao chieh k'e ching* (The correct and unified ritual text, the scripture of the teachings, precepts and regulations of the Celestial Masters) (Harvard-Yenching index (HY) 788; 3rd. cen. C.E.).

> If you do not remember the Tao, the Tao will not remember you. Therefore common people and [Taoist] officers, male and female, you should all put your affairs in order, cultivate your character, purify yourselves, think on your masters and uphold the Tao [the term here includes both the cosmic Tao and the teachings of the sect]. The customs of the world are shallow, so you husbands and wives, fathers and sons in your households should together be devoted to and preserve [the Way]... You should be pure, upright and filial, obey the Tao, reverence your master, pay ritual homage to the souls of the dead, and accord with the gods. (pp. 14b-15a)

There are also injunctions in this text that, "each household should transform itself," so as to practice all the principles of morality (p. 18a), and that prohibit male and female sect officials from appointing themselves to office (p.16b). This whole text is directed to women as well as men as a matter of course, and hence all of its teachings apply to the roles and responsibilities of women.

2. *San-t'ien nei-chieh ching* (Scriptures of the inner explanation of the three heavens (HY 1196, 5th cen.).

A passage describing the first Celestial Master Chang (2nd cen. C.E.) says:

> He set up twenty-four parish districts [in the area of present Sichuan province], and put in office male and female officials and libationers to be in charge of the correct laws and rituals of the Three Heavens [the new dispensation revealed by the Most High Lord Lao]. In transforming the people and receiving households [the work of conversion] they used five pecks of rice as a pledge of sincerity. They converted 10,000 households in 100 days; people came in clouds. For administration they made regulations and documents that were complete and effective in every way, and handed them over to their descendants to transmit through the generations as national preceptors [intended as religious advisers to emperors]. When laws and rituals were established, then humans and spirits were in security and peace. [Master] Chang subsequently ascended to heaven in broad daylight and personally received the office of Celestial Master. The son of the Celestial Master Chang Heng and his grandson Chang Lu, with their wives, were released from the corpse and ascended to heaven. So, there were three [Celestial] Masters and their wives. Since the three Masters ascended, libationers of the various parishes have transmitted the laws and rituals of the Tao. (1:6a)

Here we see women involved in founding the Taoist tradition.

3. *Cheng-i fa-wen T'ai-shang wai-lu i* (Text of the correct and unified ritual teachings, protocol for the exterior registers of the Most High) HY 1233 (5th cen.).

This text begins: "Male and female Masters all establish parish districts. Being of honored or humble position, worshipping and showing reverence, advancing and stopping, [all] depend on the regulations..."

Then follows a section titled, "Important registers received by five types of women." Registers are lists of the titles of gods who protect devotees, written on talismans worn at the waist. The five types of women are:

a) Unmarried daughters dwelling at home. Here they are to obey the instructions of their parents and receive ritual teaching from [Taoist] mistresses/masters. When taking leave of their parents they are to inform the [Taoist] official of their district responsible for the livelihood of the people, male and female. [They are to say],

"Grateful for the weighty kindness of the Tao from which I obtained life, I, an unmarried daughter, in such and such a year, with a devoted mind take pleasure in the Tao. Although I am ignorant I embolden myself to advance, and now take refuge at the master's gate [among his or her disciples]. I beg you to bestow success upon [my quest]; relying on the ritual teaching, I maintain belief and sincerity, and offer these phrases to be heard. I request to receive such and such a register and to devote myself to religious practice according to the ritual teaching. Bowing down I desire that [you] enlightened master/mistress, will deign to give me permission. Respectfully uttered."

All those who receive the ritual teaching while living at home, when they are about to be married should announce it to their master/mistress. If their master is not home, they should report it in memorial form to one of high virtue of the same Tao. If the woman must go to the family of her husband she should submit another report.

In all cases when she enters her husband's household she should tell her husband what register she has received. Her husband announces this to his parents, and goes to his master to inform him. The woman should only change her surname, and is not allowed to change the writing of it (?) (*wen*; could this be a misprint for *ming*, "given name"?). When she is at home she is called by her father's surname, when she meets others [marries] she is called by her husband's surname.

b) Daughters who leave home. Daughters who put forward their own destiny (*t'ing-ming*) and do not wish to meet others [marry] should announce to their parents that they are going to leave home to study the Way. Some establish another cloister [of their own]; some join the disciples of a master. Male masters who live alone are not permitted to accept female disciples. If a master is married she is called Mistress (*shih-mu*). When female disciples come they are to rely on a mistress. If there is no mistress they can turn to an unmarried woman master (*nü-shih*). An unmarried woman master leaves home, is devoted to her task, makes her thoughts harmonious, and follows a master to receive a register...

There follows the text of the vow taken by such an unmarried woman master, announced to the local Taoist officer:

"[I], daughter so and so, was born at such and such a time and date. The sins of my previous karma being weighty, when I was born I received a female body. I am weak and ignorant and do not wish to marry. In my parents home there is no way for me to study. Now I vow to devote my life and take refuge at the master's gate. I will exhaust my strength in sincerity and devotion, and will exert myself in sprinkling and sweeping [a standard phrase for entering disciples, male and female]. For my whole life I will continue the light, [offering] incense morning and evening. I will not dare to feel regret halfway through, and will not backslide. I will carry out this pledge in accord with the regulations. I offer up these phrases, hoping only that [you], enlightened master, will deign to bestow upon me a successful result. Respectfully uttered."

c) Married women. There are many reasons why women marry. Some do not wish to marry, but in obedience to superiors [parents] are compelled to do so. Some are taken by force by aristocratic and powerful secular households. Some attend on and uphold the ritual teaching. Some have nothing to worship. [Registers] previously received should be immediately returned to their master/mistress. The master should instruct them that if their husband upholds the Tao they should give up and change their original surname. If [the woman] has not yet received a register she should follow (accord with) her husband in receiving one. When husband and wife have the same master and the master goes some distance away, she can go to one of high virtue and give him or her allegiance according to the regulations, saying,

"[I], the wife of a local man named so and so, born at such and such a date and time, fortunately due to my past karma have been able to uphold the great Tao. Although I have been given the weakness of a woman, I have been able to rely on the people of the Tao. Just now I am expressing to the utmost my sincere devotion [to the Tao] while I attend to holding the basket and broom [work as a housewife]. I look up to the Tao to extend my life, praising its marvelous transformations; overcome with gratitude for its profound blessings, may I forever fill the role of a 'seed person' [a member of the elect, waiting for Lord Lao to return], diligently rely on the ritual teaching, and offer pledges of my sincerity and faith. I offer up these phrases, requesting to receive such and such a register. I hope that [you], enlightened master/mistress, will deign to grant permission. Respectfully stated."

Here we see that a married Taoist woman could have a complete religious status of her own.

d) Single women. This category refers to several kinds of women: widows who have vowed not to remarry, those of advanced years who have not married, those who are old with no sons, those who are wealthy and not willing to go [out to marry], and those who are poor and no one has asked for, or too sick to go. Such women can enroll with a master or mistress. Here again the text of a vow is supplied, similar in tone to those translated above, confessing sin, and petitioning to join with a master and receive a register.

e) Daughters who return to live at home. This category refers to women whose husbands have died, who have transgressed one of the seven grounds for divorce, or whose horoscopes are incompatible with those of their husbands, to the point that they are forced to live apart. Such women who cannot support themselves return to their original families, and, "...bound about with anxieties and afflictions, take refuge at a master's gate," Their vow of allegiance is similar to that of unmarried daughters living at home. (pp. 1-3a)

There are other references in this text as well to male and female masters, and all the rituals in it appear to be intended for devotees of both sexes.

There are scattered references to women in other early Taoist texts, concerning such matters as taking vows, exchanging registers with husbands at marriage, and wearing ritual robes. In general in these texts women are assumed to be an integral part of the Taoist ritual system.

Another interesting but less direct source for understanding the role of Taoist women is biographies of female immortals; living women who attain sainthood through piety and good works. There is a collection of sixteen such biographies, all short, in the *Yün-chi ch'i-ch'ien* (HY 1026), an 11th century collection of Taoist texts compiled for the emperor. Though these stories are presented in what for us is legendary form, they do give some indication of what was understood as possible for exceptional Taoist women. Most of these stories are set in the Eastern Chin dynasty (317-420 C.E.). This is not the place for a detailed discussion of this material, but one can note that the women involved were both commoners and the wives or daughters of officials who studied the Tao with such devotion that they attracted the aid of immortals. One is described as a childless widow who became an innkeeper. She made her guests feel at home, and cared for the sick. As a result she was visited by an immortal.

One woman attained the Tao because of her compassion for birds and animals, for which she put out grain on the snow in winter. Of another we are told that she,

> ...had compassion and love for others, constantly did good deeds in secret, and even loved and protected mantises and other small creatures. Through studying the Tao she became an immortal, and now lives in a cave on Mt. Sung. (p. 1608)

One woman began as a pious Buddhist who

> ...daily sprinkled and swept the floor before Buddha images, and frequently vowed her deep desire for the Tao of immortality. After she had attained it she sang so beautifully that wild birds gathered in front of her to hover and dance, moved by her profound sincerity. (p. 1609)

We also read of a female Taoist priest, of a woman who was good at exorcism, who though several hundred years old still looked twenty-five, of women hermits who regularly communed with immortals, and of a married woman who lived alone because of illness, daily reciting the *Yellow Court Scripture* (an important text of internal visualization and meditation) three times. As a result female immortals descended to visit and instruct her. Most of these women lived alone and were aided by female immortals. (*chüan* 115, pp. 1607-1616 in Vol. III of the Taipei Tzu-yu Publishing Co. edition (1978).)

In a recent article Suzanne Cahill describes the Mother Queen of the West as the patron deity of aristocratic women during the T'ang dynasty (618-907). The literary evidence for this is poems, most written by men, but a few written by women themselves, including a prostitute who became a Taoist nun. These poems are in high literary style, with much comparison of court women with the Queen Mother's divine attendants, but there are references as well to women who go to the Mother's paradise at death, to palace ladies who take religious vows and become nuns, and to women performers of Taoist ritual music. The Queen Mother is referred to as the chief guide to immortality for women, who refer to her intimately as "Amah." There are few details, but enough to indicate a cult of the Queen Mother of the West available specifically to women.[9]

There is evidence in later Taoist history of women who were leaders, teachers, and nuns. One was Tsu Shu (fl. 889-904), who was one of the formulators of the Ch'ing-wei (Clarified Tenuity) Taoist tradition. Scriptures and teachings attributed to her were transmitted through several generations of female leaders.

A woman named Sun Pu-erh was one of the "Seven Perfected" (Immortals) of the Ch'üan-chen Taoist tradition in the 12th century. She was the wife of Ma Yü, who in turn was a close disciple of Wang Che (1112-1170), the founder of the Ch'üan-chen school. After she and her husband both became disciples they separated. Sun acquired a following of her own, and became a model for other Taoist women ascetics. There are records of many other Ch'üan-chen Taoist nuns as well.[10]

By the early fifth century, if not before, some Taoists had developed methods for nourishing the body's vital force, *ch'i*, through ritual sexual intercourse. For the most part this was a matter of stimulating and purifying the *yang ch'i* of the male through successive intercourse with a number of women without ejaculating semen. At the point of climax the man was supposed to press the base of the penis with his hand, grinding his teeth in great determination, thus diverting the semen up a conduit in the back to the head, which was a receptacle for storing refined vital essence, the liquid of immortality. This ritual could be carried out only on certain days of the year, after a period of purification. It was to be practiced with young women in the household, preferably between the ages of fourteen and nineteen, changing partners as frequently as possible. For a time there was also a communal sexual ritual called *ho-ch'i* "the blending of vital breath" in which members of Taoist congregations exchanged partners.

Though the emphasis is on the attaining of immortality by men, some texts indicate that women too could benefit from these practices. It appears that all adult members could join in the communal rituals, and all of those who did were promised healing, forgiveness of sins, and protection from hostile forces. In some texts discussing private sexual rituals it is noted that women who know their secrets can also benefit; indeed, men are enjoined to avoid such women! In one detailed description it is clear that both partners can gain immortality:

> After they have concentrated and purified their thoughts, then a man and woman may practice together the art that leads to longevity. This method must be kept secret, it must be transmitted only to adepts. It allows a man and a woman together to activate their *ch'i* and the man to nurture his semen and the woman her "blood." This is not a heterodox method; it concentrates on activating *yin* and strengthening *yang*. If this discipline is practised in the correct manner, then the *ch'i* fluid shall spread like clouds throughout the body, the seed will solidify and become harmonious, and soon all those who practise it, whether young or old, shall become [vigorous] like adolescents.
>
> ...
>
> The elixir thus formed [in the bodies of the two participants] if nurtured for a hundred days, will become transcendental. And if this discipline is continued over a very long period, then it will become a natural habit, the method for living long and attaining Immortality.[11]

In sum, during its first several centuries the Taoist tradition gave a relatively high level of support to the religious role of women. Their role in later Taoism appears to have been reduced, though future research may modify that judgment. In later centuries the women religious leaders that I know of were almost all from the realm of popular religion, to be discussed below.

Women in Chinese Buddhism

Buddhism has always included lay members of both sexes, and, according to early accounts, an order of nuns began in the Buddha's lifetime, but the defining core of the tradition has always been controlled by celibate male monks. The religious goal of these monks is to escape the emotional and social bonds of ordinary life in order to attain a supreme state of detachment, freedom and inner peace. To further this goal, monks are expected to leave the household life as fathers, husbands, and sons and join an all male community designed to minimize competition, temptation, and sexual stimulation. In such a community women are perceived as a threat because they represent the social and sexual life the monks are trying to deny. Because of this tension, early Buddhist texts portray women as emotional temptresses with powerful sexual desires, though the desires of men are strongly criticized as well.

Male monastics continued to control the Mahāyāna Buddhist tradition that became dominant in China after the second century C.E., but Mahāyāna theory is non-dualistic and egalitarian. An enlightened perspective sees all things as fundamentally one because of their shared emptiness, that is, their lack of independent being and permanent distinguishing characteristics. In this perspective, eventually all dualities disappear, including that between male and female. Unfortunately, however, despite this generous theory, Mahāyāna

Buddhist monks continued to be influenced by the old attitudes toward women, who were still seen as sensual threats to the quest for Nirvāṇa. For the most part Mahāyāna texts maintain that before women can attain the status of bodhisattvas or Buddhas they must change their sex.

The varied images of women in Mahāyāna literature have been admirably discussed by Diana Paul, so there is no need for detailed treatment here. Her own perspective is summed up in the introduction:

> Like Judaism and Christianity, Buddhism is an overwhelmingly male-created institution dominated by a patriarchal power structure. As a consequence of this male dominance, the feminine is frequently associated with the secular, powerless, profane, and imperfect. Male Buddhists, like male religious leaders in other cultures, established normative behavior for women by creating certain ideals of femininity. At the same time, men's opportunities for interaction with women were minimized by the restrictions of devout practice. In early Buddhist monastic communities, interaction with laywomen was necessary for economic support but otherwise avoided. When we find texts in which the sacred is represented as masculine while the profane or imperfect is represented as feminine, we have a polarization that suggests both internal psychological conflicts and external social barriers between the sexes.[12]

Diana Paul's *Women in Buddhism* is essentially a translation of texts with introduction and commentary, thematically arranged, beginning with depictions of women as evil temptresses, coupled with sharp criticisms of men as weak sensualists easily led astray. There follow sections on women as mothers, nuns, and pious daughters. The succeeding chapters are on a women who became bodhisattvas with and without sexual transformation, on the celestial bodhisattva Kuan-yin, and on queen Śrīmālā who becomes a Buddha in her own right. The images discussed move from negative to positive, and leave one with the conclusion that despite its faults the Mahāyāna perspective on women is more affirmative than that of many other religious traditions.

The issue before us here, however, is not literary images of women but their actual participation in religious activities. Mahāyāna texts are addressed to all beings in the universe, including lay men and women, described in Chinese translation as "good men" and "believing women" (*shan-nan*, *hsin-nü*, Sanskrit *upāsaka*, *upāsikā*), so it is clear that female piety is assumed and encouraged. For most Chinese women such piety involved offering prayers and incense to Buddha images, reciting the names of Buddhas and bodhisattvas to invoke their aid, and participating in such temple festivals as the one marking the Buddha's birthday on the eighth day of the fourth lunar month. Women also joined in pilgrimages to famous monastery temples. Women make up the majority of lay Buddhist devotees in China today, as can easily be seen in any visit to a living temple. The recent study of the Kuan-yin cult on P'u-t'o shan off the Zhejiang coast by Chün-fang Yü of Rutgers University has demonstrated anew the central importance of women in Chinese Buddhism.[13]

There is no doubt that lay women have been active supporters of Chinese Buddhism for centuries, but they are not often mentioned in the sources. However, Buddhist scriptures composed in China from the fifth to eight centuries emphasize that their message is for all, men and women alike, a spirit well summed up in the *Life Protecting Sūtra* (*Hu shen-ming ching*, *Taishō* 2866):

> The Buddhist Way must be studied, and the dharma of the scriptures must be read. That I am now a Buddha is due only to accumulated studies. As for the wonderful dharma of the Mahāyāna, without regard to sex or status, those who hear this scripture will be protected by all the Buddhas, and will obtain all they desire. (85:1327a)

The *Hsiao fa-mieh chin ching* (*The Smaller Sūtra on the Complete Extinction of the Dharma*, *Taishō* 2874) promises that in the turmoil at the end of the age, "Girls and married women will all attain the Way, diligently progress as one, and so can avoid these calamities" (85:1358c). A similar indigenous text from the same time (fifth century) notes that,

> When the dharma is about to be extinguished women will be zealous, constantly doing meritorious deeds, [while] men will be lazy and indifferent, will not engage in religious discourses, will look on monks as manure, and will not have believing minds.[14]

In the fifth century many Chinese Buddhists believed that the age of the decline of the dharma had begun, so comments like these may reflect actual situations of the time.

There is some evidence for women disciples of Ch'an masters, while Buddhist women were active in lay societies of the Sung dynasty (960-1279), led by monks. These societies ranged in membership from a few score to several thousands, including both men and women, gentry and commoners. They were devoted to reciting the names of the Buddhas, reciting and copying scriptures, carving images, and providing vegetarian feasts for monks and laity. Records of these societies mention women members as a matter of course, and we know of at least one group composed of fifteen women, "devoted to the promotion of friendship among women."[15]

Women's activities in these Sung Buddhist societies were important antecedents of their activities in popular religious sects later on.

In addition to these references to ordinary women there are many royal ladies who patronized Chinese Buddhism as early as the fourth century. Two empresses of the Eastern Chin dynasty founded nunneries in Jiankang (modern Nanjing); later empresses did the same, and also invited famous monks to preach and perform rituals in the palace. The most famous empress to actively support Buddhism was Wu Tse-t'ien (625-705) who interrupted the T'ang dynasty and founded her own, the Chou, from 690-705. Empress Wu had monasteries built all over China, rock images carved, and scriptures printed and distributed. Her efforts were anticipated by the wife of Emperor Wen of the preceding Sui dynasty (581-618) who actively encourage her husband's support of the T'ien-t'ai school. Thomas Shiyu Li and Susan Naquin have recently published an article that describes in detail the support of royal women for a Buddhist temple outside Beijing in the Ch'ing period. To discuss this topic further would take us too far afield, but it is one that deserves attention, and for which references should be relatively easy to find because of the prominence of the women involved.[16]

The first Chinese nun was ordained in 317 C.E., beginning a tradition which has continued to exist until today. In the fifth century two delegations of Singhalese nuns came to China and helped establish a truly orthodox lineage through ordination by Indian masters in the presence of other nuns. A text edited in 516, the *Pi-ch'iu-ni chuan* (*Lives of Nuns*) provides information about nuns from upper-class and educated families in the region of Jiankang. Most of these exceptional women were literate in Buddhist texts and active preachers and organizers. A few were renowned for their mastery of certain scriptures, their devotion to meditation, and their ability to visualize Buddhist paradises while in trance states. Their reasons for becoming nuns are given as devotion to Buddhism in early life, refusal to marry, illness, and grief at the loss of a parent. Convents were also a refuge for women who had been abandoned or orphaned during the destructive civil wars of the fourth and fifth centuries. Chinese nuns can still be observed in Taiwan and the mainland, living in small convents and carrying out daily rituals of recitation.[17]

Women in Family and Village Popular Religion

A major tradition that took its early modern shape during the Sung period was popular religion in the family and village, the religion of the whole population except those who specifically opted out of it, such as orthodox Taoist priests, Buddhist monks, and Confucian scholars and state officials in their public roles. (Indeed, this might better be called "common religion.")

While popular religion came to include deities, concepts, and values from Taoism, Buddhism, and Confucianism, where it is still active it is above all a local religion that provides a focus for community life and hope in the face of difficulties. It can be defined by its location in the midst of ordinary social life, its pantheon of personified deities, views of afterlife, demonology, and characteristic specialists and rituals.

This popular tradition is based on ancestor veneration and the cult of household gods. Beyond the household its rituals are performed at shrines for locality gods and at village temples. Temples are residences of the gods, where they are most easily available and ready to accept petitions and offerings of food and incense.

Women have always been an integral part of popular religion as performers of household rituals, worshippers at village temples, participants in pilgrimages, and spirit-mediums. Hence, to a large extent to discuss the role of women in this tradition is to discuss the tradition itself. Most participants in modern popular religion are women, and one suspects this has long been the case.

Married women with male children are considered full members of their family and lineage and as such have primary responsibility for offering incense and food to family ancestors and household deities. They also participate in annual festivals, as mourners at funerals, and as worshippers and preparers of food at rituals of community renewal (*chiao*). Such women can become ancestors worshipped by their descendants.

Within the larger religious realm there are cults of female deities of particular concern to women, particularly those deities involved with bringing children. In addition, there is some evidence that women have their own understandings of what they are doing in ritual, different from that of men.

In a recent article on the social contexts of the goddess T'ien Hou (Empress of Heaven = Ma Tsu) in the Hongkong New Territories, James Watson emphasizes her role as a symbol of territorial control and lineage power. He adds, however, that this understanding is that of men, and continues:

> Women, as indicated earlier, have a very different vision of T'ien Hou from that held by any category of men—so different, in fact, that one begins to wonder if we are dealing with the same deity. Women play no role whatsoever in the formal organization of the temple cults, not even to the extent of forming a women's auxiliary to complement the activities of their husbands and fathers. For women the worship of T'ien Hou is usually defined in personal or family terms. Wives appear at the annual festivals with individual sets of offerings, which they present to the goddess on behalf of their households. Men never make these presentations, as they are said to be "too busy" attending to the collective rituals associated with the cult.[18]

In addition to this difference of perspective, the role of women in family and village popular religion is restricted in two ways. First, they do not usually found or manage village temples, or serve on councils of local elders that decide on temple leadership, repairs, and special festivals. However, a woman spirit-medium can be in charge of the shrine to her helper deity, either in her home or by the roadside. In the Macao village of Tai-pa, for example, there is a small temple to Kuan-yin run by an elderly woman; perhaps it is a remnant of what was once more common elsewhere as well.

A second restriction on the religious activities of women is based on their supposed pollution due to menstrual flow and the blood of childbirth. Menstruating women and those who have recently given birth are not allowed to enter temples, because their blood is believed to offend the gods. Though children are demanded by the family, and a woman must give birth in order to become a full member of society, the act of giving birth is considered a polluting sin that automatically condemns a woman to a bloody pool in purgatory! After she dies a son must arrange for a special ritual to symbolically release her suffering soul.[19]

Francis Hsü notes that the birth of a child calls for special rituals performed by women. A pregnant woman must observe several taboos, such as not looking at images of deities with animal heads, or at the sun and moon in eclipse. She consults a diviner before giving the baby a name chosen to ward off evil influences. A difficult labor may be due to a local ghost who is struggling to replace the baby's soul with its own and thus obtain a new body. In such a case, women in some areas propitiate the ghost with food, incense, and paper money offered at a spot it is believed to haunt.

The birth of a healthy child is celebrated with offerings to the ancestors, the kitchen god, and the deities on the family altar, and to the locality god (T'u-ti kung). The offerings are to report the birth and express gratitude for it. In west China the offering to the locality god is usually made by the baby's grandmother. Francis Hsü has described this ritual in some detail.[20]

In Cantonese families a diviner is asked to cast a horoscope for the baby; if it clashes with that of its mother, it may become ill or die young. In such a situation one remedy is to bond the child to someone else—a relative, a spirit-medium, a god, a sacred stone or tree; anything that will deflect bad fortune from the child. The mother is responsible for arranging this ritual adoption, and for making regular offerings to the deity involved, or visits and gifts if the protector is a person. This is again the kind of religious activity particularly carried out by women.[21] At the Wong Tai Sin temple in Kowloon one can see many women making offerings for this purpose, and confirming the results with divination sticks.

Women in Popular Religious Sects

By the early fourteenth century another form of popular religion appeared, the voluntary association or sect that could be joined by individuals from different families and villages. These sects developed out of lay Buddhist societies in the twelfth century, but their structure owed much to late Han religious associations and their popular Taoist successors, Buddhist eschatological movements from the fifth century on, and Manichaeism. By the sixteenth century the sects were characterised by predominantly lay membership and leadership, hierarchical organization, active proselytism, congregational rituals, possession of their own scripture texts, and mutual economic support. For the most part the sects simply provided a congregational alternative to village popular religion, an alternative that offered mutual support and assurance, an additional path to religious merit, and a means of going directly to paradise at death, without passing through purgatory.

In these popular religious sects women had higher relative status than anywhere else in traditional Chinese society and religion. They were not only active members from the beginnings of the sectarian tradition, but could also be congregational leaders and teachers, or even the founders of new groups. This role was facilitated by a mythology based on a supreme goddess, the creator and mother of all, in which male and female children have equal religious status. This Eternal Mother is superior to all other deities, including the Buddhas and the Jade Emperor. She waits in her paradise, sending messages to her lost children to return home. Some women sect leaders were believed to be her incarnations. The positive role of women in the popular sects was also supported by a series of scriptures related to them in which determined religious women are the chief protagonists. Born to auspicious signs, these women at an early age are attracted to Buddhist piety, maintain vegetarian diets, and vow to become nuns. They resist all family pressures to marry, and leave home in apparent disgrace, but go on to become heroic religious figures. In the end they convert their stubborn families, and are revealed to have become gods or bodhisattvas. In areas of south China there were groups of pious lay women who recited and transmitted these scriptures, women who had resisted marriage and now lived a communal life together. Similar "lay nuns" may be found in residential temples in Zhejiang province today, and no doubt elsewhere as well. Recent research by David Jordan and myself has revealed that women continue to have an important role in popular religious sects in Taiwan, as congregation leaders, spirit-writers, members of scripture chanting groups, altar women, and active worshippers. Some of them have their own distinctive interpretations of sect teaching and ritual, as do the T'ien Hou devotees observed by James Watson.

From the beginning the sources note that sect membership included women, in part because male devotees married and sometimes brought along their families when they joined. The presence of women scandalized orthodox Confucian scholars and celibate Buddhist monks, who repeatedly mention it as evidence for the vulgarity and heresy of the sects. An early fourteenth century source written by an orthodox Buddhist monk notes that in White Lotus congregations, "men and women mix together in confusion, thus disrupting proper human relationships," and that, "Though commoners, they presume to call themselves 'living Buddha Tathāgatas', with women given the title of 'Buddha mother great beings'."[22]

In a 1981 article I summarized the evidence for women with important positions in popular religious sects, including leaders of armed uprisings, congregation heads, teachers with both men and women as their pupils, and a sixteenth century nun who wrote five vernacular scripture texts of her own.[23] More detailed comments can be found in Susan Naquin's excellent study of a sectarian uprising in north China in 1813. She notes that there were no restrictions concerning who could join a sect, and that women as well as men could transmit its teachings.[24]

Women in Sectarian Scriptures (pao-chüan)

Of the many different types of Chinese vernacular literature one was developed primarily in the popular religious sects, a form of scripture text called *pao-chüan* "precious volumes." The first dateable sectarian *pao-chüan* appeared in the early 16th century, drawn from a variety of earlier resources, but written in relatively simple language promising aid and deliverance for all men and women of whatever status. These books are egalitarian and non-sexist in tone throughout.

There are several types of *pao-chüan* content, ranging from straightforward religious and moral teaching to stories that express the same values, but in more dramatic form. The doctrinal texts are addressed to "good men" and "pious women" as a matter of course, while many of the stories include women characters and are clearly addressed to all those willing to listen. In some of the story *pao-chüan* heroic religious women are the major actors. The earliest book of this type is the *Hsiang-shan pao-chüan* (Fragrant mountain *pao-chüan*), the first form of which appeared in the twelfth century, with antecedents going back to the seventh. This text opens with an introduction describing its origin and purpose, and then proceeds to the story of a young princess named Miao-shan, who, after a long struggle, becomes enlightened and discovers that in fact she is Kuan-yin. This story in effect provides mythic background for the cult of Kuan-yin of 1000 eyes and arms, who sees and aids all.[25]

The story of Miao-shan became a model for later accounts of similar heroic women, such as that in the *Liu Hsiang pao-chüan* (*The pao-chüan* of Fragrance Liu), which is discussed at length in my article on "Values in Chinese Sectarian Literature," cited above. The earliest edition of this book known to me was published in the late eighteenth century. It concerns a pious young woman who refuses to consummate her marriage and goes off on her own as a religious teacher. In the end she saves her husband's evil family, and convinces him and his second wife (forced on him by his mother) to join her in a life of celibate meditation. At death they go the Western Pure Land, where the Buddha Amitābha predicts they will become gods.

In the *Liu Hsiang pao-chüan* there is a long sermon by the old nun who converts Fragrance to Buddhism, and this sermon in turn includes a short *pao-chüan* called the "Pregnancy *pao-chüan*." Both sermon and text show a keen awareness of the situation of women in late traditional China and give strong support to refusing marriage. The nun notes that:

> ...when a boy is born, his mother is joyous, the neighbors all congratulate her, the relatives are happy, and father and mother love the child as if he were a precious jewel. When he grows up he studies, and perhaps becomes wealthy, honored, and famous throughout the world. When he goes out he is honored; when he returns home his wife and concubines diligently look after him. As a husband he fulfills his aims and honors his ancestors.
>
> ...

However, when a girl is born, everyone hates her, and no on in the household rejoices. "We women (*wo nü tzu*) are despised for troubling our mothers' bodies. Our parents must bring us up, but when a girl grows up she abandons her parents and is married to another" (*chüan* 1, pp. 4b-5a).

...

> By giving birth to children she befouls the heaven and earth,
> and offends the river god by washing bloody skirts.
>
> ...
>
> If she is on good terms with her mother-in-law she can visit her mother every year or so.
> But if she is not in accord with her other-in-law's wishes,
> she is never able to return to her mother's home.
> She thinks of the pain in the hearts of her parents, and of when she will be able to repay their kindness.

> No matter how many plans you might have, women have always submitted to others and served them.
> This is because of serious sins in their former existences. (*chüan* 1, p. 6a)
>
> ...
>
> When a woman is married to a husband for her whole life she is controlled by him. All her joys and sorrows derive from him. After they are married she necessarily suffers the pains of childbirth, and cannot avoid the sin of offending the sun, moon, and stars with a flow of blood. Now I will speak with you in more detail about the sufferings women endure in childbirth. (*chüan* 1, pp. 6b-7a)

Then follows a description of ten different forms of childbirth brought on as retribution for past sins, including several forms of birth in which the hands or feet come out first, or which involve entanglement in the mother's viscera, stillbirth, and so on. The theme is repeated that menstrual blood and the blood of childbirth offend the gods. The nun continues:

> Now the suffering of giving birth which I have discussed, the suffering of ten months of pregnancy and of three years of nursing, and after birth, the bitter toil day and night of exchanging dry and wet [clothing], these are what is called, "in loving a child, there is nothing parents won't do." (*chüan* 1, p. 9a)

The nun then recites the *Pregnancy Pao-Chüan* (*Huai-t'ai pao-chüan*), which is a detailed month-by-month account of the pains and anxieties of pregnancy. (*chüan* 1, pp. 9a-12b)

The explicit conclusion of this text is that children should repay the suffering and pain their parents have gone through by maintaining a vegetarian diet and reciting the Buddhas' names. (*chüan* 1, p. 12a) It seems reasonable to suggest, however, that such material might have led some women to question marriage itself, as did those described by Marjorie Topley in her "Marriage Resistance in Rural Kwangtung." Topley writes,

> Aimed expressly at women was the "precious volume" (*pao-chüan*) which contained biographies of model women.... Many of my informants had "precious volumes"... which further emphasize that refusing to marry is not morally wrong...

These books were read by women who lived in "girls' houses" or joined religious sects that "stressed sexual equality." Most of these women were involved in making silk, and hence had independent means of support. Thus, there was a specific social context in which books such as the *Liu Hsiang pao-chüan* made sense, that of religious voluntary associations in which unmarried women played an important or dominant role.[26]

Though the explicit ethical values supported in the *Liu Hsiang pao-chüan* are quite conventional, the chief implicit value is not, because at a basic level this text is devoted to the courage, freedom and salvation of women. Hsiang nü (Fragrance) is a full-scale religious heroine with great strength of conviction and powers of persuasion, just as Miao-shan was. She firmly remonstrates with her social superiors, and eventually brings them all around to her side. She endures the worst insults and beatings and yet remains ready to forgive. She breaks social custom by insisting on her own betrothal agreement, without an intermediary. She opposes that most established of traditional values, obtaining office through the civil service examination system. When she is eventually driven out of her husband's home, she develops her own vocation as a religious preacher and leader. And in the end she succeeds, and all the rest depend on her for deliverance.

From the social point of view, perhaps what is most important is that Hsiang nü never really has a normal marriage. The text does not say that she didn't sleep with her husband in their few days together, but she certainly remained celibate thereafter. What she values is meditation, not sex and children. There is in this text, then, a strong implicit resistance to marriage and all the toil and submission it requires. This is made abundantly clear in the sermon preached by the old nun, which contains a long section on the suffering and dangers of pregnancy and childbirth and other difficulties a wife must endure. To be sure, the point is made that these are all grounds for being filial to one's own mother, and that a woman should be especially pious so as to be reborn a man. But the resentment is strong, and the implication not far off that it is better not to marry at all, as the nun herself had not.[27]

Another *pao-chüan* in my collection is based on a similar story, the *Hsiu-nü pao-chüan* (The *pao-chüan* of daughter Elegance) (19th cen.). This is a lively tale about another heroic girl, pious from an early age, who is abducted and forced to become a concubine. She refuses to sleep with her husband, despite repeated beatings by her mother-in-law. She converts a maid in the family to Buddhism, and they meditate and worship every night. For this both are beaten unconscious with a club. Elegance then helps the maid escape, for which she herself is again beaten unconscious. When she recovers she is tied to a pillar, where boiling water is poured over her until she dies. Her soul goes to purgatory, but because of her piety is soon released, and a female Taoist immortal is sent to earth to resurrect her body. She returns to her husband's home, greeted by gods and ancestral spirits along the way. She releases all of her husband's ancestors from purgatory. When she reaches home she tells her mother-in-law the whole story, but when the older woman asks what the form of her own next life will be, Elegance tells her it will be as a domestic animal (a karmic punishment for her sins). At this the mother-in-law flies into a rage and beats her again, but now the blows have no effect. Elegance finally orders disease-causing demons to attack her husband and his mother, and then leaves. When she returns two weeks later her husband begs her to heal him; she says she will, on three conditions: first, that he stop charging a doubled rate of interest on loans; and second, that he maintain a vegetarian diet, be a good person, provide food for monks, repair bridges, roads, and rest houses, aid the poor and be compassionate. The third condition is that she be allowed to go home to her parents. She makes her mother-in-law agree to the same conditions, then heals them both by ordering the demons to leave. In the end, all the evil people in the story are either rehabilitated or punished.

When she returns home, Elegance preaches a sermon exhorting Buddhist piety and good works. It begins:

> [Since] I am a woman I don't read books and am not thoroughly versed in the scriptures, so what I say will not be literary and polished. I simply urge people to do good, maintain a vegetarian diet, recite the names of the Buddhas, and explain the Way. Now I will first preach about the glorious rewards of those in the thirty-three heavens, and the bitter sufferings of those in the eighteen [courts of] purgatory... (p. 58b)

In the end she and her parents are reborn in Amitābha's paradise.

Texts such as this are the high point of feminist thought in traditional China. Nowhere else do we find such a clear affirmation that women can attain superior status and power.

The end result of the long sectarian tradition of affirming the religious role of women may be seen in contemporary popular congregations in Taiwan, where women serve as leaders, spirit-mediums, and ritualists, and make up a substantial portion of active members. Since a description of all this is readily available in a recent book by David Jordan and me, I see no reason to discuss it at length here. Suffice it to note that in this book there are discussions of women in the early spirit-writing tradition (pp. 38-39), of Eternal Mother mythology (pp. 57-63, 123), the *Earth Mother Scripture* (pp. 72-74), the calling and work of a woman spirit-writer (pp. 149-165), and of dreams and visions of women sect members (pp. 174-212). The material on dreams and visions includes a discussion of two women who developed a sub-cult of their own, based on revelations made available only to them.[28]

Concluding Comments

This paper is intended as a preliminary inventory of what one historian of Chinese religions has learned so far about the activities of women in that history.[29]

Sources for learning about the roles of women are few and far between, but at least we know enough to suggest topics for further research, including all those noted in this paper. The most important single step is to become aware of the issue, to look for references to women, and be conscious of how much their role has been ignored. It is astounding that the lives and activities of half the Chinese population are so little mentioned in the sources. One must literally go through piles of notes and texts to find just a few nuggets here or there. To ignore actors in history is to deny them of what little immortality they might have, but in the Chinese case as in most others, such immortality has been limited almost entirely to men. Though the lives of all depended on them, it is as if women were not there. There are profound ethical issues at stake here for contemporary scholars.

The study of women in Chinese religions is also a study of their place in the culture as a whole, so continued research in this area can contribute to a more balanced understanding of the realities of China, past and present. There is also ample material for comparing Chinese women with women in other traditional cultures, a comparison I have begun to make in the case of the popular religious sects discussed above.[30]

From the material presented here one can see that in the history of Chinese religions most women had a subordinate role, but a few struggled to establish their own perspective and vocation. Through our research we can try to help them find their voices again.

Notes

1. The translation of *Analects* 17: 25 is taken from that of D.C.Lau, *The Analects of Confucius* (Harmondsworth: Penguin Books Ltd., 1979), p. 148. For discussions of the Queen Mother of the West see Michael Loewe, *Ways to Paradise: The Chinese Quest for Immortality* (London: George Allen and Unwin, 1979), pp. 86-126. See also Suzanne Cahill, "Performers and Female Taoist Adepts: Hsi Wang Mu as the Patron Deity of Women in Medieval China," *Journal of the American Oriental Society* 106.1: 155-168 (January-March, 1986). On other Taoist female deities, see Edward H. Schafer, *The Divine Woman* (Berkeley: University of California Press, 1973). For good recent summaries of Confucian attitudes toward women see Richard W. Guisso, "Thunder Over the Lake: The Five Classics and the Perception of Women in Early China," in Richard W. Guisso and Stanley Johannesen, eds.; *Women in China: Current Directions in Historical Scholarship* (Youngstown, New York: Philo Press, 1981), pp. 47-61, and Theresa Kelleher, "Confucianism," in Arvind Sharma, ed., *Women in World Religions* (Albany: State University of New York Press, 1987), pp. 135-159.

For a more positive assessment of the attitude of some Neo-Confucian scholars toward women, see Tu Wei-ming, "On Neo-Confucianism and Human Relatedness," in George A. De Vos and Takao Sofue, eds., *Religion and the Family in East Asia* (Berkeley: University of California Press, 1984), pp. 111-125.

2. Professor Ken'ichi Takashima, University of British Columbia, personal communication, June 23, 1988; Chou Hung-hsiang, "Fu-x Ladies of the Shang Dynasty," *Monumenta Serica* XXIX: 346-390, and K.C. Chang, ed., *Studies of Shang Archaeology* (New Haven: Yale University Press, 1986), pp. 103-140 (articles by Chang Cheng-lang and Chang Ping-ch'üan). I am grateful to Prof. Takashima for these references.

3. *Li-Ki*, tr. James Legge, in Max Müller, ed., *Sacred Books of the East* (London: The Clarendon Press, 1885), xxviii: 33, 74-75, 238-241. This material is discussed in Lester James Bilsky, *The State Religion of Ancient China* (Taipei: The Chinese Association for Folklore, 1975), I: 76-83. For the silkworm cult, see Dieter Kuhn, "Tracing a Chinese Legend: In Search of the Identity of the 'First Sericulturalist'," *T'oung Pao* LXX: 213-245 (1984).

4. J.J. m. de Groot, *The Religious System of China* (Leiden, E.J. Brill, 1892-1910), VI: 1191, citing *Kuo Yü* 18, *Ch'u Yü, hsia*, pp. 559-560 in the 1978 Shanghai Guji chubanshe edition. Translation modified by D.O. Introductory material here is drawn from Daniel L.Overmyer, "Chinese Religion: An Overview," in *The Encyclopedia of Religion* (New York: Macmillan Publishing Co., 1987), 3:257-289. For the activities of female shamans at the Han court see Ssu-ma Ch'ien, *Records of the Grand Historian of China* trans. Burton Watson, (New York, Columbia University Press, 1961), II: 32, 42-43.

5. Groot, *Religious System*, VI: 1209-1210, citing Wang Fu, *Chien fu lun, chüan* 3, number 12, pp. 143-144 in the 1978 Shanghai Guji chubanshe edition.

6. Jack M. Potter, "Cantonese Shamanism," in Arthur P. Wolf, ed., *Religion and Ritual in Chinese Society* (Stanford: Stanford University Press, 1974), pp. 207-231. This article is very much worth reading for its detailed transcriptions of seance conversations.
7. The most comprehensive discussion of modern Chinese shamanism is by Alan J.A. Elliott, *Chinese Spirit-medium Cults in Singapore* (London: University of London Press, 1955).
8. Henri Maspero, *Taoism and Chinese Religion*. Trans. by Frank A. Kierman, Jr., (Amherst, University of Massachusetts Press, 1981), p. 378. Originally published in French in 1971.
9. See the reference to Professor Cahill's article in note 1 above.
10. Judith Boltz, *A Survey of Taoist Literature, Tenth to Seventeenth Centuries* (Berkeley: Institute of East Asian Studies, 1987), pp. 38, 69-70, 155. See also Chen Yüan, *Nan Sung ch'u Hopei hsin Tao-chiao k'ao* (The New Taoism in the Northern Provinces at the Beginning of the Southern Sung), Beijing, 1958), pp. 42-49. Professors Julian Pas and Man Kam Leung of the University of Saskatchewan are translating this book into English: I am grateful to Prof. Pas for this reference.
11. Maspero, *Taoism and Chinese Religion*, pp. 517-541. R.H. van Gulik, *Sexual Life in Ancient China* (Leiden: E.J. Brill, 1961), pp. 197-200. The quoted passage may be found on p. 199. Its source is the *Yun-chi ch'i-ch'ien*, Vol. 27, *chüan* 105; p. 1435 in Vol. III of the 1978 Taipei reprint.
12. Diana Paul, *Women in Buddhism: Images of the Feminine in Mahayana Tradition* (Berkeley: Asian Humanities Press, 1979), pp. xiii-xiv.
13. Chung-fang Yü, oral report and video tape, Harvard workshop on Chinese religions, April, 1988. The film of pilgrimage women prostrating themselves every few steps is most moving.
14. *Fa-mieh chin ching* (*Sūtra on the Complete Extinction of the Dharma*), *Taishō* 396 12: 1119a. For a discussion of these Chinese indigenous scriptures see Daniel L. Overmyer, "Buddhism in the Trenches: Attitudes Toward Popular Religion in Chinese Scriptures Found at Tun-huang," *Harvard Journal of Asiatic Studies* 50.1:197-222 (June 1990).
15. Kenneth K.S. Ch'en, *The Chinese Transformation of Buddhism* (Princeton: Princeton University Press, 1973), p. 288.

See also the discussion of these societies in Daniel L. Overmyer, *Folk Buddhist Religion: Dissenting Sects in Late Traditional China* (Cambridge, MA: Harvard University Press, 1976), pp. 85-89. On Ch'an women, see Miriam L. Levering, "Lin-chi (Rinzai) Ch'an and Gender: The Rhetoric of Equality and the Rhetoric of Heroism" (unpublished paper, 1988), and her article "The Dragon Girl and the Abbess of Mo-shan: Gender and Status in the Ch'an Buddhist Tradition," in *The Journal of the International Association of Buddhist Studies* 5.1.19-35 (1982).
16. For the Empress Wu see C.P. Fitzgerald, *The Empress Wu* (London: Cresset Press, 1968); Antonino Forte, *Political Propaganda and Ideology in*

China at the End of the Seventh Century (Naples: Instituto Universitario Orientale, 1976), and Diana Paul, "Empress Wu and the Historians: A Tyrant and Saint of Classical China," in Nancy Auer Falk and Rita M. Gross, eds., *Unspoken Worlds: Women's Religious Lives in Non-Western Cultures* (San Francisco: Harper and Row, Publishers, 1980), pp. 191-206.

On imperial support of Buddhism during the Sui see Arthur F. Wright, *The Sui Dynasty: the Unification of China, AD 581-617* (New York: Alfred A. Knopf, 1978).

The article by Li Shiyu and Susan Naquin is, "The Baoming Temple: Religion and the Throne in Ming and Qing China," *Harvard Journal of Asiatic Studies*, 48: 1.131-188 (June 1988).

17. On Chinese Buddhist nuns see Kathryn A. Tsai, "The Chinese Buddhist Monastic Order for Women: The First Two Centuries," in Guisso and Johannesen, eds., *Women in China*, pp. 1-20; and Nancy Schuster, "Striking a Balance: Women and Images of Women in Early Chinese Buddhism," in Yvonne Yazbeck Haddad and Ellison Banks Findly, *Women, Religion and Social Change* (Albany, NY: State University of New York Press, 1985), pp. 87-111.

18. James L. Watson, "Standardizing the Gods: The Promotion of T'ien Hou ('Empress of Heaven') Along the South China Coast," in David Johnson, Andrew J. Nathan and Evelyn S. Rawski, eds., *Popular Culture in Late Imperial China* (Berkeley: University of California Press, 1985), pp. 320-321. On this point see also Margery Wolf, "China and Gendered Anthropology: Some Notes Toward Integration," (Durham, NC: Department of Anthropology, Duke University, 1985), pp. 14-15.

19. On women as a source of ritual pollution see Marjorie Topley, "Cosmic Antagonisms: A Mother-Child Syndrome," in Arthur P. Wolf, ed., *Religion and Ritual in Chinese Society* (Stanford, CA: Stanford University Press, 1974), pp. 233-249; Emily M. Ahern, "The Power and Pollution of Chinese Women," in Margery Wolf and Roxane Witke, *Women in Chinese Society* (Stanford, CA: Stanford University Press, 1975), pp. 193-214; Cordia Chu, "Menstrual Beliefs and Practices of Chinese Women" (unpublished paper, 1977); and Gary Seaman, "The Sexual Politics of Karmic Retribution," in Emily Martin Ahern and Hill Gates, eds., *The Anthropology of Taiwan Society* (Stanford, CA: Stanford University Press, 1981), pp. 381-396. See also the film by Gary Seaman of the ritual for releasing a mother's soul from the pool of blood, "Breaking the Blood Bowl" (Far Eastern Audio Visuals, 1974).

20. Francis L.K. Hsü, *Under the Ancestors' Shadow: Kinship, Personality and Social Mobility in Village China*. Revised and expanded edition (Garden City, NY: Doubleday and Co. Ltd., 1967, pp. 200-203. First published in 1948.

21. Topley, "Cosmic Antagonisms," pp. 241-245.

22. For this passage and a discussion of other sources for early White Lotus history, see Daniel L. Overmyer, "Alternatives: Popular Religious Sects in Chinese Society," *Modern China* 7.2:169-184 (April 1981).

23. Overmyer, "Alternatives"; for the scripture writing nun see Li and Naquin, "The Baoming Temple."

24. Susan Naquin, *Millenarian Rebellion in China: The Eight Trigrams Uprising of 1813* (New Haven and London: Yale University Press, 1976), pp. 38-42. For a good summary of women in popular religious sects see Yu Songqing, *Ming Qing Bai-lian jiao yan-jiu* (A study of Ming and Qing White Lotus sects), (Chengdu, Sichuan ren-min chubanshe, 1987), pp. 295-311.
25. Daniel L. Overmyer, "*Pao-chüan*: Types and Transformations" (unpublished paper, 1978), pp. 7-14; Glen Dudbridge, *The Legend of Miao-shan* (London: Ithaca Press, 1978). See also Daniel L. Overmyer, "Values in Chinese Sectarian Literature: Ming and Ch'ing *Pao-chüan*," in Johnson, Nathan, and Rawski, eds., *Popular Culture*, pp. 219-254.
26. Overmyer, "Values," pp. 245-253. From the third paragraph of 110 to the middle of 111 this material is quoted from the "Values" article. For associations of unmarried women see, Marjorie Topley, "Marriage Resistance in Rural Kwangtung," in Wolf and Witke, eds., *Women in Chinese Society*, pp. 71-76. For other discussions by Dr. Topley of these and similar groups see her "Chinese Women's Vegetarian Houses in Singapore," *Journal of the Malayan Branch of the Royal Asiatic Society* 27.1:51-67 (1954); Topley, "The Great Way of Former Heaven: A Group of Chinese Secret Religious Sects," *Bulletin of the School of Oriental and African Studies*, 26.2:362-392 (June 1963); and Topley and James Hayes, "Notes on Some Vegetarian Halls in Hong Kong Belonging to the Sect of the Hsien-t'ien tao: The Way of Former Heaven," *Journal of the Hong Kong Branch of the Royal Asiatic Society* 8: 135-148 (1968).
27. This paragraph is quoted from Overmyer, "Values," pp. 250-251
28. David K. Jordan and Daniel L. Overmyer, *The Flying Phoenix: Aspects of Chinese Sectarianism in Taiwan* (Princeton: Princeton University Press, 1986).
29. For further information, see for example an interesting account of a charismatic woman religious leader who was the daughter of a Ming official, in Ann Waltner, "T'an-yang-tzu and Wang Shih-chen: Visionary and Bureaucrat in the Late Ming," *Late Imperial China* 8.1:105-133 (June 1987).
30. On this see Overmyer, "Values," pp. 228-229.

Research for this article concluded in the summer of 1988.

List of Characters

Chang Tao-ling
張道陵
chen-hsing pu-huai
真性不壞
Chen Yuan, Nan Jung ch'u Hopei Hsin Tao-chiao Kiao
陳垣，南宋初河北新道教考
Cheng-i fa-wen T'ai-shang wai-lu i
正一法文太上外籙儀
Cheng-i fa-wen T'ien-shih chiao chieh k'e ching
正一法文天師教戒科經
ch'i
氣
chiao
醮
Ch'ien-fu lun
潛夫論
Chin-tan tao
金丹道
Ch'ing-wei
清微
Chüan
卷
Ch'üan-chen
全真
fen
分
Fu Hao
婦好
ho-ch'i
和氣
hsi
覡
Hsi-mu
西母
Hsiang-shan pao-chüan
香山寶卷
Hsiao fa-mieh chin ching
小法滅盡經
Hsing-lin
興林
Hsiu-nü pao-chüan
秀女寶卷
Hu shen-ming ching
護身命經
Huai-t'ai pao-chüan
懷胎寶卷
Kuan-shih-yin
觀世音
Kuo Yü
國語
li (Chinese mile)
里
Li-chi
禮記
Ling-kuang sheng-mu
靈光聖母
Liu Hsiang pao-chüan
劉香寶卷
Liu Kung
劉龔
Lo Ch'ing
羅清
Ma-tsu
媽祖
Ma Yü
馬鈺
Mao Tzu-yüan
茅子元
Mi-le fo
彌勒佛
Miao-shan
妙善
Miao-chuang
妙莊
Miao-shu
妙書
ming
名
Miao-yin
妙音
Nan Pi-tao
南畢道
ni-huan
泥丸(洹)
nü-shih
女師
pao-chüan
寶卷
Pi-ch'iu-ni chuan
比丘尼傳

p'in 品

Pu-ning 不佞

San-t'ien nei-chieh ching 三天内戒經

shan-nan, hsin-nü 善男信女

Shang-ch'ing 上清

Shang-ti 上帝

shen 神

shih-mu 師母

Sun Pu-erh 孫不二

T'an-yang-tzu 曇陽子

Tao-tsang 道藏

Ti-tsang 地藏

T'ien 天

T'ien Hou 天后

T'ien Hou Niang-niang 天后娘娘

T'ien-t'ai 天台

t'ing-ming 挺命

T'u-ti kung 土地公

Tsu Shu 祖舒

Tung-mu 東母

Wang Che 王嚞

Wang Fu 王符

Wang Shih-chen 王世貞

Wong Taai Sin 黃大仙

wen 文

wo nü-tzu 我女子

wu 巫

Wu-sheng lao-mu 無生老母

Wu Ting 武丁

Wu Tse-t'ien 武則天

Yu Songqing, *Ming Qing Bai-lian jiao yan-jiu* 喻松 明清白蓮教研究

Yün-chi ch'i-chien 雲笈七籤

An Enquiry Into the Sino-Indian Buddhist Debate in Tibet

W. Pachow
University of Iowa

It appears to be a natural phenomenon that our opinions differ from one another. This is exemplified in the polls and in elections. In an election, if the winner achieves a majority of 50.5 per cent of the votes, and the loser's percentage is 49.5, it may mean the former is lucky enough to be successful. But it does not necessarily mean that he is absolutely right and the other absolutely wrong. By this yardstick one may trace the source of debates, disputes, conflicts and wars. They share a common concern of trying to express something, but differ in intensity and the manner in which it is expressed. If war should break out between two groups of people, the consequences would be terrible. If it is a debate, it may mean an exhibition of eloquence, and its outcome could not be very serious or harmful. Based on this consideration we may say that debate is a healthy way of expression. It is preferable to an act of violence.

In Buddhist literature we find that Gautama Buddha on many occasions held discourses or discussions with contemporary religious leaders. He exhibited great wisdom and winning eloquence to gain victory over his opponents, and many of them eventually became his disciples. The *Dīgha-Nikāya* contains many sūtras of this nature.[1] His discussions with other people may be termed "conversation of the wise", in that one will never get angry over whether or not one is victorious or being defeated by the argument of one's opponents. When King Milinda expressed the wish to discuss matters with Nāgasena, the latter insisted that it should be in the style of "conversation of the wise," but not that of "conversation of the kings."[2] Over the centuries there are instances concerning debates between the Buddhists and other Indian religious sects. Among the Buddhists Nāgārjuna and Ārya Deva were great experts who defeated many of their opponents in public debates.[3] This tradition continued in later times.

Of special interest to us is the fact that when Hsüan-tsang was studying at the Nālanda University in India, he encountered philosophical confrontation with Buddhist scholars like Siṁhaprabhāsa and Chandrasiṁha. Later, at the request of King Śīlāditya, he represented that university and was ready to discuss the subtlety of Mahāyāna Buddhism with Prajñāgupta, a Hīnayāna teacher of the Saṁmitīya sect. It was about this time that a pundit of the Lokāyatika sect challenged the scholars of the Nālanda University, saying that he would forfeit his head if anyone could defeat him on his forty tenets. Hsüan-tsang accepted the challenge, and in the presence of Śīlabhadra, president of the Nālanda University and other scholars, he methodically disarmed his opponent's argument. The loser acknowledged defeat and was about to carry out his promise of forfeiting his own head. However, Hsüan-tsang accepted him as his personal attendant instead. His "*Hui-tsung-lun*" (A Treatise on the Conference of Doctrines) and "*P'o ê-chien lun*" (A Treatise on Destroying Evil Views) were composed in this connection.[4]

The foregoing instances, from the time of the Buddha to the seventh century, indicate that friendly discussions or debates among the Buddhists themselves or in relation to other religious groups were a normal phenomenon. Indeed, there were many debates over the centuries, and only the important ones were recorded. This assumption could be applicable to the Sino-Indian Buddhist debate which took place in Tibet in the eighth century. Being a rare occasion in Tibetan history, it was recorded in both Tibetan and Chinese documents. We shall examine the authenticity of the event in the following sections.

1. Was there a Sino-Indian Buddhist debate?

We assume that most of us know something about the Buddhist debate that took place either in Lhasa or at bSam Yas in the second half of the eighth century. The confronting parties were Mo-ho-yen (Mahāyāna) or Hva-san from China and Kamalaśīla, a disciple of Śāntarakshita from India. The focus of the dispute was that the Chinese Ch'an practice was not in accordance with the traditional Buddhism from India. Scholars such as Paul Demiéville, G. Tucci, David Snellgrove, A.K. Warder, R.A. Stein and Ueyama Daishun and others made careful investigations of this topic,[5] and the Tibetan and Chinese works such as *A History of Buddhism*[6], *The Genealogy of Kings of Tibet*[7] and *Chêng-li chüeh* (A Ratification of Suddenly Realizing the Right Principles of Mahāyāna).[8] The last name in the list was discovered from the Tun-huang caves and it was attributed to Mo-ho-yen. The authors of these documents assert that there was a Buddhist debate between the Chinese and Indian teachers. However, there are other scholars who hold a different view saying "that the Indian Kamalaśīla and the Chinese Hva-shang Mahāyāna never met, and that their confrontation is an invention of the later Tibetan historians." This view was attributed to Yoshirō Imaeda and supported by H. Guenther in his book review.[9] Thus we face an important issue; namely, was there really a Sino-Indian Buddhist debate held in Tibet? If so, when? Before we attempt to answer the question, we would like to trace the possibilities which might have led to the event in question.

The introduction of Buddhism to Tibet from both India and China took place in the seventh century during the reign of King Srong-brtsan-sgam-po. The Chinese teachers who went there were mostly Ch'an masters, and they emphasized the doctrine of sudden enlightenment. On the other hand, the Indian teachers promoted the traditional Buddhism based on analytic wisdom. Because of these differences, the former was known as the sect of Sudden Enlightenment (Tun-mên p'ai, Tibetan: Ston-min pa) and the latter the sect of Gradual Realization (Chien-mên p'ai, Tibetan: Rtsen-min pa). During the reign of King Khri-srong-lde-brtsan (died in 797) there occurred great activities for the development of Buddhism. For instance, Indian teachers such as Śāntarakshita, Padmasaṃbhava, Kamalaśīla and others were invited to Tibet, Buddhist Sanskrit texts were translated into Tibetan, Buddhist ordination was officially performed, the bSam Yas monastery was constructed (ca. 763-775), stūpas were built and students were sent to India to study Sanskrit, linguistics and other sciences.[10] In the course of time, Buddhism was firmly established in Tibet. But owing to the different traditions coming from India and China there appeared uneasiness among the Tibetan followers. Eventually there emerged noticeable friction between them which in turn brought about the official debate between the Indian and Chinese teachers under the sponsorship of King Khri-srong-lde-brtsan. The *History of Buddhism* by Bu-ston describes this event in great depth. The outcome of the debate was that the Chinese party headed by Mo-ho-yen was defeated and he was deported from Tibet.[11]

In addition to the Tibetan sources, we have the *Chêng-li chüeh* of Mo-ho-yen from Tun-huang. It gives us a different account of the story. It states the date of his visit to Tibet, a brief description of the opponent and the result of the debate. We regard this text to be of great historical significance, in that it confirms the Tibetan tradition regarding the debate; and it gives us a definite date of the said event.

In regard to the date of the debate, there is strong evidence to indicate that it took place in 781, or between 780-782, rather than 792-794, as suggested by Demiéville. This is substantiated by the statements found in the introduction to the *Chêng-li-chüeh.*[12] The author of this text says that when Sha-chou (including Tun-huang) was captured by the Tibetans, the Tsan-po (King of Tibet) extended his invitation to the Śramaṇa Mahāyāna to go there and preach the teaching of Ch'an (or dhyāna). When he arrived at Lhasa many people inquired about the method of Ch'an. The date for the fall of Sha-chou, according to Chinese documents such as *Yüan-ho-Chün-hsien chih* and *Hsi-yo-sui-tao chi*, was "the second year of Chien-chung"[13] (781). It is possible that the debate did not take place in the early months of 781, although both Indian pundits and Mahāyāna, the Chinese teacher (or Mahāyāna Hva san), were invited to Tibet. However, the smothered fire of disharmony may have been planted for a very long time. It exploded only at this juncture. The prophesy[14] made by Śāntarakshita years ago was an unmistakable indication. The introduction[15] to the *Chêng-li chüeh* informs us that at the beginning of the year of the monkey (780) Mahāyāna was informed of the complaint made by Indian monks that 'Sudden Enlightenment' taught by the Chinese teachers was not the teaching of the Buddha; therefore, it should be prohibited. The message was conveyed to Mahāyāna by the King himself. Consequently, he proposed to the King that a debate with the Hīnayāna teachers in the form of written questions might be arranged. The Indian teachers took a long time to prepare a lengthy list of queries with the intention of exposing the blemish spots of their opponents. Later, the two parties confronted each other. Mahāyāna Hva-san was able to defend his position in making suitable responses. The monks from India were defeated in the discussion. However, they incited the ministers to form a faction in order to discredit and slander the practice of Ch'an. Some Tibetan disciples of Mahāyāna committed suicide by burning, killing or letting themselves fall from a lofty cliff as a means of protest against such action. As a sequel, on the 15th day of the first month in the year of the dog (782) the King issued a decree saying, "The doctrine of Ch'an preached by Mahāyāna is fully in accord with the Canonical texts and free from any errors. From now on, members of the Order and laity may study and practice it."

The above-noted outline is the Chinese version of the debate. It has shown one side of the story, but it may not be the whole truth. One may suspect the suicidal action of the disciples of Mahāyāna. If their party was rally victorious, then that action was unnecessary. The significance of this account lies in the fact that there was indeed a debate between the Chinese and Indian parties in Tibet in 781. Probably, the Ch'an sect was defeated and temporarily suspended in that year. At the beginning of 782 the ban was officially lifted.

On the basis of both Tibetan and Chinese documents we are inclined to think that there was a Sino-Indian Buddhist debate, or even debates in Tibet on the differences of Buddhist doctrines. The date for the event seems to be 781 or during 780-82, or 792-94 as suggested by other scholars.

2. The place of the debate

If we accept the proposition that the Sino-Indian Buddhist debate was an authentic event which took place in the fourth quarter of the eighth century, our next question is related to the location in which it was held. There are two possibilities. One was Lhasa. It was stated in the *Chêng-li chüeh* that Mo-ho-yen travelled to that city to teach the method of dhyāna practices.[16] Paul Demiéville supported this site as the title of his work *Le Concile de Lhasa* indicates. The other place mentioned was bSam Yas. G. Tucci was a strong advocate for this location. His rationale was that the cultural and religious centers of Tibet in the eighth and ninth centuries were "at Yar Klun, where the old palaces, and the tombs of kings were located, or in Bragmar (dmar), a little to the north of bSam Yas."[17] Based on this observation, probably bSam Yas was the spot where the debate took place. Moreover, bSam Yas was famed for its grand monastery bearing that name. We are informed that it took more than twelve years to get the construction completed. Possibly the debate was held within the monastery.

3. *The main topics of the debate*

Our next enquiry would be the subject matter which was debated by the participating parties. Of course, the main concern was related to the differences between the sudden enlightenment theory represented by Mo-ho-yen, and the traditional Buddhist doctrines of gradual realization represented by Kamalaśīla. Bu-ston in his *History of Buddhism* recorded the views of both parties.[18] Given below is a condensed outline.

1. The propositions of the Chinese Mo-ho-yen:

   a) Good or evil deeds may result in blissful or evil births respectively.

   b) These deeds (whether good or evil) will not help anyone to gain deliverance from Saṁsāra.

   c) Anyone who observes the practices of no-thought or inclinations can be delivered from Saṁsāra.

   d) The absence of thought will bring about the non-perception of the reality of separate entities.

   e) Being in a state of non-perception of the reality one is able to attain Buddhahood instantaneously.

   f) A Bodhisattva has attained the 10th stage.

2. The objections from Kamalaśīla's party:

   a) The theory of absence of thought means the rejection of the highest analytic wisdom. It is non-constructive, similar to a person in a swoon or at the time of intoxication. Such being the case, one will not possess the cognition of non-substantiality, nor will he be able to remove the obscurations. Also, he will not extirpate the passions.

   b) One may attain to Buddhahood by possessing the Highest Wisdom—That means one reflects and discriminates.

   c) It is impossible to attain to Buddhahood at once, just as one walks step by step when one ascends a mountain.

   d) When passing through gradual training on the ten stages, one attains to Buddhahood by means of the ten virtues, and

   e) For a long time after the passing away of the Buddha, there was no dissenting points in the teaching.

The essence of Mo-ho-yen's thesis as noted above is that the effect of karma would operate in normal existence, but it would not enable one to be liberated from saṁsāra. On the other hand, the practice of thoughtlessness would help one achieve that goal. Besides, it would bring about non-perception of phenomena, reality, and thereby one may suddenly attain to Buddhahood. Undoubtedly, this theory could be easily traced to the *Platform Scripture* of Hui-nêng, the sixth patriarch of the Ch'an school.[19] In brief, it is concerned with karma, saṁsāra, absence of thought and sudden enlightenment. In the *Chêng-li chüeh* there are many questions and answers concerning concepts such as "not to attain to any dharma is the highest bodhi." "not to speak means to preach the dharma," "to be freed from all characteristics means the identity of the Buddhas," the nature of the conventional and transcendental truths and differences between the Buddha-nature and ātman and so forth.[20] It is a sizable composition of about 11,000

Chinese words. It cites many Mahāyāna sūtras such as *Vajracchedikā*, *The Lotus*, *The Laṅkāvatāra*, *The Hua-yen*, *The Nirvāṇa*, and others. Most of the questions and answers in this text did not appear in Bu-ston's account. Perhaps, he merely recorded the barest outline of the debate.

The main objections from Kamalaśīla's party focused on the irrationality of thoughtlessness and sudden enlightenment. They emphasized that without analytic wisdom one could no longer recognize evil from good, and thus it could hinder the progress of religious cultivation. They also stressed the importance of gradual realization, taking one step at a time, and the practice of the ten virtues.

Reviewing the arguments of the two parties based on Tibetan and Chinese sources, we notice that they confirm the principles of the Ch'an school and the traditional Indian Buddhist teachings. There is no evidence to indicate that the said debate was "an invention of the later Tibetan historians." Even if that claim is substantiated, how could one account for the fact that in the *Chêng-li chüeh* the Chinese party was said to be victorious? That claim could not arise if there were no debate. Further, one could not say that the Chinese document from Tun-huang was fabricated by the Tibetan historians!

In conclusion, we are inclined to think that there was a debate, or a series of written questions and answers being communicated between the Indian teachers and Mo-ho-yen from China. It took place around 781, although 792-94 has been suggested by others. The purpose of the debate was to decide which of the two schools taught the correct teachings of the Buddha. The result was that the Indian party was the winner, and Mo-ho-yen the loser; hence the promotion of Ch'an was temporarily suspended. But the ban was lifted at the beginning of 782. Moreover, the manner in which the debate was conducted appeared to be fair and friendly. The rule being prescribed for the occasion was that the loser should offer a wreath of flowers to the winner and be deported from Tibet.[21] Such being the case, it does not appear that there was a need for anyone to invent a story. Therefore, we believe that there was a Sino-Indian Buddhist debate.

Notes

1. T.W. & C.A.F. Rhys Davids, trans., *The Dialogues of the Buddha* (London: H. Frowde, 1899-1921), in three volumes.
2. H.C. Warren, trans., *Buddhism in Translation* (Cambridge, Mass: Harvard University, 1896), p. 128.
3. See *Life of Nāgārjuna* in *Taishō* T. 2047, vol. 50, p. 184c-185a; *Life of Ārya Deva*, Ibid., T. 2048, pp. 186-87. However, these biographies are blended with lengendary accounts.
4. See *Life of Hsüan-tsang*, in *Taisho* T. 2053, vol. 50, pp. 244b-45b.
5. Paul Demiéville, *Le Concile de Lhasa* (Paris: Imprimerie Nationale de France, 1952); Giuseppe Tucci, *Minor Buddhist Texts* (Rome: Instituto Italiano per Il Medio ed Estremo Orient, 1958), part 2, pp. 26,32, 36, 40, 41, 52, 65 and 82; David Snellgrove, *A Cultural History of Tibet* (New York: Frederick A. Praeger, 1968), pp. 73, 77, and 275; A.K. Warder, *Indian Buddhism* (Delhi: Motilal Banarsidass, 1970), pp. 476-77; R.A. Stein, *Tibetan Civilization* (Stanford: Stanford University Press, 1972), p. 67; Ueyama Daishun, "Donkō to Tonko bukkyōgaku" (T'an-k'uang and Buddhist Studies at Tun-huang), in *Tōhōgakuho* (1964) XXXV, p. 151.
6. Bu-ston, *A History of Buddhism*, trans. by E.E. Obermiller (Heidelberg: 1931), in 2 parts, pp. 192-96.
7. Wang I-luan, trans. *Hsi-tsang wang-t'ung chi* (Shanghai: The Commercial Press, 1955), pp. 62-63.
8. See Pelliot Collection, p. 4646 or the photo copy attached to Demiéville's *Le Concile de Lhasa*.
9. See Herbert V. Guenther's book-review of *Tibet: A Handbook* in *Journal of Asian Studies* XXXVII (1978), p. 503.
10. Wang I-luan, op. cit. pp. 64-76; W. Pachow, *A Study of the Twenty-two Dialogues on Mahāyāna Buddhism* (Taipei: Chinese Culture, 1979), pp. 34-38.
11. Bu-ston, op. cit. p. 193.
12. Pelliot and Demiéville, op. cit., f. 154A-154B.
13. Su Yin-hui, *Tun-huang lun chi* (A Collection of Essays on Tun-huang) (Taipei: The Student Book Co., 1967), pp. 218, 215-230.
14. Bu-ston, op. cit., p. 191.
15. Demiéville, op. cit., f. 127b, 128a.
16. Ibid., f. 154a-b.
17. Tucci, op. cit., p. 177.
18. Bu-ston, op. cit., pp. 193-95.
19. Wing-tsit Chan, trans., *The Platform Scripture* (New York: St. John University Press, 1963), pp. 49, 51-53, 85, 87, 89.
20. Demiéville, op. cit., f. 131a-b, 132b, 136b, 142a.
21. Bu-ston, op. cit., p. 193.

Bragmar 郎瑪

Chien-men p'ai 漸門派

Chen-li chüeh 頓悟大乘正理決

Hsi-you-sui-tao chi 西域水道記

Hsüan-tsang 玄奘

Hua-yen 華嚴

Hui-nêng 慧能

Hva-san 和尚

Hui-tsang-lun 會宗論

Kamalaśīla 蓮華戒

Mo-ho-yen 摩訶衍

Platform Scripture 六祖法寶壇經

P'o e-chien lun 破惡見論

Padmasambhava 蓮華生

Santarakshita 寂護

Śīlabhadra 戒賢

Tun-men p'ai 頓門派

Tun-huang 敦煌

Tsan-po 贊普

Ueyama 上山大峻

The Human Gods of China
New Perspectives on the Chinese Pantheon

J.F. Pas
University of Saskatchewan

Introduction

How very human are the deities of the Chinese people! Their origin and rise to prominence are often shrouded in mystery; their yielding of spiritual power is often as shaky and transitory as that of political leaders. Occasionally, like some political leaders, they make a comeback: in the People's Republic of China, gods and goddesses and Buddhas have regained some of their ancient prestige since the late seventies.

Looking at the various Chinese pantheons, one is overwhelmed by their complexity. They reflect the complexity of Chinese religion itself. Again the plural, "religions", is more adequate, since more than one religious tradition has shaped the religious consciousness of the Chinese people. Even admitting that some mutual absorption and borrowing have occurred, one must yet recognize an independent, autonomous status for the Taoist and Buddhist pantheons, and a less clearly defined, yet real autonomy for the pantheon of the Popular Religion, and perhaps of Confucianism.

The common worshipper is not always clearly aware of these differences, and is not even able to identify many of the statues of deities enthroned in the temples. The major ones they would be able to recognize, but all the lower ranking gods and goddesses are just there to receive incense and offerings of fruit and to bestow favours on the devotees, even if they do not know their names.

The purpose of this essay is not to enumerate and describe all the deities worshiped in China. Some studies made by western scholars can still be consulted effectively in this regard. (I think especially of Maspero's long article in *Asiatic Mythology*.) Several Chinese monographs have been published in recent years. My objective is rather to discuss certain aspects of the Chinese pantheons, which have been more or less neglected and to emphasize new perspectives that have to be looked at more carefully in the light of recent developments in the study of Chinese religion. The "human" character of the Chinese deities is a very fascinating dimension in such a study: like human beings, the gods have birthdays, families, careers, titles, temperaments, and authority. They fit into some kind of hierarchical structure, on which their precise function and special appeal very often depend.

First of all, what is the meaning of "pantheon"?

The word *pantheon* (from the Greek *pan*, "all" and *theos*, "a god") originally indicated a specific temple built in Rome in 27 B.C., dedicated to all the gods worshipped by the Romans. Derived from this, the word can also mean "the gods of a people taken collectively".[1] The term "gods" is sometimes used loosely, so that a pantheon can very well be a set of deities or holy beings of a transcendent nature, who serve as symbols and objects of worship of a particular group of people. Whereas the Greek and Roman pantheons were closely associated with particular peoples, the Chinese pantheons only partially do so. In China we face a very complex situation. The Greek and Roman gods are almost entirely mythical creations, but the Chinese deities or spirits are not always; many of them are deified historical personages.

It has been a western concern to "arrange" these pantheons into some kind of structured hierarchy: it is a desire for classification and order. Otherwise one is faced with a sense of great confusion, easily leading toward contempt, as when Maspero refers to this "unheard-of swarm of gods and spirits of every kind, an innumerable rabble".[2] (*Asiatic Mythology*, p. 263) Numerous as the Chinese deities are, with some effort it is quite possible to create some order among them, or to classify them into some categories. As I said, this is perhaps only a concern of western scholars. The Chinese worshipper does not care too much for classification: his only expectation is to receive help in a particular situation. Rank and hierarchy do not matter, as long as the deity possesses enough *ling* ("spiritual potency") and is willing to bestow it on the worshipper.

In recent years several Chinese scholars have made new contributions to the study of their pantheons and in an effort to create order in the chaos, they have proposed new categories of classification. Three works were published in Taiwan, one in the People's Republic of China.

The first model is proposed by Ch'i Te-tsai in *Taiwan miao-shen chuan* (*TMSC*) [Biographies and Legends of Deities (worshipped) in Taiwan Temples], 1979. The author divides the pantheon into seven categories:

(i) sage philosophers and culture heroes (*sheng-che ying-lieh*): 89 personalities.
(ii) holy worthies of Buddhism (*Fo-men sheng-chün*): 33 personalities
(iii) deities of nature worship (*tzu-jan shu-wu*)[3]: 31 personalities
(iv) deities of the folk religion (*t'ung-su hsin-yang*): 54 personalities

(v) spirits of the earth (or spirits of heaven and earth?): (*hsiang-t'u shen-shih*): 79 personalities
(vi) oppressive ghosts, not receiving sacrifices [from their descendants] (*wu-szu kui-li*): 29 personalities
(vii) anonymous spirits, enshrined in temples, but whose origin is unknown (*tai-k'ao miao-shen*): 55 listings.

The second categorization is found in Fan P'ing-shan's *Chung-kuo sheng-ming kai-lun* (*SMKL*) [A General Discussion of the Gods of China], 1979. He divides the pantheon into six groups:

(i) gods of the origins (*yüan-shih shen-ming*): 9 personalities: P'an-ku, the Taoist Triad of Three T'ien-tsün, Wu-Lao (Tung-wang kung, Hsi-wang mu, Huang-Lao, Shui-ching, Ch'ih-ching).
(ii) gods of heaven and spirits of earth (*t'ien-shen ti-shih*): 18 names, of which some may be collective deities.
(iii) gods of the human realm (*jen-ching shen-ming*): 15 names, including gods of the household.
(iv) saints (sages) and immortals (*shen-hsien*): 21 names.
(v) legendary deities (*ch'uan-chi shen-ming*): 19 names.
(vi) Holy Ones of Buddhism (*Fo-shen*): 8 names.

The third Taiwan publication is of a different nature. Chui Yün-yen. *Taiwan min-chien hsin-yang chu-shen chuan.* (*TMHC*) [Biographies of the Deities of Taiwan Folk Religion], 1984. It does not categorize but lists 413 deities arranged according to their birthdays within the twelve months of the lunar calendar.

The mainland publication is the most recent one. Authored by Lü Dzongli and Liu Qun, *Zhongguo minjian zhushen* (*MJZS*) [The Popular Deities of China] (1986), it is 924 pages long and divided into ten parts. Unfortunately, it does not have chapter headings, which would indicate the author's rationale of categorization. It is up to the reader to try and discover for himself the standards used for making up the ten groups. The following is then, tentatively, my own interpretation:

(i) The Supreme deities: Three Pure Ones of Taoism, Yü-huang Ta-ti; the Buddha(s).
(ii) Ancient deities, gods of heaven, star deities.
(iii) Fertility and household deities (Hou-t'u, Ch'eng-huang, T'u-ti, door gods, kitchen god).
(iv) Nature deities: Five mountains, especially Tung-yüeh, River deities, Dragon kings.
(v) Minor nature spirits.
(vi) More nature spirits.
(vii) Deities to assist in daily life and in the after-life: gods of epidemics, gods of healing, spirits in the netherworld (Yen-lo-wang, Ti-tsang wang), some apotheosized heroes (like Kuan-shen Ta-ti).
(viii) Gods of daily life: wealth, happiness, professions.
(ix) Taoist deities, such as Heavenly Master Chang, the Eight Immortals.

(x) Buddhist Saints: Kuan-yin, Mi-lo-fo, Buddha Amita, the Arhats (*lohan*).

Although this encyclopedic volume contains a mass of useful information about many deities, its system of categorization is not well thought out. It shows, however, that a fully logical, consistent way of grouping the Chinese pantheons is probably inconceivable.

To compare and contrast the above three Chinese models with just one example of western scholarship, we can look at Henri Maspero's classification in "Mythology of Modern China":[4] he does not divide the pantheon into a clear number of categories, but just lists the following groupings: supreme gods; gods of nature; gods of heavenly ministries or boards; gods of administrative districts; household gods; gods in Buddhist temples; gods of trades and professions; gods charged with watching over mankind individually; and gods of other worlds (hells and paradises).

These models each have their own relative justification, but the criteria used or implied are not totally convincing, and the categories are not always clearly differentiated.

In an attempt to arrive at a better type of categorization, one can be inspired by two guidelines: one either follows the total historical development of Chinese religion through the ages and then discusses the pantheons of each major historic period (horizontal); or one studies one by one the various religious traditions: the ancient religion, Confucianism, Taoism, Buddhism, Folk Religion (vertical). Since the growth of the pantheons is intimately linked with the development of their respective religion, the second method seems to be preferable. Each method has its advantages and shortcomings.

Therefore, taking into account as much as possible the data provided by previous researchers, and partially reflected in the above cited modern works, I'll propose the following categorization:

a) The gods of ancient times (prehistoric and early historic)
b) The gods of later times: the "Three Teachings": Confucianism, Taoism, Buddhism
c) The deities of the Popular Religion
d) A discussion of ancestors and ghosts.

Once again, my purpose is not to provide complete lists of the gods and goddesses, sages and saints, nor to provide a complete profile for each member of the pantheon (the best I can do is to refer to relevant literature), but to build a solid framework through which categorization of the Chinese pantheons becomes internally consistent and externally intelligible.

Categorization of the Pantheons

1. *The Gods of Ancient Times*

Supreme Deities: *Ti* (*Shang-ti*) of the Shang period; *T'ien* or *Huang-t'ien* (August Heaven) of the Chou dynasty. In early writings the two are sometimes combined and seen as functional synonyms: *Huang-t'ien Shang-ti*;

Nature Gods: thunder, lightning, rain (dragon-kings), wind, sun, moon, stars (perhaps Shang period, but certainly of Chou times);

Earth Gods: fertility spirits: soil, grain, sovereign Earth, rivers, mountains (probably Shang period or even from prehistoric times; certainly Chou);

Ancestral spirits (Shang and Chou): possibly evil spirits or *kui* (since Chou?); *Ti* or *Shang-ti* of Shang period may have started as first royal ancestor of the clan.

Animal Spirits: very likely rooted in totemism and/or shamanism.

Many of these deities or spirits continue to exist in later times' myths, legends and theories about them are amplified; their importance and worship are susceptible to changes, even to decline.

2. *The Gods of Later Times*

Although the traditional concept of *san chiao* ("three teachings", rather than "three religions") has been strongly criticized as perhaps too elitist, old-fashioned, irrelevant, or even as an abstraction, yet it must be reaffirmed that each of these three has had an autonomous existence. All three are clearly distinct, and even if one can point out some similarities between them, it does not mean identity. Their existence and recognition of their existence does not diminish the great importance of the Folk Religion as another autonomous system. It is not the place here to discuss the thorny problem of *san-chiao* versus popular religion.

a) *Confucianism and Imperial (or State) Cult*

These two are certainly not one and the same, but their objects of worship do occasionally overlap. Confucian writings extol the virtues of culture heroes and sage kings and praise them as models of virtue and ideal political leadership. In general, however, they are not deified.

TMSC lists here: Confucius, Kuan-kung, P'an-ku, Nü-kua, Shen-nung, Huang-ti, San-kuan, Chang T'ien-shih, Pao-kung, P'eng-tsu and many others. The majority of the remaining ones do not belong here.

SMKL has: Fu-hsi, Shen-nung, Huang-ti, San-kuan (also identified with Yao, Shun and Yü), K'ung-tzu, Kuan-ti, Lu-pan, and some famous pioneers and generals.

MJZS shows some interesting changes: whereas San-Kuan and Kuan-ti have been retained, a host of famous mythical figures are missing: no more culture heroes, no more K'ung-tzu. Cult figures like Kuan-ti are examples of the bridge between Confucianism and the State cult. Although Kuan-ti is not a Confucian personality, the state and the state bureaucracy promoted his cult for its ethical symbolism. Kuan-ti was seen as a model of loyalty and overall civic virtue and his cult was used as a powerful instrument to encourage these virtues amongst the people.

b) *Taoism*

Early Taoism adopted many of the traditional nature deities, but also created a set of their own: Szu-ming, god of alchemy and master of destiny, is one of the earliest Taoist creations. Then Lao-tzu and the Yellow Emperor were deified as Huang-Lao. Followed some Taoist triads: T'ai-I, T'ien-I, and Ti-I, and 36,000 spirits within the human body who also control the macrocosm. A new triad eventually replaced the former one: the Three Heavenly Worthies (*T'ien-tsun*): Yüan-shih, Ling-pao and Tao-te (the third one is the apotheosis of Lao-tzu). The second trinity was followed (but not fully replaced) by a new one: the Three Pure Ones (San-ch'ing), who are certainly different from the Three rulers (San-Kuan) of religious Taoism.

Within the growth of inner alchemy, the Taoist gods were multiplied on a grandiose scale, "mass-production", as H. Welch humorously remarks.[5] Many of them appear in some basic Taoist scriptures and play an important role in Taoist meditation techniques, especially those advocated by Mao-shan Taoism.[6]

c) *Buddhism*

Here is a case of worshipping transcendent beings who are not technically "gods", but rather like "incarnations" of the ultimate Buddha-nature in the form of Buddhas and bodhisattvas. The latter also assume a place of high eminence in the folk religion.

The Buddhist cult objects are not that numerous. Although hundreds of mythical Buddhas and bodhisattvas appear in some of the sutras, those who gained popularity among Buddhist devotees are only a handful. Among the Buddhas figure Shakyamuni, the historical founder of Buddhism, and mythical creations such as Buddha Amita, residing in the Western Land of Happiness, and the Buddha of Healing. These three are often seen as a trinity in temples.

Among the bodhisattvas, only a few well-known figures are seen over and over again: Kuan-yin, or Kuan-shih-yin, Mi-lo-fo (Maitreya), P'u-hsien, Wen-shu and Titsang wang.

Among the Buddhist saints some are outstanding; Chi-kung (the "crazy" monk), always an attractive figure because of his humour;[7] and Bodhidharma, usually called Ta-mo (or "dharma") have penetrated into the folk religion. The Buddhist saints, prototypes of the Taoist Immortals, have been grouped into sets of 16 or 18 (seen in many temples), or even larger sets of 500, which can still be seen in some monasteries in China.

3. *Deities of the Popular Religion*

The pantheon of the folk religion displays the greatest variety, and also causes the greatest confusion. The deities do apparently not like to be regimented and organized into neat rows. Leaving aside, for the time being, ghosts and ancestors, who together with the real deities populate the spiritual universe of the Chinese, we must try to find some criteria of classification. The results of former scholars must be taken into account.

Assuming the validity of what appears to be a general consensus amongst scholars, namely that there is a hierarchical structure in the heavenly bureaucracy, we must examine how such a hierarchy can be worked out in practical terms. Hierarchy implies a supreme authority at the top, some intermediate levels, and a whole gamut of lower levels. On which level one should place individual deities is not per se clear but both popular practice, field observation, and specialized studies are helpful guides to formulate a workable hypothesis.

a) *At the top*, we must of course place *T'ien* (Heaven). Although his formal worship was strictly reserved to the emperors, the common people privately worshipped Heaven as *T'ien-kung* (Lord Heaven) or *T'ien Lao-yeh* (Granddad Heaven, Venerable Old Man Heaven). Sometimes one meets the combination *Huang-t'ien Hou-t'u* (August Heaven and Queen Earth) as the primordial divine pair. It is often stated that *T'ien-kung* has been assimilated with *Yü-huang Ta-ti*, the Jade Emperor, who is Heaven in a more concrete and personalized form. Whatever the case may be, the Jade Emperor is ranked as the supreme deity of the Folk Religion, but he has also strong links with Taoism.

In most Chinese temples one sees a large bronze incense burner placed in the outer courtyard near the entrance gate of the major hall: this is where the worshippers put their first incense stick, as an act of homage to *T'ien-kung*. But otherwise, in the minds of the devotees, there is quite a distance between this superior deity and the daily concerns of the people.

b) *At the intermediate level* one finds a great number of deities of varying majesty and power, which are more often approached by the people. Their ranks are not all the same, and one can easily divide them into three sub-levels. This reflects what I believe to be the people's own mind, who do see some hierarchical differentiation among their gods.

It is very difficult, however, to be accurate, and one has to be very cautious. For instance, extreme popularity of a particular deity does not necessarily prove its higher ranking. Consideration of career making and of the local, regional, and national spread of a cult must also be taken into account.

With these cautions in mind, we may then proceed and group a large number of deities in one of the three sub-levels: higher, middle and lower.

(i) *higher middle level*: here I like to place deities of heavenly boards or ministries and some personified gods of nature, including star gods and dragon-kings. Individual deities like the Three Rulers (*San-kuan*): Sun and Moon (Yin and Yang, seen as deities); the god of the Eastern Peak (*Tung-yüeh* or T'ai-shan) and Yen-lo Wang, who is the Ruler of the netherworld; Hsüan-t'ien Ta-ti or god of the Pole Star (also called Chen-wu Ta-ti, Pei-chi Ta-ti or Shang-ti Kung); and Tou-mu (Earth Mother), would be included here. Most of these gods are of a mythical nature or are personified natural forces. In the human world they can be compared with high government officials, directors of boards, or even provincial governors.

(ii) *middle middle level*: here could be listed deified human beings of great achievement and special miraculous power whose cults have become very popular. Although most were originally historical figures, their cults are overgrown with later legends. Examples are: Queen of Heaven (Ma-tsu). Kuan-ti or Kuan-kung, Pao-sheng Ta-ti (although of regional importance only). Parallel with them we could list here some of the mythical emperors or culture heroes.

(iii) *lower middle level*: this category includes the greatest number of deities, many of them very close to the people: city gods, gods of trades and professions, patrons of business, protectors of health, childbirth, and gods of healing or protection against epidemics, patrons of the literary and military arts, and gods of general human happiness (*san-fu*). Many of these deities are apotheosized human beings, but some are rather mythical in origin. The city god indicates a rank or office rather than one individual: this position is in fact occupied simultaneously by many individuals of great reputation in different locations.

In the human world, their counterparts can be seen in the various local officials.

c) *at the lowest level*: we find the mass of humble gods or rather 'spirits' which are closest to daily life: the household gods, the gods of the kitchen (stove), of the bedroom, of wealth, of the privy and the extremely popular spirits of the local soil (*T'u-ti-kung*), as well as the door gods, guardians of the house. Some of these have a historical base, and reflect human personalities of some real, but lower achievement, whereas others are rather mythical. The spirits of the soil, similar to the city gods, are a function or office, rather than one individual. Within this group also fall minor nature spirits, viz. some animal or tree-spirits, or spirits of "strange" phenomena such as rock-spirits.

Many questions can be raised when looking at this arrangement. The importance of one particular deity is subject to fluctuations, not only due to imperial decrees, but also depending upon individual or group interest. For example, Ma-tsu can be considered as a deity of higher middle category, whereas for some present-day temple organizations, Kuan-ti, called *Kuan-shen Ti-chün*, would certainly be placed on the top level.

Since the deities included in this three-level scheme are, by definition, only those belonging to the popular religion, others have been omitted: the Taoist deities, Buddhas and bodhisattvas (and perhaps the Immortals) would fall within the middle group. Buddhist and Taoist saints (arhats, and ordinary immortals) seem to belong to the lower level, and are technically not "deities" but "saints" or "sages" (see below).

The above categorization reflects what I believe to be the view of the majority of worshippers; it is open to questioning and challenge: gods are still being promoted and demoted today (at least in the minds of worshippers ... and scholars), and individuals may put the spirit of the earth on a higher level than many a famous culture hero. Some Christians would have a greater devotion to the Virgin Mary than to her divine Son, or some would prefer going to mass on Tuesdays to honour St. Anthony rather than on Sundays. Leaving this flexibility, the above categorization has its definite usefulness in ordering the chaos of the supernatural world.

4. *A Discussion of Ancestors and Ghosts*

These two groups, although very important in the total world view of the Chinese believer, do not strictly belong to the pantheons. They are not divine beings. As in the human bureaucracy again, there are government officials, and there are private citizens. Amongst the latter, the ghosts are on the boundaries of normal society, or even downright outcasts. They have been compared to beggars. Ancestors belong to the spirit-world but are only venerated by their own descendants. A funeral is a family affair; it takes place in or near the home of the deceased (or in a funeral hall today), never in a community temple. Moreover, ancestor spirits are not strictly immortal: they will be offered sacrifices, as long as the descendants remember them. At some point in time, their tablets will be removed from the home shrine and placed in a common clan ancestral temple. Therefore, ancestors belong to the family religion, rather than to the community religion as such. They cannot be called gods in the strict sense.

Ghosts qualify even less to be considered deities. They are closer to ancestral spirits but with the understanding that they are lonely spirits: they do not have descendants to carry on sacrifices, or they have died a premature or violent death and bear a grudge against the living. These ghosts or *kui*, have been identified with the *preta* or hungry ghosts of the Buddhist tradition, and since medieval times, have received lavish banquets at least once a year.[8]

The attitude of most Chinese people is one of fear and uneasiness rather than positive respect. Ghosts are the beggars of the spirit-world and must be appeased lest they come back and harm the living. Again, it is clear that one cannot put them on the same level as the deities. It is ironical that people seem to spend more ritual time in propitiating ghosts and cancel their evil influences than worshipping and praying to the gods proper.

Human Characteristics

The Chinese people have created their gods and goddesses in their own (idealized) images and likenesses, and have endowed them with quasi-human, but slightly idealized, powers and attributes. They are the mandarins and ministers of the spirit-world.

Except for the "supreme beings", the ancient gods of nature and fertility, and the Buddhas and bodhisattvas, most of the gods and goddesses, and what one should call "saints" rather than deities, have been created by man in historic times. The processes of deification or canonization have not been uniform (see below) but include euhemerization and legend building in many instances.

Some mythical beings and truly historical personages of exceptional significance have been exalted to the rank of divine hierarchy. But in doing so, the Chinese have often provided them with purely human paraphernalia: they have birthdays; they enjoy family life with wives and children; they live in sumptuous residences, sometimes palaces; they possess wealth and influence over other spirits, especially over evil spirits, as well as over human beings; they have body guards and servants, sometimes even armies of spirit-soldiers, and are carried around in sedan chairs. When a divine image is paraded around a city or village to inspect his/her territory, it is a procession similar to that of a great mandarin on the move. Finally, the deities have temperaments and even tempers.

This detail is extremely important when it comes to dealing with them (see below, under relationships).

That the deities (and saints) of the Chinese pantheon imitate many features of human career-making and bureaucracy is very well known. However, generalities are easily stated, but specific details are often missing. The pantheon is not an exact replica of the imperial hierarchy. For instance, the traditional ranking of officials into nine categories does not seem to apply to the divine hierarchy. On earth, appointments were made by the imperial government usually after candidates had successfully passed civil or military examinations. Appointments in the supernatural administration are not so uniform. Sometimes one reads that every year, at the occasion of the (lunar) New Year, the Supreme Lord Yü-huang or Jade Emperor reviews his administrative personnel: gods are then promoted or demoted according to their demonstrated merits or demerits. There are, however, cases in literature and history where gods are appointed by the earthly emperors, by religious leaders, or even by popular acclamation. Emperors may also bestow special honours and titles on gods of unusual merit. One can thus see that the record is not clear and that generalizing statements tend to be misleading.

A close examination of the titles given to many deities is very revealing: it shows that there is some hierarchical structure, but also that it is not too rigorous, quite different from the imperial hierarchy.

In this examination, the "supreme beings" will be left out: they are often identified with the creative energies of the cosmos and are beyond human manipulation. As for the lower ranking deities, the many titles given to them reflect somehow their divine status and enforce the common view that they are conceived of in a pattern similar to that of the imperial hierarchy.

General terms used to refer to divine spirits are *shen* and *shen-ming*: "spirits" and "bright spirits" (compare with Hindu *devas*: "shining ones"). More rarely one encounters *shen-ch'i*, "spirits or gods of heaven and earth". Among the common people one also hears *Fo* (literally "Buddha") and *p'u-sa* ("bodhisattva") not just to refer to the Buddhist cult figures, but even to the gods of the folk religion. Especially *p'u-sa* is frequently used as a practical synonym of *shen*.

In temple worship, the major deity enthroned on the central altar, and usually the patron deity of the community, is called *chu-shen*, "master-deity", in contrast with the *p'ei-ou shen*, the "auxiliary or accompanying deities", installed on side altars (Compare with "master-guest" and "accompanying guests" at a Chinese banquet.)

Among the higher ranks in the celestial hierarchy, one finds titles like *Ta-ti*, "Great Lord", or perhaps "Great Emperor", "Great Ruler"; *Ti*, "Lord"; *Sheng-ti*, "Holy Lord.

Parallel with those, and probably of similar status are:

T'ien-chün	Heavenly Monarch
Ti-chün	Lord Monarch
Hsing-chün	Star Monarch

Chen-chün	True Monarch
Lang-chün	Master Monarch
Chün	Monarch
T'ien-tsun	Heavenly Honourable
T'ien-fu Ti-mu	Father Heaven and Mother Earth

Among the family members of those high ranking celestial officials are listed divine spouses, princes, and princesses:

T'ien-shang Sheng-mu	Holy Mother in Heaven (commonly named *Ma-tsu*, ancestral aunt)
Mu	Mother
Lao-mu	Old Mother
T'ien-Fei	Heavenly Concubine (= Holy Mother)
T'ien Hou	Heavenly Queen (= Holy Mother)
Niang-niang	Lady
T'ai-tzu	Prince
Kung-chu	Princess

The following series of titles seem to be of a slightly lower rank but exceptions are possible. The titles are parallel to human titles of nobility and relate to *wang* (king), *chu* (lord), *kung* (duke), *hou* (marquis), and *po* (earl):

Wang	King, Prince, Lord
Sheng-wang	Holy King
Ta-wang	Great King
Tsun-wang	Honourable King
Ta-wang-kung	Great Lordly King
En-wang	King-Benefactor
T'ien-wang	Heavenly King
Lung-wang	Dragon King
Wang-yeh	Royal Master, Respected Master
Chu	Lord
En-chu	Lord-Benefactor
Chiao-chu	Lord-Founder, Religious Founder, Master of the Doctrine
Kung	Duke
Wen-kung	Literary Duke
Kung-yeh	Respected Duke
Hou-kung	Duke-Marquis
Kung-tsu	Duke-Ancestor
Hou	Marquis
Sheng-hou	Holy Marquis
Tsun-hou	Honorable Marquis
Po	Earl
Ch'ien-sui	(literally: 'thousand years') His Highness

Another series of titles do not refer to any rank of rulership or nobility but seem to be given to famous teachers (perhaps honorary, like 'Doctor honoris causa'), and to other meritorious persons, familiarly called *yeh*, 'uncle, old man, ...'. Added to these two which occur most frequently, are a few other titles.

Shih	Teacher
Tsu-shih	Ancestral Teacher, Founder
Ming-shih	Bright Teacher
T'ai-shih	Great Teacher
Hsien-shih	First Teacher
T'ien-shih	Heavenly Teacher (refers to Chang Tao-ling and successors: 'Heavenly Master sect' of Taoism)
Tsu	Ancestor (cf. *Fo-tsu*, Buddhist ancestor or ancestral Buddha, title of Kuan-yin in the popular religion)
Lao-tsu	Old Ancestor
Hsien-tsu	Ancestor-Immortal (see also above *Kung-tsu*)
Yeh	Respected (old man)
Shen-yeh	Respected Spirit
Shih-yeh	Respected Scholar
Shih-yeh	Respected Ambassador
Ti-yeh	Respected Lord (see above) see also above *wang-yeh*; and below *chiang-yeh*
Ta-sheng	Great Saint
Ta-hsien	Great Immortal
Ta-shih	Great Ambassador
Hsien-sheng	"First-Born", Sir

Among the military officials, the most remarkable and numerous are the generals and marshals:

Chiang-chun	General
Ta chiang-chun	Great General
Chiang-chun wang	King-General, or General King
Yüan-shuai	Marshall
Ju-shuai	Lord-marshall

Among the female deities of lower rank, are the following titles:

Fu or *Fu-jen*	Lady, Spouse
Fei	Consort
Niang	Lady, Aunt
Hsüan-nü	Mysterious Female
Hsien-ku	Female Immortal, Fairy
Ma	Mother
Wang-ma	Royal Mother
Chen-chieh-ma	Faithful (chaste) Widow
Chieh	Elder Sister

Although we have left Buddhist objects of worship out of our discussion, for reasons of comparisons it is important to note the variety of titles used in this context.

Fo	Buddha
Ku-fo	Old (ancient) Buddha
P'u-sa	Bodhisattva
Fo-tsu	(see above) literally Ancestral Buddha, in fact it is an epithet for Kuan-yin
Wang	King, Prince, applied to Bodhisattva Ti-tsang
Sheng	Saint
Ming-wang	Bright King
Tsu-shih	Ancestral Teacher
Ho-shang	Monk
Lo-han	Arhat, Saint
Kung	Duke or Honorary Title "Uncle"
Tsun-wang	Honourable King
T'ien-nü	Heavenly Maiden
T'ung-tzu	(Heavenly) Youth

For reasons to be mentioned later (see the discussion about "ghosts becoming gods"), we must include the terminology used in the folk religion when referring to several groups of "ghosts", *kui*. The following titles point to different types of rationalization:

You-ying-kung	Duke Responding to Prayers
You-ying-ma	Goddess Responding to Prayers
Ta-chung-yeh	Public Old Man?
Ta-chung-ma	Public Mother?
I-min-yeh	
Pai-hsing-kung	

Besides these titles, there are several others given to ghosts for reasons of 'spiritual diplomacy' (see below), such as "duke, great king, marshall", etc. The more common titles given to ghosts are the following:

kui	Ghost, Evil Spirit
Mo	Evil ghost (also combined, *mo-kui)*
kui-shen	Spirits (in general, includes both good and evil spirits
erh-kui	Hungry Ghosts
hao hsiung-ti	Literally "Good Brothers", euphemism for "Hungry ghosts"
k'u-hun	Lonely Spirit, Orphan Spirit
hsieh-shen	"Demonic Spirit", evil ghosts manifesting themselves as good spirits
yao-kuai	Evil Fairy
yao-ching	Evil Fairy
hsiao-shen	"Little God"
hsiao-niang	"Little Maid"
nü-hun	Female Spirit
shui-kui	Water Ghost

The great variety of these titles and appellations is amazing and testifies to the great imagination of the Chinese worshippers. But one conclusion is quite obvious: there is a hierarchy of authority implied in the nomenclature. Yet, one should be careful: the distinctions of functions and levels of official positions are not so clearcut as is often believed. In that respect, the divine hierarchy is not totally similar to its human counterpart. Some authors have greatly overstated the case, as for example:

> The different gods are positive bureaucrats with a strict hierarchy of rank and with clearly defined powers. They keep registers, make reports, issue directives, with a regard to formalities and a superabundance of papers which the most pedantic administration on earth might well envy.[9]

The overstatement refers to the "strict hierarchy" and "clearly defined powers". The belief system and the terminology used within it do not warrant this conclusion. For instance, *wang*, king or prince, seems to be a higher position in the human realm than *kung*, duke. Yet Kuan Kung is for all practical purposes, a higher deity than many others called *wang*. Powers are not always clearly defined and frequently overlap: several deities are responsible for health; some deities once had particular functions but these gradually extended so as to make them "general purpose" protectors. Examples are Ma-tsu and even Kuan Kung.

The variety of titles does however point to the fact that there is a divine hierarchy, that the gods and goddesses or divine spirits all obey the highest ranking god (in the popular religion), the Jade Emperor. But the clear distinction of offices and responsibilities does not literally copy the human administration. There is probably room left for the imagination of the worshipper and for the use of "spiritual diplomacy".

Since these titles do not often indicate the precise status of a particular deity compared to others, one needs other criteria to supplement them. Without going into detail, I'd list the following: origin, popularity and spiritual power (*ling*); number and size of temples, extent and type of worship (for example the type of spirit-money offered); iconography; function; official patronage. Used in combination, sometimes with caution, one can gain a fairly accurate idea of the rank of a particular deity in the heavenly administration. Most of these criteria have been implicitly used in establishing the various levels described above.

What is perhaps a more decisive characteristic of the 'human' aspect of China's deities, is the way relationships between human beings and their gods are portrayed in literature or take place in the realities of daily life. Toward the deities of the highest level, an attitude of respect and worship prevails: they receive lavish sacrifices, are approached with humble prayers of supplication, forgiveness and thanksgiving. This is exemplified in the traditional imperial sacrifices to Heaven, and, in a different but parallel way, in the great sacrificial rites of renewal performed by Taoist priests to honour the Three Heavenly Honoured Ones. The deities (and spirits or saints) of the lower levels are approached in quite different ways by the common people. People's attitudes toward them reflect, or rather imitate, their ways of behaving toward various categories of their fellow-men. When a person approaches a deity he/she usually has a very concrete motive in mind: the obtaining of some material favour. The way in which this favour is requested depends very much on the relationship between the two principals involved.. In human society parents usually give orders to their young children. Social equals may request favours in a polite way, sometimes with insistence, up to the point of insolence. At other times they may use flattery, promises, and, if that does not work, threats which can include feelings of bitterness and anger. In extreme cases, and especially toward inferiors or enemies, one might use violence or torture. Toward one's superiors one is more cautious and polite, but flattery, gifts, and even bribery often accompany the request for a favour.

It appears that most of these human social relationships also apply to man's attitude toward his gods. The efficacy of a particular god's response to human prayers constitutes his/her *ling* or spiritual potency and reputation. In daily worship, people burn incense to their gods, offer fruit and other kinds of food and wine, and present 'paper' money to accompany their prayers and make them more effective.

Examples abound in the literature of cases in which gods are not only requested to help, but are sometimes threatened, coerced, or at least exhorted with reason and arguments. A few cases should suffice to illustrate the general principle:

(i) Many worshippers ask divine favours and make vows in return for a prayer granted.

(ii) Sometimes the god's statue is exposed to the heat of the sun in the marketplace in order to force him to send rain in cases of protracted drought.[10]

(iii) There is a hilarious example in the biography of the Sung Poet-statesman Su Tung-po who went to pray for rain in a mountain temple:

> On the south of the Wei River there is a high mountain range, generally known as the Tsinling Mountains, and in this range the highest and best-known peak is the majestic Taipo. On top of the Taipo Mountain, in front of a Taoist temple, there was a little pool where lived the God of Rain, a "dragon" who could disguise himself in the form of any small fish. Su tung-po went up to this temple and prayed. He pleaded for the farmers, but, like a good lawyer, he tried to make the Dragon God see that a drought or famine was not to the god's own interests. After flattering the god a little, he said in the official prayer, "there has been no rain or snow since last winter. Thou knowest well that the people's lives depend upon their crops. If it doesn't rain now, there will be a famine; the people will starve and be forced to become bandits. This is not only my personal duty as a magistrate to prevent: as a spirit, thou shouldst not stand quietly by and do nothing about it. His Imperial Majesty has conferred upon thee the different honours, and we have kept up the sacrifices, all for this day when we may need thee. Wilt thou please listen and fulfil thy obligation to His Majesty?"[11]

(iv) The god's displeasure and human promises to mend evil ways is the sequel to the above story. After Su's prayer, there was still no rain. He eventually discovered that a Sung dynasty emperor had declared the god a count, whereas during the earlier T'ang period, he had been a duke. This was equivalent to degradation and had caused the god's anger. After Su wrote to the court for reconsideration, the rain finally came.[12] Many more examples like this can be found in literary sources.

People's attitudes toward ghosts and ancestors are somewhat different. Ghosts are certainly not cherished or respected, rather they are feared, but because of their powers, they are still treated with caution. People often treat them in ways that resemble the treatment of beggars and bandits (and in some societies, policemen) in the human world. Rather than merely chasing them away, they are offered some food and drink (bandits and policemen are bribed) in the hope that they will leave people in peace. Even rituals of exorcism are sometimes conceived of in this way. Rather than displaying only a simple show of spiritual power that results in expelling the evil spirit, Chinese exorcists usually also give the spirit a meal and some (pocket) money. In the case of some higher-placed but potentially obnoxious spirits, they are even feasted (wined and dined) before being finally chased away. It is, once again, a "humane" way of dealing with the spiritual forces, in which some concessions are made. (The Gospel has a similar story: Jesus cast out a horde of devils, but allowed them to enter into a herd of swine.)

Towards their ancestors, the Chinese are both respectful and pragmatic. They cherish the memory of their deceased kin, but do not shrink back from "using" their ancestors' bones to their own advantage. This is certainly a way of manipulating the supernatural for one's own worldly benefits.

One final application of the general principle of human/spiritual interaction can be seen in the powers of Taoist priests. While it is common experience that human beings in a position of authority are able to manipulate and control those below them, it is similarly believed that Taoist priests are able to control various divine spirits and summon them to the world of men in order to bestow spiritual blessings. The hierarchical rank of a priest increases as the number of deities under his control expands. This is also a general principle in exorcism: evil spirits, and even benevolent deities are expelled through the supernatural help of higher spirits. The more spirits a priest controls, the more effective he will be as an exorcist. There is a report of a Taoist master who chased away from the temple a lower ranking but popular deity, Third Prince, who had entered the premises during a ceremony without the priest's permission.[13]

Origin or "Birth of the gods"

In most general terms, one can state that the Chinese deities were born in the minds of the Chinese people. Some of them had a factual or historical base to start with, but legend builders, religionists and worshippers embroidered the historical facts so that in the end, history and myth are imperceptibly interwoven.

The details of these various processes are very complicated. First, one has to take into account the "three teachings" (*san chiao*) each with its own pantheon; next, one cannot treat all the deities or spirits in an identical way: there is, it appears, although this impression has to be verified, a variety of ways in which individual deities or spirits are "born"; the proportion of history and legend may greatly vary. In the third place, the categorization of deities, which was discussed above, is not at all clear, otherwise one would have neat groups of deities whose origins would be very similar, if not identical. Therefore, instead of helping, those lists are often an obstacle creating more confusion.

It is not my intention to discuss the origin of religion in general, nor of Chinese religions in particular. The only objective here is to discover and analyze the various ways in which Chinese deities or spirits, more in particular those of the folk religion, have probably come into subjective existence. ("Subjective" here means that one must leave out their objective existence, or "true" existence. This question cannot even be asked in our present context.) The origins of belief in Heaven (*T'ien*) or *Shang-ti* belong to prehistory; so do the origins of belief in most nature deities, including the gods of fertility and the origin of the ancestor cult. One may speculate here about animistic, totemistic, and shamanistic beginnings, but it remains pure speculation.

The gods of Taoism and Buddhism, on the other hand, can be more closely examined. There are historical clues about their creation, and, in general terms, one can propose the mythologizing tendency (instinct?) of the respective religious communities as the creative force behind the Buddhas, bodhisattvas, Taoist deities and immortals. Many of the mythical sage-rulers are probably culture heroes, who were later endowed with true human personalities: this is the opposite of the euhemeristic phenomenon, a characteristic of the more rationally oriented Confucian scholars.[14] Of course, one single factor does not usually explain the origin and later evolution of one cult figure. For example, *Huang-ti* or the Yellow Emperor is a complex figure: the achievements attributed to him make him appear as a culture hero; later on he was apotheosized together with Lao-tzu into a divine being (he still is an important Taoist deity today), but perhaps his origins can be found in a localized clan figure, that outgrew its limited boundaries and gradually became more universal.[15] Separate studies should be undertaken about each of the sage kings and mythical beings to unravel the various influences and factors involved in their final *Gestalten*: Shen-nung, Fu-hsi, Nü-kua, Yao, Shun, Yü, etc. Their genesis and final configurations may have a lot in common, but there certainly are also individual characteristics assigned to each of them.

When we come to our more important and most interesting target, the gods and goddesses of the folk religion, we are faced with a phenomenon that is rightly called euhemerism or mythologizing, but this latter term is rather ambiguous. It is the phenomenon that many of the deities of the Chinese popular pantheon were historical personages to begin with, but have later on, for a variety of reasons, been elevated to super-human status or become deified. (This is one reason why I keep talking about the "human" gods of China.) Once again, each deity or cult figure deserves a separate study since, besides similarities in their genesis, there are also many differences.

Rather than discussing abstract principles, we should examine some concrete examples. Only then can inductive rules be established. If one looks at the divine objects of worship most popular in Taiwan today, one has a good starting point. According to Lin Heng-tao,[16] the popularity of a particular deity can be evaluated by means of the number of temples dedicated to this deity. Once the popularity level is established, one can further investigate the origin of the cult. Here follows a list of the fifteen most popular cult figures in modern Taiwan (list established in 1960); they all have at least 50 temples dedicated to them. Altogether they "own" 3,303 out of 4,220 temples.

	Name of Deity	*Number of Temples*
1.	Wang Yeh (Royal Master)	717
2.	Kuan-yin	441
3.	Ma-tsu	383
4.	T'u-ti-kung (Local Spirit of the Soil)	327
5.	Shakyamuni (Historical Buddha)	306
6.	Hsüan-t'ien Ta-ti (Lord of Pole Star)	266
7.	Kuan Kung or Kuan-ti	192
8.	Pao-sheng Ta-ti (God of Healing)	140
9.	San-shan-kuo wang (Three Mountain Gods)	124
10.	Third Prince, or Na-ch'o	94
11.	Shen-nung Ta-ti (Culture Hero, Agriculture)	80
12.	Ch'ing-shui Tsu-shih (Fukien Buddhist Monk)	63
13.	San-kuan Ta-ti (Lords of Three Realms)	60
14.	K'ai-t'ai Sheng-wang (Koxinga, Pioneer Settler of Taiwan)	57
15.	K'ai-chang Sheng-wang (Pioneer god of Changchou in Fukien province)	53
		3,300

We are not discussing here the popularity level of particular deities, but the origin of their cults. Therefore, (2) and (5) can be left out since they are Buddhist cult objects. The remaining 13 belong essentially to the folk religion, although they have definite connections with either Taoism (6,13), Buddhism (12), or Confucianism-State cult (7). Moreover, the cult of T'u-ti-kung (4) and Shen-nung (11) can also be ignored here: their cults have roots in prehistoric times as one type of fertility cults or culture heroes.

The remaining deities are thus open for discussion: Wang-yeh, Ma-tsu, Kuan-ti, Pao-sheng Ta-ti, San-shan-kuo wang, Third Prince, Ch'ing-shui Tsu-shih, K'ai-t'ai sheng-wang and K'ai-chang Sheng-wang. But let us keep the series intact for a moment and briefly indicate the nature of their origins:

1.	Wang-yeh	historic roots plus legend
2.	Kuan-yin	mythological

3.	Ma-tsu	historic roots plus legend
4.	T'u-ti-kung	mythic (fertility cult)
5.	Shakyamuni	historic roots plus myth
6.	Hsüan-t'ien Ta-ti	mythic (stellar deity)
7.	Kuan-ti	historic roots plus legend
8.	Pao-sheng Ta-ti	historic roots plus legend
9.	San-shan-kuo wang	(not certain, probably nature deities)
10.	Third Prince	mythic
11.	Shen-nung Ta-ti	culture hero, mythic
12.	Ch'ing-shui tsu-shi	historic roots plus legend
13.	San-kuan Ta-ti	mythic (deities of Three Worlds)
14.	K'ai-t'ai	historic roots plus legend
15.	K'ai-chang	historic roots plus legend

Summarizing the above table, it is easy to see that there are (at least) four processes of deification at work in the Chinese religion (probably more):

1. "created" mythology-deities born from literary fiction: Third Prince.
2. culture hero and mythology: Shen-nung
3. historic roots plus mythology: Shakyamuni
4. historic roots plus legend: Wang-yeh, Ma-tsu, Kuan-ti

Focussing on the fourth group, which most directly relates to the folk religion, one can easily notice their human origins. These deities were originally true historical personages, whose biographies can be studied, although later legendary accretions make it sometimes extremely difficult to separate historical facts from legends. Among the clearest examples figure deities such as Kuan-ti or Kuan Kung; from a popular warrior during the Three Kingdoms period, he became a legendary hero, glorified in literature and opera. Having become a model of loyalty to his king, he became the patron saint of the military (not the "god of war" as many authors have called him), and even of businessmen. Today he is a major cult figure among spirit-writing associations: one group has even elevated him to the highest top of the pantheon: the successor of Yü-huang Ta-ti, and renamed him Kuan-sheng Ti-chün. In the course of time, emperors bestowed special titles upon him, from "Duke" Kung (Kuan Kung), he became Kuan-ti, "Lord Kuan" (or "Emperor" Kuan).[17]

One of the most intriguing groups of deities are the *wang-yeh* ("Royal Princes"), especially worshipped in southern Taiwan, but who originated on the southeast coast of China (Fukien and Kwangtung) where they used to be called *wen-wang* ("Lords of pestilence"). The number of temples dedicated to them hits the top of the list: 717. This is however, somehow misleading. The *wang-yeh* group consists of 132 individual deities (98 of them are found in Taiwan worship)[18] each with their own family name, which betray their original human roots. They are worshipped especially as protectors against epidemics. In Taiwan, the most popular ones are worshipped together in groups of five (surnamed Li, Ch'ih, Wu, Chu, and Fan) or three (surnamed Chu, Ch'ih and Li). As individual deities, Su-fu *wang-yeh* seems to be the most popular one, especially among the medium cults.[19] According to some legends, they would have been 360 loyal officers of the Han or T'ang dynasty,[20] but that is probably purely legendary.

Each case of "deified human being" has to be carefully investigated to discover the many possible variations on the same theme. Some cases have already been mentioned in earlier studies of Chinese religion; I'd like to refer to the works of C.K. Yang and D.C. Graham. The latter states:

> Many of the gods whose images are worshipped are noted national heroes, such as Kuan-ti, Yo-fei, and Chu-ko Liang, commemoration being actually a motive for deification. Of course there is the idea that they have supernatural power and that if worshipped they will use this superhuman potency for the benefit of the worshippers.
>
> Many of the gods who are deified men are patron deities of the occupations pursued by these men when living.[21] The deification of men has gone on until very recent years. (Several cases are mentioned.)[22]

All the examples cited by Graham refer to persons deified by the local people on account of their good government or of their generosity; moreover three of the four had been deified during their lifetimes.

When C.K. Yang discusses the "cults of deified men", he divides them into two categories: "cults of nationally prominent personalities who were worshipped throughout the country, and local cults of figures whose temples were found only in certain localities".[23]

Both types of temples, Yang goes on, are found in every community, but the number of temples devoted to deceased local figures (more rarely to living men) was the higher. An example of a national cult figure is Kuan Yü,[24] others cited are Ma Yüan of Han times and Yo Fei of the Sung Dynasty. We already know about Kuan Yü or Kuan-ti; more interesting are the cults of local deified persons:

> ...every Chinese community had a number of cults dedicated to local leaders and officials who in their lifetime had prominently served the public interest, sometimes by sacrificing their lives and fortunes. These were the men (and occasionally women, as pointed out by Shryock) who served as virtuous examples for later generations because of their great deeds, and who acquired a sacred character in the eyes of the public by being enshrined in a temple.[25]

Yang further mentions the example of "two military commanders who died" in Chekiang during the opium war of 1841-42 and whose influence continued throughout the French invasion of 1881-82. This case presents a well-documented and modern example of how a cult arises and develops "through the building of sanctuaries, public sacrifices, bestowing of imperial honours, and a whole set of mythological lore woven around the two military figures..."[26]

The reason why I felt it necessary to discuss this particular process of deification in greater detail is to set the stage for the discussion of one more type of cult formation, which has been proposed in recent years as an alternative type of deification in China: the transformation of a ghost into a god. Philip

Baity appears to be one of the pioneers of this theory, but he was followed by Steven Harrell, and more cautiously, by Alvin Cohen.[27]

Baity is the most outspoken of the three when he states that "Gods begin as 'hungry ghosts' and are gradually transformed by sacrifices into deities ...".[28] He seems to say that this is the normal process of deification, since ghosts are seen as childless, with no descendants to sacrifice to them, and are, as a result, free to serve and protect the whole community rather than just their own family. Ancestor cult is thus seen as an obstacle to a more widely spread cult.

There are several problems with this theory, some of them implied in contradictory statements of Baity himself; for instance:

> The fact that most gods were created by the worship of the dead was not only repellent to the maxims of Confucian orthodoxy, but in addition would have been repugnant to the sensibilities of the villagers and the folk tradition and their insistence on the separation of the dead ghosts and the living gods.[29]

The wide gulf between deities and ghosts has been already mentioned above and makes it unlikely that transformation of ghosts into deities would be the normal process. As I commented in a review article on Baity's book:

> None of [the gods studied by the author in his research area], can be proven to have developed from a 'withered corpse'; on the contrary, several of them were historical personages of much fame, who had been great leaders in their life-time and almost certainly led a normal life within a family. If a deceased person of great merit to the community cannot become a cult object because he has posterity, then by the same token, a great official cannot serve the community at large during his lifetime either. Family ties are not necessarily an obstacle either for government service or for cult formation. When the people start worshipping a great person after his death, they do not worship him as an ancestor but as a great person who transcends the limitation of his family.[30]

One can add that when historical human beings become deified, it often happens quite some time after their death, so that the ancestral ties may have become very loose or even forgotten. In other cases, a person continues to receive ancestral sacrifices in the clan temple, but because his role has outgrown the family framework, he is also worshipped by a wider community. Confucius certainly is such a case.

That ghosts in exceptional cases are elevated to higher ranks of worship cannot be denied. But much more historical study is needed to verify and refine such a thesis.[31]. One crucial issue at stake here is who the 'ghosts' of Baity are. In China, there are several types; first, the mass of so-called 'hungry ghosts' (assimilation of ancient *kui* with the Buddhist inspired *preta*): they are anonymous ghosts and feasted regularly during the ghost festival and on other special occasions. These are not eligible to the status of deity. Rather, after being freed from their ghostly condition, they will be reincarnated as sentient beings.

Besides these, and in the mind of the Chinese people very distinct from them, are ghosts like *yu-ying-kung* or *ta-chung ma* ("public mother"?) who receive roadside offerings after their bones have been accidentally found and buried by farmers.[32] They also are anonymous ghosts, who are given adulatory names for reasons of spiritual diplomacy. Small, local cults may arise near those shrines. But do they ever rise to the status of real deities?

Then there is another category of ghosts, who were known to the community during their lifetime. They may be individuals or groups,[33] who may have died a violent, unnatural or premature death and are believed to seek revenge on society. They may be individuals who had a long life but lived on the verge of society as loners, semi-outcasts, yet feared as powerful. I would believe that only such ghosts have a change to become deities, after sacrifices to them, made mostly out of fear, prove to be effective. In such a case, *ling* is the best guarantee of cult-formation; like saints in Christianity become saints if they could perform miracles. Perhaps such ghosts are making a point: those who were outcasts during their life, were perhaps already during their life persons of great power; a developing cult may then be seen as a rectification of an injustice. In other words, spiritual value does not always coincide with socially acceptable norms.

My conclusion in this particular matter is that much more study is necessary: Baity did some field work research, but his historical foundation was too weak. The two aspects have to be more fully investigated.

Conclusions

One firm conclusion to be drawn from the above study is that to determine "who is who?" and "who is where?" in the spirit world of the Chinese people is a most difficult enterprise. Yet it is not hopeless. Maspero's outcry is an exaggeration, and if he had looked more closely to the pantheon of the Catholic Church, he would have also been perplexed and astonished by the parallels. Besides the Three Persons of the Trinity who constitute the supreme deity, there is also Jesus Christ, god-and-man. Then there is Mary, Jesus' Mother, and the twelve or thirteen, or perhaps fourteen apostles, the four evangelists (not including the apocrypha), then the saints of all kinds, martyrs, confessors, abbots, Church fathers, holy virgins, great and small, famous or obscure, universal or local. Many are real historical figures, others only legendary. But do not forget the Old Testament: patriarchs, judges, kings, prophets, and other holy persons. Then there are all the nine choruses of angelic beings: angels, archangels, (Michael, Gabriel, Raphael, Uriel, ...) and the seven other ranks of angelic figures. There are also the guardian angels, one for each human being living on earth. Alas! there are also *kui*, the devils like Lucifer, Beelzebub and his innumerable host of minor devils, frightening and powerful. There is also a hierarchy and also, surprisingly, a process of promotion (and demotion). Saints used to be acclaimed by the faithful, now they are "processed" by the Vatican, going through a painful and long procedure of beatification and canonization. Although saints are made by God's divine grace, the Church on earth decides who has really been godlike, who has reached the ideal of Christian perfection. The Church of Rome would never canonize a Protestant or a Moslem!

The confusion about the Chinese pantheon is just a bit worse than that concerning the Roman Catholic pantheon. Incidentally, one finds movements of iconoclasm in both religions. Much could be clarified about the Chinese pantheon if the distinctions of Supreme Being versus subordinate spirits (nature spirits) and versus canonized human "saints" were clear and consistent. If such principles prevailed, things would be simplified. Looking at the pantheon from a comparative viewpoint, there is not much difference in essence, only in the details and in quantity. The Chinese pantheon is much more elaborate, partly because more than one religion has contributed to its divine personnel, and partly because Chinese religion did not have a central religious authority to curb the popular fantasy. That is what perhaps best explains the so-called confusion: the popular imagination, unbridled, uncontrolled by a higher religious authority, followed its own instincts and created new "idols" or "ideals" to worship and to ask favours from in the people's harsh struggle for survival. Possibly the people's access to those many supernatural helpers, contributed to their mental and physical survival: the gods were more benign than the government officials!

Another parallel with the Christian pantheon comes to mind: in the Middle Ages, many saints were invoked to help in specific situations: St. Anthony, in order to find lost property; St. Barbara, to obtain a good death; St. Christopher (now demoted, since he was not historical!), for protection during travel; St. Rochus, against pestilence, etc. We can see parallel functions exercised by Chinese saints—each has his/her own competence and is worshipped for particular needs.

Moreover, another analogy between Chinese and Christian pantheons is their use of stereotyped iconography making it possible to recognize the identity of a saint or a deity.

As mentioned above, both the Christian Church and Chinese religion have known periods of iconoclasm. In Catholicism, the latest but not too violent wave of reformation concerning the saints took place around Vatican Council II. The saints had become irrelevant to religious life and were also seen as obstacles to ecumenical dialogue with protestant Churches (as if saints were greater obstacles than infallible popes!). In China, the wave of hatred against religion in the 1960's resulted in the destruction of many religious artifacts and books, and many deities have probably been sent into oblivion. Yet the cult of deities continues, not only in Taiwan and other areas of large Chinese settlements, but even on the Chinese mainland.[34] The flourishing of religious life in Taiwan and the vigourous temple building within the last twenty years seems to be an eloquent refutation of the Marxist thesis that religion would die out spontaneously once people's economic problems have been solved. Moreover, growing affluence perhaps creates stronger religious aspirations: there is more material well-being, but new frustrations arise with it and that may create the need for stronger supernatural protection. As communities in Taiwan and everywhere in the developing and developed world are being divided, there is a new need for unifying symbols: the "old" gods and goddesses who can demonstrate their *ling* will remain popular as symbols of community cohesion.

In this whole process of change, perhaps many small, local spirits will fall along the roadside, but the overall cult of deities and the extreme caution to appease the malevolent ghosts will remain as strong as ever, if not stronger.

Buddhist Monk Chi-Kung
(Sung Dynasty)

Buddhist Monk Bodhidharma
Founder of Ch'an Buddhism
in China (6th C.A.D.).

Sage Emperor Yao
(2357-2255 B.C.?)

Sage Emperor Shun
(2255-2205 B.C.)

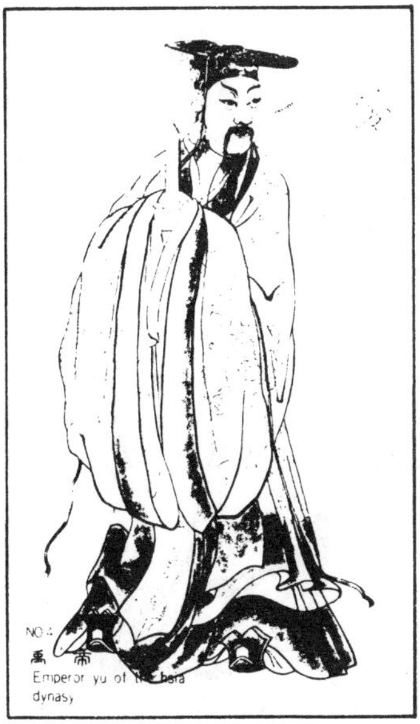

Sage Emperor Yü, Founder
of HSIA Dynasty
(2205-2197 B.C.?)

T'ang, Founder of Shang
Dynasty

Duke of Chou, Solidified the Chou Dynasty

K'ung-fu-tzu: Great Master K'ung (551-479 B.C.)

King Wen of the Chou Dynasty. Rearranged the 8 Diagrams of I-Ching.

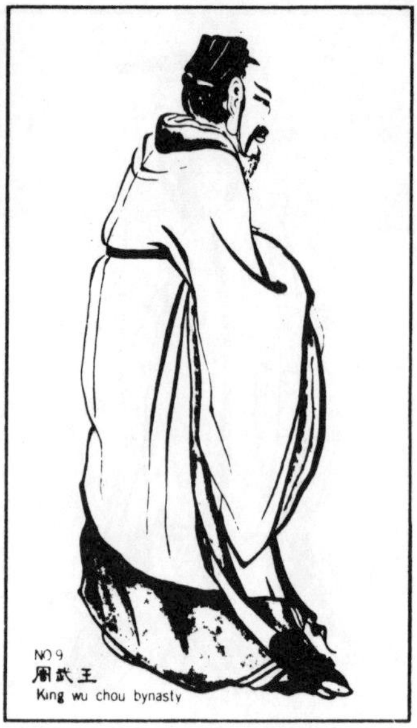

King Wu, of the Chou, Founder of the Dynasty.

Notes

1. Webster's *New 20th Century Dictionary*.
2. *Asiatic Mythology*, p. 263.
3. Literally all kinds of nature creatures.
4. *Asiatic Mythology*, pp. 252-384.
5. H. Welch. *Taoism. The Parting of the Way*, p. 107.
6. See Isabelle Robinet. *Méditation Taoiste*.
7. Recently Chi-kung has become extremely popular among lottery-gamblers in Taiwan. He reveals the lucky lottery numbers.
8. S. Teiser. *The Ghost Festival*.
9. Ou-I-Tai. "Chinese Mythology", p. 380.
10. See Eberhard. *Folk Tales of China*, pp. 113-116; and A. Cohen, "Coercing the Rain Deities in Ancient China:, *History of Religions* 17 (1978), 244-265.
11. Lin Yutang. *The Gay Genius*, p. 61.
12. Lin Yutang. *The Gay Genius*, pp. 61-62.
13. M. Saso. *The Teachings of Taoist Master Chuang*, pp. 120-121.
14. "Euhemerism" is the "theory that the gods of mythology were deified human beings", and "that myths are based on traditional accounts of real people and events" (Webster's *New World Dictionary*.) The theory was proposed by Euhemeros in 4th century B.C. Greece.
15. Jan Yün-hua. "The Change of Images: The Yellow Emperor in Ancient Chinese Literature".
16. *TSM*, pp. 36-37.
17. See P. Duara. "Superscribing Symbols".
18. Lin Heng-tao. *Taiwan Min-su lun-chi*, p. 69.
19. Liu Chih-wan. "The Temple of the Gods of Epidemics in Taiwan".
20. Lin, p. 69.
21. D.C. Graham. *Folk Religion in Southwest China*, p. 176. He mentions Tu-k'ang, Shen-nung, Lu-pan, Chang-yeh, Chang-huang, Wen-ch'ang, Confucius, Ts'ang-chih; Hua-t'o.
22. *Ibid.*, pp. 176-177.
23. C.K. Yang. *Religion in Chinese Society*, p. 159.
24. Yang, pp. 159-161.
25. Yang, p. 161.
26. Yang, p. 171. (For more detailed discussion, see pp. 168-173.
27. P. Baity. *Religion in a Chinese Town*, Ch. 6, "The Genesis of Gods", pp. 238-269. S. Harrell, "When a Ghost Becomes a God". A. Cohen, "Coercing the Rain Deities".
28. Baity. *Religion*, p. 249.
29. *Ibid.*, p. 248.
30. J. Pas. "Chinese Religion Rediscussed", p. 172.
31. A. Cohen. "Coercing the Rain Deities".
32. L. Thompson. "Yu-ying-kung".

33. I remember a mass grave erected by the local people near Kaohsiung: buried here were several scores of young working girls, drowned when their ferry sank near the Kaohsiung harbour. The grave was built to pacify their spirits and protect the community against retaliation.

34. See J.P. Pas, Editor. *The Turning of the Tide*. Hong Kong; Royal Asiatic Society & Hong Kong University Press, 1989.

Bibliography

Baity, Philip C. "The Genesis of Gods in Taiwanese Folk Religion: A Preliminary Analysis", *Proceedings of the American Academy of Religion*, 1974, pp. 33-47.

Baity, Philip C. *Religion in a Chinese Town*. Taipei, 1975.

Baity, Philip C. "The Ranking of Gods in Chinese Folk Religion", *Asian Folklore Studies* 36 (1977), 75-84.

Bredon, Juliet and Igor Mitrophanow. *The Moon Year. A Record of Chinese Customs and Festivals*. New York: Paragon Book Reprint Corp., 1966 (1st Edition: Shanghai, 1927).

Burckhardt, V.R. *Chinese Creeds and Customs* (3 Vols.). Hong Kong: South China Morning Post Ltd., 1953-58, Taipei Reprint: 1969.

Chamberlain, Jonathan. *Chinese Gods*. Hong Kong: Long Island Publishers, 1983.

Cohen, Alvin. "Coercing the Rain Deities in Ancient China", *History of Religions* 17 (1978), 244-265.

Day, Clarence B. *Chinese Peasant Cults, Being a Study of Chinese Paper Gods*. Shanghai: Kelly & Walsh Ltd., 1940. Reprint: Taipei: Ch'eng Wen Publishing Co., 1969.

Doré, Henri. *Researches into Chinese Superstitions* (Vol. 6). Taipei Reprint, 1966.

Duara, Prasenjit. "Superscribing Symbols: The Myth of Guandi, Chinese God of War". *JAS* 47 (1988), 778-795.

Eberhard, Wolfram. Tr. & Ed. *Folktales of China*. Chicago: University of Chicago Press, 1965 (1st Edition: London: Kegan Paul, 1937).

Goodrich, Anne Swann. *The Peking Temple of the Eastern Peak*. Nagoya (Japan): Monumenta Serica, 1964.

Graham, D.C. *Folk Religion in Southwest China*. Washington D.C., 1961.

Grube, Wilhelm. Tr. *Feng-shen-yen-i, Die Metamorphosen der Götter*, (Ch. 1-46, & Summary of Ch. 47-100 by Herbert Mueller), 2 vols. Taipei: Ch'eng Wen Co. Reprint, 1970.

de Harlez, Charles. *Le Livre des Esprits et des Immortels. Essai de Mythologie Chinoise* (Mémoires de l'Académie Royale des Sciences, des Lettres et des Beaux-Arts de Belgique, Tome 51). Brussels, 1893.

Harrell, Steven. "When a Ghost Becomes a God", pp. 193-206 in A.P. Wolf, Ed., *Religion and Ritual in Chinese Society*. Stanford University Press, 1974.

Hodous, Lewis. *Folkways in China*. London: A. Probsthain, 1929.

Jan Yün-hua. "The Change of Images: The Yellow Emperor in Ancient Chinese Literature". *JOS* 19 (1981), 117-137.

Lin, Yutang. *The Gay Genius. The Life and Times of Su Tungpo*. New York: The John Day Co., 1947.

Maspero, Henri. "The Mythology of Ancient China", pp. 252-384 in J. Hackin, *et al, Asiatic Mythology*. New York: T.Y. Crowell Co., n.d.; Reprinted in 1963.

Ou-I-Tai. "Chinese Mythology", pp. 379-402 in *New Larousse Encyclopaedia of Mythology*. London, 1968 (1st Edition, 1959).

Pas, J.F. "Chinese Religion Rediscussed" (Review Article of Baity. *Religion in a Chinese Town*. Taipei, 1975). *JRAS*, Hong Kong Branch, 19 (1979), 149-175.

Robinet, Isabelle. *Méditation Taoiste*. Collection "Mystiques et Religions". Paris: Dervy Livres, 1979.

Saso, Michael. *The Teachings of Taoist Master Chuang*. New Haven: Yale University Press, 1978.

Teiser, Stephen F. *The Ghost Festival in Medieval China*. Princeton: Princeton University Press, 1988.

Thompson, Laurence G. *Chinese Religion: An Introduction*. Encino & Belmont, California: Dickenson Publishing Co., 1978 (4th Edition) (1st Edition: 1969, 2nd Edition: 1975).

Thompson, Laurence G. *Chinese Religion in Western Languages: A Comprehensive and Classified Bibliography of Publications in English, French and German Through 1980*. Tucson, Arizona: University of Arizona Press, 1985 (published for the Association for Asian Studies).

Thompson, L. "Yu-ying-kung: The Cult of Bereaved Spirits in Taiwan". pp. 267-277 in L. Thompson, ed. *Studia Asiatica. Essays in Felicitation of Professor Ch'en Shou-yi*. San Francisco, 1975.

Welch, Holmes. *Taoism: The Parting of the Way*. Boston: Beacon Press, 1957 & 1966.

Yang, C.K. *Religion in Chinese Society*. Berkeley & Los Angeles: University of California Press, 1961.

Chinese Sources

Ch'i, Te-tsai. *Taiwan miao-shen chuan* (*TMSC*) ["Biographies and Legends of Spirits (Worshipped) in Taiwan Temples"]. Toulin, Yünlin County (Taiwan): Hsin-t'ung Bookstore, 1979.

Chui Yün-yen. *Taiwan min-chien hsin-yang chu-shen chuan*. [Biographies of the Deities of Taiwan Folk Religion], Taipei, 1984.

Fang, P'ing-shan. *Chung-kuo shen-ming kai-lun* (*SMKL*) ["Introduction to the Deities of China"]. Taipei: Hsin wen feng Publishing Co., 1979.

Ling, Heng-tao. "Taiwan min-chien hsin-yang te shen-ming" ["Deities of Taiwan Folk Belief"], pp. 67-89. In: *Taiwan min-su lun-chi* (*TMSL*) ["Essays on Popular Customs of Taiwan"]. Taiwan-sheng wen-hsien, 1977.

Lin, Heng-tao. *Taiwan Szu-miao Ta-ch'üan* (*TSM*) ["Complete List of Taiwan Temples"], Taipei, 1974.

Liu Chih-wan. "The Temple of the Gods of Epidemics in Taiwan". *Bulletin of the Institute of Ethnology* (Academia Sinica, Taipei), No. 22, 1966, pp. 53-95. (Chinese, with English summary, pp. 93-95.

Lü Dzongli and Liu Qun. *Zhongguo minjian zhushen* (*ZMZ*) ["The Popular Deities of China"]. Shijiazhuang (China): People's Press, 1987.

List of Characters

Chang T'ien-shih 張天師
chen-chieh-ma 貞節媽
chen-chün 真君
Chen-wu Ta-ti 真武大帝
Ch'eng-huang 城隍
Chi-kung 濟公
chiang-chün 將軍
chiang-chün wang 將軍王
chiang-yeh 將爺
chiao-chu 教主
chieh 姐
ch'ien-sui 千歲
Chou (dynasty) 周
chu 主
chu-shen 主神
chün 君
ch'uan-chi shen-ming 傳奇神明
en-chu 恩主
en-wang 恩王
erh-kui 餓鬼
fei 妃
Fo 佛
Fo-men sheng-chün 佛門聖君
Fo-shen 佛神
Fo-tsu 佛祖
fu 夫
Fu-hsi 伏羲
fu-jen 夫人
hao hsiung-ti 好兄弟
ho-shang 和尚
hou 侯
hou-kung 侯公
Hou-t'u 后土
Hsi-wang mu 西王母
hsiang-t'u shen-shih 鄉土神祇
hsiao-niang 小娘
hsiao-shen 小神
hsieh-shen 邪神
hsien-ku 仙姑
hsien-sheng 先生
hsien-shih 先師, 仙師
hsien-tsu 仙祖
hsing-chün 星君
hsüan-nü 玄女

Hsüan-t'ien Ta-ti 玄天大帝

Huang-Lao 黃老

Huang-t'ien 皇天

Huang-t'ien Hou-t'u 皇天后土

Huang-ti 黃帝

i-min-yeh 義民爺

jen-ching shen-ming 人境神明

ku-hun 孤魂

K'ung-tzu 孔子

ku-Fo 古佛

Kuan-kung 關公

Kuan-sheng Ti-chün 關聖帝君

Kuan-shih-yin 觀世音

Kuan-ti 關帝

Kuan-yin 觀音

kui 鬼

kui-shen 鬼神

kung 公

kung-chu 公主

kung-tsu 公祖

kung-yeh 公爺

lang-chün 郎君

lao-mu 老母

lao-tsu 老祖

ling 靈

Ling-pao T'ien-tsun 靈寶天尊

lohan 羅漢

Lu-pan 魯班

lung-wang 龍王

ma 媽

Ma-tsu 媽祖

Mi-lo-Fo 彌勒佛

ming-shih 明師

ming-wang 明王

mo (mo-kui) 魔鬼

mu 母

niang 娘

niang-niang 娘娘

nü-hun 女魂

Nü-kua 女媧

P'an-ku 盤古

pai-hsing-kung 百姓公

Pao-kung 包公

Pao-sheng Ta-ti 保生大帝

Pei-chi Ta-ti 北極大帝
P'ei-ou shen 陪偶神
P'eng-tsu 彭祖
po 伯
P'u-hsien 普賢
p'u-sa 菩薩
San-ch'ing 三清
san-chiao 三教
san-fu 三福
San-kuan 三官
Shang (dynasty) 商
Shang-ti 上帝
Shang-ti Kung 上帝公
shen 神
shen-ming 神明
Shen-nung 神農
shen-yeh 神爺
sheng 聖
sheng-che ying-lieh 聖哲英烈
sheng-hou 聖侯
sheng-hsien 聖賢
Sheng-ti 聖帝
sheng-wang 聖王
shih 師
shih yeh 師爺
shih-yeh 使爺
shui-kui 水鬼
Shun 舜
Szu-ming 司命
ta-chiang-chün 大將軍
ta-chung yeh 大眾爺
ta-chung-ma 大眾媽
ta-hsien 大仙
Ta-mo 達摩
ta-sheng 大聖
ta-shih 大使
Ta-ti 大帝
ta-wang 大王
ta-wang-kung 大王公
T'ai-I 太一
tai-k'ao miao-shen 待考廟神
t'ai-shih 太師
t'ai-tzu 太子
Tao-te t'ien-tsun 道德天尊

Ti 帝

ti-chün 帝君

Ti-I 地一

Ti-tsang wang 地藏王

ti-yeh 帝爺

T'ien 天

T'ien Lao-yeh 天老爺

t'ien-chün 天君

T'ien-fei 天妃

T'ien-fu Ti-mu 天父地母

T'ien-I 天一

T'ien-kung 天公

t'ien-nü 天女

T'ien-shang Sheng-mu 天上聖母

T'ien-shen ti-shih 天神地祇

t'ien-shih 天師

T'ien-tsun 天尊

t'ien-wang 天王

Tou-mu 斗母

tsu 祖

tsu-shih 祖師

tsun-hou 尊侯

tsun-wang 尊王

T'u-ti (T'u-ti-kung) 土地公

t'ung-su hsin-yang 通俗信仰

t'ung-tzu 童子

Tung-wang kung 東王公

Tung-yüeh 東嶽

tzu-jan shu-wu 自然庶物

wang 王

wang-ma 王媽

wang-yeh 王爺

wen-kung 文公

Wen-shu 文殊

wu-lao 五老

wu-szu kui-li 無祀鬼厲

Yao 堯

yao-ching 妖精

yao-kuai 妖怪

yeh 爺

Yen-lo wang 閻羅王

you-ying-kung 有應公

you-ying-ma 有應媽

Yü 禹

Yü-huang Ta-ti 玉皇大帝

yüan-shih shen-ming 原始神明

Yüan-shih T'ien-tsun 元始天尊

yüan-shuai 元帥

The Strange Case of the Overdue Book: A Study in the Fortuity of Textual Transmission

Harold D. Roth
Brown University

Introduction

It is all too infrequently that present-day scholars take the time to reflect upon how the texts we analyze and interpret from times long past have traversed the centuries to arrive on our bookshelves. When one takes into account the many generations of human beings who have participated in the transmission of any given ancient text, the vagaries of their lives, the many different social and political upheavals and their impact on the libraries of individuals and governments, it is rather amazing that we possess as many ancient texts as we do. It is not often that we can study in detail the fortuitous series of events associated with the transmission of a particular text because the requisite historical information has simply not survived. Fortunately, this is not the case with one important edition of the Han Dynasty Taoist compendium, the *Huai-nan Tzu*.

In the following article I would like to trace the circuitous route by which the sole extant witness to this edition has reached the twentieth century. Although it may seem rather astonishing, it is perhaps not all that unusual to find that the reason this witness has survived is because one of the greatest textual critics of the Ch'ing Dynasty took his time in returning a borrowed book. In studying the history of this particular edition we will also be able to examine the impact its transmission has had on the quality of its readings, and hence on our ability to understand the text itself. For it is most certainly the case that textual transmission involves textual transformation.[1]

The Northern Sung Edition

The oldest extant complete edition of the *Huai-nan Tzu* is the one known as the "Northern Sung small-character edition," which is available today in the facsimile found in the *Ssu-pu ts'ung-k'an*. As is true of the other eighty-four extant complete editions of this text, it is in the lineage of the composite recension, which is a conflation of thirteen chapters from the original Kao Yu (ca. 160-220) text and commentary, and eight chapters from the original Hsü Shen (58-148) text and commentary.[2] This particular edition preserves evidence of its conflated ancestry: despite bearing the title of the independent Kao Yu recension, *Huai-nan hung-lieh chieh*, and containing Kao's Preface, the title pages of two chapters, 10 and 21, bear the title of the independent Hsü Shen recension, *Huai-nan hung-lieh chien-ku*.

The consistent use of taboo characters throughout the edition from the reign of the Sung Dynasty Emperor Jen-tsung (1023-64) allows us to approximate the date of publication as 1050. The reported presence of one taboo character from the reign of the Southern Sung Emperor Hsiao-tsung (1163-90) on the first page of Chapter 18 does not challenge this conclusion, but rather indicates that this page was probably repaired at the later time.[3] The ancestry of this particular edition remains shrouded in mystery. All that can be safely said is that it comes from a distinctly different lineage of editions than the fragment of the T'ang Dynasty manuscript found in Japan in the 1930's, and seems to represent a later stage in the transmission of the text.[4]

In an era when collectors passionately searched for rapidly disappearing Sung editions, this edition of the *Huai-nan Tzu* was avidly sought after and lavishly praised by those few who were able to examine it. The famous bibliophile Huang P'ei-lieh (1763-1825) wrote of it:

> Recently the Hanlin Junior Compiler Wang Po-shen (Yin-chih) of Kao Yu edited this book (the *Huai-nan Tzu*) and wrote to me saying, 'I have made an exhaustive search (for editions) and could find none better than the Liu Chi edition.' The Liu Chi re-edition of the Taoist Canon edition is inferior to this Sung block-print edition by a distance that cannot be measured. How much more is this so of its superiority over the other editions?[5]

A later owner, Yang I-tseng (1787-1856), called it "the most refined and rare of all editions", and the scholar Ch'en Huan (1786-1863) said it was "the most excellent edition of the *Huai-nan Tzu*."[6]

Despite these highly favourable assessments of the Northern Sung edition, modern scholars have found much to criticize in it, as I will examine below in the final section. The reason for this discrepancy of opinion can be found in the complex history of this edition during the past two centuries, which to this point has not been fully investigated.[7] In order to unravel this history it is necessary to distinguish between the original exemplar owned by Huang P'ei-lieh, and the various copies that were made of this exemplar during the nineteenth century. It is also important to remember that the extant *Ssu-pu ts'ung-k'an* facsimile is based on one of the copies, not on the original exemplar.

Transmission of the Original Exemplar

The original exemplar of the Northern Sung edition was for the most part unknown to the community of scholars and collectors until it was acquired by the famous bibliophile Huang P'ei-lieh[8] from his friend, the Yangchow book-merchant T'ao Wen-hui, (*tzu*: Wu-liu).[9] It was previously included in the collection of the Textile Commissioner of Nanking, Ts'ao Yin (1658-1712) whose family belonged to a company of bond servants of the Manchu Plain White Banner.[10] Due to his great wealth and high official position Ts'ao was able to develop an extensive collection of rare books. The catalogue of this collection, the *Lien-t'ing shu-mu* contains a listing for an edition of the *Huai-nan Tzu* in 12 volumes, contained in one case.[11] These are the same numbers possessed by the exemplar of Huang P'ei-lieh, and so there is no doubt that the one listed in Ts'ao's catalogue is the same as that purchased a century later by Huang.[12] Ts'ao did not realize the value of his possession since he only lists it as an "old edition".

The evidence for the transmission of this exemplar before Ts'ao acquired it is somewhat sparse and has been overlooked by previous scholarship. It consists of a note on the seals imprinted in the original exemplar written by a collector who owned it after Huang, Yang Shao-ho (1828-75).[13] Listing the seals in the order in which they were imprinted, Yang mentions the two seals that precede those of Ts'ao Yin and his family. These seals read "Wang-shih Yen-chao" and "Wang-shih chia," respectively.[14]

An extensive search of bibliographical sources from the Sung through the Ch'ing reveals no men with the surname of "Wang" and personal name "Yen-chao". However there are two men named "Wang" whose courtesy name is "Yen-chao".

The first of these is Wang Han-chih (1054-1123) a native of Ch'ang-shan (in Chekiang Province) who later moved to Tan-t'u, a city in Kiangsu Province near Yanchow.[15] Han-chih, a *chin-shih* of 1073, had a long and successful official career, rising to the post of Vice-Minister of the Ministry of Works. His biographies note that his petition in response to an Imperial proclamation to local officials requesting suggestions on planning the finances for the construction and maintenance of roads was adopted. This had a particularly salutory effect on his official career, moving him from a prefectural posting into the central government administration. No mention is made of any particular literary or philosophical interests. His official career is rather busy and does not suggest that he had the leisure time to build a collection of books.

The second possible owner is Wang K'o-ming (1112-78), a native of the Lo-p'ing district of Jao-chou, Kiangsi Province, who in later life settled in the Wu-ch'eng district of Hu-chou, Chekiang Province.[16] K'o-ming was from an official's family, and is said to have drawn great satisfaction from literary studies. Because he was born with an ailment affecting his spleen and stomach that worsened as he got older, he delved deeply into medical studies. As a result he not only cured his affliction but became a physician as well. His fame spread quickly when he succeeded in controlling an epidemic in the army of Chang Tzu-kai, enabling them to decisively defeat the Chin at Hai-chou. In his official career he rose to a position in the Medical Institute of the Imperial Household.

While there is no totally justifiable reason to prefer one of these men as the earliest known owner of the Northern Sung exemplar, the biographical evidence is somewhat suggestive. Assuming the families of both men continued to live in their home districts, both districts are reasonably close to Nanking and Yangchow, where Ts'ao Yin collected his library. There is nothing in the biographies of Wang Han-chih to suggest that he had either the time or the interest to acquire an exemplar of the *Huai-nan Tzu*. However Wang K'o-ming's interest in literature and medicine, and the fact that *Huai-nan Tzu* is part of the philosophical milieu from which the underlying philosophy of Chinese medicine emerged, makes him the more likely of the two.[17] Furthermore, the evidence that the title page of chapter 18 in the original exemplar contains the taboo character *shen* from the reign of Hsiao-tsung (1163-89) means that it was replaced at this time.[18] Replacement of damaged pages is an activity that often arises from either the sale or acquisition of a book. If this is so, then K'o-ming must have been the owner because only he was alive at this time.

Further evidence to corroborate this conclusion is found in the Mao I-kuei edition of the *Huai-nan Tzu* (1580). Mao's co-editor, Wen Po, was a native of the same district of Wu-ch'eng to which Wang K'o-ming retired. There is also a distinct possibility that one of the editions used by these men was a twenty-one chapter Sung edition.[19] Perhaps Wen Po borrowed this exemplar from the descendants of Wang K'o-ming, or perhaps he bought it but did not place his seal on it. Whatever the case, it must have remained in the Wang family for at least four—if not five—centuries, until it was acquired by Ts 'ao Yin.

After its acquisition by Ts'ao there is little evidence that the Northern Sung exemplar circulated among any of the burgeoning new group of scholars who, during the eighteenth century, were turning their attention to the critical study and reconstruction of Han texts and commentaries.[20] During the entire eighteenth century there is only one scholar who made use of the Northern Sung edition. The scholar is Shen Ta-ch'eng (1700-71), who used it to collate a Ming edition, probably the Mao I-kuei.[21] Because Ts'ao's collection was probably kept in Yangchow, it is likely Shen made use of it at the time that he and his senior, the famous Han Learning scholar Hui Tung (1697-1758), were employed by the Salt Commissioner of Yangchow (1754-57).[22] The fact that Hui Tung's collation notes were recorded in Shen's hand-collated exemplar supports this.

Following Ts'ao Yin's death the family fortunes declined and never again achieved the heights set by Yin himself. Ts'ao's collection was passed on within his family during the eighteenth century. Part of it was sold to a nephew, a certain Ch'ang-ling (*chin-shih*, 1723).[23] During the Chia-ch'ing period (1796-1821) Ch'ang sold off part of the collection to Huang P'ei-lieh. The exemplar of the Northern Sung edition was probably included in Huang's purchase.

The precise date of Huang's acquisition of this exemplar cannot be ascertained. However we can make a reasonable approximation from the testimony of two sources.

The first is a colophon by Huang, dated November 5-6, 1801 and attached to a manuscript exemplar of a 28 *chüan Huai-nan Tzu* edition once owned by the famous art critic Chang Ch'ou (1577-1643).[24] In this Huang tells of his desire to collate this exemplar with the Sung printed edition. Therefore he must have owned the Sung edition by 1801.

The second source is from a collection of bibliographical notes culled from the diary of Niu Shu-yü (1760-1827) entitled *Fei-shih jih-chi ch'ao*.[25] In an entry for the date July 4, 1796, Niu tells of a visit to the house of his friend Huang during which he viewed a number of rare editions. Included among these was a Sung edition of the *Huai-nan Tzu*.

Therefore, based on these two sources, 1796 is the terminal date for Huang's acquisition of the Northern Sung exemplar.[26]

This original exemplar remained within the collection of Huang for more than twenty years. A note dated May 1816 was written when Huang had just finished using it to collate his 28 *chüan Huai-nan Tzu* edition.[27] This is the last known date for Huang's possession of the exemplar. His eyesight was failing; his fortunes were declining; and he was finally forced to sell off a large section of his library to his fellow townsman Wang Shih-chung. By 1820 the original exemplar had passed into the collection of Wang, which was called the I-yün-ching she.[28]

In 1848 Yang I-tseng (1787-1856), a native of Liao-ch'eng in Shantung was appointed Director General of the Southern portion of the Grand Canal.[29] During the subsequent four years Yang purchased a major portion of the collection of Wang Shih-chung. Using the official boats of the Grain Transport he shipped these books north to his library in Shantung, the Hai-yüan ko. Yang remained at his post and organized the defense of the Canal against the Taiping rebels. He died in office in 1856. Among the works he thus saved from destruction was the original exemplar of the Northern Sung *Huai-nan Tzu* edition.

Yang's library became one of the two principal collections of the latter half of the nineteenth century.[30] It passed on to his son Yang Shao-ho (1818-75)[31] who between 1864 and 1869 wrote a catalogue of the entire collection, with special notes on the Sung and Yüan editions. Published in 1871, this catalogue, the *Ying-shu yü-lu* is a valuable source of information on the transmission of the Northern Sung edition.[32]

On the death of Yang Shao-ho the collection passed to his son Yang Pao-i (1854-1910). Being without an heir and fearful of the fate of his great collection, Pao-i wrote a new catalogue, took a handful of the most valuable editions with him to Tientsin, and turned the remainder over to the Shangtung Provincial Government. Though the government retained control, the collection was kept in the Hai-yüan ko.[33] In 1929-30 the army of the warlord Wang Chin-fa occupied Liao-ch'eng and centered its headquarters in this library. Most of the works contained therein were either stolen or destroyed. By some unknown path, the Northern Sung exemplar found its way into the Dairen Library of the Research Department of the Japanese South Manchurian Railway Company.[34]

Diagram 1

THE TRANSMISSION OF THE EXEMPLAR
OF THE NORTHERN SUNG EDITION

Owner		*Date*
Original printing		c.1050
Wang K'o-ming and descendants		c.1160-1695
Ts'ao Yin and descendants		1695-1796
Huang P'ei-lieh		1796-c.1819
Wang Shih-chung		1819-c.1850
Yang I-tseng	Hai-yūan ko Library	1850-1911
Yang Shao-ho		
Yang Pao-i		
Hai-yūan ko as administered by the Shantung Provincial Governemnt		1911-1929
Hai-yūan ko occupied by the army of Warlord Wang Chin-fa		1929-1930
Library of the Southern Manchurian Railroad Company, Dairen		c.1930-1945
Russia		1945-present

This was the official scholarly arm of the government of the Japanese occupation state of Manchukuo. At the close of World War II, the library was occupied by the invading Russian Army and its valuable editions, probably including the Northern Sung exemplar, were removed to Russia.[35] The original exemplar of the Northern Sung *Huai-nan Tzu* has not to this point reemerged. It has, for all intents and purposes, been lost. Were it not for the copies made during the nineteenth century, we would no longer have testimony to this valuable edition.

The Copies of the Original Exemplar

The facsimile of the Northern Sung edition published in the *Ssu-pu ts'ung-k'an* owes its existence to historical accident. Were it not for an instance of irresponsible book borrowing, all witnesses to this edition would be lost. The story of its origins begins with Huang P'ei-lieh's acquisition of the original exemplar in 1796. At this time Ku Kuang-ch'i (1776-1835), a brilliant but impoverished scholar who throughout his life earned his living by working in the collections of others, was employed by Huang.[36] Also at this time the most renowned textual scholar of the Ch'ing Dynasty, Wang Nien-sun (1744-1832) and his eldest son Yin-chih (1766-1834), a superb scholar in his own right, were just completing a major work, the *Kuang-ya shu-cheng*, and beginning another, *Tu-shu tsa-chih.*[37] One of the philosophical texts that the two Wangs were emending in this latter work was the *Huai-nan Tzu.*

The fame of Huang's collection did not escape the notice of the two Wangs, who were working some 800 miles away in Peking. In 1796 they had borrowed a Sung edition of the *Kuang-ya* from Huang while completing their study of this text.[38] Sometime between then and 1801, Wang Yin-chih sent a letter to Huang soliciting his assistance in locating rare editions of the *Huai-nan Tzu*.[39] Apparently Huang never replied.

Later, in 1801, when Huang was in Peking, Yin-chih, having failed to get a response to his letter, urged Huang instead to collate his *Huai-nan Tzu* editions and share the results.[40] This prompted Huang to begin work collating his 28 *chüan* manuscript edition with his Northern Sung exemplar. However, as Huang later wrote, various other projects intervened and prevented him from completing this work until 1816. In the end Huang never allowed anyone else to work with his rare Sung *Huai-nan Tzu*. This is certainly unfortunate because it no doubt hindered the research of the two Wangs. However it seems that Huang did have some justification for refusing their request for help.

To begin with, we know that Huang possessed no *fu-pen*, or duplicate working copy, of his Northern Sung *Huai-nan Tzu*.[41] Understandably he was reluctant to permit the original exemplar to be sent over 800 miles away to Peking or to even be used extensively on his own premises for fear of losing or damaging it. Furthermore we also know that Huang had reason to distrust the reliability of Wang Yin-chih as a borrower of books.

It seems that in 1796 when the two Wangs borrowed Huang's rare exemplar of an edition of the *Kuang-ya*, they borrowed it through an intermediary named Sung Ting-chih. Later when their work was published, Huang suspected that it derived primarily from his exemplar, which after five years had still not been returned to him. Apparently one purpose of his visit to Peking in 1801 was to recover his missing book. However Wang Yin-chih did not have it. He claimed to have given it to Sung Ting-chih to return to Huang. It wasn't until over a year after this incident that Huang was able to track down Sung Ting-chih and get back his exemplar.[42] Thus it is easy to understand why Wang Yin-chih didn't press his request to borrow *Huai-nan Tzu* editions from Huang when he saw him in Peking in 1801.

It is undoubtedly due to this incident of the overdue book that today we possess the *Ssu-pu ts'ung-k'an* copy of the original exemplar. The two Wangs, unable to obtain the Northern Sung exemplar from Huang, completed the *Huai-nan Tzu* section of *Tu-shu tsa-chih* without it in 1816.[43] But they still cherished the hope of one day being able to examine it. In the meantime Huang P'ei-lieh was forced by mounting debts to sell off parts of his great collection to his fellow townsman Wang Shih-chung. The original exemplar of the Northern Sung *Huai-nan Tzu* was sold between 1817 and 1819.

In 1819, Wang Yin-chih sent a copy of the *Huai-nan Tzu* section of *Tu-shu tsa-chih* to Ku Kuang-ch'i, requesting the latter's comments and hoping that Ku could provide him notes on the superior readings of the Northern Sung edition.[44] At the time Ku possessed a hand-collated exemplar of the Chuang K'uei-chi *Huai-nan Tzu* edition of 1788 on which he recorded all textual variants from the Taoist Canon edition of 1445, which he borrowed from the collection of Yüan T'ing-t'ao in 1794. Ku added to this hand-collated exemplar reference marks to *Tu-shu tsa-chih*.[45] In August 1820, Ku was able to borrow the original Northern Sung exemplar from Wang Shih-chung and he used it to once again collate his Chuang exemplar.[46] In the process, as a favour to Wang Shih-chung, he reconstructed five missing pages, inserted them in their proper place (see Plate II), repaired out of order sections, and also wrote a colophon that was inserted in the Northern Sung exemplar in which he presented fifty-two examples of its superior readings.[47] In this colophon Ku expressed his admiration for the superb work of Wang Nien-sun, whose emendations are quite often in complete agreement with readings in the Northern Sung exemplar. Furthermore he clearly stated his intention to make a copy of this exemplar and send it to Wang Nien-sun in Peking.[48] While there is evidence that he did make such a copy, he never sent it. As we shall see, he ended up selling it to a man named Hu Yü-t'ang. Instead, Ku sent his collation notes on the superior readings in the Northern Sung exemplar to Wang Yin-chih, who rearranged these and added them as a supplement to the *Huai-nan Tzu* section of *Tu-shu tsa-chih* the following year.[49]

Probably due in no small part to Ku's laudatory comments, Wang Nien-sun finally obtained the permission of Wang Shih-chung to make a copy of the original exemplar. Wang gave the responsibility for this task to his best student, Ch'en Huan, who, like Wang Shih-chung, was a native of Ch'ang-chou in Kiangsu.[50] Ch'en then asked Chin Yu-mei to make a traced facsimile, and he stored it in his own collection, the San-pai shu-she, presumably to do further research on it before sending it to Wang in Peking. He discusses this in an 1824 preface that was attached to his facsimile copy:[51]

> This Northern Sung edition was formerly stored in the Pai-Sung i-ch'an collection of Huang Jao-p'u (P'ei-lieh). Later it went to the collection of Wang Liang-yüan (Shih-chung) of the same city (i.e., Ch'ang-chou). Mr. Wang Huai-tsu (Nien-sun) of Kao-yu entrusted me with the task of borrowing and copying it and sending it to him in Peking. Then I asked Mr. Chin Yu-mei to make a traced facsimile, and I stored it in the San-pai shu-she. The exemplar from which Ku Chien-p'in (Kuang-ch'i) made a traced facsimile copy, and increased its value to 40 silver dollars, is this one. April 1824, written by Ch'en Huan.[52]

Ironically, ten years later it was to this highly-valued facsimile made by Ku Kuang-ch'i that Ch'en had to turn in order to finally complete his textual research on the *Huai-nan Tzu*. He borrowed it from its purchaser, Hu Yü-t'ang to emend the illegible characters in his own facsimile.

> The Northern Sung edition of the *Huai-nan Tzu* in 21 *chüan* is the most rare edition. Formerly it was stored in the Shih-li-chü collection of Huang Chu-cheng (P'ei-lieh) of Soochow. Later it went to Mr. Wang (Shih-chung) of Shang-t'ang. Minister Wang (Nien-sun) had it borrowed and copied, and asked me to collate it. Many of the characters were indecipherable (due to damage). Collation and comparison were rather difficult. I did not get along with Mr. Wang (Shih-chung). Thus I was unable to inspect and copy his books. This was a constant regret for me.

> Ku P'in-weng (Kuang-ch'i) once had a traced facsimile, which he praised as being of high quality. Mr. Hu Yü-t'ang purchased it for 40 silver dollars. It was exactly like the original exemplar that was stored in the Shih-li-chü (of Huang P'ie-lieh). Now I have borrowed this facsimile from Yü-t'ang to use for collating. I once again see how valuable it is. Also, because Mr. Lan-lin (Ch'en Cheng-chih) wrote me with a request to do this, I am using it to collate his Chuang edition for him. ...April 1834.[53]

Thus Ch'en Huan was able to use the high-quality facsimile of Ku Kuang-ch'i to improve the readings in the copy that was made for him by Chin Yu-mei that contained many indecipherable characters. Unfortunately, the valuable facsimile of Ku Kuang-chi and Ch'en's facsimile have both failed to survive. However before Ch'en's copy was lost, Liu Lü-fen (*hao*: Mao-sheng) (1827-79) made his own traced facsimile of it. His brief colophon simply says:

> In 1871 I borrowed this book and the copying was begun. It continued until completion on March 12, 1872.
>
> Written by Liu Lü-fen of Chiang-shan at the Wu-men Publishing Company.[54]

Liu's copy later became part of the Han-fen lou in Shanghai, the library of the Commercial Press. It is now in the Peking Library. In 1920, a photolithographed facsimile copy was made by the Commercial Press and included in the first series of the *Ssu-pu ts'ung-k'an*. This *Ssu-pu ts'ung-k'an* edition was reproduced by I-wen Publishing Company in Taipei in 1974. Through these latter two editions the original Northern Sung exemplar of the *Huai-nan Tzu* is accessible today.

This research contains several new conclusions. Contrary to previous scholarship, Chin Yu-mei and Wang Nien-sun never owned their own facsimiles of the original exemplar.[55] Chin did, in 1824, make a copy for Ch'en Huan, but it remained with Ch'en and was never sent to Wang.[56] In 1834, Ch'en borrowed the superior traced facsimile of Ku Kuang-ch'i in which Ku had replaced the five pages missing from the original exemplar. He used this to improve the readings of his own facsimile. Evidence for this can be seen in the extant *Ssu-pu ts'ung-k'an* edition, which is copied from Liu Lü-fen's tracing of Ch'en's facsimile: there are five pages that have obviously been replaced (compare Plates I and II). Ch'en's facsimile is thus the result of the copying and editing work of three scholars: Chin Yu-mei, Ch'en, and Ku Kuang-ch'i.

The copies of Ku Kuang-ch'i and Ch'en Huan are no longer extant. The original exemplar is probably lost. The sole surviving witness to the Northern Sung *Huai-nan Tzu*, the *Ssu-pu ts'ung-k'an* edition, is a copy, twice-removed, of Ch'en Huan's facsimile. This edition owes its existence to the incident of the overdue book borrowed from Huang P'ei-lieh by Wang Yin-chih. If Wang had been a more responsible borrower it is likely Huang P'ei-lieh would have loaned him the original exemplar in 1801, thus making the later copying work of Chin Yu-mei, on which the *Ssu-pu ts'ung-k'an* edition is ultimately based, unnecessary.

Diagram 2

The Copies of the Original Exemplar

Wang Shih-chung
(owner of original exemplar, 1819-50)
(now lost)

Ch'en Huan (1824)
(made by Chin Yu-mei)
improved in 1834 by collating
with Ku's copy
(now lost)

Ku Kuang-ch'i (1820)
sold to Hu Yü-t'ang
(now lost)

Liu Lü-fen (1872)
(Now in Han-fen lou)

Ssu-pu ts'ung-k'an (1920)

Finally there were four hand-collated exemplars that recorded readings from the Northern Sung edition. They were written by Shen Ta-ch'eng (1757), Huang P'ei-lieh (1816), Ku Kuang-ch'i (1820) and Ch'en Huan (1834). The latter two are still in existence.[57] Ku's hand collated exemplar is discussed in the following section. Ch'en Huan's is the one he completed at the request of Ch'en Cheng-chih, as mentioned in the April 1834 colophon quoted above on page ?.

Textual Errors in the Ssu-pu ts'ung-k'an *Edition*

As we have seen, the greatest textual scholar of his time, Wang Nien-sun, was never able to study the original exemplar of the Northern Sung *Huai-nan Tzu*. However we have the work of four men who did carefully examine it. As we have seen above, two men who actually owned the book, Huang P'ei-lieh and Yang I-tseng, and one scholar who owned a traced facsimile, Ch'en Huan, regarded it as the best edition of the *Huai-nan Tzu*. But of the four only Ku Kuang-ch'i provided textual evidence to support his claims of excellence. In the colophon he wrote in 1820, when he borrowed and repaired the original exemplar for Wang Shih-chung, he lists 52 examples of its superior readings. These have been included in the supplement to *Tu-shu tsa-chih*. In this colophon, Ku says:

> This is truly the best of the extant editions. For example.... From the above items one can see that this edition is far above the Taoist Canon edition to say nothing of the others. As for its commentary, the places where it can correct the mistakes in the other editions cannot be enumerated. Of these I don't even provide a description....[58]

This is high praise indeed, for in *Tu-shu tsa-chih*, Wang Nien-sun calls the Taoist Canon edition the best he was able to examine.[59]

However modern scholars are not as enthusiastic about the Northern Sung edition. Wu Tse-yü acknowledges the excellent readings, but also notices a considerable number of errors.[60] In their praise for this edition, he says, Ku and Yang are guilty of "seeing the gold and ignoring the sand" that is more pervasive. Yü Ta-ch'eng echoes this:

> In looking at this book, there are enough textual errors and common forms of characters to be critical of. To spread out sand and only pick out the gold, this resides in (the eye of) the reader.[61]

Both scholars mention its similarity to the Taoist Canon edition. Yü thinks this Taoist Canon edition either comes directly from the Northern Sung edition, or that both come from the same ancestor.

Wang Shu-min also notes the affinity between these two editions. However he does not share the others' pessimism about the overall quality of the Northern Sung:

> I have completed a detailed comparison of the facsimile copy of the Northern Sung edition in the *Ssu-pu ts'ung-k'an* and the Taoist Canon edition, and from this I understand that the Taoist Canon edition is based on the Northern Sung. From time to time there are excellent readings in the Northern Sung edition that the Taoist Canon does not have. Thus the Northern Sung is superior to the Taoist Canon. It is regrettable that within it there are rather many errors.[62]

Cheng Liang-shu concurs with his teacher Wang Shu-min. He cites several of Ku Kuang-ch'i's examples of superior readings in the Northern Sung edition, then adds more that Ku did not mention. He also praises the condition of the commentary and adds that Wu Ch'eng-shih, the only scholar to write a textualcriticism of the commentary, based some of his emendations on the *Ssu-pu ts'ung-k'an* edition. However, he also takes note of the many simple errors in this edition.[63]

While it is easy to understand how the collectors Huang and Yang would not care to write about the mistaken readings in their prized possession, it is not that easy to understand how a scholar as competent as Ku Kuang-ch'i could have ignored so striking a feature. I think that the disparity in the assessments by Ku and by the modern scholars can be attributed to the fact that Ku worked on the original exemplar, while today only a thrice-removed facsimile exists, the *Ssu-pu ts'ung-k'an* edition.

I have already noted the difficulty that Ch'en Huan had in using the Chin Yu-mei copy for collating purposes. Many of the characters were indecipherable. While it is true that Ch'en improved this copy by collating it with the superior facsimile of Ku Kuang-ch'i, it is also true that the original exemplar of the Northern Sung edition contained many damaged and indecipherable characters. This is noted by Huang P'ei-lieh in a colophon written upon completion of his project of collating the original exemplar with his 28 *chüan* manuscript edition:

> In the Sung block-print edition the characters are small. Also many are damaged. Moreover the printing is indecipherable in some places. Therefore collation was difficult....[64]

However the extant *Ssu-pu ts'ung-k'an* edition, which is based on a copy, twice removed, of the original exemplar, does not have this problem. At some point along the line of copying during the nineteenth century someone had to interpret and clarify these damaged and indecipherable characters. In the process, undoubtedly, some were interpreted erroneously. Therefore the modern copies contain more of these simple errors than did the original.

I do not mean to suggest that the original exemplar studied by Ku was entirely free of errors. One glance at Ku's hand-collated exemplar of the Chuang K'uei-chi edition (facsimile reprint, *CKTCH*), on which he indicated errors in the Northern Sung exemplar, shows this claim to be unfounded. I only mean to say that during the activities of the several men who made copies, the number of errors in the text increased, and thus became a much more striking feature than it was to Ku.

Perhaps a few examples of the kind of errors being discussed will help clarify this. In the collation I did of the *Ching-shen* chapter (no. 7), I found a comparatively high number of very simple copyist's errors. For example, at *Ssu-pu ts'ung-k'an*, 2bl, I found the compound 面氣, clearly an error for 血氣 which occurs later on the page in its correct form. In the commentary at 2a10 五星 is mistakenly written as 吾工, because the copyist mistook the top part of 星 for the bottom part of 吾.

This kind of simple copyist's error occurs rather often. In the recently published mechanical facsimile of the copy of the Ku Kuang-ch'i hand-collated exemplar (see Plate III), all variants between the original Northern Sung exemplar and the Chuang K'uei-chi edition that is being collated are carefully written down. Some of the simple copyist's errors are recorded. Some are not. In the *Ching-shen* chapter, of the twenty variants between the *Ssu-pu ts'ung-k'an* and all other editions, seven are not noted by Ku. All are simple copyists' errors.

Ssu-pu ts'ung-k'an

1b10 坐 : error for 生
2a11 變 : error for 發
2b1 乎 : error for 手
3b3 揔 : error for 總
4a3 上 : error for 土
6a4 君 : error for 居
8a5 神 : error for 坤

Furthermore there are lacunae totalling six graphs of text, two of commentary on p. 12b in the *Ssu-pu ts'ung-k'an* edition that are also noted by Ku. I can only conclude from this that any errors not written down by Ku must have entered the *Ssu-pu ts'ung-k'an* edition due to the activity of the copyists, Chin Yu-mei and Liu Lü-fen.[65]

Therefore the discrepancy of opinion between the Ch'ing and modern scholars about the overall quality of the Northern Sung edition is, to a considerable extent, the result of the fact that the sole surviving witness to this edition, the *Ssu-pu ts'ung-k'an* facsimile, is a thrice-removed copy into which textual errors that were not in the original exemplar were introduced by nineteenth-century copyists. The modern assessment of the value of the Northern Sung edition is thus not based on the edition itself. Those who wish to prepare a modern critical edition of the *Huai-nan Tzu* must check textual variants in the *Ssu-pu ts'ung-k'an* edition against those recorded in the Ku Kuang-ch'i hand-collated exemplar. Until this is done, scholars who use the *Ssu-pu ts'ung-k'an* edition should take note of this problem.

The story of the original exemplar and copies of the Northern Sung *Huai-nan Tzu* edition demonstrates the extent to which historical accident has played a significant role in textual transmission and the textual transformation which inevitably accompanies it. It reminds us one again that we cannot take for granted either the presence on our bookshelves or the testimony and reliability of any single edition of an ancient text, no matter how old that edition may be.

List of Abbreviations for the Notes

CKTHC *Chung-kuo tzu-hsüeh ming-chu chi-ch'eng* 中國子學名著集成. Taipei, 1977.

ECCP Arthur Hummel (ed.), *Eminent Chinese of the Ch'ing Period*. Washington, D.C.: United States Government Printing Office, 1943.

HFLSL *Han-fen-lou chin-yü shu-lu* 涵芬樓燼餘書錄. Peking, 1951.

HNT *Huai-nan Tzu* 淮南子.

HNTCL Cheng Liang-shu 鄭良樹, *Huai-nan Tzu chiao-li* 淮南子斠理. Taipei: Chia-hsin Cement Company Cultural Foundation, 1969.

HNTSL Wu Tse-yü 武則虞, "*Huai-nan Tzu shu-lu*" 淮南子書錄. *Wen-shih* 文史 2 (1963), 291-314.

HNWSK Yü Ta-ch'eng 于大成, "*Huai-nan Wang shu-k'ao* 淮南王書考." In Yü Ta-ch'eng, *Huai-nan lun-wen san-chung* 淮南論文三種. Taipei: Wen-shih-che ch'u-p'an-she 文史哲出版社, 1975, pp. 1-56.

JPTSTC Huang P'ei-lieh 黃丕烈, *Jao-p'u ts'ang-shu t'i-chih* 蕘圃藏書題識. Compiled by Miao Ch'üan-sun 繆荃孫, Chang Yü 章鈺, and Wu Ch'ang-shou 吳昌綬. Privately printed, 1919. Reprinted in SMTP.

LTMJTP Chiang Liang-fu 姜亮夫, *Li-tai ming-jen nien-li pei-chuan tsung-piao* 歷代名人年里碑傳綜表. Shanghai, 1937. Reprint: Taipei, 1976.

PSICL Huang P'ei-lieh, *Pai Sung i-ch'an lu* 百宋一廛錄. In Chang Chün-heng 張鈞衡, *Shih-yüan ts'ung-shu* 適園叢書. Privately printed, 1914.

SB Wolfgang Franke (ed.), *Sung Biographies*. Munich, 1976. 宋代名人錄

SJCSY *Sung-jen chuan-chi tzu-liao so-yin* 宋人傳記資料索引. Taipei, 1975.

SMTP Wang Tao-jung 王道榮 (compiler), *Shu-mu ts'ung-p'ien* 書目叢編. Taipei: Kuang-wen 廣文, 1967.

SPTK *Ssu-pu ts'ung-k'an* . Shanghai: Commercial Press, 1920.

TSTC Wang Nien-sun 王念孫 and Wang Yin-chih 王引之, *Tu-shu tsa-chih* 讀書雜誌. Privately printed between 1812 and 1832. Reprint of 1870 edition, Taipei: Shih-chieh, 1963.

YSYL Yang Shao-ho 楊紹和 (compiler), *Ying-shu yü-lu* 楹書隅錄. Privately printed, 1871. Reprinted by Yang Pao-i 楊保彝, 1895, and Tung K'ang 董康 in 1911. Reprint of 1911 edition in *SMTP*.

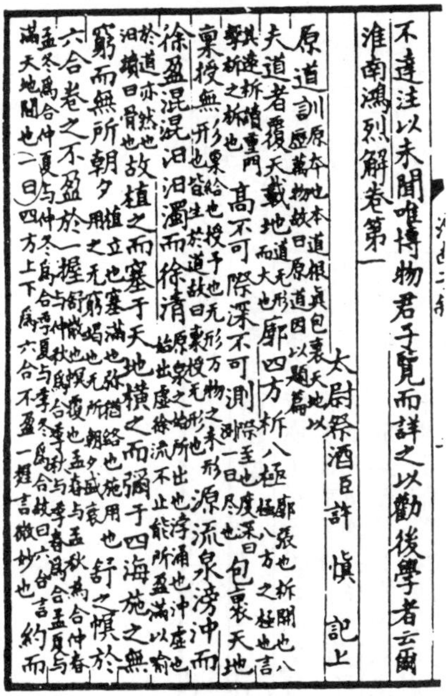

不達注以未聞唯博物君子覽而詳之以勸後學者云爾

淮南鴻烈解卷第一

原道訓 [原本也本道根真包裹天地以歷萬物故曰原道因以題篇] 太尉祭酒臣許慎記上

夫道者覆天載地 [道無形而大也] 廓四方柝八極 [廓張也柝開也八極八方之極也言其遠之柝者之柝也] 高不可際深不可測 [際一至也測盡也度深曰測] 包裹天地稟授無形 [稟給也授予也無形萬物之未形也皆生於道故曰稟授無形] 源流泉浡沖而徐盈混混汩汩濁而徐清 [原泉始出虛徐流不止也浡涌也沖虛也能以虛所盈滿] 故植之而塞于天地橫之而彌于四海施之無窮而無所朝夕 舒之幎於六合卷之不盈於一握 約而

Plate I: The Northern Sung Edition Liu Lü-fen Traced Facsimile (1872). Reproduced in the *Ssu-pu ts'ung-k'an.* chapter 1, folio 2, verso.

美而美不失故祭祀思親不求福饗賓修敬不思德唯弗

求者能有之 [言不求而所求至也] 處尊位者以有公道而無私說故

稱尊焉不稱賢也有大地者以有常術而無鈐謀故稱平

焉不稱也內無暴事以離怨於百姓外無賢行以見忌於

諸侯上下之禮襲而不離而爲論者莫然不見所觀焉此

所謂藏無形者非藏無形孰能形之 [形形而言見也] 三代之所道

者因也故禹決江河因水也后稷播種樹穀因地也湯武

平暴亂因時也故天下可得而不可取也 [不可强取] 霸王可受

而不可求也在智則人與之訟在力則人與之爭未有使

人無智者 [言己不能使人無智也] 有使人不能用其智於己者也

[illegible] 未有使人無力者有使人不能施其力於己者

也 [言己不能使人無以智力加於己] 此兩者常在久見故君賢不

Plate II: The Northern Sung Ed. (SPTK). One of the five pages replaced by Ku Kuang-ch'i. ch. 14, folio 8, recto.

宋本每半葉十二行每行廿二字注每行廿五字

道藏本重校

道藏本每半頁五行三十七字正統十年十一月十一日雕

淮南鴻烈解叙

漢涿郡高誘撰

淮南王名安厲王長子也長高皇帝之孫也其母趙氏

女遷吉按漢書淮南王傳不云趙氏女而云其弟趙兼爲趙王張敖美人高皇帝

七年討韓信於銅鞮信亡走匈奴上遂北至樓煩還過

趙不禮趙王趙王獻美女趙氏女遷吉按感云獻美人趙氏女此女字疑譌

得幸有身趙王不敢內之於宮爲築舍于外及貫高等

謀反發覺并逮治王盡收王家及美人趙氏女亦與焉

吏以得幸有身聞上上方怒趙王未理也趙美人弟兼

因辟陽侯審食其言之呂后呂后不肯白辟陽侯亦不

强爭及趙美人生男恚而自殺吏奉男詣上上命呂后

1

Plate III: The Ku Kuang-ch'i Hand-collated Exemplar (1820) Facsimile of Hsü Tsai-heng (1898). Reproduced in the *Chung-kuo tzu-hsüeh ming-chu chi-ch'eng* (1977). Kao Yu Preface, folio 1, recto.

Notes

1. I would like to define several important terms. A "text" is the unique complex of ideas created by an author. An "edition" is a distinct record of a text, whether it is a handwritten manuscript or it is printed. An "exemplar" is one particular impression of a printed edition or the actual manuscript of a handwritten edition. A "hand-collated exemplar" is an exemplar of a printed edition on which a scholar recorded his annotations, which frequently include both collations with other editions and textual emendations. A "facsimile" is either a traced or mechanically reproduced copy of an exemplar in which the format and arrangement of that exemplar is duplicated.

2. For details on these two commentaries and their merging, see my book, *The Textual History of the Huai-nan Tzu* (Ann Arbor: Association for Asian Studies [forthcoming]), Chapters 2 and 4.

3. The presence of the taboo character *shen* (written without a final stroke) was initially reported by the late Ch'ing bibliophile Yang Shao-ho in the catalogue of his family's collection, *YSYL*, p. 42b. He concludes from this that the page in question was added later. However in the *SPTK* edition this taboo is not observed. As we shall see this is far from the sole discrepancy between the original exemplar of the Northern Sung edition and the *SPTK* facsimile.

4. The T'ang manuscript fragment, which contains about one-half of Chapter 15, was found on the back of a silk scroll containing Heian court poetry. For a detailed analysis of its provenance and value, see Wang Shu-min, *Chu-tzu chiao-cheng* (Taipei: Shih-chieh, 1963), pp. 565-72. It is also discussed in Roth, *op. cit.*, Chapters 3 and 4.

5. Huang P'ei-lieh, *PSICL*, p. 27a.

6. Yang Shao-ho, *YSYL*, p. 41a; *HFLSL*, 3/40a.

7. A number of twentieth-century scholars have investigated certain aspects of the history of this edition, but their conclusions have been incomplete and sometimes inaccurate. Wu Tse-yü, *HNTSL*, pp. 295-6, and Cheng Liang-shu, *HNTCL*, p. 331, state that three scholars owned traced facsimiles, Chin Yu-mei, Wang Nien-sun, and Liu Lü-fen (*qqv.*). As we shall see, Chin and Wang never owned their own copies. They also accurately state that three scholars used the original exemplar for collation with other editions, Shen Ta-ch'eng, Ku Kuang-ch'i, and Ch'en Huan (qqv.), although Ch'en's involvement was considerably greater than this. Yü Ta-ch'eng, *HNWSK*, pp. 21-2, limits his discussion to Liu Lü-fen's copy and its provenance, and ignores the others. The brief discussion by LeBlanc is based on Yü and adds several factual errors, which I will correct below in the notes. See Charles LeBlanc, *Huai-nan Tzu: Philosophical Synthesis in Early Han Thought* (Hong Kong: Hong Kong University Press, 1985), pp. 62-3. Kuraishi Takeshiro, ("*Enanji* no Rekishi", *Shinagaku* 3 (1923): 348-51) presents a perceptive analysis, although my own conclusions differ somewhat from his.

8. *ECCP*, pp. 340-41. Huang was a native of Ch'ang-chou district in the city of Soochow, Kiangsu Province. He was a *chü-jen* of 1788, but failed the higher

exams and bought an official position. He finally retired from the civil service to a life of book collecting, beginning in 1789. He specialized in Sung editions and had a special library, the Pai-Sung i-ch'an, to house them. He himself wrote, or hired others to write, notes on his editions. Huang's notes are very highly respected and studied by collectors and students of bibliography.

9. See Huang's note in the collection of his notes *JPTSTC*, 5/19b.

10. *ECCP*, pp. 740-2. A complete and penetrating analysis of the bondservant and bannerman organizations as exemplified in the life of the family of Ts'ao Yin can be found in Jonathan Spence, *Ts'ao Yin and the K'ang-hsi Emperor: Bondservant and Master* (New Haven: Yale University Press, 1966).

The Plain White Banner was one of the top three divisions of the Manchu Army, each controlled by a Prince. Ts'ao Yin's great grandfather was captured by the Manchus when Shen-yang fell in 1621 and made a bondservant in this Banner. These bondservants and their descendants came to be the first and most trusted Chinese allies of the Manchu rulers, and as such were often favoured in the selection of officials.

Ts'ao Yin's grandfather held the very lucrative position of Salt Commissioner of Chekiang until his death in 1658, and so amassed a considerable fortune.

Ts'ao Yin's father, Ts'ao Hsi, was textile commissioner in Nanking, 1663-84. Ts'ao Yin himself held positions as textile commissioner in Soochow, 1690-92, Nanking, 1692-1712, and Salt Commissioner of Liang-huai in Yangchow. While in these positions, he was the trusted ally of the K'ang-hsi Emperor, performing various tasks, spying on officials, and actually hosting the Emperor on four visits to the South.

In Nanking Ts'ao hosted a group of scholars that included Chu I-tsun (1629-1709, *ECCP*, 182-4). He also established a printing house and published excellent editions of his rare books that are still highly valued. Ts'ao Yin most likely acquired the *HNT* around the turn of the eighteenth century.

The Dream of the Red Chamber was written by Yin's grandson about the lives of this family during its zenith of wealth and power under Ts'ao Yin.

11. The *Lien-t'ing shu-mu* is reprinted from the Ts'ao family manuscript in *Kuo-li Pei-p'ing t'u-shu-kuan kuan-k'an* (1931) vol. 4, no. 6, pp. 81-106; vol. 5, no. 1, pp. 77-102; vol. 5, no. 2, pp. 87-96; vol. 5, no. 3, pp. 91-110. The listing of the *HNT* is found at 5/1, p. 80.

12. Huang clearly states this in a collection of notes on his Sung editions first written in 1803, just after he moved them into the special library built to house them. See *PSICL*, p. 27a.

13. *YSYL* is the catalogue of this collection. It is discussed below in note 32.

14. *YSYL*, p. 41b.

15. For biographies of Han-chih, see *Sung-shih*, 347/5b, *SJCSY*, p. 237.

16. For biographies of K'o-ming see *Sung-shih*, 462/15a, *SJCSY*, p. 293, and *SB*, pp. 1114-5 (written by Manfred Porkert).

SB and *LTMJTP*, p. 277 give K'o-ming's dates as 1069-1135. *SJCSY* says 1112-78. However the general Chang Tzu-kai, whose army K'o-ming cured of the plague, was active between 1140 and 1170. (See *SJCSY*, p. 2342, *Sung-shih, chüan* 369). Thus the latter date must be correct.

The errors in *SB* and *LTMJTP* must be based on the mistake in K'o-ming's biography in the *Sung-shih*. There his death date is given as Shao-hsing 5 (1135), age 67, even though this very same biography says he was active during the Shao-hsing (1131-63) and Ch'ien-tao (1163-74) reign periods. The correct date of death should be Ch'un-hsi 5 (1178).

17. The first Chinese medical treatise, the *Huang-ti nei-ching ssu-wen* is a contemporary of the *HNT*. The two works share a basic philosophical stance and a series of interrelated technical terms. See especially *HNT*, Chapters 1, 2, 3, 7, 20. For further information on this topic see the brilliant pioneering study by Manfred Porkert, *The Theoretical Foundations of Chinese Medicine* (Cambridge: MIT Press, 1974), pp. 18, 20, 191.

18. See above, note 3.

19. Roth, *op. cit.*, Chapter 9.

20. Though not a part of this group of "Han Learning" scholars, the famous scholar and collector Ch'ien Tseng (1629-1701, *ECCP*, 156-8) owned a traced facsimile copy of a twenty-one *chüan* Sung block-print edition of the *HNT* that might have been copied from Ts'ao Yin's Northern Sung exemplar.

In the 1926 Ch'ang-shou edition of the catalogue of Ch'ien's library that was compiled and edited by Chang Yü (1865-1937) and entitled *Ch'ien Tsun-wang tu-shu min-ch'iu-chi chiao-cheng*, the note on this facsimile of a Sung block-print *HNT* is at *chüan* 3A, pp. 20b-21a.

According to *ECCP*, Ch'ien wrote the original catalogue between 1669 and 1684. It was first published in 1726. Chang Yü's edition is a compilation of several earlier editions that contains complete annotations by Chang and earlier editors on each entry. It is principally based on the edition of Kuan T'ing-fen (1797-1880).

Ch'ien Tseng was a good friend of another famous scholar and collector, Chu I-tsun (1629-1709, *ECCP* 182-4), who was in turn an associate of Ts'ao Yin. It is known that Ch'ien and Chu were strong advocates of the new practice of borrowing rare editions and making traced copies for one's own library. Both men hired calligraphers who were well-versed in this practice. Chu greatly improved his own collection by copying rare works from Ch'ien. Furthermore Ts'ao Yin also participated in this practice, borrowing and copying rare works from Chu's library.

Ch'ien's note does not indicate the source of his traced facsimile of the Sung printed *HNT*. However the fact that these men borrowed and copied each other's rare books makes it quite possible that the source of Ch'ien's facsimile was the Northern Sung exemplar of Ts'ao Yin. Unfortunately, without any further evidence we cannot definitely establish that the source of Ch'ien's facsimile was Ts'ao's exemplar. In fact, almost two hundred years ago, Huang P'ei-lieh thought of this possibility but found himself also unable to decide.

Ch'ien's facsimile was used to collate a twenty-eight *chüan HNT* that was later part of the collection of Yang I-tseng (see *YSYL* p. 44a). The note attached to this exemplar is dated May, 1782, but the author's name is lost. Ch'ien's facsimile was purchased by Sung Chih-shan (fl. ca.1820) from the famous Yangchow book merchant T'ao Wu-liu, the very man who sold the Northern Sung exemplar to Huang P'ei-lieh.

It was missing the first volume that contained *chüan* 1-4. In 1819 Kuan T'ing-fen located and purchased the missing volume, intending to give it to Sung. But the person with whom he sent it died en route and the volume was lost. The remainder of Ch'ien's facsimile is also no longer extant.

In addition to *ECCP*, information on the relationships between Ch'ien, Chu and Ts'ao can be found in the following works: Cheuk-Woon Taam, *The Development of Chinese Libraries 1644-1911* (Shanghai, 1935, rep., San Francisco: Chinese Materials Center, 1977), pp. 48-50, 60-61; Ch'en Teng-yüan, *Chung-kuo tien-chi shih* (Taipei, 1971), pp. 322-323, 394-396; and Chu Chia-hua, *Chung-kuo tsang-shu-chia k'ao-lüeh* (Hangchow, 1929), pp. 25a, 88a, 133b.

21. Wu Tse-yü, *HNTSL*, p. 301. The biography of Shen can be found in Ch'ien I-chi, *Kuo-ch'ao Pei-chuan-chi* (Privately printed, 1893), *chüan* 141.

22. *ECCP*, p. 357.

23. *ECCP*, p. 743.

24. L. C. Goodrich and C.Y. Fang (editors), *Dictionary of Ming Biography* (New York, 1976), p. 51.

25. *ECCP*, p. 593. Collected and printed by Yao Wei-tsu of Kuei-an in 1881.

26. Therefore LeBlanc's (p. 62) assertion that Huang obtained the Northern Sung edition in 1815 is incorrect.

27. Huang, *JPTSTC*, 5/20a.

28. *ECCP*, p. 341. *YSYL*, 3/41b contains a colophon by Ku Kuang-ch'i that was written on a separate sheet and included in the original exemplar of the Northern Sung edition. Dated September 1820, it states that Ku borrowed the exemplar from Wang Shih-chung.

29. *ECCP* pp. 888-89, and the introduction to *YSYL*.

30. The other was the library of Ch'ü Yung (fl. a. 1805-60), the T'ieh-ch'in t'ung chien lou, in Ch'ang-shu district, Kiangsu province (*ECCP*, p. 34). The two were referred to by the set phrase "Ch'ü in the South, Yang in the North."

31. *ECCP*, p. 889.

32. The supplement to the *YSYL* also contains copies of all the colophons of books in the Yang collection that had previously been part of the collection of Huang P'ei-lieh and Wang Shih-chung. These copies were made in 1871 by Yang Shao-ho's son, Pao-i, when the *YSYL* was initially published by Shao-ho.

In 1895 Yang Pao-i republished the work. Later, the printing blocks were scattered. Tung K'ang obtained the remaining two-thirds, supplemented the losses, and published a new edition in 1911.

It was republished in 1967 in Taipei as part of the series *Shu-mu ts'ung-p'ien*. Its four volumes are based on the edition of 1911.

33. The catalogue Pao-i compiled in 1909 lists 3,700 works in 208,300 *chüan*, including 464 Sung and Yüan editions in 11,328 *chüan*. It was published in 1931 by the Shantung Provincial Library.

None of the catalogues of this collection records the library at its full height. Unfortunately, 40-50% of its contents were destroyed in March 1861, when the Nien rebels attacked the western region of Fei-ch'eng, Shantung. (c.f. *YSYL, Introduction*)

34. The source for this information is Wu Tse-yü, *HNTSL*, p. 295-6. For details on the Dairen Library see John Young, *The Research Activities of the South Manchurian Railway Company 1907-45* (New York: Columbia University Press, 1966.)

The catalogue of the Japanese Manchukuo Dairen Library does not contain a listing of this exemplar. The catalogue, entitled *Dairen Toshokan Wakan tosho bunrui mokuroku*, was published in Ta-lien by the South Machurian Railway Company in early 1927. Hence the Northern Sung exemplar must have become part of the collection at a later date, probably after the Hai-yüan ko of the Yang family had been occupied in 1929-30.

35. I am indebted to Professor D.C. Lau of the Chinese University of Hong Kong for pointing out to me the meaning of Wu's statement that the Northern Sung exemplar was "taken out of the country." Wu says, "Fifteen years ago I heard it had been taken out of the country."

Wu wrote this in 1962. At this time, as Prof. Lau pointed out, China and Russia were still on friendly terms. Therefore, Wu had to be chary of any phrase that could be interpreted as criticism of Russia. If it had been taken elsewhere Wu would have been able to state it clearly. Young, *op. cit.*, pp. 33-34, mentions that the Russians were particularly interested in the rare Chinese books in the Dairen Library, all of which they confiscated. The rumour that years later they were returned as cultural assets has not been substantiated.

36. *ECCP*, 417-419. Ku lived at Huang's estate from 1794 to 1801, collating works from the latter's collection and helping him to identify genuine Sung editions.

37. *ECCP*, pp. 829-31, 841-2.

38. Huang, *JPTSTC*, *Introduction*, p. 3.

39. Huang, *PSICL*, p. 27a quotes part of the letter. See also Kuraishi, *op. cit.*, pp. 348-9.

40. See Huang's note dated November 5-6, 1801 in *JPTSTC* 5/19a-20a.

41. *PSICL* p. 27a.

42. *JPTSTC*, *Introduction*, p.2.

43. *TSTC*, written by Wang Nien-sun and son Wang Yin-shih, is generally acknowledged to be the greatest work of textual criticism of the nineteenth century. It contains emendations to all major classical texts. Wang Nien-sun's last note in *TSTC* is dated January 19, 1816. See 9/22/29a.

44. See the introduction to the supplement to the *HNT* section of *TSTC*, p. 1. This supplement, written by Wang Yin-chih, is dated January, 1821. It is entitled "Ku-chiao Huai-nan Tzu ko-t'iao."

45. We are fortunate to possess a copy of Ku's hand-collated exemplar in *CKTHC*, vol. 85. For Ku's note see p. 14. Also, in *JPTSTC*, 5/19a, Huang P'ei-lieh says that Ku borrowed the *Tao-tsang* edition to collate the Chuang K'uei-chi edition, and that Huang himself copied Ku's collation notes.
46. See Ku's note about this. *CKTHC*, vol. 85, p. 783.
47. Quoted in the catalogue of the later owner of the original exemplar, Yang I-tseng, *YSYL*, pp. 39a-41b. Colophon is dated September 7-16, 1820.
48. *YSYL*, p. 416.
49. See *TSTC*, ch. 9, supplement pp. 1-14. Yin-chih discusses his correspondence with Ku in a brief preface. Yin-chih's arrangement differs from that in Ku's colophon. Also it includes some passages not noted in the colophon and omits some that are. These changes must have been made by Ku since Yin-chih did not have the original exemplar to use. Small-case comments are by Yin-chih.
50. Ch'en Huan, *tzu*: Shih-fu, studio name: San-pai t'ang, studied with Tuan Yü-tsai (1735-1815, *ECCP*, 782-4) before becoming one of the most advanced pupils of Wang Nien-sun and his son Yin-chih. For his biography, see *Ch'ing-shih lieh-chuan* (Taipei: Chung-hua, 1962), 69/67b-69a.
51. This preface is inserted at the beginning of the *SPTK* edition of the *HNT*.
52. This preface is also quoted in full in the catalogue of the remaining works in the Han-fen lou, the *HFLSL*, p. 3/39b. Ch'en was not friendly with the owner of the original exemplar, Wang Shih-chung. (See the following colophon of 1834.) This must have been one of the reasons he asked another man, Chin Yu-mei to copy it. According to the *Li-tai jen-wu pieh-shu chü-ch'u ming t'ung-chien* (Taipei, 1962), p. 13, Ch'en Huan's studio name was San-pai t'ang. Therefore his library must have been the San-pai shu-she referred to in the preface of 1824.
53. This colophon is attached to a hand-collated exemplar of the Chuang K'uei-chi edition that Ch'en himself prepared on behalf of his friend, the bibliophile Ch'en Cheng-chih (*tzu*: Lan-lin). It is preserved in the *HFLSL*, p. 3/40a. This exemplar was later owned by T'an Hsien (1830-1901), who lent it to three of the most prominent textual scholars of the late Ch'ing: Chao Chih-chien (1829-84), T'ao Fang-ch'i (1845-84) and Sun I-jang (1848-1908).
54. *HFLSL*, 3/39b. The biography of Liu Lü-fen is found in Miao Ch'üan-sun, *Hsü pei-chuan-chi* (Privately printed, 1910), *chüan* 45.
55. See above, note 7.
56. This conclusion is further corroborated by the chronological biography of Wang Nien-sun and his son Yin-chih. Fang Chun-chi, *Kao-yu Wang-shih fu-tzu hsüeh chih yen-chiu* (Taipei, 1974), pp. 1-42, records the topics of correspondence between Ch'en and Yin-chih between 1824-34; no mention is made of the *HNT*. Also there is no record of Wang having received a copy of the *HNT* from anyone during this period.

This should not be at all surprising. Wang Nien-sun completed his research on the *HNT* in 1816. Yin-chih added the supplement to *TSTC*, ch. 9 in 1821. It contained Ku Kuang-ch'i's collation notes of the best readings from the original exemplar. With these notes to supplement the omissions in the earlier research, the two Wangs could justifiably feel that their research on the *HNT* was complete. Indeed, Wang's biography shows both men to have been occupied with other works during this time.

This conclusion, that Ch'en retained this copy, is corroborated by the fact that his most renowned pupil, Kuan Ch'ing-ssu, used a copy of the original Northern Sung exemplar in some research of his own in 1858. This is discussed below in note 65. Kuan must have obtained the copy from Ch'en.

Finally in 1872, Liu Lü-fen made his facsimile at the Wu-men Publishing Co. This is located in Wu-hsien, a neighbouring town to Ch'en's home of Ch'ang-shou in the Soochow area of Kiangsu Province.

57. The above discussion should correct several errors in LeBlanc, pp. 62-3. The first is that Huang P'ei-lieh obtained the Northern Sung exemplar in 1815, and was planning, with a group of friends, to prepare a new edition of the *HNT*. The historical evidence shows that the only person who wanted to prepare a new edition was T'ao Wu-liu (see Huang's note of October 1801 in *JPTSTC*, 5/19b); and of course Huang obtained his Northern Sung exemplar in 1796. Second, LeBlanc states that Ku used his own traced facsimile to collate an exemplar of the Chuang K'uei-chi edition. The truth is that Ku used the original Northern Sung exemplar to do this. Third, the date of the Chuang K'uei-chi edition is 1788, not 1789 (Ch'ien-lung 53). Finally the original Northern Sung exemplar was stored in the Library of the South Manchurian Railway Company in Ta-lien, (Japanese: Dairen) not in the "Dairen University Library". In fact Wu Tse-yü notes that a Japanese scholar, Shimada Yoshimi wrote an essay that must have been based on the colophon of Ku that was inserted in the original Northern Sung exemplar and later recorded in *YSYL*. This essay was printed by the Dairen Library of the South Manchurian Railway Co. See Wu, *HNTSL*, p. 296.

58. *YSYL*, p. 39a-41a.

59. *TSTC*, 9/22, p. 1.

60. Wu Tse-yü, *HNTSL*, p. 296.

61. Yü Ta-ch'eng, *HNWSK*, p. 22.

62. Wang Shu-min, *op. cit.*, p. 565.

63. Cheng Liang-shu, *HNTCL*, pp. 331-2.

64. *JPTSTC*, p. 19b (April 27, 1816).

65. Actually the situation is a bit more complex than I have described. The *CKTHC* reprint of the Ku Kuang-ch'i hand collated exemplar is a facsimile reproduction of a copy made in 1898 by Hsü Tsai-heng. Hsü's copy was, in turn, a facsimile of a copy made in 1858 by Kuan Ch'ing-ssu of the original Ku exemplar. Kuan Ch'ing-ssu was Ch'en Huan's best student (see *Ch'ing-shih lieh-chuan*, 69/67b-69a). After he copied out Ku's full collation notes he then checked them against a copy of the Northern exemplar. I assume that since he was Ch'en's best student, he must have used Ch'en's copy. Whenever he came to a variant between the basic Chuang edition and Ch'en's Northern Sung facsimile copy *that was not* previously noted by Ku Kuang-chi, he wrote

it down. Sometimes (e.g., pp. 33, 42, 47, 52) he added "Chi-yeh chi" ("written by Chi-yeh"). Chi-yeh was his courtesy name.

Now there are many of these notes by Kuan. What they indicate to me is not the carelessness of Ku's scholarship, but the fact that the facsimile Kuan saw (i.e. Ch'en Huan's) already contained differences from the original exemplar that Ku consulted. Often Kuan's notes indicate characters whose form is almost identical to one in the text, but which is written slightly differently. This is a sure sign that the difference was introduced by a copyist who attempted to clarify an illegible or damaged character. Therefore, there must already have been variants between the original exemplar and the copy of Ch'en Huan.

Ch'en Huan's copy was in turn copied by Liu Lü-fen, and is the basis of the extant editions. The seven copyist's errors that I have pointed out in Chapter 7 must have all been made by Liu Lü-fen when he interpreted illegible graphs in Ch'en's facsimile. None of them is recorded by either Ku or Kuan. Therefore these seven were not in either the original or in Ch'en's copy.

From this it can be seen that errors were introduced into modern editions by the copyists who were forced to interpret illegible graphs, first in the original exemplar, and then in the Ch'en copy.

List of Characters

Chang Ch'ou 張丑

Chang Tzu-kai 張子蓋

Chang Yü 張鈺

Chao Chih-chien 趙之謙

Ch'ang-ling 昌齡

Ch'ang-shan 常山

Ch'ang-shou 長洲

Cheng Liang-shu 鄭良樹

Ch'en Cheng-chih 陳徵之

Ch'en Huan 陳奐

Ch'en Teng-yüan 陳登原

Chi-yeh chi 吉也記

Ch'ien Tseng 錢曾

Ch'ien I-chi 錢儀吉

Ch'ien Tsun-wang tu-shu min-ch'iu-chi chiao-cheng 錢遵王讀書敏求記校證

Chin Yu-mei 金友梅

Ch'ing-shih lieh-chuan 清史列傳

Chu Chia-hua 朱家驊

Chu I-tsun 朱彝尊

Chu-tzu chiao-cheng 諸子斠證

Chuang K'uei-chi 莊逵吉

Chung-kuo tien-chi-shih 中國典籍史

Chung-kuo tsang-shu-chia k'ao-lüeh 中國藏書家考略

Ch'ü Yung 瞿鏞

Dairen Toshokan Wakan tosho bunrui mokuroku 大連圖書館和漢圖書分類目錄

Enanji no Rekishi 淮南子の歷史

Fang Chun-chi 方俊吉

Fei-shih jih-chi ch'ao 匪石日記鈔

fu-pen 副本

Hai-chou 海州

Hai-yüan ko 海源閣

Hsü pei-chuan-chi 續碑傳記

Hsü Shen 許慎

Hsü Tsai-heng 許在衡

Hu Yü-t'ang 胡雨塘

Hu-chou 湖州

Huai-nan Tzu 淮南子

Huai-nan hung-lieh chieh 淮南鴻烈解

Huai-nan hung-lieh chien ku 淮南鴻烈閒詁

Huang P'ei-Lieh 黃丕烈

Huang-ti nei-ching ssu-wen 黃帝內經素問

Hui tung 惠棟

I-yün-ching she 藝芸精舍

Jao-chou 饒州

Kao Yu 高誘

Kao-yu Wang-shih fu-tzu hsüeh chih yen-chiu 高郵王氏父子學之研究

Ku Kuang-ch'i 顧廣圻

Ku-chiao Huai-nan Tzu ko-t'iao 顧校淮南子各條

Kuan Ch'ing-ssu 管慶祺

Kuan T'ing-fen 管庭芬

Kuang-ya shu-cheng 廣雅疏證

Kuo-ch'ao Pei-chuan-chi 國朝碑傳集

Kuo-li Pei-p'ing t'u-shu kuan kuan-k'an 國立北平圖書館館刊

Kuraishi Takeshiro 倉石武四郎

Lan-lin 蘭鄰

Li-tai jen-wu pieh-shu chü-ch'u ming t'ung-chien 歷代人物別署居處名通檢

Lien-t'ing shu-mu 楝亭書目

Liu Lü-fen 劉履芬

Lo-p'ing hsien 樂平縣

Mao I-kuei 茅一桂

Mao-sheng 泖生

Miao Ch'üan-sun 繆荃孫

Niu Shu-yü 鈕樹玉

San-pai shu-she 三百書舍

San-pai t'ang 三百堂

shen 慎

Shen Ta-ch'eng 沈大成

Shih-fu 碩甫 or 石甫

Shimada Yoshimi 島田好

Shinagaku 支那學

Sun I-jang 孫詒讓

Sung Chih-shan 宋芝山

Sung Ting-chih 宋定之

Taam, Cheuk-Woon 譚卓垣

Tan-t'u 丹徒

Tu-shu tsa-chih 讀書雜誌

Tuan Yü-tsai 段玉裁

T'an Hsien 譚獻

T'ao Fang-ch'i 陶方琦

T'ao Wen-hui 陶蘊輝

T'ao Wu-liu 陶五柳

T'ieh-ch'in t'ung chien lou 鉄琴銅劍樓

Ts'ao Hsi 曹璽

Ts'ao Yin 曹寅

Tung K'ang 董康

Wang Chin-fa 王金發

Wang Han-chih 王漢之

Wang K'o-ming 王克明

Wang Nien-sun 王念孫

Wang Shih-chung 王士鍾

Wang-shih chia 王氏家

Wang-shih Yen-chao 王氏彥昭

Wang Shu-min 王叔岷

Wang Ying-chih 王引之

Wen Po 温博

Wu-ch'eng hsien 烏程縣

Wu Ch'eng-shih 吳承石

Wu Tse-yü 吳則虞

Wu-hsien 吳縣

Wu-liu 五柳

Yang I-tseng 楊以增

Yang Pao-i 楊保彝

Yang Shao-ho 楊紹和

Yao Wei-tsu 姚慰祖

Ying-shu yü-lu 楹書隅錄

Yü Liang-shu 于大成

Yüan T'ing-t'ao 袁廷檮

Monks and the Relic Cult in the *Mahāparinibbānasutta*: An Old Misunderstanding in Regard to Monastic Buddhism

Gregory Schopen
University of Texas at Austin

It is almost always instructive to look at the actual evidence for what are taken to be "established facts" in the history of Indian Buddhism. If nothing else, such an exercise makes it painfully obvious that most of those "established facts" totter precariously on very fragile foundations. One example only will concern us here.

It is—and has been—constantly asserted that there was in Early Buddhism a fundamental difference between the religious activities of monks and the religious activities of lay persons, especially in regard to worship and participation in cult. Moreover, this fundamental difference is said to distinguish not only the religious lives of monks from the religious lives of lay persons in Early Buddhism, it is also said to distinguish the Mahāyāna monk from his non-Mahāyāna co-religionists. All of this is, of course, asserted as "fact" and far-reaching implications are made to follow from it. But this "fact"—as I have pointed out several times now—stands in jarring contrast to everything we know from Indian epigraphy and archeology.[1] It is, indeed, the accumulating weight of this epigraphical and archeological material which in the first instance forces us to re-examine the evidence on which the "fact" of this asserted difference is founded. That evidence—not surprisingly given the history of Buddhist Studies—turns out to be exclusively literary. But it is not just exclusively literary evidence on which this fact rests: it rests entirely, it seems, on a less than careful reading of a single passage of a single text. The passage in question is, of course, *Mahāparinibbāna-Sutta* V.10:

kathaṃ mayaṃ bhante tathāgatassa sarīre paṭipajjāmāti

avyāvaṭā tumhe ānanda hotha tathāgatassa sarīrapujāya, iṅgha tumhe ānanda sadatthe ghaṭatha, sadattham anuyuñjatha, sadatthe appamattā ātāpino pahitattā viharatha. sant' ānanda khattiya-paṇḍitā pi brāhmaṇa-paṇḍitā pi gahapati-paṇḍitā pi tathāgate abhippasannā te tathāgatassa sarīra-pūjaṃ karissantīti.[2]

This—in Rhys Davids' still standard English translation of the passage—appears as:

"'What are we to do, lord, with the remains of the Tathāgata?'

'Hinder not yourselves, Ānanda, by honouring the remains of the Tathāgata. Be zealous, I beseech you, Ānanda, in your own behalf! Devote yourselves to your own good! Be earnest, be zealous, be intent on your own good! There are wise men, Ānanda, among the nobles, among the brahmins, among the heads of houses, who are firm believers in the Tathāgata; and they will do due honour to the remains of the Tathāgata'."[3]

This single, short passage, probably one of the most frequently quoted passages of Buddhist canonical literature, has been taken to establish, for example, that "śarīrapūjā, the worship of relics, is the concern of the laity and not the bhikṣusaṃgha,"[4] that "advanced monks were not to occupy themselves with such worship of stūpas," and that "the worship of stūpas should be left to the laity alone."[5] But, even if we bracket the distinct possibility raised by Professor Bareau that this passage—and a number of related passages—are 'later' interpolations in the *Mahāparinibbāna-sutta*,[6] the passage *as we have it* simply will not support the conclusions modern scholars have drawn from it.[7] First of all, there is no reference anywhere in the passage to monks. The injunction, if it is an injunction, is addressed to Ānanda, not to all monks. It is true that plural pronominal and verbal forms are used in the Pāli version of this passage. But if the plural forms are used there as inclusive of the category "monk," then they should be used in that same way at, for example, *Mahāparinibbāna* V.7 where the same thing occurs. That, however, as the context makes absolutely clear, is out of the question since the plural *mayaṃ*, "we," is actually used there in such a way as to *exclude* 'monks in different districts'. Likewise at VI.1 where a 1st person plural form of the pronoun is used Rhys Davids himself recognized that it could not be intended to include all monks: he translates *siyā kho pan' ānanda tumhākam evam assa* as "'It may be, Ānanda, that *in some of you* the thought may arise.'" Moreover, when in the *Mahāparinibbāna-sutta* we actually find explicit reference to rules governing the *Saṅgha* as a whole—as we do in the passage dealing with the abolishment of the "lesser and minor precepts" at VI.3—it is explicitly stated to be a matter for the entire *Saṅgha*. But these considerations, though consistently overlooked, may not necessarily be—in the end—the most important ones. The fact would remain that even if it could somehow be argued that the injunction was intended for the entire *Saṅgha* it would still be difficult to establish that that injunction had anything to do with the *stūpa* or relic cult.

There has been more than the usual degree of inconsistency in translating the text of the injunction and virtually no attempt to determine the precise meaning of the term *śarīra-pūjā* as it is used there. Even the great de la Vallée Poussin gives at least four different translations of the injunction, two of them in the same book:

> "Ne vous occupez pas du culte de mes reliques."[8]
> "Ne vous occupez pas des funérailles."[9]
> "Ne vous occupez pas du culte des reliques."[9]
> "Ne vous préoccupez pas d'honorer mon corps."[10]

This kind of inconsistency—which can slip so easily into confusion—is still with us. Recently, for example, Prof. A. Hirakawa said:

> "During the early period of Buddhism offerings to the Buddha's relics (*śarīra-pūjā*) were made by laymen. According to the Mahāparinibbāna Suttanta, the Buddha was asked by Ānanda what type of ceremony should be held for the Buddha's remains. The Buddha replied, 'you should strive for the true goal [*sadattha*] of emancipation [*vimokṣa*].' The Buddha thus prohibited monks from having any connection with his funeral ceremonies and instead called upon wise and pious lay believers to conduct the ceremonies."[11]

Here in four sentences *śarīra-pūjā* is glossed in three different ways: as 'offerings to relics,' as 'ceremony for remains,' and as 'funeral ceremonies.'

The problem, of course, with de la Vallée Poussin's and Prof. Hirakawa's treatment is, as it is with virtually all treatments of the passage, that they make no attempt to establish the precise meaning of *śarīra-pūjā* and, as a consequence, may be inadvertently conflating what are typologically two quite distinct things: *funeral ceremonies and cult activity directed towards relics or reliquaries are fundamentally different forms of religious behavior.* In this instance the texts—*as we have them*—seem clearer than their interpreters.

In arguing for his interpretation of the curious statement at the end of the *Ahraurā* version of Aśoka's first minor rock edict K.R. Norman says "that in Sanskrit *śarīra* in the singular means 'body,' not 'relics,' which is its meaning in the plural."[12] That the same holds for the Pāli *sarīra* in the *Mahāparinibbāna-sutta* is, uncharacteristically, beyond doubt. Before a certain point in the narrative the term is never used in the plural, always in the singular, and can only mean "body": at V.2, for example, the trees burst into bloom out of season and scatter their flowers on *the body* of the dying, but not yet dead, Buddha (*te tathāgatassa sarīraṃ okiranti*); at V.11 the *body* of a *cakkavattin* is said to be wrapped "in a new cloth" (*cakkavattissa sarīraṃ ahatena vatthena veṭhenti*); at VI.13 the Mallas are said to have approached the *body* "with dancing and hymns, and music, and with garlands and perfumes" (*yena bhagavato sarīraṃ ten' upasaṃkamiṃsu, upasaṃkamitvā bhagavato sarīraṃ naccehi gītehi... pūjentā*); at VI.18 the *body* is said to have been wrapped (*bhagavato sarīraṃ veṭhetvā*), placed on the pyre (*bhagavato sarīraṃ citakaṃ āropesuṃ*), etc. Wherever, therefore, the term *sarīra* occurs in the singular in the *Mahāparinibbāna* it unambiguously means *body*, and it occurs in the singular throughout the entire description of the actual funeral. It is in fact only after the funeral proper, only after the cremation, that we find *sarīra* in the plural and it is only here that the text could be speaking about "relics." We can actually watch—at VI.23—the transition in both grammatical number and meaning as it takes place in a single paragraph. The only question that remains, then, is which of the two possible meanings of *sarīra* is in play in the injunction delivered to Ānanda.

Since the text of the injunction uses *sarīra* in compound—*avy āvaṭā tumhe ānanda hotha tathāgatassa sarīra-pujāya*—we have no formal indication of the implied grammatical number and, therefore, of the intended meaning of *sarīra*. But even in the absence of a formal indicator, the contextual indication is virtually certain. The injunction is not an unsolicited declaration. It is a response or answer to a very specific question and the question itself does have the formal indication of grammatical number that we need. The question is put in the following form: *kathaṃ mayaṃ bhante tathāgatassa sarīre paṭipajjāmāti*. *sarīre* here is almost certainly a locative singular used in the sense of "in regard to" exactly as in the immediately preceding *mātugāme* which is constructed with the same verb: *kathaṃ mayaṃ bhante mātugāme paṭipajjāmāti* (V.9). Rhys Davids translates the latter by "How are we to conduct ourselves, lord, with regard to womankind?" If the construction of the question leading to our injunction is analogous, and if *sarīre* there is in the locative singular, it would accordingly have to be translated: "How are we to conduct ourselves in regard to the body of the Tathāgata?" To argue that *sarīre* is not a locative singular, moreover, would be difficult. The only other thing it could be, as far as I know, is an accusative plural, but there is much against this. A neuter accusative plural in *-e*—though found on occasion elsewhere—would be distinctly out of place in the language of the *Mahāparinibbāna-sutta*;[13] when *sarīra* occurs elsewhere in the *Mahāparinibbāna-sutta* in the accusative plural—and it does so at least five times—it always occurs with the "normal" neuter plural ending *- āni*; in the one other instance where *sarīre* occurs in the final sections of the *Mahāparinibbāna-sutta* it forms a part of a locative absolute so there can be no doubt about its interpretation (*daḍḍhe kho pana bhagavato sarīre*, VI.23).

All of this is only to say that it seems virtually certain that Ānanda, in his question, was not asking about his or anyone else's participation in the relic cult. He was asking about how the *body* of the Buddha should be treated *immediately* after his death, about that which we would call the "funeral arrangements".[14] But if the question is about funeral arrangements, it is at best disingenuous to suggest that the answer and the injunction is about something else. In fact the text of the injunction itself also seems to indicate that *sarīrapūjā*, the activity Ānanda was not to be preoccupied with, was intended only to refer to funeral activities.

The text says at V.11 that the body of the Tathāgata is to be treated in the same way as the body of a Wheel-turning king is treated. It is this that the "wise men… among the nobles, among the brahmins, among the heads of houses" are to do and that Ānanda is not to be overly concerned with. But the treatment accorded to the body of a dead king which is detailed in the Pāli text makes no reference either to relics or to an ongoing cult. The *sarīra-pūja* of a dead king's body described in the text involves the following steps: the body is wrapped elaborately in cloth; the body is then placed in an "oil vessel of iron"; a funeral pyre is built; the body is cremated and a *stūpa* is built. That is all. "This is the way they treat the body of a wheel-turning king, Ānanda," the text says, and then goes on:

> yathā kho ānanda rañño cakkavattissa sarīre paṭipajjanti evaṃ tathāgatassa sarīre paṭipajjitabbaṃ. cātummahāpathe tathāgatassa thūpo kātabbo. tattha ye mālaṃ vā gandhaṃ vā vaṇṇakaṃ vā āropessanti abhivādessanti vā cittaṃ vā pasādessanti tesaṃ taṃ bhavissati dīgharattaṃ hitāya sukhāya.
>
> As indeed, Ānanda, they proceed in regard to the body of a wheel-turning king, so in regard to the body of the Tathāgata the procedure is to be followed. At the main crossroads a stūpa of the Tathāgata is to be made. Who will take a garland or perfume or paint there, or will salute, or will cause their mind to be tranquil, that will be for their benefit and ease for a long time.

It may be of some importance to note the shift in verbal forms that takes place in this passage since that shift would seem to indicate that the final sentence was not intended as a part of the instructions concerning the treatment of the Buddha's body and that, therefore, the activities it describes were not thought to form a part of *sarīra-pūja*. When the text refers to what is to be done in regard to the body of the Buddha it uses future passive participles to indicate what must be done by the wise laymen who will perform the *sarīra-pūjā*: the procedure followed in regard to a deceased king *is to be followed* in regard to the Buddha; a *stūpa is to be made*. These are clear injunctions in both grammar and sense. But the injunctions end here. The final sentence, which contains the only references in the passage to what might be called cult practices, constitutes not an injunction, but a statement about the future. The text shifts from future passive participles with an imperative sense to simple futures; from "it is to be done" to "those who will do." Notice too that the final sentence also introduces a new grammatical subject: context suggests that the injunctions are addressed to the wise laymen who will perform the *sarīra-pūjā*; but the subject of the final sentence is the indefinite *ye* which Rhys Davids renders by "whosoever." All of this, again, would appear to indicate that all those activities which we associate with an ongoing relic cult did not—for the author of our text—form a part of *sarīra-pūjā*, and that *sarīra-pūjā* was used to refer only to funereal activities that began with the wrapping of the body and ended with cremation and constructing a *stūpa* and had—like the injunction as a whole—nothing to do with relics. That this was, indeed, the original meaning of *sarīra-pūjā* is in fact further demonstrated by a number of passages in Hīnayāna literature where we have clear references to monastic funerals.

In an interesting passage from the *Mūlasarvāstivāda-vinaya* we find, for example:

> "Again on that occasion another monk, being sick, died in his cell. Having brought him to the burning ground, having performed *the worship of the body*, that monk was burnt. Then the monks returned to the

monastery (...*sa bhikṣur ādahanaṃ nītvā śarīra-pūjāṃ kṛtvā dagdhas, tato vihāram āgatā*).[15]

To this passage from the *Mūlasarvāstivāda-vinaya* we might add another from the same source:

"Again on that occasion another monk died. The monks, having carried out his body, having simply thrown it into the burning grounds (...*tan 'bhinirhṛtya evam eva śmaśāne chorayitvā*), returned to the monastery. The distributor of robes entered the dead monk's cell saying 'I distribute the bowl and robe.' He—the dead monk—having been reborn among non-human beings appeared there wielding a club. He said: 'until you perform *the worship of the body* for me (*yāvan mama śarīra-pūjāṃ kurutha*), do you now distribute (my) bowl and robe?'

The monks ask the Blessed One concerning this matter.

The Blessed One said: 'By the monks *the worship of the body* for the deceased is first to be performed (*bhikṣubhis tasya pūrvaṃ śarīra-pūjā karttavyeti*). After that the bowl and robe are to be distributed.'"[16]

Both of these passages enumerate a sequence of activities involved in the disposal of the body of a monk who has died in his cell. In both it is clear that *śarīra-pūjā*—whatever it involved—took place after the body had been removed and taken to the cremation ground, but before it was cremated, before there could have been anything like what we call relics. It is again fairly certain that *śarīra-pūjā* involved the ritual handling or treatment of the body prior to cremation since the second passage contrasts it with—and insists that it replace—'simply throwing the body into the burning ground.' That it is *the body* and not relics that is the object of this treatment is both clear here and made even more explicit elsewhere.

The forty-eighth *Avadāna* of the *Avadānaśataka* looks very much like a literary elaboration of the much simpler narratives concerning the disposal of the monastic dead found in the *Mūlasarvāstivāda-vinaya*, two examples of which have already been cited. It leaves us in no doubt as to the object toward which *śarīra-pūjā* is directed. It says a certain monk:

...kālagataḥ svake layane preteṣūpapannaḥ | tato 'sya sabrahmacāribhir muṇḍikāṃ gaṇḍīṃ parāhatya śarīrābhinirhāraḥ kṛtaṃ | tato 'sya śarīre śarīrapūjāṃ kṛtvā vihāram āgatāḥ |

"...died and was reborn in his own cell as a hungry ghost (*shi nas rang gi gnas khang du yi dags su skyes so*). Then his fellow monks, having struck the *muṇḍikā* gong ("la cloche funèbre"), performed the removal of the body. Then, having performed the worship of the body on his body, they returned to the monastery."[17]

Virtually every element of this passage from the *Avadānaśataka* also occurs in the *Mūlasarvāstivāda-vinaya*. The "*muṇḍikā* gong," or "cloche funèbre,"[18] for example, is referred to in the latter more intelligibly as the *mṛta-gaṇḍī* or "gong for the dead."[19] It is, however, not just the elements of the funeral procedure which are essentially the same in the two works; the sequence in which they are said to occur is also basically the same. It is, therefore, significant that where the *Mūlasarvāstivada-vinaya* has *śarīra-pūjāṃ kṛtvā*, "having performed the worship of the body," the *Avadānaśataka* has corresponding to it the even more explicit *śarīre śarīra-pūjāṃ kṛtvā*, "having performed the worship of the body on his body." This construction leaves no doubt about the object of the *pūjā* involved.[20] Nor is this in doubt in another instance where the construction is used. In the Sanskrit version of the *Mahāparinirvāṇa-sūtra* (48.8) when Mahākāśyapa meets an Ājīvika coming from Kuśinagarī he asks him if he knows his teacher. The Ājīvika answers: *jāne / śramaṇo gautamaḥ / parinirvṛtas te āyuṣmañ chāstā / adya (gate saptāhe va)rtate śarīre śarīra-pūjā*: "I know him. He is the Śramaṇa Gautama. But sir, your teacher is dead. For seven days now the worship of the body on his body is performed."[21] But since the Buddha had not yet been cremated, it is here not just the construction, but the context too that makes it certain that *śarīra-pūjā* was understood to be an activity directed toward the body of the deceased which took place after the individual's death, but before or as a part of his cremation. It could not, therefore, have anything to do with relics for the simple reason that there were none.

All of this is richly confirmed by a variety of other passages as well. In the account of the funeral of Mahāprajāpatī and her companions found in the *Vinaya-kṣudraka-vastu* of the *Mūlasarvāstivāda-vinaya*, for example, in which prominent monks come from afar to undertake the full performance of the worship of her body (*de'i lus la mchod pa lhag par bya ba la brtson par byas*), the text says: "Then, having performed the great worship and having removed the bodies, they set the biers down at an appropriate and isolated spot (*de nas mchod pa chen po byas te khyer nas sa phyogs bar skabs dben par khyogs rnams bzhag go*). Only after the great worship was performed and the bodies removed did the cremation take place (*de nas ... bsregs so*).[22] In the terse account of the end of Aśoka found in the *Divyāvadāna*, the text says that the ministers thought of enthroning the new king only "after having carried out (Aśoka's body) on dark blue and yellow biers, after having performed the worship of the body, and after having cremated him (*yāvad amātyair nīlapītābhiḥ śivikābhir nirharitvā śarīra-pūjāṃ kṛtvā dhmāpayitvā rājānaṃ pratiṣṭhāpayiṣyāma iti*).[23] Here again "worship of the body" precedes cremation; it takes place before in fact there could be any relics. But if these passages make it clear that *śarīra-pūjā* took place before there could have been anything like a relic, still other passages make it clear that it also took place prior to the erection of a *stūpa*. In the *Saṅghabhedavastu* of the *Mūlasarvāstivāda-vinaya*, in a description of events that followed the death of a former Buddha, the text says: "A great crowd of people, after having performed the worship of the body in regard to his body, established a great *stūpa* on an isolated spot" (*tasya mahājanakāyena śarīre śarīra-pūjāṃ kṛtvā viviktāvakāśe pṛthivīpradeśe mahān stūpaḥ pratiṣṭhāpitaḥ*).[24] Similarly, in the description of events that followed the death of a series of former Buddhas found in the *Avadānaśataka*—a description that is repeated at least eleven times—the text says: "The king ..., after having performed the worship of the body in regard to the body of the Blessed One, established a *stūpa* a *yojana* in circumference, etc." (*tato rājñā .... bhagavataḥ śarīre śarīra-pūjāṃ kṛtvā samantayojanastūpaś catūratnamayaḥ pratiṣṭhāpitaḥ krośam uccatvena*).[25] Significantly in several instances this statement is completed with the phrase "and a festival of the *stūpa* was instituted" (*stūpamahaś ca prajñaptaḥ*). In all these cases then, *śarīra-pūjā* could not possibly have been thought to be connected with activity in regard to *stūpa*s since it was only after *śarīra-pūjā* had been completed that a *stūpa* was established. Moreover, in those cases in which it was said that "a festival of the *stūpa* was instituted"—and therefore something like an ongoing cult—this too took place after *śarīra-pūjā* had been performed. *śarīra-pūjā* did not form a part of any ongoing activity.

We might consider here one final and perhaps particularly interesting passage from the Sanskrit text of the *Mahāparinirvāṇa-sūtra* (49.15). When, in this version, Mahākāśyapa approaches the funeral pyre of the Buddha he takes the lid off the oil vessel, removes the cloths wrapped around the body, and "pays reverence to the uncovered body of the Blessed One" (*bhagavataḥ śarīram avigopitaṃ vandate*). Then the following thought occurs to him: *yan nv ahaṃ svayam eva bhagavataḥ śarīra-pūjāyām autsukyam āpadyeya*; "what if I myself, indeed, were to be zealous in regard to the worship of the body of the Blessed One." Having thought this, he brings other cloths, wraps the body with them, puts it back into the vessel, closes the lid, makes a(nother) pyre, and stands to one side. That is all. It is apparently just this sequence of activities which the text intends by the term *śarīra-pūjā*. Although it looks to us like "worship," even what Mahākāśyapa does in regard to the body when he has initially uncovered it is not included; that activity is expressed by a completely different word: *vandate*.

It is also important to note that in the Sanskrit text Mahākāśyapa does precisely what Ānanda is earlier told not to be concerned with, and the two passages use virtually the same words. Ānanda's question is expressed as *kathaṃ vayaṃ... bhagavataḥ śarīra-pūjāyām autsukyam āpadyemahi* (36.2) and the injunction as *alpotsukas tvam ānanda bhava śarīra-pūjāyāḥ...* (36.3), while Kāśyapa's intention appears as *yan nv ahaṃ svayam eva bhagavataḥ śarīra-pūjāyām autsukyam āpadyeya* (49.19). Since we know what Kāśyapa did when he involved himself in *śarīra-pūjā* we also know quite precisely what Ānanda was not to be concerned with and, again, it has nothing to do with the relic cult.[26] But since the Sanskrit text goes to the trouble to point out that Kāśyapa was a monk of the highest standing, one of only four *Mahāsthavira*s alive at the time (49.16), and since it is precisely this *Mahāsthavira* who is said to have engaged in *śarīra-pūjā*, we also know that it is extremely unlikely that the authors of the text understood the earlier injunction addressed to Ānanda to apply to all monks or to forbid monastic involvement in such activity. In fact, if there were any restrictions on participation in *śarīra-pūjā* they appear from the Sanskrit text to have been of a very different order. Since, again, the Sanskrit text takes the trouble to point out that Kāsyapa was not only one of only four *Mahāsthaviras*, but was also—in Buddhist monastic terms—rich and famous,[27] and since he involved himself actively in what Ānanda was counselled not to, the text may be suggesting almost the opposite of what we would expect: it may be suggesting that participation in that part of monastic funerals known as *śarīra-pūjā* was—in at least important funerals—the prerogative of advanced, high status monks.[28] Since Ānanda, at this stage, appears to have been neither, this may only confirm from an unexpected angle that the injunction addressed to him was fundamentally *ad hominem*.

All of the evidence we have, then, would seem to argue for the fact that *śarīra-pūjā* did not originally mean "worship of relics" and did not have anything to do with a relic cult. It would seem to strongly suggest—if not establish—that originally it referred to that part of the funeral ceremony which took place primarily between the time of death and the cremation and construction of a *stūpa*, and involved primarily what we would call preparation of the body. The construction of a *stūpa*—if it is included at all—signalled the end of *śarīra-pūjā*, not its beginnings. But if the available evidence suggests that *śarīra-pūjā* was not connected with an ongoing relic cult, that same evidence suggests that the injunction concerning it that was delivered to Ānanda was not intended to apply to all monks. This last is confirmed from an unexpected source.

The injunction delivered to Ānanda created problems, apparently, for the later Theravāda tradition. It reappears as one lemma of an interesting dilemma in the Fourth Book of the *Milindapañha*. This dilemma is particularly important for our discussion since it allows us to see at least something of how the injunction was understood in Śri Lanka in about the 5th Century C.E.[29] In presenting the dilemma Milinda points out that the Buddha said both "Do not you, Ānanda, be occupied with honouring the Tathāgata's bodily remains," and—in *Vimānavatthu* 82. vs.8—"Venerate that relic of him who is to be venerated (*pūjetha naṃ pūjaniyassa dhātuṃ*); by doing so you will go from here to heaven."[30] It is clear from just this much that by the time this Book was added to the *Milinda* a change in the meaning of *sarīra-pūjā* had occurred; it is clear by the way in which the dilemma is framed that *sarīra-pūjā* was now considered equivalent to 'venerating a relic,' and could now mean that. But it is also clear from Nāgasena's response that even then, and even when taken to refer to relic worship, the injunction addressed to Ānanda had not yet been understood to apply to all monks. If the injunction had already been understood to apply to all monks, or if this interpretation had been widely or fully accepted, Milinda's dilemma could not have arisen and Nāgasena's response would have made no sense.

The response of Nāgasena comes in the following form:

bhāsitam p'etaṃ mahārāja bhagavatā: abyāvaṭā tumhe ānanda hotha tathāgatassa sarīrapūjāyāti. puna ca bhaṇitaṃ:

pūjetha naṃ pūjaniyassa dhātuṃ
evaṃkarā saggam ito gamissathāti

tañ ca pana na sabbesaṃ. jinaputtānaṃ yeva ārabbha bhaṇitaṃ: abyāvaṭā tumhe ānanda hotha tathāgatassa sarīrapūjāyāti. akammaṃ h'etaṃ mahārāja jinaputtānaṃ yad idaṃ pūjā; sammasanaṃ saṅkhārānaṃ, yoniso manasikāro, satipaṭṭhānānupassanā, ārammaṇa-sāraggāho, kilesayuddhaṃ sadatthamanuyuñjanā, etaṃ jinaputtānaṃ karaṇīyaṃ; avasesānaṃ devamanussānaṃ pūjā karaṇīyā.

Taking into account the new meaning attributed to *sarīra-pūjā* this can be translated as:

"Great King, this was indeed spoken by the Blessed One: 'you, Ānanda, should not be concerned with worshipping the relics of the Tathāgata!' And again it was said (by him):

'Worship the relic of one who is to be worshipped!
acting thus, you will go from here to heaven.'

But that (which was said) was not (intended) for everyone. Only in reference to the sons of the Conqueror was it said: 'you, Ānanda, should not be concerned with worshipping the relics of the Tathāgata!' For this, Great King, is not an action for the sons of the Conqueror, namely: worship. Thoroughly understanding the conditioned; concentrating the mind; realizing the establishment of mindfulness; taking hold of the most excellent foundations; destroying the impurities; pursuing the highest goal—this is what is to be done by sons of the Conqueror. By the remainder of gods and men worship is to be performed."

The primary purpose of this passage and of the elaborate series of metaphors which follows it is readily apparent. Its primary, if not sole purpose was to establish the meaning of the injunction delivered to Ānanda by establishing to whom that injunction was to apply. The mere fact that this was a "dilemma" can, again, only mean that at the time that this passage was written that had not yet been established, it had not been determined that—as modern scholarship would have it—the injunction was meant for all monks. In fact—and this is the significance of the passage—even this late book of the *Milinda* does not understand the passage in this way. According to the *Milinda* the injunction did not apply to monks, but to what it calls *jinaputtas*, "sons of the Conqueror." But, first of all, this could not have been the intention of the original injunction since the *Dīgha* as a whole is completely ignorant of such a "group." "The compound [*jinaputta*] appears to occur," according to Horner, "three times in Buddv. [=*Buddhavaṃsa*], but nowhere else in the Pāli Canon."[31] Moreover, what little we know about this term comes from a single passage in the *Madhuratthavilāsinī*, a commentary on the *Buddhavaṃsa* which, in Horner's words, "is late."[32] It says simply: *jinaputtā ti dīpaṅkarassa satthuno sāvakā*: "the sons of the Conqueror means the disciples of the Teacher Dīpaṅkara."[33] The equation *jinaputta* = *sāvaka* is, of course, not terribly helpful. It has recently been pointed out that it is not always easy to determine who was understood to be included in the category *sāvaka*, that it certainly included monks—but by no means, perhaps, all monks—and certainly, at times, included some laymen.[34] The group designated *sāvaka* is not therefore certainly coterminous with the group designated *bhikkhu* and—given its vagueness—the group designated *jinaputta* seems even less so. It would as a consequence be difficult to argue even that the author of this Book of the *Milinda* was moving *towards* the modern interpretation which wants to see in the injunction a prohibition of monastic involvement in the relic cult. But even if this argument were to be made, it would have to be conceded that even he is yet a long way from any precision in articulating it. That interpretation, even as late as the Fourth Book of the *Milinda*, simply has not yet been made. Had it been the "dilemma" would not have arisen; had it been the author of Book Four, instead of using a term like *jinaputta*, could have simply used the word *bhikkhu*. The fact that he did not is important; the fact that he used a metaphoric epithet rather than an ecclesiastical title may also be.

bhikkhu and *jinaputta* are fundamentally different kinds of designations. *bhikkhu* is a title conferred on an individual as a result of having undergone a set of formal ecclesiastical procedures for induction into a particular group. It designates his formal membership in that group and that membership is not subject to interpretation or opinion. It is subject to recognized procedure. Anyone who undergoes the procedure is a monk. The same, of course, is not true of an epithet like *jinaputta*, if for no other reason than it obviously cannot be taken literally. An individual so designated cannot literally be "a son of the Conqueror." Moreover, there are no formally recognized procedures that make one such a "son," and no formally recognized criteria for determining membership in this "group." It, in effect, does not designate membership in a particular group but conformity to an ideal notion of what the religiosity of a follower of the Buddha—whether that follower be a layman or a monk—ought to be. This, of course, is decidedly a matter of interpretation and not a matter of ecclesiastical procedure. It may well be, then, that the author of the Fourth Book of the *Milinda* saw in the injunction addressed to Ānanda support for *his* view that *pūjā* was not an activity of what he thought was a *true* monk, but even he could not see in it support for the view that it prohibited all monks from such activity. The contrast for him, in fact, continues to be not that between social groups (laymen and monks), but that between different styles of religiosity (meditative and devotional), and a particular religious style has not yet been identified exclusively with any particular group.

***

It would seem, then, that if the arguments and observations presented here turn out to be even approximately correct we will be required to admit that a good deal of what has been said about early monastic Buddhism is based on a misunderstanding. If *sarīra-pūjā* in the *Mahāparinibbāna-sutta* has nothing to do with relics or an ongoing cult of relics, then the only textual basis for asserting that monks were not allowed to be involved with either disappears. If the "injunction" concerning *sarīra-pūjā*—however the latter be precisely understood—was not addressed to all monks, then once again we are left without any warrant for one of our favorite claims, and we must re-think what we thought we knew about the acultic character of early monastic Buddhism.

Once again, it seems, we have encountered material—this time literary—which appears to suggest that our view of the Indian Buddhist monk is in need of more than a little revision.[35]

Notes

1. See especially G. Schopen, "Two Problems in the History of Indian Buddhism: The Layman/Monk Distinction and the Doctrines of the Transference of Merit," *Studien zur Indologie und Iranistik* 10 (1985) 23ff; Schopen, "The Stūpa Cult and the Extant Pāli Vinaya," *Journal of the Pāli Text Society* 13 (1989) 24ff.
2. T.W. Rhys Davids & J.E. Carpenter, *The Dīgha Nikāya*, Vol. II (London: 1903) 141. All references to the Pāli text are to this edition.
3. T.W. and C.A.F. Rhys Davids, *Dialogues of the Buddha*, Part II (London: 1910) 154.
4. A. Hirakawa, "The Rise of Mahāyāna Buddhism and Its Relationship to the Worship of Stupas," *Memoirs of the Toyo Bunko* 22 (1963) 102.
5. N. Dutt, "Popular Buddhism," *The Indian Historical Quarterly* 21 (1945) 250-51.
6. A. Bareau, "La composition et les étapes de la formation progressive du mahāparinirvāṇa-sūtra ancien," *Bulletin de l'école française d'extrême-orient* 66 (1979) 45-103.
7. As a small sample—and it is only that—of these "conclusions" see H. Oldenberg, *Buddha. Sein Leben, seine Lehre, seine Gemeinde* (Berlin: 1897) 428; N. Dutt, "Place of Laity in Early Buddhism," *The Indian Historical Quarterly* 21 (1945) 164; Ét. Lamotte, "Le bouddhisme des läics," *Studies in Indology and Buddhology. Presented in Honour of Professor Susumi Yamaguchi on the Occasion of his Sixtieth Birthday* (Kyoto: 1955) 80; Lamotte, *Histoire du bouddhisme indien* (Louvain: 1958) 81; D.L. Snellgrove, "Śākyamuni's Final Nirvāṇa," *Bulletin of the School of Oriental and African Studies* 36 (1973) 410; A. Bareau, "Le parinirvāṇa du buddha et la naissance de la religion bouddhique," *Bulletin de l'école française d'extrême-orient* 61 (1974) 283-84; G. Nagao, "The Architectural Tradition in Buddhist Monasticism," in *Studies in History of Buddhism*, ed. A.K. Narain (Delhi: 1980) 193-94; M. Wijayaratna, *Le moine bouddhiste. selon les textes du theravāda* (Paris: 1983) 183; R. Gombrich, *Theravada Buddhism. A Social History from Ancient Benares to Modern Colombo* (London & New York: 1988) 119-24; (see also the works cited in notes 4 & 5 above and notes 8-11 below); etc.
8. L. de La Vallée-Poussin, *Nirvāṇa* (Paris: 1924) 7.
9. L. de La Vallée-Poussin, *Le dogme et la philosophie du bouddhisme* (Paris: 1930) 64; 191.
10. L. de La Vallée-Poussin, *L'inde aux temps des mauryas et des barbares, grecs, scythes, parthes et yue-tchi* (Paris: 1930) 141.
11. A. Hirakawa, "Stupa Worship," in *The Encyclopedia of Religion*, ed. M. Eliade, Vol.14 (New York: 1987) 93.
12. K.R. Norman, "Notes on the Ahraurā Version of Aśoka's First Minor Rock Edict," *Indo-Iranian Journal* 26 (1983) 278.
13. W. Geiger, *Pāli Literature and Language*, trans. by B. Ghosh (Calcutta: 1943) § 78.7; see also *Mahāparinibbāna* V.11 quoted below.

14. This seems clear as well in *Mahāparinibbāna* V.17 where Ānanda tries to dissuade the Buddha from passing away in Kusinārā.
15. R. Vira & L. Chandra, *Gilgit Buddhist Manuscripts* (*Facsimile Edition*), Part 6 (New Delhi: 1974) fol.852.8; N. Dutt, *Gilgit Manuscripts*, Vol. III, Part 2 (Srinigar: 1942) 127.13; *The Tibetan Tripiṭaka* (*Peking Edition*), ed. D.T. Suzuki, Vol. 41 (Tokyo-Kyoto: 1955) 281-1-1: *de'i tshe dge slong nad pa zhig gnas khang du shi nas de dge slong rnams kyis dur khrod du khyer te ro la mchod pa byas bsregs nas de nas gtsug lag khang du lhags pa dang* /.
16. Vira & Chandra, *Gilgit Buddhist Manuscripts*, Part 6, fol.852.6ff; Dutt, *Gilgit Manuscripts*, Vol. III, Part 2, 127.4ff; *Tibetan Tripiṭaka* (*Peking*), Vol. 41, 280-5-6ff: *de'i tshe dge slong zhig shi nas dge slong rnams kyis de phyung ste / dur khrod du de bzhin du bor nas ... re shig kho bo'i ro la mchod pa yang ma byas par ... dge slong rnams kyis sngar de'i ro la mchod pa byas la ...* This and the preceding passage are two of a series of interesting passages dealing with monastic funerals that occur in the *Mūlasarvāstivāda-vinaya*; I am now working on a detailed study of this material.
17. J.S. Speyer (ed.), *Avadānaçataka. A Century of Edifying Tales belonging to the Hīnayāna* (St. Petersburg: 1906-09, repr. The Hague: 1958) i 271.15ff; *Tibetan Tripiṭaka* (*Peking*), Vol. 40, 184-1-8ff. On the 'sectarian affiliation of the *Avadānaśataka* see, most recently, J.-U. Hartmann, "Zur Frage der Schulzugehörigkeit des Avadānaśataka," in *Zur Schulzugehörigkeit von Werken der Hīnayāna-Literatur*, hrsg. H. Bechert, Erster Teil (Göttingen: 1985) 219-24.
18. So L. Feer, *Avadāna-Çataka. Cent légendes bouddhiques* (Annales du musée guimet, t. XVIII) (Paris: 1891) 185.
19. Dutt, *Gilgit Manuscripts*, Vol. III, Part 2, 120.6ff.
20. For similar 'cognate' constructions see R. Gnoli, *The Gilgit Manuscript of the Saṅghabhedavastu. Being the 17th and Last Section of the Vinaya of the Mūlasarvāstivādin*, Part I (Serie Orientale Roma XLIX,1) (Roma: 1977) 59.18: *atithīnām atithipūjā kartavyā* (the reading here, however, is not absolutely certain; see 59 n.b); N. Dutt, *Gilgit Manuscripts*, Vol. III, Part IV (Calcutta: 1950) 177.9: *jñātīnāṃ vā jñātipūjā na kriyate*, etc.
21. For the Sanskrit text of the *Mahāparinirvāna-sūtra* I refer throughout to the edition in E. Waldschmidt, *Das Mahāparinirvānasūtra. Text in Sanskrit und Tibetisch, verglichen mit dem Pāli nebst einer Übersetzung der chinesischen Entsprechung im Vinaya der Mūlasarvāstivādins*, t.I-III (Berlin: 1950-51)—all references are to the paragraph numbers imposed on the text by Waldschmidt.
22. For the Tibetan text of the *Vinaya-kṣudraka-vastu* I have used the 'edition' in *The Sde-Dge Mtshal-par Bka'-'Gyur. A Facsimile Edition of the 18th Century Redaction of Si-Tu Chos-Kyi-'Byuṅ-Gnas Prepared under the Direction of H.H. the 16th Rgyal-Dbaṅ Karma-Pa*, Vol. 10 (Delhi: 1977): the account of the death of Mahāprajāpatī is found at fol.224.6ff.
23. E.B. Cowell & R.A. Neil (eds.), *The Divyāvadāna. A Collection of Early Buddhist Legends* (Cambridge: 1886) 433.13-16; S. Mukhopadhyaya (ed.), *The*

Aśokāvadāna. Sanskrit Text compared with Chinese Versions (New Delhi: 1963) 132.7—the text is cited from the latter; for variants see 132 n.6.

24. Gnoli, *The Gilgit Manuscript of the Saṅghabhedavastu*, Part I, 161.14.

25. Speyer, *Avadānaçataka*, i 349.6, 352.16, 357.3, 361.14, 365.13, 369.18, 373.10, 377.12, 383.2, 387.5; ii 5.17.

26. It is worth noting here that in the Sanskrit text of the "injunction" singular pronominal and verbal forms are used and it is clearly addressed to Ānanda alone.

27. *...āyuṣmān mahākāśyapo jñāto ma(hā)puṇyo lābhī cīvarapiṇḍapāta-śayan(āsana)gl(ā)napratyayabhaiṣajyapariṣkārāṇāṃ*, 49.17.

28. On Mahākāśyapa's place in the text as a whole see Bareau, "La composition et les étapes de la formation progressive du mahāparinirvāṇasūtra ancien," 70ff; Professor Bareau refers to the incidents involving Kāśyapa as "la série des récits inventés par les auteurs de *Vinayapiṭaka* pour glorifier Mahākāśyapa".

29. In dating the section in the *Milinda* in which our passage occurs thus I follow P. Demiéville, "Les versions chinoises du milindapañha," *Bulletin de l'école française d'extrême-orient* 24 (1924) 34-35; Lamotte, *Histoire du bouddhisme indien*, 465; I.B. Horner, *Milinda's Questions*, Vol. I (London: 1963) xxx-xxxi; cf. the discussion in K.R. Norman, *Pāli Literature. Including the Canonical Literature in Prakrit and Sanskrit of All the Hīnayāna Schools of Buddhism* (*A History of Indian Literature*, ed. J. Gonda, Vol. VII, Fasc.2) (Wiesbaden: 1983) 110-13.

30. The text cited here and throughout is from V. Trenckner (ed.), *The Milindapañho. Being Dialogues between King Milinda and the Buddhist Sage Nāgasena* (London: 1880) 177ff; the translation here is from Horner, *Milinda's Questions*, i 249ff.

31. Horner, *Milinda's Questions*, i 250 n.1.

32. I.B. Horner (ed.), *Madhuratthavilāsinī. The Commentary on Buddhavaṃsa of Bhadantācariya Buddhadatta Mahāthera* (London: 1946) vi.

33. Horner, *Madhuratthavilāsinī*, 99; I.B. Horner, *The Clarifier of the Sweet Meaning (Madhuratthavilāsinī). Commentary on the Chronicle of Buddhas (Buddhavaṃsa) by Buddhadatta Thera* (London: 1978) 142.

34. P. Masefield, *Divine Revelation in Pali Buddhism* (London: 1986) 1-36. Masefield's conclusions are not infrequently overstated and problematic but he clearly shows that the Pāli texts will not support a simple equation of *sāvaka* and *bhikkhu*.

35. cf. G. Schopen, "Filial Piety and the Monk in the Practice of Indian Buddhism: A Question of 'Sinicization' Viewed from the Other Side," *T'oung Pao* 70 (1984) 110-26; Schopen, "On Monks, Nuns and 'Vulgar' Practices: The Introduction of the Image Cult into Indian Buddhism," *Artibus Asiae* 49.1/2 (1988/89) 153-68.

THE MAITREYA IMAGE IN SHICHENG AND GUANDING'S BIOGRAPHY OF ZHIYI

Koichi Shinohara
McMaster University

1. Introduction

Guanding's (561-632) biography of Zhiyi (539-598),[1] and other early biographies largely based on Guanding's work, report that Zhiyi ended his life in front of the large Maitreya image at Shicheng.[2] In this paper I would like to examine this account by Guanding and compare it with other stories associated with the Maitreya image at Shicheng preserved elsewhere. Such a comparison might throw some light on the circumstances of Zhiyi's death and the nature of Guanding's account of this event that was to prove particularly influential in later years.[3]

In this investigation I am primarily interested in the nature of Guanding's biography. I am interested in studying traditional biographies of religious figures as religious literature in their own right, and not simply as sources for a critical and historical reconstruction of the lives of these figures. From this point of view I have for some time been studying Chinese biographies of Buddhist monks ("biographies of eminent monks"), paying particular attention to their sources and the manner in which the biographies were "constructed"—for the most part after the death of their subjects. I am particularly interested in the relationship between miracle stories and religious biographies.[4]

A variety of early sources relevant to the study of Zhiyi's biography has been preserved in a collection of historical documents concerning the early history of the Tiantai community called *Guoqing bolu*.[5] Since this work, which Zhiji had begun but was unable to finish before his death, was also completed by Guanding, there is a possibility that Guanding might have adjusted its contents according to his distinctive conception of Zhiyi's life.[6] Nevertheless, these sources are useful for examining the manner in which his important disciple Guanding composed his highly ideological account of Zhiyi's life, relying heavily on a variety of miracle stories woven into the biography itself. Further light can be thrown on the nature of those miracle stories that center around Buddha images and that are found at crucial turning points in Guanding's account by comparing them with other accounts of the miracles associated with the same images that may be found elsewhere. In this paper I focus on the well-established account of Zhiyi's death in front of the Maitreya image in Shicheng and compare it with other stories about this image that have been preserved. One important reason for choosing this focus is the discrepancy between Guanding's account and the underlying theme of the other miracle stories associated with the image: whereas Guanding's stories insist that Zhiyi knew beforehand that he was to die in front of the image, other stories associated with the image indicate that it was often the recipient of fervent pleas for a cure from sickness; these stories suggest that Zhiyi too might have been requesting the image to cure his illness. This discrepancy in turn serves to highlight the ideological and "constructed" character of Guanding's biography.

2. *Guanding's account of Zhiyi's death in front of the Shicheng image*

Guanding devotes a long passage (195c5-196b27) to the description of Zhiyi's death. The first part of this description is devoted to a story of Zhiyi's return to Mt. Tiantai and a miraculous visit of a deity, known to Zhiyi from an earlier encounter, and from whom Zhiyi learned about his approaching death. Let me begin my discussion by briefly summarizing the story about this visit of a deity.

One night, when a bright moon illumined the floor, Zhiyi sat alone and gave a long lecture as if someone had asked a question about a difficult problem. Attendant monk Zhixi (558-629)[7] said to him the next morning, "I don't understand what I saw last night". Zhiyi answered, "I had a dream. First a strong wind suddenly rose and destroyed a treasure *stupa*. Then a foreign monk (*fanseng*) said to me, 'A man's spiritual capacity may be compared to fire wood; the spiritual function of illumination may be compared to the fire; the secondary assistance (*pangzhu*) may be compared to the wind. When these three conditions are met, the path of transformation is in operation ("one's teaching work is successful"?). During the night (many years ago when we met) on top of the Huading peak, we agreed on (my always being with you at your side) like a shadow or an echo. The capacity and function are about to be exhausted; the secondary assistance has also ceased (i.e., the three conditions mentioned above are about to be lost). Therefore, I came to tell you about this.' I also saw the Master of the Nanyue and Meditation Master Xi[8] who asked me to lecture on the teaching. So, I said to myself, 'All other teachings are clear and one can study them by oneself. Only the teaching of the Three Contemplations and Three Wisdoms must first be taught face to face'. After I finished lecturing on the teaching, they said to me, 'The other realm is decorated and put in order (to welcome you). We have been waiting for you for a long time. The karmic condition dictates that you must go. We shall send you over there.' I paid respect to them and accepted their judgement. The sign of death has now been given. I remember the dream I had as a young man in which it was said that I should end my life here.[9] This is the reason why I was always happy to return to this mountain. I have now been miraculously informed (of my approaching death). My death will occur in the near future. After I die, place my corpse in the place I have specified on the south-western peak.[10] Place stones around the corpse and plant pine trees to cover the grave pit. Build two white *stupas*, so that those who see them may give rise to the aspiration for enlightenment."[11]

The ruler[12] had returned in the tenth month and sent Gao Xiaoxin into the mountain to bring Zhiyi back. Zhiyi distributed his possessions to be given to the poor; he marked the location of temple buildings with sticks, and drew a diagram of the manner in which the temple was to be built; he instructed the monks, saying, "The temple will be built according to these instructions. I can see its staircases rising awe-inspiringly right in front of my eyes, but the building will be completed after my death. I will not see it, but you will see it. Later, you shall build the temple, following these instructions." Disciples doubted the veracity of this prediction and said, "This mountain is very steep. How could a temple be built on this mountain?" Zhiyi answered, "It's not a small project. It will be managed by the prince's family (*wang jia*, which could also be read as Wang family)." Monks present heard these words together, but speculated differently about their meaning. Some said that the word *wang* is a surname; others said that the word means the king of gods; still others said that it refers to the king of the state. Many views were debated loudly, but no consensus emerged. Now (when Guanding is writing this biography), the matter has been settled by what actually happened; we all know what the Master meant earlier. It meant the "king" in the sense of the imperial ruler of the state.[13]

In the first half of this long passage the "foreign monk" (*fanseng*) mentions the incident on the Huading peak. The incident on the Huading peak is described in detail in an earlier passage in Guanding's biography describing Zhiyi's first visit to Mt. Tiantai (193b1-16). There the same figure is described as the "supernatural monk" (*shenseng*) who appeared to Zhiyi after his conquest of the monsters on the Huading peak, taught him the teaching of One Real Truth (*yi shi di*) and promised to be with him all the time after that incident. The meaning of these stories seems clear: Zhiyi's teaching attained its distinctive identity and uniqueness while he was on Mt. Tiantai for the first time, and came to an end when he returned to the same mountain for the second time at the end of his life; when he went back to Tiantai, Zhiyi became fully aware that he was soon to die.

The second half of this passage focuses on the close relationship between Zhiyi's life and the building of the Guoqing temple on Mount Tiantai shortly after his death. I have spelled out in greater detail elsewhere what I would regard as the basic framework of Guanding's biography of Zhiyi: the life of Zhiyi was constructed very carefully as the story of the emergence of the Tiantai community with the support of the Sui ruler Yangdi.[14] The emergence of the community and the ruler's support were said to have been predicted a long time before they occurred; the implication is that these events were predetermined and inevitable. Zhiyi's experience on the Huading peak that occurred shortly after his first entry into Mt. Tiantai and the building of the Guoqingsi there shortly after Zhiyi's death were both crucial elements in this general framework. Here the story of Zhiyi's death is tightly incorporated into this basic framework through references to these events; it also shares their character of being predetermined. Zhiyi's death needed to occur at the time it did, during his last visit to Mt. Tiantai and before the construction of the Guoqing temple, and Zhiyi was himself fully aware of the inevitability of his death at this time.

In the subsequent section in Guanding's biography which describes the immediate circumstances of Zhiyi's death a Maitreya image appears and plays an important role.

Zhiyi followed Gao Xiaoxin, whom Prince Guang, Zhiyi's secular patron, had sent, and started on the journey to Jiangdu, the city where Prince Guang, who rose meteorically in power after Zhiyi's death and became the second Sui-emperor Yangdi, lived. When they arrived at Shicheng in Shanxian, Zhiyi said that he was ill. Zhiyi said to his disciple Zhiyue (544-611)[15], "The great prince wanted me to come. I could not disobey his words, and so I came. I know that my life is to end here. Therefore, we should not proceed any further. Shicheng is at the Western gate of the Tiantai mountains. The great Buddha (located there) is the miraculous image of the future Buddha (Maitreya). It is a good location to attend to last things mindfully. Divide my robes, bowls, and other implements into two sets and offer one to Maitreya (ie., the stone image) and use the other to meet the needs of the monastic community."[16] After saying these words, Zhiyi lay down on his right side, facing West, and recited the names of Amitabha, Prajna, and Avalokitesvara.

After rejecting medicine and food, Zhiyi dictated his will, wrote 46 characters with his own hands, and left his incense burner with the pattern of lotus flowers and the *ruyi* made of rhinoceros horn to the great king. Zhiyi asked his one bowl and three robes to be cleaned and to have two scriptures (*erbu jing*) recited so that these scriptures would be the last sounds that he heard and reflected upon in this life. These scriptures were the Lotus and *Wuliang shou* scriptures, and Zhiyi then listened to them as they were recited, uttering certain phrases. When the scriptures were being recited, an official of Wu Region, Zhang Da and others, accompanied by five people, saw the vision of a great Buddha, twice as large as the stone image. Its light filled the mountain and entered into the hall. Some monks had an auspicious dream and others saw extraordinary manifestations. Even though they had these experiences in different places, the experiences occurred at this same time.

Zhiyi's final instructions included an exchange with his disciple Zhilang, in which he comments, answering one of Zhilang's questions, that his teachers and friends were coming to him in the company of Avalokitesvara. After these instructions, Zhiyi said to the monastic officer, "When a man's life ends, you hear the sound of the bell. He increases his concentration, and his breathing becomes slow and extended. When he stops breathing, that is his end. Why should we wait until the body cools down and then sound the bell? As for the worldly practice of uttering the loud sound of crying and wearing funeral dresses, you should not adopt these practices." After saying these words, Zhiyi uttered the names of the three treasures; he looked as if he was entering a meditative state. At the *wei* hour (2:00 am) on the 24th day of the 11th month of the 17th year of the Kaihuang period, sixty year cycle designation *dingsi* (598), he passed away. He was in his 60th year, and in his 40th year as a monk.

According to this account by Guanding, Zhiyi who had known from earlier miraculous conversations with the foreign monk, his teacher Nanyue, and his former disciple Faxi, that he was going to end his life shortly, chose the site of the great Buddha image in Shicheng as the location of his death. The Shicheng image was a Maitreya image, and Zhiyi appears to have presented to it half of his remaining possessions at the time of his death. Later when the *Wuliangshou jing* was recited in front of Zhiyi, miracles occurred around the image and elsewhere.

3. The text of Zhiyi's vow (Guoqing bolu, no. 64)

The *Guoqing bolu* contains a very important document composed by Zhiyi himself that concerns the Shicheng image. It is a letter to Prince Guang dated the 21st day of the 11th month of the 17th year of Kaihuang (598), namely, three days before his death, in which Zhiyi requests the prince to repair important objects of worship located in three places: to bring together the images of Vipasyin and Kasyapa in the Wu Commandary and restore them to their original form (these images were originally found together), to repair the Asoka *stupa* at Mao District, and to redecorate the ten *zhang* tall Maitreya image at Shan District with gold leaves.[17] This letter, designated as *Fayuan shuwen* and preserved as the 64th item in the *Guoqing bolu*, is referred to as the "the text of a vow" (*Fayuan shu*) in another very important letter by Zhiyi to Prince Guang.[18]

The document begins as a letter in which Zhiyi requests Prince Guang to repair these objects of worship located in the three diffrent places.[19] But this short paragraph is then followed by a statement that "Zhiyi respectfully speaks". Zhiyi begins the long section following this phrase by commenting on the importance of the images and the shortcomings of his own life, and then makes the following statement: "Happily I encountered an illustrious age when the rulers (of the Sui dynasty) became the pillar of the Buddhist world which spread the blessing of the Teaching everywhere like the sun. Relying on the imperial virtue, and receiving the support of the power of the multitude, and in order to encourage those who enjoy right karmic conditions, I vow to repair the objects in the three places—first, to promote and glorify the Teaching of the Three Buddhas, second, to protect the land of the Great Sui, and third, looking downward, for the sake of all sentient beings in the world." The passage continues describing the benefit of repairing the *stupa* and images in terms of the three categories mentioned, that of benefits to the Buddhas, the emperor, and the people.

A new theme is then introduced: Zhiyi says that he had entertained this thought of repairing the *stupa* and the images for a long time, but had never had the opportunity to realize his desire. Now, his illness has become more grave and he is approaching his death ("journey to the West"); he certainly does not hold any attachment to his physical body that was to be compared with a jar of poison[20] or a fragile earthen ware; his life had already been given to the Three Treasures earlier. After this comment, Zhiyi then puts a question or a request to "a deity" (*weishen*): "If my life is to survive this illness, and if I am capable of good deeds and will not stain the Buddha's Teaching, then please remove this sickness soon and let me fulfil my vow quickly and completely. If my life, though not completely ended, is full of obstructions posed by Mara, and I am to do a great deal of damage to those endowed with good capacities, and stain and disturb the Buddha's Teaching, then there is no reason that I should remain in this world; please (*yuan*) let my life end, and after my life ends, pass my various vows (concerning the repair of the *stupa* and images) on to someone who remains behind (*houren*; probably a reference to Prince Guang),[21] and let him carry out the work of repair in an orderly fashion. I beg that the restoration of the Three Treasures (here probably referring to the *stupa* and images in question) be completed quickly."

Zhiyi then states that he had made this vow earlier at the Jinguangming daozhang hall at Folong, and that he was making the vow for the second time in front of the stone image of Shicheng.

The letter that began with a request to Prince Guang to repair the sacred objects in three locations appears to end with Zhiyi's fervent request to the stone image. The vow described in this document has a complex structure: on one level, the vow is a vow to repair the objects of worship in the three locations of Wu Commandary, Mao District, and Shan District. This may have been the vow that he had made earlier at Folong and is repeating here. On a different level, however, Zhiyi is making a related but slightly different vow. Having stopped in front of the stone image at Shicheng and realizing the graveness of his illness, Zhiyi is making a twofold request to the stone image: if he is to live, let him complete the task set forth in the previous vow quickly himself; if he is not to live, let someone else, that is, Prince Guang carry out the task quickly and successfully.

Focusing on the fact that the vow is made in front of the Shicheng image, I interpret the meaning of this second level of the vow as follows. Realizing the gravity of his illness, Zhiyi wanted to live and made the vow in front of the large image, promising that if he could live he would repair the image. This might have been the immediate context of the vow. References to the other two places where Zhiyi promised to repair the sacred objects associated with King Asoka would in this interpretation have been secondary. Zhiyi may possibly have been trying to enhance the importance of the Shicheng image by placing it in the company of a very well-known Asoka *stupa* and image. If we read the immediate context of Zhiyi's vow in this way, then the meaning of the second part of his request may be interpreted as follows. Zhiyi is here speaking both to the stone image and to Prince Guang: he promised the stone image that even if he died, the repair would be completed (this weakens the force of his first vow, but makes it less of a matter of crude *do ut des*); he at the same time emphasizes the importance of the request to Prince Guang by saying that it was a promise he had personally made to the stone image.

Why did Zhiyi write a special letter to Prince Guang only three days before his death concerning the repair of one Asoka *stupa* and two images? Repairing *stupa*s and images was indeed a meritorious act and one may answer the question by saying that this letter simply confirms Zhiyi's eagerness to perform meritorious deeds. But why did Zhiyi repeat the vow at this crucial point in time? There may well have been a more immediate and urgent reason. By reading this complex document in the manner proposed above, we can answer these questions more coherently: Zhiyi was not ready to die, and realizing the gravity of his illness, he was trying steadfastedly, even three days before his death, to obtain a miraculous cure from an image. It is thus natural that the vow was made so close to his death: the more serious the situation, the more likely Zhiyi must have been to resort to this dramatic measure.

Guanding's biography noted that Zhiyi presented his possessions to Maitreya. Later, Guanding records a series of miracles involving this image: Zhang Da and others had a vision of a large Buddha, twice the size of this image; its light filled the mountain.[22] These stories may have been related to the making of the vow mentioned in the *Guoqing bolu*, document no. 64. Zhiyi made the vow and presented his possessions to the image; later, the miracle may have been believed to have occurred in response to Zhiyi's request.

We have noted above that in his *Biezhuan* biography, Guanding describes Zhiyi's death as an event that Zhiyi himself knew was about to take place. Even before he travelled to Shicheng, Zhiyi is said to have made necessary preparations for his death, choosing the site of the later Guoqingsi temple, and predicting how it was to be built later; he then chose Shicheng as the site of his death. In contrast, the *Fayuan shuwen* projects a different picture of Zhiyi in front of the image. Zhiyi here does not seem to have been fully prepared to die at that time; rather, he describes the image in very favorable terms by grouping it with other well-known Asoka images, and suggests that if he recovers from the illness, he will repair the image.

We have noted earlier that we can no longer assume that all documents in the *Guoqing bolu* are historically reliable and free from editorial distortions. Yet, the fact that the description in the *Fayuan shuwen* diverges from that in Guanding's description of the same events in the *Biezhuan* appears to indicate that the *Fayuan shuwen* account is at least free of an editorical revision in Guanding's hand. A brief review of the tradition associated with the Shicheng image also suggests that the *Fayuan shuwen* account may be closer to the actual historical circumstances, and it was Guanding who revised this existing account rather extensively in his description of Zhiyi's life in the *Biezhuan*.

4. Stories about the Shicheng image

Let us now turn to a brief survey of the stories concerning the Shicheng image that are found in other sources; indeed their content lends support to the analysis of Zhiyi's vow that I have just offered. The image at Shan District is described as "a stone image of Maitreya, ten *zhang* tall" in the *Guoqing bolu*, document no. 64 (line 2,3). In the official inscription for Zhiyi compiled by Liu Guyan (*Guoqing bolu*, document no. 93), the compiler of the inscription, Liu Guyan, describes the image as a stone image, one hundred *zhi* tall and covered with gold leaf, and says that the image was created by Prince Yuanxiang of Nanping, *taizai* of Liang (l.108). This title refers to Xiao Wei, the eighth son of Wendi of the Liang dynasty and a brother of Wudi; he first bore the title of Prince of Jian'an.[23] The location is given here in greater detail: "in the Shicheng temple to the east of Shan" (l. 107).

a. The Gaoseng zhuan story

The *Gaoseng zhuan* biography of Senghu (412ab) is for the most part a story of the stone image of Maitreya, ten *zhang* tall, at the Yinyuesi temple of Shicheng mountain. Senghu was originally a man of Shan[24] in Kuaiji. He later lived at the Yinyuesi temple in the Shicheng mountain. There was a cliff of rock, undisturbed by worldly visitors, to the north of the temple. The cliff went straight up to a height of more than ten *zhang* (about 25 meters). In the middle of the cliff was a pattern that looked like the representation of flames and light on Buddhist images. There were bushes and trees on top of the cliff, and their twisting trunks cast shadows over the cliff. Senghu frequently went to the wall, and then saw bright light illumininating it and heard instrumental music and songs of praise. Because of this he held an incense burner and made the vow to carve the mountain cliff and make a stone image ten *zhang* in height there. This image was respectfully to copy the appearance of Maitreya 1,000 *zhi* (about 240 meters) tall; it would enable all those sentient beings whose karmic conditions were suitable to see what it would be like when Maitreya Buddha appeared as predicted in the scriptures on three future occasions to preach and bring salvation to them.[25] During the Jianwu period of the Southern Qi dynasty (494-497),[26] Senghu gathered monks and laymen (to form the community in support of this project) and began carving the image. After several years, when only the rough outline of the face of the image had been carved, Senghu became ill and died. Just before his death, he made the vow saying that his project was not something that anyone could finish in one life time, and that he would complete the project in his second incarnation.

Later, a monk Sengshu resumed the project, but for lack of resources, he was unable to bring it to completion. In the sixth year of the Tianjian period (of the Liang dynasty; 502-519) Lu Xian of the Wu Commandary, who had the position of the Director of Shifeng, had left the city to which he had been assigned and was returning to the capital. He was spending the night at Shanji (same as Shan District?). The wind began to blow and it started to rain; it became very dark. Lu Xian was frightened, and only half asleep (*jiamei*). Suddenly, three monks (*daoren*, "men of the Way") appeared in a dream and said to him, "Your knowledge and trustworthiness are correct and firmly established, and you are naturally safe and at peace. The honourable one of Jian'an (referring to Xiao Wei) is suffering from illness and he is not yet cured. If you can arrange to have the stone image started by Senghu brought to completion, the prince will regain his health. Miraculous communication is not unreal. You ought to get the work started." Xian returned to the capital, but after a year, he forgot about this earlier dream. Later, when he was going out of the city gate, he saw a monk and said to him, "Will you let us hear you give a lecture at my place and stay overnight?" The monk replied by saying, "Do you still remember the matter about the Prince of Jian'an I entrusted to you last year at Shanji?" Xian was then frightened, and said, "I don't remember". The man of the Way said laughing, "You should think about it carefully", and took his leave. Xian realized that this monk was not an ordinary monk and went after him quickly, but after 100 steps, the monk suddenly disappeared. Xian suddenly understood the meaning of the monk's statements, and remembered the earlier dream. The monk was the third monk among those whom he saw in Shanji. Xian then ran to the Prince of Jian'an. The prince reported the story to the emperor. The emperor then ordered the Vinaya master Sengyou to take charge of the matter of the image.[27] The faith of the Prince was increased, and overjoyed he made offerings and vowed to complete the work of building the image.

The day before Sengyou arrived, a monk at the (Yinyue?) temple had a dream in which a great deity wearing a black robe followed by an army of powerful soldiers stood at the site of the cave in which the image was being carved, and they discussed numbers (?). The next day the Vinaya master You appeared. Such was the miraculous nature of this event. The cave for the image that Senghu had carved was too shallow. It had to be carved further for a length of five *zhang* (about 12 meters). Then the head dress was carved. After that the torso was carved and the polishing of the torso was about to be completed. In the middle of the night the place of the character *wan* changed its colour to red and became raised. On the chest of the present image, the place of the character *wan* is still not covered with gold leaf, and the red colour remains. The work on the image began in the 12th year of Tianjian (513) and ended in the spring of the 15th year of Tianjian (516). In the sitting position the image is five *zhang* tall; standing up it is ten *zhang* tall.[28] In front of the image cave, a three story platform was built; a temple gate and other buildings were also constructed, and a community of monks was established for the purpose for serving the image... After the image was completed, Prince of Jian'an's sickness slowly disappeared.

We have noted above that in Liu Guyan's inscription the Shicheng image is said to have been built by Prince Yuanxiang of Nanping, *taizai* of Liang, and that this prince had the title of Prince of Jian'an. The stone image in Senghu's biography is also said to be that of Maitreya (a14), ten *zhang* tall (a13), located in the Shicheng mountain (a9) or in Shan District (a23). There is little doubt that the Shicheng image that is mentioned in Guanding's biography and in Zhiyi's letter to Prince Guang is identical with the image in Senghu's biography. Two major themes in the story about this image in Senghu's biography are of particular interest to us here. First, the relationship between this image and Prince Jian'an is described here as a story of a cure. Liu Guyan's reference to the same prince as the person who originally built the image indicates that this image was known widely as the image closely associated with this prince, and thus, the reputation of this image as an image of miraculous cure may also have been well-established. If this were the case, then our interpretation suggested above that Zhiyi may have appealed to this image for a cure from his own illness becomes more plausible.

The second theme that bears on our discussion is that of the long history behind this image. According to the *Gaoseng zhuan*, the construction of this image was started earlier by monk Senghu, and Prince Jian'an only helped to bring the task to completion many years after the monk's death by arranging to have the famous monk Sengyou placed in change of the project. In his complex statement about the vow discussed in some detail above, Zhiyi appeared to realize that he might not be able to fulfil his promise to repair the image and is instructing his patron Prince Guang to bring the task to completion. If Zhiyi was familiar with the long story about this image now preserved in the *Gaoseng zhuan*, he might have understood his own situation of having promised to repair the image but being prevented from fulfilling the promise because of his illness as a situation similar to that which obtained when the image was first constructed. In both cases illness was to be cured when the work on the image was completed; in both cases, however, it was going to be secular princes who were to bring the tasks to completion, and the monks who started the task were not going to be able to complete them.

b. Daoxuan's story in the Xu gaoseng zhuan *biography of Sengming*

Daoxuan's various collections of image miracle stories contain passages on this image at Shicheng in the Shan District. Thus we can examine the later developments of the stories about the stone image of Senghu by consulting these passages. In the list of image miracle stories attached at the end of the biography of Sengming, Daoxuan tells the story of Senghu's stone image (693c15-28).

More recently under the Northern Qi dynasty of the Gao family, monk Senghu was single-minded in following the Way, but rather than cultivating the path of wisdom, he made the vow to build a stone image of the height of eight *zhang*. Everybody wondered how such a massive project could be carried out. Later in a valley to the north of his temple he found a large rock which was eight *zhang* long. He then hired a rock carver and began the work of carving the image. The carver worked around the rock and roughly finished carving the front of the torso, but the back was still uncarved and facing the ground. The carver used six implements[29] and tried to lift the rock, but he could not move it. Then overnight the rock had turned itself over. Thus, the carver finished the work and moved the image to the image hall.

On the day when Jinzhou[30] was to fall (in the year 576)[31], the image sweated and the sweat flowed on the ground. When the (Northern) Zhou soldiers entered (Northern Qi) and burnt down many Buddhist temples, this image alone did not change its appearance (or, did not show fear?). The soldiers wanted to tear it down. Over sixty people and oxen pulled it, but it would not move. Suddenly a strange monk appeared and hitting the ground with bricks and wood, built a fort around it. The work was completed in a very short period of time, and then the monk disappeared. The image later appeared in a dream of a pious layman and said, "I have pains in my fingers". After waking up, the man looked at the image. Seeing that two of its fingers were damaged, he repaired them. In the tenth year of Kaihuang (590), a thief stole the flag and parasol decorating the image. Then, the thief dreamt that a man, eight *zhang* tall (about 20 meters) came into his room and accused him. The thief was frightened and apologized for his crime. The image still exists, and the story is found in the *Jingyiji* and various records of monks.

The location of the image is not explicitly stated, but it must have been Jinzhou, since the story about the soldiers trying to tear it down is told in connection with the fall of Jinzhou and the invasion of Zhou soldiers into Qi. Since Jinzhou here is clearly a different location from the Shicheng in the Shan District in which the image in Zhiyi's biography and that in the *Gaoseng zhuan* story of Senghu's image was situated, the story about Senghu's image reported in this *Xu Gaoseng zhuan* passage is about a different image from the one we have examining here. Yet, there are obvious parallels: both are tall stone images, though the height of the two images is given slightly differently; the name of the monk who originally worked on the images is given as Senghu. Perhaps a separate story about Senghu's image developed in a different location under the influence of the *Gaoseng zhuan* story, and Daoxuan picked up that story and recorded it in this collection of miracle stories. Earlier in a discussion of miracle stories associated with Huida, I noted that the geographical setting of Huida's story expanded with Daoxuan from a narrow area in Southern China to a much wider circle including North West China.[32] The shift in the location in the story of Senghu's image have resulted from the same tendency in Daoxuan's work concerning miracle stories. One other notable feature about this version of the Senghu image story is the similarity between this story and other stories associated with Asoka images: stories about the extraordinary weight and its miraculous capacity to escape plundering in a conquered city are most notable.[33]

c. The Ji shenzhou sanbao gantong lu *story*

Daoxuan records the story of the stone image in the Shan District in the *Ji shenzhou sanbao gantong lu* as an appendix to the story about the eight *zhang* tall golden image at the Guangzhai temple (419c-420a).[34]

The image was originally produced by King Asoka at the beginning of Chinese history (*song qu*). Earlier Meditation Master Tanguang arrived from the north. He travelled along mountains and rivers and made nature the dwelling place of his spiritual life. Seeing the beauty of this mountain, he built a grass hut at the top of the peak. He heard heavenly music in the sky and a voice which said, "This is a land of the Buddha. How come you are making a vegetable garden here?" Hearing this Guang moved southward to the Tiantai mountain. Later, he built a Buddha image. He worked over many years but could not complete the work. (And Tanguang died?)

When Prince Jian'an of the Liang dynasty was ill, it was communicated through a dream that if one could build a stone image at Shan District, then his illness would be cured. Consequently, the Vinaya master Sengyou was invited to come to the mountain. Sengyou disliked the shape and construction of the earlier image that Tanguang had worked on, considering it as too provincial and vulgar. While he was still thinking about it incessantly, in the middle of the night, the mountain collapsed, and an image appeared inside. Only the head was showing, and the body below the neck was still buried in the rock. As they carved the rock, the stone pieces flew away, and the image at the base appeared. This perfectly shaped image was hidden in the rock all the time. Liu Xie wrote an inscription, and it is placed at the site of the image.[35]

There is little doubt that the image in this story is identical with the Shicheng image we have been studying here. It was the image in Shan District that was completed by Sengyou and its completion cured Prince Jian'an's illness. In this story the image is for the first time said explicitly to have been originally produced by King Asoka. Interestingly, the name of the monk who began the work on this image is given as Tanguang, and not as Senghu as in the *Gaoseng zhuan* biography. Thus, if we follow Daoxuan's account alone, Senghu who is associated with a different image in a different location has nothing to do with the Asoka image in Shan District. What was one story in the *Gaoseng zhuan* appears to have split into two in Daoxuan's collections.

Tanguang was closely associated with the Tiantai mountain. We have seen earlier that the name Tanguang was mentioned in connection with the story of Zhiyi's first visit to the Tiantai mountain in Guanding's *Biezhuan*. The *Gaoseng zhuan* biography of Jin Sengguang (395c) states that the latter was also known as Tanguang and says that this monk went to the Shicheng mountain in Shan (District) during the Yonghe period of the Jin dynasty (345-356). He first stayed in a rock cave in the southern part of the mountain, but later was told by a mountain deity in a dream to move to the Hanshishan mountain in Zhang'an District. Others built thatched huts next to his residence and the community expanded. These buildings evolved into a temple, which was later called Yinyue.[36] He lived in the mountain for 53 years and died at the end of the Taiyuan period of the Jin dynasty (376-396) at the age of 110.[37]

In Daoxuan's *Ji shenzhou sanbao gantong lu*, the connection between the Shicheng image and the Tiantai mountain received even greater emphasis by its new connection with Tanguang. One theme that remained constant was the story that connects the completion of the massive project of building this image with the cure of Prince Jian'an's illness. Daoxuan compiled this collection over 50 years after Zhiyi's death and Guanding's compilation of Zhiyi's biography. If this theme remained closely associated with the Shicheng image at that time, even though the earlier stories associated with this image had gone through a number of changes, it seems quite plausible that both Zhiyi and Guanding were quite familiar with this story about the image as an image known for its power of miraculous cure.[38]

5. Concluding comments

In an earlier paper I suggested that the death of Zhiyi must have been a profoundly "liminal" incident for the Tiantai community.[39] The effort of the community to adjust itself to the new situation was furthermore affected profoundly by the meteoric rise of its principal lay sponsor Prince Guang. Zhiyi died on the 24th day of the 11th month of the 17th year of the Kaihuang period of the Sui dynasty (*Biezhuan*, 196b26,27). This date translates into January 7, 598 in the solar calendar. Prince Guang became the crown prince in the year 600 and then rose to the throne in the 604 as Emperor Yangdi. The temple which had been built in Zhiyi's honour[40] was give the name "Guoqingsi" by an imperial edict issued on the 29th day of the tenth month of the first year of Daye (606).[41] Ikeda suggests the date of Liu Guyan's inscription for Zhiyi, titled the "the inscription for the Guoqingsi temple issued by an imperial edict" (*Guoqing bolu*, no. 93) as the third year of the Daye period (607). These dates suggests that the fortunes of the Tiantai community must have risen dramatically after Zhiyi's death, and these years must have been a rather heady time for this community.

A large number of miracle stories are recorded from this period. I pointed out in my earlier article that the basic framework of Guanding's biography, which appears to have been compiled between the years 601 and 605, was constructed by several stories of miraculous events that were said to have occurred at important turning points in Zhiyi's life.[42] A comparison of the miracle stories reported in earlier sources and the stories used to construct the basic framework in Guanding's biography indicates that Guanding must have chosen several stories that were widely known and suitable to his purposes and used these stories as crucial reference points in constructing the framework of his biography. A complex and subtle process of choice must have been made in this context to choose stories that were suitable for Guanding's purposes from the larger pool of available stories and reject others that were not suitable.

The brief review above of the stories associated with the stone image of Maitreya at Shicheng in the Shan District indicates that this image was known as an image capable of miraculous cure. The discussion of the text of the vow that Zhiyi made in front of this image suggested that three days before his death Zhiyi might indeed have been requesting a miraculous cure from this image. As we noted earlier, this theme of Zhiyi (and probably others accompanying him) requesting a miraculous cure of his illness from this stone image is entirely absent in Guanding's biography. According to the account in this biography Zhiyi had received a message from his protective deity that he was to die shortly and himself chose the site of this image as the place where he was to end his life. Would it be entirely inappropriate to speculate that in writing the story about Zhiyi's death, Guanding was confronted with the inconvenient fact that Zhiyi's attempt to secure a miraculous cure from a Maitreya image at Shicheng, known widely for its capacity confer such cure, had failed, and that Guanding had to develop a different set of miraculous stories to explain the timing of Zhiyi's death?

In his discussion of Zhiyi's death Sato Tetsuei commented briefly on the fact that the *Biezhuan*'s description was characterized by dual emphases on the faith in the Lotus sutra and the faith in Amitabha Buddha and that early sources often mention that Amitabha, Avalokitesvara, and Mahasthamaprapta appeared to Zhiyi to welcome him into the other world.[43] Since these figures are more closely associated with the theme of death and rebirth in the Pure Land, it is tempting to speculate that the connection between Zhiyi's death and the Maitreya image in Shicheng, known for its association with the theme of miraculous cure was deemphasized in the stories that developed about Zhiyi's death in the Tiantai community and these stories replaced that theme with an emphasis on stories about Zhiyi's rebirth.

(The research for this paper was carried out with the assistance of a grant from the Social Sciences and Humanities Council of Canada.)

Notes

1. Zhiyi's dates are given in most modern works as 538-597. These dates appear to have been calculated as follows: Guanding's biography gives date of Zhiyi's death as the 24th day of the 11th month of the 17th year of the Kaihuang period (*Taisho daizokyo*, vol. 50, p. 196b26, 27). Zhiyi was said to have been sixty years old at the time of his death. Though the Taisho edition of the *Xu gaoseng zhuan*, based on the Korean edition, gives the date of Zhiyi's death slightly differently, as the 22nd day, the variant reading in the majority of other editions consulted by the editors of the Taisho edition, gives the same date as Guanding's biography, ie., the 24th day. Daoxuan's *Xu gaoseng zhuan* biography states that Zhiyi was sixty-seven years old at the time of his death (567b25). If we adopt the solar calendar date for the 17th year of the Kaihuang period as 597 and, taking account of the traditional Chinese way of counting age, subtract 59 from 597, we can arrive at Zhiyi's dates as 538 to 597, the dates generally given in modern sources. Strictly speaking, however, the lunar and solar years do not correspond with each other perfectly and, most importantly for our purposes, the 24th day of the 11th month of the 17th year of the Kaihuang period happens to correspond to January 8th of the solar year 598 (See Xie Zhongsan and Ouyang Yi, *A Sino-Western Calendar for Two Thousand Years 1-2000 A.D.*, Taipei, 1966, p. 120.) If we follow the same procedure as above, following Guanding's view that Zhiyi was sixty years old at the time of his death, we can propose the year 539 as the date of Zhiyi's birth.

2. *Sui tiantai zhizhe dashi biezhuan* by Guanding, *Taisho daizokyo*, vol. 50, pp. 194a9-b26; *Tiantai guoqingsi zhizhe chanshi beiwen* by Liu Guyan, Ikeda Rosan, *Kokusei hyakuroku no kenkyu* (Tokyo, 1982), p. 467-468, ll. 107-118; *Xu gaoseng zhuan*, *zhuan* 17, *Taisho daizokyo*, vol. 50, pp. 567a25-b24. Shicheng is located in the Shan District and the image is sometimes identified as the great stone image in Shan district (*shanxian dashifo*, *Ji shenzhou sanbao gantong lu*, *Taisho daizokyo* vol. 52, 419c17.)

3. Zhiyi's biography was discussed in detail in Leon Hurvitz, *Chih-i (538-597): An Introduction to the Life and Ideas of a Chinese Buddhist Monk*, *Mélanges chinois e bouddhiques*, publié par L'Institut Belge des hautes Etudes Chinoises, Douzième volume: 1960-1962 (Bruxelles, Juillet 1962). The emphasis in this discussion is on the critical reconstruction of Zhiyi's life. Guanding's biography, while recognized as indispensable for this reconstruction, is treated with caution "because of Kuan-ting's *Tendenz*" (p. 100). Sato Tetsuei's biography of Zhiyi in the beginning section of his monumental *Tendai daishi no kenkyu* (Kyoto, 1961), pp. 28-73 shares the same basic orientation: it is also an attempt to reconstruct Zhiyi's biography based on a critical examination of sources. I have completed a preliminary study of Guanding's biography of Zhiyi and presented its summary at the annual meeting of the Canadian Society for the Study of Religion in Quebec City in June, 1989 ("Guanding's Biography of Zhiyi: Its Framework and the three Miraculous Images"). The present paper is based on one section of this larger study.

4. I have published a preliminary study of Chinese Buddhist biographies in an article entitled "Two Sources of Chinese Buddhist Biographies: *Stupa* Inscriptions and Miracle Stories", in Phyllis Granoff and Koichi Shinohara, *Monks and Magicians: Religious Biographies in Asia*, (Oakville, Ontario, 1988), pp. 119-228.

5. *Taisho daizokyo*, vol. 46, pp. 793-823. A detailed study of this work with an annotated Japanese translation was recently published by Ikeda Rosan: *Kokusei hyakuroku no kenkyu, ibid.*

6. Hirai Shun'ei, in *Hokke mongu no seiritsu nikansuru kenkyu* (Tokyo, 1985), recently suggested that the comments on Zhiyi's commentaries on the Vimalakirti sutra that are found in the *Guoqing bolu* might have been inserted in historical records in order to strengthen the view that Guanding and later the Tiantai community wished to maintain; in this manner they may have been trying connect the version of these commentaries they produced directly to Zhiyi himself. Hirai's arguments, found in pp. 45-52 in his important work, are summarized in detail in Ikeda Rosan's riview in *Komazawa daigaku bukkyogakubu ronshu*, 16 (1985), pp. 414-434. The comment on the reliablity of the *Guoqing bolu* appears in p. 49 in Hirai's work and p. 419a in Ikeda's summary. Although certain parts of the records in the *Guoqing bolu*, particularly those related to the compilation of Zhiyi's works recorded and edited by Guanding, might have been manipulated by Guanding, we might nevertheless be justified in taking other parts of the records, especially those directly related to Zhiyi's biography and yet not in harmony with Guanding's biography, as faithful reproductions of earlier historical records. It is also possible that these records might reflect the divergent, and possibly earlier, views of the Tiantai community. The information that the collection of documents originally started by Zhiji was later completed as *Guoqing bolu* by Guanding is given in Guanding's preface, *Kosei hyakuroku no kenkyu*, p. 129. See also Ikeda's comment in pp. 13-14 in the same work.

7. His biography is found in the *Xu gaoseng zhuan*, *zhuan* 19, *Taisho daizokyo*, vol. 50, p. 582a-583a.

8. The *Issaikyo (shidenbu)*, vol. 10, p. 609, n. 98 identifies this figure as Faxi who became Zhiyi's disciple at age 60. His short biography is found in *Fozu tongji*, 197. The monk was already dead at the time the incident at the Tiantai mountain described in the present passage took place, and that may have been the reason why his name was mentioned in this context.

9. Ref., 191b26.

10. Later in the biography (196c6) Guanding notes that Zhiyi was buried at the place specified by Zhiyi, presumably referring to the same location as the place mentioned here.

11. 195c12-25. For a translation of the last section of this passage, see Hurvitz, *ibid*., p. 169.

12. The term *huangshang* ("emperor") is used here to refer to Prince Guang of Jin. The prince became the emperor in the year 604. So, if the term is meant to

mean the emperor here, this would indicate that the passage in its present form was written after that date.

13. 195c28-18. *Guoqing bolu*, no. 69, line. 5,6 also refers to the story about the construction of the temple building. This document in the *Guoqing bolu* bears the date of the 15th day of the second month of the 18th year of Kaihuang [598], showing that the idea of this story existed by that time, ie., only two and a half months after Zhiyi's death.

14. "Guanding's biography of Zhiyi: Its Framework and the Three Miraculous Images", *ibid.*

15. Zhiyue's biography is found in the *Xu gaoseng zhuan, zhuan* 17, *Taisho daizokyo*, p. 570c-571a.

16. Uemura Shincho, in his translation of the *Biezhuan* in the *Kokuyaku issaikyo* (Tokyo, 1967, p. 611, n. 9), explains that the latter refers to the expenses for the funeral.

17. In an earlier article I discussed in some detail the traditions associated with the Asoka *stupa* in the Mao District and the stone images in the Wu Commandary, also believed to have been related to King Asoka. See "Two Sources of Chinese Buddhist Biographies", *ibid.*, p.163-167.

18. This letter preserved in the *Guoqing bolu*, document no. 65 is Zhiyi's testament written in the form of a letter to Prince Guang. It contains a long autobiographical passage that describes Zhiyi's life in a very different tone from that of existing biographies. I plan to discuss this letter in greater detail on a different occasion, in order to comment on different dynamics of biographies and autobiographies and further to highlight the constructed character of both types of writings. The reference to the *Fayuan shu* is found in l. 64.

19. Ikeda Rosan recently published a study of the *Guoqing bolu* entitled *Kokusei hyakuroku no kenkyu* (Tokyo, 1892). Ikeda presents in this volume a critical and punctuated edition of the text, principally based on the Taisho edition, together with detailed notes and the translation of the text. My discussion of the materials from the *Guoqing bolu* here, particularly the summary of the document no. 64 given below, is heavily indebted to Ikeda's work.

20. The expression *duqi*, translated here as "jar of poison" also appears in Guanding's *Biezhuan* biography (196a20): Zhiyi is said to have used this expression in his oral reply turning down a meal; he then dictated his will, which probably refers to the document preserved as the 66th document in the *Guoqing bolu*. Guanding may have taken the expression "*duqi*" from the *Fayuan shuwen*, and used it in composing his description of Zhiyi's state just before he dictated his will to Prince Guang.

21. As we noted above, the document that contains the text of the vow, namely, *Guoqing bolu*, no. 64, is written as a letter to Prince Guang and begins with a request to the Prince to repair the three sites in question. Another document, Zhiyi's testament written in the form of a letter to Prince Guang (*Guoqing bolu*, document no. 65, pp. 363-379), mentions the text of the vow under examination here in the list of requests that he had left for the prince (line 64). Prince Guang's reply to this latter letter, now written in the form of a letter he

wrote to the Tiantai community upon receiving the news about Zhiyi's death (*Guoqing bolu*, document no. 66, pp. 379-389), refers to the list of requests that Zhiyi had made in his testament and promises to carry out the projects Zhiyi had requested. The sites where repair work (*zhuangshi*) is required are given here as the Mao District *stupa*, stone images in Wu Commandary, the Maitreya image in Shan District (ie., the Shicheng image), and the location where Zhiyi died (p. 380, ll. 40-42). It seems appropriate, in view of the fact that Zhiyi had left the text of the vow to the prince himself in a letter that begins with a request to repair these sites, and that the prince later promised to carry out the repair work, that Zhiyi was referring to Prince Guang by the expression *houren* ("someone left behind") in this passage of the text of the vow.

22. 196b1,2.

23. His biography is found in the *Liangshu*, *zhuan* 22 (pp. 346-48).

24. Written with the same character as Shanxian (Shan District) above and probably refers to the same location.

25. Maitreya's preaching on three future occasions is mentioned in the *Fo shuo mile xiasheng jing* (Taisho n. 453), *Taisho daizokyo*, vol. 14, p. 422bc, *Fo shuo mile xiasheng chengfo jing* (Taisho, n. 454), *ibid*., 425b, and *Fo shuo mile xiasheng jing* (Taisho, n. 455), *ibid*., 427c.

26. Taisho edition, which reproduces the text of the *Gaoseng zhuan* found in the Korean edition, gives the name of the dynasty as "Northern Qi", but lists the variant reading "Qi dynasty" found in Song, Yuan, Ming and Kunaicho editions. The Northern Qi dynasty lasted between 550 and 577, but never used the era name Jianwu. Since the story later gives the date of the sixth year of the Tianjian period (507-508) as the date on which a crucial event possibly many years after Senghu's death occurs, the dynasty in question could not have been the Northern Qi, but rather must have been the Qi or Southern Qi dynasty which lasted 479-502. There was a Jianwu period under the Southern Qi dynasty; the period lasted 494-497.

27. Sengyou's biography mentions Shanxian's stone image along with the great images of Guangzhai and of Sheshan as images the Sengyou built (402c19). The story of the great image in the Guangzhai temple is told in Fayue's biography (412c-413a). The imperial order placing Sengyou in change of this image is mentioned in 412c28,19. See also 413b7,9 for further comments on the Guangzhai temple image.

28. The meaning of this sentence is unclear. Were there two images?

29. The meaning of the expression *liu ju* in 693c19 is not clear. I am here tentatively assuming that it means "six implements", assuming these implements to be a variety of common tools for moving heavy objects.

30. Northern Qi used this name for a city, earlier called Pingyangfu under the Northern Wei dynasty, in the Shanxi province. The city was also called Jinzhou under the Tang dynasty. See Morohashi, 5, 863, 4.

31. Jinzhou under the rule of Northern Qi was conquered by Northern Zhou forces in the tenth month of the fifth year of the Jiande period according to the Northern Zhou calendar (the seventh year of the Wuping period according to the

Northern Qi calendar; the tenth month of this year was in the year 576 according to the Western calendar). The description of this incident is found in the second part of the chronicle of the rule of the emperor Wu in the sixth fascicle of the dynastic history of Northern Zhou (*Zhou shu*, p. 95); the event is also mentioned briefly in the chronicle of the last ruler of the Northern Qi dynasty in the eighth fascicle of the dynastic history (*Beiqi shu*, p. 109).

32. "Two Sources...", *Ibid.*, p. 179.

33. For example a story about the unusual weight of images is told about the two stone images in Wu Commandary ("Two Sources...", *ibid.*, 165; *Ji shenzhou sanbao gantong lu*, *Taisho daizokyo*, vol. 52, 414a and *Fayuan zhulin*, *Taisho daizokyo*, vol. 53, 383a) and the story about the Asoka image of Manjusri in Mt. Lu discovered by Tao Kan (*Ji shenzhou sanbao gantong lu*, 417b and *Fayuan zhulin*, 386b). The Tao Kan image stories in the *Ji shenzhou sanbao gantong lu* include a story about an old monk to whom the image spoke miraculously, ordering him to stay in the temple after others had left because of rampant bandit activities: when rebel soldiers entered the city and attempted to decapitate the monk, the image miraculously protected him. We might note that the Manjusri image in Mt. Lu is also mentioned in Guanding's biography of Zhiyi, *Sui tiantai zhizhe dashi biezhuan*, 194c5-8. Here the mountain in which the image was housed was spared of disturbance and burning when rebellion occurred in a neighbouring city. The story about the image's weight is also told in Guanding's biography of the Asoka image in the Changsha temple (*Gaoseng zhuan*, 356a: the biography of Tanyi; see also the earlier *Mingseng zhuan* biography of Tanyi, preserved in the *Meisodensho*, *Zokuzokyo* / *Xu zang jing*, vol. 134, p. 7Ba). The *Xu gaoseng zhuan* story about this image includes a story about a fire which miraculously did not burn the building that housed this image (692c).

34. This same passage is also found in the *Fayuan zhulin*, 389b. I have recently completed three articles on the sources of the *Ji shenzhou sanbao gantong lu*: "The *Ji shenzhou sanbao gantong lu* ("Collected Records of Three Treasure Miracles in China"): Some Exploratory Notes", *Kalyana-Mitta: Professor Hajime Nakamura Felicitation Volume* (Delhi: Indian Books Centre, 1991); "Dao-xuan's Collection of Miracle Stories about 'Supernatural Monks' (*Shen-seng gan-dong lu*): An Analysis of its Sources", *Chung-hwa Buddhist Journal* Vol. 3 (April, 1990), pp. 319-380; "A Source Analysis of the *Ruijing lu* ("Records of Miraculous Scriptures"), *The Journal of the International Association of Buddhist Studies* (forthcoming).

35. The text of Liu Xie's inscription is preserved in the *Yiwen leiju*, *juan* 76, Shanghai guji qubanshe edition (n.d.), pp. 1302-1303. Liu Xie's inscription is also mentioned in Zhipan's comment on this image in the *Fozu tongji*, 347a.

36. Yinyuesi at the Shicheng mountain was the name of the temple in which Senghu lived according to the *Gaoseng zhuan*, 412a9.

37. Guanding's *Biezhuan* also mentions the name Bai Daoyou in connection with the story of Zhiyi's first visit to the Tiantai mountain (193a8). This name

must refer to the monk called Zhu Tanyou whose biography is given in the *Gaoseng zhuan*, 395c-396a. His biography is rather similar to that of Tanguang briefly summarized above. Daoxuan's work *Shijia fangzhi* contains a story of Zhu Tanyou which mentions a supernatural temple in the Tiantai mountain (972c22-973a1). This same story is found as a story of Jin Taoyou or Zhu Daoyou in the *Ji shenzhou sanbao gantong lu*, 423b-c17. We might at this point note the earlier connection between Shicheng and Zhidun. A brief comment on this connection is found in Hayashi Denho, *Chugoku bokkyo shiseki yosetsu*, vol. 1 (Kyoto, 1979), p. 53.

38. The stone image at Shicheng is mentioned in three passages (347a, 389c and 467c) in Zhipan's comment on this image in the *Fozu tongji*, compiled in the course of the 12 years between the sixth year of Baoyou (1258) and the sixth year of Xianchun (1269)(the information concerning these dates is found in 129c). Thus the image and the stories about it appear to have been well-known during the Song period. The passage in 347a, after summarizing the stories about this image in the *Gaoseng zhuan* and the *Xu gaoseng zhuan* with some additional details, notes that the Vinaya Master Daoxuan of the Tang period met a heavenly deity (*tianshen*) who said to him "The Master (referring to Daoxuan?) is a later incarnation (*houshen*) of Senghu, Sengshu, and Sengyou". For this reason, the passage continues, the image was called "*sansheng shifo*", which may be translated as the "stone Buddha of three lives" or the "stone Buddha which has been born three times". The point of this story is not entirely clear. The phraseology in this passage suggests that the "Master" (*shi*) who is said to be the later incarnation is indeed Daoxuan himself, and reminds us of the story in Daoxuan's biography in the *Song gaoseng zhuan* in which Daoxuan's mother after conceiving him miraculously was told by a foreign monk who appeared in a dream that the child she conceived was the Vinaya Master Sengyou of the Liang period (790b). We might also recall Senghu's statement in the *Gaoseng zhuan* biography that he would complete his project of carving the image in question in his next incarnation (412a17,18). In the *Gaoseng zhuan* biography this statement is immediately followed by a statement which says that Sengshu later continued Senghu's project, but could not complete it again. There may an implicit suggestion here that Sengshu was a later incarnation of Senghu. Since the project was eventually completed by Sengyou, some might have believed that Sengyou also was a reincarnation of Senghu, and the image might have been called by the name given in this passage in the sense that it was completed in the course of three lives, those of Senghu, Sengshu, and Sengyou. The deity's words to Daoxuan might simply have been connecting the two stories which were originally entirely independent of each other: one story was about the Shicheng image which established that Sengyou was a reincarnation of Senghu and Sengshu, and the other story was a biographical story about Daoxuan, which indicated that Daoxuan was the reincarnation of Sengyou. If this was the case, there may not have been any logical connection between the words of the heavenly deity to Daoxuan, explaining that he was the fourth reincarnation of Senghu and the fact that the image was called the "stone

Buddha of three lives", even though 347a passage in the *Fozu tongji* uses the conjunction "therefore" (*gu*) in this context. It is also possible that the heavenly deity's words to Daoxuan were spoken on an occasion when the Shicheng image was not the topic of conversation. It may have been Zhipan who introduced this story in the context of a discussion of the Shicheng image.

The story of the statement that a heavenly deity made to Daoxuan about this image is also told in another passage in the *Fozu tongji* located in 467b in an abbreviated form. Here the words of the deity are given without the reference to the "Master", and the words may be read as saying that the stone image itself is the later incarnation (or bodily representation) of Senghu, Sengshu, and Sengyou. It is a little easier to harmonize this reading of the deity's statement with the information given immediately after it, which states that the image was called the "stone Buddha of three lives" or the "stone Buddha which has been born three times". The designation then might refer to the fact that the three monks produced the same stone image on three different occasions.

The passage in 389c reports that the Wuyue ruler Qian Liu established the Ruixiang temple at the Shicheng mountain and offered it to the "stone image of three lives" or the "stone image that had been born three times" (*sansheng shixiang*). This reference might indicate that the image was in fact known later as an image of "three lives".

The note following this passage mentions several sources including a work called,"*Tianren gantong zhuan* (Stories of Miraculous Communications between Gods and Men?)". This latter work may have been a record of widely known incidents of Daoxuan's miraculous conversations with deities. Although the best known record of this conversation in a work called "*Daoxuan lushi gantong lu*" (T. 2107) or the "*Luxiang gantong zhuan* (T. 1898) does not include a story about this image, references to Daoxuan's exchanges with deities in the *Fayuan zhulin* indicates that a larger body of records of these incidents might have existed earlier. I am currently preparing a study of the stories about Daoxuan's exchanges with deities.

39. "Guanding's Biography of Zhiyi: Its Framework and the Three Miraculous Images", *ibid*.

40. *Guoqing bolu*, no. 87, line 1 (Ikeda, *ibid*., p. 450).

41. *Guoqing bolu*, no. 89, lines 10, 11, 14, and 15 (Ikeda, *ibid*., p. 453). See also *Guoqing bolu*, no. 90, lines 2 and 3 (Ikeda, *ibid*., 458.

42. Guanding's colophon (197c18,19) indicates that his work on the *Biezhuan* biography began with a conversation with Liu Guyan which took place in the 21st year of the Kaihuang period (which is identical with the first year of the Renshou period, the year 601). An informal biography of Zhiyi (*Xingzhuang*, an "account of conducts") compiled by Guanding is mentioned in one document preserved in the *Guoqing bolu* (no. 86). This *Guoqing bolu* document records the conversations between the messenger from the Tiantai community and court officials; the conversation in which the *Xingzhuang* is mentioned is said to have taken place on the 20th day of the 10th month of the first year of Daye (605)(Ikeda, *Kokusei hyakuroku no kenkyu*, *ibid*., 14, p. 443, line 7 and p. 444

line 30). Since the *Xingzhuang* appears to be identical with the *Biezhuan*, the latter had been completed by the year 605.

43. Sato Tetsuei, *ibid.*, pp. 64-66. The references to Amitabha, Avalokitesvara, and Mahasthamaprapta appear in *Biezhuan*, 196b5, *Guoqing bolu*, 66 (lines 9, 10; Ikeda, p. 379), 67 (lines 12, Ikeda, p. 390), 68 (line 10, Ikeda, p. 68).

List of Characters

Bai Daoyou 白道猷

Beiqi shu 北齊書

Biezhuan 別傳

Baoyou 寶祐

Changsha 長沙

daoren 道人

Daoxuan 道宣

Daoxuan lushi gantong lu 道宣律師感通錄

Daye 大業

dingsi 丁巳

erbu jing 二部經

Fayuan shuwen 發願疏文

Fayuan shu 發願疏

fanseng 梵僧

Faxi 法喜

Fayuan zhulin 法苑珠林

Fayue 法悅

Folong 佛龍

Fo shuo mile xiasheng jing 佛說彌勒下生經

Fo shuo mile xiasheng chengfo jing 佛說彌勒下生成佛經

Fozu tongji 佛祖統紀

Gao 高

Gao Xiaoxin 高孝信

Gaoseng zhuan 高僧傳

gu 故

Guang 廣

Guangzhai 光宅

Guanding 灌頂

Guoqing 國清

Guoqing bolu 國清百錄

Hanshishan 寒石山

houren 後人

Huading 華頂

Ikeda Rosan 池田魯參

Issaikyo (shidenbu) 一切經

Ji shenzhou sanbao gantong lu 集神州三寶感通錄

Jiangdu 江都

Jian'an 建安

Jiande 建德

Jianwu 建武

jiamei 假寐

Jin 晋

Jin Sengguang 帛僧光

Jingyi ji 旌異記

Jinguangming daozhang 金光明道場

Jinzhou 晋州

Kai-huang 開皇

Kokusei hyakuroku no kenkyu 國清百録の研究

Kokuyaku issaikyo 國訳一切経

Kuaiji 會稽

Liang 梁

Liang shu 梁書

Liu Guyan 柳顧言

Liu Xie 劉勰

Lu 盧

Lu Xian 陸咸

Luxiang gantong zhuan 律相感通傳

Mao 鄮

Meisodensho 名僧傳抄

Mingseng zhuan 名僧傳

Nanping 南平

Nanyue 南嶽

pang zhu 傍助

Qi 齊

Qian Liu 錢鏐

Renshou 仁壽

rui 如意

Ruijing lu 瑞經錄

Ruixiang 瑞相

sansheng shifo 三生石佛

sansheng shixiang 三生石像

Sato Tetsuei 佐藤哲英

Senghu 僧護

Sengming 僧明

Sengshu 僧淑

Sengyou 僧祐

Shan 剡

Shanji 剡溪

Shanxian 剡縣

shanxian dashifo 剡縣大石佛

shen seng 神僧

Sheshan 攝山

shi 師

Shicheng 石城

Shifeng 始豐

Shijia fangzhi 釋迦方志

Song gaoseng zhuan 宋高僧傳

song qu 宋初

Sui 隋

Sui tiantai zhizhe dashi biezhuan
隋天台智者大師別傳

Taisho daizokyo 大正大藏經

Taiyuan 太元

taizai 太宰

Tang 唐

Tanguang 曇光

Tanyi 曇翼

Tao Kan 陶侃

Tendai daishi no kenkyu
天台大師の研究

Tianjian 天監

Tianren gantong zhuan 天人感通傳

tianshen 天神

Tiantai 天台

Tiantai guoqingsi zhizhe chanshi beiwen
天台國清寺智者禪師別傳

Uemura Shincho 上村真肇

wan 萬

Wang 王

wang jia 王家

wei 未

weishen 威神

Wendi 文帝

Wu 吳

Wu* 武

Wudi 武帝

Wuliangshou jing 無量壽經

Wuliang shou 無量壽

Wuping 武平

Wuyue 吳越

Xi 喜

Xian 咸

Xianchun 咸淳

Xiao Wei 蕭偉

Xing zhuang 行狀

Xu gaoseng zhuan 續高僧傳

Yangdi 楊帝

yi shi di 一實諦

Yinyue 隱嶽

Yinyuesi 隱嶽寺

You 祐

yuan 願

Yuanxiang 元襄

Zhang Da 張達

zhang 丈

Zhang'an 章安

Zhilang 智朗

Zhipan 志磐

Zhixi 智晞

Zhiyi 智顗

Zhou 周

Zhou shu 周書

Zhu Tanyou 竺曇猷

zhuan 卷

zhuang shi 裝飾

Zokuzokyo / Xu zang jing 續藏經

RECENT DEVELOPMENTS IN THE TEXT CRITICAL STUDY OF THE PLATFORM SCRIPTURE

Ryosho Tanaka
Komazawa University

1. Introduction

According to the Tun-huang text S 5475, Hui-neng of Ts'ao-ch'i, the sixth patriarch of Chinese *ch'an* Buddhism, conferred precepts and preached to monks and laymen at the Precept Platform of the Ta-fan-ssu temple of Shao-chou. The record (*ching*, *sutra*) of this sermon compiled by his disciple Fa-hai is generally called "the Platform Scripture of the Sixth Patriarch" (*liu-tzu t'an-ching*).[1] Scholars of *ch'an* Buddhism have been greatly interested in this record and there exist a large number of studies on this subject.[2] We can glimpse the scale of existing scholarship on this topic by the fact that 41 books, 57 philological articles, and 28 articles with a variety of emphases are listed as studies of the Platform Scripture in Appendix II in *Eno Kenkyu* (A Study of Hui-neng), the recent work that was the result of the joint efforts of the Zenshushi Kenkyukai (*Ch'an* history research team) of Komazawa University.[3] In this paper I would like to review some of the recent examples of this large body of scholarly literature.

The history of the study of the Platform Scripture has been discussed by other scholars on several occasions in the past. One recent and important example is Yanagida Seizan's comprehensive discussion in 32 pages in a volume that appeared in 1980, *Tonko Butten to Zen* (Buddhist literature from Tunhuang and *ch'an*).[4] In this paper I will concentrate on more recent developments in the study of the text of the Platform Scripture.

The text of the Platform Scripture exists in more than ten variant versions, including the oldest existing version that is found in the Tunhuang text S 5475. These variant versions are systematically ordered into three groups: the Tunhuang text, Hui-hsin text, and Ch'i-sung text. There is a general consensus that this basic threefold classification may be further developed into a fivefold list by adding two derivative texts: (1) the Te-yi text that appears to have been compiled using an old manuscript from the Tunhuang text group and the Ch'i-sung text as its basis, and (2) the Tsung-pao text that was primarily based on the Ch'i-sung text.[5] Recently, previously unknown texts belonging to earlier layers in this fivefold classification of the texts of the Platform Scripture have been discovered, and important studies of these texts have been published. My review of recent developments in the textual study of the Platform Scripture will focus on these new discoveries.

2. *Kinzan Tenneiji Text*

This text was mentioned first in the *Wakanjo becchibon mokuroku* (*Catalogue of Special Collections [Chinese and Japanese Works]*), published in 1936 by Tohoku Imperial University, and then again apparently on the basis of the information given in that catalogue, in the *Shinsan zenseki mokuroku (Newly Compiled Catalogue of Zen Buddhist Literature)*, published in 1962 by the Library of Komazawa University. The existence of this text has, therefore, been known for some time, but no serious scholarly attention has been paid to it. The manuscript in question is kept in a special collection called Kano Library and is designated as a rare book by the Tohoku University Library. Shiina Koyu had an opportunity to examine and photocopy this manuscript, and published a report of his bibliographical study.[6] A photographic reproduction of this text may be found in Yanagida Seizan's *Rokuso Dangyo shohon shusei (Variant Versions of the Platform Scripture)* to be discussed below. Here I will comment on the general character of this text on the basis of Shiina's report.

This text is divided into two parts (*jo* and *ge*) and said to be a manuscript produced during the Kamakura period. Its title is given as "*Shao-chou Ts'ao-ch'i-shan Liu-tsu-shih t'an-ching*" in a form that is identical with the title of the Daijoji text. Its relationship with the Daijoji text is made clearer in the following collophon found at the bottom of the cover (*zhih*) of the manuscript.[7] The second part of this colophon contains a statement entrusting this text to a disciple (the disciple may have been Sokyo). This paragraph may be summarized as follows:

> This text of the Platform Scripture consists of two fascicles and was discovered in a secret treasure box that was kept in the storage building of Kinzan Tenneiji Temple. The versions of the Platform Scripture that are read widely at the present time vary from each other extensively, and diverge from the original text. Students can not help but be puzzled by these divergences. The only exception is the text that has been kept secretly in the temple of the Soto sect, Daijoji in Kaga (present Ishikawa Prefecture). This Daijoji text is believed to preserve the original text of the Platform Scripture. When I compared the two fascicle version of the Kinzan Tenneiji Temple with it, the two versions matched perfectly character for character. The only regret was that a few sheets were missing in this two fascicle version. I copied these pages from the Daijoji text and made this two fascicle version complete by

adding them to it. Please make sure that this text will not ever be lost. I entrust this to your safe keeping.

The first part of the collophon informs us that this task of supplementing missing sentences was performed by the monk Hakuei Egyoku who resided at the Kinzan Tenneiji during the first ten days in the seventh month of the fourth year of Enkyo period (1747).[8]

Shiina reports that this Kinzan Tenneiji temple is an old temple of the Myoshinji School of the Rinzai sect that is located in Fukuchiyama city in Kyoto district. The temple was first established by Guchu Shukyu (-1409) in the fourth year of the Teiji period (1365), and Hakuei Egyoku was the eighth patriarch of this temple. An examination of the calligraphy indicates that sections supplemented by Egyoku are probably found in the second fascicle: from the second sheet to the second line in the fifth sheet and from the seventh to the ninth sheets. The text orginally consisted of 25 sheets in the first fascicle including the preface and the 38 sheets in the second fascicle. Shiina suggested that the first fascicle consisted of 21 sheets including the preface, that the section supplemented by Egyoku was found in the second and third sheets in the second fascicle, and that eleven sheets from the fourth to fourteenth sheets in the second fascicle were now missing.[9] This analysis needs to be corrected.

As we noted above, the content of this text matches that of the Daijoji text for the most part. One important issue pointed out by Shiina is the lineage of the "transmission of the lamp" among patriarchs in the West that is found in the section called "*shih yi, chiao-shih shih-seng ch'uan-fa*". The list in the Daijoji text is identical with the list that was first established in the *Pao-lin chuan* (801), ie., the theory of 28 Western patriarchs of the Vasumitra tradition. This list was then adopted in subsequent histories of the "transmission of the lamp", and thus became the standard paradigm of the "transmission of the lamp" in *ch'an*/Zen Buddhism. By contrast, the Kinzan Tenneiji text gives a distinct list that stands closer to the list in the Tunhuang text. The five older texts of the Platform Scripture, including the Shinpukuji text to be discussed below, list the following patriachs in the section of the transmission under consideration here.

Tunhuang text	Shinpukuji t.	Tenneiji t.	Koshoji t.	Daijoji t.
Ananda	Ananda	Ananda	Ananda	Ananda
Madhyantika	Madhyantika		Madhyantika	
Sanavasa	Sanavasa	Sanavasa	Sanavasa	Sanavasa
Upagupta	Upagupta	Upagupta	Upagupta	Upagupta
Dhrtaka	Dhrtaka	Dhrtaka	Dhrtaka	Dhrtaka
				Miccaka
				Vasumitra
Buddhanandi	Buddhanandi	Buddhanandi	Buddhanandi	Buddhanandi
Simha bhiksu	Simha bhiksu	Simha bhiksu	Simha biksu	Simha biksu
Sanavasa	Sanavasa	Sanavasa*	Basiasita	Basiasita
Upagupta*	Upagupta**	Upagupta**	Upagupta**	Punyamitra
Sangharaksa	Vasumitra*	Vasumitra*	Vasumitra*	Prajnatara

Subhamitra	Sangharaksa*	Sangharaksa*	Sangharaksa*	
Bodhidharma	Bodhidharma	Bodhidharma	Bodhidharma	Bodhidharma

(* and ** indicate alternate forms in which the names are given in Chinese characters.)

The list in the Kinzan Tenneiji text is similar to the list in the Daijoji text in only one respect: both fail to mention Madhayantika. The list in the Kinzan Tenneiji text is otherwise closer to the list in the Tunhuang text: both the list in the Tunhuang text and that in the Tenneiji text fail to mention Miccaka and Vasumitra mentioned in the list in the Daijoji text; in the second half of the list after Simha biksu, the Daijoji text diverges from the others and follows the *Pao-lin chuan* tradition, while the others follow the list in the Tunhuang text more closely. Both the list in the Tenneiji text and that in the Shinpukuji text reverse the order between Sangharaksa and Vasumitra (Subhamitra) from that given in the Tunhuang text. Since both the list in the Shinpukuji text and that in the Tunhuang text mention Madhyantika, who is not mentioned in the list in the Tenneiji text, we may conclude that the Shinpukuji text is closer to the Tunhuang text. The first half of the list in the Koshoji text follows the corresponding part of the list in the Tunhuang text, but the second half of the list in the Koshoji text, ie., the section after Simha biksu, reveals its transitional character—Sanavasa is here confused with Basiasita as in the list in the Daijoji text.

Shiina reports that the transmission verses of the six partriarchs in China cannot be discussed comparatively since the sheets that recorded the relevant section in the Kinzan Tenneiji text are missing.[10] In fact no such sheets existed to begin with. Though the Tunhuang text records transmission verses for all six patriarchs in China, all the other texts only record the transmission verses of Bodhidharma and Hui-neng, and fail to give the transmission verses for any of the other patriarchs.

The appearance of the Kinzan Tenneiji text makes it possible to go behind the Daijoji text: the comparison between the two texts enables us to reconstruct and restore in more perfect form the text dated to the sixth year of Cheng-he (1116) that lay behind these two existing texts. In this sense the Kinzan Tenneiji text is extremely valuable as a new source in the study of the Platform Scripture.

3. The Publication of the Rokuso dangyo shohon shusei *and the* Eno kenkyu

We have noted above that the Kinzan Tenneiji text is kept as a rare book in the special collection called Kano Library in the Library of Tohoku University. It is therefore not easily accessible to a general readership. The original copies of other important texts of the Platform Scripture, such as the Tunhuang text S 5475 located in the British Library, are similarly inaccessible. Recent technological developments in photographically based printing have changed this situation: we are now able to examine the photographic copies of these manuscripts published in book form. Important texts of the Platform Scripture were collected and published in 1976 under the title *Rokuso dangyo shohon shusei (Manuscripts and Printed Editions of the Platform Scripture of the Sixth Patriarch)* edited by Yanagida Seizan.[11] This work contains the following items:

Complete texts:

(1) the Tunhuang text, one fascicle (manuscript; S 5475 in the British Library)
(2) the Koshoji text, two fascicles (printed edition; located in the Koshoji temple in Horikawa, Kyoto; reproduced by Suzuki Teitaro)
(3) the Kinzan Tenneiji text, two fascicles (manuscript copied during the Kamakura period; located in the Kano Library, Tohoku University Library)
(4) the Daijoji text, two fascicles (*jo/t'ieh*) (manuscript copied during the Kamakura period, property of the Daijoji temple in Kanazawa and located at the Prefectural Art Museum of Ishikawa Prefecture)
(5) the Kao-li text, one fascicle (printed in the ninth year of the Kuang-hsü period [1883] and published by the Chia-yeh-shan Hai-yin-ssu temple in Korea; the copy in possession of Anayama Sumiko, Fukuoka)
(6) the southern collection text, Ming edition, one fascicle (printed at the Kaiyuji temple in Kikugawa-cho, Yamaguchi Prefecture)
(7) the Cheng-t'ung text, Ming edition, one fascicle (manuscript based on the Cheng-t'ung text printed in the fourth year of Cheng-t'ung [1439] during the Ming period, in possession of Yanagida Seizan)
(8) the Chen-p'u reprint edition text, Ch'ing period, one fascicle (printed in the *ping-chen* year (1676?) during the Ch'ing period, in possession of Yanagida Seizan)
(9) the Ts'ao-ch'i original text, one fascicle (printed in the third year of Hoei [1706] in Japan, in possession of Yanagida Seizan)
(10) the popular text, one fascicle (manuscript copied during the Edo period in Japan, in possession of Yanagida Seizan)
(11) the Chin-ling k'e-ching-ch'u text, one fascicle (printed in the 18th year of the Chung-hua min-kuo [1929], in possession of Yanagida Seizan)

Appendices:

A. Fragments
(1) the Kanazawa Bunko text, fragment (manuscript copied during the Kamakura period, located in the Kanazawa Bunko library)
(2) the Hsi-hsia translation (1), fragment (manuscript, located in the Peking National Library)
(3) the Hsi-hsia translation (2), fragment (manuscript, located in Ryukoku University Library)
(4) the Ts'ao-ch'i ta-shih chuan, one fascicle (manuscript, property of the Hieizan Enryakuji temple in Otsu, located in the Nara National Museum, reproduced by Kokeiso)
B. Articles
Yanagida Seizan, "Bibliographical explanation"
Kawakami Tenzan, "On the Platform Scripture in Hsi-hsia translation" (In Japanese), originally published in the *Shina bukkyo shigaku*, vol. 2, no. 3 (September, 1938).

Yanagida Seizan, "The Platform Scripture of the Sixth Patriarch as a Scripture of Mahayana Precepts", originally published in the *Indogaku bukkyogaku kenkyu*, vol. 12, no. 1 (January, 1964).
The *Rokuso dangyo shohon shusei* is thus an extremely valuable publication. It provides photographic reproductions of important texts of the Platform Scripture; it brings together other relevant materials for the study of the Platform Scripture and also includes some major scholarly discussion of this subject.

In March, 1978, roughly two years after the publication of the *Rokuso dangyo shohon shusei*, the Zen History Seminar ("*zenshushi kenkyukai*") at Komazawa University collected the results of our joint research project that had been underway for about eight years and published the large volume mentioned at the start of this paper that is entitled, the *Eno kenkyu* (A Study of Hui-neng).[12] As its subtitle "Preliminary studies on the biography and the sources on Hui-neng" makes clear, its content consists of two sections: the first section entitled "Studies" consists of studies of the biography of Hui-neng and the second section entitled "Sources" is a study of the sources for the study of Hui-neng and is broader in scope. The "Study" section consists of two chapters. The first chapter is devoted to presenting the critical edition accompanied by an annotated translation of a basic source for the study of Hui-neng's biography, "*Ts'ao-ch'i ta-shih chuan*". The second chapter is devoted to an analysis of eighteen works that enable us to trace how Hui-neng's biography changed during the 600 years beginning with the *I-fa t'a-chi* (676) and the *Yüan-ch'i wai-chi* (1291) that was appended to the *Tsung-pao* text of the Platform scripture. These sources are examined in terms of their contents; the examination focuses on some 53 items. The "Sources" section consists of three chapters. The first chapter contains a synoptic edition of the five texts of the Platform scripture, and the second chapter a critical edition of the *Chin-kang ching chieh-yi* based on six texts. The third chapter is titled "A compilation of sources for the study of Hui-neng" and reproduces relevant passages from 116 works. Finally, a chronological table of historical events relevant for the study of Hui-neng and a bibliography of secondry literature are appended. We decided to exclude from the book materials that relate exclusively to the study of Hui-neng's thought, but it does contain materials that are relevant to virtually all other subjects that touch upon the study of Hui-neng. Yet, it is still a "preliminary study", and the "study of Hui-neng" based on the materials prepared in this volume remains to be written.

The *Eno kenkyu* makes two contributions to the study of the text of the Platform scripture. The first chapter of its "Sources" section, as I noted above, contains a synoptic edition of the five texts of the Platform scripture. It also contains a bibliographical introduction entitled "General Remarks on the Platform Scripture of the Sixth Patriarch". The five texts chosen for synoptic comparison are (1) the Tunhuang text, ie., the oldest existing text of the Platform scripture that is kept at the British Library, (2) the Daijoji text, which is believed to have been copied during the Kamakura period and is ultimately based on the Hui-hsin text group, (3) the Koshoji text, which represents the

Gozan edition text, (4) the Te-yi text that was published by Chia-yeh-shan Hai-yin-ssu in the 9th year of the Kuang-hsü period of Kao-li (1883) and is believed to be ultimately based on the Ch'i-sung text, and (5) the Tsung-pao text that is found in the *fu* box of the Northern collection of the Ming edition of the Tripitaka, published in the 37th year of Wan-li period (1609). These texts are placed side by side using the breakdown of the Platform scripture into 92 sections that D.T. Suzuki used earlier in editing the Tunhuang text of this work. The *Rokuso dangyo shohon shusei* edited by Yanagida Seizan enables us to examine the original manuscripts and printed editions paying attention to the caligraphy and the appearance of the original documents; the synoptic edition of the Platform scripture ("*Rokuso dangyo gohon taisho*") in the *Eno kenkyu* highlights the differences in the contents of the highly variant versions represented in the five texts. Virtually all relevant information concerning the sources for studying the text of the Platform scripture are thus now available in an easily accessible form in these two works.

4. The Discovery of the Shinpukuji text.

Earlier in the section on the Kinzan Tenneiji text I presented a list comparing the names of Indian patriarchs mentioned in different textual traditions, and included in this list the relevant information from the Shinpukuji text. The discovery of this text was made public in October, 1978. The text was discovered by Ito Takatoshi of Komazawa University and through the arrangements made by Ito, Ishii Shudo of Komazawa University conducted a thorough investigation of this text and published the results.[13] Ishii reproduced the Shinpukuji text in his article and discussed it in detail commenting on its form, lineage, and other notable features. My comments on the Shinpukuji text here are based on Ishii's report.

The Shinpukuji temple is a major temple that belongs to the Chizan School of the Shingon Sect located in the Naka-ku District of Nagoya city. The Shinpukuji Library in which the new text of the Platform Scripture was discovered is housed in the Hoshoin of the Shinpukuji temple. Two catalogues of the works preserved in the Shinpukuji Library have been published: the "*Shinpukuji zenpon mokuroku*", edited by Kuroita Katsumi in October, 1935 lists 241 works; the "*Shinpukuji zenpon mokuroku zokushu*" published in May, 1936 mentions 580 items. However, the text of the Platform scripture discovered recently is not mentioned in either of these catalogues, and Ito who specializes in the study of the San-lun school discovered it accidentally in the course of his search for materials related to the San-lun school preserved in the Library.

The Shinpukuji text is a hand copied manuscript bound into two booklets. Ishii believes that the manuscript was probably copied during the Nanbokucho period (1337-1392) but possibly even earlier during the last years of the Kamakura period (1192-1333). The outside covers of both booklets bear the title "*Liu-tzu t'an-ching (The Platform Scritpure of the Sixth Patriarch)*"; inside the booklet the title is given in the second fascicle as "*Liu-tzu t'an-ching, chüan hsia (Platform Scripture of the Sixth Patriarch, Part II)*", but no corresponding title is found in the booklet containing the first fascicle; at the end of each fascicle the appropriate title is given as "*Liu-tsu t'an-ching, chüan shang (The Platform Scripture of the Sixth Patriarch, Part I*" and "*Liu-tsu t'an-ching, chüan hsia*" respectively and the preface by Hui-hsin and the postscript by Chou Hsi-ku are appended. Hui-hsin's preface is also found in the Koshoji text, which also carries the preface by Ch'ao Tzu-chien. Both the Daijoji text and the Kinzan Tenneiji text are based on the Hui-hsin text, but Hui-hsin's preface are missing in these texts, and the preface by Ts'un-chung is found in its place.

The postscript by Chou Hsi-ku which was originally attached to a printed edition and gives its date as the eighth day of the tenth year of the fifth year of the Ta-chung-hsiang-fu period (1012) is unique to this text and is particularly noteworthy.[14] Isshi clarifies the significance of this postscript by refering to Hu Shih's discussion in "*T'an-ching k'ao chih erh—Pa nihon kyoto horikawa koshoji ts'ang pei-sung hui-hsin pen t'an-ching ying-yin pen*".[15] There Hu Shih first mentions the passage on the Platform Scripture in the 16th fascicle of the Chü-chou text of the *Chün-chai tu-shu chih* prepared by Ch'ao Kung-wu. Ch'ao Kung-wu copied this work and wrote a preface in the twenty-first year of the Shao-hsing period (1151). Two years later in the twenty-third year of the Shao-hsing period (1153) Ch'ao Tzu-chien printed the Ch'i-chou text. This Ch'i-chou text is the original on which the Koshoji text was based. Both Ch'ao Kung-wu and Ch'ao Tzu-chien were seventh generation descendants of Ch'ao Chiung; Cha'ao Kung-wu was the paternal cousin ("*tang-ti*") of Ch'ao Tzu-chien. This passage mentions the Platform Scripture in three fascicles compiled by Hui-hsin which contained 16 sections and carried a preface by Chou Hsi-fu.[16] On the basis of this information Hu Shih suggested that the Hui-hsin text accompanied with a preface by Chou Hsi-ku, namely the tradition of the text to which the Shinpukuji text belongs, existed in three fascicles and with 16 sections at one time. Furthermore, sometime during the 120 year period between the ninth year of the T'ien-sheng period (1031) when Ch'ao Chiung copied the manuscript and the twenty-first year of the Shao-hsiang period (1151), someone must have reorganized Hui-hsin's text of the Platform Scripture in two fascicles and containing 11 sections into a text in three fascicles and containing 16 sections. Hu Shih speculated that the three fascicle text might have been the Ch'i-sung text that the monk Ch'i-sung produced in the third year of the Chih-he period (1056) of the Northern Sung dynasty.

Ishii notes that the discovery of the Shinpukuji text enables us to reject this speculation by Hu Shih. The Shinpukuji text accompanied by Chou Hsi-ku's postscript is obviously related closely to the Hui-hsin text mentioned in Ch'ao Kung-wu's *Chün-chai tu-shu chih* and in other sources based on it mentioned by Hu Shih, for example, the bibliography in the *Wen-hsien t'ung-k'ao* by Ma Tuan-lin. Hu Shih appears to have been misled by some scribal errors: the text mentioned in the sources quoted by Hu Shih must have been in two fascicles; the "sixteen sections" must have been a mistake for "eleven sections". The "preface by Chou Hsi-fu" must refer to the "postscript" composed by Chou Hsi-ku. Chou Hsi-ku's postscript informs us that the Shinpukuji text was based on the Hui-hsin text printed in the tenth month of the fifth year of the Ta-chung-hsiang-fu period (1012).

Ishii examined the prefaces to other texts belonging to the Hui-hsin text group and established the transmission of the Hui-hsin text as follows:

1) Hui-hsin learned that students were discouraged by the cumbersomeness of the old text of the Platform Scripture and established the original Hui-hsin text consisting of two fascicles and divided into eleven sections on the *hsin-hai* or the 23rd day of the *juei-pin* month in the *t'ai-sui ting-mao* year, *ie*., the 23rd day of the fifth month of the fifth year of the Ch'ien-te period (967).

2) Scholars have noted that there are some differences between the names given to the eleven sections in the Daijoji text and those in the Koshoji text and that the Daijoji text preserves the older names. The Shinpukuji text uses the same old names that the Daijoji text uses, but adds the word "*mon/men* (gate)" to each of the eleven names. These names found in the Shinpukuji text provide us with additional evidence for reconstructing the titles and the contents of the 11 sections of the original Hui-hsin text.

3) Accoring to Ch'ao Tzu-chien's preface to the Koshoji text, he learned the existence of the manuscript of the Hui-hsin text which Ch'ao Chiung (951-1034), his ancestor going back seven generations, had seen on sixteen separate occasions in the ninth year of the T'ien-sheng period (1031) when he was 81 years old; His seventh generation descendant, Ch'ao Tzu-chien became a Deputy Governor in the Ch'i-chou Commandary, and met the governor Kao-kung shih-yü. In the course of their conversation the topic of the manuscript of the Platform Scripture that Ch'ao Chiung saw came up. Since Ch'i-chou was the memorable place where the Sixth Patriarch had received the robe of transmission, Kao-kung said that a copy of the Platform Scripture ought to be available there. And so it was that Ch'ao Tzu-chien punctuated the text and printed it on the 20th day of the sixth month of the 23rd year of the Shao-hsing period (1153). Thus, as Hu Shih pointed out earlier, the two prefaces to the Koshoji text, one by Hui-hsin and the other by Ch'ao Tzu-chien, enable us to reconstruct the lineage of the Koshoji text as follows:

Hui-hsin text (the fifth year of the Ch'ien-te period [967]) → Ch'ao Chiung's manuscript (the nineth year of the T'ien-sheng period [1031]) → the text printed by Ch'ao Tzu-chien in Ch'i-chou (the 23rd year of the Shao-hsing period [1153]) → Gozan reprint text → Koshoji text.

4) The original version of the Shinpukuji text came into being in the fifth year of the Ta-chung-hsiang-fu period (1012). It is important to note that this text thus appeared earlier than Ch'ao Chiung's manuscript (the nineth year of the T'ien-sheng period [1031]), or the Ch'i-sung text in three fascicles (the third year of the Chih-he period [1056]), which was said to have been based on an old text in Ts'ao-ch'i and transmitted later through the Te-yi text and the Tsung-pao text. The *Ts'ao ch'i liu-tsu ta-shih t'an-ching ("The Platform Scripture of the Great Master, the Sixth Patriarch of Ts'ao-ch'i")*, mentioned in Chou Hsi-ku's postscript, was a hand-copied manuscript. The Shinpukuji text group may have been the oldest printed version of the Hui-hsin text.

5) Both the Daijoji text and the Kinzan Tenneiji text were based on Ts'un-chung's reprint edition dated the sixth year of the Chih-he period (1116). The Kinzan Tenneiji text, which preserves the old colophon, appears to represent the old form of the text more closely. The analysis of the patriarchal lineage presented above showed that the Daijoji text had gone through further editorial changes. Furthermore, Chou Hsi-ku's text was printed earlier in the fifth year of the Ta-chung-hsiang-fu period (1012) than Ts'un-chung's reprint text (dated 1116). We may assume that the former must have preserved the original Hui-hsin text more faithfully. Chou Hsi-ku's text is the original on which the Shinpukuji text is based.

Taking these considerations into account, a diagram describing the transmission of the variant versions of the Platform Scripture may be drawn (Appendix II).

Certain distinctive features of the content of the Shinpukuji text show that this text stands much closer to the Kinzan Tenneiji text and the Daijoji text than to the Koshoji text. Relevant evidence for this analysis includes the reference to Hui-neng as "*mou-chia*", the treatment of the exchange over wind and banner, the exchange with Hui-ming, and the reference to the posthumous title of "Zen master Ta-chien". The comparison of the patriarchal lineage given in the Shinpukuji text with those in other texts, on the other hand, shows that it is closest to that given in the Kinzan Tenneiji text. The difference between the list in the Shinpukuji text and the list in the Koshoji text is greater, and the difference between the list in the Shinpukuji text and the list in the Daijoji text is the greatest.

At the end of Ishii's article, the text of the Shinpukuji text is reproduced using the framework proposed in the *Eno kenkyu (A Study of Hui-neng)*.

5. Reconstruction of the Hui-hsin text and the hypothesis concerning the Ch'i-sung text

Important advances were made in the study of the Hui-hsin text group thanks to the discovery of the Shinpukuji text which appears to preserve the original form of the Hui-hsin text more faithfully. Following his article announcing the discovery of the Shinpukuji text and publishing the text, Ishii Shudo continued his work on this subject and attempted to reconstruct the original Hui-hsin text of the Platform Scripture. The newly discovered Shinpukuji edition was used as the basis for this reconstruction, and four other texts that belong to the Hui-hsin text group were consulted; these four texts were the Kinzan Tenneiji text, the Daijoji text, the Koshoji text, and the text printed by Nakano Inchiuemon in the eighth year of the Kan'ei period (1631). The reconstructed text was then compared to the Tunhuang text.[17]

A five text synoptic edition of the Platform Scripture that reproduced the Tunhuang text, the Daijoji text, the Koshoji text, Te-yi text, and Tsung-pao text side by side had been included in the *Eno Kenyu (A Study of Hui-neng)* published earlier. Ishii's new contribution carried the work that lay behind this synoptic edition one step further. Two of the five texts included in the synoptic text in the *Eno Kenkyu (A Study of Hui-neng)* edition are derived from a common ancestry, ie., the original Hui-hsin text. This original Hui-hsin text is reconstructed in Ishii's new contribution on the basis of the Shinpukuji text and compared with the Tunhuang text. Following the basic framework used in the synoptic edition in the *Eno Kenkyu (A Study of Hui-neng)*, the Tunhuang edition and the reconstructed Hui-hsin text are given synoptically: the former in the top half of the page and the latter in the bottom half of the page; variant readings of the Hui-hsin group texts are noted and the Japanese reading of the texts given in the top and bottom halves of the page are given independently. The editorial note mentions the works consulted in editing the texts and producing their Japanese reading: Philip B. Yampolski, *The Platform Sutra of the Sixth Patriarch*[18] and Yanagida Seizan, *Zen Goroku*[19] and for the Koshoji edition, Nakagawa Taka, *Rokuso dankyo*.[20] Thus, Ishii's article reproduces the oldest existent text of the Platform Scripture that is accessible to us, ie., the Tunhuang text dated around 790 and the second oldest Hui-hsin text dated 967 and gives their Japanese reading in a convenient synoptic format, facilitating detailed comparative discussion of the text of the Platform Scripture.

No copy of the Hui-hsin text itself is known to us. The text reconstructed in the manner described above is no more than a scholar's hypothetical reconstruction. The other important early text of the Platform Scripture, ie., the Ch'i-sung text which constitutes the origin of the later expanded "popular" text of the Platform Scripture, also has been lost to us. Having thrown considerable light on the original form of the Hui-hsin text, Ishii moved on to an investigation that resulted in a hypothesis concerning the origin of the Ch'i-sung text.[21]

As Hu Shih pointed out, the existence of the three fascicle text of the Plaform Scripture edited by Fo-jih Ch'i-sung (1007-1072) of the Yün-men School is known from the "*Liu-tsu fa-pao chi hsü*" compiled in the third year of the Chih-he period by Lang Chien. This preface is found in the eleventh fascicle of Ch'i-sung's *Hsin-chin wen-chi.* Hu Shih discussed the Ch'i-sung text in two articles: "*T'an-ching k'ao chih yi: Pa ts'ao-chi ta-shih pieh-chuan*" (January, 1930) and "*T'an-ching k'ao chih erh: Pa nihon kyoto horikawa koshoji ts'ang pei-sung hui-hsin-pen t'an-ching ying-yin*" (April, 1934). Hu Shih's views are examined in Ishii's article in the light of the newly discovered materials from the Hui-hsin text group.

The last half of Lang Ch'ien's preface records that Ch'i-sung obtained an old Ts'ao-ch'i text in the third year of the Chih-he period (1056) and by editing this text produced the Ch'i-sung text of the Platform Scripture that consisted of three fascicles. We may assume therefore that if we can determine the identity of this "old Ts'ao-ch'i text", we will be able to learn a good deal of concrete information about the nature of the Ch'i-sung text. The Ming edition of the Platform Scripture mentions a prediction concerning the bodhisattvas who were to come from the east seventy years after the death of Hui-neng.[22] Hu Shih suggested that this prediction comes from the "*Ts'ao-ch'i ta-shih chuan*" that appeared around the year 781, and argued that this "*Ts'ao-*

ch'i ta-shih chuan" was the "old Ts'ao-ch'i text" in question. Ishii lists relevant quotations from the "*Ts'ao-ch'i ta-shih chuan*", "*Tsu-t'ang chi*", "*Ching-te ch'uan-teng lu*", "*Ch'uan-fa cheng-tsung chi*", and the Tsung-pao text of the Platform Scripture and draws the following conclusion: the prediction concerning the activities of the two bodhisattvas who appear 70 years after the death of Hui-neng does indeed first appear in the "*Ts'ao-ch'i ta-shih chuan*", but the Tsung-pao text of the Platform Scripture is based not on the "*Ts'ao-ch'i ta-shih chuan*" but on the Transmission of the Lamp literature, particularly on the *Ching-teng ch'uan-teng lu* on which the text relies most closely. Furthermore, all four examples that Hu Shih mentioned in order to prove its reliance on the "*Ts'ao-ch'i ta-shih chuan*" are drawn from the Transmission of the Lamp literature, such as the *Ching-te chuan-teng lu*. Thus, it is possible that the "*Ts'ao-ch'i ta-shih chuan*" may have been quoted indirectly in the Ch'i-sung text. But the "old Ts'ao-ch'i text" must doubtlessly have been a version of the Platform Scripture and not the "*Ts'ao-ch'i ta-shih chuan*". Ishii suggests that the version of the Platform Scripture in question might have been a manuscript of the Hui-hsin text.[23]

Concerning the content of the Ch'i-sung text in three fascicles Hu shih first suggested that this text was based on the old text of the Platform Scripture (represented in the Tunhuang manuscript) and the "*Ts'ao-ch'i ta-shih pieh chuan*". Later, after learning the existence of the Koshoji text, he came to believe that Ch'i-sung text in three fascicles was based on the Hui-hsin text (represented in the Koshoji text) in two fascicles and the "*Ts'ao-ch'i ta-shih chuan*" in one fascicle. As we noted earlier, Hu Shih also speculated that the Hui-hsin text mentioned in the *Chün-chai tu-shu chih* that consisted of three fascicles, divided into 16 sections, and containing a preface by Chou Hsi-ku (the original *Chün-chai tu-shu chih* text gives the name as Hsi-fu) might have been the Ch'i-sung text. But the discovery of the Shinpukuji text containing Hui-hsin's preface and Chou Hsi-ku's postscript dated the fifth year of the Ta-chung-hsiang-fu period (1012) showed that the Hui-hsin text in three fascicles and divided into 16 sections did not exist at all. The "three fascicles" and "sixteen sections" mentioned in the *Chün-chai tu-shu chih* are scribal errors for "two fascicles" and "eleven sections" respectively. Hui-hsin's preface speaks of "dividing the text into two fascicles and unfolding it into eleven sections". Thus, the editorial organization into two fascicles and eleven subsections was Hui-hsin's contribution and the distinctiveness of this text was found in this organization.

As for the content of the Ch'i-sung text in three fascicles, Ishii suggested the following: Ch'i-sung used the Hui-hsin text in two fascicles and eleven sections as his basis; he then added to this basic text the words of instruction associated with such figures as Liu Chih-lüeh, Fa-hai, Chih-ch'e, Chih-t'ung, Chih-tao, Hsing-ssu, Huai-jang, Hsüan-chüeh, Chih-huang, and Wo-lun taken from the *Ching-te ch'uan-teng lu* and other related sources; the Tsung-pao text shows how these materials were added. The Tun-huang and Hui-hsin texts presuppose a situation in which Ch'an Buddhism was dominated by the descendants of the ten great disciples of Hui-neng, ie., Fa-hai, Chih-ch'eng, Fa-ta, Shen-hui, Chih-ch'ang, Chih*-t'ung, Chih-ch'e, Chih-tao, Fa-chen, and Fa-ju. Ch'an Buddhism at the time of Ch'i-sung was by contrast dominated by different leaders, ie., those who belonged to the Nan-yüeh and Ch'ing-yüan groups. Ch'i-sung therefore found it necessary to include words of instruction attributed to Huai-jang of Nan-yüeh and Hsing-ssu of Ch'ing-yüan, and since these words were not found in the *"Ts'ao-ch'i ta-shih chuan"*, he must have supplied them from the Transmission of the Lamp literature. This supplementary material filled one fascicle, and therefore the length of the entire text was expanded to three fascicles.

Ishii further suggested that the lineage of transmission among Indian patriarchs presented in the Ch'i-sung text must have been the Vasumitra lineage based on the *Pao-lin chuan*. Ch'i-sung advocated this list in his *Ch'uan-fa cheng-tsung chi (Record of the Correct Transmission of the Buddha's Teaching)* and elsewhere. Hu Shih suggested that the shift from the Sunavasa lineage to the Vasumitra lineage must have occurred with the Ch'i-sung text. Ishii evaluated Hu Shih's view on this point positively, and argued that the introduction of this shift must have been the most important motive that led Ch'i-sung to edit the two fascicle Platform Scripture into the three fascicle version. Ch'i-sung wrote extensively in defending the "correctness" of the "transmission of the Buddha's teaching" in the Ch'an tradition and answering the criticisms that scholastic circles directed against the Ch'an theory of partriarchal transmission. Ch'i-sung, however, also found the Hui-hsin text unsatisfactory. Ishii believed that this was the context in which the Ch'i-sung text first emerged. Ishii further highlighted the uniqueness of the Ch'i-sung text by noting the following points. Shen-hui's influence had disappeared in this text. The Platform Scripture lost its character as a text of transmission: the work which originally had the character of a sermon preaching the Precept of Formlessness was transformed into a more general collection of a variety of sermons.

The discovery of the Shinpukuji text that preserved the original form of the Hui-hsin text threw considerable light on the history of the Platform Scripture. We are now able to trace more concretely how the history of the emergence and later transformations of the Platform Scripture reflect the different stages in the development of Ch'an Buddhism and its thought.

6. The Discovery of the new Tunhuang text

When we speak about the Tunhuang text of the Platform Scripture, we generally take it for granted that we are refering to the text in the Tunhuang manuscript S 5475, a text identified by Yabuki Keiki while he was inspecting the Tunhuang materials in the British Library for the second time between 1922 and 1923. This text is often treated as the only copy of the Platform Scripture that was found in the Tunhuang library, and its importance is emphasized in the light of this situation. However, the existance of other Tunhuang texts of the

Platform Scripture has been known and references have been made to them from time to time.

The *Tun-huang yi-shu tsung-mu so-yin* published in May, 1962 by the Shang-wu yin-shu-kuan in Beijing contains a section called "4. *Tun-huang yi-shu san-lu*". The second item in this section is designated as "*Lü-shun po-wu-kuan so-ts'un tun-huang chih fo-chiao ching-tien (Buddhist scriptures from Tunhuang in possession of the Lü-shun museum)*". This list was based on the periodical *T'u-shu-kuan-hsüeh chi-k'an*, Vol. 1, no. 4. The item 0179 in this section is described as "*Nan-tsung ting-chiao (tsui-shang ta-ch'eng mo-ho-pan-jo po-lo-mi-to ching*".[24] This text probably refers to a version of the Platform Scripture. The character "*ting*" ("top") in the phrase "*nan-tsung ting-chiao*" is probably a mistake for "*tun*" ("sudden"), and the title "*tsui-shang ta-ch'eng mo-ho-pan-jo po-lo-mi-to ching*" matches perfectly with the first part of the title of the existing Tunhuang text of the Platform Scripture, ie., S 5475. We can infer that this text was identified and taken out of Tunhuang by the Otani expeditionary party and was later kept at the Lü-hsun museum. Nothing is known, however, about the later circumstances of the Lü-shun museum, and the present location of the Buddhist scriptures from Tunhuang in its possession. Thus, it is not possible to pursue the investigation of this text any further.

The existence of another Tunhuang text of the Platform Scripture had been reported even earlier. The Hsiang Ta's "*Hsi-cheng hsiao-chi*" published in the *Kuo-hsüeh chi-k'an*, Vol. 7, no. 1 (July, 1970) mentions a text in possession of Jen Tzu-yi. The "*Hsi-cheng hsiao-chi*" is the record of the investigation of old manuscripts that Hsiang Ta, then a professor of Beijing University, conducted on several occasions in Tunhuang. Yanagida discusses this work in his article in the *Tonko butten to Zen* mentioned earlier. The relevant section of this discussion may be summaried as follows.[25] Hsiang Ta's comments:

> Jen Tzu-yi owned some manuscripts of sutras found in the Tunhuang caves. Hsiang Ta was shown these manuscripts: six *chüan* of hand copied scriptures and three books of fragments. In addition, there was a booklet consisting of 93 sheets. This booklet contained four works: the "*P'u-t'i-ta-mo nan-tsung ting shih-fei lun*", the "*Nan-yang ho-shang tun-chiao chieh-t'o ch'an-men chih-liao-hsing t'an-yü*", the "*Nan-tsung tun-chiao tsui-shang ta-ch'eng t'an-ching*" as well as the commentary on the "*Ching-kang pan-jo po-lo-mi-to hsin-ching*" by Shen-hsiu's disciple Ching-chüeh. Except for the 12 lines in one sheet at the beginning of the "*Ting shih-fei lun*", all works were complete and at the very end there was a collophon by monk Kuang-fan which lacked one sheet... This material in possession of Jen Tzu-yi is undoubtedly a manuscript copied during the Five Dynasties or early Sung period, and the format that copies six lines in a half page follows the format of the Sung edition. The "*Nan-tsung ting shih-fei lun*" in this collection enables us to supplement the missing parts of the texts of the same work in British and French collections. The "*Nan-yang ho-shang t'an-yü*" in this collection is a complete text; there is a fragment of this work in Beijing

Library. The text of the Platform Scripture here can be compared with the manuscripts in England and France. The Heart Sutra (*hsin ching*) with a commentary by Ching-chüeh has a preface by Li Chih-fei, indicating that this commentary was composed in the 15th year of the K'ai-yüan period. Ching-chüeh was a disciple of Shen-hsiu. Since this work has been missing in the tripitaka for a long time, this will enable us to throw some light on the doctrines of the Northern school of gradual teaching. All four works included in this collection are important sources for the study of Ch'an Buddhism.

The "British and French collections" mentioned in connection with the "*P'u-t'i-ta-mo nan-tsung ting shih-fei lun*" here ought to be corrected as "French" and the "England and France" mentioned in connection with the "Platform Scriptrue" ought to be changed to "England". Yet, Hsiang Ta's concluding remark that these four works constitute extremely valuable source materials is certainly appropriate. Hsiang Ta included this record of his investigations in the *T'ang-tai Ch'ang-an yü Hsi-yü wen-ming* that he published in April, 1957 from the Hsin-hua shu-tien, but did not comment on what happened to this booklet later.

During his visit to Beijing Yanagida enquired about this material at Beijing Library and the Chinese Academy of Social Sciences. Later, Ch'ang Shu-hung, the Director of the Tunhuang Institute (*tun-huang wen-wu yen-chiu so*) who visited Japan in November, 1979, responded to Yanagida's question about this material as follows: the location of the original material is unknown; but he had seen the same material in possession of Jen Tzu-yi that Hsiang Ta saw earlier, and he owns a photographic copy of the material. He thus indicated that textual critical work based on photographic copies of relevant works may become possible in the near future.

The present location of this text became known through a recent publication, *Tun-huang t'u-lu-fan wen-hsien yen-chiu lun-chi (Essays in the Study of Literary Findings from Tunhuang and Turfan)*, volume 3 (Beijing-ta-hsüeh ch'u-pan-she, February, 1986). In a section entitled, "*Tun-huang hsien po-wu-kuan ts'ang tun-huang yi-shu mu lu (Catalogy of Tunhuang Manuscripts in Tunhuang Prefectural Museum)*" in this volume the Tunhuang Museum listed and described the 78 items of Tunhuang manuscripts in its possession. A work with the title "*Nan-tsung tun-chiao tsui-shang ta-ch'eng po-jo po-lo-mi ching*" appears at the seventy-seventh item in this list and a short description of this work is provided.

Yang Tseng-wen, professor in charge of Buddhist studies, Institute for the Study of World Religions, Chinese Academy of Social Sciences, learned about this manuscript in the same year, and, after examining this manuscript on the basis of a photographic copy provided by the Tunhuang Museum, reported on his findings at the Second Japan-China Conference on the Study of Buddhism in October, 1987.[26] The report begins with a brief description of the manuscript containing four kinds of *ch'an* works that is in possession of the Tunhuang Museum (to be called Tunhuang Museum manuscript below) and the circumstances that led Yang to investigate this manuscript. A survey of the study on Tunhuang *ch'an* manuscripts conducted by Japanese and Chinese scholars in the past sixty years follows. A subsection entitled "The Discovery and Study of the Tunhuang text of the Platform Scripture" provides a summary history of the scholarship on the widely known Tunhuang manuscript of the Platform Scripture. The following section entitled, "The Academic Value of the Tunhuang Museum manuscript (Jen Tzu-yi manuscript) of the Plaform Scripture, *Nan-tusng ting shih-fei lun*, and other works" gives the summary of Yang's findings. Important items in this summary include the following points.

1) The Tunhuang Museum manuscript no. 077 was originally discovered by Jen Tzu-yi in 1935 in the temple at the top of the Ch'ien-fo-shan mountain in Tunhuang. In addition to the four *ch'an* works mentioned earlier by Hsiang Ta, the manuscript also contains the *Nan-tsung ting hsieh-cheng wu-keng-chuan*, probably composed by Shen-hui, and one five-character poem appended to it.

2) The Tunhuang Museum text of the Platform Scripture consists of 42 sheets (84 pages). Each half-sheet contains six lines, and each line 25 characters. Altogether the text contains around 12,000 characters. Its title and content are identical with those of the well-known Tunhuang manuscript (S 5475). This text belongs to the same group of the texts of the Platform Scripture as the manuscript S 5475.

3) Yang reports that the well-known Tunhuang text S 5475 lacks three lines, altogether 68 characters, and the meaning of the passages where these characters are missing is unclear. These three lines are preserved in the Tunhuang Museum text, and thus the latter enables us to restore the original form of these passages.

Example 1.

In a passage in which Hui-neng is lecturing on meditation, the Tunhuang text S 5475 gives, "*shan-chih-shih, yü wu chi ch'eng chih*". However, *yü* ("to meet") is a mistake for "*yü**" ("ignorant"), and 18 characters are missing in the S 5475 following this character. The Tunhuang Museum text gives the passage as "*shan-chih-shih, yü*-jen chih-jen, fo-hsing pen yi wu ch'a-pieh, chih yü mi-wu, mi chi whe wu, wu chi ch'eng chih*".

Example 2.

In a passage where Hung-jen orders his disciples to write a verse, the Tunhuang S 5475 text gives an unintelligible phrase "*huo chi chi*". The Tunhuang Museum text gives the phrase as "*huo chi tso*", and the meaning is clear here ("Make the verse quickly").

Example 3.

The meaning of the expression "*fo-hsin chung-sheng*" in one passage in the Tunhuang S 5475 text is obscure. This passage that reads: "*tan shih fo-hsin chung-sheng, chi neng shih fo*" (translated as "they have only to know that the Buddha mind is within sentient beings; then they will be able to know the Buddha" by P. Yampolski[27]) in S 5475 is given as "*tan shih chung-sheng, chi neng shih fo* (Only if they know sentient beings, do they immediately know the Buddha)" in the Tunhuang Museum text. This suggests that the two extra characters "*fo-hsin*" in S 5475 were added by mistake.

4) The Tunhuang text S 5475 and the Tunhuang Museum text were copied from manuscripts that belong to the same group. This group of manuscripts represents what may be designated as the original Tunhuang text. This original Tunhuang text was transmitted from Fa-hai through Tao-chi to Wu-chen. The text contains the story about "determining which was the correct Buddhist teaching and which not" twenty years after Hui-neng's death and also gives the names of the twenty-eight patriarchs in detail. On the basis of this evidence, Yang concludes that this original Tunhuang text was a revised version of the Platform Scripture produced by a disciple of Shen-hui or someone who had been under Shen-hui's influence; this revised version came into existence after the original text compiled by Fa-hai had circulated for some time. Yang suggests that the original Tunhuang text came into being during the period between the twentieth year of K'ai-yüan (732) and the appearance of the *Pao-lin chuan* in the 17th year of Chen-yüan (801).

Yang gives the transmission of the early text that lies behind the Hui-hsin text of the early Sung ("Hui-hsin's original text" in the sense of the text used by Hui-hsin) as Fa-hai through Chih-tao through Pi-an through Wu-chen to Yüan-hui. Hui-hsin's preface states that this text contained more sentences ("cumbersome"). This text thus contained materials added later to the original Tunhuang text. Yang hypothetically gives the date of this text as early or middle ninth century. The text that circulated widely at the time when Ch'i-sung (1007-1072) revised the text of the Platform Scripture was characterized as "vulgar, cumbersome, and disparate in writing" (Lang Chien's preface). Yang believes that this text must have been "Hui-hsin's original text", ie., the text that Hui-hsin used in producing his own text, and not the Hui-hsin text itself which resulted from editing this "Hui-hsin's original text" into the text in two fascicles and divided into eleven sections. Yang then notes that the text that Ch'i-sung produced through his revision does not exists any more, but that the Te-yi text and the Tsung-pao text from the Yüan period as well as the "original Ts'ao-ch'i text" from the Ming period belong to the group of texts that trace their origin to Ch'i-sung's text.

The Tunhuang text S 5475 is notorious for its poor quality. The newly discovered Tunhuang Museum text enables us to conduct new critical discussions of the early Tunhuang text. Furthermore, what we have seen above indicates that the benefit of the new text will not be confined to this contribution: it will also enrich immeasurably our discussion of broader issues in the study of the Platform Scripture. Yang reports that the Tunhuang Museum text will be published from the Wen-wu ch'u-pan-she under the title, *Tun-huang hsien po-wu-kuan so-ts'ang t'ang-mo wu-tai hsieh-pen "t'an-ching", "nan-tsung ting shih-fei lun" teng ch'an-tsung wen-hsien yen-chiu* in a near future. We look forward eagerly to the appearance of this work.

7. Conclusion

We have reviewed the remarkable developments in the text critical study of the Platform Scripture. We have confined our attention to the discussion of newly discovered texts. There remain a number of major questions that await elucidation in the study of the Platform Scripture. These questions include, for example, the question of the origin of the Platform Scriptrue on which Yaganida proposed a daring hypothesis in the past,[28] and the questions closely related to this issue concerning Hui-neng's biography and his thought.

APPENDIX I

1. The colophons of the Tenninji Text: 延享四丁卯七月上澣，再修表帙而備足闕文缺字，金山天寧常住，現白英惠玉記焉。

此壇經全部二卷，出于金山寶藏秘函之中矣。今流布于世叢林壇經，舊刊新刻不一，或多或省，分門字數皆失。本經之正者間有之，末流之學者，不能無疑於其間也。特秘賀北洞宗大乘禪寺寫本壇經，用為正本傳焉。今次此二冊考合之，不違一字，只有闕紙數枚為恨而已。幸得賀北正本寫書，而書加而備足之，永莫廢失。至囑。

2. Chou Hsi-ku's postscript:

後敘

余賞公暇，信覽曹溪六祖大師壇經，導化迷愚之人，令識本心，見本性，自悟成佛，莫向外求。言直理玄，法法非法，不可思議。乃勸諸善，雕印經受持，獲大功德，無以菩提者也。

大中祥符五年歲次壬子十月八日，傳教弟子宣德郎守尚書屯田員外郎騎都尉賜緋魚袋周希古敘。都勸緣廣教院主僧保昌。金花山人嚴放外書。滝西卓海 刊字。

3. The passage from the *Chün-chai tu-shu-chih* quoted by Hu Shih:

六祖壇經三卷 右唐僧惠昕撰，記僧盧慧能學佛本末。慧能號六祖。凡十六門，周希復有序。

4. The prediction passage in the Ming edition of the Platform Scripture:

吾去七十年，有二菩薩從東方來，一出家，一在家，同時興化，建立吾宗，締緝伽藍，昌隆法嗣。

APPENDIX II

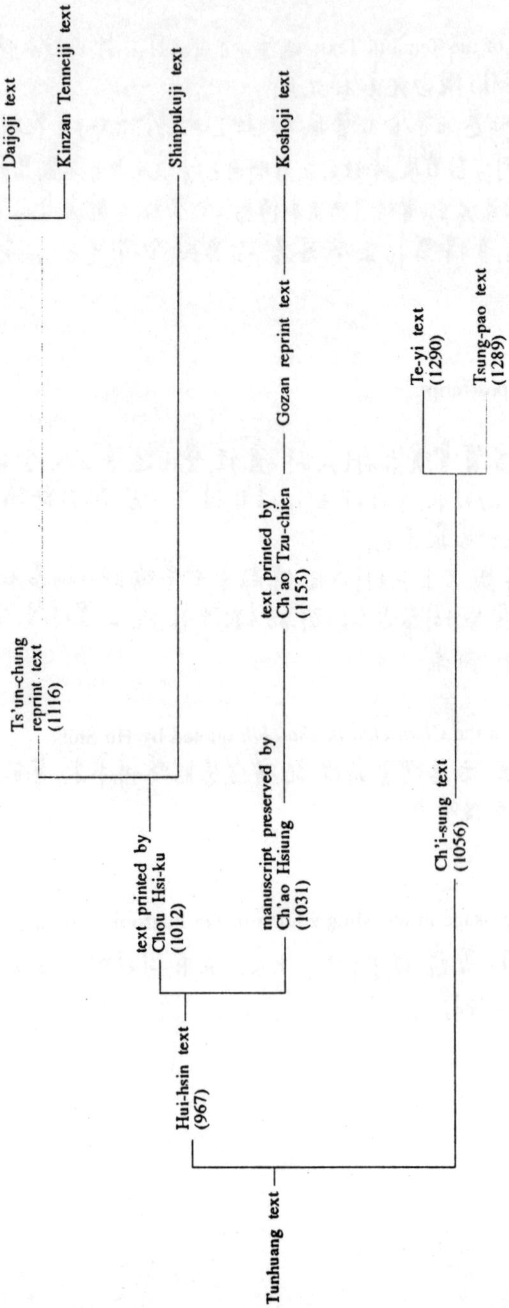
Tunhuang text
Hui-hsin text (967)
text printed by Chou Hsi-ku (1012)
manuscript preserved by Ch'ao Hsiung (1031)
Ts'un-chung reprint text (1116)
Daijoji text
Kinzan Tenneiji text
Shinpukuji text
text printed by Ch'ao Tzu-chien (1153)
Gozan reprint text
Koshoji text
Ch'i-sung text (1056)
Te-yi text (1290)
Tsung-pao text (1289)

NOTES

1. Here I am calling this work "*t'an-ching*" (Platform Scripture) following Ui Hakuju's usage. Ui called his study of this text in his work "*Dankyo ko*", ie., "Reflections on Platform Scripture" refering to the text as *dangyo/t'an-ching*. See Ui, *Daini Zenshushi kenkyu* (Tokyo: Iwanami, 1941), Chapter 1. p. 1.
2. This text has often been treated as a topic that every scholar must study. Ui, for example, stated in his preface to the study of this text that "Students of the history of *ch'an* Buddhism must *without fail* investigate this Platform Scripture at least at one point in their work..." (emphasis by Tanaka). Ui, Hakuju, *ibid.*, p. 1.
3. Komazawa Daigaku Zenshushi Kenkyukai, *Eno kenkyu*, Tokyo: Taishukan, 1978.
4. Yanagida Seizan, "Issues Surrounding the Tunhuang Text of the Platform Scripture" (in Japanese), Shinohara Hisao and Tanaka Ryosho (eds.), *Tonko butten to zen*, Koza Tonko series, no. 8, Tokyo: Daito shuppansha, 1980, pp. 19-50.
5. Ref., *Eno kenkyu, Ibid.*, p. 398. A diagram represening the relationship among variant versions ("*Ihon keitozu*") is found in p. 399.
6. Shiina Koyu, "On the Kinzan Tenneiji Text of the Platform Scripture" (in Japanese), *Indogaku Bukkyogaku Kenkyu*, Vol. 23, no. 2, pp. 291-295.
7. Yanagida Seizan (ed.), *Rokuso Dangyo shohon shusei*, Kyoto: Chubun shuppansha, 1976, p. 67.
8. The original text of these colophons are found in Appendix I.
9. Shiina, *ibid.*, p. 292.
10. *Ibid.* p. 293.
11. *Rokuso dangyo shohon shusei*, *ibid.* This work was published as the seventh volume of the ten volume series entitled *Zengaku sosho* under the general editorship of Yanagida Seizan.
12. See footnote 3 above for facts of publication.
13. Ishii Shudo, "A New Manuscript of the Liu-tsu t'an-ching discovered by Ito Taketoshi in the Shinpukuji Temple: Its Relationship to the Hui-hsin Text" (in Japanese), *Komazawa daigaku bukkyogakubu ronshu (Journal of Buddhist Studies)*, no. 10, November, 1979, pp. 74-111.
14. The original text of this postscript is found in Appendix I.
15. Yanagida Seizan, ed., *Koseki zengakuan* (Chubun shuppansha, June, 1975), pp. 79-80.
16. The relevant passage is reproduced in Chinese in Appendix I.
17. The result of this attempt was published as "A Study of Hui-hsin's text of the Platform Scripture: its text reconstructed and compared with the Tunhuang text" (in Japanese) in two issues of the *Komazawa daigaku bukkyogakubu ronshu*, no. 11 (November, 1980), pp. 96-138, and no. 12 (October, 1981), pp. 68-132.
18. Columbia University Press, 1967

19. *Sekai no meicho series: zoku 3* (Chuokoronsha, October, 1974), pp. 93-179.
20. *Zen no Goroku* series (Chikuma shobo, February, 1976), pp. 1-201.
21. The outcome of this investigation was published in his article entitled, "A Hypothesis concerning the Ch'i-sung text of the Platform Scripture" (in Japanese), *Shugaku kenkyu*, no. 23 (March, 1981), pp. 202-208. This article appeared in March, 1981 after the first part of his study of the Hui-hsin text, "A Study of Hui-hsin's text of the Platform Scripture: its text reconstructed and compared with the Tunhuang text" had appeared in the *Komazawa daigaku bukkyogakubu ronshu*, no. 11 (November, 1980) but before the publication of the second part of this same article in no. 12 (October, 1981) issue of the same periodical. Prof. Ishii, however, first completed his study of the Hui-hsin text and then investigated the Ch'i-sung text.
22. The original text is found in the Appendix I.
23. In Contrast Prof. Lou Yü-lieh of Beijing University agrees with Hu Shih's view that identifies the "old Ts'ao-ch'i text" that Ch'i-sung obtained with the *Ts'ao-ch'i ta-shih chuan* and develops his argument from the viewpoint that "the Ch'i-sung text was a composite version based on Hui-hsin text (or possibly the Tunhuang text) and the *Ts'ao-ch'i ta-shih chuan*". See his article, "On the Tunhuang text of the Platform Scripture, the *Ts'ao-ch'i ta-shih chuan*, and the Early Ch'an Thought" (in Japanese), *Matsugaoka bunko kenkyu nenpo*, no. 2, February, 1988, p. 2.
24. p. 317.
25. *ibid.*, p. 35-36.
26. Yang's paper was entitled "On Chinese and Japanese Studies of Tunhuang Ch'an Buddhist Literature with Some Comments on the Academic Value of the Manuscripts of the Platform Scripture, the *Nan-tsung ting shih-fei lun*, and other works in the Tunhuang Museum". A Japanese translation prepared by Mugiya Kunio of this paper is found in the October 23rd, 1987 issue (no. 23706, pp. 10-12) of the *Chugai nippo*, published by the Chugainipposha that sponsored this conference from the Japanese side.
27. *Ibid.*, 180.
28. Yanagida Seizan, *Shoki zenshu shisho no kenkyu* (Kyoto, 1967), pp. 148-212, 253-278.

(Translated by Koichi Shinohara).

List of Characters

Anayama Sumiko 穴山寿美子

Beijing-ta-hsüeh ch'u-pan-she 北京大學出版社

ch'an 禪

Ch'ang Shu-hung 常書鴻

Ch'ao Chiung 晁迥

Ch'ao Kung-wu 晁公武

Ch'ao Tzu-chien 晁子健

Chen-p'u 真樸

Cheng-he 政和

Cheng-t'ung 正統

Chen-yüan 貞元

Ch'i-chou 蘄州

Ch'i-sung 契嵩

Chia-yeh-shan Hai-yin-ssu 伽耶山海印寺

Ch'ien-te 乾德

Chih-ch'ang 知常

Chih-ch'e 志徹

Chih-ch'eng 志誠

Chih-he 至和

Chih-huang 智隍

Chih-t'ung 智通

Chih*-t'ung 知通

Chih-tao 志道

Chikuma shobo 筑摩書房

Chin-kang ching chieh-yi 金剛經解義

Chin-ling k'e-ching-ch'u 金陵刻經處

ching 經

Ching-chüeh 淨覺

Ching-kang pan-jo po-lo-mi-to hsin-ching 金剛般若波羅蜜多心經

Ching-te ch'uan-teng lu 景德傳燈錄

Ch'ing 清

Ch'ing-yüan 青原

Chizan 智山

Chou Hsi-fu 周希復

Chou Hsi-ku 周希古

Chü-chou 衢州

chüan hsia 卷下

chüan shang 卷上

Ch'uan-fa cheng-tsung chi 傳法正統記

Chubun shuppansha 中文出版社

Chugai nippo 中外日報

Chugainipposha 中外日報社

Chün-chai tu-shu chih 群齋讀書志

Chung-hua min-kuo 中華民國

Chuokoronsha 中央公論社

Daijoji 大乗寺

Daini Zenshushi kenkyu 第二禅宗史研究

Daito shuppansha 大東出版社

Dankyo ko 壇經考

Edo 江戸

Enkyo 延享

Eno kenkyu 慧能研究

Fa-chen 法珍

Fa-hai 法海

Fa-ju 法如

Fa-ta 法達

fo-hsin 佛心

fo-hsin chung-sheng 佛心衆生

Fo-jih Ch'i-sung 佛日契嵩

fu 扶

Fukuchiyama 福知山

Fukuoka 福岡

ge 下

gozan 五山

Guchu Shukyu 愚中周及

Hakuei Egyoku 白英慧玉

Hieizan Enryakuji 比叡山延曆寺

Hoei 寶永

Horikawa 堀川

Hoshoin 寶生院

Hsi-cheng hsiao-chi 西征小記

Hsi-hsia 西夏

Hsiang Ta 向達

hsin ching 心經

Hsin-chin wen-chi 鐔津文集

hsin-hai 辛亥

Hsin-hua shu-tien 新華書店

Hsing-ssu 行思

Hsüan-chüeh 玄覺

Hu Shih 胡適

Huai-jang 懷讓

Hui-Hsin 惠昕

Hui-ming 慧明

Hui-neng 慧能

huo chi tso 火急作

huo chi chi 火急急

I-fa t'a-chi 瘞髪塔記

Ihon keitozu 異本系統圖

Indogaku bukkyogaku kenkyu 印度學仏教學研究

Ishii Shudo 石井修道

Ishikawa 石川

Ito Takatoshi shi hakken no shinpukuji bunko shozo no rokusodangyo no shokai--ekinbon rokusodangyo 伊藤隆寿氏發現の真福寺所藏の「六祖壇經」の紹介一惠昕本「六祖壇經」の祖本との関連 tono kanren

Ito Takatoshi 伊藤隆寿

Jen Tzu-yi 任子宜

jo/*t'ieh* 帖

jo 上

juei-pin 蕤賓

K'ai-yüan 開元

Kaga 加賀

Kaiyuji 快友寺

Kamakura 鎌倉

Kanazawa 金沢

Kan'ei 寛永

Kanazawa Bunko 金沢文庫

Kano 狩野

Kao-kung shih-yü 高公世史

Kao-li 高麗

Kawakami Tenzan 川上天山

Kikugawa-cho 菊川町

Kinzan Tenneiji 金山天寧寺

Kinzan tenneiji kyuzo rokusodangyo nitsuite 金山天寧寺舊藏「六祖壇經」について

Kokeiso 古徑莊

Komazawa 駒沢

Komazawa daigaku bukkyogakubu ronshu 駒沢大學佛教學部論集

Komazawa Daigaku Zenshushi Kenkyukai 駒沢大學禪宗史研究會

Koseki zengakuan 胡適禪學案

Koshoji 興聖寺

Koza Tonko 講座「敦煌」

Kuang-fan 光範

Kuang-hsü 光緒

Kuo-hsüeh chi-k'an 國學季刊

Kuroita Katsumi 黒板勝美

Lang Chien 郎簡

Li Chih-fei 李知非

Liu Chih-lüeh 劉志略

Liu-tsu fa-pao chi hsü 六祖法寶記敍

liu-tzu t'an-ching 六祖壇經

Lou Yü-lieh 樓宇烈

Lü-hsun 旅順

Lü-shun po-wu-kuan so-ts'un tun-huang chih fo-chiao ching-tien
旅順博物館所存敦煌之佛教經典

Ma Tuan-lin 馬端臨

Matsugaoka bunko kenkyu nenpo 松ケ岡文庫研究年報

Ming 明

mon/men 門

mou-chia 某甲

Mugiya Kunio 麥谷邦夫

Myoshinji 妙心寺

Nagoya 名古屋

Naka-ku 中區

Nakagawa Taka 中川孝

Nakano Inchiuemon 中野市右衛門

Nan-tsung ting shih-fei lun 南宗定是非論

nan-tsung ting-chiao 南宗頓教

Nan-tsung tun-chiao tsui-shang ta-ch'eng po-jo po-lo-mi ching
南宗頓教最上大乘摩訶般若波羅密多經

Nan-tsung ting hsieh-cheng wu-keng-chuan 南宗定邪正五更轉

Nan-tsung tun-chiao tsui-shang ta-ch'eng t'an-ching 南宗頓教最上大乘壇經

Nan-yang ho-shang tun-chiao chieh-t'o ch'an-men chih-liao-hsing t'an-yü
南陽和上頓教解脫禪門直了性壇語

Nan-yang ho-shang t'an-yü 南陽和上壇語

Nan-yüeh 南嶽

Nanbokucho 南北朝

Nara 奈良

Otani 大谷

Otsu 大津

P'u-t'i-ta-mo nan-tsung ting shih-fei lun 菩提達摩南宗定是非論

Pao-lin chuan 寶林傳

Pi-an 彼岸

ping-chen 丙辰

Rinzai 臨濟

Rokuso dankyo 六祖壇經

Rokuso Dangyo shohon shusei 六祖壇經諸本集成

Rokuso dangyo gohon taisho 六祖壇經五本對照

Ryukoku 竜谷

San-lun 三論

Sekai no meicho 世界の名著

shan-chih-shih, yü*-jen chih-jen, fo-hsing pen yi wu ch'a-pieh, chih yü mi-wu, mi chi whe wu, wu chi ch'eng chih
善知識，愚人智人，佛性本亦無差別，只緣迷悟，迷即為悟，悟即成智

shan-chih-shih, yü wu chi ch'eng chih 善知識，遇悟即成智

Shang-wu yin-shu-kuan 商務印書館

Shao-chou 韶州

Shao-chou Ts'ao-ch'i-shan Liu-tsu-shih t'an-ching 韶州曹溪六祖師壇經

Shao-hsing 紹興

Shen-hsiu 神秀

Shen-hui 神會

shih yi, chiao-shih shih-seng ch'uan-fa 十一，教示十僧傳法

Shiina Koyu 椎名宏雄

Shina bukkyo shigaku 支那佛教史學

Shingon 真言

Shinohara Hisao 篠原壽雄

Shinpukuji zenpon mokuroku zokushu 真福寺善本目錄續輯

Shinpukuji zenpon mokuroku 真福寺善本目錄

Shinpukuji 真福寺

Shinsan zenseki mokuroku 新纂禪籍目錄

Shugaku kenkyu 宗學研究

Sokyo 祖鏡

Soto 曹洞

Sung 宋

Suzuki Teitaro 鈴木貞太郎

Ta-chien 大鑑

Ta-chung-hsiang-fu 大中祥符

Ta-fan-ssu 大梵寺

Taishukan 大修館

t'ai-sui ting-mao 太歲丁卯

tan shih chung-sheng, chi neng shih fo 但識衆生 即能識佛

tan shih fo-hsin chung-sheng, chi neng shih fo 但識佛心即能識佛

T'an-ching k'ao chih erh--Pa nihon kyoto horikawa koshoji ts'ang pei-sung hui-hsin pen t'an-ching ying-yin pen
壇經考之二 —跋日本京都堀川興聖寺藏北宋惠昕本壇經影印本

t'an-ching 壇經

T'an-ching k'ao chih yi: Pa ts'ao-chi ta-shih pieh-chuan
壇經考之一：跋曹溪大師別傳

Tanaka Ryosho 田中良昭

tang-ti 堂弟

T'ang-tai Ch'ang-an yü Hsi-yü wen-ming 唐代長安與西域文明

Tao-chi 道際

Te-yi 德異

Teiji 貞治

T'ien-sheng 天聖

ting 頂

Ting shih-fei lun 定是非論

Tonko Butten to Zen 敦煌佛典と禪

Tonkobon Rokuso Dangyo no shomondai 敦煌本六祖壇經の諸問題

Ts'ao-ch'i 曹溪

Ts'ao ch'i liu-tsu ta-shih t'an-ching 曹溪六祖大師壇經

Ts'ao-ch'i ta-shih chuan 曹溪大師傳

Tsu-t'ang chi 祖堂集

tsui-shang ta-ch'eng mo-ho-pan-jo po-lo-mi-to ching 最上大乘摩訶般若波羅蜜經

Ts'un-chung 存中

Tsung-pao 宗寶

T'u-shu-kuan-hsüeh chi-k'an 圖書館學季刊

tun 頓

Tun-huang 敦煌

Tun-huang yi-shu tsung-mu so-yin 敦煌遺書總目索引

Tun-huang hsien po-wu-kuan so-ts'ang t'ang-mo wu-tai hsieh-pen "t'an-ching",
敦煌縣博物館所藏唐末五代寫本「壇經」
"nan-tsung ting shih-fei lun" teng ch'an-tsung wen-hsien yen-chiu
「南宗定是非論」等禪宗文獻研究

tun-huang wen-wu yen-chiu so 敦煌文物研究所

Tun-huang t'u-lu-fan wen-hsien yen-chiu lun-chi 敦煌吐魯番文獻研究論集

Tun-huang hsien po-wu-kuan ts'ang tun-huang yi-shu mu lu
敦煌縣博物館藏敦煌遺書目錄

Tun-huang yi-shu san-lu 敦煌遺書散錄

Ui Hakuju 宇井伯寿

Wakanjo becchibon mokuroku 和漢書別置本目錄

Wan-li 萬曆

Wen-hsien t'ung-k'ao 文獻通考

Wen-wu ch'u-pan-she 文物出版社

Wo-lun 臥輪

Wu-chen 悟真

Yabuki Keiki 矢吹慶輝

Yamaguchi 山口

Yanagida Seizan 柳田聖山

Yang Tseng-wen 楊曾文

yü 遇

yü* 愚

Yüan 元

Yüan-ch'i wai-chi 緣起外記

Yüan-hui 圓會

Yün-men 雲門

Zengoroku 禪語錄

Zen no Goroku 禪の語錄

Zengaku sosho 禪學叢書

zenshushi kenkyukai 禪宗史研究會

zhih 帙

The Development of Chinese Culture: Some Comments in Light of the Study of the Introduction of Indian Buddhism into China

Tang Yijie
Beijing University

In the *Historical Records* (*Shiji*) there is a saying: "Those who, living today, are interested in the ancient Way as the mirror in which they see themselves reflected are different (from ordinary people)". Jia Yi, in "On the Past of the Qin Dynasty" (*Guoqin lun*), quoted a proverb: "Remembrance of the past is the teacher of the future". Past things cannot be taken in their entirety as models of future things; however, is it not possible to analyze and examine the course of past history, find some regularity behind certain phenomena, and let that regularity serve a frame of reference in terms of which to think about the present? If the answer to this question were simply negative, then there would be no point in studying history and reflecting upon it. Therefore, I think there is some truth in the saying: "Remembrance of the past is the teacher of the future".

In the course of the development of Chinese history, there were three major occasions when a foreign culture was introduced into China. 1) The introduction of Indian culture after the first century, A.D. The Indian culture that was introduced consisted principally of Indian Buddhism and influenced Chinese culture profoundly. 2) The introduction of Western civilization that began in the seventeenth century (the middle of the Ming dynasty period). This consisted principally of the efforts of Western missionaries such as Matteo Ricci to introduce Western civilization. 3) The introduction of Marxism after the May Fourth Movement.

The historical conditions of these three events were different. These introductions of a foreign culture occurred in different periods in Chinese history; the nature of the cultures introduced and the manner in which they were introduced were also different. Consequently, these three events had different effects on Chinese culture. It is a major enterprise to investigate this matter comprehensively, and such an enterprise is beyond the limits of my ability. In this paper I would like only to discuss the historical example of the introduction of Buddhism, and examine certain phenomena that appear after the foreign culture that has been introduced comes into contact with the native culture. I would also like to see whether an examination of these phenomena can provide us with some meaningful insights regarding the more general issue of the introduction of a foreign culture.

Generally speaking, the introduction of Indian Buddhism involved the following stages: first, Buddhism attached itself to the native culture so that it could spread; secondly, certain contradictions and conflicts arose between Buddhism and traditional Chinese culture; finally, Buddhism was assimilated by Chinese culture and contributed on a large scale to the further development of Chinese culture. I would like to comment briefly on each of these stages.

I

When Indian culture was first introduced into China, it attached itself to the native Chinese culture so that it could spread and exert its influence. When Buddhism was introduced into China in the Han Dynasty period (206, B.C.-220), it was attached to the native Chinese "techniques of the Way" or "Taoist techniques" (*daoshu* or *fangshu*). During the Wei and Jin Dynasties (220-419), when the metaphysical speculation of the "profound learning" (*xuanxue*) was popular, "Buddha" and "Emperor Huang and Lao Zi" were treated as similar entities. The Prince of Chu "read the sayings of Emperor Huang and Lao Zi and honored the Buddha's temple (*rensi*)." (*Houhan shu*, chapter 42). Emperor Huan (reign years: 147-167) also built shrines for Emperor Huang and Lao Zi as well as for the Buddha in his palace (*Houhan shu*, chapter 30B, *Xiang Kai zhuan*).

At that time even Buddhists themselves called their teaching "techniques of the Way (*daoshu*)." In the essay, "On the Resolution of Puzzles" (*Lihuo lun*), Mou Zi treats Buddhism as one of the ninety-six types of techniques of the Way: "There are ninety-six different kinds of spiritual Ways (*dao*). If you look for the august and great, none surpasses the Way of the Buddha (*fodao*)." In the *Scripture in Forty-Two Chapters* (*Sishi'erzhangjing*), Buddhism is also called "the Way of Buddha (*fodao*)" by its Buddhist author.

The content of Buddhist teaching at that time was mainly summarized by such theses as "the imperishability of the soul" and "moral retribution of causes and consequences". There does not seem to have been any understanding of the teaching of "no self" in Indian Buddhism. The idea of "the imperishability of the soul" had existed indigenously in Chinese philosophy, where it took the various forms of "theories about ghosts" (*yougui lun*). In the *Book of Poetry* there is a saying that the human spirit goes to heaven after passing away (*Sanhou zaitian, Daya, Fuwang*). In the *Huainan Zi* it is said that "body can die, but the spirit cannot die" (*Jingshen xun*). In opposition to these thoughts, during the Han Dynasty period Huan Tan developed a theory that "when the body is dead the spirit is also dead." Wang Chong (27-90?) also said, "A person who is dead does not become a ghost." Nevertheless, the theory that "the imperishability of the soul" can be achieved by certain physical and spiritual cultivation was native to Chinese philosophy.

As for "moral retribution of causes and consequences," though there are differences between the discussions in Buddhism and native Chinese philosophy, the Buddhist idea which was popular in the Han Dynasty was consistent with the native Chinese idea of "good deeds produce happiness and licentiousness, misfortune" (*Fushan, huoyin*). The *Book of Changes* (*Yijing*) says, "A family which accumulates good deeds is bound to have a lot of happiness; a family which fails to accumulate good deeds is bound to have misfortunes."

Toward the end of the Han Dynasty period and around the beginning of the Wei Dynasty period (220-265) numerous new translations of Buddhist scriptures appeared. Buddhism spread in China in two major streams: one was the school of An Shigao, which taught Hinayana Buddhism and emphasized the method of meditation; another was the school of Zhi Loujiachen (Skt., Lokakṣema?), which taught Mahayana Buddhism and lectured on the Perfection of Wisdom philosophy. An Shigao translated many Buddhist scriptures. His most influential translations were the *Ānāpāna Sūtra* (*Anban shouyi jing*) and the *Yinchiru jing* (*skandha-dhātu-āyatana-sūtra*?). The *Ānāpāna sūtra* discussed the techniques of breath control, which was similar to the breath control techniques of Chinese Taoists and those who followed the cult of immortals (*shenxian*). The *Yinchiru jing* explained Buddhist terms and concepts and was similar to the commentarial scholarship of scriptures that flourished during the Han Dynasty period.

The *Yinchiru jing* took the concept of "original breath (*yuan qi*)" as its basic category and developed a theory of the universe and human life; *yuan qi* was said to be the same as the "five elements" (*wuxing*). It also discussed the Buddhist theory of "five accumulations" (*wuyin*, an earlier term used to translate *skandha*, which was later translated as *wuyun*), treating the five categories of form (*se*, or *rūpa*), feeling (*shou*, or *vedanā*), perception (*xiang*, or *samjñāna*), volition (*xing*, or *saṃskāra*), and consciousness (*shi*, or *vijñāna*) as the effects of the Five Elements. From these examples we can detect that An Shigao advocated the Hinayana method of meditation; it is also clear that he attached Buddhism to the teachings of the "techniques of the Way" (*daoshu*) that were prevalent in China and explained Buddhism using as his model these teachings about the technique of the Way.

The school of Zhi Loujiachen taught the Mahayana learning of the Perfection of Wisdom; it believed that the basic principle of life is "the mind (or spirit, *shen*) reverting to the original truth (*benzhen*)" and becoming one with the "Way". Here we can see the influence of the Taoist thought of the *Lao Zi* and the *Zhuang Zi*. The second generation disciple of Zhi Loujiachen, Zhi Qian, translated the *Prajñāpāramitā sūtra* ("Perfection of Wisdom scripture") into Chinese, giving its title as the "Scripture of Salvation into the Infinite Through Great Brightness" (*Daming du wuji jing*). The word "*prajñā*" in the title was here translated as "great brightness (*daming*)". The word "brightness (*ming*)" must have been taken in the sense of the statement "Knowledge of the constant is known as discernment (or brightness, *ming*)" in the *Lao Zi* (chapter 16). The word "*pāramitā*" was translated as "salvation into the infinite (*du wuji*)". This expression must similarly refer to the state of union with the "Way" ("Return to the Infinite", *Lao Zi*, chapter 28).

During the Wei and the Jin Dynasties, the ontology of the "profound learning" metaphysics based on the Taoist thought in the *Lao Zi* and the *Zhuang Zi* was very popular. The central issue of "profound learning" metaphysics was the question of the relationship between the Root (*ben*) and the Branches (*mo*) and between Being (*you*) and Nonbeing (*wu*). The central issue of the Buddhist teaching of the Perfection of Wisdom (*prajñā*) was the question of Emptiness (*kong*) and Existence (*you*, "Being"). Thus the Buddhist discussion was somewhat similar to that of the "profound learning" metaphysics. It was for this reason that many Buddhists of that time used the "profound learning" metaphysics to interpret Buddhist philosophy, even going so far as to use the so-called methods of "matching concepts (*ge yi*)" and "linking similar things (*lian lei*)."

Dao'an once said: "Among the twelve categories of Buddhist scriptures that of the *pimuluo* (meaning *pifuluo*, ie., *vaipulya* which probably meant Mahayana) scriptures is most popular; this was because the *Vaipulya* scripture's teaching of 'forgetting both existence and nonexistence' was similar the thought taught in the land in the *Lao Zi* and the *Zhuang Zi*." Here we can see that this famous teacher of that time already recognized that the popularity of Buddhism depended on its being understood in light of the thought of the *Lao Zi* and the *Zhuang Zi*.

There is a passage in the "Letters and Scholarship" section of the *New Account of Tales of the World* (*Shishuo xinyu*): "During the Zhengshi era (240-249), Wang Bi (226-249) and He Yan (ca. 190-249) had favored profound and transcendent (*xuansheng*) conversations about the *Lao Zi* and the *Zhuang Zi*, and after that the world set great store by them. But at the time of the crossing of the Yangze River (307-312) Buddhist doctrines became especially popular." (quoted in Liu Xiaobiao's commentary).

In the beginning of the Eastern Jin Dynasty (317-419), the study of "*prajñā*" became extremely popular and the so-called "six schools and seven sects" (*liujia qizong*) developed. The issue that they were interested in was essentially the question of the relationship between the Root (*ben*) and the Branches (*mo*) and between Being (*you*) and Nonbeing (*wu*). What is called the "teaching of the Original Nonbeing" (*benwu yi*) inherited and developed further the teaching that "valued Nonbeing" (*guiwu*) taught by Wang Bi and He Yan; the "teaching of Annihilating Mind" (*xinwu yi*) was similar to Ji Kang and Ruan Ji's idea of "No Mind" (*wuxin*); the "teaching of Matter As Such" (*jise yi*) is related to Guo Xiang's thought of "Exalting Being" (*chongyou*)

Why did all of this occur? I think any culture has its conservative elements, which gives that culture a resistance to foreign cultures. Thus, foreign cultures must first adjust themselves to the native culture and attach themselves to it. Those parts which are similar to the native culture will then spread easily; those parts which are alien to the native culture will then be slowly assimilated by the native culture and thereby influence the native culture.

II

As it spread broadly after the Eastern Jin Dynasty, Indian Buddhism gave rise to contradictions and conflicts between the traditional Chinese culture and the imported Indian culture. Yet in the midst of these contradictions and conflicts Indian Buddhism contributed to the further development of Chinese culture.

In the early years of the Eastern Jin Dynasty, the Buddhist teaching of Perfection of Wisdom (*prajñā*) attached itself to the "profound learning" metaphysics based on the *Lao Zi* and the *Zhuang Zi*; this position may be called the "Buddhist profound learning metaphysics (*foxuan*)". By the end of the Eastern Jin Dynasty and the beginning of the Liu Song Dynasty, other schools of Buddhism, both Hinayana and Mahayana, started to be introduced; they offered a variety of interpretations of the Buddhist scriptures, and exegetical scholarship on scriptures developed.

In the final analysis, Indian culture and native Chinese culture represent two distinct and different types of cultural traditions. Indian culture could not remain permanently attached to Chinese culture.

By the end of the Eastern Jin Dynasty period and later, numerous translations of Buddhist scriptures appeared, and these translations became more and more systematic. At the same time the superiority of some aspects of Indian culture over traditional Chinese culture became evident. Contradictions and conflicts inevitably arose between the two different cultural traditions.

The translation of Buddhist scriptures into Chinese began in the Han Dynasty period. According to the Kaiyuan catalogue of Buddhist scriptures, about 1420 volumes of Buddhist scriptures were translated during the roughly 250 years between the Han Dynasty and the Western Jin Dynasty. But during the Eastern Jin Dynasty (if we include the activities in the northern dynasties of Later Qin, Western Qin, Former Liang, and Norther Liang), about 1716 volumes of Buddhist scriptures were translated. More scriptures were translated during these 100 years than during the 250 years that preceded them. Particularly noteworthy in this context are Kumārajīva's precise translations of Mahayana and Hinayana scriptures, monastic rules, and doctrinal treatises; these translations enabled readers to understand the original meaning of the teachings that were representative of Indian Buddhist culture. By that time, not only foreign monks, but also Chinese monks had attained a relatively correct understanding of Buddhism which tallied with the original Indian meaning of its teachings. As they achieved a relatively correct understanding of Buddhism, new problems confronted these Buddhists: should they continue to understand Buddhism in terms of Chinese culture, or should they teach Buddhism in China according to the original meaning of its teaching? Thus began the inevitable conflicts between these two different types of cultures.

During the Southern and Northern Dynasties period (420-589), the conflicts between Buddhism and native Chinese culture occurred in many fields. These conflicts surfaced as problems of political and economic interests; they also appeared as problems in the fields of philosophy, religion, and ethics.

An important historical work has been preserved for us, and this work provides us with the broad outline of the contradictions and conflicts between Indian Buddhism and traditional Chinese culture during this period. This work is the *Hongming ji*. Through this work we can glimpse the issues that arose at that time: the controversy over the immortality or mortality of the spirit (or soul, *shen*); the controversy over karmic retribution, which involved the philosophical issue of moral causality (*yinguo*, "causes and consequences") vs. preordained fate (*ziran*; "our preordained nature [*xingming*] is self-so"); the relation between Emptiness and Existence; the controversy over the question whether monks should pay respect to the ruler, which involved the issue of this-worldly or other-worldly ethics (*chushi*; *rushi*); the relationship between human beings and other "sentient beings" (*sattva*). He Chengtian, basing himself on the *Book of Changes*, maintained that human beings, Heaven and Earth are three distinct entities, and criticized Buddhists for failing to make these distinctions, treating human beings and other sentient beings on the same level. This issue was related to the defence of the Confucian tradition.

There was also a controversy about Chinese culture and foreign cultures. He Chengtian, in "Reply to Zong Bin", wrote: "Chinese people and foreigners are naturally different, and this difference is rooted in their different natures (*xing**). Chinese people are endowed with a clear and harmonious nature, and are capable of humane sentiments and upholding correct morality; therefore Duke of Zhou and Confucius taught them the teaching of human nature and learning; foreigners are endowed with a violent nature and are greedy and full of anger; therefore Śākyamunī imposed on them the discipline of the five precepts." Gu Huan, in his "On Chinese and Foreigners" (*Yixia lun*), also claimed that China is the country of "rites and morality" (*liyi*) and that therefore we should not abandon the Chinese ways and imitate foreign countries. The principle on which he based his argument was roughly the same as that of He Chengtian.

During this period Emperor Wu in the North Chou Dynasty ordered the persecution of Buddhism, not only for political and economic reasons, but also for cultural reasons. In this period the contradictions and conflicts between Buddhism and Taoism, which was the traditional religion of the Chinese people, also became acute. First, there was the controversy about the theory that Lao Zi transformed himself into a foreign teacher (the Buddha); this was then followed by the controversies over death and rebirth, body and mind (*shen*, "spirit"), as well as the controversy about the relationship between Chinese and foreign cultures.

All these controversies were expressions of the contradictions and conflicts between two different types of cultures. Some of these controversies continued right into the Sui and Tang Dynasties (581-617; 618-907). I will not comment on them further here.

It is clear from the situation described above that after two different types of cultures come into contact with each other, contradictions and conflicts inevitably arise. One important question is how to deal with these contradictions and conflicts: either to repel foreign cultures using political power, or to remain amidst these contradictions and conflicts and absorb and assimilate what is good in the foreign culture. This is a large question. From the Southern and Northern Dynasties (420-589) to the Sui and Tang Dynasties there were contradictions and conflicts between Indian culture and the native Chinese culture. In my opinion Chinese people did not reject the foreign culture, but rather absorbed and digested the foreign culture as much as possible. This attitude showed the confidence of the nation as well the values of its own culture.

The experience of these contradictions and conflicts and the continued assimilation of Indian culture into traditional Chinese culture that resulted from it contributed forcefully to the development of Chinese culture. During this period, Chinese culture flourished in philosophy, literature, architecture, technology and even medicine. There is no doubt that all these accomplishments were related to the way in which Indian culture was treated in China at that time.

III

Indian Buddhism was gradually assimilated by Chinese culture after the Sui and Tang Dynasties. First Sinified Buddhist schools were established. By the Song Dynasty (960-1279) Buddhism had become a part of traditional Chinese culture and was completely blended into it—Buddhism evolved into the Neo-Confucian Philosophy of Principle (*lixue*) of the Song and Ming Dynasties.

Among the several schools of Buddhism that appeared during the Sui and Tang Dynasties, the Tiantai School, Huayan School, and Chan School were in fact Sinified schools of Buddhism. The central issues that these three schools concentrated on were the problem of the relationship between mind (*xin*) and human nature (or essence)(*xing**) and the problem of the relationship between principle (*li*) and fact (*shi*). The problem of the relationship between mind and human nature had always been an important issue in traditional Chinese philosophy, in which the discussion of this issue can be traced back to Confucius and especially to Mencius. When Mencius talked about "giving full realization to his mind" (*jinxin*), "understanding his own nature" (*zhixing*), and "knowing heaven" (*zhitian*) side by side in one sentence, he was clearly touching upon the issue of nature and mind.

The above-mentioned three schools of Buddhism all discussed the issues of Buddha nature (*foxing*) and the original mind (*benxin*). The Chan School was specially interested in the issue of mind and human nature. According to the Chan School the Buddha nature is identical with the original mind; the Chan School in fact had developed the indigenous Chinese discussion of mind and human nature in a new context from one particular perspective.

As for the problem of principle and fact, the Hua-yen School talked about the "free and harmonious interpenetration between principle (*li*) and fact (*shi*)(*lishi wu'ai*)" and the "free and harmonious interpenetration among facts (*shishi wu'ai*)." This discussion was not unrelated to the "profound learning" metaphysics of the Wei and Jin Dynasties, since the idea of "the identity of the substance (*ti*) and function (*yong*)" had already existed in the "profound learning" metaphysics of that time. For example, Wang Bi once claimed that "Nonbeing is the cause of Being." He also said, "Although [Heaven and Earth]• are engaged in great undertakings and have great wealth in possessing the myriad things, each thing still has its own character. Although it is valuable to have Nonbeing as its function, nevertheless there cannot be substance without Nonbeing."(Commentary on the *Lao Zi*, chapter 38). Both these statements explain the relationship between Being and Nonbeing on the basis of "the identity of substance and function". The idea of the "free and harmonious interpenetration between principle (*li*) and fact (*shi*)" is thus related to Wang Bi's thought. On the other hand, the idea of the "free and harmonious interpenetration among facts (*shishi wu'ai*)" was influenced by Guo Xiang's theory of "self-transformation of things" (*duhualun*).

In China, the Huayan school and Chan school have had the most influence on Chinese philosophy. This was because they represented Sinified Buddhism. By contrast, the Faxiang school only lasted about thirty years, in spite of the fact that it was promoted by the famous Xuanzang. This was because the Faxiang school was purely Indian Buddhism.

In the Song Dynasty the Neo-Confucian Philosophy of Principle (*lixue*) opposed Buddhism, and from the longer perspective of the development of Chinese philosophy, this Neo-Confucian Philosophy of Principle took over the place that Buddhism had occupied earlier. This development was not a matter of accident, either. We can understand the reasons behind this development in a coherent way. From the beginning traditional Chinese thought has been "this-worldly" (*rushi*); in other words it has focussed on the realization of "ordering the state and pacifying the entire world (*zhiguo ping tianxia*)". This basic orientation differed fundamentally from that of "other-worldly" (*chushi*) Buddhist thought. However, even in traditional Chinese thought questions such as "What is the basis for the establishment of a perfect society?", and "How are we to realize the ideal of the 'ordering of the state and pacifying the entire world'?" became very important.

In this connection the concept of "Heavenly principle (*tianli*)" was introduced. Cheng Hao said, "There are many things in my learning that I have received from others, but the two character phrase *tianli* ("heavenly principle") is derived from my own experience." The *tianli* ("heavenly principle") is not *kongli* ("empty principle" or "principle of emptiness") but rather *shili* ("substantial principle" or "principle of the real"); it is the "virtue that expresses perfection." As for the relation between "Heaven (*tian*)" and "Man (*ren*)" (or *renxing*, ie., the nature of human being), Neo-Confucianists either claim that "The nature is the principle (*Xing ji li*)," or state that "The mind is the principle (*Xin ji li*)". Both these statements refer to the issue of the relation of the mind and the human nature. Thus this issue was a basic question in Neo-Confucianism.

In both the Neo-Confucian positions expressed in these theses (" Nature is the principle" and "The mind is the principle"), the question of the relationship between Heaven and human beings arises. Consequently, the Neo-Confucian thinkers established in their ontology "the unity of Heaven and human beings". The Cheng brothers described the relation between Heaven and human beings by the statement "The substance (*ti*) and the function (*yong*) share the same source; what is manifest (*xian*) and what is subtle (*wei*) are not separated from each other". Zhu Xi described this relationship of Heaven and human beings using the thesis "Every human being has his Great Ultimate (*taiji*), and every object has its Great Ultimate". Lu Jiuyuan says "the Universe is my mind and my mind is the Universe". And Wang Shouren spoke about the identity of Heaven and human beings (*tianren yiti*) when he stated, "The mind is the principle. When we say mind, we are at the same time referring to all of Heaven, Earth, and myriad things."

When the ideal that "the Heaven and human beings become one being" is perfectly realized, the project of "ordering the state and pacifying the entire world" is also realized; from the perspective of perfecting an individual human being, what is required is to manifest the "Heavenly principle" in himself. In order to manifest the "Heavenly principle" in himself, a person must raise the standard of his morality to the point where the unity of knowledge and action is achieved, and he must engage in the spiritual cultivation of his own mind. An important linkage developed in this sphere of mind cultivation between the Neo-Confucian Philosophy of Principle during the Song (960-1279) and Ming (1368-1661) periods and the spiritual cultivation and practice of Chan Buddhism that had flourished earlier. However, the goal of the moral practice of Neo-Confucianism was not to enable the individual to achieve Buddhahood, but to realize their ideal of a harmonious society. Neo-Confucianism criticized Buddhism on the one hand, and absorbed and assimilated Buddhism on the other, and in this way developed for Chinese philosophy a system that was even closer to perfection; this system contained an ontology, a theory of value and a philosophy of life.

In the period starting from the Han Dynasty (206 B.C.-220) and ending with the Song and Ming Dynasties, Chinese philosophy experienced the impact of a foreign culture, and completed a course of development that may be described by the formula of thesis, antithesis, and synthesis. The three developments we have examined above may be understood as expressions of this threefold formula of historical development. The encounter and assimilation of Indian Buddhism was the first example of this kind in the history of Chinese philosophy.

What can we learn from this process? I believe that there are at least four lessons.

1) The process of the absorption of Indian culture into Chinese culture lasted several hundred years. This shows that the absorption and assimilation of one culture into another cannot be accomplished overnight, but that it requires a certain duration of time and certain conditions. We can say the following on the

basis of the example of the introduction of Indian culture: although Indian Buddhism was very popular between the first and the tenth century, traditional Chinese culture also revealed its great vitality; each of the three stages of thesis, antithesis, and synthesis pointed to the places where the vitality of traditional Chinese culture lay and showed in what sense it was valuable; each of these stages showed how traditional Chinese culture dared to welcome a foreign culture into its midst, and how effective it was in absorbing and assimilating it. From this example, we can conclude that the attitude of "openness" towards foreign cultures is a sign of the vitality of the national culture. The capacity of a culture to assimilate a foreign culture is an important condition for the more rapid growth of that culture. Foreign cultures act as stimuli for the development of the native culture. When a vigorous culture faces the challenges of a foreign culture, not only does it not reject outright that culture, but it assimilates the foreign culture, in order to foster its own healthy development. Such viewpoints as "cultural relativism" (*benwei wenhua*) and "nativism" (or "national essence ideology", *guocui zhuyi*) not only stifle the development of Chinese national culture; they are themselves expressions of the decline of that culture.

2) This analysis of the phenomena which appeared after the encounter of native Chinese culture with Indian culture is a product of our current understanding. At the time this process of historical development occurred, people who were directly involved in this development were not aware of what we know today with hindsight, namely that the development went through a series of distinctive stages. When we study these stages of development today, we can recognize the following phenomena: at one stage in the introduction of a foreign culture, the foreign culture frequently spontaneously adjusts itself to the needs of the native culture in a variety of ways and searches for points of integration with the native culture. For example, during the Han Dynasty period, Buddhism emphasized such slogans as "the imperishability of the soul" and "moral retribution of causes and consequences"; later, it also adjusted itself to the "profound learning" metaphysics of the Wei and Jin Dynasties and advocated the "Buddhist metaphysics of profound learning (*foxuan*)". It was by no means simply a matter of accident that these developments occurred at that time.

Can we then say that this kind of development constitutes a certain universal law? I believe we can. If a foreign culture takes the place of the native culture (or a certain part of that culture) instead of adjusting itself to the native culture, it will then have negated everything about the native culture (or the corresponding part of that culture.) This will result for the host country in cutting off its own history and in abandoning the spirit upon which the existence of its own nationality has depended over a very long period. In this case, the foreign culture becomes something imposed by force on the people or the nation to which the foreign culture was introduced. Consequently, that foreign culture remains a rootless culture and could hardly survive over a long period of time there.

If, after a foreign culture has been introduced, a native culture is able self-consciously and deliberately to seek out the points of integration between itself and the foreign culture, and to let that foreign culture adjust quickly and smoothly to the needs of the development of the people and the nation to which it has been introduced, the situation will be different. Not only will the development of the native culture be enriched, but the native culture will also be able to generate under the impact of the foreign culture new possibilities for reorienting some of the areas of its development.

3) Every culture has its own distinctive characteristics which distinguish it from other cultures. If it is to exist as an unique culture its fundamental characteristics must be protected; otherwise it will become a thing of the past and not continue as a real culture that functions in real life. Compared with Indian Buddhism, the most evident characteristic of traditional Chinese culture is that it teaches us how to realize the ideal of "ordering the state and pacifying the entire world." Such a "this-worldly" spirit differs completely from the "other-worldly" spirit of Indian Buddhism. After being introduced to China, Indian Buddhism exerted profound influences on the social life of Chinese people; it changed many aspects of the social life of Chinese people. But the basic "this-worldy" spirit of Chinese culture has never been changed by the imported Indian culture. Hence, Chinese culture as an independent cultural system continued to exist and be developed.

Whether traditional Chinese culture can be further developed in the future thus depends on two factors: first, it must be able to keep its own distinctive characteristics; secondly, it must also be brave in assimilating foreign cultures in order to meet the developmental needs of actual social life. The first of these two conditions allows for the expression of the unique and distinctive value of a particular traditional culture. If a culture is unable to keep its own characteristics, it will vanish from the stage of history. The second condition gives expression to the fact that if a vigorous culture preserves its distinctive characteristics, and at the same time is also able to follow contemporary developments and assimilate new things, it is then bound to be able to develop further. If a culture loses its capacity for assimilating new things, it can no longer continue to exist as a culture which keeps its own characteristics. The history of the development of traditional Chinese culture illustrates that Chinese culture fulfilled these two conditions in the course of its history.

4) After the introduction of Indian culture into China, there was a period in which the influence of Buddhism in daily life was greater than that of the native Chinese culture. The bibliographical chapter in the *History of the Sui Dynasty* (*Suishu, Jingjizhi*) says that since Emperors promoted Buddhism, it developed so greatly that "everyone admired Buddhism. The copies of Buddhist scriptures that circulated among ordinary people were a hundred times more numerous than those of the Six Classics." Thus, many of the new developments in Chinese culture during the Sui and the Tang Dynasties were connected with Buddhism. Many famous thinkers during that time were monks and some of the Buddhist schools contributed to the development of Chinese philosophy. This situation may represent phenomena that necessarily occur at one stage after two different

traditions of culture have remained in contact with each other over a long period.

However, Chinese Buddhist schools and sects did not develop in the direction of forcefully adapting the spirit of social life in China to the demands of Indian culture; on the contrary, Buddhism developed in the direction of Sinification. It is particularly important to note in this context that the distinctively "religious" characteristic of Buddhism was destroyed by the emergence of Chan Buddhism. Chan taught that you not only do not have to recite scriptures and pray to the Buddha; you may also swear at the Buddha and patriarchs. Furthermore, according to Chan, the ideal of becoming the Buddha can be realized in daily life. In this sense, the place of Buddhism is taken by traditional Chinese culture: "Carrying water and chopping fire wood—without exception these are all spiritual paths." It will require only one more step beyond this in order to reach the position that "serving the father and serving the ruler" is the way of becoming a sage and a wise man. Once this step is taken, traditional Chinese culture has replaced Buddhism completely.

At present, the development of history demands that we place the question "how should Chinese culture develop?" again on the agenda for our discussion of contemporary issues. Our nation is again placed under the impact of various intellectual trends of Western culture: how are we to reflect upon the value of traditional Chinese culture, how are we to reform and develop it further so that it will adapt to the currently unfolding trends of modernization? In order to do justice to these questions, we must continuously explore and meet new challenges. We have discussed the introduction of Buddhism to China, and described the variety of phenomena that appeared after our native culture experienced the impact of a foreign culture. This exploration ought to serve as a very important reference point for studying the future development of Chinese culture.

(Translated by Koichi Shinohara)

List of Characters

An Shigao 安世高
Anban shouyi jing 安般守意經
ben 本
benwei wenhua 本位文化
benwu yi 本無意
benxin 本心
benzhen 本真
Chan 禪
Cheng 程
Cheng Hao 程顥
chongyou 崇有
Chu 楚
chushi 出世
daming 大明
Daming du wuji jing 大明度無極經
dao 道
daoshu 道術
Daya 大雅
du wuji 度無極
duhualun 獨化論
fangshu 方術
Faxiang 法相
fodao 佛道
foxing 佛性
foxuan 佛玄
Fushan, huoyin 福善禍淫
Fuwang 父王
ge yi 格義
Gu Huan 顧歡
guiwu 貴無
Guoqin lun 過秦論
Guo Xiang 郭象
guocui zhuyi 國粹主義
He Yan 何晏
He Chengtian 何承天
Hongming ji 弘明集
Houhan shu 後漢書
Huainan Zi 淮南子
Huan Tan 桓譚
Huan 桓
Huang 黃
Huayan 華嚴
Ji Kang 嵇康
Jia Yi 賈誼

Jingjizhi 經籍志
Jingshen xun 精神訓
jinxin 盡心
jise yi 即色義
Kaiyuan 開元
kong 空
kongli 空理
Lao Zi 老子
li 理
lian lei 連類
Lihuo lun 理惑論
lishi wu'ai 理事無碍
Liu Xiaobiao 劉孝標
liujia qizong 六家七宗
lixue 理學
liyi 禮義
Lu Jiuyuan 陸九淵
ming 明
mo 末
Mou Zi 牟子
Pinaye xu 毗奈耶序
ren 人
rensi 仁祠
renxing 人性
Ruan Ji 阮籍
rushi 入世
Sanhou zaitian 三后在天
se 色
shen 神
shenxian 神仙
shi 事
Shiji 史記
shili 實理
shishi wu'ai 事事無礙
Shishuo xinyu 世說新語
shou 受
sishi'erzhangjing 四十二章經
Suishu 隋書
taiji 太極
ti 體
tian 天
tianli 天理
tianren yiti 天人一體
Tiantai 天台

Wang Bi 王弼

Wang Shouren 王守仁

Wang Chong 王充

wei 微

wu 無

wuxin 無心

wuxing 五行

wuyin 五陰

wuyun 五蘊

xian 顯

Xiang Kai zhuan 襄楷傳

xiang 想

Xin ji li 心即理

xin 心

xing 行

xing* 性

Xing ji li 性即理

xingming 性命

xinwu yi 心無義

Xuanzang 玄奘

xuansheng 玄勝

xuanxue 玄學

Yijing 易經

Yinchiru jing 陰持入經

yinguo 因果

Yixia lun 夷夏論

yong 用

you 有

yougui lun 有鬼論

yuan qi 元氣

Zhengshi 正始

Zhi Qian 支謙

Zhi Loujiachen 支婁迦讖

zhiguo ping tianxia 治國平天下

zhitian 知天

zhixing 知性

Zhu Xi 朱熹

Zhuang Zi 莊子

ziran 自然

Zong Bin 宗炳

A New Look at the Earliest Chinese Buddhist Texts

E. Zürcher
Rijksuniversiteit te Leiden

1. Introductory remarks

The Chinese Buddhist texts that on the basis of internal and external evidence may be ascribed to the "embryonic phase" of Chinese Buddhism—the second and early third century AD—constitute a corpus of writing materials roughly equal to one-third of the *Hou Han shu.* If we compare this large body of archaic Chinese Buddhist scriptures with the few bits of available information on the historical aspects of Han Buddhism, or with the pitiful amount of original source materials on Han Taoism (or, indeed,on any other aspect of religious life of that period), it is obvious that, at least as far as the scriptural evidence is concerned, we might be tempted to conclude that Buddhism is by far the most richly documented sector of Later Han spiritual life. At first sight it would seem possible to analyse the doctrinal *contents* of these texts in order to fill in the empty contours of Han Buddhism: what the first generations of Chinese devotees believed is to be found in the scriptures.

This, of course, is a methodological error. In spite of all the changes and adaptations which the scriptures may have undergone in the course of translation, they basically remained intrusions from another civilization, containing an enormous range of concepts, rules, literary images and religious lore which, once introduced into China, lost their original degree of cohesion and integration. Some elements in a scripture could—for a variety of reasons—"catch on" and become productive factors in Chinese Buddhism, whereas other notions figuring in the same text would remain alien and undigested.[1] The argument that the fact that certain scripture was selected for translation implies a conscious choice of the translator and therefore to some extent reflects the predilections of the Chinese public does not hold good either, for that choice may have depended on other factors as well: the foreign masters produced the texts that they happened to have memorized before their arrival in China, or that were available as manuscripts. In general, as far as actual impact and productivity are concerned, we have to use other criteria, such as the occurrence of certain notions in the earliest commentaries, prefaces and colophons and in certain passages that, as far as we can judge, did not figure in the original text and were added for the benefit of a Chinese audience. Some of the ideas we find there also play a central role in the scriptural texts, such as the concepts of impermanence and causation, the elimination of desire, the elusive and dangerous nature of uncontrolled thought and the need to control it by means of psychic exercises. Such ideas may indeed be recognized as central concepts in Han Buddhism. But the mere fact that a certain theme figures in a translated Han scripture may certainly not be taken to mean that it was part of the Chinese religious experience.

There is, however, another possible approach that may yield some new, if indirect, clues: an analysis of the formal aspects of these texts, and an attempt to define their linguistic, terminological and stylistic features. Since I have presented a survey of the linguistic peculiarities of the earliest Buddhist translations elsewhere,[2] I shall in this article confine myself to a very brief summary of the purely linguistic features, and concentrate on matters of terminology and style. In doing so, I shall not go into the complicated textual relations between earlier and later Chinese versions, nor shall I make any detailed comparisons between these ancient translations and their extant Pāli and Sanskrit parallels. The question will be to what extent, and in what ways, these archaic translations can be made to yield information about the intellectual and social context of the very first stage of Chinese Buddhism, when it still was an obscure subcultural religion in extramural Luoyang.

In order to do so, we must first clearly define the corpus of texts that can be accepted as genuine. This is a sad necessity, for Chinese Buddhist bibliographers through the ages have been ever more generous in their attributions—in the successive bibliographies the number of works attributed to An Shigao has grown from 34 to 179, and those "by Lokakṣema" from 7 to 23!

The criteria for selection are the following:

(1) In general, no attention has been paid to attributions made later than the fourth century AD. This means that in most cases I have relied on what is considered the best authority regarding archaic translations: the *Zongli zhongjing mulu*, completed by the scholar-monk and eminent bibliographer Dao'an in 374 AD.[3] To some extent I have also been guided by information drawn from the early fourth century bibliographer Zhi Mindu.

(2) Wherever possible, corroborating evidence has been drawn from textual glosses, from contemporary or very early colophons and prefaces, and from the fact that certain scriptures are quoted or referred to in the earliest Chinese Buddhist commentaries,[4] or have been the basis of secondary, "polished" recensions that were produced shortly after the end of the Han.

(3) On the basis of (1) and (2), some "landmarks"—unquestionably authentic products of certain translators—could be established, e.g. T 224 *Daoxing jing* attributed by Dao'an to Lokakṣema; mentioned as Lokakṣema's work in Dao'an's preface to the same scripture; confirmed by a contemporary

colophon dated October 26, 179 AD supplying details about place and circumstances of translation, names of collaborators, etc.), or T 602 *Anban shouyi jing* (attributed by Dao'an to An Shigao; often quoted in the earliest [first half 3rd century] Chinese commentaries; preface by Kang Senghui ca. 250 AD mentioning An Shigao as the translator, and supplying names of Chinese devotees from the school of An Shigao who transmitted the scripture).

(4) These "landmarks" were subjected to terminological and stylistic analysis in order to define a number of distinctive lexical and stylistic features peculiar to certain translators' teams.

(5) The other extant scriptures attributed by Dao'an and Zhi Mindu to Han translators were re-examined in the light of (4); as a result, two of these had to be eliminated.

This critical selection has yielded a body of 29 texts that may be considered genuine Han translations, made at Luoyang by five different translators' teams between 150 and 220 AC. Their titles are listed in the Appendix to this article; for reasons of space the detailed bibliographical data concerning each text have been omitted.

2. *The 'scriptural idiom'*

Anybody who even casually has looked into an early Chinese Buddhist text must have been struck by the very peculiar kind of language used in it—a literary medium that differs as much from standard classical Chinese as it does, rather surprisingly, from the fairly regular classical language of the earliest Taoist documents.[5] In some scriptures this particular idiom prevails throughout; in other cases we find various degrees of *wenyan* admixtures: classical stylistic features such as a regular four-syllable prosodic pattern the use of Chinese-type parallelism, and archaisms such as *si* for "this" and *jue* as a third person possessive pronoun. It is obvious that we have to do with a "scriptural idiom" serving as the vehicle of a marginal literature written for a special type of readership.

It cannot be doubted that this idiom largely reflects the vernacular language of the period, the more so since many features that are characteristic of our texts agree with the findings of scholars in the field of Chinese historical linguistics.[6] However, it should be pointed out that the source materials used by such scholars (such as Zhao Qi's second-century Mencius commentary; selected passages from early dynastic histories, and *Shishuo xinyu*) fully belong to the sphere of the cultured elite and therefore are written in a standard *wenyan* that only occasionally contains some vernacular elements, especially in direct speech. The Buddhist materials exhibit those features to a much greater extent, and in this respect by far surpass any secular text. The elements of living speech, which in secular literature are no more than vernacular intrusions embedded in a mass of classical idiom, here play a dominating role.

Yet it would be a gross simplification to regard this early Buddhist scriptural idiom as a completely faithful reflection of Late Han vernacular. We have to consider the influence of various distorting factors.

In the first place, with one or possibly two exceptions[7] we are dealing with translations, and sometimes we find distortions, especially at the syntactic level, that must be due to the non-Chinese (Indian) original. One interesting case is the frequent use of the vocative. In native Chinese literary prose, where it is rather uncommon, it invariably is placed in isolation at the beginning of the sentence. In Buddhist texts it is often inserted awkwardly somewhere in the first part of the sentence, thereby giving rise to such monstrosities as *Rushi, Shelifu, zhufo* ..."And so, Śāriputra, all Buddhas ...". Another curious case may be the use of the particle *yi* meaning "and" in enumerations, possibly under the influence of Indian *ca* or *athavā*. In general, however, this type of distorting influence is only rarely found. The archaic translations are very free and seldom aim at word-for-word rendering, as clearly can be observed in the translation of stereotyped formulas of which the Indian original can be defined with certainty.

In the second place, we often find distortions due to prosodic patterns, especially in the somewhat more "sophisticated" scriptures. It is well-known that Chinese literary prose of the second and third century shows a marked preference for the four-syllable line. To take one example from contemporary secular literature: the *Shenjian* by Xun Yue (ca. 200 AD) shows a distribution in which 52% is made up of four-syllable clauses, against 17.3% three-syllable, and 15.5% five-syllable groups. In some Buddhist texts the four-syllable pattern reaches the same proportions, and the habit is clearly growing with the development, in the course of several decades, of a conventionalized Chinese "scriptural style". The phenomenon has been described by Yoshikawa (1958) and Hrdličková (1958). It is obvious that in such texts the translator may tend to reduce binomes to monosyllables, to expand monosyllabic forms into uncommon or even artificial binomes, to drop verbal complements, or to insert meaningless particles, all this in order to make the narrative fit into the Procrustes bed of the four-syllable pattern.

And, finally, we can assume that the vernacular character of the scriptural idiom was weakened by the very fact of its being written down in a script which had become fully adapted to a largely artificial monosyllabic literary language. Its distorting effects, such as cases of artificial "mono-syllabization", can occasionally be observed in our texts.

Some characteristic features of an archaic, largely vernacular text—Lokakṣema's translation of the *Prajñāpāramitā in 8000 stanzas* (*Aṣṭasāhasrikā-prajñāpāramitā*) of 179 AD[8]—can be shown by comparing it with parallel passages as they occur in a much more polished mid-third century version ascribed to Zhi Qian.[9] A single example may suffice. The loud wailings of the Bodhisattva Sadāprarudita ("Always Weeping") are compared with the laments of a poor victim of injustice.

Lokaksema:

亦無有菩薩所行法則，
用是故甚大愁憂，啼哭而行

譬如人有過於大王所
其財產悉入縣官

父母及身皆閉在牢獄
其人啼哭愁憂不可言

薩陀波倫菩薩愁憂
啼哭如是

"And also there was no norm-and-rule practised by the Bodhisattvas,
and because of that reason he was very much grieved, and he wept and wailed as he went.
It sounded like a man who has committed a transgression at the great king's residence—his property is all confiscated by the authorities,[10]
and his parents and he himself are locked up in prison—
that man will weep and wail and be grieved in such a way as cannot be told: in the same way the Bodhisattva Sadāprarudita was grieved, and wept and wailed."

Zhi Qian:

國無開士 所行淨法
是故哀慟
如人有過 於國王所
財產悉沒
父母及身 閉於牢獄

"Nor was there in (that) land the pure norm practised by the Revealers.
Therefore he grieved,
like a man who has committed a transgression at the king's residence—his property is all confiscated,
and his parents and he himself are locked in prison."

Here we see the "polisher" at work in various ways: proper names have been translated rather than transcribed (*kaishi* instead of *pusa*), or even left out (as in the case of the cumbrous *Satuobolun*) if the context is clear enough. Binominal forms are often replaced by monosyllables (*wu* for *wuyou*; *fa* for *faze*; *mo* for *moru*; the bisyllable *laoyue* is maintained *metri causa!*); "vulgar" expressions have been replaced by more regular forms (*shigu* for *yongshigu*); the narrative has been concentrated by leaving out irrelevant words and phrases (including the Homeric elaboration of the simile: "that man will weep …") and finally the whole passage, which in the Han version does not show any metric regularity, is forced into a rigid four-syllable pattern.

Zhi Qian's polished version of the *Aṣṭasāhasrikā* is an invaluable yardstick by which "vulgar" (hence probably vernacular) elements can be set apart, and the ways and degrees of stylistic adaptation can be defined in the products of various translators' teams.

3. Linguistic features

As I said above, a number of linguistic traits of the archaic Chinese translations have been described by me elsewhere. Here I shall only mention a number of salient features without textual examples, for which the reader may be referred to the article mentioned in note 2. Some of the most salient features are

- An abundant use of binomes (even in an adverbial position, like *huanfu* "again");
- verbal compositions with direction complement (*songchu* "to send out"; *shequ* "to reject");
- a very strong reduction of forms in the pronominal system (e.g. personal pronouns virtually being reduced to *wo* and *ru*);
- the very frequent use of plural suffixes, both simple (*-deng*, *-bei*, *-cao*) and composite (*-caodeng*, once even *-caodenbei*);
- the obsolescence of the nominal sentence AB *ye* and the development of copula *shi*.

We can conclude that the language of the earliest Buddhist translations is based on a substrate that in a somewhat formalized way reflects the second century spoken language of the metropolitan area. This substrate forms a clearly recognizable system that deviates from the literary language in a very consistent way.

4. Terminological and stylistic features

The distinctive features of the vernacular substrate figure in every text on our list, but they do not do so to the same extent. In some cases it really forms the substance of the text, without any clearly recognizable classical admixtures; on the other end of the scale we find some texts in which it merely "filters through", being distorted by classical fossilized forms, rhythmical patterns (both in prose and in unrhymed verse), Chinese-type parallelism and other stylistic embellishments. There are, moreover, considerable differences in the ways in which various translators rendered foreign proper names and Buddhist technical expressions: very different Chinese equivalents have been coined (or borrowed from other sources) to render the same foreign name or concept, and some translators obviously tried to find Chinese terms for everything, whereas others prefer to make frequent use of transcription.

A closer look at those differences in style and terminology will allow us to define certain "schools" of translators; and on the basis of bibliographical and historical evidence these can be arranged in a chronological order. This in turn may enable us to trace the steps of a gradual process of sinization, eventually resulting in the formation of a distinctly Chinese Buddhist "scriptural style".

(a) *Terminology and style: schools and stages of development.*

Chinese Buddhism starts with a mysterious embryonic phase about which very little is known. There is a gap of about eight decades between the first unquestionable sign of Buddhism in China (65 AD) and the arrival of An Shigao in Luoyang (148 AD) that marks the beginning of regular translation activities. We do not know any literary product of that primeval period; the traditions concerning the so-called *Sūtra in Forty-two Chapters* (*Sishierzhang jing*) supposedly translated under Emperor Ming, are utterly unreliable, and even the most archaic of the many extant versions is probably of post-Han date.[11] Secular sources supply a few bits of very early terminology which are vastly different from anything we know. Terms like *futu* for *buddha*, *sangmen* for *śramaṇa*, *yipusai* for *upāsaka*[12] are nowhere found in extant Buddhist translations. There is no evidence of any connection between this embryonic Buddhism, with its quaint terminology and its puzzling relations with court and courtiers, and the activities initiated by An Shigao.

The oldest and most primitive nucleus in our materials is formed by the sixteen short scriptures which may be regarded as genuine products of An Shigao and his collaborators. It is a very homogeneous group of texts, clearly recognizable by their linguistic and stylistic features. The language is erratic, crude, full of vulgarisms, often chaotic to the point of unintelligibility. There is a marked preference for translation of technical terms (making free use of non-Buddhist Chinese pseudo-equivalents such as *dao dizi* for *bhikṣu* and *dushi wuwei* for *nirvāṇa*), whereas foreign proper names are mostly transcribed. The style is strikingly "un-Chinese". There is no trace of any concession to Chinese literary taste (or of any familiarity with it): no tendency to impose prosodic patterns on the narrative; no syntactic parallelism; no use of typical fossilized *wenyan* elements. Versified passages are rendered in prose, even when introduced by the words "The following is said in *gāthās*".[13] The works of this type were produced roughly between 150 and 170 AD.

In the next phase (ca. 170-190 AD), the Indo-Scythian Lokakṣema and his collaborators produced a number of translations, seven of which have been preserved. These again form a distinct and very homogeneous type, very different from the products of An Shigao and his school. The language is more natural and intelligible than that of An Shigao; in certain narrative passages it may reach a high level of fluency and liveliness, with abundant use of vernacular elements. On the other hand, Lokakṣema's versions are characterized by a preference for transcriptions of both proper names and technical terms that frequently overburden the narrative with phonetic renderings of up to twelve syllables. There is no sign of Chinese-type literary embellishment. However, we observe the first beginnings of Chinese unrhymed Buddhist verse, made, as it were, with some hesitation: in the same text some originally metrical portions are rendered in prose, whereas other versified passages have been translated into Chinese *gāthās* of 5, 6 or 7 syllables.[14]

Somewhat later, in the 'eighties of the second century, and apparently working in isolation from Lokakṣema's team, the Parthian An Xuan and his Chinese collaborator Yan Foutiao produced the "mirror of the Dharma", *Fajing jing* (T 322). This scripture again represents a very distinct type of translation technique. The terminology is very original and differs completely from that of An Shigao and Lokakṣema. Virtually all proper names and technical terms have been translated (sometimes in somewhat bizarre ways: *gougang* for *srota-āpanna*; *dadao* for *mahāyāna*; *shujin* for *bhikṣu*; *miao* for *vihāra*) and there is some admixture of typical *wenyan* elements. The prose is sometimes prosodic.

A third generation of translators was active near the end of the second and in the early third century AD. The first of these was the Indo-Scythian Zhi Yao whose *Chengju guangming dingyi jing* (T 630) again appears to be a highly individual creation. All proper names and technical terms are rendered by Chinese equivalents which do not occur in the works of earlier translators. Most striking is the literary style of this work. The language is more classical than that of any other Han Buddhist text; the prosodical four-syllable pattern is carried to extremes (comprising more than 60% of the prose narrative), and there are many examples of the purest Chinese-type parallelism;[15] *gāthās* are rendered in unrhymed verse.

In the early years of the third century, two or possibly three translators, the Sogdian Kang Mengxiang and the Indians Zhu Dali and Zhu Tanguo (Mahābala and Dharmaphala?) made a Chinese version of a *Life of the Buddha*, the two parts of which were produced as two distinct scriptures (T 184: *Xiuxing benqi jing*, and T 196: *Zhong benqi jing*). In these works, the literary influence is very marked: frequent use of *wenyan* elements and stylistic embellishment, Chinese-type parallelism, and a very regular prosodic pattern. The *gāthās* are rendered in unrhymed verse of varying lengths, often with great sophistication. The new element is terminological syncretism. Foreign names and Buddhist expressions are rendered by means of a mixed vocabulary borrowed from various earlier translators, resulting in a great variety of forms that serves a double purpose: to avoid monotony, and to enable the translator to conform to the four-syllable pattern by choosing a prosodically suitable rendering. From a literary point of view these two Buddha biographies are no doubt the most sophisticated products of Han buddhism. Shortly after the fall of the Han (in the period 220-250 AD) the whole of T 184 and the first part of T 196, together with some passages drawn from two other sources, were combined and re-edited by Zhi Qian under the title *Taizi ruiying benqi jing* (T 185). As incorporated into this composite narrative, the Han account of the Buddha's life was for centuries to remain one of the most popular texts of early Chinese Buddhism.

(b) *Early buddhist scriptural style: the process of sinization*

The pattern that emerges from this chronological survey is very clear. Even in this very early period of Chinese Buddhism, we observe a process of gradual digestion of the literary "alien bodies" that were introduced from outside into the world of Chinese civilization. A common semi-literary idiom, deeply influenced by the vernacular, became increasingly conventionalized by the formation of a whole set of typically Chinese stylistic and terminological features. As early as the third century AD a distinctly Chinese Buddhist "scriptural style" had developed, as different from Chinese secular literature as from its Indian prototypes; in its turn it became frozen into a kind of canonical language and divorced from the living language.

Several forces were at work in shaping the terminological and stylistic conventions of this vast literature: the persisting influence of the Indian original; the influence of classical Chinese; the role of the translator's personal inventivity in creating new forms and ways of expression or in borrowing them from other sources.

At the level of terminology, it is quite clear that the translators, faced with the problem of faithfully rendering non-Chinese names and terms, in the Later Han period oscillated between two extremes: maximum adherence to the Indian original (hence maximal transliteration, of which Lokakṣema's *Daoxing jing*, T 224, with its monstrosities like *pusa-mohesa-moheyan-sengnie*: *bodhisattva-mahāsattva-mahāyāna-saṃnāha-saṃnaddha* is the most glaring example), or maximum intelligibility (hence total translation, even avoiding such well-known borrowings as *biqiu* (*bhikṣu*) and *nihuan* (*nirvāṇa*), and replacing them with Chinese "equivalents" like *chujin* and *miedu*). But in the end both extremes disappeared. In the late third century a mixed vocabulary had crystallized, in which both transcriptions and translation played their part, in a rather consistent way.

As far as translating names and terms is concerned, independent invention and borrowing both played important roles. In many cases we recognize the fruits of personal inventiveness. Expressions like *shanlai* "welcome" (= *svāgata*), *rulai* "thus-come" (*tathāgata*) and *zuxingzi* "son of good family" (*kulaputra*) obviously are neologisms; so are also some curious mixed translations like *hengsha*, "sand of the Ganges" (*gaṅgānadīvālukā*) and *chatu*, "field, region" (*kṣetra*). In some cases we have to do with misguided creativity, probably based on wrong information supplied by the foreign master: *du*, "crossing" for *pāramitā* is based on a false etymology (*param* + *ita*, "gone beyond"), and *weicengyou*, for "marvellous" (*adbhuta*) is derived from a misinterpretation of a Prākrit form (*abbuta*, mistaken for *abhūta* "not become").

The use of Chinese native terminology in rendering Buddhist ideas will be discussed more extensively in the next section. Here it will suffice to say that, in general, terminological borrowings clearly derived from the Confucian tradition are rare; that some basic terms have obviously been taken over from popular Taoism, and in a number of interesting and puzzling cases the Chinese redactors appear to have drawn their inspiration from obscure local cults and beliefs with which they were somehow associated—a fact that in one case is supported by epigraphical evidence.

But here again the extremes have been obliterated in the course of the process we are describing. The most glaring Taoist borrowings eventually disappeared from the scriptural idiom. For *nirvāṇa* the older Chinese "equivalents" were supplanted by a transcription, and *pusa* took the place of *mingshi* and *kaishi*. Lokakṣema's remarkable *trouvaille benwu* for *tathatā* ("suchness", indicating the metaphysical Emptiness underlying all phenomenal existence) was rejected in favour of the neologism *zhenru*. Thus, Buddhist terminology gradually gained its own identity, and the wild experiments of the founding fathers never were repeated.

At the level of style and composition we see that analogous forces at work in shaping a fairly uniform scriptural style, and here the pattern is even more clear.

As far as the influence of the Indian original is concerned, it is obvious that the first translators' teams were, so to speak, helplessly and passively undergoing the impact of these literary intrusions from another world. *Wenyan* conventions and stylistic features may have been unknown to them, but even if they had had some classical training, they may have been unable to apply it to a body of texts so completely alien to Chinese literary tradition.

Gradually, however, some features of Chinese literary style and composition were introduced by the successive generations of translators. The most striking example is the increasing use of the prosodic four-syllable pattern in prose, a stylistic convention that played a dominating role in secular classical literature of the period. The stages are very clear: total absence in the works of An Shigao and Lokakṣema, occasional appearance in the 'eighties of the second century (An Xuan, T 322); universal application in the latest Han translations. It was to remain dominant in all later Chinese Buddhist scriptures.

The same holds good for one of the most characteristic features of Chinese classical composition: the rigid pattern of paired sentences showing semantic and syntactic parallelism. It can nowhere be found in the earliest translations, not even in the *Fajing jing* by An Xuan which otherwise contains quite a number of *wenyan* elements. It only appears at the end of the second and in the early third century in the texts that also in other respects are deeply influenced by Chinese literary conventions.

The case of what may be considered as the most characteristic feature of Chinese scriptural idiom, the so-called "prosimetric form",[16] is somewhat different: here we have to do not with a one-way intrusion of Chinese stylistic conventions into an emerging scriptural idiom, but with the formation of a *new* stylistic device, developed under the stimulus of the Indian example, and, as far as we know, not inspired by any pre-existing Chinese literary pattern. Alternation of prose and versified passages (*gāthās*, sometimes translated as *song*, sometimes transcribed as *jie* or *jue**) formed an integral part of the Indian literary tradition. Sometimes they are placed at the end of a sermon, summarizing its essential content; in other cases (particularly in scholastic treatises) they introduce the work as a whole (laudatory stanzas addressed to the Buddha, the Dharma and the Saṅgha), or they precede the individual sections of the work in the form of extremely concentrated mnemonic verses (*kārikā*). Mostly, however, they are embedded in a continuous narrative. In a prose context, the versified portions often render direct speech, being introduced by such formulas as "and then, speaking in *gāthās*, he said ...". But direct speech may also end somewhere in the middle of the hymn, which then goes on to describe other happenings in verse, or, on the contrary, only a part of the *oratio recta* may have *gāthā* form, the prose monologue or prose dialogue suddenly turning into verse, and from verse into prose again.

All these were elements of a great foreign literary tradition which, once transplanted into China, had to find its own means of expression. The complicated patterns of Indian metre could not be expressed in Chinese, and it was equally impossible to retain the original palmodic melodies to which the *gāthās* had to be sung. Both the metric form of the text and the musical form of the recitative had to be adapted to the nature of the Chinese language and the conventions of Chinese musical art.

This process started early, and our Han materials allow us to observe its various stages. In the very first phase (An Shigao and his collaborators) the translators evidently were at a loss what to do with the *gāthās*. The introductory stanzas of the *Daodi jing* (T 607) are rendered in clumsy prose, and in several other texts of this school the words "the following is said in *gāthās*" are followed, somewhat paradoxically, by passages in prose.

One generation later, Lokakṣema occasionally attempts to introduce Chinese unrhymed stanzas, whereas in other passages—even in the same scripture—verse is turned into prose. Anyhow, by this occasional use of unrhymed Chinese verse Lokakṣema introduced a literary device that would for centuries remain characteristic of Chinese "scriptural style". As such it was a step of momentous importance, for the prosimetric style to which he (or rather his Chinese collaborators) had given the start was to find its way, via Buddhist *bianwen* and their secular counterparts, into later Chinese popular literature, where it would survive till modern times.

It is unknown whether this Chinese response to the Indian *gāthās* tradition was a free invention or a borrowing from an unknown native source. Two of Lokakṣema's collaborators are known to have been patrons of some obscure local cult, and it would be tantalizing to suppose that through them some kind of popular incantation may have been introduced into the translation work in which they themselves were engaged. But this is pure speculation. For all we know, earlier and contemporary Chinese lyrics were universally characterized by the use of rhyme (it is true that a number of Odes of the *Song* section of the *Book of Songs* are rhymeless, but even granting the fact that *gāthās* are often called *song*, it would be too far-fetched to regard this as more than coincidental; *song*, for *gāthā*, obviously just means "laudatory hymn"). Taoist hymns and other versified texts cannot have been a source of inspiration (even if we suppose that such texts existed as early as the second century AD), for in early Taoist scriptures the stanzas invariably are rhyming, even in texts that are deeply influenced by the Buddhist scriptural style.

The Chinese device thus created was very simple. Han scriptures contain stanzas of four, five or seven syllables. Cases of *enjambement* are very rare: in general, each verse forms either a full independent sentence (e.g., *xin qi xiang ze chi*) or at least a well-defined clause forming part of a more complex sentence (e.g. *Song shi sanmei shi/sile zuo shamen*). The short (3, 4 or 5 syllable) lines just consist of so many syllables without any further internal prosodical pattern. In 7-syllable *gāthās*, however, we observe an interesting phenomenon, no doubt inspired by secular poetry: there is a distinct attempt to put a caesura after the fourth syllable, even in the earliest examples.[17]

After the first attempts by Lokakṣema's team, we see how the prosimetric form becomes more sophisticated. It culminates, as far as Han scriptures are concerned, in the Buddha biographies of the early third century (T 184 and T

196), which contain several dozens of versified passages. Whereas in the earlies specimens (Lokakṣema, Zhi Yao) the *gāthā* passages are mere "blocks" of direct speech, we find here all patterns of alternation (direct speech turning into description, and the reverse, within a single poetic passage) which lend a special flavour to the narrative. It would not be an exaggeration to say that the epic description of the Buddha's struggle with Māra in T 184 in liveliness and dramatic power far surpasses anything written in Chinese secular literature of the period.

A third area of invention and experiment was created by the necessity to render the numerous stereotyped formulas and standard passages found in every Buddhist text. In their original form the Indian *clichés* are completely stereotyped elements, a kind of literary modules that may range from one sentence or short paragraph (e.g. the well-known opening and closing sentences of any *sūtra* or the formula describing how a person politely inquires after the Buddha's health) to whole passages (such as the elaborate description of the happy reign of a Universal King, or the long sequence beginning with the Buddha emitting a radiance that pervades the whole universe and then smiling, and finally uttering the prophecy of someone's future Buddhahood).

In trying to coin suitable Chinese equivalents, the earliest translators show two tendencies, both of which bear the stamp of "Chinese taste": condensation and variation. In rendering the literary *clichés* the translators (or rather the Chinese redactors) time and again appear to have made concessions to the Chinese predilection for terse and concentrated description by leaving out stages, cutting out unessential elements, and thus reducing the Indian luxuriant verbosity of the original. In the same way, there is a strong tendency to avoid the monotonous effect of another characteristic feature of the Indian scriptural style: the verbatim repetition of whole passages, by introducing a certain amount of diversification and irregularity. The Chinese eventually did create a number of formulas (thus the opening words *Evaṃ maya śrūtam* "So I have heard" soon became *wen rushi*, since the late fourth century—probably for metric reasons—supplanted by *rushi wo wen*), but in the early period such formulas never were as rigidly stereotyped as their Indian prototypes, and in the same translated scripture we often find various alternative forms and longer or shorter versions of the same *cliché*.

The process of sinization which we have traced in terminology, style and composition thus resulted in the formation of a distinctly Chinese form of literary expression; in its essential features this scriptural style had already become conventionalized in the early third century—barely seventy years after An Shigao's first primitive attempts. In this respect, as in so many others, the Han experience has been decisive.

5. The Chinese audience

We may start from two self-evident facts: we are dealing with products of translation, and those translated *sūtras* were written down. Both facts have a whole range of implications which cannot be elaborated here. For our present subject it is important to note that, in the first place, the translation effort, which appears to have started soon after An Shigao's arrival at Luoyang around 148 AD and which was quite productive (yielding, according to Dao'an, some seventy *juan* of Chinese versions in the first forty years), implies that there must have been a Chinese *clientèle* large enough to warrant such an undertaking. And, secondly, the production of such a considerable body of written texts is highly significant. We do not know to what extent oral propagation played a role as well, but the very existence of our texts proves that Buddhism primarily addressed itself to an educated minority.

On the other hand, the linguistic and stylistic features make clear that when dealing with these archaic scriptures we are very far removed from the literary culture of the true elite. In most texts the language is rather primitive and clumsy; the vocabulary is limited and repetitive, and seen in the more "sophisticated" scriptures we hardly find any conventional expressions borrowed from the Chinese high-class literary tradition.

We may conclude that these texts circulated among a public of Chinese lay devotees with rudimentary schooling, standing outside the elite of scholar-officials, but sufficiently literate to read these texts with their limited vocabulary and their unadorned style. In the context of the urban society of Later Han times, one may think of a sub-elite of clerks and copyists, the lowest fringe of the bureaucracy, and traders and artisans. The propagation of Buddhism at the intermediate level would also explain why the official historical records do not contain a single reference to this "Church of Luoyang", and why there is no evidence of any connection between the hybrid court Buddhism mentioned in secular historiography and the activities of the Buddhist missionaries at Luoyang.

There probably were no fully ordained Chinese monks before the third century AD.[18] However, this does not mean that the scriptures offered to the Chinese devotees were limited to the kind of "edifying texts" that were primarily destined to be read by the lay public. On the contrary: most Han scriptures are highly technical and scholastic, and they treat subjects that normally belong to the practice of monastic Buddhism, such as *dhyāna* exercises, respiratory techniques, numerical categories, themes of contemplation, and the constituent elements of the pseudo-personality. Lay believers apparently took part in such exercises—in fact, around the middle of the third century a certain Chen Hui, no doubt a layman, is known to have expounded the highly scholastic *Yin chi ru jing* and the treatise on "Respiratory Concentration", *Anban shouyi jing*, both translated by An Shigao.[19]

It therefore seems that the fundamental distinction between monastic and lay Buddhism had not yet taken shape, as far as the Chinese believers were concerned. There are, however, some signs indicating that among the laity itself there was a certain diversity of interests, some believers being attracted by the simple and easily digestible teachings of lay Buddhism, and other by the *arcana* of Buddhist scholasticism and contemplation.

6. The believers and the experts

If we inventorize the stylistic and terminological features of the extant Han scriptures, there are four texts that form a distinctive category of their own.

(1) T 322 "The *sūtra* of the Mirror of the Doctrine", *Fajing jing*, translated by An Xuan, ca. 180 AD;

(2) T 630, "The *sūtra* on the Mental Fixation of Integral Illumination", *Chengju guangming dingyi jing*, attributed to the late second century translator Zhi Yao.

Both texts are characterized by a considerable number of classical admixtures, a very idiosyncratic terminology (e.g. *chujin* and *chue* for *bhikṣu*), and, above all, the fact that the translators have done their utmost to translate everything into Chinese, even including proper names such as *Wenwu guo* for Śrāvastī. This peculiarity—which by itself would already suggest an attempt to cater to the taste of a fairly cultured "non-professional" public—becomes even more relevant if we look at the contents of T322 and T680: they are the only Han scriptures in which a detailed description is given of the moral duties and devotional practices of the lay believer, or, as T 322 calls him, "the Bodhisattva who practices the Way while staying in the household".

(3) T 184, "The *sūtra* on the Origin of (Religious) Practice", *Xiuxing benqi jing*, and

(4) T196, "The Middle (Part) of the *sūtra* on the Origin (of Religious Practice)", *Zhong benqi jing*, both translated by the Sogdian Kang Mengxiang, with the assistance of the Indian monks Zhu Dali and Zhu Tanguo, around 200 AD.[20]

The two texts, which contain an account of the Buddha's career from the prophecy of his future Buddhahood under Dīpaṃkara to the middle part of his ministration, actually form one continuous narrative. The style is rather literary, with many *wenyan* elements and a regular rhythmic four-syllable pattern. The quality of Kang Mengxiang's style, its "grace and fluency"[21] is quite conspicuous; the combined text of T184/T196 no doubt forms the most readable, and even enjoyable, part of archaic Chinese Buddhist literature. The religious message of the narrative is simple and direct: feats of supernatural power, moral rules, edifying anecdotes, and stories about the retribution of sins. Purely doctrinal matters play a minor role.

We can conclude that these scriptures constitute the "popularizing sector" in Han Buddhist literature—elementary texts written in a semi-classical style, preaching a rather simple kind of morality: the Three Refuges; the Five Rules of lay Buddhism; devotion; love towards all creatures; the impermanence of all things, and the inevitability of karmic retribution. The texts sharply contrast with the other prevailing type of Han scriptures: the much more vernacular and generally abstruse scriptures of a more specialized nature, which emphasize mental discipline and *dhyāna* practices, respiratory techniques, the ecstatic "visualization" of Buddhas, the contemplation of the impure, the eradication of all desire (*chu yu*) and of all uncontrolled mental activity (*xinyi*).

It may well be that the latter type of scriptures reflects the interests of another group of devotees within the same subculture: not the simple *upāsakas* looking for moral guidelines and a new type of religious piety, but the active practicants attracted by a master like An Shigao, who already in his life-time appears to have been regarded as a powerful magician.[22]

7. Buddhism and indigenous Chinese traditions: the exotic alternative

In spite of occasional (and surprisingly rare) terminological borrowings from Confucian and Taoist lore, the most striking aspect of Han Buddhism is its novelty. The view that Buddhism was accepted because it, in certain ways, accorded with indigenous traditions must be rejected; Buddhism was attractive not because it sounded familiar, but because it was something basically new. Certain concepts and practices bore a superficial resemblance to Taoist notions, but the basic difference in orientation and application must have been obvious right from the start. In Taoism, breath control serves to accumulate the vital essence inside the body; in Buddhism, *ānāpāna* is practised as a mental tranquilizer before entering meditation. In Taoism, sexual techniques are used as a means to achieve salvation; in Buddhism, all desire—and sexual desire in particular—is a negative force; rebirth as a woman is the result of karmic sin, and the female body is an instrument of moral destruction.[23] And, most important of all, the Taoist belief in the possibility of bodily immortality is incompatible with the Buddhist idea that *all* bodily existence—even that of the gods—is transitory and doomed to decay. And here, again, the opposition appears to be reflected by the written language, for the hybrid, semi-vernacular idiom of the Buddhist texts completely differs from the simple but regular *wenyan* of the earliest Taoist scriptures and commentaries.

If Han Buddhism, in its most essential aspects, was not a variant from but rather a distinct alternative to Taoism, the same must be said of its relation to Confucian ethics. It is true that lay morality includes a number of rules that basically accord with Confucian norms of social behaviour: observing ones' duties towards relatives and other dependents; temperance; sincerity in social relations, and indifference to worldly praise or blame. But even in the two scriptures which exclusively deal with the moral and religious duties of the Buddhist layman, the essential message is hardly compatible with Confucian ethics. In all his actions, the lay devotee should consider the transitoriness of all things and the inanity of all worldly relations.[24] Even when serving his parents and showing love to his children he should regard the household as a prison and his relatives as dangerous enemies.[25] He should train himself to feel no special attachment to his nearest kin, for his love should go to all creatures: and, after all, why love your son more than all those fellow-creatures in the world, who may have been your sons and daughters in innumerable former lives?[26] Far from accommodating with the rules of Confucian social ethics, Han Buddhism preached a detached attitude towards even the nearest relatives, coupled with an ideal of "universal love" far more radical and comprehensive than anything that could be found in traditional Chinese thought.

The same universalistic and non-familial kind of morality is found time and again in T 630. In the fifty-five moral rules for lay devotees (fifteen for high officials, ten for commoners, twenty-five for noble ladies, and ten for common women) the specific virtues of family life (filial piety, brotherly love, etc.) which form the very heart of Confucian ethics, are hardly touched upon. Only in the rules for "noble ladies" the theme of her obligations towards husband and near relatives are mentioned in passing. For the rest the full emphasis is on ethical behaviour towards the world at large, or towards specific groups of people beyond the family (the poor and destitute; servants and slaves; the people under one's jurisdiction; even sinners who should be kindly treated and converted).

Here, again, we may find a most un-Confucian position of Buddhist lay ethics reflected in the terminology of our scriptures, in which clear Confucian borrowings are extremely rare.

But are we not, after all, on a wrong track by trying to define the ideological position of Han Buddhism in terms of the easy dichotomy "Confucian/Taoist"? Chinese society of the second century AD—and for centuries afterwards—was not a "Confucian society" as we know it from late imperial times. Confucianism was represented by an extremely small elite—a very thin top layer, under which there was an immense variety of local beliefs, cults and religious practices.

In many cases these may have been variations within a common fund of religious and magical lore without any special affinity either to Confucianism or to Taoism. In fact, the terminology of Buddhist texts contains a number of quaint Chinese "equivalents" that look like borrowings from unknown sources of Chinese religious lore. What is the background of the very common archaic term *yin*, "dark(ening) element"(?), as used for *skandha*, the constituent parts of the human person? Why is the universal ruler (*cakravartin*) referred to as a "flying emperor", *feixing huangdi*? Why are the gods (*deva*) called *tian*? Is the term "subterranean prison", *diyu*, a Buddhist neologism, or does it reflect some popular belief concerning the fate of sinners after death? It may well be that further analysis of archaic Buddhist terminology will teach us more about this unexplored zone of Han popular religion.

If one would try to indicate, in most general terms, what may have been the special appeal of a doctrine that so clearly rejected some of the most firmly established ideas of the age, the answer probably would lie in the Buddhist preoccupation with Impermanence, its (sometimes almost morbid) insistence on the transitoriness of all pleasure, on death and decay, and mental purification as the only way to escape from it.

As Yoshikawa Kōjirō has shown,[27] the awareness of impermanence, the "fleeting life" with its sorrows and sad partings, had become a dominant theme in the Late Han period. Buddhism showed how this *vanitas* forms the very substance of all existence, and, at the same time, offered a way out which was comparatively simple: eternity could be gained by the radical destruction of all desire.

It did so, in this very early phase, without any tendency to compromise. It was not the semi-Taoist mongrel which it is sometimes held to be: on the contrary, it was not yet domesticated. It may therefore have recruited its first followers not from the many who expected familiar answers, but rather from marginal elements who were prepared to break with tradition. Therefore it was, in spite of its almost microscopic scale, a ferment in Late Han society. As a radically alternative way to individual salvation it reminds one of those alien and obscure cults which at the other end of the Euro-Asiatic continent, and roughly in the same period, became popular all over the Roman empire, and even of the "orientalizing" sub-cultures of our own age. The universality of the phenomenon may, after all, justify the attention we have given to the very first stage of Chinese Buddhism—that tiny exotic plant flowering on the ruins of the Han empire.

Notes

1. To give only one example: the ideal of supporting oneself by food-begging never became popular in China, in spite of the fact that it is very often referred to in the scriptures as an essential part of the monastic life.
2. "Late Han Vernacular Elements in the Earliest Buddhist Translation", *Journal of the Chinese Language Teacher's Association* 12.2 (October, 1977),. pp. 177-203.
3. Cf. my *Buddhist Conquest of China*, Leiden, 1959, pp. 30-31.
4. The first commentaries that quote or refer to Chinese Buddhist scriptures are T1694 *Yin chi ru jing zhu* (glosses on An Shigao's *Yin chi ru jing*, T 603, by a certain Chen Hui), and the anonymous glosses in the first chapter of T225, *Da mingdu jing*, wrongly attributed to Zhi Qian (cf. Lewis R. Lancaster, "The Chinese Translation of the *Aṣṭasāhasrikā-prajñāpāramitā-sūtra* attributed to Chih Ch'ien", *Monumenta Serica* 28 (1969), pp. 246-257).
5. The "Inscription of Laozi" (*Laozi ming*) of 165/166 AD by Bian Shao (incorporated in the *Lishi* by Hong Gua, ed., *Sibu congkan* p. 3.1a) is obviously a product of court literature, written in the over-ornate rhetoric style that was commonly used for such commenorative inscriptions. The *Liexian zhuan*, certainly not by Liu Xiang, but probably a Han work (as it is quoted twice by Ying Shao in his *Hanshu* commentary, second half second century AD), is written in regular *wenyan* without any trace of "vulgar" language. But even the three texts that at least by some scholars are associated with late Han popular Taoism: the *Taiping jing* and the *Xiang'er* and *Heshang Gong* commentaries on *Laozi*, are all written in a simple and artless but rather regular *wenyan*, and do not show any feature characteristic of the language of archaic Buddhist scriptures.
6. Cf. W.A.C.H. Dobson, *Late Han Chinese*, Toronto, 1964; Ushijima Tokuji, *Kango bumpō ron: chūko-hen*; Yoshikawa Kōjirō, "*Sesetsu-shingo* no bunsho", *Tōhōgaku* (Kyoto 10.2, 1939, pp. 86-110 (English translation by Glen Baxter, "The *Shih-shuo hsin-yü* and Six Dynasties Prose Style", *HJAS* 18, 1955, pp. 124-242); *id.*, "Rikuchō joji shōki", in Yoshikawa's Collected Works, *Yoshikawa Kōjirō zenshū*, vol. 7, Tokyo 1968, pp. 473-598; *id.*, *Bussetsu Muryōjugyō no bunshō*; Hong Cheng, "Lun Nanbeichao yiqian Hanyu de xici", *Yuyan yanjiu* 2, 1957, pp. 1-22; Liu Shiru, "Lüe lun Wei Jin Nanbeichao zidongci 'shi'-zi de yongfa", *Zhongguo yuyan* 66.12 (1957), p. 19-24.
7. T 1508 *Ahan koujie shi'er yinyuan jing*, which, as indicated by the title, appears to be an "oral explanation" of the Chain of Causation and some other related scholastic subjects, and T 602 *Da anban shouyi jing*, which partly consists of an early commentary on a text translated by An Shigao.
8. T224 *Daoxing jing*.
9. The work no doubt dates from the mid-third century, but it shows certain terminological peculiarities that plead against the attribution to Zhi Qian. Cf. the article by L.R. Lancaster referred to in note 4.

10. The term *xianguan* is used many times in Buddhist texts, and there invariably refers to the administrative officers, "the authorities", quite distinct from the supreme power of the sovereign (*wang*, *dawang*). This is even quite explicit in T 630 (*Chengju guangming dingyi jing*), p. 457.1: "If there is a worthy born into a noble family, who (later) is charged with general supervision over the (local) administrators ..." (*ruo you xianshi, sheng yu zhongxing zhi jia, tongling xianguan...*), and, *ib.*: "If a worthy has by his birth a (karmic) affinity with the administration .. ." (i.c. is destined to become a high official): (*xianshi sheng you xianguan zhi yinyuan...*). It is nowhere used for the person of the emperor, as is occasionally done in secular Han texts.
11. The text as we find it in the Korean recension of the Taishō canon (T 784) possibly is a redaction made by Zhi Qian in the period 220-250 AD; cf. Tang Yongtong, *Han Wei liang Jin nanbeichao fojiao shi*, Shanghai, 1938, pp. 38-39.
12. **b'jiəu-d'uo; *sang-mu*ən; **i-p'uo-s*ək.
13. *Conghou shuojue* (**dz'iwät* apparently is a transcription of *gāthā*; the initial remains puzzling) in T150; cf. in T 607 the curious formula *Conghou fushushuo*, "The following is said in a bound (=metrical?) way". The common *jie* (**g'iät*) for *gāthā* occurs for the first time in Lokakṣema's *Banzhou sanmei jing* (T 418).
14. The Korean recension of T 418 is the only one in which the *prose* parts which render the *gāthās* of the original have been preserved (T 418, p. 906.1-2 and 907.2-3); in the other redactions they have been transposed into Chinese *gāthās* as well.
15. E.g. T 630, p. 453.2, a passage which reads like a Chinese essay:

"whilst dwelling in the house of instability/
his mind thinks of the protection (afforded by) Expediency"
"whilst staying in the pit of snakes/
his mind contemplates on the path of Abandonment ...

椅不固之屋，心思方便之護；
坐蛇蚖之地，心念捨遠之徑。
"

and so on, through a series of nine couples of paired phrases, interrupted, in true parallel style, by the words *Shigu kaishi*, "Therefore the Revealer ...", after which the 5-6 metre is resumed. 是故開士
16. For this term see V. Hrdličková, "The first translations of Buddhist sūtras in Chinese literature and their place in the development of story-telling", *Archiv Orientální* 26, 1958, pp. 114-144.
17. Clearly observable in the seven-syllable *gāthās* in Lokakṣema's *Banzhou sanmei jing* (T 418) of 179 AD, e.g. (p. 611.2),

般舟三昧經：佛語阿難，汝見不；五百人等在〃立；其心歡然歌頌曰：我等亦當逮得法

etc.
18. According to *Gaoseng zhuan* (T 2059, p. 324.3) An Xuan's collaborator Yan Foutiao was *śramaṇa*, a fully ordained monk. However, in the corresponding passage in *Chu sanzang ji ji* (T 2145, p. 96.1) it is only said that he had

"left the household", *chujia*, an expression that is also used for one who has joined the Order as a novice. In fact, the only work which he has produced independently was a treatise on the "Ten Rules for the Novice", cf. *Buddhist Conquest*, pp. 55-56.

19. Cf. note 4 above, and *Buddhist Conquest*, pp. 53-54.

20. The *Xiuxing benqi jing* is not mentioned by Sengyou in his *Chu sanzang ji ji*, but the authenticity of the text as a late Han translation is beyond all doubt. In the first place it forms a continuous whole with T 196 (the last paragraph of T 184 actually is repeated *verbatim* at the beginning of T 196); in the second place, its early date is proved by the fact that many passages from it have been incorporated into Zhi Qian's "polished" version of the Buddha's life (T 185, *Taizi ruiying benqi jing*), and, thirdly, the text contains a number of glosses introduced by the words *Han yan*..., which points to a date before 220 AD. T 196 is explicitly attributed to Kang Mengxiang and Zhu Tanguo in *Gaoseng zhuan* I, p. 324.3, probably on the basis of an early colophon.

21. Remark made by Dao'an, *yiyi liubian*, reported in *Chu sanzang ji ji* XIII, p. 96.1

22. An Shigao's biography in *CSDJJ* and *GSZ* is a mosaic of miraculous stories, some of which are extremely interesting. But some of An Shigao's supernatural powers (such as telling the future and understanding the language of the birds) are already described in Kang Senghui's preface to the *Anban shouyi jing* (*CSDJJ* VI 43.2), and this information was no doubt supplied by the three devotees from An Shigao's school who transmitted the scripture to him. And in an anonymous preface (the author only refers to himself as Mi—apparently his personal name) to Chen Hui's early third century commentary on the *Yin chi ru jing* (T 1694 p. 9.2), again from the same school, An Shigao is referred to as "a bodhisattva of universal manifestations" (*An hou Shigao zhe puxian pusa ye*). This may be mere rhetoric—but it could also be related to the curious stories about An Shigao's miraculous adventures in North, Central, and South China, in successive lives, such as we find in his GSZ "biography".

23. The female lay devotee should perform her religious observance three times a day, and each time "she should devoutly implore (the Buddha), always wishing to get rid of her female body" (致心懇惻常願離於女人之身 TT 630, p. 457.2).

24. T 322, p. 16.2-3.

25. T 322, p. 17.2-28.1.

26. T 322, p. 18.1-3.

27. Notably in his brilliant analysis of the *Nineteen Old Poems* and their persistent theme of "sorrow at the passing of time": "*Suii no hiai (Koshi jūkyūshu no shudai)*", *Chūgoku bungakuhō*, 14, 1961, pp. 1-21.

Appendix
Buddhist Texts of the Later Han Period

I. Translations made by An Shigao (active ca. 150-170 AD)

I.1 T 13 *(Chang ahan) shi baofa jing*, 1 ch.
Classification of terms in groups of ten, with short explanation.

I.2 T 14 *Ren ben yu sheng jing*, 1 ch.
Explanation of the twelve members of the Chain of Causation.

I.3 T 31 *Yiqie liu she shou yin jing*, 1 ch.
Very short text explaining the way to extirpate the Impurities (*āsrava*).

I.4 T 32 *Si di jing*, 1 ch.
Exposition of the Four Noble Truths.

I.5 T 36 *Ben xiang yi zhi jing*, 1 ch.
Causal series leading from "bad company", via "unbelief", "wrong thoughts" ... to "desire", and the opposite series, leading from "good company" to "emancipation".

I.6 T 48 *Shi fa fei fa jing*, 1 ch.
Examples showing how the viruous monk will never boast of his religious attainments, and how he who is lacking in virtue will become arrogant, to his own detriment.

I.7 T 57 *Lou fenbu jing*, 1 ch.
Scholastic enumeration of the Impurities, Sense-desires, Feelings, Perceptions, etc., together with their causal factors and their bad consequences.

I.8 T 98 *Pu fayi jing*, 1 ch.
Various series of 12, 20, 16... etc. factors, every series being either conducive or obstructive to Emancipation.

I.9 T 112 *Ba zheng dao jing*, 1 ch.
The eight bad ways of action and the eight good ways of action that constitute the Eightfold Path.

I.10 T 150 *Qi chu san guan jing*, 2 ch.
A collection of 47 very short *sūtras*, 30 or which have their Pāli counterparts in the *Aṅguttara-nikāya*. Various numerical series of phenomena, actions, attitudes, and human types.

I.11 T 602 *Da anban shouyi jing*, 2 ch.
Treatise describing the practice of "Respiratory Concentration" (*ānāpāna-smṛti*), together with a commentary that has become inextricably mixed up with the text.

I.12 T 603 *Yin chi ru jing*, 1 ch.
Scholastic compendium dealing with sense-perception, the four bases of supernatural power, the five powers, etc.

I.13 T605 *Chanxing faxiang jing*, 1 ch.
Very short text containing a list of themes for contemplation.

I.14 T 607 *Daodi jing*, 1 ch.
Primitive translation of Saṅgharakṣa's *Yogācārabhūmi*, a treatise on *dhyāna*.

I.15 T 792 *(Fo shuo) fa shou chen jing*, 1 ch.
Very short text explaining how sexual desire obstructs the way to insight and true happiness.

I.16 T 1508 *Ahan koujie shi'er yinyuan jing*, 1 ch.
Commonly, but no doubt wrongly, attributed to An Xuan; the attribution to An Shigao made by Dao'an is substantiated by the terminology. An exegetical work explaining, *inter alia*, the Chain of Causation, the composition and functions of the body, the elements as the causes of diseases, etc.

II. Translations by Zhi Loujiachen (? Lokakṣema) (active ca. 170-190 AD)

II.1 T 224 *Daoxing (banruo) jing*, 10 ch.
The earliest translation of the "Perfection of wisdom in Eight Thousand Stanzas", *Aṣṭasāhasrikā-prajñāpāramitā*; the title is borrowed from the heading of the first chapter (*Daoxing pin*).

II.2 T 280 *(Fo shuo) dousha jing*, 1 ch.
Short *sūtra* containing a description of the miraculous apparition of Buddhas and Bodhisattvas from all directions of space and an enumeration of their names. The title is unexplained.

II.3 T 313 *Achu fo guo jing*, 1 ch.
"Pure Land"-type *sūtra* devoted to the glorification of Akṣobhya, the Buddha of the Eastern Paradise.

II.4 T 418 *Banzhou sanmei jing*, 3 ch.
The earliest version of the *Bhadrapāla-sūtra* (the title is a transcription of *Pratyutpanna-samādhi-sūtra*), dealing with the power of this *samādhi* that enables the devotee to visualize the Buddha Amitābha. Only the Korean recension of T 418 represents Lokakṣema's original translation; the other recensions contain a great number of interpolations and variants that probably were borrowed from a late third century version by Dharmarakṣa. In the Taishō canon this text is preceded by a shorter version (T 417, 1 ch.) with the same title and also bearing the name of Lokakṣema. Internal evidence proves that it actually is a later "polished" extract based upon T 418. A detailed study of the complicated textual problems is found in Paul Harrison, *The Pratyutpanna-buddha-saṃmukhāvasthita-samādhi-sūtra, an annotated English translation of the Tibetan version* (PhD. dissertation, A.N.U.), Canberra, 1979, Appendix A, esp. pp.200-235. Harrison concludes that chapters 1-6 of the Korean recension go back to Lokaksema's original translation; that the prose of chapters 7-26 of all recensions may with some hesitation also be attributed to Lokakṣema, but that the *gāthās* are the work of a somewhat later hand. The text, with

which chapters 1-6 have been conflated is another early version; its attribution to Dharmaraksa is rejected by Harrison on stylistic grounds.

II.5 T 458 *Wenshushili wen pusa shu jing*, 1 ch.
Exposition of the stages of the Bodhisattva career, explained in terms of the doctrine of universal Emptiness. The *sūtra* shows an interesting affinity with the *Vimalakīrti-nirdeśa.*

II.6 T 350 *Yi ri moni bao jing*, 1 ch.
Archaic translation of the *Kāśyapaparivarta*, about the Bodhisattva career and the doctrine of Emptiness.

II.7 T 626 *Azheshi wang jing*, 2 ch.
Mahāyāna treatment of the theme of King Ajātaśatru of Magadha being tortured by remorse after having killed his father; he is converted by the Bodhisattva Mañjuśrī.

II.8 T 807 *(Fo shuo) neizang bai bao jing*, 1 ch.
A mahāyānistic interpretation of the Buddha's life as a series of "magical performances" intended to lead all beings to salvation.

III. Translation by An Xuan and Yan Foutiao (active ca. 180 AD)

III.1 T 322*Fajing jing*, 1 ch.
Earliest translation of the *Ugra(datta)-paripṛcchā*, in which the Buddha explains the duties of the lay believer to the householder Ugra(datta), in Mahāyānistic terms.

IV. Translations by Kang Mengziang, Zhu Dali (? Mahābala) and Zhu Tanguo (? Dharmapala) (active ca. 200 AD)

IV.1 T 184*Xiuxing benqi jing*, 2 ch.
Account of the early part of the Buddha's career, from the prophecy of his future Buddhahood under Dīpaṃkara to the happenings in the first days after his Enlightenment.

IV.2 TT 196*Zhong benqi jing*, 2 ch.
Actually the second half of a continuous "life of the Buddha", of which T 184 is the first part. Account of the middle part of the Buddha's career, and some later episodes.

V. Translation attributed to Zhi Yao (late second century)

V.1 T 630 *Chengju guangming dingyi jing*, 1 ch.
Mahāyāna scripture treating two different subjects. The first part is devoted to the Six Perfections (*pāramitā*) and the "Mental Concentration of Integral Illumination". The second part contains a description of the moral and religious duties of various classes of lay devotees.

VI. Three archaic texts with doubtful attributions.

VI.1 T 105*Wu yin piyu jing*, 1 ch.

Very short text containing a number of stereotyped similes illustrating the unreality of the five constituent elements (*skandha*) of the pseudo-person. Attributed by Dao'an to An Shigao. The text is no doubt archaic, but style and terminology are definitly not those of An Shigao and his team.

VI.2 T 109*Zhuan falun jing*, 1 ch.

Archaic translation of the Buddha's first sermon held at Benares, with an introductory passage that does not appear in any other known version. Attributed by Dao'an to An Shigao, but the text contains stylistic features and *wenyan* admixtures that do not normally appear in An Shigao's translations.

VI.3 T 624*Dunzhentuoluo suo wen rulai sanmei jing*, 3 ch.

Archaic translation of the *Druma-kiṃnararāja-paripṛcchā*. Very elaborate text, largely consisting of numerical series, in which both the Buddha and King Druma (the ruler of the semi-human beings called *kiṃnara*) explain and glorify the Bodhisattva career and the Mahāyāna doctrine of universal Emptiness. The scripture culminates in the prophecy of King Druma's future Buddahood. Listed as "lost" by Sengyou (CSTJJ II, p. 6.2); in the *Kaiyuan shijiao lu* of 730 AD and later catalogues it is again mentioned as an existing text attributed to Lokakṣema. In view of the style and terminology it may certainly be regarded as a Han scripture, albeit with some hesitation as regards its attribution to Lokakṣema.

List of Characters

Achu fo guo jing 阿閦佛國經

Ahan koujie shi'er yinyauan jing
阿含口解十二因緣經

An Xuan 安玄

An Shigao 安世高

Anban shouyi jing 安般守意經

Azheshi wang jing 阿闍世王經

Ba zheng dao jing 八正道經

Banzhou sanmei jing 般舟三昧經

-bei 輩

Ben xiang yi zhi jing
本相猗(v. 倚)致經

benwu 本無

Bian Shao 邊韶

biqiu 比丘

Bussetsu Muryōjugyō no bunshō
佛說無量壽經の文章

-cao 曹

Chanxing faxiang jing 禪行法想經

(Chang ahan) shi baofa jing
(長阿含)十報法經

chatu 剎土

Chen Hui 陳慧

Chengju guangming dingyi jing
成具光明定意經

chu yu 除欲

chue 除惡

chujia 出家

chujin 除饉

conghou shuojue 從後說絕

conghou fushushuo 從後縛束說

Da anban shouyi jing 大安般守意經

Da mingdu jing 大明度經

da-dao 大道

dao dizi 道弟子

Dao'an 道安

Daodi jing 道地經

Daoxing (banruo) jing 道行(般若)經

Daoxing jing 道行經

Daoxing pin 道行品

dawang 大王

-deng 等

di 帝

diyu 地獄

du 度

Dunzhentuoluo suo wen rulai sanmei jing 伅真陀羅所問如來三昧經

dushi wuwei 度世無為

*dz'iwät 绝

fa 法

Fajing jing 法鏡經

faze 法則

feixing huangdi 飛行皇帝

(Fo shuo) dousha jing (佛說)兜沙經

(Fo shuo) fa shou chen jing (佛說)法受塵經

(Fo shuo) neizang bai bao jing (佛說)內藏百寶經

futu 浮屠

gougang 溝港

Han Wei liang Jin nanbeichao fojiao shi 漢魏兩晉南北朝佛教史

Han yan... 漢言

hengsha 恒沙

Hesang Gong 河上公

Hong Cheng 洪誠

Hong Gua 洪适

huanfu 還復

jie 偈

jie (*g'iät) 偈

jue 厥

jue* 絕

kaishi 開士

Kang Mengxiang 康孟詳

Kango bumpō ron: chūko-hen 漢語文法論：中古編

laoyue 牢獄

Laozi ming 老子銘

Liexian zhuan 列仙傳

Lishi 隸釋

Liu Shiru 劉世儒

Lou fenbu jing 漏分布經

Lüe lun Wei Jin Nanbeichao zidongci 'shi'-zi de yongfa 略論魏晉南北朝繫動詞「是」字的用法

Lun Nanbeichao yiqian Hanyu de xici 論南北朝以前漢語的繫詞

Mi 宓

miao 廟

miedu 滅度

mingshi 明士

mo 沒

moru 沒入

nihuan 泥洹

Pu fəyi jing 普法義經

pusa 菩薩

pusa-mohesa-moheyan-sengnie
菩薩摩訶薩摩訶衍僧那僧涅

Qi chu san guan jing 七出三觀經

Ren ben yu sheng jing 人本欲生經

Rikuchō joji shōki 六朝助字小記

ru 汝

rulai 如來

Rushi, shelifu, zhufo
如是, 舍利弗, 諸佛

rushi wo wen 如是我聞

Satuobolun 薩陀波倫

sangmen 桑門

Sengyou 僧祐

Sesetsu-shingo no bunsho
世說新語の文章

shanlai 善來

Shenjian 申鑑

shequ 捨去

shi 是

Shi fa fei fa jing 是法非法經

shigu 是故

Shigu kaishi 是故開士

Shishuo xinyu 世說新語

Shou yi 守意

Si di jing 四地經

si 斯

Sishierzhang jing 四十二章經

song 頌

songchu 送出

Suii no hiai (Koshi jukyushu no shudai)
推移の悲哀 (古詩十九首の主題)

Taiping jing 太平經

Taizi ruiying benqi jing
太子瑞應本起經

Tang Yongtong 湯用彤

tian 天

Ushijima Tokuji 牛島德次

wang 王

weicengyou 未曾有

wen rushi 聞如是

Wenshushili wen pusa shu jing 文殊師利問菩薩署經

Wenwu guo 聞物國

wo 我

wu 無

Wu yin piyu jing 五陰譬喻經

wuyou 無有

Xiang'er 想爾

xianguan 縣官

xin qi xiang ze chi 心起想則癡

xinyi 心意

Xiuxing benqi jing 修行本起經

Xun Yue 荀悅

Yan Foutiao 嚴浮調

ye 也

yi 亦

yin 陰

Yi ri moni bao jing 遺日摩尼寶經

Yin chi ru jing 陰持入經

Yin chi ru jing zhu 陰持入經注

Ying Shao 應劭

yipusai 伊蒲塞

Yiqie liu she shou yin jing 一切流攝守因經

yiyi liubian 奕奕流便

yongshigu 用是故

Yoshikawa Kōjirō 吉川幸次郎

Yoshikawa Kōjirō zenshu 吉川幸次郎全集

Zhao Qi 趙岐

zhenru 真如

Zhi Loujiachen 支婁迦讖

Zhi Mindu 支敏度

Zhi Qian 支謙

Zhi Yao 支曜

Zhong benqi jing 中本起經

Zhu Dali 竺大力

Zhu Tanguo 竺曇果

Zhuan falun jing 轉法輪經

Zongli zhongjing mulu 總理眾經目錄

zuxingzi 族姓子

BOOKS OF RELATED INTEREST FROM NAB

SUKHMANI SAHEB: TREASURE OF BLISS

A Poetic rendering in English of some selected verses from Sukhmani Saheb

—Bharat Bhooshan

This book presents poetic rendering in English of some of the most poignant verses from the Sukhmani Saheb. It will have special value and significance to those who are looking for an introduction to this Holy Scripture but are constrained either for want of time or because of their inability to understand the language and style of the original text.

ISBN: 81-7822-258-2

ISLAM

An Historical Introduction

—Gerhard Endress

This highly acclaimed survey provides a thoughtful and concise account of all aspects of Islam in history. Written in clear and accessible language—and featuring a chronology of political and cultural events from the rise of Islam to the twentieth century—this is the essential introduction to Islamic history and culture.

ISBN: 81-7822-156-x

UNDERSTANDINGISLAM

—Frithjof Schuon

Religion, Schuon believes, is to guide humankind to a spiritual level on which all problems are seen and solved through man's faith upon the eternal wisdom of the Creator. This is a book that elucidates the essence of Islam, comparing it with the world-view of Christianity and other religious traditions.

ISBN: 81-7822-151-9

BEYOND RELIGION

Meditations on Man's True Nature

—Robert Powell

What are 'meditations'? Numerous meditations are possible and helpful, but there is only one of supreme importance; it is the meditation on the theme 'Who am I?' This leads eventually to the recognition that one is the Unicity, the Totality or the Consciousness Itself, beyond all limitations and divisions. It essentially consists of eternal watchfulness, the witnessing of the consciousness everlastingly falling back into seeing events as variations on the theme of body-mind identification.

ISBN: 81-7822-139-x

THE FIRST AND BEST BUDDHIST TEACHINGS

Sutta Nipata Selections and Inspired Essays

—Susunaga Weeraperuma

Susunaga Weeraperuma's faithful and masterly rendering of the Sutta Nipata—the oldest sacred book in the Buddhist literature—deepens our understanding of the teachings. An eminent writer in the field of Buddhism, he has lucidly expressed the ancient wisdom using a contemporary idiom. Great philosophical and psychological insights abound this collection of essays. Additional essays address various issus of deep concern and offer practical solutions—on depression, facing death, growing old, finding happiness or world peace.

ISBN: 81-7822-257-4

EMBRACING HEAVEN & EARTH

The Liberation Teachings for Enlightenment

—Andrew Cohen

A book of extraordinary spiritual intelligence, challenging the reader to participate in the ultimate revolution: to abandon the security of the known for the thrill of the unknown, which is Enlightenment.

ISBN: 81-7822-218-3